"Open Thou Mine Eyes"

Defending the Old Testament in Latter-day Saint Doctrine

Proceedings from the
2025 FAIR Virtual Conference
and Additional Papers

Edited by:

Jared Riddick
Sarah N. Allen
Spencer Kraus
Trevor Holyoak

Fair
2025

Copyright © 2025 by The Foundation for Apologetic Information and Research, Inc.

All rights reserved. No part of this publication may be reproduced, stored in a retrieval system, or transmitted in any form or by any means—electronic, mechanical, photocopying, recording, or otherwise—without the prior written permission of the publisher, except for brief quotations used in scholarly or critical reviews.

"Open Thou Mine Eyes": Defending the Old Testament in Latter-day Saint Doctrine

Edited by Jared Riddick, Sarah N. Allen, Spencer Kraus, and Trevor Holyoak

Proceedings from Ancient Truths for Modern Faith: Defending the Old Testament in Latter-day Saint Doctrine, held October 9th–11th 2025, in American Fork, UT.

Cover Image: "Open Thou Mine Eyes: Psalm 119:18" by Amberlea Erekson Smoot
Cover Design: Jared Riddick
Interior Design and Typesetting: Jared Riddick
Copyediting: Jared Riddick, Sarah N. Allen, Spencer Kraus

ISBN (dust-jacket hardcover): 979-8-9993242-8-3
Library of Congress Control Number: 2025951430
First edition: December 2025

Published by:
    FAIR
    PO Box 491677
    Redding, CA 96049
    United States
    fairlatterdaysaints.org

Produced and published in the United States of America

For permissions, academic inquiries, or bulk orders, contact: dbeck@fairlatterdaysaints.org

The views expressed in each chapter are those of the individual authors and do not necessarily reflect those of the editors, FAIR, or the Church of Jesus Christ of Latter-day Saints.

This anthology is a scholarly work. Every effort has been made to properly attribute sources and permissions.

Table of Contents

Editor's Introduction   v

Understanding the Old Testament Today

1. Focal Lenses for In-Depth Understanding of the Old Testament   1
   Kerry Muhlestein

2. The Old Testament within the Expanded Latter-day Saint Canon: Interpretive Straitjacket or Parachute?   31
   T. Benjamin Spackman

3. Defending the Old Testament: Ancient Israel's Offering to the World   60
   Daniel Ellsworth

4. Defending Josiah   79
   Allen Hansen

Covenants, Commandments, and God's People

5. From Sinai to Salt Lake: Sacred Promises, Reimagined for a New Dispensation   131
   Jennifer Roach Lees

6. Justifying Joshua: A Restoration Theodicy for the Conquest of Canaan   143
   Paul Bryner

7. The Israelite Cultural Background of Nephite Polygamy   186
   Matthew Roper

8. "Even as Moses Did": The Use of the Exodus Narrative in Mosiah 11–18   229
   Sara Riley

Symbols, Worship, and Divine Power

9. Hold to the … Serpent Wand?   246
   John S. Thompson

10. Who Shall Ascend Into the Hill of the Lord?: An Old Testament Framework for Understanding the Exclusive Nature of the Temple   261
    Tyler Golightly

11. In the Beginning: Grounding Joseph Smith's Cosmology in Genesis 1   274
Stephen O. Smoot

12. Out of the Dust Re-Examined: The Literary Function of Necromantic Imagery in the Book of Mormon   305
Amanda Colleen Brown-Mather

13. Master Mahan: Legend(s) of Cain in the Latter Day Saint Tradition   323
Christopher James Blythe

Prophets, Promise, and Fulfillment

14. "They Did Contain the Five Books of Moses": Source Criticism and the Contents of the Plates of Brass   345
Neal Rappleye

15. Does Isaiah's Description of the Righteous Servant Refer to Jesus Christ?   388
Jeffrey M. Bradshaw

16. The Historical Jonah   430
John Gee

17. "To Seal the Children to the Fathers": Ancient and Modern Traditions of Elijah's Return   446
Spencer Kraus

About the Contributors   468
Image Credits   473
Subject Index   475

Editor's Introduction

This has been the third year that FAIR has held our annual Virtual Conference — centered around the volume of scripture to be covered in the upcoming "Come, Follow Me" year — and it feels like we are just getting started, with each year better than the last. For its size alone (never mind the large chronological and cultural gap) the Old Testament is always a daunting prospect of study for Latter-day Saints, and there's a tendency for many to throw up their hands and not drink as deeply as we would in a Book of Mormon or Doctrine and Covenants year. It just seems to be too much.

In our own small way, in addition to our usual video and annual conference offerings, we at FAIR wanted to help change that a bit this year. As a young missionary, I can vividly recall inhaling the Old Testament in full for the first time. As I read each morning and evening, to appropriate a phrase from one fictional teacher, I felt that I was taking my first steps into a larger world. The other standard works, especially the Book of Mormon, made more sense to me than ever before. That is an experience that I hope can be replicated for every Latter-day Saint this upcoming "Come, Follow Me" year, as the Church again begins their study of the Old Testament.

In the spring of 2025, as our panel reviewed submissions for the then-upcoming conference, there was a building excitement for what we would have to offer this year. As I scrolled through abstracts, sitting in a Pennsylvania restaurant, I found myself looking forward to seeing the presentations, and to digging into them in print while working with my co-editors on this volume. It has been an immensely rewarding experience, and one that I hope readers of this book will also enjoy.

This book contains seventeen fascinating papers that will expand and deepen your appreciation of the Old Testament. Fourteen of them were presented at our October 2025 virtual conference, with three excellent further additions that we decided to recruit afterwards.

In our keynote presentation, BYU professor Kerry Muhlestein discussed employing four "focal lenses" to overcome modern challenges to understanding the Old Testament, centered on seeing it as family history, a story of God's anger and His mercy, rich in symbolism, and ultimately, a foundation of the covenant.

Next, T. Benjamin Spackman discusses how our expanded canon functions as an interpretive "parachute" offering a flexible, faithful engagement that embraces the inspired — but human — nature of scripture while rejecting rigid, inherited assumptions that could bind us. Moving from there, Daniel Ellsworth defends the enduring value of the Old Testament by encouraging us to prioritize core Restored doctrines of the Gospel, and reminding us that it is unnecessary to defend questionable literalisms or interpretations that exclude the Lord as a motivating force.

In his article, Allen Hansen pushes back against modern critical views of King Josiah, portraying him as a righteous restorer of Israel's covenant that counteracted idolatrous influence, and ultimately became a tragic hero that was loyal to the Lord. Jennifer Roach Lees examines three covenants — the Noahic, Abrahamic, and Mosaic — as expressions of a continuous divine pattern, demonstrating that modern revelations recontextualize and expand, rather than merely restore, the meaning and application of ancient sacred promises.

Paul Bryner navigates the difficult topic of the conquest of Canaan and the problem of pain within the book of Joshua, while Matthew Roper contextualizes polygamy in the ancient Near East and Law of Moses, demonstrating that the condemnation of Nephite plural marriage in the Book of Mormon stemmed from their violation of the specific "Law of Lehi" and the misuse of the examples of Kings David and Solomon. Sara Riley explores the fascinating study of Exodus motifs in the Book of Mormon, with compelling intertextual parallels between that narrative and Mosiah 11–18, arguing that Abinadi and Alma are intentionally cast in Mosaic roles to underscore themes of deliverance, covenant renewal, and prophetic legitimacy.

John S. Thompson explains how ancient Egyptian symbolism, where the rod equals the word of a deity, illuminates scriptural imagery, linking the brazen serpent to divine power and the iron rod to mastering the serpent of chaos. In an ever-relevant theme in this era of expanded temple construction, Tyler Golightly analyzes the Old

Testament framework of sacred space and holiness, concluding that the exclusive nature of modern Latter-day Saint temples — often paraphrased as sacred, not secret — is part of an enduring divine pattern that necessitates worthiness and preparation to encounter God.

From there, Stephen O. Smoot details how Genesis 1 supports core Latter-day Saint doctrines like creation from pre-existent matter and divine plurality. In a fascinating analysis, Amanda Colleen Brown-Mather examines how Book of Mormon prophets radically reinterpret Isaiah 29:4's necromantic — a word that we do not see often used in Latter-day Saint circles — "voice from the dust" imagery, transforming the metaphor of divination into a symbol of divine redemption and prophetic word transcending the grave. Diving into the world of Latter-day Saint folklore, Christopher James Blythe looks at interpretations surrounding Cain — ranging from Joseph Smith's "Master Mahan" to fundamentalist theories of serpent parentage — to illustrate the ways that members of the Restoration movements have historically engaged in speculative theology to fill silence in the scriptural record.

In his examination, Neal Rappleye contests the late-dating scholarship for the Pentateuch, arguing that linguistic and archaeological evidence places the compilation of the "five books of Moses" firmly before the exile, and thus supporting the historical plausibility of Nephi's brass plates. Jeffrey M. Bradshaw affirms that belief in Isaiah 53's Righteous Servant as Jesus Christ is well-founded in ancient traditions and scripture, and notes how the Book of Mormon decisively resolves historical uncertainty regarding the Servant's identity and suffering mission. In a look at a much-neglected book, John Gee argues for the historicity of the book of Jonah, correlating the mass repentance in Nineveh with an unexplained historical period of Assyrian imperial decline, lending surprising archaeological consistency to the text.

Finally, capping off the volume much as the subject of his paper does the Old Testament, Spencer Kraus explores Malachi's prophecy concerning Elijah's return, arguing that Joseph Smith's and Moroni's unique renderings function as prophetic commentary clarifying the restoration of the indispensable sealing power for binding families in the latter days.

This book is a labor of hundreds of hours of labor from dedicated disciple-scholars. It is one of many great offerings to support Latter-day Saint study of the Old Testament this upcoming year. I am grateful in particular for the work of my co-editors, Sarah N. Allen, Spencer Kraus, and Trevor Holyoak, as well as David Harper, who volunteered many hours in the capacity of a research assistant, helping authors with tracking down sources. We hope that these essays will help to open your eyes to the world of the Old Testament, and how a dedicated study of it will serve as a blessing in your personal journeys to "feast upon the words of Christ" and seek to better know our Savior and His gospel.

Jared Riddick
December 2025

1

FOCAL LENSES FOR IN-DEPTH UNDERSTANDING OF THE OLD TESTAMENT

KERRY MUHLESTEIN

Many modern readers struggle to connect with the Old Testament, viewing it as distant, violent, or confusing due to significant cultural and temporal gaps. Unlocking its spiritual power requires intentionally swapping modern perspectives for "focal lenses" that clarify the text's original intent. First, viewing the narrative as personal family history transforms it from a foreign record into a shared heritage. Second, reading the "whole story" reveals a God who employs both fierce anger and tender mercy to reclaim His children, extending redemption even beyond physical death. Third, developing "symbol literacy" allows readers to decode the profound lessons hidden in ancient actions and rituals that legalistic modern minds often miss. Finally, applying the lens of the "covenant" exposes the text's central theme: a relentless God who uses every tool—including scattering and gathering—to forge an unbreakable relationship with humanity. These perspective shifts reveal a book of urgent, living theology.

I am glad to be part of this conference. I love the work that FAIR does, and I'm glad to be talking to you about studying the Old Testament.

In my opinion, there is so much more power, richness, and depth to get out of this book than any of us are currently accessing. I believe we are just scratching the surface. What the Old Testament can offer us is beautiful, and so I want to spend my time helping all of us get even more out of it.

When I think of the Old Testament, I think of a painting I love from the Sistine Chapel. In many ways, it represents the story of the

Old Testament. The depiction is of God reaching out to Adam, while Adam lackadaisically almost reaches back. It depicts God yearning to be with us, energetically reaching out to us, while we are mixed in our feelings about reaching back to Him. As a result of this situation, God will plead with us again and again, asking us to please "turn" or "return to Me." In response, both ancient and modern humankind lazily reach forth our hands, not quite turning to God.

In too many ways, that is the story of the Old Testament. Sadly, it is also often the story of our interaction with the Old Testament. Some of us love it, some are afraid of it, and no one cares about it as much as they should. As a result, none of us are getting as much out of it as we should be. Perhaps we all fill a role similar to Adam in the Sistine Chapel painting. In effect, we say "Oh, if you can reach me through the Old Testament, God, then go ahead and do it. But I'm not going to put a lot of effort into it."

I want us to do better this year. There is so much to get out of the Old Testament! Here I will speak about how we bring different interpretive lenses with us to our study. These can sometimes distort the way we see and understand that book of scripture. It's not enough to just take off the incorrect lenses we have. We need to put on some new ones that will open up the teachings of this inspired book.

My eyeglasses are currently dirty, and I need a new prescription. I will be going in a few hours to get one. But that does not mean I can just take these old glasses off. If I just remove them now, then, yes, I am not seeing things with the wrong prescription, but I also will not be seeing anything clearly either. I need that new set of glasses to really see better. Similarly, we will need to put on our new interpretive lenses, our correct interpretive lenses, when we study the Old Testament.

OBSTACLES TO UNDERSTANDING THE OLD TESTAMENT

Let us look at some of the incorrect lenses, or obstacles, to understanding the Old Testament in our day.

The Gaps of Time and Context

An obvious gap is time; a tremendous amount of time has gone by between the stories and the writings of the Old Testament and our own day. That means that we know less than we would like about some of the peripheral information which could help us understand it.

In contrast, think of what we have available as we study the Doctrine and Covenants in our *Come, Follow Me* reading this last year. The amount of resources provided is staggering. When we study any given revelation, there is a vast and wonderful amount of information just a few screen touches away.

In comparison, because Latter-day Saints often know so much less about ancient historical and cultural contexts, there are very few Old Testament resources to teach us about the specific context of any given chapter. It represents a real obstacle in understanding the Old Testament, and of course, this leads to some of these other obstacles we will look at now.

We know some of the history of the world of the Old Testament, but at the same time, there is so much that we do not understand. While this is a genuine hurdle, we often fail to take advantage of the knowledge we do have. We actually know a great deal about many of the stories contained in the Bible, but we tend to look at them in isolation, causing us to fail to see how those stories fit into the broader biblical picture.

We understand a Bible story better when we add context. From the Assyrians, Babylonians, Egyptians, and others — through archaeology, historical records, historical depictions, and other sources — we learn a great deal that we can easily use to help us better understand specific biblical stories. Yet we often neglect them. We need to put on these lenses of available history, archaeology, geography, and culture, which can open up so much more of the Old Testament for us.

The Gap of Ancient Culture

As mentioned, ancient culture is an important element to consider here. I will provide an example to illustrate. Many of us live in a highly sterilized world: most of us do not kill and dress our food, we have not participated in wars, and we have not had people attack our homes.

That's not the case for the people in the Old Testament.

They often had to defend themselves if they were going to survive. Most of them experienced some violence, and participated in small- or large-scale wars or defense. Most of them were slaughtering animals. They were familiar with blood, with death, and with violence in ways we are not. That cultural gap is sometimes shocking and surprising to us. We need to learn to put ourselves in their place. That is going to be crucial in achieving a better understanding of the Old Testament.

The Lens of Modern Sensibilities

Too often, our modern, sterilized sensibilities are shocked by violent elements that were part of everyday life for the people about whom we are reading. That shock removes us so far from the story that we fail to identify with the lives of the people we are studying.

Along these lines, there is a modern way of thinking that is an obstacle in our Old Testament study. I will return to this when we discuss symbolism but let me say at the outset that we often have a modern Western, post-Scientific Revolution way of thinking that is wholly different from the way they thought. If we refuse to try to see things from their perspective, then we will fail to learn much of what we could learn. We must do better at putting ourselves in their shoes and their mindsets.

This resistance sometimes prevents us from seeing what they are saying. We are so sure that those who are in the past are primitive in the way that they think that we ignore their teachings and refuse to give them credit for profound ideas.

The Lens of the Restoration

Let us also be clear that, as members of the Church of Jesus Christ of Latter-day Saints, we have a very specific interpretive lens which we often use in our scripture study, but perhaps not as much as we could.

That is the lens, not only of Christianity, but of restored Christianity. We are so fortunate to have texts like the Book of Moses, which is the Joseph Smith Translation of the first part of Genesis, and texts like the Book of Abraham. Through these books we can see that Christ and God's gospel have been here from the very beginning. From the days of Adam, the Gospel has been taught.

That should change the way we understand the Old Testament. This does not mean that everyone in the Old Testament always understood the Gospel. Often, Israel was in varying states of apostasy, which means that throughout their history they did not necessarily have the same understanding we do in this Dispensation of the Fulness of Times.

Yet there are clearly kernels of the Gospel to be found. Still, because of the Books of Moses and Abraham, we know that, from the beginning of time, God was teaching His children about the Savior and the way to be saved and return to Him. This knowledge changes the way we understand God and His interactions with His children.

The author's recently published commentary

Helpful Resources for Study

With all of that in mind, let us also just give you an idea of some resources that are easily available to you. You will be familiar with many resources, but there are some which you may not be familiar with that I have helped put together.

One is OutofthedDust.org. Because I'm not a web developer, the aesthetics may be lacking, but the content is good. Beyond that, on my podcast, "**The Scriptures are Real**," you can find a tremendous amount of resources for understanding the Old Testament. Of course, there are many podcasts that can be helpful for you, but I hope to just make you aware that "The Scriptures Are Real" is a podcast that aims to provide you with a deluge of helpful information and perspectives about the Old Testament. We hope to make it a resource where you can get what you need to understand the Old Testament throughout the year.

Additionally, there are dozens and dozens of publications. I, and others, have new books coming out this year that are aimed at helping you to better understand the Old Testament. I would encourage you to avail yourself of all the opportunities you can find that are helpful for you and that you have time for.

Focal Lens #1: The Old Testament is Family History

Let us start by looking at one specific interpretive lens: I hope we think of the Old Testament as family history.

If one were to look north while standing on the grounds of Nabi Samwil, just north of Jerusalem, you would see the hills of Ephraim on the far horizon. Beyond that, there are lands of inheritance for the other tribes of Israel. All of us should identify with the House of Israel, whether by adoption or literal descent. Once we make a covenant, we are of the House of Israel, and the Old Testament becomes our family history. If you were at Nabi Samwil, you would be looking at your homeland, and that should affect you in some way. You should start to recognize and realize that when you think of family history, you should not just think of great-great grandma Mildred, but also great-great-great grandma Sarah, Rebekah, and Rachel.

The Old Testament is our story, and when we think of it that way, it changes the way we read it. It suddenly becomes less a foreign territory, less other, less about someone else. It becomes our story, something that belongs to us, and which we belong to, so we start to identify more with the Old Testament.

Putting on this specific interpretive lens and thinking of the Old Testament this way will be a big part of your unlocking the Old Testament.

Focal Lens #2: Seeing the Whole Story

I want to emphasize that the Old Testament gives us a fuller story than we are often used to. For example, it tells us more about God than we are sometimes expecting. We will address that in just a moment — the whole story of how God works with His children.

Embracing the "Warts and All"

The Old Testament often gives us the whole story, warts and all. It does not give us a sanitized story.

In contrast, think of the Book of Mormon. It is a wonderful book of scripture, the most correct book on earth, but it is sometimes intentionally sanitized. In fact, the prophet Mormon even tells us he is sanitizing it, that he does not want to put some things in the record because of how terrible they are (Mormon 5:8). That means that we do not necessarily get the full picture of the good and the bad done by some of its great leaders and people. Although, in some cases, such as the mistakes of Alma the Younger and the sons of Mosiah, we do.

The Old Testament is consistently good at painting the full picture, in telling us the great and bad things, the triumphs and the struggles which the people went through. This is not unlike the Doctrine and Covenants, in that it consistently tells us when the prophet Joseph needs to repent.

We need to embrace that rather than say, "I don't know, that's iffy about Jacob" or something along those lines. We should say, "Look at the struggles Jacob is having. Look at the struggles Abraham is having. Look at the struggles Eli is having." Think of Samson, David, and others. Look at their struggles and be able to recognize that good people will still have struggles. Sometimes people who could be great do not succeed because they give in to their vices — as in the case of Samson — but we can look at the stories and recognize that these are people like ourselves.

Life is messy, but in the middle of messiness, people can come to God. It's a beautiful part of the Old Testament.

Understanding the Whole Story of God

I want to spend some time emphasizing the whole story of who God is. As members of the Church of Jesus Christ of Latter-day Saints, we have a very unique perspective on this. When I teach the Pearl of Great Price, after giving my students some history of how we got the book, we usually start with Moses chapter 1.

It is very rare for the first question from my students to not be "who is speaking here?" This seems to be because we understand the speaker to be Jehovah, and we understand Jehovah to be Jesus Christ, and yet He's speaking about Jesus Christ as His Son. That often confuses my students.

Jehovah: Revealing the Father

This is Jehovah that we are reading about, and we should think of Jehovah in a very specific way, especially in the Old Testament.

After the Resurrection, it is different, but in the Old Testament, there is a very specific way to think of Jehovah; that is Jesus Christ acting for and in behalf of His Father. It is called divine investiture of authority, and it is a principle that I am sure you are familiar with. They were even more familiar with it in the ancient world; there we find representatives from one kingdom coming to another, and speaking as if they were the king of the other country. No one truly thought they were, but they treated them as if they were, because that is the way they did business. Rulers often invested someone to act on their behalf. Thus, they understood the principle of investiture in the ancient world, and this should help us understand Jehovah.

After the Fall, we are cut off from the presence of God. He does not interact with us directly, but rather interacts with us through an intermediary. Further, we interact with Him, including even in our prayers, through an intermediary. That intermediary is Jesus Christ. In the Old Testament, in His role as intermediary, Christ speaks as if He is the Father because that is what He has been asked to do. His role is to act for and in behalf of God. We will understand the Old Testament text best if we are reading the text as if it is God the Father speaking and acting, knowing in the back of our minds that it is Jehovah, His Son Jesus Christ, representing God to us.

Realizing this should cause us to pause and ask some profound questions. For example, who is Jehovah really?

Jehovah is Christ, whose primary job is to reveal the Father to us. Eventually He will do this by bringing us into the Father's presence. In the interim — and this is what He talks about more than anything else in the Gospels, especially in the Book of John — Christ reveals the Father to us by doing what the Father would do, saying what the Father would say, and acting the way the Father would act. We learn about the nature of our Father by seeing the nature of Jehovah, who is acting so much like the Father that we can come to know the Father by coming to know Him.

Thus it is intended that we think of the Father as we read about Jehovah. It is good to remember that it is Jesus Christ, it helps us understand who He is and His role as a Redeemer. But Jehovah wants to reveal the Father to us; He wants to act in the same way the Father would act, and He wants us to be thinking of the Father. He is clear about that in the Gospel of John (see John 5:19).

To be clear and add emphasis: all of this means we should be thinking of the Father as we read the Old Testament, while also thinking of Christ. I do not want to take the Savior out of this picture — please do not misunderstand me — but let us not take the Father out of the picture either, because that's not what Christ tells us to do. Let us keep the Father in focus.

This is Jehovah, or Christ, acting for and on behalf of His Father, and intending for us to think of the Father and learn about the nature of the Father. In this way, we are blessed to read the Old Testament and simultaneously learn about the nature of the Father and His Beloved Son.

The Nature of Jehovah: Anger and Mercy

Now we can come to the question, what is Jehovah like? This is a useful question. We want to know the nature of both the Father and the Son. As we learn about One, we learn about the Other. What do we learn about Jehovah's nature?

The Old Testament will teach us a tremendous amount about that topic. Again, we should put our Restoration interpretive lens on as we learn about Jehovah. What does the Restoration teach us, especially using the Joseph Smith Translation of the Bible, especially the Book of Moses? There are several key elements we must take note of, and, as we do so, I think we will find that some of the problems which many Christians have with the nature of God are resolved.

In Moses 7:34, during Enoch's vision of the Great Flood, it says: "And the fire of my indignation is kindled against them, and in my hot displeasure will I send in the floods upon them, for my fierce anger is kindled against them."

That's about as wrathy as it gets. This is an upset God. We will come back to the idea of an angry or an upset God, but part of the way that we can understand this concept is by continuing to just a few verses later, where He says:

> But behold, their [the people in Noah's day] sins shall be upon the heads of their fathers. Satan shall be their father,

and misery shall be their doom. And the whole heaven shall weep over them, even all the workmanship of mine hands. Wherefore should not the heavens weep, seeing these shall suffer? (Moses 7:37).

Reading these two passages allows us to see that God is simultaneously experiencing both anger and sorrow over the misery and suffering of His children. This includes the suffering that they are bringing upon themselves, and the suffering which He will bring upon them as He brings in the floods. That helps us understand who God is. His anger is a tool, and His punishments are also a tool to bring his children back to Him. As we discuss looking at the whole story, we are going to look at that more.

Let me be clear about this, I have had many students who are uncomfortable as they read the Old Testament. They read Isaiah, who testifies so beautifully of Christ, but also speaks of God being angry, upset, and full of wrath. I have had students say, "That's not God."

We must recognize that this is God telling us what He looks like and who He is. That is one of the interpretive lenses we must use, and it can be difficult for us. We often do not allow God to tell us what He is like, but instead insist that He be the way that we expect Him to be. As an example, when He presents himself to us in this story and others, He has both anger and mercy.

There is a key passage that helps illuminate this. In Jeremiah 3:12, God says that He *is* merciful, or has *hesed*. He continues by saying He does not *maintain*, or *keep*, or *hold*, anger forever (Jeremiah 3:12, translation mine). This is an important distinction. God *is* merciful, and anger is something He does or holds. One is an attribute, the other is something He does because of His attributes. At the same time, I have come to conclude that His anger is not like my anger. As a being who has a fallen nature, I do not think I am capable of feeling the kind of anger that God does.

It is important to note that God does the act of anger, and that He does it in a way that I am not capable of. This is an act that is not for me to emulate. He seems to be able to do, hold, keep, or act out anger in a godly way, which is beyond my ability. I cannot equate my anger with God's, but I also can't pretend that God does not have anger just because it does not match mine, and thus does not match my idea of what God is like. There is always an element of fallen nature in my anger that is not appropriate. I have to believe and have faith that a divine being has a different anger, and that it is always associated with love and bringing His children where they need to be.

When juxtaposing the verses from Moses 7 we quoted above, we see this mixture. Jehovah is someone who loves His children and also will have to save His children, sometimes by removing their oppressors and sometimes by punishing them. Let us keep that in mind as we learn about the nature of Jehovah by reading the Old Testament and Restoration passages in the Old Testament.

In a latter-day revelation, speaking about the Saints who have endured terrible things in Missouri, we find a powerful principle which will help us understand many Old Testament stories.

> Verily I say unto you concerning your brethren who have been afflicted and persecuted and cast out from the land of their inheritance. I, the Lord, have suffered the affliction to come upon them, wherewith they have been afflicted in consequence of their transgressions. Yet I will own them, and they shall be mine in that day, when I shall come to make up my jewels. Therefore, they must needs be chastened and tried, even as Abraham, who was commanded to offer up his only son…

A few verses later, the Lord continues:

> …they were slow to hearken under the voice of the Lord their God. Therefore, the Lord their God is slow to hearken unto their prayers, to answer them in the day of their trouble. In the day of their peace, they esteemed lightly my counsel, but in the day of their trouble of necessity, they feel after me. Verily, I say unto you, notwithstanding their sins, my bowels are filled with compassion towards them. I will not utterly cast them off; and in the day of wrath, I will remember mercy (Doctrine and Covenants 101:1-4, 7-9).

That sentiment could be applied to almost every story in the Old Testament. I hope that reading it in a more familiar language — the Doctrine and Covenants has a language that just resonates more with us in our modern times — will help us recognize what Jehovah is doing in the Old Testament and what His motives, His nature, and His character are. He punishes to correct us and draw us to Him, but He does not cast us off and He is ever ready to extend mercy.

That is the story of the Old Testament. It saturates the entire book.

Letting God Define Himself

What do you expect God to be like? Before you continue reading, take a moment to think about that. What do you expect God to be like? Then ask whether this expectation creates a set of blinders that you will not even realize you are wearing.

Does it make it so there are certain things we just won't see?

I have seen this play out repeatedly. For example, I have had Old Testament students who have said, "This can't be Jehovah. That's not what He's like." In the New Testament, "That can't be Christ. That's not the way He talks."

I have read countless times, even in Latter-day Saint publications, where someone has said, "this is how Christ did things," and then they talk about things that He did not do. Or they will say, "Christ always teaches this way," and then they start talking about a certain teaching principle, seemingly not noticing that He taught in different ways dozens of times.

We often think the Savior should be a certain way, and then we read that expectation into the text. Then when the text presents something different, we try to turn a blind eye. It colors the way that we see everything, and soon there are things that we cannot see correctly, because we are trying to find God behaving and speaking the way that we think He should behave or speak.

It is far better to let God present Himself the way that He wants to present Himself.

Read the scriptures without blinders, without lenses that color it, without your expectations, and find out what is actually in there, and then ask yourself, why does God want me to see Him this way?

When you do, you will find that God is more magnificent, powerful, loving, and merciful than you have ever thought. It is just not always in the ways that we expected. Too often, we try to limit Him, and give ourselves a watered-down God created in our image — or in the image we would like Him to be — rather than Him creating us in His image and teaching us what He is actually like.

This is something we struggle with, and I hope you will look at how God does present Himself in the Old Testament.

The Divine Warrior and the Savior

This concept is well-portrayed in several chapters in Isaiah.

In Isaiah 27, God describes Himself as having a great and terrible sword. Jehovah is using this sword to battle Leviathan, the chaos monster that represents all that Satan would have undone in God's creation to make everything terrible and miserable for us. Interestingly, just two chapters prior, in Isaiah 25, Jehovah describes Himself as wiping away all of our tears.

I find that my students are not comfortable with Jehovah being described as having and using a great sword. In the Old Testament, He is frequently described as a man of war, or as a divine warrior. My students and many others do not like that. We do not want God to be a warrior. We want Him to be someone who is just wiping away tears. Yet, I would say that it is important for us to understand that Christ has the ability to deliver us. Why can He deliver us? Because He is a divine warrior; He fights for us in so many different ways.

One of those ways was suffering for all of our sins, and thus conquering death, but He will also fight for us by removing our oppressors. That is a prominent theme in Isaiah, especially its latter portions: Jehovah will remove those who oppress. He first pleads with them to stop oppressing, and if they do not stop, He removes and punishes the oppressors. That is why He can deliver us; the reason that Christ can reach out and wipe away our tears with one hand is because, in the other hand, He holds a great and terrible and a mighty sword. It is critical for us to recognize this interrelationship.

In my experience of asking people about their faith in Christ as a Savior, I have found that many struggle in answering what a Savior is. The most common answer I receive is, "He is my friend, He is there for me." That is a good and important thing, but that is not what a Savior is. A Savior is someone who saves you from whatever is trying to conquer you, and He can do that only by conquering whatever it is that is trying to conquer you.

If we do not recognize Christ's ability to be victorious, His ability to conquer, His supremacy as the divine warrior, then we cannot have faith that He can deliver us from everything we need to be delivered from. Misunderstanding this will induce anxiety and fear. If we will not understand how much Jehovah — Jesus Christ, sent on behalf of the Father — can deliver us, then we have cause to be afraid. We need to understand that Christ has fought the fight, won the victory, and has conquered on our behalf. He is our Savior. That allows Him to be there for us, and to wipe away our tears.

That is a lens we need to put on as we study the Old Testament.

Reading Beyond the "End" of the Story

There is a wide-angle lens we must use as we study the Old Testament. I want to encourage us to see the whole story; to see the big picture, not just a little part of it. We too often isolate a part, and do not read the whole thing.

Allow me to provide some examples of what I am talking about.

First, let us first remember the age-old idea of a group of blind people trying to determine what an elephant looks like. The old story tells of several blind men who each touch a different part of an elephant. One grabs the trunk, another the leg, another the tail — each convinced he knows what the creature must be like. Their descriptions don't match because each man has only a small piece of the truth. The parable reminds us how easily our perspective can be limited, and how important it is to look for the fuller picture.

The Old Testament helps us see the whole story, but we will not be able to take advantage of this if we continue to read its various parts in isolation. The Old Testament should be read in conjunction with the Restoration. For example, the story of Noah and the Ark.

We know that in Noah's day the world was wicked. The people were thinking of only evil continually (Moses 8:22); they were without affection and hated their own blood (Moses 7:33). As a result of this, they were all oppressing each other. "The whole earth was filled with violence" is another phrase we see, in Genesis 6:13. They were all oppressing one another; there was no opportunity for truth, for freedom, for a lack of oppression, or for moving forward righteously.

As a result, God removed all those oppressors in this horrific story called the Flood, where eight souls survived, and everyone else did not. That is devastating. We are grateful for the eight souls that survived, that humanity could continue, and that we can be descended from those eight souls. Still, it is devastating to think of all those who died.

Fortunately, we should not think that this is the end of the story. We learn from Doctrine and Covenants Section 138 that Jesus Christ specifically went to those souls in the Spirit World who died during the Flood. He brought the gospel specifically to them, and organized it being taught to them. That tells us that, as terrible and as wicked as they were, and as much as God had to remove them from this part of the story, that was not the end of the story. They still had another chance.

We need to remember that the story does not end, even with death. So often death happens in the Old Testament, and it seems so shocking to us, and we forget that for God, it is moving us from one room to another; from one part of what we are doing to another, where He can work with us again. It is crucial to remember that God works with us in this way, across various spheres of existence, and He looks at a much larger picture than we can see.

This example can help us understand the Conquest, another time of tremendous violence where whole nations were to be destroyed, though that is not what ended up happening. Again, we know that these people were wicked. While we get allusions to this from the Bible, we learn more from some simple verses in 1 Nephi 17, where Nephi tells us that they had been wicked and that they had rejected every word that had been preached unto them (1 Nephi 17:33–35).

This tells us that God had been reaching out to them, preaching to them, and they had rejected His pleadings. They had become wicked, and so they were to be removed. While we do not have the story of the Savior going to them in the Spirit World, I am certain they were given another chance just as the people in the days of Noah. Remembering the Flood narrative and applying it to this story helps us look, not just at a part, but rather at the whole story. Even the part that we do not know much about.

Let us consider a few other examples.

First, we examine the story of Hosea and Gomer, where we know that Gomer is a harlot. She might have been forced to be a harlot, because she is redeemed by Hosea, which indicates that she was not free while a harlot. The timing is not completely clear there, but it seems — in my opinion — that he buys her out of slavery, where she has been a harlot. Hosea then marries her, and she has children with him, and then she plays the harlot again. And why did she? Because she liked the payments she got as a harlot.

That is us too often, isn't it? This is another of our lenses. We will talk later about symbolism and applying it to ourselves. As we do so in this story, we see that too often it is a story about us, where God redeems us, and then we say, "I like that other stuff," and we go back to our sins like a sow wallowing in the mire.

So, what happens in the story? Well, God tells Hosea what He will do. He says:

> Therefore, will I return and take away my corn in the time thereof, and my wine in the season thereof, and will recover my wool and my flax given to cover her nakedness. I will also cause all of her mirth to cease (Hosea 2:9–11).

God is telling Hosea that He will ensure that Gomer will not be happy anymore. "And I will destroy her vines and her fig trees, whereof she hath said, 'These are rewards that my lovers have given me'" (Hosea 2:12). In other words, the Lord says, "Well, if she's going to play the harlot and she's doing it because she likes this stuff, and she thinks that it makes her life exciting, or fun, I'm going to take away all of it. She won't get this stuff. She's not going to have the excitement and the fun. I'm going to make her life miserable."

Then He says very specifically, "So that she will recognize how good it was when she was with you, Hosea, and will come back to you" (paraphrase of Hosea 2:7). And then He compares that to the house of Israel. And He says:

> It shall come to pass that in that day, I will hear, sayeth the Lord, I will hear the heavens, and they shall hear the earth, and the earth shall hear the corn, and the wine, and the oil, and they shall hold Jezreel. And I will sow her unto me in the earth, and I will have mercy upon her that had not obtained mercy. And I will say to them which were not my people, thou art my people, and they shall say, thou art my God (Hosea 2:22–23).

He is punishing Gomer and, by symbolic extension, Israel, including each of us. He is allegorizing that story to Israel and saying, "I will punish Israel, but it's only so that they will realize that they need to come back to me, and I will let them come back. I will plead with them to come back and accept them back and say, You are my people, and you can say that I am your God." That's the end of that story; it does not end at the punishment phase, it ends at the "come back" phase. We are going to see that *this* is the story of the Old Testament.

In Isaiah 55:7, we read, "Let the wicked forsake his way, and let the unrighteous man his thoughts, and let him return unto the Lord, and

He will have mercy upon him, and to our God, for He will abundantly pardon." What a beautiful phrase! This is the plea we find more than any other plea in the Old Testament, "Return unto me" or "return unto the Lord." He just pleads with us again, and again, and again. In Ezekiel 16, we read:

> But now when I passed by thee and looked upon thee, behold thy time was in the time of love, and I spread my wing over thee and covered thy nakedness. Yea, I swear unto thee and entered into a covenant with thee, sayeth the Lord God, and you became mine (Ezekiel 16:8, translation mine).

We hear that from a God who will keep working with us. If we read the whole story, we will read that even after we rebel, it is still a time of love, a time for Him to take us in, and make us His.

Let us consider another example along these lines. This is from the book of Ezekiel. We find this several places there, but in Ezekiel 18:27, it says:

> Again, when the wicked man turneth away from his wickedness that He hath committed, and doeth that which is lawful and right, He shall save his soul alive, because He considereth and turneth away from all his transgressions that He hath committed, He shall surely live, He shall not die.

Moving forward a few verses to Ezekiel 18:31, we see a plea:

> Cast away from you all your transgressions whereby you have transgressed, and make you a new heart, and a new spirit. For why will ye die, O house of Israel? For I have no pleasure in the death of him that dieth, saith Lord God, wherefore, turn yourselves and live ye.

This is His plea, and what He is saying will eventually happen, and if we keep reading the book of Ezekiel, we see that this will eventually happen for all.

If we read the whole story, God keeps pleading. Not only does He keep pleading, but eventually, He is successful. That is what we find when we read the whole story. Let us not forget that. The Lord is always pleading for us to come back, and that is how the story will end:

> For I am the Lord. I change not. Therefore, ye sons of Jacob, are not consumed. Even from the days of your father's, ye are gone away from mine ordinances and have not kept them. Return unto me, and I will return unto you, sayeth the Lord of hosts (Malachi 3:6-7).

That is at the very end of the Old Testament. If we keep reading the whole story, that is what we will find: a God who punishes us to help us return to Him, who is ever pleading for us to return, and who is ever willing to accept us when we do.

Focal Lens #3: The Lens of Symbols

Let us consider another interpretive lens, that of symbols. The ancient Israelites were a very symbol-oriented people. They saw the world through them, and that is difficult for us. We sometimes forget the power that lies in symbols. When something is conveyed to us via symbols, we remember it better; they reach into our hearts and souls and emote more with us. Symbolism touches our emotions and yields many layers of meaning. Orson F. Whitney once said, "God teaches by symbols. It's his favorite method of teaching,"[1] and I agree with that.

The Cultural Gap in Symbol Literacy

There is a cultural distance between us and ancient Israel, and this is one of the biggest cultural differences. We dwell in an increasingly legalistic society; we want one thing to mean one thing and one thing only. That is how it has to be in a legal document. We do not want something to be taken in more than one way, but symbols are intended for that, so we increasingly dislike them.

We are inheritors of a Protestant culture, one which divorced itself from Catholicism. Catholicism has many symbolic actions and rituals within it, and so Protestants distanced themselves from that. That trajectory continues today, and we understand symbols, and symbolic actions, less and less. That is the place we are at culturally, and it presents a huge danger for us, because my generation is less culturally literate than my grandparents' generation and my children's generation is less symbolically-literate than mine.

That is a problem because the gospel is laden with symbols. All of our ordinances have symbols, especially the temple, which is full of ordinances that employ symbols. And the less symbol-literate our youth are, the less comfortable they will be in the temple, the more it will seem odd to them. I have heard of young adults who have said as they come out of their first time in the temple, "that felt like a cult."

---

1. Orson F. Whitney, "Latter-Day Saint Ideals and Institutions," *Improvement Era* 30, no.10 (August 1927): 861.

Well, that's because they are symbol-illiterate. We need to work at teaching our youth to be symbol-literate, and to be familiar with symbolic actions. We will have to become symbol-literate ourselves to do that. We need to start getting better at recognizing the power of symbols, and looking for them, especially symbolic action. Studying the Old Testament this year is the perfect place to work on that together.

The scriptures are rife with symbols. There are literary symbols, but there are even more symbols that are conveyed by actions. These are things that God did, actions He had His prophets engage in, or events that happened as He orchestrated history. That is one type of symbolic action. To understand the Old Testament, we must be constantly looking for meanings behind actions and stories.

Symbolic Action in the Exodus Narrative

Let us look at an example from the Exodus narrative, which is entirely steeped in symbolic action. There was a literal Exodus, although we only receive a simplified and stylized rendition of the story. In fact, I think God brought the Exodus about in a way that conveys rich and tremendous symbolism, and then it was written about in a skillful way which informs us of the events, but does so in a way that highlights the symbols which carry profound lessons.[2] It is designed to teach many things, including the story of each of us leaving the world behind, coming and making covenants with God, and then coming into His presence, whether represented by either meeting God at Mount Sinai or by entering the promised land — symbolic of our true promised land, the Celestial Kingdom.[3]

In order to get more out of the Old Testament, we need to develop within ourselves the art of being able to see and appreciate the actual story, but simultaneously not letting that appreciation distract us from recognizing the lessons conveyed by that story and its symbols.

---

2. Kerry Muhlestein, "'What I Will Do to Pharaoh': The Plagues Viewed as a Divine Confrontation with Pharaoh," in Daniel L. Belnap and Aaron P. Schade, eds., *From Creation to Sinai: The Old Testament Through the Lens of the Restoration* (Provo, UT: Religious Studies Center, Brigham Young University; Salt Lake City: Deseret Book Company, 2021), 447–482.
3. Kerry Muhlestein, "Israel, Exodus, Atonement, and Us," in *Covenants, Prophecies, and Hymns of the Old Testament,* ed. Victor Ludlow (Provo, UT: Brigham Young University Press, 2001), 89–100.

Case Study: Miriam's Leprosy and the Whole Story

There is one particular story within the Exodus narrative that can help us see both the symbolism and the importance of reading the whole story.

During the wilderness sojourn, Aaron and Miriam confronted Moses with the idea that he had taken too much upon himself, suggesting that they should have a greater share in the leadership (Numbers 12:2). This is during a time where Israel — as in the days of Joseph Smith — was trying to figure out what it meant to be led by a prophet of God.

They had just been told everyone should be a prophet (Numbers 11:29); inspiration was flooding forth for everyone. In both dispensations, the outpouring of the Spirit created some confusion about how the idea of everyone receiving inspiration interacted with a hierarchy of one person speaking to all Israel on behalf of God.

In our dispensation, during that period of confusion, Hiram Page thought he could receive revelation for the Church as well (Doctrine and Covenants 28). In Moses's era, it is manifest in several ways, including this instance when Aaron and Miriam challenged him about their ability to have the Lord speak through them. They recognized that they received inspiration, but they confused that with the right to speak on behalf of God to the entire congregation. This left God with a choice.

If it had been our day, Moses could have addressed the problem by delivering a wonderful and persuasive sermon; he could have taught all the correct principles, and that would have been persuasive enough for us. However, in their day, if Moses had only orally taught them what was incorrect about their public challenge, it would not have been enough. Israel would have naturally seen the little confrontation as a symbolic action, and if no corresponding action had been part of the answer, then the people would not have recognized that there was an answer at all. They would have interpreted this as Aaron and Miriam being right, and Moses being wrong. In order for the lesson that needed to be taught to be heard by Israel, it had to be taught through a symbolic action.

God responded with a visible and powerful symbolic action that taught more than a thousand words could have: Miriam was struck with leprosy. Leprosy made her ritually impure. To be clear, she was ritually unclean, not actually spiritually unclean, but ritually unclean. This meant she could not participate in any of the rituals that were symbolically about approaching God.

Symbolically, Miriam being struck with leprosy taught all Israel that when you challenge the authority of God's prophet — when you don't accept God's prophet — you have distanced yourself from God. They learned that you cannot approach God when you are not listening to the prophet. That is a powerful lesson; it was better for Miriam to be struck with leprosy than that all of Israel should perish and dwindle in unbelief because they did not believe the prophet (see 1 Nephi 4:13).

We will witness that principle repeatedly in the Old Testament; God will smite someone, teaching through symbolic action what needs to be taught, because it was more important to save the nation and not have them dwindle in unbelief, than it was to spare one person temporary pain or difficulty.

This concept should remind us of the lesson which God taught Nephi when he commanded him to kill Laban (see 1 Nephi 4). The principle applies in numerous situations, including the one that Aaron and Miriam created when they publicly challenged Moses. As a result, Miriam was struck with leprosy. That carried an important lesson in and of itself, and often that is where readers stop.

Let us, as careful readers, remember to examine the whole story. What happens after the leprosy? The entire camp of Israel waited, Miriam apparently repented, and the Lord quickly healed her. This seems to have taken place almost immediately. Yet, there was a period where Miriam needed to wait for a week before she could engage in the ritual which would make her ritually pure again. As she waited, the entire camp of Israel waited for her. They did not leave Miriam behind, they waited as long as was necessary. Then, when she could be with them again, they moved on.

Think of the symbolism behind that story. If we stop reading and thinking when Miriam was struck with leprosy, it could seem like a story of a rather capricious God. But when we look at the whole story, we see a God who is willing to teach, and who is also merciful, willing to wait as long as is necessary to not leave us behind. Rather, God patiently waits for us to be ready, so that He can bring us along on our journey, if we are only willing to come with Him.

That is reading the whole story, and simultaneously carefully examining the symbolism behind it. Combining these two lenses is a crucial key to understanding the Old Testament, and it is one that we must develop, and then help others acquire. We could elaborate at great length on this point, using example after example. Instead, we will examine one other fundamental lens that must be applied if we are to understand the Old Testament.

Focal Lens #4: The Lens of the Covenant

That is the lens of the covenant. When we understand what the covenant is, and start looking for covenant language, we can see and understand so many more things that are happening in the scriptures. For a moment, let us carefully apply this covenant lens, letting it color the way we read the Old Testament.

Covenant, Family, and Relationship

As we do so, we need to think about how much the covenant is about the family. In many ways, the story of the Old Testament — in fact the story of all scripture — is about trying to make the entire world part of God's family, and this lens helps us see how covenants bring families together and are administered through them.

Let us begin by remembering that the Old Testament is a story of families, from beginning to end. It begins with Adam and Eve and the advent of their family. Noah and his family are the next major story, followed by Abraham and all of the messy, difficult things that come as part of his family story. Next, we encounter Isaac, then Jacob and the messy things with his family, followed by Joseph, and so on. There is always a mess; you get the picture. The Old Testament focuses on family, and these stories are about real families trying to come together and come to God in the midst of flawed human beings in difficult circumstances.

With this in mind, what can we learn about covenants as we read this story of families in the Old Testament? How can we recognize covenants in the scriptures?[4] In order to develop this skill, we first need

---

4. You can find more about this in Kerry Muhlestein, *Insights and Inspirations from the Old Testament* (American Fork, UT: Covenant Communications,

to understand our greatest obligation under the covenant. That is to love God; it is to love God with everything we have and are.

If there is something we should learn from this being our greatest obligation, I believe it is this: the greatest obligation in the covenant demonstrates what the crux of the covenant is. The crux of the covenant is relationship. We cannot elaborate on this here, but the more I study the covenant, the more I realize that relationship is the governing principle and everything else in the covenant stems from there.[5]

First, it is about having a relationship with God. It is about loving God and Him loving us. We need to recognize why God wants a relationship with us, and that is because He is our Father and He loves us. The whole point of the Plan of Salvation is to enable us to have a closer relationship with Him, by being more like Him, and allowing us to have the joy that comes from Him, and from having that relationship with Him. President Russell M. Nelson taught us about this, "if we let God prevail in our lives, that covenant will lead us closer and closer to him. All covenants are intended to be binding. They create a relationship with everlasting ties."[6] Jenet Erikson taught, "We are deeply relational beings, designed not for independence, but for radical dependence and connection."[7] Our most important and meaningful connection is with God.

Let us remember that and go back to President Nelson's teachings, "Once you and I have made a covenant with God, our relationship with him becomes much closer than before our covenant. Now we are bound together. ... Each of us has a special place in God's heart. He has high hopes for us."[8] Think of that! Think of the hopes God has for each of us and the special place we have in God's heart because we are bound together. That is what the covenant is about.

2025), and Kerry Muhlestein, "Recognizing the Everlasting Covenant in the Scriptures," *Religious Educator*, 21, no. 2 (2020), 41–71.

5. See Kerry Muhlestein, *God Will Prevail: Ancient Covenants, Modern Blessings, and the Gathering of Israel* (American Fork, UT: Covenant Communications, 2021), 7; and Kerry Muhlestein, *The Easter Connection: Made Whole with God through Christ* (American Fork, UT: Covenant Communications, 2024).
6. Russell M. Nelson, "The Everlasting Covenant," *Liahona* (October 2022), 5.
7. Jenet Erickson, "Designed for Covenant Relationships," BYU Devotional, November 8, 2022, online at speeches.byu.edu.
8. Nelson, "The Everlasting Covenant," 6.

President Nelson also taught us that "making a covenant with God changes our relationship with Him forever. It blesses us with an extra measure of love and mercy. It affects who we are and how God will help us become what we can become."[9] That is beautiful. So, who are we? Well, we know that our primary identity should be that we are a child of God, and a child of the covenant, and a disciple of Christ. All of those come together in the Old Testament beautifully.

Hesed: *The Heart of the Covenant Relationship*

This special relationship and special love and mercy which President Nelson was talking about is *hesed*. *Hesed* is a Hebrew word that denotes a special loyalty and love available within the covenant. It is available because of the closer relationship.[10] It is not that God doesn't want to extend this to everyone. He does. In fact, He desperately wants to extend it to everyone. We are trying to get everyone on both sides of the veil to be part of the covenant, so they can have this special relationship with God.

Yet the fact of the matter is that there are some things that grow out of a deeper relationship that are not possible if that relationship is not created and nourished. *Hesed* might be the most important thing that grows out of that deeper relationship with God.

Isaiah speaks about it this way on behalf of God, "For the mountain shall depart, and the hills be removed, but my kindness shall not depart from thee, neither shall the covenant of my peace be removed from thee, sayeth the Lord that hath mercy on thee" (Isaiah 54:10).

Literally this passage reads that the Lord's *hesed* will not depart, no matter what. Isaiah is telling us that it is more likely the mountains pack up and leave than it is that God will stop having *hesed* with us. That is what *hesed* is, an unending loyalty that extends mercy and love to us.

In Jeremiah 31:3, the Lord says, "Yea, I have loved thee with an everlasting love. Therefore with lovingkindness [*hesed*], have I drawn thee." President Russell M. Nelson said, "*Hesed* is a special love and mercy that God feels for and extends to those who have made a cov-

---

9. Nelson, "The Everlasting Covenant," 10.
10. Muhlestein, *God Will Prevail,* 9–12.

enant with Him, and we reciprocate with *hesed* for Him."[11] That is beautiful, is it not?

That is about our relationship. Marriage is important and real, and at the same time, it is a symbol that teaches us about our covenant relationship with God. Within the relationship you create in marriage, there is bound to be greater love and loyalty than outside of that relationship. That is what happens in a covenant relationship with God.

Our second great covenantal obligation is to love our neighbor as ourselves. That is also about relationships. When you remember that, and read the Old Testament with this lens — that God is trying to help us have and deepen our relationship with Him and with each other, and that this is the point of everything that's going on in the Old Testament — then you will start to draw more out of the Old Testament.

A Summary of Covenant Blessings

If we are going to start to see the Old Testament through a covenant lens, then we must briefly summarize, at a 30,000 foot view, the blessings and obligations of the covenant. The most salient elements for our purposes are:

1. Have a higher relationship with God.
2. This allows us to prosper.
3. Then we need a place to prosper, so we must have a land to prosper in.
4. Once we're prospering, people want to take the gains of prosperity from us, so God will protect us.
5. With all of this in place, we can support having huge posterity.
6. Finally God will gather us and our posterity to Him.
7. Eventually that gathering will be into a fully unified relationship with Him. We can call that exaltation.

If we remember these key high-level points, they create a lens that allows us to see the covenant in the scriptures. Applying this lens will cause us to see covenant everywhere in scriptures. It radically changes the depth that we can gain from the Old Testament.

Looking for Covenant Promises

President Russell M. Nelson once made an invitation:

---

11. Nelson, "Everlasting Covenant," 6.

> As you study your scriptures during the next six months, I encourage you to make a list of all that the Lord has promised He will do for covenant Israel. I think you will be astounded. Ponder these promises. Talk about them with your family and friends. Then live and watch for these promises to be fulfilled in your own life.[12]

That is a fantastic lens to use in your study of the Old Testament this year: look for the promises extended to Israel. If you begin to recognize what they are, start to list them, or talk about how they work in your life, on its own, that lens will help you gather more out of the Old Testament than almost anything else you can do.

The Covenant Corruption Cycle

It will also be helpful to look at the covenant cycles we will see in the Old Testament. What happens when we do not keep the covenant? You do not just fail to receive the covenant blessings. Instead, God will reverse those blessings. In the Old Testament, that is called a covenant cursing. When we think of covenant cursings — or covenant reversals — we realize that those who break the covenant do not just experience the absence of prosperity, they experience destitution. They do not simply fail to have numerous posterity, they lose even the posterity which they have, and become small.

The Lord reverses covenant blessings when the covenant is broken. Why? Just as he taught Hosea, He does this so that we will recognize how much we need Him and return to Him.

I refer to this as the covenant corruption cycle. Sometimes, it is called the pride cycle, or the idolatry cycle. This cycle can be seen in all of scripture, and has different manifestations in different countries, cultures, and nations. Still, in the end, it is always about the covenant. When we are not keeping the covenant, we keep corrupting it, and then we just keep spinning down and up, down and up. As we examine the scriptures with the covenant lens on, we will see that cycle repeated in every era and clime.

Recognizing Covenant Phrases

If you look for covenant phrases, you will also better see and understand the covenant in the Old Testament. These phrases stem

---

12. Russell M. Nelson, "Let God Prevail," *Ensign* (November 2020), 95.

from the blessings listed above. They are a shorthand for letting the reader know that the writer is speaking about the covenant. When a reader recognizes a phrase that alludes to, or evokes one of the blessings, or its corresponding cursing, that reader will realize that the writer is referring to the covenant.

For example, anytime God or any of the prophets use the phrase "my people" or "His people," we are witnessing the primary way God speaks about His covenant relationship with His children. If a reader takes note of phrases about someone being God's people, or His being their God, that reader can be sure that they are reading a covenant passage.

Similarly, when we read about multiplying, making it so Israel has more seed, or that Israel is prospering or being protected by God, or anything along those lines, we should recognize that the writer is talking about the covenant. When we read about a promised land, we are reading about the covenant.

It may be helpful to look at one example.

Most readers have probably heard the commandment "Thou shalt honor thy Father and thy mother" (Exodus 20:12). They may even remember the associated promise or blessing with that command: "that thy days may be long in the land which the Lord thy God giveth thee." I hope that by now you recognize what we just read.

In essence, the command is associated with the covenant promise of keeping the promised land. This means that when God gave that commandment, He was making a specific reference to the covenant. This means that we have just encountered a shorthand phrase for saying, "honor your father and your mother so that I can give you all the covenant blessings." This is what happens when we read the Old Testament with a covenant lens. It changes even little things like this basic commandment. It doesn't mean we shouldn't ask why that specific phrase was used. It means that we should examine both why the specific covenant promise of having a long life in a promised land will happen from keeping this commandment, and simultaneously we should think about how this commandment is part of the covenant and how covenant blessings flow from keeping that commandment.

Similarly, when God speaks about conquering others, or being protected from being conquered, those are covenant phrases. We should recognize that the Lord is talking about the covenant. When

He says, "Come return to me" or "return to the covenant," obviously, then he is talking about the covenant.

I once collected and published as many examples as I could find of any variations of the phrase "my people," "thy people," or "His people" in the scriptures. There were eight-and-a-half pages of a summary of God talking about doing something for His people.[13] It was amazing.

In fact, as I was reading it for the audio version, it was a day where I just learned about some terrible things that had happened to a dear loved one and terrible things that that loved one had done. It was a depressing day, one of the worst days of my life — probably the worst day of my life at that point. Then I went and read these blessings, and it became a tremendously wonderful and comforting experience. I no longer feared for my loved one after reading all the blessings and mercies that God was promising that loved one, and it came because I recognized the covenant phrases from God saying, "We are His people."

After collecting passages that used the phrase "my people," I looked for what was being most often spoken about in connection with that phrase. The concept most strongly associated with being God's people was that of redemption. There is something powerful just in that realization, is there not? Do you see the kinds of things that can happen when you start to recognize covenant phrases in the scriptures? It is a powerful lens.

Examples of Covenant Language in Scripture

A few more examples will be illustrative. When Isaiah says that we need to "enlarge our tents and strengthen our stakes" (Isaiah 54:2), what he is saying is we must do that because suddenly we are going to have a multitude of children.

If we read the whole context of that verse, Isaiah is teaching that, at some future point, Israel will have a more numerous offspring than they had before. As a result, Israel will need a larger tent in which to live. When viewed through a covenant lens, and recognizing that numerous posterity is a covenant blessing, we realize that what Isaiah is really saying is, "At this point I am pouring covenant blessings out upon you because you are keeping the covenant."

---

13. Kerry Muhlestein, *Finding Promised Blessings on the Covenant Path* (American Fork, UT: Covenant Communications, 2023), 16–28.

Another example of Isaiah's use of covenant phrases is one that people often mistake for something else. Isaiah says, "Woe unto those who build houses one close to another" (Isaiah 5:8). When I was younger, I thought this meant that God really did not like duplexes or apartment buildings. This was woefully wrong. Instead, if you read the whole passage, Isaiah is saying, "You had built many houses, one next to another, because you had such numerous offspring. But now they will be desolate. No one will live in them."

This is a way of saying that instead of the covenant blessing of a large posterity, Israel would experience the covenant cursing of having a very small posterity. When you recognize this, you realize what He's saying is, "Woe unto you because you were experiencing covenant blessings, and then you broke the covenant, so now you're not receiving those blessings."

Conclusion: All Lenses on the Gathering of Israel

Summing up may best be done by looking at one final thing. We have looked at the blessings promised for covenant keepers, but here we will carefully examine a specific illustrative set. In the list of promised covenantal blessings, the combination of a specific set is important. Having a higher relationship with God, prospering, having a promised land, having innumerable posterity, and receiving *hesed* from God, combine to mean that when Israel strays, God will gather them. Elsewise said, when God scatters Israel for breaking the covenant, because He has promised them these blessings, He will gather them if they will consent to return to Him.

This means that the scattering and gathering of Israel is one of the lenses we should always have on when reading the Old Testament. We will best understand and apply this lens if we combine all the other lenses we have talked about. If we come to understand the nature of God, and look at the whole story, see and understand symbols — especially symbolic actions — and recognize covenant language, we start to see promises and examples of gathering throughout every layer of the Old Testament.

Perhaps we can see this best from a big picture view of the gathering.

God scattered the Northern tribes in about 720 BC. It would be easy to think that this is the end of their story, but if we look at the big picture we see that it is not. God promised a gathering, and He began that gathering in about 1830 AD, when the Book of Mormon was published and the Church was organized. This represents a 2,500 year cycle.

If it takes God 2,500 years to bring Israel back to Him, then that is what it takes. God is not daunted by the timeline, He plays the long game and takes as much time as works best. Looking at the gathering this way helps us recognize that the story is not over yet; God is continuing to work with us. He will gather Israel in, even if it takes Him 2,500 years. He will work with us for 2,500 years if necessary, because that is how long it took to humble Israel to the point where they were willing to return to Him. Their story is symbolically yours as a covenant holder, and the covenant mercy He extends to the entire House of Israel is applied to you as a covenant holder.

That is the story of the Old Testament. That is putting on enough interpretive lenses that we are able to draw out of the Old Testament some of the power that God wants us to get out of it.

This is an edited transcript of the presentation, broadcast on October 9, 2025.

2

THE OLD TESTAMENT WITHIN THE EXPANDED LATTER-DAY SAINT CANON

INTERPRETIVE STRAITJACKET OR PARACHUTE?

T. BENJAMIN SPACKMAN

Does modern revelation force believers into a corner, binding them to literal interpretations of ancient texts, or does it offer a rescue from such rigidity? Common assumptions often treat scripture as a static "divine encyclopedia" wherein nothing more than a surface reading is necessary to understand it. This approach, inherited from nineteenth-century Protestantism, effectively turns the expanded canon into an interpretive "straitjacket," creating conflicts with historical and scientific reality. However, a careful examination of Restoration scripture and history reveals a different pattern: revelation as a dynamic, ongoing process involving active human participation. By embracing the principles of divine accommodation, historical context, and the reality of human error within prophetic writings, the text shifts from a source of dogmatic restriction to a flexible tool for navigating complexity. Rather than demanding adherence to impossible literalism, modern revelation functions as a "parachute," allowing for a faithful, intellectually honest engagement with the Old Testament that honors both its divine inspiration and its human origins.

When it comes to understanding ancient scripture, does modern revelation — both our expanded canon beyond the Bible as well as the interpretive *magisterium*[1] of Church leaders — function more as

---

1. That is, Latter-day Saints reject *sola scriptura*; Church leaders collectively — not individually — make authoritative interpretations of scripture binding on the Saints. See T. Benjamin Spackman, "LDS Bible Scholar: We Don't Play by Protestant Rules," *Keystone* podcast, hosted by David Snell, 30 September

a straitjacket, binding us to difficult Old Testament interpretations? For example, could modern revelation commit us to young-earth creationism or the strict Mosaic authorship of Genesis? Or does modern revelation function more like a parachute, something to help us out of interpretive crises and difficult passages of the Old Testament? In this article, I argue in favor of the parachute model, which entails an understanding of several aspects of Latter-day Saint history, teachings, and assumptions about the nature of revelation, scripture, and interpretation.

In 1958, quoting the late President Anthony W. Ivins, President Hugh B. Brown said that "it is our misinterpretation of the word of the Lord that leads us into trouble."[2] If true, then the practical question we should be asking ourselves is, "How do we avoid misinterpreting scripture?"

The answer begins, as with many Sacrament meeting talks, with defining our terms. We will start with "interpretation." Interpretation is nothing more than attributing *meaning* to the text; what you think it means, what you think the author was trying to say to some ancient audience. It is important to understand that we are all interpreting all the time; it is impossible *not* to interpret, though we can do so more consciously and carefully.

We all bring different assumptions, knowledge, and background to the scriptural text when we are interpreting, and those things shape our understanding. Ofttimes, when we find ourselves disagreeing with someone else about a scripture, it is because we are each bringing different assumptions, knowledge, or experiences to the scriptural text. Learning to recognize what we have brought, and how it shapes our understanding is an important part of responsible interpretation.

Assumptions and conceptions are all the more powerful because they are implicit, invisible, or taken for granted; it is why we call them "assumptions." Our unconscious inheritance of them makes them more difficult to identify and evaluate. They are the intellectual air we breathe, and the conceptual water we swim in.

There are two key assumptions that will result in very different interpretations, which will be our initial focus. These are: (1) the

---

2024, online at keystonelds.com.
2. Hugh B. Brown, "What is Man and What May He Become?" in *The Instructor* 93, no. 6, (June 1958): 174.

nature of scripture and (2) how we ought to understand its original prophetic message, i.e. by what approach or method, if any.

Assumptions: The Nature of Scripture

Setting aside questions of "mistranslation" (per the Eighth Article of Faith), does scripture represent one single perspective or multiple?

If scripture represents a single divine perspective, it entails that prophets function, in essence, as divine scribes who contribute little themselves; it gives us a concept of scripture as univocal — God's perspective — scripture as quasi-inerrant encyclopedia of static eternal truths of doctrine, history, and science.

I term this the "divine encyclopedia" model.

On the other hand, is scripture authored from a divinely inspired but human perspective?

If so, scripture would be multi-vocal, as it would partially reflect the perspectives of prophets in their own time, place, culture, language, and degree of knowledge. If this is our assumption, then we operate with a concept of scripture which allows for multiple perspectives; line-upon-line, progressive revelation; expanding and correcting partial or incomplete truths; and cultural assumptions.

We might call this the "inspired human author" model of scripture.

Assumptions: The Nature of Interpretation

How ought we to understand scripture? What method, if any, puts us into the mindset of the prophetic author or ancient audience, or is that not important? How accessible is its original meaning(s), as intended by its prophetic authors or editors?

Let us make explicit here that Christian and Jewish history acknowledged at least four kinds of interpretation that could co-exist with each other,[3] and Latter-day Saints at least two: original meaning and a personal spiritual meaning of application. This has been discussed profitably in the *Church News*,[4] and President Dallin H. Oaks

---

3. In Christian terms, these were the *tropological, allegorical, anagogical,* and *literal*, the latter referring to the historical/contextual authorial-intended meaning. See Alister E. McGrath, *Reformation Thought*, 4th ed. (Wiley Blackwell, 2012), 103–105.
4. Aubrey Eyre, "2 BYU religion professors weigh in on why 'Come, Follow Me'

acknowledges this duality. "Scripture is not limited to what it meant when it was written, but may also include what that scripture means to a reader today."[5]

Our interest here lies not in the inspired personal meanings which may vary for each individual, but in that meaning that originates from the inspired scriptural authors. When introducing "Come, Follow Me" in the *Church News* in 2019, BYU professor Gaye Strathearn taught that Latter-day Saints need both:

> Noting the importance of understanding the context in which the scriptures were written and the intentions behind what was included by their authors, Strathearn explained that a two-fold interpretation is necessary to increase spiritual and practical understanding of the scriptures and their doctrines. … [Readers] need to understand how to interpret the text 1) according to the text itself — including the authors who wrote it — as well as 2) interpret the text in a way that is personal and applies to them currently as individuals and families.[6]

The focus of this paper is not to instruct on spiritual likening and personal application, but original meaning. Some assume that *that* meaning of scripture is plain and self-evident, immediately accessible to all sincere seekers at face-value, even through translation, after thousands of years, and without any real need for context(s). I term this "plain reading." This approach represents a very democratic and populist way of reading, because it makes scripture — again, the original meaning, at least — accessible to all equally; on the other hand, it also represents a very decontextualized approach which fails to understand the nature of communication.

In our daily chats, texts, emails, and Sunday sermons, the speaker and audience share a time, place, culture, language, situation, and very often, worldview. Because they share those things, much is assumed between the two and can go without being said.[7] Gaps and unstated

---

should be just the beginning of your gospel study," *Church News*, 25 February 2019, online at thechurchnews.com.
5. Dallin H. Oaks, "Scripture Reading and Revelation," *Ensign* (January 1995): 8.
6. Eyre, "2 BYU religion professors weigh in," online at thechurchnews.com.
7. See E. Randolph Richards and Brandon J. O'Brien, *Misreading Scripture with Western Eyes: Removing Cultural Blinders to Better Understand the Bible* (Downers Grove, IL: IVP Press, 2013) and E. Randolph Richards and Richard James, *Misreading Scripture with Individualist Eyes: Patronage, Honor, and*

framings or facts are filled in from the shared cognitive environment. "Plain reading" assumes that nothing that went "without being said" was necessary for communication. Indeed, "plain reading" assumes that everything necessary for understanding was recorded, and assumes further that those other elements do not significantly shape the message. What God used to inspire Moses, Paul, or Nephi (or even Joseph Smith) was so universal and non-specific in content that we can understand it today, exactly the same way, merely by reading the words in English. The problem is that "plain reading" tends to fill in the scriptural gaps — what went without being said — with *modern* assumptions and *modern* knowledge, not those shared between ancient speaker and audience. This innocently "wrests scripture" by unintentionally recontextualizing it as a modern text, not an ancient one.

The alternative to "plain reading" acknowledges the necessity of recovering unstated contexts, stepping outside our own cultural assumptions and knowledge to try to see through ancient eyes; original meaning entails attention to unstated contexts, careful attention to history, and translation. I term this "contextual reading."

The Intellectual Milieu of the Restoration and Its Effects on Latter-day Saint Assumptions

In 1830, every member of the Church, including Joseph Smith, was a convert. Any returned missionary knows that emerging from the waters of baptism does not entail some kind of memory-wipe and Matrix-like download of the *Gospel Principles* manual. Rather, the convert's preexisting assumptions, beliefs, and cultural norms are likely to remain, now with the overlay of whatever Gospel teachings they have internalized.

In 1830, most converts came from a conservative American Protestant background, and similarly brought their preexisting assumptions, beliefs, frameworks, and cultural norms with them. This intellectual inheritance included both general ideas about the nature of scripture and interpretation as well as specific interpretations of passages and their implications. Two of these common to nineteenth-century

---

Shame in the Biblical World (Downers Grove, IL: IVP Academic, 2020) for good discussion of this.

American Protestants carried over into Latter-day Saint thought, such as that Africans were descended from Cain and thus cursed with black skin and slavery, and that the Roman Catholic Church constituted the "whore of all the earth" or "Church of the Devil."

With these invisibly-inherited conceptions absorbed by some Latter-day Saints, it is not surprising that some found these inherited interpretations "confirmed" by their reading of the the Book of Mormon and Pearl of Great Price. Later, more careful reading of these passages, which the Church has published, would demonstrate that scripture did not actually fit those inherited views.[8] This intellectual inheritance also included more abstract ideas, such as conceptions of the nature of scripture and its interpretation. Because of the strongly American Protestant context of the Restoration, Latter-day Saints inherited a tendency towards both the "divine encyclopedia" model of scripture and the "plain reading" model of interpretation.

Fortunately, a number of Latter-day Saint scholars have explicitly identified some of these tendencies and inherited assumptions.[9] Gordon Irving notes that today these ideas would likely be termed "fundamentalist," a loaded and shifting term that requires some unpacking.[10] In a 2014 blogpost titled "The Next Generation's Faith Crisis," Latter-day Saint biblical scholar Julie Smith identified nine assumptions still common to Latter-day Saints.[11] Note how these express aspects of the "divine encyclopedia" and "plain reading" models.

---

8. For example, on the Catholic issue, Stephen E. Robinson corrected the misreading of 1 Nephi 13–14 in "Warring Against the Saints of God," *Ensign* (January 1988): 34–39. A longer version appeared as "Early Christianity and 1 Nephi 13–14," in *The Book of Mormon: First Nephi, The Doctrinal Foundation*, ed. Monte S. Nyman and Charles D. Tate Jr. (Provo, UT: Religious Studies Center, Brigham Young University, 1988),177–191. On the race issue, see the relevant Gospel Topics essays on the website for The Church of Jesus Christ of Latter-day Saints, churchofjesuschrist.org
9. See especially Philip Barlow, *Mormons and the Bible: The Place of the Latter-day Saints in American Religion*, updated ed. (New York: Oxford University Press, 2013).
10. Gordon Irving, "The Mormons and the Bible in the 1830s," *BYU Studies* 13, no. 4 (1973): 1–14.
11. Julie M. Smith, "The Next Generation's Faith Crisis," *Times & Seasons* blog, 31 October 2014, online at archive.timesandseasons.org.

1. The doctrine taught in the scriptures has always been the same throughout history.
2. Writers of scripture and other church leaders have always taught exactly the same doctrines.
3. The simple, surface meaning of the text is the correct one
4. The text as you read it reflects precisely how it was originally written.
5. There is no historical, cultural, or literary background that you need in order to understand the text.
6. Every detail of the scriptures is literally, historically true and accurate.
7. The same word always means the same thing in the scriptures.
8. The author and date commonly attributed to the book in question are always accurate.
9. Nothing in the Bible reflects the cultural biases of the authors.

Many Latter-day Saints have transferred the unwittingly inherited Protestant ideas of inerrant inspiration from the Bible onto modern prophets and modern revelation. Some are prone to mock Evangelicals who say "God said it, I believe it, that settles it." Unfortunately, some of us then turn around and say, "Well of course the *Bible* hasn't been 'translated correctly' but modern revelation says it, I believe it, that settles it." Those who do so are embodying the "fundamentalist" assumptions enumerated by Barlow, Irving, and Smith: the "divine encyclopedia" and "plain reading" approaches. Such was the Restoration's intellectual inheritance.

On the basis of Church publications and teachings, I argue that the position of the Church is that scriptures are written from inspired human perspectives, and that historical, cultural, and literary contexts are necessary to understand their original message. This position implicitly rejects the "divine encyclopedia" and "plain reading" approaches. Understanding that this is the Church's model frees us from difficult and restrictive interpretive positions (the "straitjacket") and offers ways to accept scripture as inspired without inherited so-called "fundamentalist" assumptions. As we closely study modern revelation, we shed that inheritance for the restored truths about the nature of scripture and interpretation that will emerge. This is wonderfully liberating, and provides a "parachute" as we approach the sometimes difficult and controversial Old Testament and its related issues in modern revelation.

The history of Latter-day Saint interpretation has been traced elsewhere, and I do not intend to do so here.[12] Rather, I wish to emphasize two things in summary.

First, that historical diversity of interpretations and perspectives among Latter-day Saint leadership (and scholars) has not always been widely known. Often the most "literal" approach — for example, "divine encyclopedia" and "plain reading" — has come to dominate common understandings. Elder Paul V. Johnson, while serving as Commissioner of Church Education, alluded to that diversity as well as to the dominance of certain strains of thought which evinced strong but unjustified certainty.

> Many of us have a difficult time dealing with ambiguity, especially in issues concerning the Church. In fact, we may be drawn to use quotes in our teaching that are definitive because they seem to dispel the ambiguity. But some quotes are definitive on issues where there is no official answer. People who are more tentative on a subject that hasn't been revealed or resolved don't get quoted as much, but may be more in line with where our current knowledge is.[13]

Second, that "current knowledge," or the current teachings of the Church regarding the nature of scripture and interpretation, is represented by the printed manuals, magazines, and other materials which are approved and distributed. To that end, I will quote or reference them extensively. In a number of cases, they follow Elder Johnson's guidance in acknowledging the uncertainty and complexity

---

12. See, for example, the previously cited works of Barlow, *Mormons and the Bible*; Irving, "Mormons and the Bible in the 1830s"; and Smith, "Next Generation's Faith Crisis." See also T. Benjamin Spackman, "(No) Death Before the Fall?: The Basis and Twentieth-Century History of Interpretation," in *The Restored Gospel of Jesus Christ and Evolution*, ed. Jamie L. Jensen, Steven L. Peck, Ugo A. Perego, and T. Benjamin Spackman (Provo, UT: College of Life Sciences, Brigham Young University, 2025), 81–115; T. Benjamin Spackman, "'The Scientist is Wrong': Joseph Fielding Smith, George McCready Price, and the Ascent of Creationist Thinking among Latter-day Saints in the Twentieth Century" (PhD. diss, Claremont Graduate University, 2024).
13. Paul V. Johnson, "A Pattern for Learning Spiritual Things," *Religious Educator* 14, no. 3 (2013): 19.

of scripture, or tacitly moving away from some of the "overclaiming" of the past. Examining current Church teachings both demonstrates an embrace of the "inspired human author" and "contextual interpretation" and provides us with a number of useful principles to keep in mind.

Principles Learned from Studying Modern Revelation

I treat the first two principles together:

(1) Prophetic co-participation in revelation and (2) Revelation as an ongoing and partial process

These related ideas begin with a concept of revelation as involving the active participation of a human prophet, and that all revelation is going to be a divine-human composite; secondly, that revelation is an ongoing and partial process, as opposed to a once-for-all singular event.

According to BYU professor Grant Underwood, a close study of the Book of Commandments and Doctrine and Covenants reveals this:

> [Joseph's] revelations were not understood as infallible texts written in stone by the finger of God; they came instead through a finite and fallible prophet who, along with his associates, was not shorn of his humanity in exercising his prophetic office. Moreover, the revelation texts were not viewed as fixed and complete, beyond revision, but as articulations that could and should be updated to reflect the ongoing flow of revelation to the church.[14]

In a BYU-Hawaii devotional, Underwood acknowledged the role of assumptions and explained:

> some Latter-day Saints may assume that the Prophet was not involved in any way whatsoever with the wording of the revelation texts, that he simply repeated word for word to describe what he heard God say to him. But our investigation has suggested otherwise. We need to see Joseph as more than a mere human fax machine through whom God communicated,

---

14. Grant Underwood, "The Dictation, Compilation, and Canonization of Joseph Smith's Revelations," in *Foundational Texts of Mormonism: Examining Major Early Sources,* ed. Mark Ashurst-McGee, Robin Scott Jensen, and Sharalyn D. Howcroft (New York: Oxford University Press, 2018), 122.

finished revelation texts composed in heaven. Joseph had a role to play in the revelatory process.[15]

In an excellent article on the process of revelation, based on close study of the Doctrine and Covenants, Steven Harper notes that:

> Joseph knew better than anyone else that the words he dictated were *both human and divine,* the voice of God clothed in the words of his own limited, early American English vocabulary. He regarded himself as a revelator whose understanding accumulated over time. Joseph recognized as a result of the revelatory *process* that the texts of his revelations were not set in stone. Rather, he felt responsible to revise and redact them to reflect his latest understanding.[16]

Joseph updated and adapted his past revelations as he received new ones. There are examples of this throughout the Doctrine and Covenants, between Genesis, Moses, and Abraham,[17] as well as between the Book of Mormon and the Joseph Smith Translation of the Bible.

In every case, confusion as to these changes and differences stems from a failure to understand the nature of revelation, conceiving of it as an event disclosure of absolute information, not a partial and ongoing process. As Doctrine and Covenants scholar Robert Woodford pointed out in the *Ensign,*

> [A] correct understanding of the nature of the revelations the Prophet Joseph Smith received and how he updated them in light of continued revelation explains why many changes occurred. Indeed, each of the sections has been edited to some degree, demonstrating that Joseph Smith did not receive all

---

15. Grant Underwood, "Relishing the Revisions: Joseph Smith and the Revelatory Process," BYU Hawaii Devotional, 13 October, 2009, online at speeches.byuh.edu. Similar analysis from Underwood appears in "Revelation, Text, and Revision: Insight from the Book of Commandments and Revelations," *BYU Studies Quarterly* 48, no. 3 (2009): 67–84.
16. Steven C. Harper, "'That They Might Come to Understanding': Revelation as Process," in *You Shall Have My Word: Exploring the Text of the Doctrine and Covenants,* ed. Scott C. Esplin, Richard O. Cowan, and Rachel Cope (Provo, UT: Religious Studies Center, Brigham Young University; Salt Lake City: Deseret Book, 2012), 31. Emphasis added.
17. For a discussion on this topic, see T. Benjamin Spackman, "A Paradoxical Preservation of Faith: LDS Creation Accounts and the Composite Nature of Revelation," *FAIR* Conference Address, Provo, UT, August 2019, online at fairlatterdaysaints.org.

these revelations as word-for-word dictations from the Lord (although he may have received some this way).[18]

Similarly, as the first Latter-day Saint scholar to closely study the Joseph Smith Translation, Robert J. Matthews[19] concluded, in an *Ensign* article, that the JST

> was not a simple, mechanical recording of divine dictum, but rather a study-and-thought *process* accompanied and prompted by revelation from the Lord. That it was a revelatory *process* is evident from statements by the Prophet and others who were personally acquainted with the work.[20]

It is not merely orthodox Latter-day Saint *scholars* who have argued that revelation involves human participation and is more of a process than event. The Church has published ten principles for answering gospel questions, each with significant elaboration.[21] These are found in the *Topics and Questions* section online; since the Overview title is "Answering Gospel Questions," I will use that as the title when I reference one of these principles or sub-principles.[22] One of the core principles therein is an explanation of "Recogniz[ing] that Revelation is a Process."[23]

> It's easy to imagine that when God wants to communicate something, He simply reaches out to Church leaders to let them know. But the history of the Restoration demonstrates

---

18. Robert J. Woodford, "How the Revelations in the Doctrine and Covenants Were Received and Compiled," *Ensign* (January 1985): 27.
19. For his work, see Robert J. Matthews, *"A Plainer Translation": Joseph Smith's Translation of the Bible, A History and Commentary* (Provo, UT: Brigham Young University Press, 1975). On the significance and history of Matthews's work on the Joseph Smith translation of the Bible, see Thomas E. Sherry, "Robert J. Matthews and the RLDS Church's Inspired Version of the Bible," in *BYU Studies Quarterly* 9, no. 2 (2010): 93–119.
20. Robert J. Matthews, as quoted by David Rolph Seely, "The Joseph Smith Translation: 'Plain and Precious Things' Restored," *Ensign* (August 1997): 11, emphasis added.
21. Ryan Jensen, Guiding principles to help answer gospel questions," *Church News*, 16 December 2023, online at thechurchnews.com.
22. The Church of Jesus Christ of Latter-day Saints, "Answering Gospel Questions," *Topics and Questions,* online at churchofjesuschrist.org.
23. The Church of Jesus Christ of Latter-day Saints, "Recognize that Revelation is a Process," *Seeking Answers to Questions,* Topics and Questions, online at churchofjesuschrist.org.

that revelation is a process of seeking to know God's will and is most often received after pondering and pleading. ... While essential gospel truths are unchanging, the Church's policies, programs, organizations, and teachings have been revealed line upon line over months, years, and decades. And the process continues.

The existence of this ongoing process emerges clearly from studying the Book of Commandments, the Doctrine and Covenants, the Joseph Smith Translation, as well as the Book of Mormon and Pearl of Great Price. If modern-day revelation is a process, in which prophets co-participate in forming, shaping, and giving voice to that revelation, and this is true from Joseph Smith down to the present, how much more so of ancient prophets?

(3) Scripture typically speaks from inspired and accommodated human perspectives

The 2026 *Come, Follow Me* manual for the Old Testament explains clearly that we should expect the cultural embeddedness of a prophet to influence the message:

> Naturally, that story is told from a certain point of view — really, certain *points* of view. ... it's inevitable that a historical account will reflect the perspective of the person or group of people writing it. This perspective includes the writers' national or ethnic ties and their cultural norms and beliefs. Knowing this can help us understand that the writers and compilers of the historical books focused on certain details while leaving out others. They made certain assumptions that others would not have made. And they came to conclusions based on these details and assumptions. *We can even see different perspectives across the books of the Bible (and sometimes within the same book).* The more we're aware of these perspectives, the better we can understand.[24]

As for multiple perspectives, *Come, Follow Me* provides an example.

> You might think of the book of Proverbs as a collection of wise counsel from loving parents. ... But Proverbs is followed by the

---

24. The Church of Jesus Christ of Latter-day Saints, "Thoughts to Keep in Mind: The Historical Books in the Old Testament," in *Come, Follow Me — For Home and Church: Old Testament 2026* (Salt Lake City: The Church of Jesus Christ of Latter-day Saints, 2025), 141, emphasis added, online at churchofjesuschrist.org.

book of Ecclesiastes, which seems to say, "It's not that simple."... the two books look at life from different perspectives.[25]

We should expect to find human perspectives within scripture for several reasons. First, we naturally interpret and understand revelation from within our own frame of reference. In 1933, Elder Stephen L. Richards of the Quorum of the Twelve Apostles used this principle to explain parts of the Old Testament which reflected limited prophetic knowledge and culturally-influenced conceptions:

> What if Hebrew prophets, conversant with only a small fraction of the surface of the earth, thinking and writing in terms of their own limited geography and tribal relations did interpret [God] in terms of a tribal king and so limit His personality and the laws of the universe under His control to the dominion with which they were familiar? *Can any interpreter, even though he be inspired, present an interpretation and conception in terms other than those with which he has had experience and acquaintance? Even under the assumption that Divinity may manifest to the prophet higher and more exalted truths than he has ever before known and unfold to his spiritual eyes visions of the past, forecasts of the future and circumstances of the utmost novelty, how will the inspired man interpret?* Manifestly, I think, in the language he knows and in the terms of expression with which his knowledge and experience have made him familiar. So is it not therefore ungenerous, unfair and unreasonable to impugn the validity and the whole worth of the Bible merely because of the limited knowledge of astronomy and geography that its writers possessed?[26]

Second, God generally commands and communicates to us in ways we are culturally conditioned to expect; He Himself adopts and communicates on our level. This concept is called "accommodation," or sometimes — focusing on God coming down to the human level — "condescension." This idea runs replete throughout all our scriptures,

---

25. The Church of Jesus Christ of Latter-day Saints, "September 7–13: 'He Shall Direct Thy Paths': Proverbs 1–4; 15–16; 22; 31; Ecclesiastes 1–3; 11–12," in *Come, Follow Me — For Home and Church: Old Testament 2026* (Salt Lake City: The Church of Jesus Christ of Latter-day Saints, 2025), 246, online at churchofjesuschrist.org.
26. Elder Stephen L. Richards, "An Open Letter to College Students," *Improvement Era* 36, no. 8 (June 1933): 453, 484, emphasis added.

Latter-day Saint history, and broader Christian and Jewish history.[27] Elder Richard Holzapfel recently explained accommodation in an article in the *Liahona*. Alluding to 2 Nephi 31:3 and Doctrine and Covenants 1:24 (among other passages), he says that God

> speaks in the cultural context of the life and time of a person or people. He communicates according to their understanding. ... the Lord kindly condescends to communicate His will in their language and culture so He can instruct and succor them.[28]

One evangelical biblical scholar summarized the concept:

> Accommodation is God's adoption of the human audience's finite and fallen perspective. Its underlying conceptual assumption is that in many cases, God does not correct our mistake in human viewpoints, but merely assumes them in order to communicate with us.[29]

Similarly, the *Answering My Gospel Questions* manual alludes to accommodation in both ancient and modern times:

> Remember that God speaks to us according to our understanding. All human beings are shaped by culture: the beliefs, customs, languages, and values we share. Cultures vary greatly from place to place and over time. God's willingness to deliver revelation that speaks to us within our cultures and according to our understanding is a beautiful truth of the Restoration. Remembering this can help us approach the scriptures and the words of past prophets with humility. God spoke to the ancient Israelites according to their ancient near-Eastern understanding. He spoke to Joseph Smith using symbols and language from his 1800s American culture.[30] And

---

27. See the many examples in T. Benjamin Spackman, "Truth, Scripture, and Interpretation: Some Precursors to Reading Genesis," *FAIR* Conference Address, Provo, UT, August 2017, online at fairlatterdaysaints.org.
28. Richard Neitzel Holzapfel, "The Lord Guides His Church According to Our Language and Understanding," *Liahona* (August 2022): digital-only content, online at churchofjesuschrist.org.
29. Kenton L. Sparks, *God's Word in Human Words: An Evangelical Appropriation of Critical Biblical Scholarship* (Grand Rapids, MI: BakerAcademic, 2008), 230–231. See Spackman, "Truth, Scripture, and Interpretation" for other references.
30. For example, regarding the relationship between Freemasonry and the temple, a church history essay reads, "There are different ways of understanding the relationship between Masonry and the temple. Some Latter-day Saints point

God communicates to us today according to our own limited capacity in ways we can understand.[31]

For example, some modern readers tend to impose modern assumptions onto the text of Genesis 1, believing it to be reveal scientific facts and modern cosmology. However, scholarly research of its ancient Near Eastern and Israelite context has led us to understand that Genesis 1 does not reflect modern cosmology, nor was its purpose to be a "scientific" revelation. The Lord accommodated the common Near Eastern understanding of the physical cosmos in order to teach other principles. He assumes the ancient Near Eastern cosmology of a flat earth with a solid dome surrounded by the cosmic chaotic waters, in order to teach the Israelites important things about the nature of the cosmos, the nature of deity, and the nature of humans in relation to them.[32]

(4) Harmonization may distort understanding

We have a natural tendency to see our own understandings reflected in the scriptures. Given our principle of "restoration", Latter-day Saints, in particular, tend to read modern doctrinal understandings back-in to earlier texts. The competing principle of "line upon line" (as well as historical contextual study) suggests that, in

---

to similarities between the format and symbols of both the endowment and Masonic rituals and those of many ancient religious ceremonies as evidence that the endowment was a restoration of an ancient ordinance. *Others note that the ideas and institutions in the culture that surrounded Joseph Smith frequently contributed to the process by which he obtained revelation.* In any event, the endowment did not simply imitate the rituals of Freemasonry. Rather, Joseph's encounter with Masonry evidently served as a catalyst for revelation," emphasis added. See The Church of Jesus Christ of Latter-day Saints, "Masonry," *Church History Topics,* online at churchofjesuschrist.org.

31. The Church of Jesus Christ of Latter-day Saints, "Recognize that Revelation is a Process," online at churchofjesuschrist.org.
32. See Joshua M. Sears, "From Biology Major to Religion Professor: Personal Reflections on Evolution," in *The Restored Gospel of Jesus Christ and Evolution*, ed. Jamie L. Jensen, Steven L. Peck, Ugo A. Perego, and T. Benjamin Spackman (Provo, UT: College of Life Sciences, Brigham Young University, 2025), 23–46; Kyle R. Greenwood, "When Worlds Collide: Scripture and Cosmology in Historical Perspective," in *The Restored Gospel of Jesus Christ and Evolution*, 49–59; Avram R. Shannon, "The Genesis Creation Account in Its Ancient Context," in *The Restored Gospel of Jesus Christ and Evolution*, 61–75.

some cases, reading past scripture through current lenses may well distort the past.

The recent *Scripture Helps: Old Testament* manual says that

> Because we live in a very different world from the people who wrote the Old Testament, we might mistakenly apply our own modern views and cultural standards to what we are reading. This can lead to misunderstandings. Make an effort to see what you are reading from the perspective of the inspired authors in their original context.[33]

Answering Gospel Questions also cautions against assuming the status quo was present in the past.

> When we study the past, we sometimes find that practices, teachings, and ideas we thought were unchanging have actually changed quite a bit. Core principles of the gospel are eternal, but the ways they are understood and expressed over time reflect the line upon line nature of revelation and the constant change of human culture. The principle of continuing revelation helps us navigate these changes.[34]

The Book of Mormon offers two examples. From close reading, it appears both that the idea of a Messiah who would save *the world*, and the existence of a Satan-like, fallen angel figure, were not commonly understood among the Israelites. Lehi receives a distinct revelation of the first (1 Nephi 1: 8 onwards, but especially v. 19), and the second comes from his reading of Isaiah (2 Nephi 2:17).[35] Neither teaching seems to stem from inheritance of a common Israelite understanding at Lehi's time. Should we take Lehi's understanding, or our current understandings, and then assume they were all present throughout the entire Old Testament period? This does not seem warranted.

---

33. The Church of Jesus Christ of Latter-day Saints, "Studying the Old Testament," *Scripture Helps: Introduction*, Scripture Helps: Old Testament (Salt Lake City: The Church of Jesus Christ of Latter-day Saints, 2025), IX, online at churchofjesuschrist.org.
34. The Church of Jesus Christ of Latter-day Saints, "Work to Understand the Past," *Seeking Answers to Questions,* Topics and Questions, online at churchofjesuschrist.org.
35. Scripture Central, "Why Did Lehi 'Suppose' the Existence of Satan?" *KnoWhy* 43, 29 February 2016, online at scripturecentral.org.

(5) Scripture is not inerrant

Latter-day Saints rarely use the term "inerrant." However, many of us have inherited inerrantist instincts, particularly regarding Latter-day Saint prophets and modern scripture.[36] Against this inherited impulse, note in general how current manuals and teachings speak about this. From *Come, Follow Me*, "in addition to being limited to a particular perspective, scriptural histories are subject to human error." Indeed,

> the inspired word of God, even though — like any work of God transmitted through mortals — [is] subject to human imperfections. ... The words of Moroni, referring to the sacred Book of Mormon record that he helped compile, are helpful here: "If there are faults they are the mistakes of men; wherefore, condemn not the things of God" (title page of the Book of Mormon). In other words, a book of scripture doesn't need to be free from human error to be the word of God.[37]

Answering My Gospel Questions notes that, while we tend to focus on the positive, we need to

> remember that humans make mistakes. When we tell stories from Church history, we tend to focus on heroic actions and happy endings. It is good to remember people when they were at their best. But we sometimes forget that Latter-day Saints of the past, including early Church leaders, were human beings. Human beings have weaknesses. They make mistakes. They sin. Remember that God uses imperfect people to accomplish His work. We can learn from both their contributions and their mistakes.[38]

We presume scripture is illustrating the ideal, providing models to follow, which Matthew Schlimm calls the "searching for saints" model.[39] (We thus get confused when we see those saintly role models

---

36. Spackman, "Paradoxical Preservation of Faith," online at fairlatterdaysaints.org.
37. The Church of Jesus Christ of Latter-day Saints, "Thoughts to Keep in Mind: Reading the Old Testament," in *Come, Follow Me — For Home and Church: Old Testament 2026* (Salt Lake City: The Church of Jesus Christ of Latter-day Saints, 2025), 11, online at churchofjesuschrist.org.
38. The Church of Jesus Christ of Latter-day Saints, "Work to Understand the Past," *Seeking Answers to Questions,* Topics and Questions, online at churchofjesuschrist.org.
39. Matthew Richard Schlimm, *This Strange and Sacred Scripture: Wrestling with the Old Testament and Its Oddities* (Grand Rapids, MI: BakerAcademic,

doing unsaintly things.) John J. Collins similarly notes "a common but ill-founded assumption that all Scripture should be edifying," that is, positive and uplifting.[40]

Whereas Mormon and Moroni sometimes insert themselves into the text via asides with a "thus we see," the Old Testament will hold up negative examples without explicitly identifying them as such. It tends to highlight these through other, more subtle, means which often do not survive translation.

Another important facet is this; humans have no option but to rely on their own limited human understanding unless and until God provides something more. Elder John A. Widtsoe spelled out what this entailed for scripture:

> When inspired writers deal with historical incidents they relate that which they have seen or that which may have been told them, unless indeed the past is opened to them by revelation.[41]

Elder Widtsoe's paradigm acknowledges the human positionality of the writer. Though inspired, a prophet's sources of knowledge remain limited to the human realm — reason, tradition, observation, culture, experience — unless God intervenes with revelation.

This applies to several Book of Mormon connections to Old Testament interpretation. For example, Nephi refers to both the "Books of Moses" and "Five Books of Moses." Is this proof that Moses both wrote Genesis through Deuteronomy and that the current text of those books is the same text which Nephi had? Does modern revelation "confirm" this?

Unless one assumes that Nephi had an unrecorded revelation on this topic, or speaks directly out of God's omniscience, this constitutes overclaiming. Nephi was hundreds of years removed from Moses. In absence of revelation, he serves as a witness only to a tradition in his time and place of Mosaic attribution, not Mosaic authorship.

The 2026 *Come, Follow Me* manual follows the Bible Dictionary in carefully stating that "These books, which are attributed to Moses, probably passed through the hands of numerous scribes and compil-

---

2015), 46.
40. John J. Collins, *Introduction to the Hebrew Bible* (Minneapolis: Fortress Press, 2004), 90.
41. John A. Widtsoe, *Evidences and Reconciliations*, arr. G. Homer Durham (Salt Lake City: Bookcraft, Inc., 1960), 127.

ers over time."[42] Nephi is a relevant data point, but not the dispositive proof sometimes claimed.

Nephi told his brothers that Moses "truly spake unto the waters of the Red Sea and they divided hither and thither, and our fathers came through, out of captivity, on dry ground, and the armies of Pharaoh did follow and were drowned in the waters of the Red Sea."

Was Nephi a direct witness to the parting of the Red Sea? No, he lived much later. Once again, Nephi is a datapoint for the existence of a particular Exodus tradition in his own time, circa 600 BC, but not a direct witness himself. Roughly speaking, Nephi was as far removed from Moses and the Exodus as we are today from the Crusades[43] or the Black Plague. His witness is not sufficient evidence to prove the recounted historicity of the Exodus, at least as it appears in our Old Testament today.

Alma the Younger referred to "the flood ... in the days of Noah" (Alma 10:22). Does this prove the reality of a worldwide flood or the historicity of Genesis 6–9? Again, the operative question is, does a prophet inherently and inevitably speak out of divine omniscience? If not, then Alma was reliant on his tradition, what he had seen and heard. Living roughly 600 years after Nephi, Alma was at an even greater remove from this earlier scriptural narrative. He apparently had a tradition like our current Genesis story, though — living in the Americas circa 82 BC — he is at a significant geographical, linguistic, chronological, and cultural remove from it.

This passage may be a witness for the presence of a flood tradition in the Book of Mormon, but it cannot witness directly to anything about Genesis or the flood itself. Alma was certainly not an eyewitness to a global flood, only a witness to an Israelite tradition in 600 BC, as passed down orally or written through Nephite cultural lines for 200 years. Can we accept the Book of Mormon as historical and inspired and still read Genesis 6–9 differently? It would seem so.

In Ether 13, Moroni summarizes some of Ether's teachings and refers offhandedly to "when the waters receded off of this land" (Ether 13:2). Many have assumed that this too is a reference to the Genesis flood, in which case the above reasoning equally applies. However,

---

42. The Church of Jesus Christ of Latter-day Saints, "Pentateuch," *Bible Dictionary*, online at churchofjesuschrist.org.
43. At least, the Fourth Crusade in 1204 AD.

note that the phrase "waters receding off this land" immediately follows mention of "the beginning of man."

Given that both Genesis 1 and other ancient Near Eastern cosmogonies begin with land emerging from cosmic waters, it is possible that the "waters receding" refers not to the waters of the flood of Noah, but rather that it was "a choice land above all other lands" from the beginning of creation, from when land first emerged from the cosmic waters.

Regarding Mosaic authorship, the Exodus and Red Sea, and the Genesis flood, the Book of Mormon authors do not seem to "have the past opened to them by revelation" (per Elder Widtsoe) on these questions, and to use them as proof in our understanding of the Old Testament interpretation relies on an assumption scripture as "divine encyclopedia."

(6) Past Scripture was Addressed to Past People, so Past Context is Crucial for Modern Readers

If God, per accommodation, speaks to people in their time, place, and circumstance, in a way they can understand, then it follows that later readers of the record of that interaction need to try to understand that time, place, and circumstance; otherwise they risk reading through modern lenses and distorting the past.

Biblical scholar John Walton expresses this pithily; scripture might be *for* us, but it was not *to* us. That is, we can certainly profit from it and be inspired by it, but we are not the primary intended audience. He writes,

> the theological message of the Bible was communicated to people who lived in the ancient Near Eastern world. If we desire to understand the theological message of the text, we will benefit by positioning it within the worldview of the ancient world rather than simply applying our own cultural perspectives.[44]

Sidney Sperry, one of the first Latter-day Saints to earn an Old Testament-related doctoral degree expressed a very similar idea in the *Ensign*:

---

44. John Walton, "Creation," in *Dictionary of the Old Testament: Pentateuch*, IVP Bible Dictionary Series, 8 vols., ed. T. Desmond Alexander and David W. Baker (Downers Grove, IL: IntervarsityPress, 2003), 1:156.

> [W]e ofttimes read our Bible as though its peoples were... American and interpret their sayings in terms of our own background and psychology. But the Bible is actually [a Near Eastern] book. It was written centuries ago by [Near Eastern] people and primarily for [Near Eastern] people.[45]

In 1945, *The Instructor* — paraphrasing President John Taylor — said, "The Bible was written for the people of its day. ... Isaiah, Ezekiel, etc. had revelations for themselves, *not us*."[46] Today, the 2026 *Come, Follow Me* manual reminds us that

> people today aren't the primary audience of the Old Testament prophets. Those prophets had immediate concerns they were addressing in their time and place — just as our latter-day prophets address our immediate concerns today. ... when you read ancient prophecies, it can help to learn about the context in which they were written.[47]

Just as General Conference talks of the 1910s largely spoke *to* the issues and *in* the American cultural idiom of that time, so, too, did Jeremiah's preaching in the seventh century BC, addressed issues of the seventh century in the cultural idiom of their time.

Context is key to understanding how the original audience would have heard God's prophets. "You can find meaningful insights about a scripture if you consider its context — the circumstances or setting of the scripture."[48] Many manuals have emphasized the role of context; for Doctrine and Covenants, the Church provided an entire volume, *Revelations in Context: The Stories Behind the Sections of the Doctrine and Covenants*, which states in its preface:

> [I]n many cases, the Doctrine and Covenants contains only half of the dialogue. ... [and] does not contain the stories behind the revelations. ... While the section headings ...

---

45. Sidney B. Sperry, "Hebrew Manners and Customs" *Ensign* (May 1972): 29.
46. John Taylor, as quoted in Russel B. Swensen, "Methods of Studying Scripture," *Instructor* 80, no. 2 (February 1945): 67.
47. The Church of Jesus Christ of Latter-day Saints, "Thoughts to Keep in Mind: Prophets and Prophecy," in *Come, Follow Me — For Home and Church: Old Testament 2026* (Salt Lake City: The Church of Jesus Christ of Latter-day Saints, 2025), 253, online at churchofjesuschrist.org.
48. The Church of Jesus Christ of Latter-day Saints, "Ideas to Improve Your Personal Scripture Study," *Scripture Study Ideas*, online at churchofjesuschrist.org.

provide some context for the revelations. ... in the Doctrine and Covenants, they don't tell the complete story.[49]

If this is true for scripture merely two centuries old, written natively in English, from a limited geography and time period, how much more is it the case for ancient scripture, translated from its original languages, from different places, times, and cultures? The Old Testament spans more than a thousand years, multiple languages and dialects,[50] places, and cultures from the Egyptian, Mesopotamian, Israelite, and Persian to name a few.

The fact that *Answering My Gospel Questions* contains a section on studying in context strongly suggests that seeking out that context is a good way to answer questions and respond to concerns.

> Place things in context. ... People in the past had different assumptions about the world than we do. ... If we want to better understand the words and actions of those in the past, we also need to understand the culture and context in which they occurred. ... understanding historical context helps to keep us from imposing our present views on people of the past in a way that prevents understanding.[51]

To paraphrase King Benjamin, "there are so many kinds of context that I cannot number them all."[52] Elder John A. Widtsoe cautioned that "one may quite as easily find himself in mistaken notions if he attempts the interpretation of the scriptures without getting a full perspective of the subject and adequate knowledge of human events that led to the giving of the scriptures, including origins and translations."[53] Never-

---

49. The Church of Jesus Christ of Latter-Day Saints, "Preface," *Revelations in Context: The Stories Behind the Sections of the Doctrine and Covenants*, ed. Matthew McBride and James Goldberg (Salt Lake City: The Church of Jesus Christ of Latter-day Saints, 2016), vii, online at churchofjesuschrist.org.
50. Here I intend Hebrew and Aramaic, as well as influences from Ugaritic, Egyptian, and Akkadian. The Hebrew changes over time even within the Old Testament (for example, Early Biblical Hebrew, Standard Biblical Hebrew, Late Biblical Hebrew), and sometimes reflects northern or southern dialects.
51. The Church of Jesus Christ of Latter-day Saints, "Work to Understand the Past," online at churchofjesuschrist.org.
52. This is a tongue-in-cheek reference to Mosiah 4:29.
53. John A. Widtsoe to the Quorum of the Twelve Apostles, 27 January 1931, *John A. Widtsoe Papers*, CR 712 2, Box 178, Folder 3, Church History Library, Salt Lake City, UT.

theless, it will be useful to enumerate a few different types of context. The Church manual *Scripture Study: Power of the Word* described several kinds of context: the time and place, the cultures, the historical contexts and settings, and the geography.[54]

Another key kind of context is *literary* context, that is, *genre*. What kind of thing are we reading? Different genres have different purposes and different conventions. If we misunderstand what type of thing we are reading, we are likely to ask the wrong questions and draw the wrong conclusions. The Christian literary scholar C. S. Lewis wrote that "The first qualification for judging any piece of workmanship from a corkscrew to a cathedral is to know what it is — what it was intended to do and how it is meant to be used."[55] Misreading poetry as prose, or parable as history will lead to misunderstanding.

Discussing the book of Genesis in particular, Walter Moberly emphasizes the importance of genre:

> You cannot put good questions and expect fruitful answers from a text apart from a grasp of the kind of material it is in the first place; misjudge the genre, and you may skew many of the things you try to do with the text.[56]

To this end, the *Come, Follow Me* manual says that "knowing what kind of book [or section] you are studying can help you understand how to study it."[57] The problem is that as non-native readers, we do not easily pick up on those markers that tell us what genre a book or section belongs to, and thus how to categorize the information it presents. Elder John A. Widtsoe recognized both the presence and problem of genre decades ago.

> As in all good books every [genre] is used in the Bible that will drive the lesson home. It contains history, poetry and allegory

---

54. See The Church of Jesus Christ of Latter-day Saints, "Studying Scripture in Context," "Bridging the Cultural Gap," "Literary Styles of Scripture," and "Scriptural Use of Symbolism," in *Scripture Study — The Power of the Word Teacher Manual,* rev. ed. (Salt Lake City: The Church of Jesus Christ of Latter-day Saints, 1992, 2001), 30–43, online at churchofjesuschrist.org.
55. C. S. Lewis, *A Preface to Paradise Lost* (New York: HarperOne, 1942), 1.
56. Walter Moberly, "How Should One Read the Early Chapters of Genesis?," in *Reading Genesis After Darwin,* ed. Stephen C. Barton and David Wilkinson (New York: Oxford Press, 2009), 5.
57. The Church of Jesus Christ of Latter-day Saints, "Reading the Old Testament," 11, online at churchofjesuschrist.org.

[and other genres]. *These are not always distinguishable, now that the centuries have passed away since the original writing.*[58]

The question of genres and history is an important one; Latter-day Saints have inherited a strong impulse to read all scripture as historical except for obvious "symbolic" or "figurative" aspects. However, this is not what scripture itself presents us. Jesuit New Testament scholar Raymond Brown observed that, "Often it is thought that inspiration makes everything history. It does not; there can be inspired poetry, drama, legend, fiction, etc."[59] Providing a specific example, Evangelical Biblical scholar Kenton Sparks wryly asserted that "Jesus's preferred genre for conveying truth was fiction."[60]

The *Scripture Helps* for 2026 says that "the Old Testament writers did not intend to provide a comprehensive historical account in their writings."[61] *Come, Follow Me* expands on this idea and tries to calibrate our expectations away from an all-history kind of scripture:

> Don't expect the Old Testament to present a thorough and precise history of humankind. That's not what the original authors and compilers were trying to create. Their larger concern was to teach something about God. ... [Some] Old Testament writers did not aim to be historical at all. Instead, they taught through works of art like poetry and literature.[62]

Come, Follow Me introduces us to several genres, one important one being poetry.

> The books of Job, Psalms, and Proverbs are almost entirely poetry, as are parts of prophetic books like Isaiah, Jeremiah,

---

58. John A. Widtsoe, *In Search of Truth: Comments on the Gospel and Modern Thought* (Salt Lake City: Deseret Book, 1930), 87, emphasis added. I have replaced Widtsoe's "literary device" with "genre," as it better describes higher-level categories like "history, poetry, and allegory" rather than, for example, alliteration, onomatopoeia, etc.
59. Raymond E. Brown, *101 Questions and Answers on the Bible* (Mahwah, NJ: Paulist Press, 1990), 31.
60. Sparks, *God's Word in Human Words*, 215.
61. The Church of Jesus Christ of Latter-day Saints, "Studying the Old Testament," 2, online at churchofjesuschrist.org.
62. The Church of Jesus Christ of Latter-day Saints, "Reading the Old Testament," 10–11, online at churchofjesuschrist.org.

and Amos. Because reading poetry is different from reading a story, understanding it often requires a different approach.⁶³

Indeed, much of prophetic literature is poetry, and visually indicated as such by its formatting in modern Bible translations, in order to help readers know when to shift reading strategies. As explained in one *Ensign* article, "Understanding Old Testament Poetry," Israelite poetry relied on parallelism, not rhyme.⁶⁴ (We should understand, however, that "poetry" does not inherently indicate "fiction" any more than "prose" indicates "historical narrative.")

To illustrate, many Latter-day Saints have been uncomfortable in the first chapter of the book of Job, wherein Satan seems to bait God into torturing Job to prove a point; all Job's children and animals die, and he himself is smitten with extremely painful illness. Some have pointed to Doctrine and Covenants 121:10 as proof of Job's historicity; as Joseph Smith suffers, the beleaguered prophet is reminded, "thou art not yet as Job."

However, in 1921, the First Presidency, while assuming Job's historicity, did allow for the possibility that the book of Job "was one of the kind prevailing in olden times, setting forth certain principles in the form of a parable, as it was with the parables of Jesus Christ when in the flesh."⁶⁵ Today, *Come, Follow Me* explicitly says, "The opening chapters of Job emphasize, in a poetic way, Satan's role as our adversary or accuser; *they don't describe an actual interaction between God and Satan.*"⁶⁶

---

63. The Church of Jesus Christ of Latter-day Saints, "Thoughts to Keep in Mind: Reading Poetry in the Old Testament," in *Come, Follow Me — For Home and Church: Old Testament 2026* (Salt Lake City: The Church of Jesus Christ of Latter-day Saints, 2025), 219, online at churchofjesuschrist.org
64. Kevin L. Barney, "Understanding Old Testament Poetry," *Ensign* (June 1990): 50–54.
65. Charles W. Penrose, for the First Presidency, to Joseph W. McMurrin, October 13, 1921. Transcript in my possession. For context, see Thomas G. Alexander, *Mormonism in Transition: A History of the Latter-day Saints, 1890–1930* (Champaign, IL: University of Illinois Press, 1986), 283.
66. The Church of Jesus Christ of Latter-day Saints, "August 10–16, "Yet Will I Trust in Him": Job 1–3; 12–14; 19; 21–24; 38–40; 42," in *Come, Follow Me — For Home and Church: Old Testament 2026* (Salt Lake City: The Church of Jesus Christ of Latter-day Saints, 2025), 222, online at churchofjesuschrist.org.

As for Doctrine and Covenants 121, a new volume from BYU Ancient Scripture professor Joshua Sears, published by Deseret Book, places Job and other such allusions into literary context.

> [W]e should be careful not to confuse an allusion with a historical evaluation. The Lord and His prophets can quote or allude to fictional characters and narratives without making a judgment about the reality of those characters and narratives outside their literary world. The Cheshire Cat has been quoted several times in General Conference, but this does not make the cat historical. ... In a similar manner, when ... the Doctrine and Covenants compares Joseph Smith to Job, we should not assume that the allusions in and of themselves confirm the historicity of those stories.[67]

Similarly, prophets in General Conference have quoted from or alluded to — to choose a few — characters from *Les Misérables*,[68] *Bambi*,[69] *The Hobbit*,[70] *Harry Potter*,[71] *The Lion King*,[72] *Cinderella*,[73] and the *Peanuts* comic-strip.[74]

(7) Intellectual Humility and Close Careful Reading

The *Answering My Gospel Questions* teachers' manual explains that "we overclaim when we assert knowledge beyond what the Lord has revealed through both ancient and modern prophets. ... We are being dogmatic when we express our opinions as if they were indisputable facts and are intolerant of ambiguity when there are not clear answers."[75]

---

67. Joshua M. Sears, *A Modern Guide to an Old Testament* (Salt Lake City: Deseret Book Company, 2025), 57.
68. Thomas S. Monson, "Bring Him Home," *Ensign* (November 2003): 59.
69. Cree-L Kofford, "Your Name is Safe in Our Home," *Ensign* (May 1999): 83.
70. Dieter F. Uchtdorf, "Your Great Adventure," *Ensign* (November 2019): 86, 89.
71. Uchtdorf, "Your Great Adventure," 90n6.
72. W. Craig Zwick, "Lord, Wilt Thou Cause That My Eyes May Be Opened," *Ensign* (November 2017): 97.
73. Thomas S. Monson, "Be Thou an Example," *Ensign* (May 2005): 114; L. Tom Perry, "Becoming Men in Whom the Spirit of God Is," *Ensign* (May 2002): 39.
74. Quentin L. Cook, "Choose Wisely," *Ensign* (November 2014): 46, 48.
75. The Church of Jesus Christ of Latter-day Saints, "How to Be Bold but Not Overbearing When Discussing the Gospel," in *Answering My Gospel Questions Teacher Manual* (Salt Lake City: The Church of Jesus Christ of Latter-day Saints, 2022), 47, online at churchofjesuschrist.org.

Certain assumptions about the nature of scripture and interpretation can lead to dogmatic overclaiming. If we approach scripture assuming it can be understood simply and obviously — at face-value — then we are likely to confuse our unconscious *interpretation* of scripture with scripture itself and thus make dogmatic claims *for* scripture which it does not itself make. We are likely to see scripture's meaning as clear, plain, and obvious; we may accuse those who may see it differently as simply "rejecting scripture" when in fact it is one's *interpretation* of scripture that is being rejected.

On the other hand, if we approach scripture remembering that it was written for people in a different time, place, culture, language, and setting, then some intellectual humility naturally emerges. Am I really understanding this the way ancient prophets intended? Have I done the necessary "work to understand the past"?[76]

As should be clear from the previous six principles and sometimes tedious quotations from current manuals and publications, the Church is advocating and modeling the "inspired human author" and "contextual reading" approaches. These lead us to seek out contexts, recognize our own modern impositions, and interpret carefully, aware of the many ways we may misunderstand.

As the "divine encyclopedia" and "plain reading" constituted the intellectual inheritance of the early Saints, there have occasionally been warnings to evaluate their writings carefully. In 1956, the First Presidency observed that "sometimes the Brethren in earlier days advanced ideas for which there is little or no direct support in the scriptures (they are largely speculative) ... [concerning] which the Lord has not yet revealed the Truth."[77] President J. Reuben Clark, in his landmark talk "When Are Church Leaders Words Entitled to the Claim of Scripture" cautioned us to be wary of "adventurous expeditions of the brethren into ... highly speculative principles and doctrines."[78]

---

76. The Church of Jesus Christ of Latter-day Saints, "Work to Understand the Past," online at churchofjesuschrist.org.
77. As quoted in Devery S. Anderson, *Bruce R. McConkie: Apostle and Polemicist, 1915–1985* (Salt Lake City: Signature Books, 2024), 70, Kindle edition.
78. As quoted by D. Todd Christofferson, "The Doctrine of Christ," *Ensign* (May 2012): 90n6.

Statements made on the basis of "plain reading" and "divine encyclopedia" approaches tend to be presented definitively, and such statements throughout Latter-day Saint history likely provided the implicit context for Elder Paul V. Johnson's statement, which bears quotation again:

> Many of us have a difficult time dealing with ambiguity, especially in issues concerning the Church. In fact, we may be drawn to use quotes in our teaching that are definitive because they seem to dispel the ambiguity. But some quotes are definitive on issues where there is no official answer. People who are more tentative on a subject that hasn't been revealed or resolved don't get quoted as much, but may be more in line with where our current knowledge is.[79]

To avoid dogmatic overclaiming, we should follow the principles modeled above by current Church publications, and read carefully and methodically. President Dallin H. Oaks once recounted a story of careful observation and avoiding overclaiming:

> I remember the reported observation of an old lawyer. As they traveled through a pastoral setting with cows grazing on green meadows, an acquaintance said, "Look at those spotted cows." The cautious lawyer observed carefully and conceded, "Yes, those cows are spotted, at least on this side."[80]

Conclusion

The principles of continuing revelation and interpretation that we learn from close study of the Restored Gospel and modern revelation, lead us away from the inherited nineteenth-century Protestant models conceptualizing scripture as a "divine encyclopedia" to be understood through "plain reading."

To the contrary, they reveal a model of scripture as a human-divine composite inspired for a particular time and place, divinely accommodated to the human level. Church materials today model a two-fold way of reading scripture, both as a disciple seeking personal inspiration and application, but also a seeker of knowledge *about* scripture and its contexts.

---

79. Johnson, "Pattern for Learning Spiritual Things": 19.
80. Dallin H. Oaks, "The Historicity of the Book of Mormon," in *Historicity and the Latter-day Saint Scriptures,* ed. Paul Y. Hoskisson (Provo, UT: Religious Studies Center, Brigham Young University, 2001), 246.

Indeed, I believe we cannot fully learn *from* scripture unless we are also trying to learn *about* scripture. The first is the act of a disciple, the latter, the approach of the scholar; it is significant that several Church leaders have tried to blur the line between the two. Elders Neal A. Maxwell, Henry B. Eyring, and others spoke of disciple-scholars,[81] and President Gordon B. Hinckley said bluntly: "There is no clearly defined line of demarcation between the spiritual and the intellectual when the intellectual is cultivated and pursued in balance with the pursuit of spiritual knowledge and strength."[82]

Understanding the principles above provides a robust way of approaching the difficulties of scripture. To paraphrase Robert Woodford, a correct understanding of the nature of the revelation and interpretation makes sense of much of the real and perceived difficulties. As Joshua Sears writes,

> If we spot contradictions, errors, biases, or different perspectives in Old Testament historical accounts, we don't need to panic. We know to expect that. Christians who believe the Bible is inerrant (without error or bias) and univocal (uniformly consistent in its perspective) often struggle with these aspects of the text, but Latter-day Saint doctrine [allows us to make sense of these.][83]

Latter-day Saint principles, derived from close study of modern revelation, function as a parachute, not a straitjacket. I believe this understanding of scripture and interpretation is closer to truth "as it really is" (Doctrine and Covenants 93:24), and that modeling these principles in our talks, families, classrooms, and pulpits will build knowledge, increase testimony, and strengthen our commitment to Christian discipleship.

---

81. For example, see Henry B. Eyring, ed., *On Becoming a Disciple-Scholar: Lectures Presented at the Brigham Young University Honors Program* (Salt Lake City: Bookcraft, 1995).
82. Gordon B. Hinckley, "Come and Partake," *Ensign* (May 1986): 48.
83. Sears, *Modern Guide*, 74.

3

DEFENDING THE OLD TESTAMENT

ANCIENT ISRAEL'S OFFERING TO THE WORLD

DANIEL ELLSWORTH

For many modern readers, the Old Testament can feel confusing, harsh, or distant — yet it remains a crucial foundation of Latter-day Saint belief. A thoughtful defense of the Old Testament begins by recognizing what does not require defending: absolute scriptural inerrancy, overly literal interpretations, or rigid assumptions about ancient narratives. The focus instead turns to core doctrines consistently affirmed through modern revelation. Meaningful engagement also requires awareness of two major challenges. One comes from academic approaches that rule out divine action from the outset, shaping conclusions about prophecy, authorship, and miracles long before evidence is considered. The other arises within the Church, when prophecy is misread, wrested from context, or applied in ways that undermine faith. By approaching the Old Testament with humility, philosophical awareness, and an understanding of ancient literary conventions, readers can better appreciate ancient Israel's sacred offering and recognize its continuing power to reveal God's purposes to His covenant people.

When we, as Latter-day Saints, speak of defending the Old Testament, there are several ways to think about the task. Our first thoughts should focus on the importance of the Old Testament in the restored gospel. In my case, this is a recent understanding. I count myself among many members of the church who grew up avoiding the Old Testament in favor of the Book of Mormon and other more "reader-friendly" works of scripture and commentary. For most of my life, the Old Testament seemed like a pile of frustratingly incoherent puzzle pieces from which I could not easily derive a clear picture. Knowing that the Book of Mormon provides robust summaries of essential Old Testament events and doctrines, I was always happy to defer to it as the path of least resistance for benefiting from the Old Testament.

But some years ago, I underwent a shift. Facing the prospect of teaching the Old Testament in Sunday School, I sensed that if I were going to open that volume and teach from it, I should first have a better understanding of precisely what I was looking at. Countless books, lectures, and podcasts later, I settled into a view of the Old Testament that now differed from my previous assumptions in important ways. As a result of that learning process, I have undergone a change in perspective about what it means as Latter-day Saints to defend the Old Testament.

When it comes to that defense, we would be wise to choose our battles. This means making distinctions between what precisely needs to be defended, versus which questions, arguments, and controversies are not our circus and not our monkeys. There are questions around the Old Testament where flags of firm conviction must be planted, and there are others where we can be more neutral and flexible.

WHAT NOT TO DEFEND

I begin with something that should bring a sense of relief for any Latter-day Saints looking to defend the Old Testament; I will review a number of items that we should expend no time and effort to defend.

First, *we do not need to defend the idea that everything in the Old Testament is a divine communication.* When we affirm that we believe the Bible to be the word of God "as far as it is translated correctly" (Articles of Faith 1:8), this is best understood as a statement of how the Bible functions. In one 1995 article, President Dallin H. Oaks explained the Latter-day Saint position:

> Some Christians accept the Bible as the one true word, completely inspired of God in its entirety. At the opposite extreme, some other Christians consider the Bible as the writings of persons who may or may not have been inspired of God, which writings have little moral authority in our day. The Latter-day Saint belief that the Bible is "the word of God as far as it is translated correctly" places us between these extremes, but this belief is not what makes us unique in Christianity.
>
> What makes us different from most other Christians in the way we read and use the Bible and other scriptures is

our belief in continuing revelation. For us, the scriptures are not the ultimate source of knowledge, but what precedes the ultimate source. The ultimate knowledge comes by revelation.[1]

To see scripture as a vehicle for revelation is perhaps the best understanding of what it means for the Bible to be the word of God. The books of the Old and New Testament are the offerings of ancient peoples who did their best to explain their experiences with God. Like the rest of the world, we have choices in how to receive those offerings. President Oaks referred to extreme views of inerrancy versus skepticism, and we are under no obligation to defend either of those extremes. We can revere the Bible as a sacred offering that has been ordained of God to reveal God's purposes for humanity, without allowing the human processes of production, transmission, and translation to diminish the value of that offering.

Second, *we do not need to defend all of our mental models of passages in the Old Testament.* We recall in the Book of Mormon the moment where Nephi read to Laman and Lemuel from the brass plates, and they responded by asking, "What meaneth these things which ye have read? Behold, are they to be understood according to things which are spiritual, which shall come to pass according to the spirit and not the flesh?" (1 Nephi 22:1). This question reveals that, even among ancient Israelites, there was an understanding that it was possible to form different mental models of scripture. In our time, Elder Bruce R. McConkie spoke of elements of the Garden of Eden narrative as being true in a figurative sense.[2]

The Old Testament was recorded using ancient conventions that modern readers sometimes struggle to understand. Ancient Israelites presented their stories using different genres of prose, polemic, allegory, satire, poetry, and more. Utilizing modern scholarship, we can sometimes gain a better sense of the mental models which they held towards the world and the labor of telling their stories. However, even the best scholarly tools will produce inconsistent views of the ancient scriptural past.

---

1. Dallin H. Oaks, "Scripture Reading and Revelation," *Ensign* (January 1995): 7, online at churchofjesuschrist.org.
2. Bruce R. McConkie, "Christ and the Creation," *Ensign* (June 1982): 9–15, online at churchofjesuschrist.org.

On questions such as the exact mechanisms used in the Creation, or the specifics of the Great Flood, it is fine for us to form our own mental models, but we would do well to hold those mental models as tentative, flexible, and open to revision. To form a rigid viewpoint on a scriptural brain teaser that is only peripheral to the gospel, and then defend that viewpoint as infallible, is an exercise in misplaced zeal, and it does not advance the cause of the Restored Gospel.

What To Defend

Knowing that when it comes to scripture there are some things that do not need defending, we now proceed to the question: *what should we defend*? I suggest that a good answer is that we should defend the "core doctrines" of the Restored Gospel. In a 2007 commentary on the Church Newsroom, we read:

> Some doctrines are more important than others and might be considered core doctrines. For example, the precise location of the Garden of Eden is far less important than doctrine about Jesus Christ and His atoning sacrifice. The mistake that public commentators often make is taking an obscure teaching that is peripheral to the Church's purpose and placing it at the very center. This is especially common among reporters or researchers who rely on how other Christians interpret Latter-day Saint doctrine.[3]

In a talk addressed to modern Latter-day Saints, Elder Neil L. Andersen offered an insight about doctrine that I consider to be helpful as we read ancient scripture. He said,

> A few question their faith when they find a statement made by a Church leader decades ago that seems incongruent with our doctrine. There is an important principle that governs the doctrine of the Church. The doctrine is taught by all 15 members of the First Presidency and Quorum of the Twelve. It is not hidden in an obscure paragraph of one talk. True principles are taught frequently and by many. Our doctrine is not difficult to find.[4]

---

3. The Church of Jesus Christ of Latter-day Saints, "Approaching Latter-Day Saint Doctrine," Church Newsroom, 3 December 2012, online at newsroom.churchofjesuschrist.org.
4. Neil L. Andersen, "Trial of Your Faith," *Ensign* (November 2012): 41, online at churchofjesuschrist.org.

The Old Testament is full of what might creatively be called "statements made by ancient church leaders." Some of those statements are going to be in harmony with doctrine that has been consistently revealed over time, and affirmed by living prophets and apostles in the present day. Other statements may simply represent an ancient writer's best understanding of a concept in their time. To illustrate, consider Lehi's epiphany after spending time studying the brass plates: "And I, Lehi, according to the things which I have read, must needs suppose that an angel of God, according to that which is written, had fallen from heaven; wherefore, he became a devil, having sought that which was evil before God" (2 Nephi 1:17).

Think of Lehi's perspective up to that point; how limited access to scripture had resulted in significant gaps in his understanding of the nature of the Adversary and opposition in the world. Sometimes, we assume that the people of scripture understood the gospel like we do today, but Lehi's experience helps us to see that ancient Israelites' understanding of God and the world around them was constrained by their lack of access to information.

This is to say that in defending the Old Testament, we should exercise caution, focusing on defending concepts in the text that rise to the level of confirmed restoration doctrine.

What Are We Defending Against?

This brings us to the next question: *when we defend the Old Testament, who or what exactly are we defending it against?*

Our first instinct might be to see ourselves as firefighters putting out the fires of criticism set by our detractors. In 2019, Elder and Sister Renlund offered a different metaphor, that of a game of whack-a-mole, where we are frantically trying to counter a never-ending series of objections to our faith.[5]

Both metaphors are useful; they illustrate that if our approach is reactive, we will never have enough time and energy to defend the faith. It is too easy for our detractors and critics to formulate and repeat objections, and frankly, many in their audiences are in a cognitively shallow space where they are unlikely to ever explore our responses to a helpful depth.

---

5. Dale G. Renlund and Ruth Renlund, "A Dented Boat and Strengthened Faith," devotional speech, 13 January 2019, online at churchofjesuschrist.org.

This is not to say that traditional defensive apologetics are not important; they definitely are. But traditional apologetics should also be paired with apologetics which explore problems of bias and worldview that shape critical views. And these should be accompanied by explorations of the basic questions of epistemology, which many of our critics strenuously avoid.

The cause of the restored gospel benefits from defenses of the Old Testament along two fronts: the first front is external attacks from nonbelievers. The second front is the work of believers — many among us — who misinterpret and wrest the Old Testament in ways that undermine the truth.

Defending Against External Attacks

Addressing the first front of attack, let us focus on the field of biblical studies. In biblical studies, the dominant paradigm is sometimes called methodological atheism, or methodological naturalism. This means that researchers adopt a set of assumptions about reality that predetermine a set of possible conclusions that do not involve God. When the Old Testament claims, for example, that Isaiah saw far into Israel's future and spoke about it, biblical scholars rule out the validity of that claim in advance. The decision to rule out that claim is not the product of scientific investigation or any other rational process; it is simply an assumption that scholars consider to be useful.

Theologian Walter Wink expressed the problem when he said that "People with an attenuated sense of what is possible will bring that conviction to the Bible and diminish it by the poverty of their own experience."[6] Philosopher Arthur Schopenhauer famously said that "Every man takes the limits of his own field of vision for the limits of the world."[7] In the use of methodological naturalism, the field of biblical studies imposes an attenuated sense of what is possible alongside an artificially narrow field of vision upon its participants. Over time, many of them come to believe that the field's methodological paradigm allows for all that is possible to see.

---

6. Walter Wink, as quoted in Craig S. Keener, *Miracles: The Credibility of the New Testament Accounts* (Grand Rapids: Baker Academic, 2011), 85.
7. Arthur Schopenhauer, *Studies in Pessimism: A Series of Essays by Arthur Schopenhauer*, trans. Thomas Bailey Saunders (London: George Allen & Company, LTD., 1913), 69.

Years ago, Alan Goff published an article where he referred to "zombie Mormon history."[8] Its basic premise is that when historiography does not account for a historian's personal factors, and does not explore the impact of personal intellectual biases, the historian is operating without the kind of self-awareness that is a prerequisite for any claim to objectivity. Without any training in philosophy, scholars end up operating like "zombies", following intellectual impulses that they never honestly examine.

Philosopher Eleonore Stump spoke of the lack of philosophical maturity in the field of biblical studies:

> Surely some detailed acquaintance with biblical criticism is crucial for understanding the religion one is attacking or defending, and the philosophical examination of Judaism and Christianity will not be done well without some attention to the best contemporary understanding of the biblical texts on which those religions are founded. On the other hand, however, the final judgement regarding historical authenticity may turn out very differently if biblical scholarship is subjected to analysis and questioning by philosophers. Many cannot survive philosophical scrutiny, and bringing philosophical analysis to bear on biblical criticism often alters the historical conclusions which can be justified by that discipline.[9]

When Stump asserts that the findings of the field of biblical studies cannot survive philosophical scrutiny, she is correct. In the field of philosophy, we utilize a number of tools to establish the validity of claims. One of those tools is basic deductive logic; another is the identification of logical fallacies that weaken or nullify the validity of a claim. Philosophy holds a deeper toolset in the subfield of epistemology that explores more foundational commitments, such as scientism, positivism, and empiricism, which artificially constrain the possibilities of researchers.

As an example, consider this statement from biblical scholar Bart Ehrman:

---

8. Alan Goff, "The Inevitability of Epistemology in Historiography: Theory, History, and Zombie Mormon History," *Interpreter: A Journal of Mormon Scripture* 9 (2014): 111–207.
9. Eleonore Stump, "Modern Biblical Scholarship, Philosophy of Religion and Traditional Christianity," *Aletheia* 1 (1985): 75–80. The article, sans page numbers, was accessed online at leaderu.com.

> If historians can only establish what probably happened, and miracles by their definition are the least probable occurrences, then more or less by definition, historians cannot establish that miracles have ever probably happened.[10]

The ending statement that "historians cannot establish that miracles have ever probably happened" is true. The tools of historiography cannot establish anything about miracles, other than the fact that people through the ages have claimed to experience them. But to frame miracles in terms of probability or likelihood is the wrong way to think about them.

To illustrate why, consider this personal anecdote. Years ago, my young daughter came to me and said there was something on the floor of my home office, and it looked like a huge spider. I went to see what she was talking about, and I found there, on the floor, a big crawfish. How in the world would a big crawfish appear on the floor of my home office? I do not have an aquarium or a pond containing crawfish, and I had not purchased any takeout meals of crawfish.

Before that moment, if someone had told me a big crawfish would mysteriously appear on the floor of my home office, I would have said that was not just unlikely or improbable: I would have said it was impossible.

But some relevant facts to consider: there is a farm pond a quarter mile away from my house. I have a cat named Tiger, who likes to hunt and bring home his "trophies", and Tiger has a cat door into my home office. Tiger is afraid of water, though, so this is where I was stumped in my quest to reconstruct the crawfish's journey to the floor of my home office. But with a little online research, I discovered that crawfish can walk out of their water habitats and move on land, sometimes over surprising distances. With this collection of facts, is it still improbable that a crawfish appeared on my home office floor?

In my twenty years of living in this home, this was the only instance of a crawfish appearing on my office floor. So, on any given day, is it probable or improbable that a crawfish will appear?

There are two ways of answering that question.

---

10. Bart D. Ehrman, *Jesus, Interrupted: Revealing the Hidden Contradictions in the Bible (And Why We Don't Know About Them)* (New York: HarperOne, 2009), 176.

The first is to simply consider how often the circumstances arise that would lead to this thing happening. If that is all that we do, we will consider the appearance of the crawfish on my office floor to be improbable. The second way to answer the question is to consider what was likely to happen with all of the right circumstances in place. With a farm pond nearby out of which emerged a land-crawling crawfish, and a cat in the area who was roaming, hunting, and eager to bring home a trophy, suddenly the appearance of the crawfish on my home office floor was not improbable at all. It was more or less inevitable.

This incident illustrates why it can be poor quality thinking to make a blanket statement that miracles are probable or improbable. Miracles either happen, or they do not. I speak from personal experience in affirming that they do. If I am right, then the likelihood of a miracle in any given instance is a question of conditions and circumstances that lead to it happening, or not. For people with direct personal experience of miracles, there is no question that they happen. So most of our discussion around miracles focuses on creating the right conditions and circumstances for them to become increasingly more possible in the world around us.

Latter-day Saint scholar Phil Barlow offered this insight:

> [Some] critics steeped in modern assumptions may exceed necessary critical thought by too facilely discounting the witness of earlier generations as self-evidently a product of wish fulfillment. Rather than suspending judgment, they may start with the post-Enlightenment assumption that miracles — say, the resurrection — cannot have happened, because such things do not happen. No one they respect has witnessed one.[11]

This tendency to assume that our mental horizons are the only ones possible goes beyond the question of miracles, into questions surrounding authorship. Consider these two statements typical of claims in biblical scholarship:

- "These verses were inserted by a later author; they were not written by Jeremiah himself."

---

11. Philip L. Barlow, "Adam and Eve in the Twenty-First Century: Navigating Conflicting Commandments in LDS Faith and Biblical Scholarship," *Studies in the Bible and Antiquity* 8 (2016): 122.

- "This chapter reflects a shift in thinking, and therefore could not have been written by Isaiah."

Now, consider those two statements, but with the addition of a frank acknowledgement of the scholar's possible personal perspective:

- "These verses were inserted by a later author; they were not written by Jeremiah himself. This is obvious to me, as they do not reflect what I personally would have said if I were in Jeremiah's situation."
- "This chapter reflects a shift in thinking, and therefore it could not have been written by Isaiah. I know this because I personally have never undergone this kind of a shift in my thinking, and therefore I cannot accept that Isaiah did."

Both of these revised statements expose the potential undeclared baggage of paradigm that pervades the claims of some biblical scholars. They might have an understanding of what *they would do* if they were an ancient prophet or scribe. They might then work backwards from those paradigm-level assumptions and, as they analyze textual and historical data, make decisions around evidence that reflect and affirm their paradigms.

Biblical scholar Robert Funk made a refreshingly honest statement about his field when he said "Methodology is not an indifferent net — it catches what it intends to catch."[12] This is not bad when we have good reasons to catch a particular thing. For example, in much of the book of Romans, we witness the apostle Paul's personal shift in methodology from a non-Christian interpretation of scripture to a new Christian interpretation of scripture. Having become an eye-witness of the risen Christ, Paul was now compelled to change his methodological net to catch new principles and concepts that were more aligned with his new reality.

But it is also possible to create methodological nets that catch and affirm misconceptions. For example, biblical scholar Steven McKenzie said, "The genre of prophecy in the Hebrew Bible was not primarily to predict the future — certainly not hundreds of years in advance — but rather to address specific social, political, and religious circumstances

---

12. Robert W. Funk, "Beyond Criticism in Quest of Literacy: The Parable of the Leaven," *Interpretation: A Journal of Bible and Theology* 25, no. 2 (April 1971): 151.

in ancient Israel and Judah. This means that there is no prediction of Christ in the Hebrew Bible."[13] This statement is an example of some of the myopic reasoning that we can find in biblical studies; McKenzie is offering a naked assertion here, not a conclusion derived from scientific or other analysis. But he presents it as a self-evident fact, when in reality all he has shown in this statement is a glimpse of his arbitrarily-chosen methodological net. And undoubtedly, his net catches exactly what it intends to catch: a de-Christianized Old Testament. McKenzie's methodological net differs from that of the apostle Paul, because Paul has personally witnessed some realities that McKenzie has not.

As another example of methodology leading to bias, think of the field of Mormon Studies and its numerous contradictory theories around the provenance of the Book of Mormon.

One theory holds that the Book of Mormon was the product of a process of automatic writing; another theory claims it is the product of plagiarism from numerous sources; another claims it was authored by people around Joseph Smith; another claims that it was the product of psychedelics; and so on. The problem for the field of Mormon Studies is that only one of their theories can be true. This means that, with each of these hypotheses, a scholar or researcher fashioned a methodological net that was intended to catch their chosen narrative, and ignore or refute other rival narratives.

Again, since only one of these theories can be true, if there are six theories around the provenance of the Book of Mormon and we assume, for the sake of argument, that one of them is true, that means five of them are incorrect. If those five theories have been produced by credible scholars casting methodological nets that use sound argumentation and rigorous scholarly evaluation of sources, then it follows that in most cases, this robust scholarly toolset is used by historical-critical scholars to give academic respectability to their incorrect narratives of history. In modern lingo, we might say that often, historical-critical scholarship is used as a toolset for alleviating the intellectual discomfort of the scholar.

---

13. Steven L. McKenzie, "Forthtelling, Not Foretelling: Biblical Prophecy," in *How to Read the Bible: History, Prophecy, Literature — Why Modern Readers Need to Know the Difference, and What It Means for Faith Today* (New York: Oxford University Press, 2005), 67.

There is a phrase used in criminal investigations: *tunnel vision*. The basic premise is that when investigating a crime, people carry a tendency to zero in on a narrative of events early in the process, which excludes a number of other viable possibilities for investigation. If an indictment emerges from an investigation plagued by tunnel vision, it is likely to result in acquittal, as a defense attorney operating free of the investigator's tunnel vision will have the ability to present the jury with other plausible narratives of the crime.

For example, imagine a criminal investigation where DNA and fingerprints are found on a weapon early in the investigation. In this case, we can assume the case has been solved definitively, and everything about the crime scene and numerous other relevant facts are justifiably seen as evidence for the narrative. But suppose that, later in the investigation, it becomes clear that the weapon had been stolen and used by an individual who wore gloves to hide their own fingerprints and DNA, and security cameras show that the initial suspect had been shopping in a store at the time the crime was committed. The second suspect then offers a full, detailed, verifiable confession. Now, suddenly, everything observed at the crime scene and all of the other facts gathered by investigators are no longer seen as evidence of the first narrative. They are now seen as evidence for the second and final narrative. When these kinds of reversals occur in criminal investigations, observers can experience a kind of intellectual whiplash.

The field of biblical studies can include a similar type of intellectual whiplash. Reading early- and mid-twentieth century studies on the authorship of the Pentateuch, for instance, we might see the voluminous evidences marshaled by researchers and conclude that the Documentary Hypothesis is a decisively established fact, the only possible explanation for the formation of that part of the biblical text. But when reading biblical scholarship from later in the twentieth century and beyond, we are likely to experience intellectual whiplash as we see how more recent scholars have thoroughly dismantled their predecessors' arguments.[14]

In an example relevant to those of us who believe in the historicity of the Book of Mormon, if we were to spend time reading scholars who

---

14. For one example, see Duane Garrett, *Rethinking Genesis: The Source and Authorship of the First Book of the Pentateuch* (Grand Rapids: Baker Book House, 1991).

have concluded there were multiple authors and textual divisions in Isaiah 40–66, we might experience intellectual whiplash when reading scholars like Shalom Paul or Benjamin Sommer, who have amassed extensive evidences that establish single authorship for all of those chapters. Consider these statements from Sommer:

> "Was there in fact a Third Isaiah or perhaps several Third Isaiahs? It seems to me that no convincing evidence has yet been marshaled to demonstrate such a thesis."

> "The even distribution of these thematic and stylistic features in Isaiah 35 and 40–66 is highly significant. It suggests that a single author wrote all these chapters, relating to older texts in a consistent fashion throughout."[15]

Now consider the views of scholar Hugh Williamson, responding to Benjamin Sommer:

> A work as stimulating as this deserves a much fuller evaluation than can be offered here. I must therefore restrict myself to just two initial reactions. In the first place, there is a danger (and Sommer is by no means alone in falling for it) that discovery of some new data may blind the critic to the force of other considerations which need to be kept alongside it. The critical conclusions which he rejects have been achieved over a long period of time and on the basis of many converging lines of evidence.[16]

Here are two scholars who both possess what is considered to be the best possible training in the tools of the field of biblical studies, and yet they cannot agree on basic questions of evidence. Why not? Repeating the insight of Robert Funk, *methodology is not an indifferent net — it catches what it intends to catch*. These two scholars intend to catch different things, so they have fashioned different methodological nets.

The reality of the field of biblical studies might be summarized as this: anytime you read mainstream, peer-reviewed studies in that field, you are reading narratives of cultural context, of authorship, of

---

15. Benjamin D. Sommer, "Appendix: Was There a Trito-Isaiah? Deutero-Isaianic Allusion and the Unity of 35, 40–66," in *A Prophet Reads Scripture: Allusion in Isaiah 40–66,* Contraversions: Jews and Other Differences, ed. Daniel Boyarkin and Chana Kronfeld (Stanford: Stanford University Press, 1998), 191, 193.
16. Hugh Williamson, "A Prophet Reads Scripture (Book Review)," *Journal of Semitic Studies* 46, no. 1 (2001): 165.

authorial intent, and more. Most of the items of evidence in support of those narratives have been discussed by numerous other scholars in the field, who have either refuted those items outright or have presented them as evidence in support of a somewhat different narrative that is in conflict with the one you are reading.

When you look at the long rows and tall shelves full of books in your university library's biblical studies section, you are seeing an enormous amount of well-researched, well-documented, rationally-argued claims that not all people in that field believe to be factually true.

That is because *most of the output of the field of biblical studies is not produced with the aim of establishing what is objectively true.* To be sure, some things in that field can be said to be true in a definitive way. Biblical scholars can make objective claims about the number of times a particular Hebrew verb is used in the Masoretic text rendition of the book of Micah, or perhaps the characters and images on an ancient artifact. Those are objective facts which cannot be rationally disputed.

But most of the output of the field of biblical studies is not of that kind. Most is analysis that reflects any number of subjective judgments informed by worldview and other personal factors. Biblical scholar Michael Legaspi frankly describes his field as "best understood as a cultural-political project shaped by the realities of the university."[17]

I repeat — it is a mistake to think of the field of biblical studies as an enterprise that is trying to tell us what is objectively true about the Bible. Compare the field of biblical studies to a game being played by scholars. When an article passes the process of peer review for a journal in biblical studies, that does not mean that the peer reviewers believe the article's contents are correct. Their approval means that they believe the article conforms to the rules of the game of biblical studies as understood and applied by that particular journal. Just as different basketball leagues have different rules, different academic journals, publishing houses, and university biblical studies departments hold to different sets of rules in the game of biblical studies.

By now it should be clear that objectivity cannot be a primary rule of the game of biblical studies. In case it is not clear, consider what biblical scholar Jacques Berlinerblau said of his discipline:

---

17. Michael C. Legaspi, *The Death of Scripture and the Rise of Biblical Studies*, Oxford Studies in Historical Theology, ed. David C. Steinmetz (New York: Oxford University Press, 2010), 7.

> The unspeakable that I allude to in my title concerns what we might label the demographic peculiarities of the academic discipline of biblical scholarship. Addressing this very issue thirty years ago, M. H. Goshen-Gottstein observed: "However we try to ignore it, practically all of us are in it because we are either Christians or Jews." In the intervening decades, very little has changed. Biblicists continue to be professing (or once-professing) Christians and Jews. They continue to ignore the fact that the relation between their own religious commitments and their scholarly subject matter is wont to generate every imaginable conflict of intellectual interest. Too, they still seem oblivious to how strange this state of affairs strikes their colleagues in the humanities and social sciences. …What results is a situation in which biblical scholarship's "secular" wing is more like a reformed religious or liberal religious wing.[18]

When Berlinerblau mentions the problem of conflicts of intellectual interest, this is not a problem when, for example, a scholar is counting usages of a particular phrase in the Septuagint book of Genesis. Those usages are simply data. However, when a scholar decides that those data are evidence of a narrative surrounding that data, we exit the realm of objectivity. A scholar's background, worldview, and any number of other personal factors will steer the scholar's adoption of that narrative over a different narrative held by other scholars who have similar training.

The Old Testament presents ancient Israelites' narratives of their history, and when a modern scholar claims to be able to give you an objective view of "what really happened instead," it is obvious that the field of biblical studies is not equipped to offer that in any reliable way.

When the reliability of the Old Testament is challenged from secular corners like some of those in the field of biblical scholarship, we would do well to assess whether the battle is worth fighting, whether anything of real doctrinal value is at stake. If it is, then we should examine the methodology, and the biases or "-isms" like naturalism and positivism, that shaped the weapon used by our metaphorical opponent. We should examine the choices in epistemology that constrain our opponent's views, and our own. What Christian philoso-

---

18. Jacques Berlinerblau, "The Unspeakable in Biblical Scholarship," in *Secularism and Biblical Studies,* ed. Roland Boer (New York: Routledge, 2014), 20, Kindle edition.

pher Peter Van Inwagen said of New Testament scholarship applies to biblical scholarship as a whole:

> First, "ordinary" Christians (Christians not trained in New Testament scholarship) have grounds for believing that the gospel stories are (essentially) historical — grounds independent of the claims of historical scholarship. Secondly, New Testament scholars have established nothing that tells against the thesis that ordinary Christians have grounds independent of historical studies for believing in the essential historicity of the gospel stories. Thirdly, ordinary Christians may therefore ignore any skeptical historical claims made by New Testament scholars with a clear intellectual conscience.[19]

This argument is sound, and it helps to clarify our grounds for belief. For example, most of our core doctrines are supported to some degree by direct modern witness testimony from prophets and ordinary Latter-day Saints. Therefore, when our opponents make subjective epistemic choices to exclude Restoration witness testimony, our efforts to defend or persuade end up playing out like a baseball team trying to score a home run on a soccer field. Different choices in epistemology leave us playing fundamentally different games on different kinds of fields with different rules and objectives.

When we really understand the various games being played in the arena of biblical studies, we are equipped to make better assessments about the real quality of its claims. After we adjust the field of biblical studies for inflation, so to speak, I suggest that very few of its narratives amount to credible attacks on the restored gospel.

Defending Against Internal Attacks

Having addressed this first front, let us move on to the second: how do we defend the Old Testament from poor interpretation by fellow Latter-day Saints?

A good rule of thumb is to hearken back to the principle that Laman and Lemuel had internalized from their own religious upbringing: it is the principle that prophecy can be interpreted in ways that are lit-

---

19. Peter Van Inwagen, "Do You Want Us to Listen to You?" in Craig Bartholomew, C. Stephen Evans, Mary Healy, and Murray Rae, eds., *"Behind" the Text: History and Biblical Interpretation*, Scripture and Hermeneutics, 8 vols., series ed. Craig Bartholomew (Grand Rapids: Zondervan, 2003), 4:85.

eral and observable, or in a conceptual way, what Laman and Lemuel referred to as being fulfilled "according to the Spirit" (1 Nephi 22:1).

Recall Ezekiel's vision of a field of bones. In that vision, Ezekiel is shown a valley full of many bones, and he is commanded to prophesy upon them. Ezekiel prophesies their resurrection, then witnesses its fulfillment before him. He is then told that the bones are the entire house of Israel.

An erroneous interpretation of this passage could lead us to undertake a search for the specific valley of bones. We might form teams of experts, combing the Levant for the site, and making theoretical calculations about what quantity of bones the field would contain if it were all the house of Israel.

Of course, that would be preposterous. In Ezekiel's vision, it was represented to him the reality that physical resurrection is part of God's plan for the restoration of His covenant people, and this was represented to him on a *conceptual* level. The vision had the purpose of conveying to Ezekiel the concept of resurrection in a way that he could understand, and the particulars of the fulfillment of this prophecy are not something that we should try to attach to a specific single moment and location in the future.

If we can understand that the Old Testament contains some prophecy intended to be conceptually interpreted, we can avoid many "doubtful disputations" (Romans 14:1). These contentious and pointless brain-teaser battles tend to arise when we lack humility about our interpretations. Defending the Old Testament involves proactively teaching the humble and careful interpretation of prophecy.

A final front of defense is to understand that much of Old Testament prophecy has applicability to us, but that does not mean it is *about* us. To illustrate why that is important, consider a recent conversation I had with an individual that referred me to Jeremiah 23's condemnation of wicked pastors:

> Woe be unto the pastors that destroy and scatter the sheep of my pasture! saith the Lord. Therefore thus saith the Lord God of Israel against the pastors that feed my people; Ye have scattered my flock, and driven them away, and have not visited them: behold, I will visit upon you the evil of your doings, saith the Lord (Jeremiah 23:1–2).

In our conversation, this individual told me that according to this passage, our current First Presidency and Quorum of the Twelve Apostles are under condemnation from God. I replied to him that no, this passage is not referring to our current church leadership. It was a statement made toward ancient Israelite spiritual leaders. The principles in Jeremiah 23 might have some general applicability to a number of situations through the ages, but when Jeremiah gave us this passage, he had his time and context in mind, not ours.

Similarly, some disaffected church members often use passages from the book of Isaiah in an attempt to give some kind of authority to their own personal murmuring toward current church leadership.

The Book of Mormon states that Isaiah prophesied to all of the house of Israel. This is sometimes erroneously interpreted to mean that every passage in Isaiah is somehow about us. That is not true. Some passages in Isaiah have direct application to our time and context while other passages do not apply. Instead, they convey general patterns and principles that all of the House of Israel can apply to their own time and context using wisdom and discernment.

Defending the Old Testament means being aware of how misinterpretations and misapplications of Old Testament prophecy can lead to apostasy, and inviting those that misunderstand to adopt better interpretations that lead to sustaining God's ordained servants today.

Conclusion

It is my hope that this paper can help Latter-day Saints to critically think through our defenses of the Old Testament: specifically, what aspects of the Old Testament we ought to defend, and the nature of the attacks that believers are likely to encounter in our day. When Latter-day Saint understanding and defenses of the Old Testament bring us into conflict with the field of biblical studies, our attention to foundational questions of worldview and personal factors, and our willingness to forthrightly articulate how those influence our own perspective, give us an opportunity to model honesty in those disagreements.

To defend the Old Testament is to defend scriptural texts that formed the basis for the religion that Jesus adhered to in mortality. To defend the Old Testament is to defend the prophetic mantle. To defend the Old Testament is to defend the value of ancient Israel's sacred offering of scripture to the world. And to defend the Old Testament carefully, intelligently, with wisdom, maturity and discernment, is to defend the Restored Gospel.

4

DEFENDING JOSIAH

ALLEN HANSEN

King Josiah is a figure of stark contradiction: revered in the Bible as a peerless reformer yet frequently dismissed by modern critics as a power-hungry zealot who invented scripture to centralize authority. This article challenges that cynical modern consensus, arguing that a robust historical and contextual analysis vindicates Josiah as a faithful restorer of Israel's covenant. Rather than a calculated political coup, his reforms were a desperate, pious response to the crushing idolatrous influence of the Neo-Assyrian empire. The text demonstrates that Josiah's actions, including the supposed "violence" of his purge, were standard ancient ritual measures to cleanse a polluted land, not the acts of a tyrant. Evidence from later Jewish and Christian traditions, as well as Restoration scripture, consistently upholds Josiah as a model of righteousness. Ultimately, Josiah emerges not as a villain, but as a tragic hero who reclaimed his nation's spiritual identity and sacrificed his life in loyalty to God.

King Josiah is a rare example of a man almost universally praised in the Bible, yet much maligned today; almost a 180° turn in appreciation. This major and dramatic divide boils down to a single issue: his reforms.

One Latter-day Saint summary sets the stage reasonably well:

> The discovery of the Book of the Law during King Josiah's reign (from 640 to 609 BC) jump-started a reform movement within Judaism. As part of this reform, Josiah carried out an aggressive shift within the popular religion — removing pagan religious institutions, eliminating sites of worship throughout Judah in order to centralize all worship at the Temple in Jerusalem, and attempting to reestablish the covenant between the Jewish people and God. These events are particularly noteworthy for LDS students of the scriptures since they occurred within the

early lifetimes of the prophets Jeremiah and Lehi, and these events influenced both their ministries and their theology. The scriptures that were being used in Jerusalem at the end of Josiah's reign, including some of the prophecies of Jeremiah and the Book of Deuteronomy (the Book of the Law) appear in the Brass Plates taken by Lehi to the New World.[1]

How one perceives these reforms tends to determine one's view of Josiah. Many in the Bible viewed Josiah as a righteous king restoring proper forms of worship and bringing his people back to the Lord. His death — an enigmatic episode — may be read as the ideal fulfillment of the *Shema* in Deuteronomy, and he is depicted as God's loyal vassal who did not hesitate to lay down his life for his Lord.

Twentieth-century biblical scholarship presented a critical view of Josiah's reign and reforms that was radically different to his depiction in the Hebrew Bible.[2] He was viewed as a figurehead of a movement pushing a new agenda, which attempted to erase earlier, legitimate forms of YHWH worship. This movement has been termed as the Deuteronomists, called after the fifth book of the Pentateuch, which was supposedly written or extensively edited by King Josiah's priests and scribes.

The studies of Margaret Barker have contributed to a Latter-day Saint view of these reforms as apostasy, with the Book of Mormon serving as a righteous rejection of them.[3] A slew of recent books and podcasts have gone farther, and taken a more extreme stance, viewing Josiah and his reforms as evil and the book of Deuteronomy itself as demonic.[4] Such a caricature is an unwarranted distortion and rests on shaky ground.

---

1. Benjamin L. McGuire, "Josiah's Reform: An Introduction," *Interpreter: A Journal of Mormon Scripture* 4 (2013): 161–163.
2. Though dated, one of the better, extensive treatments of the critical position remains Moshe Weinfeld, *Deuteronomy and the Deuteronomic School* (Oxford: Clarendon Press, 1972).
3. The classic treatment remains Kevin Christensen, "Paradigms Regained: A Survey of Margaret Barker's Scholarship and Its Significance for Mormon Studies," *Foundation for Ancient Research and Mormon Studies Occasional Papers* 2 (2001): 1–94. See also his recent survey, "Twenty Years After 'Paradigms Regained,' Part 1: The Ongoing, Plain, and Precious Significance of Margaret Barker's Scholarship for Latter-day Saint Studies," *Interpreter: A Journal of Latter-day Saint Faith and Scholarship* 54 (2022): 1–64.
4. David Butler, *In the Language of Adam* (Plain and Precious Publishing, 2024),

The book of Deuteronomy was important to the New Testament, the Book of Mormon, and the Doctrine and Covenants.[5] So much in scripture would be missing and incomprehensible without it, and we cannot afford to discard it based on unsubstantiated speculation and conspiracy theories. Instead, Latter-day Saints must apply a critical approach, which does not seek to discard the Bible or any of its books, but to better understand them on their own terms, as a product of their times.

Ultimately, overtly negative and simplistic views damage our ability to learn from the scriptures. As a paradigm, it is a dead end.[6] We need not return to a naive view of the Bible to appreciate Josiah's role as

---

and Jonah Barnes, *The Key to the Keystone* (Plain and Precious Publishing, 2024). The interested reader may find multiple such podcasts by searching the names of either author.

5. See Matthias Henze and David Lincicum, eds., *Israel's Scriptures in Early Christian Writings: The Use of the Old Testament in the New* (Grand Rapids, MI: Eerdmans, 2023), 767–794; Gregory Steven Dundas, *Mormon's Record: The Historical Message of the Book of Mormon* (Provo, UT: Religious Studies Center, Brigham Young University; Salt Lake City: Deseret Book, 2024), 175–211, 289–324, but esp. 300–306. No study of Deuteronomy in the Doctrine and Covenants exists that I am aware of. For now, see Doctrine and Covenants 84:39–62 for examples of both the language of Deuteronomy ("For you shall live by every word that proceedeth forth from the mouth of God") and its characteristic themes, such as covenant, heeding, hearkening, and being blessed for that or cursed for disobeying. It may be significant that Section 84 deals with the call to go to a new land of promise and build a new covenant Zion there.

6. One of Kevin Christensen's valuable contributions to church scholarship is to recognize the importance of paradigms. "In debates about religion, background theory is the issue, fundamental assumptions and basic concepts are at stake, and therefore, the dependence of measurement and observation on those assumptions is crucial. This theory-dependence was exactly the reason for, and substance of, my whole approach. It is why I cited the Parable of the Sower and the Parable of the Wine Bottles. It's why I cite Kuhn and Barbour and Goff.... The whole concept of paradigm debate and the influence of theory on experiment design, testing, and interpretation has also been a prominent theme in my LDS writings since my first publication in 1990. And Stephenson's conspicuous failure to address that basic underlying premise means that the beam in his own eye remains in place to obscure his vision. Everything that follows in his essay suffers thereby." Kevin Christensen, "Image is Everything: Pay No Attention to the Man Behind the Curtain," *Interpreter: A Journal of Mormon Scripture* 17 (2016): 99–150.

a righteous king and the book of Deuteronomy as valuable scripture. Even if there were excesses, these reforms were still necessary and an overall positive.

We can fully endorse William Hamblin's view that, "I believe Josiah's reform of the temple cult was both necessary and inspired and was not in itself the cause of a temple apostasy."[7]

Time and Place

The Why

There is a wonderful quote from Frank Herbert's *Dune*.

> To begin your study of the life of Muad'Dib, then take care that you first place him in his **time:** born in the 57th year of the Padishah Emperor, Shaddam IV. And take the most special care that you locate Muad'Dib in his **place:** the planet Arrakis. Do not be deceived by the fact that he was born on Caladan and lived his first fifteen years there. Arrakis, the planet known as Dune, is forever his place.[8]

Historical context is time and place. Herbert adapted this from an insight in Lesley Blanch's now largely forgotten history of the Russian conquest of the Caucasus and the Muslim leader of the resistance: Imam Shamyl. "Thus, in writing of Shamyl, we must place him first in his time — the first half of the nineteenth century, and then in his

---

7. William J. Hamblin, "Vindicating Josiah," *Interpreter: A Journal of Mormon Scripture* 4 (2013): 165–176. Hamblin did not believe nothing was lost, just that the reforms did not create an apostasy, and that overall, they were needed. While I may differ in degree on what was lost, I find his position entirely reasonable. Neal Rappleye explores what some of these excesses may have looked like in the context of Lehi's family dynamics. See Neal Rappleye, "The Deuteronomist Reforms and Lehi's Family Dynamics: A Social Context for the Rebellions of Laman and Lemuel," *Interpreter: A Journal of Mormon Scripture* 16 (2015): 87–99. Another possible example of what was lost is discussed in Neal Rappleye, "Serpents of Fire and Brass: A Contextual Study of the Brazen Serpent Tradition in the Book of Mormon," *Interpreter: A Journal of Latter-day Saint Faith and Scholarship* 50 (2022): 217–298. Neal Rappleye is a good friend and co-author, and I am indebted to his many insights over the years on Deuteronomy, the Deuteronomists, and much more.
8. Frank Herbert, *Dune* (Philadelphia: Chilton Books, 1965), 3. Paul is the charismatic, sympathetic and ruthless villain of the story, which I obviously do not view as holding true for Josiah. No comparison between the figures is intended.

place — the mountains — and then, in turn, we must place those mountains in their frame."[9]

The Caucasuses are nestled in between two seas and hemmed in by Russia to the north and the then-Ottoman and Persian empires to the southwest and southeast, respectively. When these empires expanded and fought each other, the Caucasuses were caught in the middle of it all.[10] Blanch was right to insist that her readers must understand the geography to understand the people and events in her history. Time and place. Politics, culture, war, economics, intellectual and religious beliefs are all part of this. This is true for history in general, no matter its subset.

Judah in the 7th Century BCE

To understand Josiah, then, we must understand him in relation to time and place. He was likely born in 648 BCE and assumed the throne around the year 640. A potential meaning of his name is YHWH strengthens or empowers.[11]

When examining a map of the Ancient Near East, one of the first things you may notice is how tiny Judah was, surrounded by bigger kingdoms and empires. The next thing is that, despite its size, Judah controlled vital trade and military routes between the empires. Assyria could not be reached by land from Egypt and vice-versa without going through Judah. The great empires always had an interest in the fortunes of that kingdom.[12]

---

9. Lesley Blanch, *The Sabres of Paradise: Conquest and Vengeance in the Caucasus* (London: John Murray, 1960), 27.
10. The Russian literature on this conflict is extensive. Important treatments in English are W. E. D. Allen and Paul Muratoff, *Caucasian Battlefields: A History of the Wars on the Turco-Caucasian Border, 1828–1921* (Cambridge: Cambridge University Press, 1953); Moshe Gammer, *Muslim Resistance to the Tsar: Shamil and the Conquest of Chechnia and Daghestan* (London: Frank Cass, 1994); Gary Hamburg, Thomas Sanders, and Ernest Tucker, eds., *Russian-Muslim Confrontation in the Caucasus: Alternative Visions of the Conflict between Imam Shamil and the Russians, 1830–1859* (Abingdon, UK: Routledge, 2004).
11. Shalom Smirin, *Josiah and His Times* (Jerusalem: Bialik Institute, 1951), 33.
12. See "Map 4" in Yohanan Aharoni, Michael Avi-Yonah, Anson F. Rainey, Ze'ev Safrai, and R. Steven Notley, *The Carta Bible Atlas*, 5th ed. (Jerusalem: Carta Jerusalem, 2011), 13.

To Judah's immediate north, the kingdom of Israel and its capital of Samaria lay in ruins, destroyed by Assyria nearly a century prior.[13] This is not to say it was a desolate wasteland; a certain number of Israelites remained, alongside administrators and colonists brought in by Assyria but the land *was* depopulated, a shadow of its former self.[14] It was also a physical reminder of broken covenants and exile, that is, spiritual death.[15]

Judah had barely escaped destruction itself. The population decreased dramatically and much of the Shephelah — the breadbasket of Judah — was taken away by Assyria and given to Gaza and other Philistine kingdoms.[16] The influx of rural and provincial refugees from Judah into Jerusalem caused an additional social upheaval, exacerbated by the arrival of Israelite refugees from the northern kingdom

---

13. Bob Becking, *The Fall of Samaria: An Historical and Archaeological Study*, Studies in the History and Culture of the Ancient Near East, 18 vols., ed. Weippert and Baruch Halpern (Leiden, NL: Brill, 1992), is an extensive study of the difficult and often contradictory material on the conquest of the Northern Kingdom. A number of approaches to this problem were suggested in a 2017 conference organized by Sheichi Hasegawa. "Despite considerable scholarly efforts over many years, the events of the last three decades of the Northern Kingdom of Israel are still hidden beneath the veil of history. A number of questions remain unresolved..." Shuichi Hasegawa, "The Last Days of the Kingdom of Israel: Introducing the Proceedings of a Multi-Disciplinary Conference," in Shuichi Hasegawa, Christoph Levin, Karen Radner, eds., *The Last Days of the Kingdom of Israel* (Berlin: De Gruyter, 2019), 1.
14. Gary N. Knoppers, "In Search of Post-Exilic Israel: Samaria after the Fall of the Northern Kingdom," in *In Search of Pre-Exilic Israel: Proceedings of the Oxford Old Testament Seminar*, ed. John Day (London: T&T Clark International, 2004), 170–171.
15. On the topic of exile as death, see Gary A. Anderson, *The Genesis of Perfection: Adam and Eve in Jewish and Christian Imagination* (Louisville, KY: Westminster John Knox Press, 2002), 121; Matthew J. Ramage, *From the Dust of the Earth: Benedict XVI, the Bible, and the Theory of Evolution* (Washington, D.C: Catholic University of America Press, 2022), 154.
16. W. Boyd Barrick, *The King and the Cemeteries: Toward a New Understanding of Josiah's Reforms* (Leiden, NL: Brill Academic, 2002), 145–146; Shuichi Hasegawa, "History and Archaeology: The Kingdom of Judah," in *The Oxford Handbook of the Books of Kings*, ed. Steven L. McKenzie and Matthieu Richelle (New York: Oxford University Press, 2024), 253; C. L. Crouch, *The Making of Israel: Cultural Diversity in the Southern Levant and the Formation of Ethnic Identity in Deuteronomy* (Leiden, NL: Brill, 1982), 71–74.

with their own culture and practices.[17] Judah's prestige and political power were vastly reduced. Under Manasseh, the kingdom regained much territory, but sunk deeper in a spiritual morass.[18]

A fuller consideration of the proximate cause is necessary: Assyrian dominance.

Assyria

Assyria was among the greatest empires that the world had ever known; it stretched from parts of modern Iran in the east, to Armenia in the north, to Arabia in the south, and at times as far west as Egypt.[19] Naturally, this was achieved by violent conquest and subjugation.

Per Mark Healy, "The Kings of Assyria were very mindful of the effectiveness of the 'invincible weapon' that existed in the form of the army they commanded. While it was never quite 'invincible', the Assyrian military was nonetheless the most effective in the Near East for over three centuries."[20]

Imagine living in the world today and not experiencing some sort of presence or influence from the United States. Though without the intensity of modern mass media and global communications, that was

---

17. See the map in Craig W. Tyson and Virginia R. Herrmann, eds., *Imperial Peripheries in the Neo-Assyrian Period* (Louisville, CO: University Press of Colorado, 2018), 1. Benjamin Toro cautions that "the Neo-Assyrian Empire was not a contiguous territory, but an imperial core dotted with 'islands' of imperial control or outlying provinces, surrounding other states, which are considered 'allies' or vassals." Benjamin Toro, *The Pax Assyriaca: The Historical Evolution of Civilisations and Archaeology of Empires* (Bicester, GB: Archaeopress Publishing, Ltd., 2022), 88. On the refugees, see Barrick, *King and the Cemeteries*, 146–159; William M. Schniedewind, *Who Really Wrote the Bible: The Story of the Scribes* (Princeton: Princeton University Press, 2024), 82–96.
18. Paul S. Evans, *Sennacherib and the War of 1812: Disputed Victory in the Assyrian Campaign of 701 BCE in Light of Military History* (London: T&T Clark, 2023), 53.
19. For a concise political and military history, see Mark Healy, *The Ancient Assyrians: Empire and Army, 883–612 BC* (Oxford: Osprey Publishing, 2023).
20. Healy, *Ancient Assyrians*, 189. A fuller consideration of the Assyrian military and its religious dynamic is found in the relevant chapters of Charlie Trimm, *Fighting for the King and the Gods: A Survey of Warfare in the Ancient Near East* (Atlanta: SBL Press, 2017).

Assyria in the Ancient Near East, and understanding that impact is crucial to understanding the Josian reforms.

Empire and war were religious imperatives in Assyria. The world was divided into a center and periphery. The center was Assyria, the abode of the gods, of civilization, and order instead of chaos. The periphery was where barbarians and demons and chaos resided, but it was rich in resources. The center had a divine mission to expand. They brought order and civilization; the periphery gave its resources.[21]

Ashur was originally the city-god of Ashur, its personification. He was a universalist god, and "the Assyrian king was "his chief priest and vicar on earth." As G. Frame points out, "the god, the city, and the land were all known by the same name."[22] Ashur took on the attributes (and households) of the earlier, more powerful gods, Enlil and Marduk, and he mandated conquest to expand the center.[23] Assyria's vassals were expected to recognize Ashur's ascendancy and suzerainty.

However, there is no evidence that Assyria directly imposed the *cult* of their gods on subjugated peoples.[24] The subjugated could keep their gods as long as they accepted the suzerainty of Assyria and its god Ashur. *Rebellion* would result in the cultic images of the gods being exiled, just like their people. The stakes of defiance were high. Make no mistake, political rebellion was always understood as a religious act. The Rassam cylinder records how inhabitants of Ekron rebelled, that is, sinned against the god Ashur. Mention of the king comes after in this section of the account and is closely tied to the god.[25] The king

---

21. Mario Liverani, *Assyria: The Imperial Mission* (University Park, PA: Eisenbrauns, 2017), 12–14.
22. Douglas R. Frayne and Johanna H. Stuckey, *A Handbook of Gods and Goddesses of the Ancient Near East: Three Thousand Deities of Anatolia, Syria, Israel, Sumer, Babylonia, Assyria, and Elam* (Winona Lake, IN: Eisenbrauns, 2021), 34.
23. Frayne and Stuckey, *Handbook of Gods and Goddesses*, 34; Liverani, *Assyria*, 12–15. Todd Uriona raised the intriguing possibility that Assyrian ideology may be referenced in Nephi's vision of the great and abominable church. Todd Uriona, "Assyria and the 'Great Church' of Nephi's Vision," *Interpreter: A Journal of Latter-day Saint Faith and Scholarship* 55 (2023): 1–30.
24. Mordechai (Morton) Cogan, *Imperialism and Religion: Assyria, Judah and Israel in the Eighth and Seventh Centuries B.C.E.* (Missoula, MT: Scholars Press; Society of Biblical Literature, 1974), 88.
25. Lines 41–48 of the Rassam cylinder. Mordechai (Morton) Cogan, *The Raging*

punished earthly rebels, their dead ancestors, *and* their gods.[26] "The tombs of their former and later kings, (who had) not revered Ashur and Ishtar, my lords, (who had) harassed my royal ancestors, I ravaged, tore down, and laid open to the sun."[27]

What is more relevant is Assyrian "soft power," or its cultural cachet and influence. Assyria was the dominant power in the world and other nations followed the trends the- Assyrians set.[28] When you are the dominant power, many begin to see things your way. Cogan suggests that Manasseh's zealous and aggressive embrace of paganism was due in part to his wife, a lady of Yotbah in Assyrian-occupied Israel.[29] As can be seen by the examples of Solomon's wives and of Jezebel and Athaliah, women were indeed a driving force in cultic reforms.[30] Be that as it may, Assyria's influence on Israel and Judah's elite was clearly deleterious. It helped resurrect older, forbidden practices and transformed the meaning of others.

For instance, horses and chariots of the sun were worshipped as part of Canaanite/Levantine religion, and YHWH worship likely incorporated much of this imagery. Ancient Israel also perceived God and his angels as riding chariots.[31] That was nothing novel, yet

---

Torrent: Documents from Assyria and Babylonia relating to Israel during the First Temple Period (Jerusalem: Carta Jerusalem, 2008), 108 [Hebrew].

26. Cogan, *Imperialism and Religion*, 22–37.
27. Steven M. Voth, "Jeremiah," in *Isaiah, Jeremiah, Lamentations, Ezekiel, Daniel*, Zondervan Illustrated Bible Backgrounds Commentary, 10 vols., ed. John H. Walton (Grand Rapids, MI: Zondervan, 2009), 4:257.
28. It must be noted that much of this came by way of Aramaean influence and participation in Assyrian belief, culture, and administration. Cogan, *Imperialism and Religion*, 83–90; Eckart Frahm, "Introduction," in Eckart Frahm, ed., *A Companion to Assyria*, Blackwell Companions to the Ancient World (Chichester, GB: John Wiley & Sons Ltd., 2017), 7.
29. Cogan, *Imperialism and Religion*, 91.
30. See Ginny Brewer-Boydston, *Good Queen Mothers, Bad Queen Mothers: The Theological Presentation of the Queen Mother in 1 and 2 Kings,* Catholic Biblical Quarterly Monograph Series 54 (Eugene, OR: Pickwick Publications, 2016), 9–15, for a helpful overview of queen-mothers in cult and politics. See also Elna K. Solvang, *A Woman's Place is in the House: Royal Women of Judah and their involvement in the House of David*, Journal for the Study of the Old Testament Supplement Series 349, ed. David J. A. Clines, Philip R. Davies, and Andrew Mein (Sheffield, GB: Sheffield Academic Press, 2003), 154–172.
31. 2 Kings 2:11, 2 Kings 6:17; Zechariah 1:8–11. Ezekiel 1 describes an elaborate

we find them taking on a new ritual prominence during the era of Assyrian ascendancy. As noted by Eynikel, "The sun and moon cults were known in Syro-Palestine before the period of the Assyrian domination, but the cults were intensified as of this period."[32] "In Judah," writes Cogan, "new forms dressed up old Canaanite ritual in a blatant assimilatory trend...."[33]

What was true in general for Levantine worship was doubly so for such images as divine chariotry. This may be understood by looking closer at Assyrian practice and imagery.

> In Assyria and Babylonia, pulling the ceremonial chariot bearing the image of Samaš, Marduk, and Adad was serious and sacred business, requiring lavish preparation. Talented artisans crafted ornate blankets with tassels and intricate harness decorations to caparison the horses formally. The priests conducted complex rituals involving hymns and incantations, some designed to be whispered into the horses' left ears, three times over, while they consumed the special offering set before them.[34]

---

vision of God riding a chariot. This imagery persisted in Judaism. See Allen Hansen and Spencer Kraus, "My Name is the Sun," in *Abraham and His Family in Scripture, History, and Tradition*, 2 vols., ed. Jeffrey M. Bradshaw, John S. Thompson, Matthew L. Bowen, and David R. Seely (Orem, UT: Interpreter Foundation; Salt Lake City: Eborn Books, 2025), 1:150–152.

32. Erik Eynikel, *The Reform of King Josiah and the Composition of the Deuteronomistic History,* Oudtestamentische Studiën, Old Testament Studies, 84 vols., ed., Archibald L. H. M. van Wieringen (Leiden, NL: Brill, 1995) 33:210. See also the fuller discussion in pages 205–211. For more on the sun cult, see Mark S. Smith, "The Near Eastern Background of Solar Language for Yahweh," *Journal of Biblical Literature* 109, no. 1 (Spring, 1990), 29–39; J. Glen Taylor, *Yahweh and the Sun: Biblical and Archaeological Evidence for Sun Worship in Ancient Israel,* Journal for the Study of the Old Testament Supplement Series 111, ed. David J. A. Clines and Philip R. Davies (Sheffield, GB: JSOT Press, 1993). Morton Smith, "Helios in Palestine," in Morton Smith, *Studies in the Cult of Yahweh,* 2 vols., ed. Shaye J. D. Cohen (Leiden, NL: Brill, 1995), 1:238–262, surveys evidence from later periods.

33. Cogan, *Imperialism and Religion*, 87–88. Cogan views that assimilatory influence as coming through Aramaic mediation.

34. Deborah O'Danie Cantrell, *The Horsemen of Israel: Horses and Chariotry in Monarchic Israel (Ninth–Eighth Centuries B.C.E.)*, History, Archaeology, and Culture of the Levant, 11 vols., ed. Jeffrey Blakely and K. Lawson Younger Jr. (Winona Lake, IN: Eisenbrauns; University Park, PA: Penn State University Press, 2011), 1:58.

We have a striking visual record of the importance of chariots in Assyrian religion:

> In a detail within Sennacherib's relief series of the battle of Lachish, two priests in tall hats are performing a ceremony before an altar within the military camp. The representation of two priests performing a ceremony in front of an incense-burner, an altar and a chariot, sometimes with divine standards, is repeated continuously.[35]

These standards stood in for the gods, who rode the chariot like the king would while conducting the war and leading the army to victory. One of the Assyrian divine epithets was *Rakib-El*, or El's charioteer (likely the sun god was meant), attesting to the importance of chariotry in religion. This deity was also the patron of the aggressively expansionist Sam'al dynasty in Aramea that was alternately foe and vassal to Assyria.[36] One of the Sam'alian kings justified his legitimacy by emphasizing that both *Rakib-El* and the king of Assyria chose him to rule. *Rakib-El* thus had clear associations with legitimate kingship and Assyrian rule or ideology and could easily fit in a Yahwistic framework. Legitimate practices and symbols could become corrupted, and their meaning change over time; yet they were not the core of Israelite belief.

Josiah's reign coincided with the drastic decline of the Assyrian empire. Ashurbanipal died sometime between 630–627 BCE. Assuming the latter date, "just 15 years after the death of this last 'great king of Assyria', the Neo-Assyrian Empire was gone...."[37]

Babylon was able to break free of Assyrian rule, and allied itself with the Medes, a new power in the region. Assyria's appeal to its Egyptian ally could not save it.[38] Nineveh, the largest city in the world, was sacked in 612, and the last king reigned only until 609 BCE

This gave Josiah a freer hand. "The general outline is clear: Josiah operated within a power vacuum that occurred because of the decline

---

35. Krzysztof Ulanowski, *The Neo-Assyrian and Greek Divination in War* (Leiden, NL: Brill, 2021), 101.
36. Frayne and Stuckey, *Handbook of Gods and Goddesses,* 300. Cogan, *Imperialism and Religion*, 88–89.
37. Healy, *Ancient Assyrians*, 177.
38. Healy, *Ancient Assyrians*, 177–185.

of the Assyrian empire."³⁹ When Josiah extended his rule to the north at Assyria's expense, it was because the empire was unable to defend its far-flung territories.⁴⁰

Egypt

Space will not allow for a detailed look into the Egyptian kingdom, so a brief overview will have to suffice. During Josiah's reign, the pharaoh Psamtik I was a member of the 26th dynasty, which had overthrown the Nubians. Assyria's yoke had been broken in, and this opened a new cultural and political moment in Egypt.

Egypt had historical claims on the Levant; it had been part of their empire. Similar to the Assyrian model, this interest was as much religious as geopolitical. "The beginning of Egyptian expansion into the Levant was justified as an exercise in 'extending the borders of Egypt' and in 'eliminating violence from the highlands.'"⁴¹

The Levant was where their ambitions lay, and likely why they came to Assyria's aid against Babylon, despite their history of conflict. A strong Babylon would frustrate Egypt's ability to control the region, whereas a weaker Assyria would be more amenable to territorial concessions.

After the fall of Assyria, Egypt exerted a powerful pull on post-Josian Judah. Babylon did not have a fraction of the influence on the region that either Assyria or Egypt did. Egypt, essentially, was reconstituting its empire, viewing Judah as a vassal. Many of the Judahite elite saw Egypt as their natural ally against Mesopotamian powers such as Babylon and the late, unlamented Assyria, much in the same way that the Scots viewed the *auld alliance* with France against England.⁴²

---

39. Bustenay Oded, ed., *2 Chronicles*, Olam HaTanach, 24 vols., 6th ed., ed. Y. Amit, A. Berlin, H. Cohen, et. al (Tel-Aviv: Divrei HaYamim Publishing, 2002), 24:260 [Hebrew].
40. Cogan, *Imperialism and Religion*, 71. How far north Josiah's effective rule extended is a matter of dispute. However, he is depicted as acting in Samaria with impunity, and that was the seat of Assyrian administration in Israel. This fits the historical picture of Assyria's downfall.
41. Liverani, *Assyria*, 13.
42. Siobhan Talbott, *Conflict, Commerce and Franco-Scottish Relations, 1560–1713*, Perspectives in Economic and Social History 28, ed. Andrew August and Jari Eloranta (New York: Routledge, 2016), 15–16. Niall Barr, *Flodden* (Stroud, GB: Tempus Publishing Group, LTD., 2003), explores the disastrous results

Cultural and historical ties were strong.[43] As Jeremiah (and, indeed, Josiah) predicted, Egyptian machinations resulted in Judah's ultimate destruction at the hands of Babylon.

Kingship

Kingship is another concept that may seem broadly familiar to modern readers, but requires some explanation if we are to more fully understand it with ancient eyes. According to Sarah Japhet, "YHWH's kingship is only realized by means of the Davidic dynasty."[44] The person of the king mattered. "[From] first to last the king or, to be more precise, the ruling member of the House of David is regarded in some way as the light or life of his people."[45]

Unlike the rest of the Ancient Near East, Israel and Judah did not consider their king as "god," though in some sense he may have been more than human.[46] At the very least, he had a unique connection to God, and stood between Him and the rest of His nation. Kingship was a corporal and sacral concept.

> Thus it is that any violent disturbance of the national life, such as that caused by a prolonged drought or an outburst of plague, may be attributed to the fact that the king himself has violated the sanctions of the group; and the whole royal house or the very nation itself may be involved with him in the condemnation which follows upon any such trespass. Correspondingly, if the nation is to prosper, the king must act as the embodiment of "righteousness." That is to say, it is first and foremost his concern to see that the behaviour of

---

the alliance had for sixteenth-century Scotland.

43. The literature on Israelite-Egyptian ties is rich. See J. Andrew Dearman, *The Book of Hosea* (Grand Rapids, MI: William B. Eerdmans Publishing Company, 2020), 39; Bernd U. Schipper, "Egypt and the Kingdom of Judah under Josiah and Jehoiakim," *Tel Aviv* 37, no. 2 (2010): 200–226.
44. Sara Japhet, *The Ideology of the Book of Chronicles and Its Place in Biblical Thought* (Winona Lake, IN: Eisenbrauns, 2009), 310.
45. Aubrey R. Johnson, *Sacral Kingship in Ancient Israel* (Cardiff: University of Wales Press, 1955), 2.
46. Nicholas Majors, *The King-Priest in Samuel* (Eugene, OR: Wipf & Stock, 2023), 3; Sigmund Mowinckel, *He That Cometh: The Messiah Concept in the Old Testament and Later Judaism*, trans. G. W. Anderson, 3rd ed. (Grand Rapids, MI: Eerdmans, 2005), 104–110.

society at large is thoroughly "righteous" and that, to this end, the sanctions of the group, particularly the nation's laws, are uniformly observed throughout the different strata of society; for it is only in this way, when the individual is restrained from doing "what is right in his own eyes," that the wellbeing of the nation, in fact its life or vitality, can be assured.[47]

Johnson observes that the king is responsible to God for the people because they are God's people. Overseeing the cult so it functioned properly was another part of the king's duties. This is analogous to how the latter-day President of the Church is responsible for temples and the endowment ceremony.

Comparative material bears this observation:

> The ancient Near Eastern temple ideology embodied a mutual relationship between king and cultus: just as the monarch assumed responsibility for the cultus, the cultus bestowed blessings upon the monarch, legitimacy not being the least of these. Expressed in this way, it might be argued that monarchies exploited the religious traditions of their nations for their own glorification. Without excluding that possibility in individual regimes, the texts reveal a different perspective: the kingship existed, at least in part, for the sake of the cultus and the cultic responsibility lay near the centre of the very concept of king.[48]

What is sometimes missed is that the king *was* the head of the priesthood on earth. Temples were his immediate concern, and the basis of his right to reign. For example, according to one Egyptian inscription, Amon chose Tutankhamen as king precisely because temples lay in ruins, and he was to restore them after the evils caused by his father Akhenaten.[49]

> From this perspective, kings are chosen to establish and maintain the cultus. Disregard for the cultic aspect of the royal vocation could be interpreted as the reason for a king's removal (as in the case of Nabonidus), just as the cultic accomplishments of a monarch or dynasty could stand as implicit proof of the wise choice of the gods.[50]

---

47. Johnson, *Sacral Kingship*, 3.
48. William Riley, *King and Cultus in Chronicles: Worship and the Reinterpretation of History* (Sheffield: Sheffield Academic Press, 1993), 159.
49. William Riley, *King and Cultus*, 160.
50. Riley, *King and Cultus*, 161.

In ancient Israel, the priest-king was not meant to replace the high-priest or the Levites. Rather "his role centers upon leading Israel with keeping all the words of the law (Deut. 17:18-20)."[51] The king ensured that the temple was "up and running," and that there were enough Levites and supplies to function properly. He was to serve during the festivals. However, unlike in Mesopotamia, the Israelite king was *not* a lawgiver, but an upholder of the law, and this is an important distinction for Josiah's reforms. The command to have a copy of the law written by the king was a strong reminder that he was not above it and that he served God, not the other way round. Doing justice does not depend on the king, conceptually; rather, he depends on it to be a king in the first place.

It is illuminating to consider some of the kingship theologies developed on ancient and biblical bases, as they offer a window to a different conceptual world.

> The idea that a ruler's will reflected God's will was ... commonplace in medieval Christian states and perhaps, if we leave aside the specifically Christian content, in almost all premodern societies. It is probably the most powerful political idea in human history, reflected for Christians even in the Lord's Prayer: "Thy will be done on earth as it is in Heaven."[52]

One medieval European writer offered a striking take on the king's identity as a deified man: "Concerning one personality, he was, by nature, an individual man: concerning his other personality, he was, by grace, a Christus, that is, a God-man."[53] Russian kingship theology also employed this idea: "Although the tsar's earthly nature is like that of every man, the power of his rank is higher, like God."[54] There is

---

51. Majors, *King-Priest in Samuel*, 70–71.
52. Daniel B. Rowland, *God, Tsar, and People: The Political Culture of Early Modern Russia* (DeKalb, IL: Northern Illinois University Press; Ithaca, NY: Cornell University Press, 2020), 383–384.
53. The Norman Anonymous, as cited in Ernst H. Kantorowicz, *The King's Two Bodies: A Study in Mediaeval Political Theology* (Princeton: Princeton University Press, 1957), 46.
54. B. A. Uspenskij and V. M. Zhivov, "Tsar and God: Semiotic Aspects of the Sacralization of the Monarch in Russia," in Boris Uspenskij and Victor Zhivov, *"Tsar and God" And Other Essays in Russian Cultural Semiotics*, trans. Marcus Levitt, David Budgen, and Liv Bliss, ed. Marcus C. Levitt (Boston: Academic Studies Press, 2012), 4.

another statement in a Russian compilation that echoes the sixth-century Byzantine writer Agapetos, but it is shockingly addressed to a *pagan* king. "To you, tsar, a mortal and perishable man, we give honor and obeisance as to one who has power, because the kingdom and the glory of this quickly perishing world is given you by God."[55]

Daniel Rowland pointed out that maintaining this image was a massive investment and undertaking: "Rulers spent large amounts of their time, and often very large amounts of precious financial resources, to demonstrate their piety, and, through good works, the connection between their will and God's will."[56] To read this too cynically is to miss a valuable insight into how people imagined God and His representatives on earth.

In medieval Ethiopia, the role of the scribes was to magnify the righteous acts of the king.[57] This was not cynical or nefarious, it was how they perceived the world and the relationship of the king to God. "In these books, the emperor is described as God's messenger and a miracle worker who can destroy his enemies by his very presence. Thus, all members of the kingdom must make obeisance to him; all who serve him will be blessed, and all who oppose him will be cursed."[58] Saint Tekele Heymanot wrote that when the emperor and his army appeared on the battlefield, "As smoke is scattered by the wind so did their enemies scatter when facing them."[59]

The Deuteronomists are not nearly as effusive. The king is important, but decidedly human, and his appearance in battle does not guarantee victory. As great as Josiah was, he was not described as anything near like God, and he would die in battle without gaining victory. It is possible that in Ethiopia this is "an aspect of the general African 'Konigskultur' ... though not denying the importance of its Christian and Old Testament roots."[60] Yet, this was also a feature of medieval

---

55. Uspenskij and Zhivov, "Tsar and God: Semiotic Aspects," 4.
56. Rowland, *God, Tsar, and People*, 368.
57. Daniel Belete, *The Gideonites: A History of the Jews of Ethiopia and Their Journey to the Land of Israel* (Ariel, IL: Belete Books, 2024), location 21–23 in the Steimatzky e-reader [Hebrew].
58. Belete, *Gideonites*, location 21.
59. Belete, *Gideonites*, location 22.
60. Edward Ullendorff, *Ethiopia and the Bible: The Schweich Lectures 1967* (London: Oxford University Press for the British Academy, 1968), 131.

European belief. However we are to understand this, it highlights a powerful contrast between Deuteronomistic kingship and other forms, and the Hebrew Bible appears to be a deliberate exception to most kingship theologies.

This should inform our understanding of the scribal project both under and after Josiah's kingship, and it cannot be emphasized enough that the biblical scribes were not shy when it came to criticizing kings, even those whom they favored.[61] The king was praised only for doing what was right before God, the temple, and the people.

What Were the Reforms?

Two Accounts

The Hebrew Bible presents us with two accounts of the reforms in 2 Kings and 2 Chronicles. The account in 2 Kings describes how Josiah discovered a book of the law while repairing the temple and launched an impressive series of reforms in the space of a year.

Despite some skepticism, the 2 Chronicles account should be preferred on historical grounds.[62] According to the Chronicler, Josiah took his sacred duties as king seriously. At age sixteen — before attaining majority — he sought after God. This phrase suggests something of his goodness and abilities even at a young age. It also seems to suggest that God formed Josiah for the purpose of restoring proper worship in

---

61. See, for example, the episode of David and Bathsheba in 2 Samuel 11–12.
62. Barrick, *King and the Cemeteries*, 17–20; Lauren A. S. Monroe, *Josiah's Reform and the Dynamics of Defilement: Israelite Rites of Violence and the Making of a Biblical Text* (New York: Oxford University Press, 2011), 15–16, 57–58; Smirin, *Josiah and His Times*, 52–58. This paper adopts a holistic, unitary approach to the Bible. The texts more often demonstrate a literary unity and logic than not. Thus, the Documentary Hypothesis and classic source criticism are not the concern here and shall not be utilized. Others are welcome to take a different approach to the question at hand. The interested reader is directed to Jeffrey L. Morrow and John S. Bergsma, *Murmuring Against Moses: The Contentious History and Contested Future of Pentateuchal Studies* (Steubenville, OH: Emmaus Academic, 2023); Gary A. Rendsburg, *How the Bible Is Written* (Peabody, MA: Hendrickson Publishers, 2019); Joshua Berman, *Ani Maamin: Biblical Criticism, Historical Truth, and the Thirteen Principles of Faith* (Jerusalem: Maggid Books; Koren Publishers, 2020). These provide a look into problems with the Documentary Hypothesis and suggest alternative approaches to biblical scholarship.

the temple, and that the young king intuitively recognized his mission. Anson Rainey noticed that the year 633 BCE was the very year Josiah married Hamutal of Libnah in the Shephelah. As this was a significant Levitical stronghold, Rainey speculated that marriage to an important Levitical family might have stimulated the reforms.[63] While impossible to prove, this may well have some truth to it. As we have seen, women were a powerful factor in cultic reforms, and priests and Levites were part of strong familial networks. Hilkiah and Shaphan, for example, were likely close relatives. The Levites also tended to be politically and religiously conservative, having a particular aversion to the northern and foreign worship introduced into Judah.[64]

> Josiah, it seems, was influenced in his youth by anti-Assyrian circles, and being of strong character knew what he must do. As king of Judah he aspired to be his own master, independent of all foreign powers. For this to happen he believed that a return to the source [of Israel's faith] and the traditions of the fathers was needed, necessitating the removal of all foreign worship from the land.[65]

This should not be viewed as a cynical power-grab: if the kingdom were not free, then by implication, God — its ultimate king — was also a subservient vassal god, unable to fulfil the most basic of promises He made to His people. The king represented His agent on earth, mirroring God's own dominion over the world. Josiah never completely achieved his goal, and he ultimately died for it.

Josiah spent the next four years of his reign enacting cultic reforms aimed at restoring proper worship of YHWH, which was expressing faith in Him. We would do well to remember that faith in God was essentially loyalty to him.

The Chronicler and 2 Kings are not as contradictory as they may seem at first glance.[66] They contain the same kind of reforms and the same events but in a differing order; Chronicles also omits what Manasseh supposedly reformed after his repentance.[67] Otherwise,

---

63. Anson F. Rainey, "The Biblical Shephelah of Judah," *Bulletin of the American Schools of Oriental Research* 251 (1983): 16.
64. Rainey, "Biblical Shephelah of Judah," 16–17.
65. Smirin, *Josiah and His Times*, 63.
66. Smirin, *Josiah and His Times*, 36, 50–58; Oded, *2 Chronicles*, 24:258 [Hebrew].
67. The rhetoric of Chronicles is contradictory on this point.

they agree in substance. There are Assyrian examples relating to the land of Israel, where the king's deeds over a lengthy period are condensed into a single year.[68]

Curiously, there is a well-known nineteenth century analogue. John Wesley Powell's popular *The Exploration of the Colorado River and Its Canyons* combined the dramatic events of his 1869 expedition with the scientific accomplishments of 1871–1874.[69] Thus, even in the modern age, strict chronological fidelity has sometimes been sacrificed for literary and rhetorical effect, as well as market demands.[70]

The Reforms

As noted by Shalom Smirin, none of Josiah's reforms had needed a book; They followed the example of prior reforms.[71] This was how the kings of Judah acted when they found the kingdom to be in serious trouble. Hezekiah, the most extensive reformer prior to Josiah, did much the same, but did not rely on a book, either (2 Kings 18:1–8). What, then, were these reforms?

William Hamblin listed three basics of Josiah's reforms:

1. Israel should worship only YHWH; Israel must not worship foreign gods.
2. Israel must not worship idols (or worship YHWH as an idol), or follow other Canaanite cultic practices.
3. To the extent they discuss it, Israel must worship only in the Jerusalem temple.[72]

Whatever quibbles there may be, overall, the schema is sound. The point was to remove the presence and worship of other gods.

---

68. Sargon II's expedition against Philistine Ashdod. See Cogan, *Imperialism and Religion*, 88–89.
69. Edward Dolnick, *Down the Great Unknown: John Wesley Powell's 1869 Journey of Discovery and Tragedy Through the Grand Canyon* (New York: HarperCollins, 2001), 290.
70. John F. Ross, *The Promise of the Grand Canyon: John Wesley Powell's Perilous Journey and His Vision for the American West* (New York: Viking, 2018), 240–241.
71. Smirin, *Josiah and His Times*, 52–54.
72. Hamblin, "Vindicating Josiah," 171–172.

Following Smirin, it can be seen that all the specifics acts of Josiah described in 2 Kings 23 describe the removal of idolatrous worship:

- v. 4: The vessels for Baal, the Asherah, and other astral deities are removed from the temple and burned.[73]
- v. 5: Idolatrous priests appointed by previous kings to offer incense to foreign gods are removed from office. A foreign term for priests is used.[74]
- v. 6: The Asherah is removed from the temple, burned, and ground to powder.

---

73. Baal was a central god of the Canaanite-Phoenician pantheon. Frayne and Stuckey, *Handbook of Gods and Goddesses*, 43–46; Michael D. Coogan and Mark S. Smith, eds., *Stories from Ancient Canaan*, 2nd ed. (Louisville, KY: Westminster John Knox Press, 2012), 97–153. There is considerable debate over the role of Asherah in ancient Israel. Mark S. Smith, *The Early History of God: Yahweh and the Other Deities in Ancient Israel* (Grand Rapids, MI: William B. Eerdmans Publishing Company; Dearborn, MI: Dove Booksellers, 2002), xxx–xxxvi, is a useful overview of the problem. The notes in Benjamin D. Sommer, *The Bodies of God and the World of Ancient Israel* (New York: Cambridge University Press, 2009), 202–205, contain remarkably helpful discussions of the secondary literature. The caution in Steve A. Wiggins, *A Reassessment of Asherah: With Further Considerations of the Goddess* (Piscataway, NJ: Gorgias Press, 2007), is commendable, and he corrects many misconceptions regarding the goddess. Pillar figurines are addressed in Erin Darby, *Interpreting Judean Pillar Figurines: Gender and Empire in Judean Apotropaic Ritual*, Forschungen zum Alten Testament 2 Reihe 69 (Tübingen, DE: Mohr Siebeck, 2014), 37–43. The classic LDS treatment remains Daniel C. Peterson, "Nephi and His Asherah: A Note on 1 Nephi 11:8–23," in *Mormons, Scripture, and the Ancient World: Studies in Honor of John L. Sorenson*, ed. Davis Bitton (Provo, UT: Foundation for Ancient Research and Mormon Studies, 1998), 191–243. Too close a connection between Asherah and our Restoration view of Heavenly Mother, as held by D. J. Butler and other podcasters, does not, in my opinion, hold up when the evidence is considered. Margaret Barker's book, *The Mother of the Lord: Volume 1: The Lady in the Temple* (London: Bloomsbury T&T Clark, 2012), has been important to these claims. An extended excursus on the flawed methodology and dubious claims in the book would exceed the scope of this paper.
74. Barrick, *King and the Cemeteries*, 66–70. Butler's suggestion that these were "veil men," "priests of the veil," or "*chomer*-priests" is entirely fanciful. Butler, *In the Language of Adam*, 310–311.

- v. 7: The houses of the *kadeshim* are smashed to pieces, which is where the women wove textile coverings for the Asherah.[75]
- vv. 8–9: The priests from all the towns of Judah are brought to Jerusalem while the *bamoth* are defiled, and in some cases, smashed to pieces.[76]
- v. 10: The *tophet* at the valley of Hinnom is defiled, which is where the Molech rites took place.[77]
- v. 11: The horses dedicated to sun worship are removed from the entrance to the temple and sent elsewhere; the chariots are burned.
- v. 12: The altars built by Ahaz and Manasseh are smashed and ground to dust.

---

75. On the role of textiles in Assyrian worship, see Salvatore Gaspa, *Textiles in the Neo-Assyrian Empire: A Study of Terminology,* Studies in Ancient Near Eastern Records, 23 vols., ed. Gonzalo Rubio (Berlin: De Gruyter, 2018), 19:186–235. Though I disagree with some of Amanda Brown's conclusions on the nature of the reforms and Huldah's role in them, her recent paper is an excellent look at what we know of the cultic weavers, and how their craft was an expression of their devotion and worship. Amanda Colleen Brown, "Material Expression and Mantic Performance: An Examination of Women's Religious Experience at the Time of Josiah," in *Material Culture and Women's Religious Experience in Antiquity: An Interdisciplinary Symposium*, ed. Mark D. Ellison, Catherine Gines Taylor, and Carolyn Osiek (London: Bloomsbury Publishing, 2021), 71–97. *Kadeshim* were likely *not* cultic prostitutes, either male or female. See Stephanie Lynn Budin, *The Myth of Sacred Prostitution in Antiquity* (New York: Cambridge University Press, 2008), 14–47.
76. *Bamoth* (sing. *bamah*) are cultic installations of some kind. The English "high places" does not particularly capture their meaning or use. W. Boyd Barrick, *BMH as Body Language: A Lexical and Iconographical Study of the Word BMH When Not a Reference to Cultic Phenomena in Biblical and Post-Biblical Hebrew,* Journal for the Study of the Old Testament Supplement Series 477, ed. Claudia V. Camp and Andrew Mein (London: T&T Clark International, 2008), 3–11.
77. On the question of Molech, whether it was a deity or form of sacrifice, the jury is still out. See Heath D. Dewrell, *Child Sacrifice in Ancient Israel* (Winona Lake, IN: Eisenbrauns, 2017), 6–36; Jon D. Levenson, *The Death and Resurrection of the Beloved Son: The Transformation of Child Sacrifice in Judaism and Christianity* (New Haven, CT: Yale University Press, 1993), 18–21. The recent Frayne and Stuckey, *Handbook of Gods and Goddesses,* 213, comes down on the side of Molech being a deity. Regardless, the rites still involved the sacrifice of children.

- v. 13: Solomon's *bamoth* in Jerusalem which are dedicated to Ashtoreth of the Sidonians, Chemosh of Moab, and Milcom of the Ammonites are defiled.[78]
- v. 14: The *masseboth* are broken and the *asherim* are cut down; human bones are put in their place.[79]
- v. 15: The Bethel altar and the *bamah* built by Jeroboam are smashed to pieces. The *bamah* and an Asherah are burned.
- vv. 16–18: While desecrating idolatrous places of worship, Josiah discovers the tomb of the prophet who rebuked Jeroboam for his idolatry. His bones are spared.
- v. 19: The houses of the *bamoth* in Samaria are treated like those of Bethel.
- v. 20: The priests who officiated at the *bamoth* of Samaria are slain upon them, using the terms for sacrifice. The *bamoth* are further defiled by burning human bones upon them
- v. 24: Josiah's deeds are recapitulated and summarized as removing the diviners and *teraphim* and other idols. All of these are illegitimate practices.[80]

The only act of the reform not aimed at removing idolatry was a positive enactment: the proper celebration of the Passover on a grand scale in Jerusalem. In this case, Josiah closely followed the instructions in Deuteronomy.[81] But what is often missed is that this holiday celebration commemorated the *establishment* of Israel as a nation upon its God-given land. To remember the deliverance from Egypt was to

---

78. See the respective entries in Frayne and Stuckey, *Handbook of Gods and Goddesses*, 35–38, 160, 211.
79. Masseboth were standing stone monuments. On their use in worship, see Theodore J. Lewis, *The Origin and Character of God: Ancient Israelite Religion through the Lens of Divinity* (New York: Oxford University Press, 2020), 335–336; Barrick, *King and the Cemeteries*, 103–105. *Asherim* (a masculine plural) are some sort of ritual object, but their meaning is uncertain. Judith M. Hadley, *The Cult of Asherah in Ancient Israel and Judah: Evidence for a Hebrew Goddess* (Cambridge: Cambridge University Press, 2000), 200–201. For the burning of bones, see Monroe, *Josiah's Reform*, 105–107.
80. On teraphim, see Karel van der Toorn, Bob Becking, and Pieter W. van der Horst, eds., *Dictionary of Deities and Demons in the Bible*, 2nd ed. (Leiden, NL: Brill, 1999), 844–850.
81. Jacob S. Licht, *Time and Holy Days in the Biblical and the Second Commonwealth Periods* (Jerusalem: The Bialik Institute, 1988), 143–147 [Hebrew].

contrast their former situation as slaves with God's power to give them a land of inheritance; it all depended on the covenant they made with him at Sinai to keep His commandments.[82] For Josiah, this would have been a highly public way to mark the renewed covenant between God and His people, and for the people to show their commitment to God. The Passover was also rich with themes of *protection* from death and destruction.[83] Josiah likely hoped to invoke that divine protection for the people.

The reforms were necessary because kings such as Manasseh had made aggressive changes to Judah's worship, installing the cult of other gods. "It may be supposed, therefore, that the King's historiographer did record historically accurate information as to the period of public inauguration of certain cults, even though he viewed all foreign cults under the general rubric Canaanite idolatry."[84]

This was true also of the former kingdom of Israel, which introduced foreign priests into the cultus as well. Many legitimate practices were corrupted in the process, and kings such as Hezekiah and Josiah acted to undo those changes.

A helpful analogy from modern culture is the renewal of wedding vows. Israel was depicted in the Bible as God's wife. Apostasy and covenant-breaking was akin to adultery.[85] The kings were removing all markers of favor or devotion to other lovers: those foreign deities and their worship.

Turning to a cultic perspective, "Josiah's actions serve to render cult places and installations forbidden points of divine access by imposing a 'skull-and-crossbones' of sorts, a warning of danger or of poison cultically construed."[86] In simpler terms, Josiah denied idolaters the use of their holy spaces by defiling them and the defilement also served as a visible reminder of the spiritual danger of idolatry.

Drawing from Latter-day Saint church history, an example is the Mormon Reformation of the 1850s. "'The Great Reformation' which spread quickly throughout the Church of Jesus Christ of Latter-day

---

82. Deuteronomy 16:1–12, especially v. 12.
83. Licht, *Time and Holy Days*, 139–140.
84. Cogan, *Imperialism and Religion*, 73.
85. Leland Ryken, James C. Wilhoit, and Tremper Longman III, eds., *Dictionary of Biblical Imagery* (Downers Grove, IL: IVP Academic, 1998), 39–40.
86. Monroe, *Josiah's Reforms*, 5.

Saints in 1856 and 1857, was a strenuous effort to promote a moral and spiritual awakening among members of the Church in Utah."[87] There is no denying that, whatever the rhetorical excesses, there was a very real need for change among the Saints and a recommitment to God. Likewise with Judah and Israel.

The prominence of the *bamoth* in the reforms contrasts with their absence in Huldah's prophecy, and it seems likely that their idolatrous use was the problematic factor rather than any centralization of worship.[88] "Huldah the prophetess does not warn against the high-places and does not call to centralize worship but reproves the nation for worshipping 'other gods.' From this it is doubtful that Josiah worked to centralize worship, or even operated on the basis of Deuteronomy at all."[89]

Symbols are not static; their meanings can change. The pentagram — whether inverted or not — was a powerful Christian symbol beginning in the Medieval era. It represented the five wounds of Christ and served to make His atoning sacrifice present among any who contemplated the image. "Thus through its close relation to Christ the pentangle becomes also a symbol of resurrection and potential divinity for humans."[90]

The pentagram was used in Christian art and architecture, including the famous Marktkirche of Hannover, as well as the stained-glass windows of the Nauvoo Temple and the exterior walls of the Salt Lake Temple. Yet, today, no one would casually decorate a church with pentagrams. Nor do teenagers who feel themselves angsty and edgy draw it for the Christian symbolism, but rather the opposite. The pentagram has been co-opted and transformed by Satanists, and the most visceral identification is now with them. As a Christian symbol, it has been retired, largely known as such only to historians and medievalists.

---

87. Howard Clair Searle, "The Mormon Reformation of 1856–1857" (Master's thesis, Brigham Young University, 1956), 1.
88. Bustenay Oded and Michael Kochman, eds., *2 Kings*, Olam HaTanach, 24 vols., 6th ed., ed. Y. Amit, A. Berlin, H. Cohen, et. al (Tel-Aviv: Divrei HaYamim Publishing, 2002), 9:193–202.
89. Oded and Kochman, *2 Kings*, 9:193.
90. Piotr Sadowski, *The Knight on His Quest: Symbolic Patterns of Transition in Sir Gawain and the Green Knight* (Newark, DE: University of Delaware Press; London: Associated University Presses, 1996), 133.

Re-educating society at large would be an uphill struggle with little hope of success. Originally entirely positive, the pentagram's visual impact is negative and to use it today is to make a statement, the wrong kind of statement at that.

Thus it was with the items that Josiah removed. Whatever their original role may have been in Israel's worship, their meaning and purpose were corrupted to the point where the immediate association in Josiah's day was one of idolatry. From the association with Baal and the hosts of heaven, it is clear that Asherah was being worshipped in her Canaanite/Syrian identity as Baal's consort or associate, and not YHWH's.

When Judah's very survival as a nation lay at stake because of its idolatrous behavior, to leave these cultic implements and places up, or to attempt reeducation, was not an option Josiah could afford.

Discovering the Book

If the cultic reforms were not motivated by the discovery of the book, then what exactly was its role in them?

Temples were the repository of both sacred books and mundane records. The concept of a dedicated, freestanding library did not yet exist. The legitimacy of any text kept in the temple would have been assumed. While the episode can be read as the discovery of a book that no one knew anything about, this it is not a particularly sound reading. Neither Hilkia, Shaphan, Josiah, nor anyone else at the court raised the question of whether the book was authentic or not. Josiah rent his clothing immediately upon hearing the book read; this was a strong act of penitence, remorse, and grief. As king, he assumed personal responsibility for the nation's sins, even those that had been committed before his birth.

Josiah's question, rather, was what the book's message meant both for the king personally and the nation collectively.

> Go ye, inquire of the LORD for me, and for the people, and for all Judah, concerning the words of this book that is found; **for great is the wrath of the LORD that is kindled against us, because our fathers have not hearkened unto the words of this book, to do according unto all that which is written concerning us** (2 Kings 22:13, emphasis added).

The book being some form of Deuteronomy is highly likely, given its focus on the consequences of breaking the covenant with God. The book may have been as short as to contain only Deuteronomy 26–29, with its list of blessings and curses pertaining to living the covenant in the promised land.[91] The description in 2 Kings is too brief to permit any decisive conclusions about the book's identity, but what is clear is that its contents terrified Josiah. He realized how severely the nation had sinned against the Lord for generations, and the book made the consequences of such feel much more vivid and real.

To see the reforms as primarily being based on Deuteronomy's call to centralize worship in Jerusalem is to miss an important detail: "In all the chapter [2 Kings 23], Jerusalem's special and unique status as the only place for cultic activity is not mentioned even once, in contrast with Deuteronomy's frequent repetition of this theme (without mentioning Jerusalem by name)."[92]

Josiah dispatched a delegation to Huldah the prophetess, headed by Hilkiah the high priest. Huldah's oracle contained both good and bad news. Josiah, for his grief and contrition before God, would escape the coming evils and die in peace. The nation, though, would reap the fearful consequences of abandoning God and choosing to worship others: "My wrath shall be kindled against this place, and it shall not be quenched."[93]

Josiah's personal greatness as king is shown by his next move. "[He] interpreted his role of reading the law and obeying the law as much larger than personal piety."[94] Instead of giving up his nation for lost, and resting on the personal promise of a peaceful death, Josiah took charge: he would have everyone enter into a new covenant.

There is again an analog in the rebaptisms of the Mormon Restoration.

> Apparently, [Jedediah] Grant had tired of preaching a reformation that never took hold; now he would require rebaptism and reconfirmation — outward signs of fealty to the thunderings of the Almighty through His chosen vessel. In

---

91. In the later Jewish division of scripture portions, Deuteronomy 26:1–29:8 is a singular unit, *parashat Ki Tavo*. The narrative unity in such a division is logical.
92. Smirin, *Josiah and His Times*, 48.
93. 2 Kings 22:17.
94. Majors, *King-Priest in Samuel*, 210.

effect, he would cut off the entire membership of the church and require them to submit to reconversion and rededication to the principles he and his colleagues had been hurling at them for years. There would be no passive Saints in the kingdom of Jedediah's stewardship. It would be all or nothing.[95]

In theory, a new covenant would take precedence over the old one, and commend the people to God for their newfound commitment to Him: a clean slate. It was a gamble that ultimately failed. The spiritual rot had set in too deep, and the people's repentance was too shallow.

Still, this is the crux of the book's discovery: it was a stark witness and reminder of the covenant. "The importance of the book is that it serves as a covenant book, that is, the commitment of the people for all generations to follow the laws and commandments written in this record of the Torah of Moses."[96]

Violence

Many later readers have been disturbed by the violence described in the narrative, be it killings, destruction of altars and cultic items, or the macabre burning of human bones. Some have taken this to an extreme, portraying Josiah as a bloodthirsty ("murder-happy") man who "smashed and killed those who disagreed" with him.[97] A number of recent books describe how supposedly "Josiah's men went burning and killing through the streets of Jerusalem."[98] The caricature, however, is untethered from reality, and is not reflected in the sources.

There is a single recorded incident when priests were killed by Josiah (2 Kings 23:19-20). These were the priests in Samaria, and were considered a foreign element imposed upon the cultus by wicked Israelite and Assyrian kings. To leave them in place would be to invite further pollution and chaos upon the land and provoke God further. This sort of violence was not something unique to Josiah or even to Deuteronomy, it was the warp and woof of holiness. What was holy had to be protected from the forces of evil, which constantly sought to pollute it, and a polluted land would spit out the inhabitants defiling

---

95. Gene A. Sessions, *Mormon Thunder: A Documentary History of Jedediah Morgan Grant* (Urbana, IL: University of Illinois Press, 1982), 207.
96. Oded, *2 Chronicles*, 24:258 [Hebrew].
97. Butler, *In the Language of Adam*, 277, 279.
98. Barnes, *Key to the Keystone*, 162. The number of pro-Latter-day Saint podcasts where such claims are made is staggering.

it.[99] In fact, the language of violence in 2 Kings 23 echoes the language of the priestly inspections of contaminated houses in Leviticus 14.[100] Lauren Monroe observed:

> References to burning, beating, scattering, casting of dust, and defiling in the reform account reflect apotropaic rites of riddance intended to contain contagion and eliminate dangerous forces perceived to be antithetical to Yahweh. Such rites are common in priestly texts of Leviticus and Numbers, but are almost entirely unattested in Deuteronomy and deuteronomistic texts.[101]

Josiah was thus fulfilling his role as the head of the priesthood and removing the forces of evil from his land and people. Otherwise, we find Josiah treating priests gently, even those directly involved in idolatrous practices.

Religion was not a private affair in the Ancient Near East but a public, communal one. It was essential to a family, village, town, region, or nation's survival.[102] Improper practices endangered the entire nation by provoking God's wrath and displeasure, as well as giving power to His divine or demonic enemies. Josiah was aiming for a decisive break with idolatry, and that is why he acted as he did.

The Ideological/Theological Aftermath

The claim is often made that the reforms changed doctrine. However, the evidence for this is weak. As noted, Josiah removed the idolatrous horses and chariot of the sun. The sun was the premier

---

99. Tikvah Frymer-Kensky, "Pollution, Purification, and Purgation in Biblical Israel," in *The Word of the Lord Shall Go Forth: Essays in Honor of David Noel Freedman in Celebration of His Sixtieth Birthday,* ed. Carol L. Meyers and M. O'Connor (Winona Lake, IN: Eisenbrauns; American Schools of Oriental Research, 1983), 329–331, 333, 336–348; Jacob Milgrom, *Leviticus 17–22: A New Translation with Introduction and Commentary,* Anchor Yale Bible Commentaries, 95 vols. (New York: Doubleday, 2000), 3A:1482, 1572, 1580, 1583.
100. Monroe, *Josiah's Reform,* 25–30.
101. Monroe, *Josiah's Reform,* 24.
102. Talal Asad, *Genealogies of Religion: Discipline and Reasons of Power in Christianity and Islam* (Baltimore: Johns Hopkins University Press, 1993), 207. Asad explains succinctly how attitudes to religion changed in modernity. "This construction of religion ensures that it is part of what is inessential to our common politics, economy, science, and morality."

god worshipped in the Levant. If the reforms were about changing doctrine, there should not be scriptures where such associations are deemed legitimate, yet the Deuteronomistic History and subsequent scriptures are teeming with them.

In 2 Kings 13:14, we read of Elisha's deathbed: "Now Elisha was fallen sick of his sickness whereof he was to die; and Joash the king of Israel came down unto him, and wept over him, and said: 'My father, my father, the chariots of Israel and the horsemen thereof!'"

Elisha then engages in a "magic" practice: he places his hands on Joash's hands while the latter shoots arrows to the east. This arrow signifies the downfall of Israel's Aramean enemies. Each arrow which strikes the ground corresponds with a victory.

In a society surrounded by pagan religions that named their gods divine charioteers, worshipped their horses, and brought chariots on campaign for the gods to ride, to call a man the chariot and riders of Israel would have come dangerously close to idolatry. Belomancy, or arrow magic, was widespread in the Ancient Near East. Arrows encapsulated attributes of the gods, and Assyrian kings also used them as votive offerings to the gods while on campaign.[103] The whole chapter is teeming with idolatrous associations which the Deuteronomists would have had to be blind to miss.

According to the logic which understands the reforms as inaugurating mass doctrinal change, such a pericope would have been anathema. This reading of the reforms is too facile, and should be rejected in favor of a more sophisticated understanding of the interplay between practice and belief.

THE BOOK OF DEUTERONOMY

What Is It?

To know somewhat of the book of Deuteronomy and its outlook is essential. First, though, a note of caution on assuming a Deuteronomistic school of thought can even be spoken of accurately today:

---

103. Ezekiel 21:26; Samuel Iwry, "New Evidence for Belomancy in Ancient Palestine and Phoenicia," *Journal of the American Oriental Society* 81, no. 1 (January–March, 1961): 27–34; Steven Winford Holloway, *Aššur is King! Aššur is King!: Religion in the Exercise of Power in the Neo-Assyrian Empire*, Culture and History of the Ancient Near East, 146 vols., ed. B. Halpern, and M. H. E. Weippert (Leiden, NL: Brill, 2002), 10:161–162.

> Indeed, "deuteronomistic" has become something of a portmanteau word so semantically overloaded in itself, and further befogged by differing understandings of the compositional development of the Book of Kings, that if "deuteronomism" ever existed in biblical Israel as a distinct point of view expressed in a distinct literary style, its characteristic features must be defined with greater precision for it to be a useful exegetical category.[104]

This is rarely done. Instead, there is much speculation on what parts of Deuteronomy were written and when, with the questions framed so as to presuppose the conclusions:

> Even the fulcrum of all this speculation — Ur-Deuteronomy — has become increasingly difficult both to differentiate from later "deuteronomistic" accretions and to date relative to pivotal material in the Former Prophets. These factors caution against taking the "Deuteronomistic History Hypothesis," in any of its permutations, as a secure premise for a compositional analysis of what for purposes of neutral identification can be called the "Kings History" (KH).[105]

Yehezkel Kaufman pushed back on common scholarly assertions on the nature of the book:

> With all the importance of the question of [Deuteronomy]'s composition in and of itself, it has no decisive bearing on the development of Israelite religion. In [Deuteronomy] there are ancient laws. Whether these laws date to the days of Moses or the judges or Solomon — we are unable to say. There is room only for conjecture. It is also possible that the book had various forms and recensions, that were only collated later. Here, too, we can only speculate.[106]

Kaufman goes on to state that overall, Deuteronomy has a unified structure and content unique to it. He objected to the Documentary Hypothesis, where Biblical books were stitched together out of different source documents like a patchwork quilt or Frankenstein's monster. "At any rate, there are no grounds for assuming that this or that narrative detail was doubled unintentionally, or was not meant to drive home an exhortation, but that somehow these doublets occurred

---

104. Barrick, *King and the Cemeteries*, 13–14.
105. Barrick, *King and the Cemeteries*, 14.
106. Yehezkel Kaufman, *The Religion of Israel, from Its Beginnings to the Babylonian Exile*, 4 vols. (Jerusalem: Bialik Institute, 1955), 1:109 [Hebrew].

solely by combining different source documents."[107] Kaufman stated that there may well have been multiple recensions of Deuteronomy before it attained its final form.[108] Of this, there is some evidence from the Septuagint and from Qumran, most famously Deuteronomy 32, which appears in several dramatically different versions.[109]

The book's title itself, and what it tells us, should also be examined. N. Tur-Sinai proposed that *mishneh torah* — the Hebrew name of Deuteronomy — means covenant or contract of the law.[110] This is fitting, as it serves to remind the people that the laws are the conditions of the covenant. That is also how Josephus, as a student of the Hebrew Bible, understood it within a Greco-Roman political context. Deuteronomy, he explained to his gentile audience, was the Jews' national constitution.[111]

What Does it Teach

To fully cover the teachings of Deuteronomy is not possible within the scope of this paper. Volumes have been written on it. What can be done is to provide a quick overview of some of its teachings which have

---

107. Kaufman, *The Religion of Israel*, 1:108 [Hebrew]. On the various attempts to split Deuteronomy into various sources and compositional layers, Kaufman wrote on page 106 that, "without 'wishful thinking' and a priori assumptions that Deuteronomy is composed of different source documents, it is very hard to consider these attempts successful. There is no clear, substantive basis for separating it into sources."
108. Kaufman, *The Religion of Israel*, 1:109 [Hebrew].
109. Though considering the Qumran *vorlage* of Deuteronomy 32:8 original, Bickerman also offered a caution. "As a matter of fact, only the printed book can produce textual uniformity." Elias J. Bickerman, "Some Notes on the Transmission of the Septuagint," in Elias J. Bickerman, *Studies of Jewish and Christian History*, 2 vols., ed. Abram Tropper (Leiden, NL: Brill, 2007): 1:156. The sons of God passage was discovered at Qumran. The Septuagint has angels of God (with a notable exception reading 'sons of God'), and the Masoretic, children of Israel. Mark S. Smith, *God in Translation: Deities in Cross-Cultural Discourse in the Biblical World* (Grand Rapids, MI: William B. Eerdmans Publishing Company, 2010), 196.
110. Naphtali Hertz Tur-Sinai, *Vol. II: The Book*, The Language and the Book, 2 vols. (Jerusalem: Bialik Institute,1950), 2:226.
111. Joshua A. Berman, *Created Equal: How the Bible Broke with Ancient Political Thought* (New York: Oxford University Press, 2008), 52.

a bearing on the question of the reforms, as they appear frequently in such debates.

Places of Worship

The idea that Deuteronomy is stating that only one temple can ever be built is problematic. While the Samaritan version echoes something similar — though more explicit in the location — neither they, nor the Jews of the early Second Temple Era saw an inherent problem in having multiple temples. Despite tensions between the groups, this did not cause a parting of ways.[112] For most of its history, the kingdom of Judah did not narrowly view the injunction in Deuteronomy, and legitimate shrines, cultic rooms, and temples continued to operate outside of Jerusalem.[113] If the current understanding of the archaeological layers of Arad is correct, then the temple there continued to function even after the reforms.[114] It is not always appreciated that while Exodus mentions multiple altars, it too presupposes a centralized worship site: the Tabernacle.

> [Rowley] was skeptical of the idea that the notion of centralization was strictly Deuteronomistic: "But it is quite unnecessary to suppose that the author of Deuteronomy must have been the first to think of the suppression of the 'high places' and the centralisation of worship."[115]

The Love of God

Deuteronomy has the love of God at the heart of its message, and it strongly binds the corporate identity of Israel to that of the priests, the king, the land, and God Himself on the basis of the covenant. Strong limits are placed on the king, who is firmly seen as a servant of God, the people, and the cultus. It is odd to imagine that a king and his court would have commissioned such a book that curtails their power. As Berman observed, other kings in the Ancient Near East "ruled by

---

112. Reinhard Pummer, *The Samaritans in Flavius Josephus,* Texts and Studies in Ancient Judaism 129 (Tübingen, DE: Mohr Siebeck, 2009), 14–15. My thanks to Spencer Kraus for this insight.
113. Avraham Faust, "Israelite Temples: Where Was Israelite Cult Not Practiced, and Why," *Religions* 10, no. 2 (2019): 106.
114. Susan Ackerman, *Under Every Green Tree: Popular Religion in Sixth-Century Judah* (Chico, CA: Scholars Press, 1992), 51.
115. As cited in Benjamin D. Thomas, *Hezekiah and the Compositional History of the Book of Kings* (Tübingen, DE: Mohr Siebeck, 2014), 15.

means of what may be called an exclusionary power strategy," meaning that *everything* was designed to concentrate power in the hands of the king alone.[116] Deuteronomy rejects any such systems.

The Divine Council

Some of the strongest material on the Divine Council is found in Deuteronomy and the Deuteronomistic History. There is no reason to think that Deuteronomy opposed the idea of prophetic involvement in its deliberations.[117] Deuteronomy 32 was even read by later Jews and

---

116. Berman, *Created Equal*, 54.
117. Peter C. Craigie has pointed out how important the divine council is to Deuteronomy 33. "The theophany at Sinai is described as having been a time of bright light with the brightness emanating from the presence of God on the mountain. With God were the members of his divine council, *holy ones* and *warriors of God*...." The assembled people also seem to affirm this. "In v. 3b, the people affirm the role of the members of the divine council in assisting Moses in his task: his (i.e., God's) holy ones are at your (i.e., Moses') hand. ... The reference is to the assistance given to Moses by members of the divine council when Moses mediated the law of God to the people at Mount Sinai." While tentative, it is a compelling reading. Peter C. Craigie, *The Book of Deuteronomy* (Grand Rapids, MI: William B. Eerdmans Publishing Company, 1976), 393. In Deuteronomy 32, Moses invokes the theogonic pair of Heaven and Earth to witness him extoll the virtues of YHWH against the fickleness and perfidy of his people when they break the covenant. Eric Peels, *The Vengeance of God: The Meaning of the Root NQM and the Function of the NQM-Texts in the Context of Divine Revelation in the Old Testament* (Leiden, NL: Brill, 1994), 134–136. There is no indication that the divine council was democratic or pluralistic, *contra* Val Larsen, "First Visions and Last Sermons: Affirming Divine Sociality, Rejecting the Greater Apostasy," *Interpreter: A Journal of Latter-day Saint Faith and Scholarship* 36 (2020): 52–53, who notes: "In their conception of God and emphasis on the Law, the Deuteronomists exhibited a centralizing, monist impulse at odds with the pluralism inherent in the council ethos. The implementation of their vision required an earthly analogue of their heavenly Solitary Sovereign, a Yahwist monarch. Thus the most important Deuteronomist was Josiah, the king. Without his leadership, the Deuteronomist revolution would have been impossible. Worship of the Abrahamic Gods of the Sôd was too entrenched and widespread to be eliminated without a strong monarch leader." As Theodore Mullen noted, "the divine council has no authority or power apart from the high god. Though a full hypostatization does not seem to have taken place, the assembly and the decree of the high god are inseparable." This is true of Canaanite and Phoenician formulations as well, and thus cannot be blamed on Deuteronomists. E. Theodore Mullen, Jr., *The Divine Council in Canaanite and Early Hebrew Literature* (Leiden, NL:

Christians as teaching deification and astralisation.[118] This reception history is a surer guide to what ancients found problematic than many modern assertions are.

An Embodied God

The God in Deuteronomy is an anthropomorphic, embodied God.

> Consequently, it is crucial to note that neither these nor any other verses in Deuteronomy claim that God is invisible or lacks a body. Rather, these verses state that God's body cannot be seen by humans because the latter are on earth while God's body is in heaven. Scholars are correct to claim that Deuteronomy's is a theology of transcendence, but emphasizing transcendence and rejecting anthropomorphism are two different things. Deuteronomy's emphasis on transcendence remains quite literal: God transcends this world in the spatial sense that He sits enthroned up there, while we are down here. Consequently, there is no reason to suspect that the book's conception of God is anything but Anthropomorphic.[119]

Day of Atonement

It has been alleged that Deuteronomy is opposed to the day of atonement, since it is omitted from the list of holidays. The reasoning is somewhat facile, given how Exodus itself omits the day from its equivalent lists[120] "A key fact to remember is that Deuteronomy's laws respond to a new context of entering the promised land. Thus, the

---

Brill, 1980), 279.

118. David A. Burnett, "A Neglected Deuteronomic Scriptural Matrix for the Nature of the Resurrection Body in 1 Corinthians 15:39–42?" in, *Scripture, Texts, and Tracings in 1 Corinthians*, ed. Linda L. Belleville and B. J. Oropeza (Lanham, MD: Lexington Books; Fortress Academic, 2019), 187–211; David A. Burnett, "So Shall Your Seed Be": Paul's Use of Genesis 15:5 in Romans 4:18 in Light of Early Jewish Deification Traditions," *Journal for the Study of Paul and His Letters* 5, no. 2 (2015): 220–226.
119. Benjamin D. Sommer, *Bodies of God*, 64.
120. Exodus 30:10 mentions an atonement made once a year over the altar, but no fixed time of year is mentioned. Exodus 23 and 34 list the same festivals as Deuteronomy 16. "The problem of the first of Tishrei is connected to the tenth of it, which is the day of atonement. Apart from Lev. 16, it is mentioned only in the two holy day lists that include the first of Tishrei as a holy day." Jacob S. Licht, *Time and Holy Days*, 107.

legal revision that Deuteronomy employs is one that contextualizes and applies older laws for living in the promised land."[121]

How Old Is It?

An early date for Deuteronomy has never been off the table in biblical studies; almost as soon as the late date was proposed, an early date was defended.[122] However, the dating remains a vexed issue. By means of illustration, "Ernest W. Nicholson has run the gamut of opinions within his career, originally affirming an eighth and seventh-century dating, before revising this opinion completely to prefer an exilic date."[123]

A fruitful line of inquiry into Deuteronomy's composition date is to interrogate its teachings on kingship, and how that may reflect its historical environment. There is a dearth of any mention of specific administrative offices and realities that would reflect the period of the late monarchy and its interests. While Deuteronomy recognizes the need for a monarchy, it seems to come from a political context different than that of monarchy.

> The King Law cannot be taken as an indication that essential parts of Deuteronomy or the Pentateuch are dependent on the Prophets. A more plausible background to the King Law should perhaps be sought in pre-monarchic circles in ancient Israel. It appears to stem from a period where Israel has not yet any direct experience with monarchy as a governmental system but would be tempted to adopt the value systems of ancient Near Eastern kingship together with the very notion of royal government.[124]

In its political aspects, there are enough indicators of Deuteronomy predating Josiah's reign that it cannot be glibly assumed that either he or his supporters wrote it. If this cannot be safely assumed,

---

121. Majors, *King-Priest in Samuel*, 207.
122. Rannfrid Irene Thelle, *Approaches to the 'Chosen Place': Accessing a Biblical Concept* (New York: T&T Clark International, 2012), 7.
123. Laura Elizabeth Quick, *Deuteronomy 28 and the Aramaic Curse Tradition* (Oxford: Oxford University Press, 2017), 135.
124. Carsten Vang, "The Non-Prophetic Background for the King Law in Deut 17:14–20," in *Paradigm Change in Pentateuchal Research*, ed. Matthias Armgardt, Benjamin Kilchör, and Markus Zehnder, Beihefte Zur Zeitschrift Fur Altorientalische Und Biblische 22 (Wiesbaden: Otto Harrassowitz, 2019), 208.

then its relationship to the reforms and any distinctive school of deuteronomists should be reconsidered.

The Deuteronomist(s)

The historian-redactor responsible for the Kings History has earned the modern moniker of Deuteronomist. Regardless of his relationship to Deuteronomy, it is worth considering what kind of man he likely was.[125] One scholar observed:

> Dtr is a skillful historian, with a deep and original understanding of the past. He is also a great writer, with a clear theological agenda. So he is a writer, a theologian, and a historian, and there is no contradiction between these definitions. ... [H]e is the most important historian of biblical times, who offered his readers a comprehensive historical picture of Israel's past, from the Exodus until the Babylonian exile. ... Dtr does not regard Israel's history as a random collection of events. Quite the opposite: he emphasizes the direct involvement of God in history. His work was not written just to teach the historical facts, although it is certainly important to him to describe the main events. He writes a moral history intended to teach his contemporaries a moral and religious lesson and to prepare them for future developments.[126]

This not only sounds like Mormon, but it could also *be* Mormon; or at least an apt description of his literary project.[127] This is not the secret, sinister cabal of conniving scribes that some have imagined.

Galil argues that the Deuteronomist redactor lived in the early Babylonian exile and reworked prior editions of scriptural books into Deuteronomy, Joshua-Kings and Jeremiah, with small additions after him. Others consider the entire corpus pre-exilic, and still others date

---

125. He would almost certainly have been a man. We have no evidence for female scribes in ancient Israel, let alone ones who composed or redacted entire books. Athalya Brenner, "Introduction," in Athalya Brenner and Fokkelien Van Dijk-Hemmes, *On Gendering Texts: Female and Male Voices in the Hebrew Bible* (Leiden, NL: E. J. Brill, 1996), 5.
126. Gershon Galil, *God's Love Story: Past, Present and Future in the Deuteronomistic Composition* (Münster, DE: Zaphon Verlag, 2022), 155.
127. I appreciate Gregory Smith sharing some turns of phrase with me. For more on the parallels between Mormon and the Deuteronomist redactors, see Gregory Dundas, *Mormon's Record*, 300–320, as well as his fuller discussion of sacral history and the Deuteronomists on pp. 175–211.

it far later to the Persian or even Hasmonean eras.[128] As mentioned, the question is vexed. Whatever the dating, the only substantive difference would be the specific historical circumstances of the redactor. As outlined by Galil, the character and value system would be relevant regardless of the chronology.

Jeremiah

The prophet Jeremiah was a contemporary of Josiah, albeit a younger one.[129] No explicit references to the reforms appear in his writings, and many have argued against any implicit ones, either.[130] This silence is a puzzle with no satisfactory answer, and no consensus has been reached despite the life of Jeremiah being one of the most studied by scholars.[131]

Perhaps a partial answer is to be found in the later Jewish apocryphal tradition that Josiah did not believe Jeremiah's accusations against the people, because he trusted too much in the genuineness of their repentance.[132] In other words, Jeremiah may have supported the need for the reforms, but was disappointed that the people's repentance was only skin-deep. There is, however, a more solid line of enquiry.

Is there anything in Jeremiah's teachings that would have conflicted with the reforms? The answer appears to be no.

Like Huldah, Jeremiah also accuses Judah of worshipping other gods, which will result in their destruction.[133] The teachings and oracles of Jeremiah abound with examples of God's anger over this dis-

---

128. Galil, *God's Love Story*, 155–156.
129. William Holladay concluded that the phrase "in the thirteenth year" really meant Jeremiah was born in that year, as he was called in the womb. This reading seems forced. William L. Holladay, *Jeremiah 1: A Commentary on the Book of the Prophet Jeremiah Chapters 1–25*, Hermeneia Commentary (Philadelphia: Fortress Press, 1986), 1–2.
130. Niels Peter Lemche, "Did a Reform like Josiah's Happen?" in *The Historian and the Bible: Essays in Honour of Lester L. Grabbe*, ed. Philip R. Davies and Diana Vikander Edelman (New York: Bloomsbury T & T Clark, 2010), 17–18.
131. William L. Holladay, *Jeremiah: Reading the Prophet in His Time — and Ours* (Minneapolis: Fortress Press, 1990), 1–2; Jack R. Lundbom, *The Early Career of the Prophet Jeremiah* (Eugene, OR: Wipf and Stock, 2012), xv–xviii.
132. See the discussion below of Babylonian Talmud, T. Ta'anit 22a-22b.
133. Jeremiah 4 and 11, among many; Oded and Kochman, *2 Kings*, 9:196.

loyal behavior. "By one count, 42 different verses in Jeremiah mention or elaborate on God's anger."[134]

Jeremiah also, at times, speaks highly of Josiah and the members of the Hilkiad and Shaphanid families. This has led some to argue that positive references to Deuteronomy and the Deuteronomist reforms were added later.[135] However, this is ad hoc reasoning, resting upon preconceived notions. J. Unterman refuted the claim that pro-Josianic passages in Jeremiah are a late addition.[136]

Jeremiah 22:15–17 contains a striking assessment of Josiah's righteousness, in contrast with that of his son, Jehoiakim.

> Shalt thou reign, because thou strivest to excel in cedar? Did not thy father eat and drink, and do justice and righteousness? Then it was well with him. He judged the cause of the poor and needy; then it was well. Is not this to know Me? saith the LORD. But thine eyes and thy heart are not but for thy covetousness, and for shedding innocent blood, and for oppression, and for violence, to do it.

According to this divine oracle delivered by the prophet, Josiah did justice, encapsulated by his treatment of widows and orphans, the most vulnerable members of ancient society.[137] The chronicler directs his readers to a corpus of laments, which includes some written by Jeremiah and others, for Josiah's death (2 Chronicles 35:25–27). This is a strong, positive reference whose authenticity cannot be easily dismissed.

---

134. Elmer A. Martens, "Toward an End to Violence: Hearing Jeremiah," in *Wrestling with the Violence of God: Soundings in the Old Testament,* ed. M. Daniel Carroll R. and J. Blair Wilgus (Winona Lake, IN: Eisenbrauns, 2015), 134.
135. J. Philip Hyatt, "Jeremiah and Deuteronomy," *Journal of Near Eastern Studies* 1, no. 2 (April 1942): 165–172.
136. Jeremiah Unterman, *From Repentance to Redemption: Jeremiah's Thought in Transition,* Journal for the Study of the Old Testament Supplement Series 54 (Sheffield, GB: JSOT Press, 1987), 26–28. On the importance of the Shaphanid family to Jeremiah, see Nicholas R. Werse, *Reconsidering the Book of the Four: The Shaping of Hosea, Amos, Micah, and Zephaniah as an Early Prophetic Collection* (Berlin: De Gruyter, 2019), 334–336.
137. Sweeney observed that the things Josiah was praised for are characteristic of Deuteronomy's legal code, and he cites further references to that code. Marvin A. Sweeney, *King Josiah of Judah: The Lost Messiah of Israel* (New York: Oxford University Press, 2001), 211.

THE DEATH OF JOSIAH

The death of Josiah is the most enigmatic episode in his life. Even ancient authors struggled with it, and 2 Kings and 2 Chronicles differ in important details. The problem stems from a contradiction between Huldah's prophesied peaceful fate for Josiah and the actual circumstances of his violent death. That death would violate the principle of divine reward and punishment. Those problems cannot be resolved here.

When Josiah was 39, Pharaoh Necho II led an expeditionary force through the land of Israel. He was moving to aid the Assyrian empire against Babylon, and Josiah barred his way.

> This was a pronounced pro-Babylonian policy based on geopolitical considerations, that shortly afterward were proven as justified: Josiah was convinced that the struggle between the principal players would not end in an Assyrian victory, and thus it was. Only, Josiah was unable to stop Pharaoh and was killed in battle.[138]

Necho II sent a message to Josiah. The language is somewhat obscure, but the overall meaning was that Necho did not intend to interfere with Josiah's kingdom, so Josiah should let him pass. His problem was with Babylon. Josiah rightly saw through this sophistry, and recognized the ultimate threat posed by a strong Egypt.

Second Chronicles' geopolitical take on the events is preferred to 2 Kings, but when it comes to the religious significance, the latter offers the better reading. The links to Deuteronomy are strong, and hold the key to the entire narrative.

The verses of Deuteronomy 6:4–5 are part of a single unit and should be read together. They are typically known as the Shema, and together form a central prayer in Judaism to this day. The unit is liturgical-confessional, meaning that it was part of the formula of public worship and expressed the core of faith and worship. The Shema was seen as a form of bearing witness or testimony, and just like the latter word, was ultimately connected to the concept of covenant. The famous declaration that "YHWH is one" uses a term frequently

---

138. Yair Hoffman, ed., *Jeremiah*, Olam HaTanach, 24 vols., 6th ed., ed. Y. Amit, A. Berlin, H. Cohen, et. al (Tel-Aviv: Divrei HaYamim Publishing, 2002), 11:121; Smirin, *Josiah and His Times*, 98–100, 102–103.

applied in the Bible to the object of one's love and thus, is deeply connected to the requirement in the next verse to love God.

> Love in the book of Deuteronomy has the particular meaning of loyalty, and a completely identical phenomenon is found in fealty oaths by Ancient Near Eastern vassals, and also in treaties from the classical world — Greek, Hellenistic, Roman — terms of love and affection express loyalty. Whereas in the rest of the ancient world "love" meant political allegiance, here it means religious allegiance. Thus, the expression "Thou shalt love YHWH thy God" should be understood as "Thou must be loyal to YHWH thy God."[139]

The combination of the terms *lev*, *nefesh* and *me'od* indicate the complete and total nature of this love and loyalty to God. *Lev* is the heart, which anciently was the seat of thought, as well as of good and evil urges. *Nefesh* is the soul, which was also used synonymously with one's life. *Me'od*, or much, plenty, was often used to mean one's power and its sources: property and possessions. This encompassed not just wealth but also might of arms.[140]

Over-familiarity with the repeated command to love God with all our heart, might, mind, and strength may obscure just how strong a demand God can make on his covenant people. In many ancient treaties, a vassal was required to assist his lord "with all his heart," which meant providing him with men and chariots — equivalent to *me'od* in Deuteronomy — and even a willingness to assist with "all his soul." That is, the vassal was required to die for his lord if necessary.[141]

This is seen in the terms that are used in 2 Kings 23:25 to praise Josiah after he was killed in battle to defend his kingdom against Pharaoh Necho II. It states that Josiah turned back to God (repented and showed him loyalty) with all his *lev*, all his *nefesh*, and all his *me'od*.

---

139. Moshe Weinfeld, *The Decalogue and the Recitation of "Shema": The Development of the Confessions* (Tel Aviv: Ha-Kibbutz Ha-Meuhad, 2001), 131 [Hebrew].
140. Hence the LXX 'strength,' δυνάμεως. For just how often this covenantal commandment is reiterated in the standard works, see Neil J. Flinders and Paul Wangemann, "A Systematic Examination of the Terms Heart, Mind, Might, and Strength as Used in the Standard Works of the Church of Jesus Christ of Latter-day Saints," *Deseret Language and Linguistic Society Symposium* 12, no. 1 (1986): 164–197.
141. Weinfeld, *The Decalogue and the Recitation of "Shema,"* 133 [Hebrew].

These are the exact trio of words used in the Shema. Josiah is shown to be God's selfless and loyal vassal who did not hesitate to lay down his life for Him in battle.

Josiah's vision of a righteous kingdom of covenant people died alongside him that day in Megiddo. Despite Egypt's best efforts, Necho II's subsequent defeat at Carchemish opened the door for Babylonian expansion to the south, and Egypt's allies were subjugated one by one. It was never again able to exercise control over the Levant until the period of the Ptolemies.

Josiah in Apocryphal and Post-Biblical Texts

How were Josiah's reforms and his own character later perceived? The question is important because such texts preserve, if not reliable history, then at least some kind of popular memory. The authors of such texts were also often perceptive readers of scripture. Scholars, such as Margaret Barker, have looked to such works for traces and echoes of unofficial or unorthodox and suppressed beliefs.[142] It is thus fair to query them as sources of collective memory, whatever their accuracy.

References are infrequent but the picture is overwhelmingly positive. Ben Sira has high praise for Josiah, linking him to one of the most memorable features of the ancient temple to those who worshipped there: incense burning.

> The name JOSIAH is like blended incense,
> made lasting by a skilled perfumer.
> Precious is his memory, like honey to the taste,
> like music at a banquet.
>
> For he grieved over our betrayals,
> and destroyed the abominable idols.
> He kept his heart fixed on God,
> and in times of lawlessness practiced virtue.
>
> Except for David, Hezekiah, and Josiah,
> they all were wicked;
> They abandoned the Law of the Most High,
> these kings of Judah, right to the very end. (Ben Sira 49, NABRE)

---

142. Margaret Barker, "What Did King Josiah Reform?" in *Glimpses of Lehi's Jerusalem*, ed. John W. Welch, David Rolph Seely, and Jo Ann H. Seely (Provo, UT: Foundation for Ancient Research and Mormon Studies, 2004), 524–542.

The praise is effusive. The art of the ancient perfumer was highly demanding, especially when combining various elements into one whole.[143] Josiah is also sweet "like honey" in a society where sweeteners were hard to come by, and he is like the "music at a banquet" (Ben Sira says wine banquet), or in other words, a symposium. That is a communal gathering where "music and conversation between good men about good things are identified as the primary route to virtue and wisdom."[144]

The reasons for this praise are that Josiah kept his heart fixed on God; practiced virtue when others did the opposite; kept to what the Lord commanded; and grieved for the people's apostasy. Most importantly, he rooted out the idols that turned men's hearts away from God. Josiah embodied virtue.

Josephus also viewed Josiah positively.

> And when he was twelve years old, he gave demonstrations of his religious and righteous behavior: for he brought the people to a sober way of living, and exhorted them to leave off the opinion they had of their idols; because they were not Gods; but to worship their own God. And by reflecting on the actions of his progenitors, he prudently corrected what they did wrong, like a very elderly man, and like one abundantly able to understand what was fit to be done: and what he found they had well done, he observed all the country over, and imitated the same. And thus he acted in following the wisdom and sagacity of his own nature, and in compliance with the advice and instruction of the elders. For by following the laws it was that he succeeded so well in the order of his government; and in piety with regard to the divine worship. And this happened because the transgressions of the former Kings were seen no more, but quite vanished away.[145]

---

143. For Ben Sira this is the temple incense, and also connected with wisdom. Martha Himmelfarb, *A Kingdom of Priests: Ancestry and Merit in Ancient Judaism* (Philadelphia: University of Pennsylvania Press, 2006), 37-38; Jan Liesen, *Full of Praise: An Exegetical Study of Sir 39, 12-35* (Leiden, NL: Brill, 1999), 135. On incense in general, see Alan Millard, "Incense - The Ancient Room Freshener: The Exegesis of Daniel 2:46," in *On Stone and Scroll: Essays in Honour of Graham Ivor Davies*, ed. James K. Aitken, Katharine J. Dell, and Brian A. Mastin (Berlin: De Gruyter, 2011), 111-121.
144. Fiona Hobden, *The Symposion in Ancient Greek Society and Thought* (Cambridge: Cambridge University Press, 2013), 41.
145. Josephus, *Antiquities of the Jews*, 10.4.1.

[Huldah] bid them go back to the King, and say, that "God had already given sentence against them, to destroy the people, and cast them out of their country, and deprive them of all the happiness they enjoyed; which sentence none could set aside by any prayers of theirs: since it was passed on account of their transgressions of the laws, and of their not having repented in so long a time: while the Prophets had exhorted them to amend, and had foretold the punishment that would ensue on their impious practices: which threatening God would certainly execute upon them: that they might be persuaded that he is God, and had not deceived them in any respect, as to what he had denounced by his Prophets: that yet, because Josiah was a righteous man, he would at present delay those calamities; but that after his death he would send on the multitude what miseries he had determined for them.[146]

When retelling the story of Josiah's death, Josephus introduces the element of fate or destiny, making the king a victim of the same forces active in a Greek tragedy. That is, his death is not because of personal wickedness or sin. "But Josiah did not admit of this request of Neco's: but put himself into a posture to hinder him from his intended march. I suppose it was destiny that pushed him on this conduct; that it might take an occasion against him."[147]

Elsewhere, Josephus wrote that "It is impossible for men to escape their fate even though they foresee it."[148] Josiah's death does not diminish his virtue or righteousness, and Josephus concludes by sharing the tradition that Jeremiah lamented his death. This is a tradition we find across various Jewish groups. "The Rabbis, as well as Josephus, understand 2 [Chronicles] 35.25 to refer to the Book of Lamentations, in which Jeremiah laments the fate of the 'anointed of the Lord' [Lamentations 4:20], by which Josiah is meant."[149]

Second Baruch, a work likely written no earlier than the beginning of the second century AD, goes further in its praise of Josiah than the Hebrew Bible does. Baruch sees a vision of bright waters.

---

146. Josephus, *Antiquities,* 10.4.2.
147. Josephus, *Antiquities,* 10.5.1.
148. Josephus, *Wars of the Jews,* 6.314, as given in Louis H. Feldman, *Josephus's Interpretation of the Bible* (Berkeley and Los Angeles: University of California Press, 1998), 195.
149. Louis Ginzberg, *Legends of the Jews,* 2 vols. (Philadelphia: Jewish Publication Society, 2003) 2:1062.

> And the tenth bright waters you have seen; that is the purity of the generation of Josiah, the king of Judah, who was the only one in his time who subjected himself to the Mighty One with his whole heart and his whole soul. He purified the country from the idols, sanctified all the vessels which were polluted, restored the offerings to the altar, raised the horn of the holy, exalted the righteous, and honored all those who were wise with understanding.[150]

The reforms and, indeed, their violence are commended in the vision.

> And he was zealous with the zeal of the Mighty One with his whole soul, and he alone was strong in the Law at that time so that he left no one un-circumcised or anyone who acted wickedly in the whole country all the days of his life. He, then, is one who shall receive reward forever and ever and be honored with the Mighty One more than many in the last time. For on his account and on account of those who are like him, the precious glories have been created and prepared which were spoken to you earlier. These are those bright waters which you have seen.[151]

A prayer which begins "even as you received the gifts of the righteous in their generations" includes Josiah among the righteous who are praised.[152]

Pseudo-Hegesippus wrote something between a commentary and a paraphrase of Josephus's *Wars*, and provided a Christian take on what he considered Josiah's exemplary death.

> What shall I say of Josiah, than whom no one was a better expounder of **religio**, despiser of death, advocate of liberty? For he, located on that regal promontory wherefrom it was possible to escape death, yet because he saw that on account of [its] grievous sins the captivity of the people of Israel was impending, embroiled himself in a foreign war, and he fled life. Neco cried out: "I have not been sent against you, but to the king of Israel." Yet he did not fall back before falling victim

---

150. A. F. J. Klijn, trans., *2 (Syriac Apocalypse of) Baruch* 66:1–2, The Old Testament Pseudepigrapha, 2 vols., ed. James H. Charlesworth (Peabody, MA: Hendrickson Academic, 2010), 1:643–644.
151. Klijn, *2 Baruch* 66:5–8, 1:644.
152. D. R. Darnell, trans., *Hellenistic Synagogal Prayers*, 6:3–10, The Old Testament Pseudepigrapha, 2 vols., ed. James H. Charlesworth (Peabody, MA: Hendrickson Academic, 2010), 2:684–685.

to the lethal point of an arrow. Cast down by this wound, he is an indication to us whether merit or chance is more influential in war. Josiah, the restorer of sacred rites, was defeated, and Neco, the most villainous of all people, was victorious, but he (Josiah), conquered, is now with the angels, and this "victor" is in torment.[153]

The Syriac Cave of Treasures continues along the same lines.

> He was eight years old when he began to rule, and he reigned in Jerusalem for thirty-one years. ... He did what is good in front of the Lord, and did everything just as his father David had, swaying neither to the right nor to the left. Pharaoh the lame killed him, he died, and his son Jehoahaz ruled after him.[154]

Other Syriac sources bear this out, and Ephrem the Syrian relates a fictional argument between Death and Satan over which of them is mightier.

> DEATH: Josiah from his youth up
> despised you, O Evil One, [II Kgs 22:1–2]
> yet even in his old age
> he could not get the better of me [II Kgs 23:29–30].[155]

Death explicitly states that Josiah despised the Devil, and thus was a righteous man, yet even he could not avoid death.

A debate over which calamities require the sounding of an alarm leads the Talmud to discuss Josiah's fatal encounter with Necho.

> **Rather, even** in a case of **a sword of peace,** when an army passes through with no intention of waging war against the Jews, but is merely on its way to another place, this is enough to obligate the court to sound the alarm, **as you do not have a greater example of a sword of peace than Pharaoh Neco.** He passed through Eretz Yisrael to wage war with Nebuchadnezzar, **and**

---

153. Carson Bay, *Biblical Heroes and Classical Culture in Christian Late Antiquity: The Historiography, Exemplarity, and Anti-Judaism of Pseudo-Hegesippus* (Cambridge: Cambridge University Press, 2023), 114–116.
154. Alexander Toepel, trans., *The Cave of Treasures* 40:11–14, *Old Testament Pseudepigrapha: More Noncanonical Scriptures,* 2 vols., ed. Richard Bauckham, James R. Davila, and Alexander Panayotov (Grand Rapids, MI: William B. Eerdmans Publishing Company, 2013), 1:570.
155. Sebastian P. Brock, *Treasure-House of Mysteries: Explorations of the Sacred Text through Poetry in the Syriac Tradition* (Yonkers, NY: St. Vladimirs Seminary Press, 2012), 230.

> nevertheless King Josiah stumbled in this matter. ... **What is the meaning of the phrase "God, Who is with me"? Rav Yehuda said** that Rav said: This is referring to Neco's **idolatry, which he brought for assistance.** ... Josiah **said: Since** he trusts in idolatry, **I will be able** to defeat **him.** ... **For what reason was Josiah punished? Because he should have consulted with** the prophet **Jeremiah to find out if he should go to war, but he did not consult** with him. **How did** Josiah **interpret** the verses of the Torah? How did they lead him to go to war? The verse states: **"Neither shall a sword go through your land"** (Leviticus 26:6). **What is** the meaning of the term: **"Sword"? If we say** that it is referring to **a sword that is not of peace, but isn't it written** earlier in the same verse: **"And I will give peace in the land"? Rather,** the verse must mean that **even a sword of peace** shall not pass through the land, and Josiah sought to prevent this occurrence, in fulfillment of the blessing. **But he did not know that his generation did not merit** these blessings, and he would therefore not receive divine assistance in this regard.[156]

That is it, a single mistake. The Talmud closes out its discussion with a story involving the prophet Jeremiah and the dying king.

> **When** Josiah **was dying, Jeremiah saw his lips moving.** Jeremiah said: **Perhaps, Heaven forbid, he is saying something improper** and complaining about God's judgment **on account of his** great **distress.** Jeremiah **bent over and heard that he was justifying God's judgment against himself.** Josiah **said: "The Lord is righteous, for I have rebelled against His word"** (Lamentations 1:18). **At that moment,** Jeremiah **began** his **eulogy** for Josiah: **"The breath of our nostrils, the anointed of the Lord,** was trapped in their pits" (Lamentations 4:20).[157]

Even when Josiah made a mistake, he was believed to have acknowledged it and still praised God. The mistake in not consulting Jeremiah before going to war against Pharaoh was just that, a mistake, not an indictment of his character or reforms. In the narrative, Josiah's humility and love for God, despite horrific physical pain[158] so moves Jeremiah that he composes an inspired lament on the spot. The

---

156. T. Ta'anit 22a-22b, *Babylonian Talmud*, Steinsaltz edition, 22 vols. (New York: Random House, 1995), 14:108–109, emphasis in the original.
157. Ta'anit 22b., *Babylonian Talmud*, 14:109, emphasis in the original.
158. The narrative says Josiah was shot through with so many arrows that he was like a sieve.

Targum of Chronicles continues this line of interpretation. "These words add to TC a depiction of Josiah as a righteous king, unwavering in his loyalty to the God of Israel, who ironically met his end as a result of an excess of faith in God."[159]

Seder Olam Rabbah is an early chronology of biblical and Jewish history. Alongside the dry listing of events, it often contains narrative details.

> (2Chr. 34:1, 2Kings 22:1) "Eight years old was Josiah when he became king and 31 years he reigned in Jerusalem. ... (2Kings 22:3) "It was in the 18th year of king Josiah 218 years." In that year, the book of the Torah was found in the Temple and in that year had Josiah made repairs to the Temple. There were from the repairs under Joash until the repairs under Josiah. And why was it necessary to repair so quickly in the days of Joash? (2Chr. 24:7) "Because of the criminal Athaliahu, her sons damaged the House of God. ..." That year, Josiah repented (2Kings. 23:25) "and before him there was no king who so wholeheartedly returned to the Eternal... ." Josiah hid the Ark as it is said (2Chr. 35:3): "He said to the Levites, the instructors of all of Israel, the ones holy to the Eternal, put the Holy Ark into the Temple built by Solomon, David's son, king of Israel, so that it cannot be carried further on the shoulders." (2Kings 23:29) "In his days there attacked Pharao Necho, the king of Egypt, against the king of Assyria on the river Euphrates; King Josiah went towards him, but he (Necho) had him (Josiah) killed as soon as he (Necho) saw (him)." (2Chr. 35:21–24) "He (Necho) had sent him messengers, saying: What have I to do with you, king of Judah ... But Josiah did not turn his face away from him ... And the archers shot at king Josiah ... So his servants transferred him to his secondary chariot and brought him to Jerusalem where he died ...." Jeremiah composed a funeral dirge about him (Threni 4:20): "The spirit of our life, the anointed of the Eternal, was caught in their pits."[160]

The *Pirkei de-Rabbi Eliezer* is in many ways closer to Second Temple apocrypha and the rewritten Bible than it is to Rabbinic Judaism. It often preserves the witness of largely independent traditions. These also praise Josiah. *Pirkei* 17:14 holds that Josiah was foreor-

---

159. Leeor Gottlieb, *Targum Chronicles and Its Place Among the Late Targums* (Leiden, NL: Brill, 2020), 351.
160. Heinrich W. Guggenheimer, *Seder Olam: The Rabbinic View of Biblical Chronology* (Lanham, MD: Jason Aronson, Inc., 1998), 210.

dained, was perfectly righteous before God, and was killed for the secret sins of his people. He was too righteous to remain among the wicked.

> Rabbi Nathaniel said: Three hundred years before the birth of Josiah, was his name mentioned, as it is said, "Behold, a child shall be born unto the house of David, Josiah by name" (1 Kings 13:2); "And he was eight years old when he began to reign" (2 Kings 22:1). What is the disposition of a lad of eight years of age? He despised the idols and broke in pieces the pillars, and smashed the images and cut down the groves. His merit was great before the Throne of Glory. Because of the evil which Israel did in secret the righteous one was gathered (to his fathers), as it is said, "For the righteous is taken away because of the evil" ([Isaiah] 57:1). || All Judah gathered together also with Jeremiah the prophet to show lovingkindness to Josiah, as it is said, "And Jeremiah lamented for Josiah, and all the singing men and the singing women spake of Josiah" (2 [Chronicles] 35:25).[161]

Apocryphal texts provide no support for any claims of wicked, corrupt reforms. If there were, it was not part of the collective memory several hundred years down the line. This is an idea that has only emerged in the modern era.

THE WITNESS OF THE RESTORATION

There are very few direct references to Josiah in the Restoration. All of them, though, view Josiah positively. While Latter-day Saints are not bound by tradition or precedent here, these do bear some weight and should be considered.

Joseph Smith would make two revisions to the Josiah narratives in his Bible "translation." The first revision is this, 2 Kings 22:2: "And he did that which was right in the sight of the Lord and walked not in all the way of David his father and turned not aside to the right hand or to the left."[162]

---

161. Gerald Friedlander, *Pirkê de Rabbi Eliezer: (the Chapters of Rabbi Eliezer the Great) According to the Text of the Manuscript Belonging to Abraham Epstein of Vienna* (New York: Bloch Publishing, 1916), 121. See also 32:6, where Josiah's divinely preordained name (*Yoshiyahu* יאשיהו) is punned upon by God as "let him be a gift" (*yaei shai hu* יאי שי הו) for the sacrificial altar.
162. Kent P. Jackson, ed., *Joseph Smith's Translation of the Bible* (Provo, UT: Religious Studies Center, Brigham Young University; BYU Press; Salt Lake

Joseph took particular care to avoid the potential for misreading the verse as meaning that Josiah engaged in any of David's sins. In the OT Revision 2 manuscript, Joseph changed the word order of 2 Chronicles 34:16 from "and brought the king word back again" to "and brought the word of the king back again." Whatever Joseph may have meant by this, he was clearly not claiming Josiah and his men created the book themselves, or that they engaged in any kind of wrongdoing.

> 2 Kings, Chapter 9–25
>
> The rest of the Seccond Book of the Kings Correct ...
>
> 2 Chronicles, Chapter 33
>
> XXXIII— Correct——
>
> 2 Chronicles, Chapter 34
>
> XXXIV— 16 Verse and Shaphan carried the book to the king, and brought the word of the king back again, saying, all that was commited to thy servants they do
>
> 2 Chroniclse, Chapter 35
>
> XXXV— Correct——[163]

Orson Pratt emphasized the importance of scriptures in many of his discourses, and Josiah was an important spiritual model for him.

> The history of the inspired writings anterior to the Babylonish captivity is very brief. The number of copies were very few. In the days of Josiah, all of the Jews seem to have been destitute of a copy of the law. During the reign of that king, in repairing the house of the Lord, a copy of the book of the law was found; and when presented to the king, he sent five messengers to Huldah, the prophetess, saying, "Go, enquire of the Lord for me, and for them that are left in Israel and in Judah, concerning the words of the book that is found." 2 [Chronicles] 34:21 The messengers returned and reported to the king that the book found was indeed a Divine revelation, and the king caused all the inhabitants of Jerusalem to be assembled to hear the words of the book. (See 2 [Chronicles] 34:1–33)
>
> For a long period previous to finding the book, the Jews had been ignorant of the Scriptures, and had fallen into the grossest idolatry. A new revelation through the prophetess

---

City: Deseret Book, 2021), 153.

163. Joseph Smith, "Old Testament Revision 2," p. 78, *Joseph Smith Papers,* online at josephsmithpapers.org.

> Huldah seems to have been sufficient to convince the king and all Israel of the divinity of the book. They must have been inclined, in that age of the world, to believe the history of the servants of God more than in this age; for now the people generally require a vast amount of evidence. The testimony of a dozen witnesses is scarcely regarded.[164]

Orson would return to this theme in his sermon, this time explicitly relating it to the Book of Mormon. He saw strong parallels between it and Josiah's reforms, all positive.

> I have already observed, through the persecutions raised against the house of Israel, their books were destroyed; yes, even the tables of stone, for some reason, were taken from them, and all Israel were left without even a copy of the law, until accidentally they happened to find one that had been hid in the house of the Lord, as I have already named; and they were so ignorant with regard to this copy that they were obliged to send for Huldah, one of the prophetesses in Israel, 2 [Chronicles] 34:22 to inquire of the Lord to know if it really was his word. They found a book, but they did not know whether it was true or false; and they thought it important that it should be determined by the immediate word of God.
>
> Why not this generation go and do likewise? Why not inquire of the Lord whether the Book of Mormon is a Divine revelation? The copy found anciently contained the words of the Lord. And the people were so rejoiced that the whole nation of Jews gathered together to hear it read, and rejoiced over it, and gave heed to its precepts. They were not like the present generation; they did not fight it, and testify all manner of evil against it, and publish lies against it; but they believed it on the testimony of the prophetess.[165]

Just as Josiah inquired of God through a prophet when he received new scripture, so too must people today when they encounter the Book of Mormon or the gospel as restored through the prophet Joseph Smith.

President Spencer W. Kimball continued this line of thought, commending Josiah as *the* model to follow.

The story of King Josiah in the Old Testament is a most

---

164. Orson Pratt, "Evidences of the Bible and Book of Mormon Compared," in *Journal of Discourses,* 26 vols., ed. G. D. Watt, J. V. Long, et al (Liverpool: Amasa Lyman, 1860), 7:23–24.
165. Orson Pratt, "Evidences of the Bible and Book of Mormon Compared," 7:24.

profitable one to "liken ... unto [our]selves." (1 [Nephi] 19:24.) To me, it is one of the finest stories in all of the scriptures.

Josiah was only eight years old when he began to reign in Judah, and although his immediate progenitors were extremely wicked, the scriptures tell us that "he did that which was right in the sight of the Lord, and walked in all the way of David his father, and turned not aside to the right hand or to the left." (2 Kings 22:2.) This is all the more surprising when we learn that by that time (just two generations before the destruction of Jerusalem in 587 B.C.) the written law of Moses had been lost and was virtually unknown, even among the priests of the temple!

But in the eighteenth year of his reign, Josiah directed that the temple be repaired. At that time Hilkiah, the high priest, found the book of the law, which Moses had placed in the ark of the covenant, and delivered it to King Josiah.

When the book of the law was read to Josiah, he "rent his clothes" and wept before the Lord....

The king then read the book before all the people, and at that time they all made a covenant to obey all the Lord's commandments "with all their heart and all their soul." (2 Kings 23:3.) Then Josiah proceeded to clean up the kingdom of Judah, removing all the idols, the groves, the high places, and all the abominations that had accumulated during the reign of his fathers, defiling the land and its people. ...

I feel strongly that we must all of us return to the scriptures just as King Josiah did and let them work mightily within us, impelling us to an unwavering determination to serve the Lord.

Josiah had the law of Moses only. In our scriptures we have the gospel of Jesus Christ in its fulness; and if a taste is sweet, in fulness there is joy.[166]

In the same vein, Elder Joseph B. Wirthlin made brief mention of Josiah in a 1990 General Conference talk.

King Josiah was a king of Judah who reigned in righteousness. When he was only eight years old, he succeeded his father as king. Scripture tells us that although he was just a boy, Josiah "did that which was right in the sight of the Lord, ... and turned not aside to the right hand or to the left" (2 [Kings] 22:2).[167]

---

166. Spencer W. Kimball, "How Rare a Possession — the Scriptures!" *Ensign* (September 1976): 4–5.
167. Joseph B. Wirthlin, "The Straight and Narrow Way," *Ensign* (November 1990): 64.

Not a single prophet, apostle, or other general authority of the Restoration is on record condemning, disparaging, or rejecting the reforms.

Conclusion

When all is said and done, Josiah was no villain, but a king who sought to do God's will and save his people. He was a human king who sought to follow God and do right by him; succeeding on a personal level, but ultimately failing to save his nation. He was a king who took his royal and priesthood duties seriously, ultimately giving his life for them. That is the best reading of the present evidence.

The hope is that enough points in favor of Josiah and his reforms have been raised here that, as scholars and students of the gospel, we can reclaim him as a positive example for our discipleship. His example matters and he was no bogeyman. Prophets, both ancient and modern, knew it.

Most arguments against him are not as solid as they may have seemed. Some are entirely baseless. At heart, the reforms were an attempt to regain Judah's independence, stop idolatry, and prevent the destruction of the kingdom. They were not meant to change the text of scripture, but to demonstrate recommitment to God and His covenant. Legitimate practices and symbols of ancient Israelite religion had been corrupted through the idolatrous influence of Assyria; the covenant was broken and Judah's very survival as a nation lay at stake because of it.

As king, Josiah was the head of the Levitical Priesthood, responsible for the proper functioning of the temple, and ensuring that his people adhered to God's law. His reforms were needed to extract Judah from the spiritual morass into which they had sunk. They came too late, and Josiah gave up his life in the service of God, fulfilling the greatest commandment.

One final hope is this; that by highlighting the positive nature of Josiah and his reforms, and how Nephite kings and prophets emulated the ideal of kingship he embodied, some of the insights in this preliminary reappraisal will be taken up by others, and lead to a better understanding of the Book of Mormon and other Restoration scripture.

5

FROM SINAI TO SALT LAKE

SACRED PROMISES, REIMAGINED FOR A NEW DISPENSATION

JENNIFER ROACH LEES

Latter-day Saints are well acquainted with covenants in the modern Church but often find Old Testament covenants difficult to interpret when they do not align directly with current practices. This can lead to viewing the Old Testament as inconsistent or less relevant to modern faith. In this article, the covenants of Noah, Abraham, and Moses are examined as expressions of a consistent pattern in God's dealings with His people — one marked by continuity, renewal, and expanding understanding. Each covenant gains new depth through later revelation, illustrating how divine promises unfold across time. Viewed in this way, the Restoration through Joseph Smith continues that same process of covenant renewal and fulfillment.

INTRODUCTION: I HAVE A WORK FOR YOU TO DO

The instructions which Joseph Smith received from Moroni in 1823 were primarily centered on the translation of the Gold Plates. The angel described the plates' location, the accompanying interpreters (later referred to as the Urim and Thummim), and the divine purpose behind their future translation. Joseph was told that he must not seek the plates for personal gain, but rather to fulfill God's work. The bulk of these conversations should be understood as the angel giving instructions to Joseph about how he was to begin his prophetic career and bring forth the Book of Mormon, but it also marked the beginning of his role in restoring lost truths. This was communicated to Joseph when Moroni quoted passages from Malachi, Isaiah, and Joel — scriptures that speak of priesthood restoration, the sealing power of Elijah, and the gathering of Israel. These references pointed beyond the translation of scripture to a broader divine agenda: the reestablishment of sacred covenants between God and His children.

Just like the Bible, the Book of Mormon is saturated with covenant language — promises of land, posterity, and divine favor contingent on obedience. Thus, while the immediate task was translation, the ultimate goal was the Restoration: priesthood authority, temple ordinances, and the covenant path that would prepare the earth for Christ's return. When Heavenly Father spoke through the angel Moroni and told Joseph, "I have a work for you to do," He meant far more than just a translation project. Joseph did not know it yet, but translating the Book of Mormon was to go hand-in-hand with restoring the covenant relationship between God and His children.

Covenants in Joseph's Day

In Joseph Smith's early nineteenth-century context, most Christians, especially those influenced by Protestant traditions, would have had a strong conceptual framework for understanding covenants, often through a theological lens shaped by Reformed or evangelical thought. Charles Spurgeon, an influential minister during Joseph's day said,

> There is no more blessed way of living than a life of dependence upon a covenant-keeping God. We do not need to worry because He cares for us; we do not need to carry burdens because He invites us to cast them upon Him.[1]

Additionally, many Christians would have understood covenants as binding spiritual agreements that involved both divine promises and human responsibilities. Simeon Ash said that the covenant of grace "the first and most firm foundation of a Christian's comfort."[2]

Baptism and communion were seen as signs, or seals, of covenant membership, and sermons frequently emphasized the importance of

---

1. Charles H. Spurgeon, *Morning and Evening: A New Edition of the Classic Devotional Based on the Holy Bible, English Standard Version*, rev. Alistair Begg (Wheaton, IL: Crossway Books, 2003), 256, the devotional for the evening of 1 September.
2. Simeon Ash, "To the Reader," in John Ball, *A Treatise on the Covenant of Grace: wherein The graduall breakings out of Gospel-grace from Adam to Christ are clearly discovered* (London: Simeon Ash, printed by G. Miller, 1645), A3:2, online at archive.org.

keeping one's covenant with God through moral living and personal conversion. While the theological vocabulary varied across different denominations, the idea that God relates to His people through covenants was deeply embedded in the religious imagination of Joseph's day. The young prophet was not inventing the concept of covenants, or even introducing it for the first time; rather, Joseph was restoring aspects of making covenants with God that had been lost.

However, confusion sometimes arises for Latter-day Saints when they turn to the Old Testament or the Book of Mormon, hoping to find outlined specifics about the practice of covenant-making in these ancient texts. One young missionary recently asked, "I'm here working to help people onto the covenant path, and the first covenant is baptism. I can easily go to 2 Nephi 31 to see the origins of baptism. But where can I go to find the origins of the other covenants we make?" This elder wanted to be pointed to a specific passage where he could see the origins of the covenants involving the Laws of Obedience, Sacrifice, the Gospel, Chastity, and Consecration.

Certainly, scriptural support can be found for the concepts behind the covenants; but we do not see those covenants being administered through a temple endowment-like setting as we do today. Alma the Younger instructed his son Corianton about the Law of Chastity, but they were not sitting in a temple making a formal covenant when he did so. Is this a problem? Should modern Latter-day Saints be concerned that the covenants we consider to be restored ancient truths are not presented in scripture in the same way that they are today?

To address this concern, this paper is primarily concerned with demonstrating that the covenants found in the Old Testament were not one-time static events intended only to be understood one way and never again be reinterpreted. Rather, they continually had their meaning renewed in subsequent contexts. In a similar way, the Restoration is not a carbon copy of some ancient point in time, but a re-articulation of eternal principles for today's Saints. When Joseph Smith restored covenants, he was not introducing something new — the idea of covenants already existed in his day — he was recontextualizing them for deeper meaning.

What Is the Meaning of This?

The Old Testament presents four major covenants, each named

after the Prophet or leader involved in the covenant. They are the Noahic, the Abrahamic, the Mosaic, and the Davidic. The Davidic covenant is outside the scope of this paper and will not be addressed herein. Those living during the times of the Old Testament and those reading it during the New Testament era, however, would have understood the word "covenant" to refer to these four covenants.

Noah

Established in Genesis 9, the Noahic Covenant represents God's enduring promise to all living creatures following the Great Flood. After Noah and his family exited the ark, God pledged never again to destroy the earth by flood. The sign of this covenant is the rainbow, set in the clouds as a visual testament of divine mercy and faithfulness. A unique feature of this covenant is that it is one-way. The Lord makes a promise to humanity that is not dependent on their faithfulness; the promise is His alone to keep. It serves as a foundational moment in biblical theology, illustrating God's grace and commitment to preserving life despite human fallibility.

While God is true to his promise to never flood the earth again, the theme would reemerge in later scripture. In Isaiah 54, God is speaking words of reconciliation to Israel over His previous anger with them. The people had persisted in their disobedience and idolatry, and He had expressed his anger to them. In verse 9, the Lord expressed, "For this is as the waters of Noah unto me: for as I have sworn that the waters of Noah should no more go over the earth; so have I sworn that I would not be wroth with thee, nor rebuke thee" (Isaiah 54:9, KJV). While the initial covenant had to do with the physical condition of the earth, here God expanded it to include the idea of His anger flooding over them.

In Hebrews 11:7, Noah is praised for his faithfulness. Here the Noahic Covenant is less about God's promises of mercy, but rather how Noah gained righteousness by participating in the covenant. "By faith Noah, when warned about things not yet seen, in holy fear built an ark to save his family. By his faith he condemned the world and became heir of the righteousness that is in keeping with faith" (Hebrews 11:7, NIV).

1 Peter 3 provides an entirely different take on the meaning of this covenant. The apostle explained that the Flood was like a baptism for

the whole earth. He saw it as a fresh start for all of humanity and a call to righteous living. Peter appealed to the suffering of Christ and implored his readers to willingly take on the suffering that may come as a result of following the Savior. For Peter, the covenant was about accepting what was given (baptism) and then choosing to live differently because of this grace, even through persecution or suffering for one's faith.

At times in scripture, different emphases have been placed on the meaning of the Noahic covenant. Sometimes it is about a literal flood of the earth, and at others, it is about the Lord promising that His mercy will outlast His anger. On some occasions, it is about obedience bringing righteousness, or about accepting suffering just as the Savior did. Each time a scriptural writer talks about this covenant, they are not erasing the previous meaning — they are adding to it. The covenant does not change with each passage; rather, it is expounded upon.

Restoring or Expanding?

We return to the question: what was Joseph Smith doing when he restored the idea of covenants? As shown, they were already well-known in his time, as shown through many writings and sermons from the era. When Joseph spoke about covenants, he was speaking to people with an already well-established understanding.

However, when the Lord spoke of the Noahic Covenant in Isaiah 54, He was also speaking into well-established ideas of what that Covenant meant. The people of Isaiah's day would have easily retold the story of Noah, and provided appropriate commentary on its exact meaning. Then, roughly 1,500 years later, God brought up the covenant again and added meaning. Another 700 years later, and He would provide additional meaning through the apostle Peter and the writer of the Epistle to the Hebrews.

No one in Israel living prior to Isaiah would have articulated that the Noahic Covenant was about the relationship between God's mercy and anger; or that it was about baptism or righteous living. They would have expressed the original meaning: the Noahic Covenant was about the Lord promising to never flood the earth again. But the meaning of the covenant did not stay static, God added layers and nuance as the circumstances of His children demanded. It is as if the Lord is writing new verses to an old song.

When the Prophet Joseph Smith begins talking about the restoration of covenants, we still have to ask, what is being restored? Is it simply that Joseph discovered an old text, dusted it off, and called it a restoration?

This does not appear to be the case.

Instead, Joseph is participating in the grand tradition of the scriptures — he allows God to use him to add a new verse to an old tune. While God has certainly established His covenants in scripture, He continues to speak in our day, and bring layers of new meaning to these promises. Joseph Smith is not simply restoring old covenants; he is helping to co-create and expand them. "It is my meditation all the day ... to know how I shall make the Saints of God comprehend the visions that roll like an overflowing surge before my mind. Oh! how I would delight to bring before you things which you never thought of!"[3]

ABRAHAM

Introduced in Genesis 12 and expanded through chapters 15 and 17, the Abrahamic Covenant marks a pivotal moment in biblical history, where God initiates a lasting promise with Abraham and his descendants.

It includes three core components:

1. the promise of land (Canaan)
2. the assurance of countless posterity ("as numerous as the stars")
3. the declaration that through Abraham's seed, "all nations of the earth shall be blessed."

This covenant is both conditional — involving Abraham's faith and obedience — and everlasting, forming the theological backbone for Israel's identity and destiny. It establishes a relationship not just based on divine favor, but on mutual commitment.

Just as with the Noahic Covenant, over time we see the Abrahamic Covenant expanded in the scriptures. The details of all of those expansions are too numerous to address here, but we see the same idea — God "adds a verse" to the song where the meaning of the covenant is added to and expounded upon. Perhaps this covenant, more than any

---

3. Joseph Smith, "Discourse, 16 April 1843, as Reported by Willard Richards," pp. 144–145, *Joseph Smith Papers*, online at josephsmithpapers.org.

of the others, illustrates the work which the Prophet Joseph Smith was doing to both restore and expand.

More, More, More

In her excellent book, *Alexander Campbell and Joseph Smith: 19th-Century Restorationists*,[4] RoseAnn Benson discussed this dynamic by contrasting Joseph Smith with another religious figure of his day. Alexander Campbell also considered himself to be one called to restore the true church, but his vision for this was very different from Joseph's. Campbell favored a minimalist, rationalist restoration — focused on stripping Christianity down to its New Testament essentials. His was a restoration of distillation. "Alexander's restorationist views focused on a rational and reasoned interpretation of the scriptures through the lens of Enlightenment philosophy," while "Joseph approached restoration through what in the 19th century was called enthusiasm."[5]

Campbell believed his restoration would bring Christianity back to the practices of the primitive church. "A restoration of the ancient order of things is all that is necessary to the happiness and usefulness of christians."[6] By this, he meant that there was a limited number of things necessary for the church to be able to function, and that there was no need to add any more. He emphasized the importance of "scripture alone," baptism, and weekly observance of the Lord's Supper. In his view, little else was needed beyond this. His restoration was to take the church to its barest essentials without any superfluous ideas or practices.

Joseph Smith could not have viewed the restoration any more differently. In one sense, Campbell used the term "restoration" in its most obvious form, to bring back something that had been lost. However, Joseph's version of "restoration" was expansive, imaginative and reve-

---

4. RoseAnn Benson, *Alexander Campbell and Joseph Smith: Nineteenth-Century Restorationists* (Provo, UT: Brigham Young University Press; Abilene, TX: Abilene Christian University, 2017).
5. RoseAnn Benson, "Campbellites and Mormonites: Competing Restoration Movements," *Interpreter: A Journal of Latter-day Saint Faith and Scholarship* 31 (2019): 236, 235.
6. Alexander Cambell, *A Restoration of the Ancient Order of Things (1824)*, rev. D. S. Burnet in the *Christian Baptist*, 7 vols. (Bethany, WV: Disciples of Christ Historical Society, 1835), 2:128, online at digitalcommons.discipleshistory.org.

latory.[7] Not only did he want to bring back ancient priesthood, covenants, and temple worship, but Joseph wanted to introduce new ideas, new scriptures, and "new verses" to the song of the original covenants in the Old Testament. This is well-illustrated by his expansion of the Abrahamic Covenant.

During the dedication of the Kirtland Temple, Joseph Smith and Oliver Cowdery received priesthood keys from a prophet referred to as Elias, who "committed the dispensation of the gospel of Abraham, saying that in us and our seed all generations after us should be blessed" (Doctrine and Covenants 110:12). This committed the Abrahamic promises to him, enabling the gathering of Israel and the sealing of families. The original Abrahamic Covenant promised that Abraham's seed would spread throughout the earth and that through him, all people would be blessed. Joseph took this covenant and specified exactly how it would happen through the sealing ordinances. What is only hinted at in the original promise to Abraham becomes specific through Joseph Smith.

Moses

Established between God and the Israelites at Mount Sinai (Exodus 19–24), the Mosaic Covenant was a conditional agreement that laid out the terms by which Israel would remain God's chosen people. It included the Ten Commandments and a broad legal code governing moral, civil, and ceremonial life. The covenant emphasized obedience: blessings would follow if Israel kept God's laws, and curses would result from disobedience. It also introduced a priesthood, sacrificial system, and sacred space (the tabernacle) to facilitate worship and atonement.

The Mosaic Covenant is a foundational moment in scriptural history, illustrating God's desire for a holy people and the challenges of human fidelity. But this covenant is different from the others discussed. It is not just modified by subsequent prophets in the future as the others were; it is essentially surpassed by the "new covenant" in Jesus Christ. For the sake of brevity, this paper will only consider the Mosaic Covenant on its own without analyzing its relationship to the new covenant.

---

7. For a general discussion of this topic, see Benson, *Alexander Campbell and Joseph Smith*, 321–338.

This covenant also differs in that the trajectory of understanding is not in how meaning is layered on top of what has been given, but in how meaning was developed by the people living it. This covenant does receive additional layers of meaning as new scriptures are written and new prophets teach the principles, but the real "change" intended here is in the life of the person called to live it.

While all Christians resonate with this covenant, Latter-day Saints can perhaps see a special kind of mirroring, similar to how they perceive themselves as a "peculiar people." In this sense of the word, "peculiar" does not mean odd or eccentric; rather, it means to be "set apart" as a people with a divine mission in this life on behalf of those who have come before.

How can we see this playing out in the Mosaic Covenant?

What Does the Mosaic Covenant Contain?

The Mosaic Covenant is a multifaceted agreement between God and the Israelites that is more than just a set of rules — it is a comprehensive framework for learning to live as God's covenant people. It includes the Ten Commandments (Exodus 20); the Book of the Covenant (Exodus 21–23), which contextualizes the Decalogue into civil and social law; ceremonial law, which teaches the people about ritual purity, priestly duties, holy days, consecration and festivals; the Sacrificial System, which details instructions for sacrifices when the laws are broken; instructions for the priesthood and tabernacle; blessings and curses that come about with obedience or disobedience; and finally, a covenant ceremony wherein the people affirm their willingness to enter into this agreement.

Modern readers sometimes read these rules and regulations and get so lost and bogged down in the details that they cannot find the theme. To be fair, many of the commandments are written for a society that is very different from theirs.

To understand further, some historical context is needed. At the beginning of the book of Exodus, God's people are enslaved to the Egyptians. God promises to rescue them, and He does. Once the people are in the desert, it becomes obvious that living as slaves in Egypt did not prepare them for living a covenant life of trusting God as He led them through the wilderness. They are not practiced in the attitudes and behaviors required to allow themselves to be led in this way. God intervenes by giving the Ten Commandments and the Law of Moses.

How God Leads Them

To illustrate this point, consider Exodus 23:19: "Do not cook a young goat in its mother's milk" (NIV). This law is given three times, in Exodus 23:19, Exodus 34:26, and Deuteronomy 14:21. The modern reader might wonder why the people need to be told multiple times to refrain from cooking a young goat in this manner — and why is this commanded in the first place?

There have been many interpretations of this verse over time, ranging from the practical to the esoteric. Rabbinic tradition used this verse to build the separation of meat and dairy in Jewish dietary law. Observant Jews today maintain separate dishes, utensils, and even sinks for meat and dairy. Their kitchens are built in such a way that you would not cook cream of mushroom soup with the same utensils and tools you would use to make a turkey sandwich. They must be separate.

Why?

As God reveals these laws for living to the people the observant reader notices that God has commands about keeping some things separate from each other. These include things such as: no intermarrying with people who are not Jews; no mixing of two types of fabric unless they are specifically instructed to do so, etc. Later, in Leviticus, along these same lines we find examples of many things God wants kept separate: there are certain things you can't touch (like dead bodies), and if you do, you will be considered unclean for a time period. Certain animals must be kept separate from other animals — some are for eating and some are not. The people must separate themselves from impure practices and unclean foods.

The Lord is trying to teach them in a way they can understand. The point of all of those purity laws ("purity" here meaning keeping this separate from that) is to help them understand that God's people are to be distinct, or to be "peculiar." They are not to mix — not because the other people groups are not God's children as well, but because God has chosen to work through one nation to bless all the other nations. They are not to mix this and that because they are to be distinct.

The whole point of keeping things separate is to give them a living example of keeping themselves separate from the false teachings and practices around them. The Lord is not being unreasonable — He is trying to shape the people into understanding that creating an idol like the golden calf is not going to help them become His people. Instead of just telling them this, He wanted them to have reminders of it all the way down to how they cook a young goat or sew a sweater. They belong to God and He can not shape them into the nation they need to be if they are following the same practices as everyone else.

God is using these rules as identity formation. A careful reading of the text reveals a God who cares about the redemption of His people. Frequently, as impatient beings, we would like redemption to be instant and complete, to be some kind of magic thing that happens to us. We do not want it to be an opportunity to live in a context where redemption can be played out by us.

After the golden calf, the Lord could have fixed everything with the Israelites and just tried to continue leading them as before, but the people would not have changed. God doesn't usually magically zap change into human beings —and He doesn't expect them to change on a dime, either. One day, they have no idea really how to trust God — and the next, they're expected to get it right every time. Not so. Instead, He provides a structure in which they can learn, over time, how to become faithful followers.

The trajectory of change is not a change to the covenant itself, or at least not at this time. It is the development of change that happens in a person who seeks to follow the covenant. Like most Christians, Latter-day Saints do not follow most of the Mosaic Covenant today; however, they do follow a set of rules and expectations intended to do the same thing — to form us as a people tasked with work to do.

Conclusion

The Mosaic, Abrahamic, and Noahic covenants each represent distinct stages in God's unfolding relationship with humanity, yet their meanings stretch far beyond the historical moments in which they were established. For Latter-day Saints, these covenants form a spiritual architecture that reveals sacred patterns over time. Rather than offering direct analogs to modern ordinances or temple covenants, these biblical agreements operate as theological templates — each illuminating principles such as obedience, lineage, divine protection, and communal identity. Importantly, Restoration scripture and modern revelation reinterpret these covenants through the lens of continued progression, portraying them as expressions of God's enduring desire to bind Himself to His people.

The layered meaning of these ancient covenants encourages Latter-day Saints to see their own spiritual journey as part of a larger covenantal narrative. As they study these foundational agreements, they gain tools for interpreting modern covenants — not in isolation, but as echoes of eternal themes. God's promise to make a people holy, preserved, and chosen reverberates through patriarchs and prophets, eventually converging in Restoration doctrine — and still being revealed today. In this way, the covenants become more than static contracts — they evolve as revelations tailored to the needs of unfolding dispensations, allowing modern Saints to find relevance and renewal in ancient words.

6

JUSTIFYING JOSHUA

A RESTORATION THEODICY FOR THE CONQUEST OF CANAAN

PAUL BRYNER

The divine command to exterminate the Canaanites in the book of Joshua presents a moral dilemma for believers who view God as perfectly good. For Latter-day Saints, this specific "problem of evil" application can be navigated through the theological lenses of restored doctrine that can mitigate the narrative's severity while justifying it regardless. First, the biblical narrative itself may be historically imprecise; archaeological evidence and internal textual contradictions suggest the conquest was likely a gradual, defensive dispossession rather than the rapid, total genocide described in the book of Joshua. Second, the principle of divine accommodation is a limitation imposed by God's character that constrains divine communication and allows for less-than-divine laws to be given to fallen cultures in a way that indemnifies God while accomplishing his purposes. Finally, the scriptural assurances of Canaanite moral culpability, paired with a safety-net scriptural assurance of divine justice, assures believers that God had justified reasons for any conduct attributable to Him. Restored doctrines help to justify God in the Joshua narrative while simultaneously steering believers towards Christ and away from violence.

Latter-day Saints are familiar with the notion of promised lands: the theme runs replete through the Old Testament, Book of Mormon, Doctrine and Covenants, and even Pearl of Great Price.[1] Divine promised lands require good behavior for tenure, so to speak, and

---

1. For example, Genesis 12:1–7; 2 Nephi 1:5–12; Ether 2:7–12; Doctrine and Covenants 38:18–22; Doctrine and Covenants 57:1–3; Abraham 2:6; Moses 6:17.

poorly behaving tenants are evicted. But that "eviction" process — the removal of entire nations from land — is an unpleasant phenomenon. In many instances, groups destroy themselves through infighting; in others, one wicked nation eliminates another.

But what are readers to make of the book of Joshua, where God's covenant people are commanded to clear the land of the Canaanites? How can this narrative be squared with our knowledge of God's goodness and power? There are no simple answers, but for Latter-day Saints, the perplexity of the story can be resolved to a degree by viewing it through the lens of the restored gospel of Jesus Christ and its doctrines. In particular, doctrines and teachings regarding biblical infallibility, Israelite and Canaanite wickedness, and an ultimate trust in God's commands allow us to reckon with one of the most perplexing questions about the Old Testament.

THEODICIES FOR THE BOOK OF JOSHUA

For millennia, Judeo-Christian and Gentile societies have tried to reconcile the goodness and power of God with the disturbing sufferings, or "evils," that have occurred throughout history and on a daily basis.[2] This question, widely known as the problem of evil, has long been used as an argument to deny the goodness, power, or even the existence of God.[3] Traditional formulations follow this pattern:

- God is perfectly good (omnibenevolent) which means he seeks to prevent evils as much as he is able.
- God is omnipotent, which means he is able to prevent all evils.
- Evil exists.[4]

Theists, or believers in God, have responded to this trilemma with arguments that justify God's goodness and power, known as "theodicies."[5] A theodicy answers the problem of evil by either rejecting or

---

2. Michael L. Peterson, ed., *The Problem of Evil: Selected Readings*, 2nd ed. (Notre Dame, IN: Notre Dame Press, 2016). The Book of Job deals with this question indirectly. The original postulation of the problem of evil, though attributed to Epicurus, is first found in Sextus Empiricus's *Outlines*.
3. For the classic version of the problem of evil critique, see J. L. Mackie, "Evil and Omnipotence," in *The Problem of Evil: Selected Readings*, ed. Michael L. Peterson, 2nd ed. (Notre Dame, IN: Notre Dame Press, 2016), 81–94.
4. Mackie, "Evil and Omnipotence," 81–82.
5. The term was coined by Gottfried Wilhelm Leibniz in his 1710 book *Theodicy*,

qualifying one or more of the three propositions. Thus, a theist might argue God's goodness does not entail that he would prevent all evils.[6] Alternatively, a theodicy might reject that God's omnipotence means that he can prevent all evils.[7] A final strategy is to reject that there are evils at all by defining an evil as *unjustified* suffering.[8] The Restored Gospel contains doctrines that work well with several existing theodicies, a topic that would require volumes to fully cover.[9]

The narrative content of the book of Joshua provides us with a unique version of the problem of evil. There is an additional premise involved — that is, the nature of the scripture itself.[10] Another unique element is that a theodicy for the book of Joshua only concerns the events surrounding the Conquest of Canaan, rather than dealing broadly with all evils. The Joshua version of the problem of evil, with four premises that cannot all be true, might read:

---

which literally means "God justification."

6. This is a "greater good" argument, like Thomas Aquinas's in *Summa Theologia* suggesting that some evil allows for greater good overall. However, this seemingly cannot be true at the same time as God's logical omnipotence, as it is logically possible to imagine greater goods without any evil. See Mackie, "Evil and Omnipotence," in *The Problem of Evil: Selected Readings*, 81–94.

7. This is typically the Latter-day Saint response, but has become more popular in other Christian circles in recent decades. See Blake T. Ostler, *Exploring Mormon Thought, Volume 4: God's Plan to Heal Evil* (Kofford, 2020). The argument is essentially that, somehow, God cannot create the best possible world while still allowing free agency. See Alvin Plantinga, "The Free Will Defense," in *The Problem of Evil: Selected Readings*, ed. Michael L. Peterson, 2nd ed. (Notre Dame, IN: Notre Dame Press, 2016), 95–129.

8. This was Augustine's approach, who argued that evil is only the privation of good and does not actually really exist. David Ray Griffin, "Augustine and the Denial of Genuine Evil," in *The Problem of Evil: Selected Readings*, ed. Michael L. Peterson, 2nd ed. (Notre Dame, IN: Notre Dame Press, 2016), 242–261.

9. For an overview and list of sources, see Scripture Central, "Why Does God Allow Bad Things to Happen? (Moroni 9:19)," *KnoWhy* 767 (December 10, 2024), online at scripturecentral.org.

10. As one evangelical author opined, "*the problem of Scripture is one permutation of the larger problem of evil*" in that, like the rest of creation, "this good creation is fallen and includes ... disorder[.]" Kenton L. Sparks, *Sacred Word, Broken Word: Biblical Authority and the Dark Side of Scripture* (Grand Rapids, MI: Eerdmans, 2012), 22.

- God is perfectly good (omnibenevolent), which means he seeks to prevent evils as much as he is able.
- God is omnipotent, which means he is able to prevent all evils.
- The divinely-commanded violence against Canaanites described in the book of Joshua are evils.
- The book of Joshua accurately describes that God commanded violence against Canaanites.[11]

As with the regular problem of evil, an argument that rejects or qualifies one of the premises constitutes a theodicy. This paper will explore probable Latter-day Saint views on each of these premises and explore the resulting theodicies.

God is Omnibenevolent

Most Latter-day Saints will probably affirm the first premise: God generally desires to prevent evil from occurring. God weeps when His children suffer and takes no pleasure in the suffering of the sinner.[12] Although we would agree that God's goodness does not preclude Him from allowing evil, we would assert that God has some larger-picture purpose in mind that minimizes suffering in the eternal scheme.

God has Qualified Omnipotence and Must Accommodate Human Shortcomings

Latter-day Saints will probably reject the second premise: there are certainly limits on God's omnipotence, but it is not necessarily clear whether this is for logical or physical reasons, like not having the ability, or if it is only based on God's chosen moral principles.[13] If

---

11. Compare the lists from Charlie Trimm, *The Destruction of the Canaanites: God, Genocide, and Biblical Interpretation* (Grand Rapids, MI: Eerdmans, 2022), 49–50.
12. Moses 7:37–40; Ezekiel 18:23.
13. Church leaders have held varying opinions about whether or not God is the author of all laws, based upon passages like Doctrine and Covenants 88:42. For a summary of these varying opinions, see James McLachlan, "Is God Subject to or the Creator of Eternal Law?," *BYU Studies Quarterly* 60, no. 3 (2021): 49–63. For a discussion of qualified omnipotence, see David L. Paulsen and Blake T. Ostler, "Sin, Suffering, and Soul-Making: Joseph Smith on the Problem of Evil," in *Revelation, Reason, and Faith: Essays in Honor of Truman G. Madsen*, ed. Donald W. Parry, Daniel C. Peterson, and Stephen D. Ricks (Foundation for Ancient Research and Mormon Studies, 2002), 258–267.

God's only restraints on divine intervention are moral principles, then presumably all evil which God permits is justified by those principles. The line is thin in scripture, though, between physical limitations and moral constraints.[14] Thus, enough ambiguity exists to assume that God is constrained to a degree by morals, physics, or both, and Latter-day Saints would likely reject this premise as true.

In the context of Joshua, the question is whether God commanded the Conquest because he was unable to give Israel its promised land in a less violent way, or at least to communicate that intent. The miracles described in the Joshua account make it unlikely that God was *physically* unable to do anything else.[15] If God can send angels at some times but not at others, then his limits on communication must be exclusively moral. It is possible that Israel's faithlessness, a moral constraint, precluded the clarity and content of the messages that they could receive. A theodicy that rejects this premise would be based on the principle of accommodation: due to God's moral laws, His revelations must meet His children where they are morally, and thus the clarity and content they can receive is limited.

If God Commanded the Conquest, He Had a Reason for Doing So

The third premise is not true if evils are defined as *unjustified* suffering. One of the primary reasons for believing that the Canaanite Conquest may have been justified is given in the text itself: the Canaanites were sufficiently wicked for God to authorize such treatment. This kind of argument asserts that, because this suffering was deserved, it is the kind of suffering that even a good God would not desire to prevent. Alternatively, these evils could be justified for other reasons that we cannot comprehend, a view called "skeptical theism," which seems to be taught in the book of Job.

---

14. God says that "honor ... is my power" (Doctrine and Covenants 29:36), and "that which is governed by law is also preserved by law and perfected and sanctified by the same" (Doctrine and Covenants 88:34).
15. The Book of Mormon suggests that lack of miracles and revelation is a sign of faithlessness, a moral factor, rather than a limitation on God's power. See Mormon 9:20.

The Book of Joshua May Inaccurately Portray the Israelite Conquest

The fourth premise, that the book of Joshua accurately describes God commanding violence, could also be challenged in several appropriate ways. The first is that there are disagreements in the Old Testament about what actually occurred. The second is that the Bible is specifically known in Restoration scripture as having a messy transmission history that makes it particularly susceptible to human error.[16] A third way, in harmony with accommodation, is Restoration scripture's description of ancient Israelites as spiritually lacking at the time of the Conquest, which could constrain how and what God communicated to them.

Synthesis of Plausible Joshua Theodicies

The arguments against the Joshua problem of evil are strongest when synthesized together. For example, when presented with the problem, a Latter-day Saint can first suggest that a surface-level reading of the text may not accurately describe what occurred: intratextual contradictions, possible exaggeration, archeological debates, and probable errors or edits have consigned the events to a degree of ambiguity. She can then note that if the events did occur as described, God's perfect nature restricts his interactions with humanity and requires accommodation of unprepared humans, resulting in imperfect laws and imperfect agents being used to carry out a divine purpose. Finally, she can argue that God's commands are always justified, whether because of Canaanite depravity as suggested in the text or for other reasons known only to God. The following sections will explore these potential justifications for the Conquest in this rearranged order.

THEODICY #1: THE BOOK OF JOSHUA MAY INACCURATELY PORTRAY THE ISRAELITE CONQUEST

This theodicy can be supported by many underlying principles discussed below: intratextual conflict regarding the purpose, manner, and scope of the Conquest; archaeological data in favor of a less-vi-

---

16. Even some non-Restoration Christians have advocated for a rejection of the concept of scriptural inerrancy to avoid the moral difficulties of Joshua. Wesley Morriston, "Did God Command Genocide? A Challenge to the Biblical Inerrantist," *Philosophia Christi* 11, no. 1 (2009): 7–26.

olent settlement by Israelites; literary exaggerations not immediately apparent; and doctrinal teachings about biblical fallibility.

Herem *in the Old Testament*

Several different Hebrew verbs are used to describe the various actions involved in the Conquest. The most significant violent verb in Joshua though, upon which much of the perceived violence hinges, is an ominous root usually translated as "utterly destroy" or "accursed": the Hebrew noun *herem* and its verb form *haram*.[17]

At the broadest level, the noun *herem* refers to an item "devoted" and set apart to God, such as for use in the temple.[18] In fact, some apologists argue that the term *only* carries this meaning, but this is unlikely because of the words that accompany *herem*. Rather, it is almost exclusively used to refer either to something cursed and devoted to God for destruction, or else the process of doing so — and often seems to imply that God performs the consigning act.[19] All items devoted in this manner are accursed and banned from being taken as personal spoils — they are God's spoils — and so people who violate this rule become victims of *herem* and other punishments themselves.[20]

Herem comes with an implicit recognition that God helped win a battle and can be seen as a weighty form of repayment, gratitude, or even sacrifice for victory.[21] Beyond *herem* of items, people and even

---

17. Ludwig Koehler, Walter Baumgartner, and Johann J. Stamm, *The Hebrew and Aramaic Lexicon of the Old Testament* [HALOT], trans. and ed. Mervyn E. J. Richardson, 2 vols. (Boston: Brill, 2001), s.vv, "I חֵרֶם, I חרם." For the best Latter-day Saint treatment of *herem*, see David Calabro, "'Thou Shalt Utterly Destroy': Understanding the Biblical Herem," in Daniel L. Belnap and Aaron P. Schade, eds., *From Wilderness to Monarchy: The Old Testament Through the Lens of the Restoration* (Provo, UT: Religious Studies Center, expected Dec. 2025).
18. For this usage, see Numbers 18:14; Ezekiel 44:29.
19. John H. Walton suggests that many of the references to *herem* in the Conquest did not necessary involve death, though this does not seem supported by the command to "save alive nothing that breatheth: But thou shalt utterly destroy [*herem*] them" (Deuteronomy 20:16–17) or the many references to being put to the sword. See John H. Walton, *The Lost World of the Israelite Conquest* (Downers Grove, IL: InterVarsity Press, 2017), 169–232.
20. Leviticus 27:28–29; Deuteronomy 7:26; Joshua 6:18; Joshua 7:1, 11–15; 1 Kings 20:42; 1 Chronicles 2:7.
21. Numbers 21:2–3; Micah 4:13.

cities can qualify to receive *herem* by worshipping idols.[22] In several passages in the Old Testament, God threatens to *herem* both Israel and other nations who are acting wickedly, whether through human agents or other means.[23] Some of these passages are quoted in the Book of Mormon.[24]

The act of *herem* is unique among forms of divine destruction in that God seems to solicit human participation. Moses expressly commanded the Israelites to *herem* not only the cities, livestock, and idols of the Canaanites, but also the entire population.[25] Moses then led the Israelites to *herem* two Amorite city-states beyond the Jordan River, in Heshbon and Bashan.[26] Joshua next led Israel across the Jordan to *herem* a number of city-states and their armies within Canaan, including "all the country of the hills, and of the south."[27] After Joshua's death, Israelite tribes later *herem* certain areas as they complete the Conquest.[28] Saul was commanded to *herem* the entire Amalekite population.[29] Although all of these events somewhat involve Israel's settlement in Canaan and are centered on Joshua, the difficulties of *herem* are not isolated to the book of Joshua.

Interestingly, *herem* is not performed exclusively by the Israelites. The biblical text suggests that God, at least symbolically, performs *herem* through Gentile nations. Even further, it also describes Gen-

---

22. Exodus 22:20; Deuteronomy 13:13–18. Cf. Exodus 32:25–29; Numbers 31:1–18, which do not use the verb *haram* but convey a similar idea.
23. Isaiah 34:1–8; Isaiah 43:28; Jeremiah 25:8–9; Jeremiah 50:21–16; Jeremiah 51:1–3; Malachi 4:6.
24. Compare to Micah 4:13 and 3 Nephi 20:19; Malachi 4:6 and 3 Nephi 25:6. Isaiah 11:15 KJV and 2 Nephi 21:15 may be mistranslating the term from a cognate verb meaning "split" or "divide." Koehler, Baumgartner, and Stamm, *HALOT*, s.v. "II חרם." For a thoughtful treatment of *herem* ideology in the Book of Mormon, see Daniel L. Belnap, "Utterly Destroyed: The Cosmology of Conflict and the *herem* in the Book of Mormon," upcoming paper, manuscript in possession of author.
25. Deuteronomy 3:21–22; Deuteronomy 7:1–26; Deuteronomy 20:1–18.
26. Numbers 21; Deuteronomy 2:24–37; Deuteronomy 3:1–22; Joshua 2:9–10. Moses's campaign also included conquests in the Transjordan and Negev, though the word *herem* is not used, even though the Midianite males were all killed. Numbers 31–32.
27. Joshua 6:1–8:29; Joshua 10:1, 8–9, 28–43; Joshua 11:1–23; Joshua 12:7–24.
28. Judges 1:16–17; 1 Kings 9:20–21; 1 Chronicles 4:41.
29. 1 Samuel 15:1–35; David later continued this in 1 Samuel 30:13–18.

tile nations performing *herem* of their own accord for their false deities.³⁰ Both a Moabite and a Sabaean inscription describe instances of *herem* — the Moabite text in particular includes eradicating an Israelite-controlled town for the deity Chemosh.³¹ But other than these examples, there are few if any instances in the Ancient Near East of nations wiping out other groups solely on the basis of religious edict.³² In general, it is much more convenient (or at least lucrative) for a state to subdue another, put them in servitude, and collect regular tribute. While it is certain that the Israelites were not the only ones with a concept of *herem*, it is unclear how widely the practice was done — it seems rather rare.

Herem has disturbed readers for millennia, and different explanations have been offered for why its unique applications are justified, misunderstood, and limited in scope.³³ Some of these will be explored below. And while it remains unlikely that *herem* carries a non-violent meaning, the possibility should be remembered as a possible justification for solving the Joshua problem of evil.

Conflicting Accounts Regarding Extent of Conquest

Scholars have long noted that the biblical text seems to contradict itself in the Conquest story, both in the degree and the speed in which the Israelites carried it out. This contradiction allows readers to select the narrative that they prefer — which, for modern Christians, is likely the option with less destruction. This discrepancy does not

---

30. Daniel 11:44; 2 Chronicles 20:23.
31. Lauren A. S. Monroe, "Israelite, Moabite and Sabaean War-ḥērem Traditions and the Forging of National Identity: Reconsidering the Sabaean Text RES 3945 in Light of Biblical and Moabite Evidence," *Vetus Testamentum* 57, no. 3 (2007), 324. Walton also points to a Hittite text describing devotion of a city as an example of *herem*, though a different lexeme is used; thus, I do not use it as an attested example. See Walton, *Lost World*, 170–172.
32. Trimm, *The Destruction of the Canaanites*, 42–45. *See also* Walton, *Lost World*, 206: "It is also worth noting, however, that the lack of ḥerem does not necessarily correspond to what we would consider a more humane treatment of enemies; all of Mesha's enemies are killed (*hrg*), even if the city they formerly occupied is not ḥerem."
33. For a review of different approaches throughout time, see Arie Versluis, "The Early Reception History of the Command to Exterminate the Canaanites," *Biblical Reception* 3 (2014): 308–329.

explain away every instance of *herem*, but it does help clarify many in the Joshua narrative.

The *herem* instructions are disturbing particularly because they do not appear defensive and instead consist of aggressive destruction of noncombatants and animals. In Deuteronomy, Moses instructed the Israelites that "thou shalt smite them, and utterly destroy [*haram*] them; thou shalt make no covenant with them, nor shew mercy unto them," (Deuteronomy 7:2) and that "thou shalt save alive nothing that breatheth: But thou shalt utterly destroy [*haram*] them" (Deuteronomy 20:16–17). The first portion of Joshua specifically records the *herem* of the cities of Jericho, Ai, Makkedah, Libnah, Lachish, Eglon, Hebron, Debir, Hazor, as well as the kings and armies of several cities — including Jerusalem.[34] More importantly, the book of Joshua makes the blanket statements that:

> So Joshua smote *all the country of the hills*, and of the south, and of the vale, and of the springs, and *all their kings: he left none remaining, but utterly destroyed all that breathed*, as the Lord God of Israel commanded. ... And *all these kings and their land did Joshua take at one time*, because the Lord God of Israel fought for Israel (Joshua 10:40–42).[35]

> So Joshua *took the whole land*, according to all that the Lord said unto Moses; and Joshua *gave it for an inheritance* unto Israel according to their divisions by their tribes. And the land rested from war (Joshua 11:23).

> And the Lord *gave unto Israel all the land* which he sware to give unto their fathers; and *they possessed it, and dwelt therein*. And the Lord gave them rest round about, according to all that he sware unto their fathers: and *there stood not a man of all their enemies before them*; the Lord delivered all their enemies into their hand. There failed not ought of any good thing which the Lord had spoken unto the house of Israel; all came to pass (Joshua 21:43–45).

The book of Joshua acknowledges that "Joshua made war a long time with all those kings," which accords well with Moses's prophecies that "I will not drive them out from before thee in one year" and "the Lord thy God will put out those nations before thee by little and

---

34. Joshua 6:1–8:29; Joshua 10:1, 8–9, 28–43; Joshua 11:1–23; Joshua 12:7–24.
35. See also Joshua 11:10–12.

little."³⁶ Even so, the timeline of the Conquest in early Joshua is much faster — and more thorough — than what is reflected in later Joshua and Judges.

In the next chapter, the Lord would tell Joshua, "Thou art old and stricken in years, and there remaineth yet very much land to be possessed ... [yet] divide thou it by lot unto the Israelites for an inheritance, as I have commanded thee" (Joshua 13:1, 6). So in Joshua 13–22, Joshua divides up the land to each tribe, though the text reaffirms that much of the allotted land has not yet been conquered, including "all the land of the Canaanites," Philistine territory, and Phoenician territory.³⁷ Several cities — or at least their kings and armies — that were said to have been defeated by Joshua are later said to not have been conquered or are described as being conquered again, such as Jerusalem, Hebron, Gezer, Megiddo, and Hazor.³⁸ The text also acknowledges that many Canaanites remain in the land for generations.³⁹

These discrepancies can be dealt with in a variety of ways. In fact, scripture itself seems to be aware of them and attempts to smooth them out somewhat. If we grant scripture the benefit of the doubt and take it literally, we could assume that Joshua generally defeated all of the Canaanites over a span of years, but not thoroughly enough for the Israelites to maintain control.

We could also assume that the descriptions of total domination of the region were simply hyperbolic rhetoric emphasizing God's power and Joshua's faithfulness. This would certainly bear similarity to other Ancient Near Eastern war accounts, a genre prone to exaggeration glorifying leaders and deities.⁴⁰ This lens is fairly persuasive

---

36. Exodus 23:29–30; Deuteronomy 7:22; Joshua 11:18.
37. Joshua 13: 2–6.
38. Jerusalem: Joshua 10:1–26; Joshua 12:10; Joshua 15:63; Judges 1:21. Hebron: Joshua 10:1–26; Joshua 14:13–15; Judges 1:10. Gezer: Joshua 10:1–26; Joshua 16:10; Judges 1:29. Megiddo: Joshua 12: 21; Judges 1:27. Hazor: Joshua 11:10–13; Judges 4:2.
39. 1 Kings 9:20–21.
40. Charlie Trimm, analyzing Egyptian and Assyrian sources, says "it appears that while ancient Near Eastern kings did not invent stories of war, they clearly recounted events with rhetorical flourishes that downplayed the negative aspects of the account, emphasized the aspects that glorified them and their gods, and employed hyperbole with respect to the extent of their victories." Trimm, *Destruction of the Canaanites*, 24. See also Patrick Q. Mason and

in explaining why the direct account of the Conquest is much more triumphant than the later narrative material and mitigates the scope of violence, though it still assumes an underlying Conquest. This theory also leaves unexplained why the Conquest narrative would suddenly shift in tone instead of presenting a thoroughly exaggerated account.

Another theory, accepted by many scholars, is that the conflicting narratives about the speed and scope of the Conquest are derived from multiple traditions, stitched together by a later editor.[41] The exact contours of the traditions are unclear, but one would be a triumphant war narrative and the other a more conservative description of generational expansion. This final theory comports best with the narrative and has particular relevance for the *type* of conquest performed by the Israelites. Because one tradition seems to have been especially violent and the other was less so, the contradictory nature of the Conquest accounts — initially a weakness of the narrative — can become a strength by allowing readers to excise unpleasantries from the narrative.

Archeological Evidence and Theological Implications

Archaeologists have explored the question of Conquest contradictions to attempt to determine which narrative is more historically accurate. Their findings definitively show the population explosion of a new group in the early Iron Age (about the time of Joshua) in Canaan's central hill country with a distinct style of homes and pottery, and an avoidance of pig meat — confident evidence of early Israel.[42] However, as William G. Dever summarizes, "Of the two accounts of the emergence of Israel in Canaan now placed back-to-back in the Hebrew Bible, Judges far more than Joshua has the ring of truth about it. Its stories of a two-century sociological and religious struggle

---

J. David Pulsipher, *Proclaim Peace: The Restoration's Answer to an Age of Conflict* (Provo, UT: Maxwell Institute, 2021), 167–168. See also Walton, *Lost World*, 206: "It is also worth noting, however, that the lack of ḥerem does not necessarily correspond to what we would consider a more humane treatment of enemies; all of Mesha's enemies are killed (hrg), even if the city they formerly occupied is not ḥerem."

41. Yair Hoffman, "The Deuteronomistic Concept of the Herem," *ZAW* (1999): 196–210.
42. William G. Dever, *Who Were the Early Israelites and Where Did They Come From?* (Grand Rapids, MI: Eerdmans, 2003), 101–128.

against the prevailing local Canaanite culture fits astonishingly well with the current archaeological facts on the ground."[43]

Archaeology suggests that, alongside the culture of potential wanderers from across the Jordan river and immigrants from Egypt, much of early Israel's material culture was in fact Canaanite.[44] This should not surprise us since Abraham was a "Syrian," the Israelites left Egypt with a "mixed multitude," Israelites entered Canaan with "thy stranger that is in thy camp," Israelites "dwelt among the Canaanites," and Israelites began worshipping Canaanite gods immediately after the death of Joshua.[45] Hebrew is closely related to the Canaanite dialects. As Ezekiel critiqued Jerusalem, "Thy birth and thy nativity is of the land of Canaan; thy father was an Amorite, and thy mother an Hittite" (Ezekiel 16:3). The concept of a migrating minority coming to dominate the local population, politically and religiously, should be familiar to all Book of Mormon readers: would we expect to find Mulekite or Nephite archaeological remains in Zarahemla?[46]

It should be acknowledged that much of this archaeological scholarship does not disparage the Bible but rather privileges some of its passages above others. In doing so, it calls into question the difficult *herem* accounts of Jericho, Ai, and a long list of other cities, providing a solution to the moral difficulties.

In sum, the archaeological trends favor a historical Israel, but with perhaps less aggressive settlement than the book of Joshua suggests.[47] However, we should be reluctant to allow archaeology to be dispositive of the question, especially when the destruction layers of cities

---

43. Dever, *Who Were the Early Israelites*, 228.
44. Dever, *Who Were the Early Israelites*, 181–182, 236–237. Faithful readers who delve into this material should be aware, though, that many archaeologists assume contrary to scripture that the Israelite tribes were simply an outgrowth of Canaanite culture rather than a massive group emigrating from Egypt. I attempt to carve a middle path of acknowledging Canaanite material culture among early Israelites while defending historical claims of scripture.
45. Exodus 12:38; Deuteronomy 26:5; Deuteronomy 29:11; Joshua 9; Judges 1:32; Judges 2:12.
46. Omni 1:17; Mosiah 25:2.
47. Past models have included a pure conquest model, peaceful infiltration model, and peasant revolt model, all of which have now largely been abandoned to suggest that much of the Israelite population was actually Canaanite. Dever, *Who Were the Early Israelites*, 153.

like Hazor and Laish seem to fit the biblical description.[48] If given the benefit of the doubt, some of these discrepancies can be smoothed out by other arguments, which prevents second-guessing the historicity of scripture. For example, several aspects of the Joshua account are miraculous, and thus it should not be surprising to believers that Conquest archaeology would defy expectation.[49] Even if archaeology can help explain away some of the violence in Joshua though, it does not explain every instance of *herem* and requires the application of other principles.

In summary, as Latter-day Saint scholars Patrick Q. Mason and J. David Pulsipher wrote:

> [Another] strategy is to interpret the Bible's violent passages using the insights of modern scholarship, which is increasingly skeptical about the historical reliability of the Hebrew Bible's accounts of genocide. Most biblical scholars have concluded that many books of the Hebrew Bible contain textual insertions and other changes by writers who lived many centuries after the events described and who frequently narrated earlier history with their own contemporary interests and dilemmas in mind.... For example, there is little archaeological or genetic evidence of a violent conquest of Canaan by Israelites; to the contrary, the data suggests that the takeover was a slow and relatively peaceful process. Therefore, scholars increasingly believe that significant parts of the military stories recorded in the book of Joshua, including the divine command to utterly destroy the Canaanites, may have been inserted by later scribes....[50]

Herem or "Defensive" Dispossession?

Similar to the discrepancies in the extent of the Israelite Conquest are those in the *kind* of conquest performed, and these two roughly correlate.[51] The early Joshua narrative that proclaimed a quick and total victory over the land of Canaan also describes the most instances of *herem* of large groups of people. These align with the violent *herem* instructions in Deuteronomy as well.

---

48. Dever, *Who Were the Early Israelites*, 210.
49. Joshua 6:20; Joshua 10:11–14.
50. Mason and Pulsipher, *Proclaim Peace*, 167.
51. Hoffman, "The Deuteronomistic Concept of the Herem," 198–201.

In contrast, several of the other passages that command the Israelite Conquest do not mention *herem* at all. Though these passages sometimes describe destruction of the Canaanites, God names Himself as the agent. The focus is instead on the land itself, with the goal of simply driving out and dispossessing the Canaanites. Any destruction is instead directed towards their idols:

> *I will cut them off.* Thou shalt not bow down to their gods, nor serve them, nor do after their works: but thou shalt utterly overthrow them, and quite break down their images.... *I will send my fear before thee, and will destroy all the people to whom thou shalt come, and I will make all thine enemies turn their backs unto thee. And I will send hornets before thee, which shall drive out* the Hivite, the Canaanite, and the Hittite, from before thee (Exodus 23:20–33).

> Defile not ye yourselves in any of these things: for in all these the nations are defiled *which I cast out before you*: And the land is defiled: therefore I do visit the iniquity thereof upon it, and *the land itself vomiteth out her inhabitants.* Ye shall therefore keep my statutes ... That the land spue not you out also, when ye defile it, *as it spued out the nations that were before you* (Leviticus 18:24–30).

> When ye are passed over Jordan into the land of Canaan; *Then ye shall drive out all the inhabitants of the land from before you*, and destroy all their pictures, and destroy all their molten images, and quite pluck down all their high places: *And ye shall dispossess the inhabitants of the land, and dwell therein*: ... But if ye will not drive out the inhabitants of the land from before you; then [they] shall vex you in the land wherein ye dwell (Numbers 33:50–56).

> And thou shalt do that which is right and good in the sight of the Lord: that it may be well with thee, and that thou mayest go in and possess the good land which the Lord sware unto thy fathers, *To cast out all thine enemies from before thee*, as the Lord hath spoken (Deuteronomy 6:18–19).

Several scholars have suggested that the original commandment was simply to dispossess, and fight only to the degree necessary — essentially reclaiming land with force rather than *herem*, and then only engaging in defensive battles.[52] The theory goes that a later editor

---

52. Richard S. Hess argues that Jericho and Ai, referred to as "cities" with "kings," were more likely military forts full of a few hundred men each, and the phrase

then rewrote or edited the story to include *herem* of the Canaanites.⁵³ A land-focused rather than *herem*-focused conquest is supported by the passages indicating Moses and Joshua tried to make peace before fighting (though obviously conflicting with the extreme Deuteronomy command to "make no covenant with them, nor shew mercy unto them").⁵⁴

Exaggeration could have inflated not only the success of the Conquest but the extent of its violence. After all, the text suggests that everyone knew the Israelites were coming into the land, and as one scholar wrote, "[w]hen a city is in danger of falling ... people do not simply wait there to be killed; they get out ... Only people who do not get out, such as the city's defenders, get killed."⁵⁵ One suggested explanation suggested by scholars is that the additional *herem* narrative was rhetoric not meant to be taken literally by readers. Richard Hess argues that the designations of men, women, and children are simply idiomatic ways of saying "all,"⁵⁶ comparable to saying "we destroyed them" when describing a sports game.

An original dispossession-focused rather than *herem*-focused Conquest has the benefit of meshing well with Nephi's description: "And after they had crossed the river Jordan he did make them mighty *unto the driving out of the children of the land, yea, unto the scattering them* to destruction" (1 Nephi 17:32). But Nephi's phrase doesn't rule out *herem*, and a conquest without it would not explain other instances

---

"men and women" is simply an idiom for "all." Richard S. Hess, "The Jericho and Ai of the Book of Joshua," in *Critical Issues in Early Israelite History*, ed. Richard S. Hess, Gerald A. Klingbeil, and Paul J. Ray Jr. (Winona Lake, IN: Eisenbrauns, 2008): 33–46. For a claim that it was defensive battles only, see Trimm, *Destruction of the Canaanites*, 74–75; Paul Copan, "Yahweh Wars and the Canaanites: Divinely-Mandated Genocide or Corporate Capital Punishment? Responses to Critics," *Philosophia Christi* 11, no.1 (2009): 82–83.

53. Hoffman, "The Deuteronomistic Concept of the Herem," 198–201; Mason and Pulsipher, *Proclaim Peace*, 167–168.
54. Numbers 21:21–25; Deuteronomy 2:26–37; Joshua 11:19–20. The examples of Rahab and the Gibeonites also show that penitent, or at least compliant and prudent, Canaanites could potentially be spared. See Joshua 2; Joshua 9; Copan, "Yahweh Wars," 75–76.
55. Copan, "Yahweh Wars," 83, quoting unpublished manuscript of John Goldingay. Compare Jeremiah 4:29; 1 Samuel 31:7.
56. Hess, "The Jericho and Ai of the Book of Joshua" : 33–46; see also Copan, "Yahweh Wars," 80.

of *herem* or why God allowed dispossession in general. However, this piece of the puzzle helps mitigate the weight of the Conquest account, and other principles can help answer the remaining questions.

The difficulties are that banishment differs from the plain meaning of the text in certain sections; the two traditions are difficult to cleanly separate; and still raise questions about justification of ethnic cleansing.[57] But these difficulties are more palatable than the *herem* of women and children, and can be further mitigated by the theodicies described below.

Biblical Fallibility

Latter-day Saints are strongly committed to the premise that scripture, and, by extension, its authors, are inspired yet fallible, especially the Bible.[58] The prophet Joseph Smith taught that Latter-day Saints believe in the Bible "as far as it is translated correctly," and that the text has been modified by "ignorant translators, careless transcribers, or designing and corrupt priests."[59] This intentional modification of the Bible, also described by Nephi, would probably have occurred long before any of the earliest attested Bible manuscripts.[60] The Old Testament was the bulk of this modified Bible. Our current Old Testament is likely smaller than the proto-Old Testament on Nephi's brass plates, which included prophets not mentioned in the modern Old Testament such as Zenos, Zenock, and Neum, as well as unknown prophecies of Joseph of Egypt.[61]

---

57. Trimm, *Destruction of the Canaanites*, 74–75, says that the killing references outnumber banishment; Copan suggests that banishment is three times as common. Certainly they have different criteria. Copan, "Yahweh Wars," 83.
58. God speaks to people according to their understanding (Doctrine and Covenants 1:24; 2 Nephi 31:3) and the Book of Mormon writers, especially Moroni, acknowledge that there may be human "faults" in the text. Book of Mormon Title Page; Mormon 8:17
59. Article of Faith 8; Joseph Smith, "History, 1838–1856, volume E-1 [1 July 1843–30 April 1844]," p. 1755, *Joseph Smith Papers*, online at josephsmithpapers.org.
60. An angel, addressing Nephi, told him "And after these plain and precious things were taken away [the Bible] goeth forth unto all the nations of the Gentiles" (1 Nephi 13:23–29). Because this seems to be describing a censorship scheme after the death of Christ, it is possible that Dead Sea Scrolls manuscripts of the Old Testament predate this editing, but it is unclear and no other manuscript candidates date close enough.
61. 1 Nephi 13:23; 1 Nephi 19:10–17; 2 Nephi 3; see also Alma 46:24–27. Nephi

Nephi makes clear that his version of the Old Testament contains some kind of Conquest narrative, but there is little evidence for what aspects of our Conquest narrative Nephi knew.[62] For example, modern scholarship has attempted to peel back editorial layers and sources within the Old Testament, including the motivations of the scribes or scribal schools who composed each theoretical layer.[63] Some efforts have been made to determine the extent that Nephi's brass plates aligned ideologically with one of the theoretical editorial sources suggested by scholarship; such efforts have been interesting but inconclusive.[64] In particular, a group of theoretical "Deuteronomic" editors are alleged to have favored passages about *herem*,[65] but Lehi's family seems to have a mixed observance of "Deuteronomic" ideals over gen-

---

writes that the brass plates included "the five books of Moses," (in the first manuscript as "Book of Moses,") though there is reason to think that his version may have had substantial differences. 1 Nephi 5:11; see Kevin L. Barney, "Reflections on the Documentary Hypothesis," *Dialogue* 33, No. 1, 57–99.

62. 1 Nephi 5:11–13; 1 Nephi 17:32–38.
63. For a useful but somewhat doctrinally-cavalier introduction to this topic and its interaction with Latter-day Saint scripture, see David E. Bokovoy, *Authoring the Old Testament: Genesis – Deuteronomy* (Salt Lake City: Greg Kofford Books, 2014); see also Alex Douglas, "David E. Bokovoy. Authoring the Old Testament: Genesis–Deuteronomy. Salt Lake City: Greg Kofford Books, 2014," *Studies in the Bible and Antiquity* 8, no. 12 (2016): 229–238. While much of this source-critical scholarship is speculative and some callously disregards Moses as a historical figure, the Books of Moses themselves openly confesses editorial work centuries after the life of Moses, making the question of editing one of degree. This includes Pentateuchal references to Moses's death, Moses as the humblest of all men, third person references to Moses generally, the Conquest in the past, the Israelite monarchy, and several statements about conditions "to this day" that would outdate Moses. See Genesis 36:31; Numbers 12:3; Deuteronomy 1:1–5; Deuteronomy 2:12; Deuteronomy 10:8; Deuteronomy 34:5–7.
64. See Kevin L. Barney, "Reflections on the Documentary Hypothesis," *Dialogue: A Journal of Mormon Thought* 33, no. 1 (Spring 2000): 57–99; John L. Sorenson, "The 'Brass Plates' and Biblical Scholarship," in *Nephite Culture and Society: Collected Papers* (Salt Lake City, UT: New Sage Books, 1997): 25-39; Sidney B. Sperry, "Some Problems of Interest Relating to the Brass Plates," *Journal of Book of Mormon Studies* 4, no. 1 (1995): 185–191; Scripture Central, "What Parts of the Old Testament Were on the Plates of Brass? (1 Nephi 5:10)," *KnoWhy* 410 (May 20, 2020), online at scripturecentral.org.
65. Hoffman, "The Deuteronomistic Concept of the Herem," 198–201.

erations.⁶⁶ Thus, one possibility is that Nephi's brass plates — presumably a more historically and doctrinally accurate antecedent to our Old Testament — may have lacked the extreme *herem* passages found in the current Old Testament in Deuteronomy and Joshua. As noted above Nephi's summary of the Conquest allows room for this to be the case.

A final question regarding the fallibility of these passages is why Joseph Smith's New Translation of the Bible did not clean up the *herem* passages. After all, it granted additional insight into other difficult Old Testament topics like the Flood, circumcision, Lot's daughters, and God hardening Pharaoh's heart.⁶⁷ However, this question is more about the nature of Joseph Smith's translation than about these particular passages.⁶⁸ If the translation simply reverted the Bible to an original state, then all unedited biblical text would be sanctioned by omission. However, enough evidence exists for us to conclude that this was not the nature of the JST in every instance. Instead, we can conclude that Joseph Smith "might have rendered a plainer translation to this, but it is sufficiently plain to suit [God's] purpose as it stands" (Doctrine and Covenants 128:18).

Caution With Challenging Scripture

Although all scripture is somewhat earthly due to its human audience, there is a doctrinal danger with taking scripture fallibility

---

66. For example, some evidence suggests that Lehi and Nephi's family traditions exemplify Deuteronomic theology, while a strong argument can be made that Laman and Lemuel's rebellious streak comes from their own Deuteronomic lens. Neal Rappleye, "The Deuteronomist Reforms and Lehi's Family Dynamics: A Social Context for the Rebellions of Laman and Lemuel," *Interpreter: A Journal of Latter-day Saint Faith and Scholarship* 16, no. 7 (2015): 87–99; Scripture Central, "How is the Use of Deuteronomy in the Book of Mormon Evidence for its Authenticity? (1 Nephi 4:34)," *KnoWhy* #428 (April 26, 2018), online at scripturecentral.org.
67. Moses 7–8; JST Genesis 14; JST Genesis 17.
68. Joseph Smith's translation of the Bible can be categorized into several different kinds of changes like revelations, doctrinal clarifications, answers to questions, and grammatical changes. S. Kent Brown, Victor L. Ludlow, Robert J. Matthews, and C. Wilfred Griggs, "The Joseph Smith Translation of the Bible: A Panel," in *Scriptures for the Modern World*, ed. Paul R. Cheesman and C. Wilfred Griggs (Provo, UT: Religious Studies Center, Brigham Young University, 1984), online at rsc.byu.edu.

and questions about the historicity of the scriptural narrative too far. Moroni warned that, regardless of the scriptural "faults of a man," we ought to be careful how we evaluate "the things of God."[69]

Yet it may be doctrinally justified to challenge aspects of the Conquest narrative precisely because it seems to contradict more authoritative scripture, weightier "things of God." This is markedly different than critiquing based on modern social norms (some of which are incidentally derived from Christian scripture, though)[70] and instead only scrutinizes contradictions within scripture. Joseph Smith, though admittedly acting under prophetic prerogative, said,

> I believe the bible as it read when it came from the pen of the original writers ... As it read[s] Gen 6 ch. 6 v. [says] 'it repented the Lord that he had made man on the earth;' ... which I do not believe.... *If any man will prove to me by one passage of Holy Writ, one item I believe, to be false, I will renounce and disclaim it* far as I have promulged it. ... Look at Heb. 6 ch. 1 v. for contradictions ... *This is a contradiction — I don't believe it*: I will render it, as it should be[.][71]

Rejecting either that the Israelites performed *herem* or that God commanded them to do it, as with Joseph Smith rejecting that God hardened Pharaoh's heart, could simply be an instance of using scripture to correct another contradictory scripture — though admittedly this must be tenuous because readers lack prophetic authority.

Christians and Jews have wondered about the correctness of *herem* for millennia, and not because of any modern ethic but because of scripture itself.[72] Fortunately, Latter-day Saints have a somewhat established hierarchy of religious authorities that can help resolve seeming contradictions — if they really are such.[73] Modern prophets generally

---

69. Mormon 8:17; Title Page of the Book of Mormon.
70. Sparks, *Sacred Word*, 39–43.
71. Joseph Smith, "History, 1838–1856, volume E-1 [1 July 1843–30 April 1844]," p. 1755, *Joseph Smith Papers*, online at josephsmithpapers.org.
72. Sparks, *Sacred Word*, 50–65.
73. The mode of Judas's death is different in Matthew and Acts but is harmonized by the JST, which might suggest that harmonization is the first thing we should attempt, especially for historical ambiguities. JST Matthew 27:6; Acts 1:18; Sparks, *Sacred Word*, 32–33.

trump the ancient ones,[74] and newer revelation generally supersedes the older.[75]

The Book of Mormon was lauded by Joseph Smith as "the most correct of any book" (albeit before the publication of the final Doctrine and Covenants or Pearl of Great Price), and thus stands as a sort of "first among equals."[76] In regards to scriptural speakers, while prophets indeed speak for God,[77] the teachings of Jesus are certainly the most infallible.[78] "Any alternative approach has the burden of explaining why Jesus should be decentered and what ought to be put in his place as the lens through which we should read and evaluate all other scripture."[79] When none of these authorities give a clear answer, the gift of the Holy Ghost may show the "truth of all things" (Moroni 10:5), the "light of Christ" in our consciences directs us without "compell[ing] in all things."[80]

Teachings of Jesus, modern prophets, and the Book of Mormon unequivocally denounce violence, or demeaning of other ethnic groups, while inviting charity.[81] The Holy Ghost and the Light of Christ lead away from violence. Though this does not mean that the

---

74. Wilford Woodruff, in *Conference Report*, Oct. 1897, pp. 22–23, quoted in *Teachings of Presidents of the Church: Joseph Smith* (Salt Lake City, UT: The Church of Jesus Christ of Latter-day Saints 2007), 198–199.
75. 2 Nephi 28:30; Doctrine and Covenants 50:24.
76. Joseph Smith, "Remarks, 28 November 1841," p. 112, *Joseph Smith Papers*, online at josephsmithpapers.org; Mason and Pulsipher, *Proclaim Peace*, 43.
77. Doctrine and Covenants 1:38.
78. Christ is a "a foundation whereon if men build they cannot fall" (Helaman 5:12).
79. Mason and Pulsipher, *Proclaim Peace*, 169.
80. Doctrine and Covenants 58:26. President Oaks describes the light of Christ first in his list of helps that God has given mankind after leaving premortality, and it is the lens through which we make all discernment. President Dallin H. Oaks, "Divine Helps for Mortality," *Liahona* (May 2025): 104–106; April 2025 General Conference; Moroni 7:16; Doctrine and Covenants 84:46. Some scholars have arrived at a similar conclusion: ultimately, we must rely on our consciences and the Spirit as we interpret scripture (though we would first defer to prophetic teachings). Sparks, *Sacred Word*, 118–121.
81. President Russell M. Nelson, "Peacemakers Needed," *Liahona* (May 2023): 98–101; Church Newsroom, "President Nelson calls upon Latter-day Saints 'to lead out in abandoning attitudes and actions of prejudice'," 4 October 2020, online at thechurchnews.com; President Dallin H. Oaks, "Love Your Enemies," *Ensign* (November 2020): 26–29.

Conquest was not justified on special grounds or did not occur, we can certainly conclude that its violence is not a general prescriptive example for Latter-day Saints to follow.

THEODICY #2: GOD HAS QUALIFIED OMNIPOTENCE AND MUST ACCOMMODATE HUMAN SHORTCOMINGS

Divine Accommodation of Israel's Knowledge

While acknowledging biblical fallibility, it is also arguable that the Bible correctly describes God's orchestration of the Canaanite displacement, but that this simultaneously *did not exhibit God's moral approval of the actions taken despite his seemingly active role*. That is, in terms of theodicy, God's character may qualify his omnipotence in a way that restricts how and what He communicates to those who are morally unprepared. In that vein, the Conquest could have been God actively utilizing a spiritually ignorant agent to bring about judgment on others, a repeated spiritual idea.

Although the Book of Mormon potentially allows for specifically-commanded violence when explicitly directed by God,[82] it teaches a general principle that "[it is] *by the wicked that the wicked are punished*; for it is the wicked that stir up the hearts of the children of men unto bloodshed" (Mormon 4:5). Isaiah teaches similarly that God used Assyria as the "rod of mine anger. ... I will send him against a hypocritical nation ... Howbeit he meaneth not so, neither doth his heart think so."[83] This example suggests that the wicked individuals who are used to bring judgment are not always or even usually aware of their role as a destructive agent of God.

Yet aside from indirect guidance, the scriptures also suggest that God can give *direct* commandments of a less-divine nature to spiritually ignorant individuals not ready for a higher commandment. In respect to Mosaic divorce laws, Jesus said, "*Moses because of the hardness of your hearts suffered you* to put away your wives: but from the

---

82. 1 Nephi 4:8–18.
83. 2 Nephi 20:5–7. This rationale also extends to biblical passages that describe the Babylonians as destroying the Assyrians under God's command, or the Persians and Medes defeating the Babylonians under Cyrus, as well as God bringing nations against his covenant people to humble them. Isaiah 13:17–19; Isaiah 44:28–45:1; Ezra 1:1–2; Jeremiah 51:11.

beginning it was not so" (Matthew 19:8). In fact, Restoration teachings suggest that Israel received its lower law, complete with a lower priesthood and lower ordinances, just before the Conquest because Israel rejected a higher law.[84] The law that remained was "the law of carnal commandments, which the Lord in his wrath caused to continue with the house of Aaron among the children of Israel" (Doctrine and Covenants 84:24–27). Although this is often emphasized as being the ordinances and rituals of the Mosaic law, it seems fair to extend this accommodation principle to other commands given to Israel during its wandering such as Conquest commands.

Thus, while the law of Moses is from God, *it is also explicitly an accommodation* to what Israel, at that time and in that cultural context, was able to accept and abide — with the ultimate purpose of pointing the way to a new covenant in some future day. One scholar calls this view of accommodation "moral-epistemic disappointment," where "critical judgement is appropriately directed at an individual agent whose behaviour we regard as morally lacking, but who was not in a historical or cultural position to think the requisite moral thought—it was outside the routine moral thinking of their day."[85]

The commands to drive out and *herem* the Canaanites are codified in several of the books of Moses, collectively referred to as the "Law" or "Torah." To the degree that they accurately reflect what Moses commanded, it should be remembered that these commands were given alongside ritual purity laws for leprosy, textiles, and kosher food laws, along with slavery laws, laws for avenging a killed family member, and a large list of animal sacrifices. All of these practices, which Christians have contextualized as being a part of the old covenant, can also be seen as accommodating Israel in its ancient culture.

Difficulties of Accommodation

Although the practice does not seem to have been widespread, *herem* is attested outside of the Bible and could very well be an accommodation borrowed from a neighboring culture. Alternatively, Canaanite *herem* could have been a darkly merciful instruction that

---

84. JST Exodus 34:1–2.
85. Miranda Fricker and Michael Brady, "The Relativism of Blame and Williams's Relativism of Distance," *Proceedings of the Aristotelian Society Supplementary Volume* LXXXIV (2010): 152–153.

controlled violence to a degree that may not have occurred if the Israelites invaded Canaan of their own accord.[86] Perhaps the Israelites were somehow unprepared to share the land, to convert the inhabitants, or lacked faith to have them driven out entirely by God. God had offered to Moses to annihilate the Israelites for their wickedness but he refused; the Conquest would not have been necessary in that case, though the death count may not have changed much.[87]

Yet one wonders why God commanded *herem* at all when he was willing to stop the earth's rotation, topple walls, and send stones from the sky as a part of the Conquest.[88] The Law of Moses was also generally a step up from its neighboring nations, which makes the accommodation principle less convincing in the case of *herem*. But it is also clear that the Israelites were not especially righteous at the time of their conquest, as Moses reminded them.[89] These principles can soften our perception of God's nature as unconditionally harsh, though it may not answer all the questions for everyone by itself.

In conjunction with a fallible scripture theodicy, God's accommodation may not have required Him to give violent commands to Israel but rather to *allow them to record the narrative as it survived in their tradition, regardless of historical or moral error*. In fact, any fallible scripture theodicy is itself an extension of a qualified omnipotence argument, because assumedly God would communicate perfectly to humanity to prevent all violence if the restrictive laws He abides allowed him to do so. These arguments could transform God's violent commands in Joshua into God merely allowing violence and allowing later scribes to depict Him as giving such commands.

Yet it would be arrogant for modern Latter-day Saints to assume moral superiority over all peoples in all periods of history, let alone God's ancient covenant people.[90] When considering ancient Israel's

---

86. Walton, *Lost World*, 173. This seems contradicted, though, by the fact that Israel could enslave others and take their women as concubines who were deemed less wicked than Canaanites. See Deuteronomy 20.
87. Exodus 32:7–14; Number 14:11–25.
88. Joshua 10.
89. Deuteronomy 9:4–5.
90. "For our own part, we cannot believe, that the ancients in all ages were so ignorant of the system of heaven as many suppose." Joseph Smith, "Letter to the Church, circa March 1834, as Published in Evening and Morning Star," p. 287, *Joseph Smith Papers*, online at josephsmithpapers.org.

immoral state or progression of revelation, Latter-day Saints cannot assert an absolute linear correlation between time and correctness because of dispensation doctrine. Certainly if some revelation is progressive, line upon line, then some revelation would be regressive. [If apostasies occurred and] truths were lost, then there has certainly been doctrinal *regression* during some periods.[91] Though the Old Testament acknowledges Israelite wickedness, it suggests that the lack of total *herem* of the Canaanites was actually because the Israelites weren't righteous enough to defeat their powerful enemy — not that *herem* was required because they weren't righteous enough.[92]

Similarly, beyond maligning the wayward early Israelites we may also insult God's ancient prophets when writing off *herem* commands of Joshua, Moses, and Samuel as simply a part of early, depraved Israel. Moses was a prototypical prophet of the Old Testament who foreshadowed Christ, held the keys of gathering Israel, was translated, saw the Lord and all of creation, and held the High Priesthood.[93] Though Moses was certainly a man of his time like all prophets, he seems to have known much more than he was permitted to teach to Israel, and any accommodations were likely more for Israel than Moses.[94] Similarly, Joshua was one of the fulfillments of Moses's successor prophecy, and the namesake of Moses's most famous successor: Jesus himself.[95] If the account is accurate, he was a faithful scout of the land of Canaan and an obedient servant of God who spoke with angels.[96] Perhaps our first assumption ought not to be that these prophets could only comprehend genocide, but that Israel itself was commanded for justified

---

91. This can also be said of the falling away after Christ's ministry, or of ancient condemnations of modern wickedness.
92. Judges 2:20–23.
93. Sparks, *Sacred Word*, 68–69; Doctrine and Covenants 84:6, 25; Doctrine and Covenants 110:11; Moses 1.
94. We know that Moses saw all of creation and had a higher law revealed to him that he could not share with Israel. Moses 1; JST Exodus 34:1–2.
95. Deuteronomy 18:15–18; Frederick W. Danker, Walter Bauer, William F. Arndt, and F. Wilbur Gingrich, *Greek-English Lexicon of the New Testament and Other Early Christian Literature*, 3rd ed. (Chicago: University of Chicago Press, 2000), s.v. "Ἰησοῦς."
96. Numbers 14:6–9; Joshua 5:13–15.

reasons, was only prepared to hear a violent message, or later distorted the message given.[97]

Ultimately, accommodation remains a valuable interpretive lens. As Puslipher and Mason wrote, "One such strategy is to recall that all scriptural instances of a direct divine command for humans to commit violence precede Christ's mortal ministry. Thus, we might attribute the statements to a God who is working with people who are living a lesser law; in other words, God meets them where they are and over time tries to get them to do better. This explanation has some merit. God's commands do seem to become less violent over the course of the Hebrew Bible."[98]

Comparison to American Colonization

In literature that critiques the violence in Joshua, comparison is often made to colonial European nations as evidence that the Conquest was evil. Regardless of the potential merits of such an argument, Latter-day Saints actually have scripture that summarizes the era of European colonization that can potentially bolster the "ignorant agent" hypothesis for the Israelites. Book of Mormon teachings valuably distinguish between God's orchestration of political victories and the morality of political entities.

An analogy can perhaps be drawn between the Canaanite Conquest in Joshua and the colonization account of the Americas found in 1 Nephi 13. Nephi's vision describes a large-scale colonization of the continents where his descendants had intermingled, including death and loss of land on a massive scale.[99] Nephi describes the colonization of the Americas in terms of God's Spirit or power and God's wrath, though Nephi will later hint that these terms may be more of a shorthand for divinely-permitted temporal prosperity than signifying divine approval of morality:

> the wrath of God is upon the seed of thy brethren ... the Spirit of God ... came down and wrought upon the man; ... the

---

97. For a contrary view of accommodation, though, see Sparks, *Sacred Word*, 53.
98. Mason and Pulsipher, *Proclaim Peace*, 165–166.
99. Presumably, this and other large-scale punishments in scripture are justified by a multi-generational corporate identity, as discussed later. Trimm, *Destruction of the Canaanites*, 90, citing Joel S. Kaminsky, "Corporate Responsibility in the Hebrew Bible," *JSOT Sup* 196 (Sheffield: Sheffield Academic, 1995).

> Spirit of God ... wrought upon other Gentiles ... the wrath of God ... was upon the seed of my brethren; and they were scattered before the Gentiles and were smitten. And I beheld the Spirit of the Lord, that it was upon the Gentiles, and they did prosper and obtain the land for their inheritance. ... the power of God was with them, and also that the wrath of God was upon all those that were gathered together against them to battle (1 Nephi 13:11–19)

Although Nephi's account initially seems to unequivocally justify the colonization, a closer reading shows that Nephi does not rejoice in this or entirely endorse it. Beyond Nephi's own emotional exclamations at the horror of what he witnessed done to his descendants,[100] he also noted that the divine empowerment enjoyed by the European Gentiles was not accompanied by, or a result of, doctrinal knowledge. Rather, Nephi declares that the inheritance of the Americas by the Gentiles — and the actions that cleared the land — were done *in conjunction with doctrinal ignorance*. In regard to the early modification of the Bible, Nephi wrote,

> [B]ecause of these things which are taken away out of the gospel of the Lamb, an exceedingly great many do stumble, yea, *insomuch that Satan hath great power over them*. Nevertheless, thou beholdest that the Gentiles who have gone forth out of captivity, and *have been lifted up by the power of God* above all other nations (1 Nephi 13:29–30).

Despite Lehi's land covenant and Satan's great power over the Gentiles, the Gentiles were empowered by God to displace American peoples. If nothing else, this seemingly contradictory appraisal of early Euro-American righteousness should caution Latter-day Saints from assuming that God approved of the *moral methods* of colonization, even if God seemed to somehow allow or facilitate it, as with the Assyrian "rod of anger."[101] Lest we think that individuals described anciently

---

100. 1 Nephi 15:5; 2 Nephi 26:7.
101. This is not to deny that many aspects of the American revolution and foundation of its unique government were providential. See Scripture Central, "How Do Latter-day Saints See God's Hand in History? (1 Nephi 13:13, 19)," *KnoWhy* 712 (January 26, 2024), online at scripturecentral.org; Roy A. Prete, ed., *The Divine in the Historical Narrative: A Latter-day Saint Perspective* (self-pub., 2021), online at godinhistory.org; Roy A. Prete, ed., *Window of Faith: Latter-day Saint Perspectives on World History* (Provo, UT: Religious Studies Center, Brigham Young University, 2005).

as having divine power or God's Spirit are always morally impeccable, several accounts from the book of Judges temper that conclusion. The "Spirit of the Lord came upon" Ehud, Jephthah, Gideon, and Samson to strengthen them in their political roles on behalf of God's covenant people, despite their unsavory behavior involving assassination, idolatry, prostitution, extreme violence, and potentially child sacrifice.[102]

The implicit condemnation of the colonization methods in the Americas can also be seen in the behavior expected in the Book of Mormon by the Gentiles *after* the Restoration has begun. God gives Gentiles many affirmative duties to reform themselves and to bless Native Americans after the Restoration begins, or else they will experience consequences comparably dire to those of American colonization.[103] Jesus, when describing what will occur to wicked modern Gentiles without repentance, even adopts Micah's violent Old Testament imagery of Israelites performing *herem*.[104]

The colonization analogy may be limited because Moses and Joshua commanded the Conquest whereas the colonization of the Americas was merely facilitated by God's Spirit and power rather than divine commands. But if the Israelites were sufficiently wicked (or the command was justified), the distinction remains irrelevant because the Israelites were minimally culpable for compliance. The effect of this argument is to suggest that God does not inspire behavior that would be especially sinful for the inspired individuals, and simply puts the responsibility on God, who must be justified on other counts such as his qualified omnipotence. What if such a process of relative ignorance was at work in the Canaanite Conquest, and it remains true that the wicked (even if less so) will destroy the wicked?

---

102. The "Spirit of the Lord came upon" Ehud, Jephthah, Gideon, and Samson to strengthen them in their political roles one behalf of God's covenant people, despite their unsavory behavior involving assassination, child sacrifice, idolatry, and prostitution, and potentially child sacrifice. See Judges 3:26; Judges 6:34; Judges 11:29; Judges 14:6, 9; Judges 15:14; Copan, "Yahweh Wars," 79.
103. 1 Nephi 14:1–6; 3 Nephi 16:10–15; 3 Nephi 20:15–20, 27–28; 3 Nephi 21:11–21; Mormon 5:20–24.
104. 3 Nephi 20:19.

Theodicy #3: If God Commanded the Conquest, He Had a Reason for Doing So

Wickedness of the Canaanites

The primary textual reason *herem* of Canaanites was deemed acceptable is that God wanted to punish and end their depravity.[105] The most specifically mentioned reason is that the Canaanite's idolatrous ways would improperly influence Israel, but this simply speaks to the extent of the Canaanite wickedness (and Israel's sensitivity to outside influence).[106] The fact that the Israelites were immediately influenced by the Canaanites, and similarly evicted from the land several generations later, shows that Canaanite influence was indeed infectious.[107]

Canaanite wickedness did not occur overnight, though. In Genesis, God informed Abram that his descendants would have to wait centuries to inherit Abram's promised land specifically because "the iniquity of the Amorites is not yet full."[108] In fact, the Canaanites contemporary with Abraham and Isaac acted respectably towards them,

---

105. A common reason suggested inside and outside the Church, similar to the Flood rationale, is that God was preventing unborn spirits from living hopeless lives. See John Taylor, *Journal of Discourses*, 26 vols., ed. D. W. Evans, Geo. F. Gibbs, et al. (Liverpool: William Budge, 1878)), 19:158–159; Morriston, "Did God Command Genocide?" 25. While this may very well be true, it is not necessarily a scriptural idea. Similarly, if taken into our own hands to decide whether another's life is worth living, the principle can echo an abortion rationale; only the divine prerogative would separate the two.
106. Exodus 23:33; Numbers 33:55; Deuteronomy 7:4; Deuteronomy 20:18; Joshua 2:1–3. Walton suggests that these two are different and that the Canaanites are not actually depicted as wicked and simply had influential idolatrous culture of an unacceptable *political* nature, but the distinction is unconvincing. Walton, *Lost World*, 33–118.
107. Judges 2:11–13.
108. Genesis 15:12–16. Walton argues that because Abram is well-acquainted with some Amorites, this is actually a comfort to Abram. Walton also argues that "iniquity" should be read as an undeserved "punishment" which is deferred indefinitely. Walton undermines his point, though, by pointing to the Sodom story, where God also tells Abram that he would not annihilate a city that had ten good people. This creative approach contradicts the weight of evidence, such as Moses's declaration that the Canaanites are wicked, and the repeated condemnation of Canaanite practices in the law codes. See Walton, *Lost World*, 50–63.

and he cooperated with Amorites.¹⁰⁹ By the days of Moses and Joshua, that iniquity had apparently become "full." Moses made it clear to the Israelites that their inheritance of the land was due to Canaanite wickedness and the patriarchs' righteousness (rather than Israel's):

> Speak not thou in thine heart, after that the Lord thy God hath cast them out from before thee, saying, For my righteousness the Lord hath brought me in to possess this land: but *for the wickedness of these nations* the Lord doth drive them out from before thee. Not for thy righteousness, or for the uprightness of thine heart, dost thou go to possess their land: but *for the wickedness of these nations* the Lord thy God doth drive them out from before thee, and that he may perform the word which the Lord sware unto thy fathers, Abraham, Isaac, and Jacob. Understand therefore, that the Lord thy God giveth thee not this good land to possess it for thy righteousness; for thou art a stiffnecked people (Deuteronomy 9:3–6).

What was this extreme wickedness that merited either total destruction or displacement? This difficult question requires an exploration of who the Canaanites were, itself a difficult question.¹¹⁰

In Genesis, Canaan is a son of Ham who is cursed due to a mysterious indiscretion of his father.¹¹¹ The text lists the nations who were understood in Genesis as descending from him, thus falling within the term "Canaanite": the Hittites, Jebusites, Amorites, Girgashites, and Hivites, among others.¹¹² The identification of the Canaanites is made more difficult by the fact that they are often listed as a separate group from those who are said to be within the Canaanite umbrella.¹¹³ For example, one of Moses' commands to clear the land of individuals refers to "seven nations greater and mightier than thou," consisting of "the Hittites, and the Girgashites, and the Amorites, and the Canaan-

---

109. Genesis 20:1–18; Genesis 21:22–34; Genesis 23:1–20; Genesis 26:1–31. See Walton, *Lost World*, 50–63.
110. Katell Berthelot, "Where May Canaanites Be Found? Canaanites, Phoenicians, and Others in Jewish Texts from the Hellenistic and Roman Period," in *The Gift of the Land and the Fate of the Canaanites in Jewish Thought*, ed. Katell Berthelot, Joseph E. David, and Marc Hirshman (New York: Oxford University Press, 2020): 1–25.
111. Genesis 9:18–27; Trimm, *Destruction of the Canaanites*, 37–38.
112. Genesis 10:15–19.
113. Genesis 15:18–21. See Numbers 13:29; cf. Deuteronomy 1:7.

ites, and the Perizzites, and the Hivites, and the Jebusites[.]"[114] Many of the references simply say "inhabitants of the land."[115]

Though the physical location of the Conquest described in Joshua is clear, the geographical extent of the Canaanite culture is not. The region of the Conquest in Joshua has not yielded texts that describe this culture, and archives from northern sites like Ugarit and Mari arguably do not reflect the Iron Age Canaanite culture described in Joshua. These archives also do not seem to display moral depravity beyond that of other Near Eastern nations, at least as gleaned from their legal, religious, and wisdom texts.[116]

The Bible itself tells us precious little about the actual sins of the Canaanites. Leviticus instructs that "after the doings of the land of Canaan, whither I bring you, shall ye not do: neither shall ye walk in their ordinances" (Leviticus 18:3). The chapter then lists prohibitions against incest, adultery, child sacrifice, and bestiality, ending with, "For all these abominations have the men of the land done, which were before you."[117] Two other passages reiterate child sacrifice as a Canaanite practice, with one also noting illicit forms of divination.[118]

Because *herem* does not seem far distant in some instances from child sacrifice, and because modern society has distanced itself from the sexual ethics of Leviticus, some have critiqued this as insufficient wickedness to justify the treatment of the Canaanites.[119] The Amarna letters describe Canaan before Joshua's time as a place with squab-

---

114. Deuteronomy 7:1. Perhaps this is similar to the nesting of titles in the Book of Mormon, where many subtribes are considered Nephites but one subtribe are Nephites proper. Jacob 1:13–14.
115. Numbers 38:50–56.
116. Richard S. Hess, "'Because of the Wickedness of These Nations' (Deut. 9:4–5)," in *For Our Good Always: Studies on the Message and Influence of Deuteronomy in Honor of Daniel I. Block*, ed. Jason S. DeRouchie, Jason Gile, and Kenneth G. Turner (Winona Lake, IN: Eisenbrauns, 2013), 17–37.
117. Leviticus 18:1–30.
118. Deuteronomy 12:31; Deuteronomy 18:9–14. Walton argues that these legal restrictions only apply to Canaanites who had little revealed knowledge, but Nephi's assertion of revealed knowledge among Canaanites makes this untenable for Latter-day Saints. See Walton, *Lost World*, 50–63; 1 Nephi 17:33–38.
119. For a stringent response to this modern attitude, see Clay Jones, "We Don't Hate Sin So We Don't Understand What Happened to the Canaanites," *Philosophia Christi* 11, no. 1 (2009): 53–72.

bling city states that conscripted laborers, fought for power, and were plagued by large bands of roving bandits.[120] Thus, some have portrayed Canaanite sin as primarily being socioeconomic oppression of the poor, which may have even motivated oppressed Canaanites to go become Israelites.[121] Though less scripturally-based, this reason can stand alongside the others.

In the Book of Mormon, Nephi leans heavily upon Canaanite wickedness as the reason for the Conquest, whether from the sources available to him or as theological "suppos[ing]" from the story of the Conquest. Nephi's analysis of the Canaanite dispossession is one of the foundational Book of Mormon passages on the doctrine of promised lands:

> And now, do ye suppose that the children of this land, who were in the land of promise, who were driven out by our fathers, *do ye suppose that they were righteous? Behold, I say unto you, Nay*. Do ye suppose that our fathers would have been more choice than they if they had been righteous? I say unto you, Nay. Behold, the Lord esteemeth all flesh in one; he that is righteous is favored of God. *But behold, this people had rejected every word of God, and they were ripe in iniquity; and the fulness of the wrath of God was upon them*; and the Lord did curse the land against them, and bless it unto our fathers; yea, he did curse it against them unto their destruction, and he did bless it unto our fathers unto their obtaining power over it. Behold, the Lord hath created the earth that it should be inhabited; and he hath created his children that they should possess it. And he raiseth up a righteous nation, and destroyeth the nations of the wicked. And he leadeth away the righteous into precious lands, and the wicked he destroyeth, and curseth the land unto them for their sakes (1 Nephi 17:33–38).

One of the difficulties in condemning the Canaanites, based solely on the biblical account, is that it does not suggest that they knew God sufficiently to merit destruction. Certainly, both the New Testament and modern revelation suggest that all the world's nations are suffi-

---

120. Dever, *Who Were the Early Israelites*, 170–189; cf. 3 Nephi 2:11; 3 Nephi 6:10–14; 3 Nephi 7:1–14, in the generation leading up to Nephite destruction at the death of Christ.
121. Dever, *Who Were the Early Israelites*, 170–189; Nicholas Wolterstorff, "Reading Joshua," in *Divine Evil*, 236–256.

ciently morally aware to be held culpable to a degree.[122] But the Book of Mormon's teachings on divinely sanctioned national obliteration seem to require a high level of knowledge of God, or at least special land covenant blessings.[123] Nephi's statement that "*this people had rejected every word of God*" suggests that the sins mentioned in the Old Testament, and probably more, were committed against this background of moral warnings from God.

Alternatively, it may have been that despite their rejection of revealed messages, the Canaanites retained a low awareness of true doctrine. In that vein, it is worth mentioning that the Canaanites were not completely destroyed and instead remained in the land to serve as a test for the Israelites. This bears similarities to the Book of Mormon Lamanites, who also possessed a lower knowledge than their neighboring nation:

> Because that this people hath transgressed my covenant which I commanded their fathers, and have not hearkened unto my voice; I also will not henceforth drive out any from before them of the nations which Joshua left when he died: *That through them I may prove Israel, whether they will keep the way of the Lord to walk therein*, as their fathers did keep it, or not. Therefore the Lord left those nations, without driving them out hastily; neither delivered he them into the hand of Joshua.[124]

Another principle to mention in regard to societal wickedness is an assumption of corporate identity.[125] This idea, which permeates both the Old Testament and Book of Mormon, suggests a general morality of society for which each member is independently accountable,

---

122. Romans 1:18–32; Romans 2:14–15; 2 Nephi 2:5; Alma 29:5–8; Doctrine and Covenants 88:7–13.
123. The Nephites, who were given greater moral knowledge, were obliterated while the Lamanites, who knew less, were spared as a nation. Outside of exceptional knowledge, the requirements for national destruction are a general ripeness in iniquity, the presence of secret combinations, and the anecdotal horrors that accompany such a decline. Alma 37:26–31; Helaman 2:13–14.
124. Judges 2:20–23; cf. 1 Nephi 2.
125. Trimm, *Destruction of the Canaanites*, 90, citing Kaminsky, "Corporate Responsibility in the Hebrew Bible." These attitudes of moral societal unity are more common outside of the Western world. See Jonathan Haidt, *The Righteous Mind: Why Good People are Divided by Politics and Religion* (New York: Vintage Books, 2012), 118–120.

and perhaps even punishable. Under corporate identity, all ancient Nephites suffer natural, economic, and political disasters as a society when they have wicked leaders — even women, children, and those with little to no social influence.[126] Corporate identity can be explained naturalistically because interrelated people will naturally affect each other.[127] Spiritual corporate identity is limited in terms of final accountability for sins of others, but multigenerational covenants continue to be a way in which God has opted to interact with humanity. This principle relates to the problem of evil generally and goes beyond the scope of this paper.

Finally, there is a difference between saying that the Canaanites were so wicked that they *had* to be destroyed and saying that their destruction was *justified*. To paraphrase Jesus, "Suppose ye that these [Canaanites] were sinners above all the [nations], because they suffered such things? I tell you, Nay: but, except ye repent, ye shall all likewise perish" (Luke 13:2–3). One scholar, defending the destruction of the Canaanites, wrote,

> Now, I am not arguing that the Canaanites were absolutely the worst specimens of humanity that ever existed, nor am I arguing that the Canaanites were the worst specimens of humanity in the ancient Near East (ANE). ... Furthermore, we should not think that God no longer judges nations today — even if we may not be able to determine this precisely.[128]

The Israelites themselves may also have merely been *justified* in eliminating the Canaanites, though the command given them makes it unlikely. In the Doctrine and Covenants, the Lord suggests that "the

---

126. For example, consider the famine in Helaman 11 and that all of Nephite society suffered from it.
127. Scripture contains conflicting statements about the accountability of children for parental decisions, which can be reconciled by separating *moral* or/*spiritual* accountability from *temporal* accountability, or *prescriptive* punishment from *descriptive* punishment. Whether or not children are spiritually punished for Adam's sins, they are certainly the recipient of whatever worldly legacy their parents pass on to them, whether prosperous or woeful. Corrupt leaders will naturally cause suffering among their own society, regardless of whether their subjects are upright. This is a naturalistic view that suggests that corporate identity blessings and curses are inherent naturally in our social systems. Exodus 20:5; Ezekiel 18:20; Article of Faith 2.
128. Copan, "Yahweh Wars," 74.

law that I gave unto mine ancients," presumably including ancient Israel, was that "they should not go out unto battle against any nation, kindred, tongue, or people, save I, the Lord, commanded them" (Doctrine and Covenants 98:33–36). Clearly the Old Testament claims that God did command the Conquest, but [the law of the ancients] also seems to assume that any command to go to war would require the opponent to first "proclaim war against them" and reject three offers of peace (Doctrine and Covenants 98:33–36). The Conquest narrative contains limited instances of Moses and Joshua offering peace but overall portrays the Israelites as proclaiming war.

Other provisions of the law of the ancients acknowledge that it is generally *more blessed* to not use justified violence when there is an option, and one's "reward shall be an hundred-fold" (Doctrine and Covenants 98:25). There is clearly a higher way in such a case. Mason and Pulsipher exhort us, "Rather than being a justified response in which our less than celestial actions can be excused, nonviolent forbearance is a sanctified (and sanctifying) response that not only helps make us more holy but also blesses future generations."[129] What that passage does not make clear is whether forbearance is a theologically sound option to a divine command of violence. Mason and Pulsipher seem to assume so in the story of Nephi when he was "constrained" to kill Laban and commanded in the imperative.[130] It remains plausible that the commands to Moses and Joshua were merely options originally, but the plain language of the text is imperative.

In summary, Book of Mormon doctrine and biblical passages suggest that the Canaanites *as a society* were indeed sufficiently worthy of destruction by God, or at least of being driven out. This doesn't explain why God included the Israelites in the destruction rather than using other means, but it can help ease concerned readers in tandem with other lenses of the restored gospel.

---

129. Mason and Pulsipher, *Proclaim Peace*, 131.
130. For an argument that Nephi had a choice, see Doctrine and Covenants 98:32; Mason and Pulsipher, *Proclaim Peace*, 46–65, 166–167. However, by Nephi's account, he was told and "constrained by the Spirit" three times to do this. 1 Nephi 4:8–18.

Reasons Beyond Understanding

As a final fallback for the perplexed reader, there is the doctrinal assurance that God's ways are just and merciful, even if beyond our comprehension, whether or not reasons are provided in scripture. If this principle is true, then either God did not command *herem* upon the Canaanites, or God did so with a sufficient reason, even if we do not yet know what that may be. This is sometimes criticized as a non-argument,[131] but it is really an appeal to God's character as witnessed in other instances throughout our lives to explain a perplexing situation.[132] In fact, church leaders have made it clear that for some difficult questions, adopting incorrect solutions for theological quandaries can be a step backwards. President Dallin H. Oaks said,

> It's not the pattern of the Lord to give reasons. We can put reasons to commandments. When we do we're on our own. … Let's [not] make the mistake that's been made in the past, here and in other areas, trying to put reasons to revelation. … *The revelations are what we sustain as the will of the Lord and that's where safety lies.*[133]

Although the text does give some reasons why the Canaanite command was given, there is also room for alternative purposes that do not need to be explicitly stated. In discussions of theodicy — arguments justifying God's goodness in the face of evils — this attitude is called "skeptical theism."[134] Skepticism is often an unfriendly word in religious circles, but the "skeptical" of skeptical theism is only skeptical about whether we can fully comprehend God's nature, especially his justice and purposes. This attitude seems to be embodied in the

---

131. Edwin Curley, "The God of Abraham, Isaac, and Jacob," in *Divine Evil? The Moral Character of the God of Abraham*, Michael Bergmann, Michael J. Murray, and Michael C. Rea (New York: Oxford University Press, 2011) 69.
132. Mark C. Murphy, "God Beyond Justice," in *Divine Evil*, 167.
133. Dallin H. Oaks cited in "Apostles Talk about Reasons for Lifting Ban," *Daily Herald* (Provo, Utah) (5 June 1988): 21 (Associated Press); reproduced with commentary in Dallin H. Oaks, *Life's Lessons Learned: Personal Reflections* (Salt Lake City: Deseret Book Company, 2011), 68–69. See also Jeffrey R. Holland, Interview, 4 March 2006, *The Mormons*, PBS, online at pbs.org. All of the above quotes may also be found online at fairlatterdaysaints.org.
134. See Alvin Plantinga, "Comments on 'Satanic Verse: Moral Chaos in Holy Writ,'" in *Divine Evil*, 109–114; Murphy, "God Beyond Justice," 150–167.

book of Job.¹³⁵ After accusing God of being unjust and calling Him to account, God appears to Job and reminds him that Job doesn't have the knowledge, experience, ability, or ethos to be calling God unjust or questioning his ways.¹³⁶

By this view, God's justice and character are to some degree a mystery that cannot be fully comprehended by mortals. As the Lord proclaims through Isaiah, "my thoughts are not your thoughts, neither are your ways my ways, saith the Lord. For as the heavens are higher than the earth, so are my ways higher than your ways, and my thoughts than your thoughts" (Isaiah 55:8–9). Jacob feels similarly: "Behold, great and marvelous are the works of the Lord. How unsearchable are the depths of the mysteries of him; and it is impossible that man should find out all his ways" (Jacob 4:8).

It is one thing to assert that God's commands may not be understood at a certain time, and another thing altogether to explain *why*. Often, critics have brought the straw man argument of "divine command theory" against Latter-day Saints, claiming that we believe God's commands are right *because* he commands them. These criticisms are especially brought against writings surrounding the Conquest, the beheading of Laban, the binding of Isaac, and early church plural marriage (including the questionable "Happiness Letter").¹³⁷

---

135. See Plantinga, "Comments on 'Satanic Verse: Moral Chaos in Holy Writ,'" 109–114.
136. Job 38:2–4.
137. For an example of these criticisms, see Mark S. Gustavson, "Scriptural Horror and the Divine Will," *Dialogue: A Journal of Mormon Thought* 21 no. 1 (Spring 1988), 72–81. The "Happiness Letter," which was attributed to Joseph Smith by a Church critic and was likely not written by Joseph, reads "That which is wrong under one circumstance, may be, and often is, right under another. God said thou shalt not kill, — at another time he said thou shalt utterly destroy. … Whatever God requires is right, no matter what it is, although we may not see the reason thereof till long after the events transpire … even things which might be considered abominable to all who do not understand the order of heaven only in part, but which, in reality, were right, because God gave and sanctioned by special revelation." Church leadership and scholarship have stepped away from quoting it as an authoritative Joseph Smith quote. Yet even this questionable quote, which is often described as divine command theory, is clearly not so because it suggests a "reason thereof" for God's actions that is simply not known at the time. "Appendix: Letter to Nancy Rigdon, circa Mid-April 1842," p. 2, *Joseph Smith Papers*, online at josephsmithpapers.org (spelling

Certainly scriptural and prophetic teachings encourage obedience to commands which are not understood, but a reason is always given. When Nephi was constrained to kill Laban — a commandment that most individuals ought to question — the Spirit gave Nephi several reasons why.[138] Scripture suggests that God's commands are done "in the wisdom of him who knoweth all things" (implying that God's acts are informed by knowledgeable *reasons*), not at the caprice of a Greek deity like Zeus.[139] In fact, prophetic teachings about God's moral laws binding Him (and perhaps predating Him) are a direct rebuttal of divine command theory.[140]

Even in instances where command reasons are not given initially, they are given to individuals who know God's ethos sufficiently for the decision to be reasonable. Abraham's binding and near-sacrifice of Isaac is another example, where 1) the purpose in the text was to test Abraham's obedience and it was revealed to him immediately before he would have complied; 2) Abraham had already had decades worth of experiences where God appeared to him before this point; and 3) according to the author of Hebrews, Abraham expected that Isaac

---

and punctuation have been standardized); Gerrit Dirkmaat, "Searching for 'Happiness': Joseph Smith's Alleged Authorship of the 1842 Letter to Nancy Rigdon," *Journal of Mormon History* 42, no. 3 (July 2016), 94–119.

138. These include the Lord delivering him to Nephi; Laban's disobedience, theft, and attempt on Nephi's life; the Lord slaying the wicked to bring about his righteous purposes; and the principle that Laban's death was better than "that a nation should dwindle and perish in unbelief" (1 Nephi 4:10–13). From these initial reasons, Nephi reasons further that getting away with the records was necessary for his future descendants to have a meaningful religious experience under the covenants he had previously received regarding Nephi's descendants' compliance to divine law (1 Nephi 4:14–18). See also John W. Welch, "Legal Perspectives on the Slaying of Laban," *Journal of Book of Mormon Studies* 1, no. 1 (1992), 119–141.

139. 2 Nephi 2:24. Rejecting divine command theory allows Latter-day Saints to sidestep Plato's "Euthyphro Dillemma" that questioned whether Greek deities could give just commands if their decisions were correct by default instead of upon some kind of principle.

140. Doctrine and Covenants 29:36; Doctrine and Covenants 88:34; Joseph Smith, "Discourse, 7 April 1844, as Published in Times and Seasons," p. 614, *Joseph Smith Papers*, online at josephsmithpapers.org. Also see McLachlan, "Is God Subject to or the Creator of Eternal Law?," 49–63.

would simply be raised from the dead anyway.[141] Adam was rewarded by God for sacrificing although his justification was "I know not, save the Lord commanded me," though Adam too had walked with God and later had the purpose explained (Moses 5:6). Certainly God must have reasons for every action, for "the day shall come when you shall comprehend even God" (Doctrine and Covenants 88:49).

Finally, modern rhetoric appropriately tends to emphasize God's love, but perhaps go too far when *foreclosing* the possibility of God ever being angered by sin or punishing anyone. One of Joseph's complaints about the creeds of his day was that they were reductive descriptions of God that put him in a box: "the creeds set up stakes, and say, 'Hitherto shalt thou come, and no further'; which I cannot subscribe to."[142] As Paul wrote when recounting the history of Israel, "Behold therefore the goodness and severity of God"(Romans 11:22). Perhaps there is some room here for humility about our knowledge, rather than simply concluding the historical and ethical incorrectness of the *herem* accounts.

Conclusion: Applying the Principles

Solving the Joshua problem of evil is not necessarily an impossible logical conclusion to arrive at when studying the isolated scenarios in Joshua. The harder challenge is foreclosing incorrect applications to other modern situations.[143] If God can justly command individuals like Abraham, Nephi, and Joshua to engage in violence, how do we draw the line today?[144] Though most Christians and Latter-day

---

141. Genesis 22:15–18; Hebrews 11:19. See also Matthew Patrick Rowley, "Child Sacrifice, Conquest and Cosmic War: On the Harmful Habitation of Biblical Texts," *Transformation* 34, no. 2 (2017): 134, "Before the text describes the command to sacrifice Isaac in Genesis 22, it shows that Abraham was miraculously validated on a national and international scale as one who hears from God. The modern mother or father who believed God told them to kill has not been — and does not even claim to be — validated in the same way as Abraham in Genesis 12–21."
142. Joseph Smith, "History, 1838–1856, volume E-1 [1 July 1843–30 April 1844]," pp. 1754–1755, *Joseph Smith Papers*, online at josephsmithpapers.org.
143. For arguments regarding the future-facing implications of these passages, see Stanley N. Gundry, ed., *Show Them No Mercy* (Grand Rapids, MI: Zondervan); Bergmann, Murray, and Rea, eds., *Divine Evil*; Randal Rauser, "'Let Nothing that Breathes Remain Alive': On the Problem of Divinely Commanded Genocide," *Philosophia Christi* 11, no. 1 (2009): 27–41.
144. See Genesis 22; 1 Nephi 4. For example, the Daybell and Lafferty murders

Saints will probably never be tempted to use these passages to justify violence, some admittedly have in the past. For example, biblical Conquest rhetoric was during the colonization of the Americas.[145]

The theodicies explored above each give different avenues for solving the Joshua problem of evil. If a believer argues that the book of Joshua (or its superficial interpretation) does not accurately depict the Conquest — an admittedly sound conclusion with a basis in scripture — then they need only disclaim Conquest historicity and the problem of *herem* is solved. But believers who accept Nephi's summary of the Conquest as more authoritative than the book of Joshua will want to accept that *some sort of Conquest occurred*, even if without *herem*.

We can assume that occasional individuals with violent delusions of grandeur will continue to cause harm inside and outside of the Church for the foreseeable future regardless of any religious rhetoric. But Latter-day Saints can defend the historicity of this narrative while making sure to reaffirm Church teachings that 1) all of God's commands, if indeed commanded, are given "for the benefit of the world; for he loveth the world" (2 Nephi 26:24); 2) God's commands ought only be heeded if they come clearly and through the proper channels; and 3) some scripture ought to be read *descriptively* instead of *prescriptively*. Joseph Smith taught these principles with clarity:

> we feel ourselves bound by the laws of God, to observe and do strictly, with all our hearts, all things *whatsoever is manifest unto us by the highest degree of testimony that God has committed us*, as written in the old and new Testament, or any where else, by any manifestation, *whereof we know that it has come from God: and has application to us*, being adapted to our situation and circumstances; age, and generation of life; and that we have a perfect, and indefeasible right, to embrace all such commandments, and do them; knowing, that *God will not command any thing, but what is peculiarly adapted in itself, to ameliorate* the condition of every man under whatever circumstances it may find him, it matters not

---

included claims of divine justification. Gustavson, "Scriptural Horror," 75; Meredith Deliso, "'Doomsday mom' Lori Daybell found guilty in murder conspiracy trial," *ABC News* (April 22, 2025, 6:12 PM), online at abcnews.go.com.

145. Alfred A. Cave, "Canaanites in a Promised Land: The American Indian and the Providential Theory of Empire," *American Indian Quarterly* 12, no. 4 (Autumn, 1988): 277–297.

what kingdom or country he may be in. And again, we believe that it is *our privilege to reject all things, whatsoever is clearly manifested to us that they do not have a bearing upon us.* Such as, for instance, it is not binding on us to build an Ark, because God commanded Noah to build one. [But] on the other hand, *"Thou shalt not kill [and the Ten Commandments]" ... we most cordially embrace, and consider them binding on us because they are adapted to our circumstances.* We believe that we have a right to revelations ... on all subjects pertaining to our spiritual welfare; if it so be that we keep his commandments, so as to render ourselves worthy in his sight.[146]

With these principles in mind, it is clear that in this last dispensation, Latter-day Saints have the privilege to reject the command to exterminate Canaanites as "not hav[ing] a bearing upon us," whereas the command not to kill is "binding on us." The "highest degree of testimony" we have received in Jesus' teachings strongly advocates nonviolence and forbearance — living like Him, and this is the behavior we ought to live by.[147]

In conclusion, if an extremely violent Conquest really did occur (and we should not conclude that it did to the degree assumed by others based on Theodicy #1), there is ample justification for it through a theory of God accommodating Israel as an ignorant instrument in his hands, or by emphasizing textual and nontextual reasons for doing so. But precisely because we are engaging in an argument that justifies an instance of violence, Latter-day Saints should be at the forefront of proclaiming peace and spreading Christ's charity so as to show that we are *not encouraging violence*.[148] Like Nephi, we will ultimately

---

146. Joseph Smith, "Letter to Isaac Galland, 22 March 1839," p. 54, *Joseph Smith Papers*, online at josephsmithpapers.org.. Thanks to Gerrit Dirkmaat for making me aware of this source.
147. Mason and Pulsipher make an intriguing distinction between imitating the mortal Christ versus the ascended Christ and the Father: They are perfected and can properly use violence, but we cannot and should not seek to imitate that aspect of their nature. Mason and Pulsipher, *Proclaim Peace*, 154–155.
148. Perhaps the best approach to the problem of evil, after all, is to worry less about why it happens and instead learn how to harness Christ's charity to prevent more suffering in the world. Reckoning with evil in one's own life and the lives of others is the "existential problem of evil." For an LDS approach to the existential problem of evil, see Paul Bryner, "A Response to Antitheodicy: Dostoevsky, Mormon, and the Problem of Evil," April 26, 2024, paper presented

declare to God at the last day, "Thy ways are just" — the real question is whether the same will be said about us (2 Nephi 26:7).

---

at *Graduate Theological Union at Berkeley at conference entitled Latter-day Saint Theology & Divine Finitude: Scripture, Revelation, The Problem of Evil & Social Justice*, Panel 3 starting at 28:15, online at youtube.com.

7

THE ISRAELITE CULTURAL BACKGROUND OF NEPHITE POLYGAMY

MATTHEW ROPER

Polygamy in the Bible and the Book of Mormon can feel puzzling or troubling to modern readers. Set against the broader ancient Near Eastern world, this discussion shows that while most marriages were monogamous, plural marriage was a socially accepted, legally regulated way to secure heirs and protect vulnerable women. Abraham and Jacob are portrayed as faithful patriarchs whose plural families became vehicles for God's covenant promises, and the Law of Moses assumes and structures polygamy rather than banning it. Royal excess, not plurality itself, lies at the heart of the condemnations of David and especially Solomon. With that backdrop, Jacob's sermon in the Book of Mormon comes into clearer focus: Nephite men are condemned not simply for having multiple wives, but for breaking the specific "Law of Lehi" mandating monogamy unless God expressly commands otherwise and for misusing David and Solomon as excuses. In the end, obedience to living revelation—not mere appeal to precedent—governs how God's people "raise up seed" in any age.

The Church of Jesus Christ of Latter-day Saints teaches that "monogamy is God's standard for marriage unless He declares otherwise (see 2 Samuel 12:7–8 and Jacob 2:27, 30)."[1] The Book of Mormon prophet Jacob's sermon at the temple, including his condemnation of polygamy among the early Nephites (Jacob 2–3), cannot be fully understood outside the context of the culture from which that people came. The plates of brass contained an account of righteous covenant ancestors, some of whom practiced polygamy. They also contained

---
1. Introduction to "Official Declaration 1," Doctrine and Covenants.

the commandments from the law of Moses and the words of other prophets which provided the foundation for a righteous social order among the children of Lehi (1 Nephi 3:20; 1 Nephi 5:11–14).

The purpose of what follows is to show how Old Testament polygamy provides context for Jacob's teachings on that occasion.[2] First, this practice will be addressed in light of the ancient Near East and the cases of two righteous patriarchs, Abraham and his grandson Jacob. Next, I will survey commandments given under the Law of Moses which relate to polygamy in ancient Israel and the accounts of kings David and Solomon in light of these laws. Jacob's condemnation of Nephite polygamy will then be discussed in light of this cultural background.

Part 1: Polygamy in the Ancient World

While most marriages in the ancient Near East and ancient Israel were likely monogamous, polygamy was considered a normal cultural practice for those whose abilities and means allowed them to provide for such a family.[3] I. Mendelsohn states, "The Deuteronomic law takes

---

2. I use the common term *polygamy* in this article although Old Testament plural marriage is more accurately defined as *polygyny*, the practice of one man having more than one wife.

3. "Polygamy, which included concubinage, allowed a household to increase its labor force and its chances to provide a living male heir to inherit the estate (Genesis 12–22). This arrangement also provided a support system for women who would not have otherwise married, widows, divorcees, and any children of the last two groups, as well as for aged parents. However, there is no explicit evidence for how the management of a household would have been carried out by two or more wives. Perhaps the favorite wife enjoyed a special status (Gen. 29:30–31; Ex. 21:10; Deut. 21:15–17; 1 Sam. 1:6), though presumably each wife had responsibility for her own children. ... In actual practice, however, polygamy seems to have been limited to the very wealthy, including especially the patriarchs (Gen. 29:15–30; 30:1–9; 36:1–5), judges (Gideon: Judg. 8:30–31), and royalty (e.g., 2 Sam. 3:2–5; 5:13; 15:16; 16:21–22; 1 Kings 11:3). Save for Samuel's father (1 Sam. 1:5–6), no comment in the entire Deuteronomic History (Samuel–Kings) had more than one wife." Leo G. Perdue, "The Israelite and Early Jewish Family: Summary and Conclusions," in *Families in Ancient Israel*, ed. Leo G. Perdue, Joseph Blenkinsopp, John J. Collins, and Carol Meyers (Louisville: Westminster John Knox Press, 1997), 185. Carol Meyers in her work on the lives of women in ancient Israel observes that generally speaking, the lifespans of women generally, and women who gave birth in particularly could be remarkably short. In light of this, she thinks

it as a matter of fact that the normal well-to-do family consisted of two wives" and that such a man "could have as many wives and concubines as he could financially support."[4] According to Bruce Vawter, "Throughout the biblical period ... polygamy is accepted without remark alike in Israel's laws and its history, though the average man more often than not continues to be shown as monogamous."[5] Consequently, "during the biblical period polygamy never came to be considered socially or morally reprehensible."[6] "Israelite law," states Philip King, "took polygamy for granted."[7] Most recently, after a thorough examination of the issue in a recent book, Ryan Stephens concludes that "Mosaic Law permits polygamy as a licit and regulated practice."[8]

Wives and Concubines

When trying to understand polygamy in antiquity, including that portrayed in the Bible, care must be taken to avoid imposing contemporary attitudes and cultural baggage upon the past, which for some may feel like a different world. As one authority on biblical culture writes:

> The practice of appealing to the Bible in support of the traditional Jewish or Christian view of marriage is understandable, but it calls for some qualification. First, theoretical or theological statements about marriage (e.g.,

---

that "it would have been a demographic impossibility for most men to have had multiple spouses." Carol Meyers, *Rediscovering Eve: Ancient Israelite Women in Context* (New York: Oxford University Press, 2013), 101.

4. I. Mendelsohn, "The Family in the Ancient Near East," *Biblical Archaeologist* 11, No, 2 (May 1948): 25.
5. Bruce Vawter, "The Biblical Theology of Divorce," *Proceedings of the Catholic Theological Society of America* 22 (1967): 225–226.
6. Vawter, "The Biblical Theology of Divorce," 226.
7. Philip J. King and Lawrence E. Stager, *Life in Biblical Israel* (Louisville: Westminster John Knox Press, 2002), 38.
8. Ryan Stephens, *Polygamy in the Law of Moses* (Lanham, MD: Lexington Books, 2024), 103. Anciently, adultery referred to sexual relations between a man and the wife of another man or a married woman with a man who was not her husband. A woman who was betrothed to a future husband was held to be under the same standard of fidelity, even if the marriage was not yet consummated. Under the Law of Moses, adultery was condemned and was a capital crime. Raymond Westbrook, "Adultery in Ancient Near Eastern Law," *Revue Biblique* 97, no. 4 (Octobre 1990): 542–580; Stephens, *Polygamy in the Law of Moses*, 113.

Gen. 2:24, about man and woman becoming one flesh) must not be mistaken for or confused with relevant social realities. Second, the physical, psychological, and emotional environment of the household at that time was quite different from that of the privatized nuclear family of today. Third, more than one form of marriage is attested, and polygamous unions occurred throughout most of the biblical period.[9]

For example, there were social and legal distinctions among wives in the ancient world, a concept that is foreign to many modern ears. When discussing polygamy, scholars will sometimes use terms such as primary or first-tier wife and secondary or second-tier wife. An example of a secondary wife would be a "concubine," a word that can lead to inaccurate ideas or assumptions. Contrary to some portrayals, a concubine — at least in ancient Israel — was not an extramarital liaison. For a righteous Israelite, according to Jeffrey Tigay, "a sexual union and the raising of children require a marital relationship that is intended to be permanent."[10] Michael Coogan explains that in the Bible a concubine "does not have its usual meaning in English of a mistress, it denotes a secondary wife, either a free woman or a slave."[11] A concubine (*pilagesh*) was a category of wife, although usually understood as a wife of second tier as compared to the primary wife.

A primary wife might be obtained through a bride price paid by the groom. She might also bring a dowry of wealth or property to the marriage. Typically, this would not be the case with a concubine who came from poorer circumstances or who may have originally been a captive or a slave prior. Stephens notes, "While a concubine may be referred to as a 'wife,' it is significant that the primary formally married wives in the narrative accounts are never referred to as a concubine."[12] Hagar is referred to as a wife (Genesis 16:3; 25:1) as well as a concubine (Genesis 25:6). Keturah is called both a wife (Genesis 25:1) and a concubine (Genesis 25:6; 1 Chronicles 1:32). Abraham's wife Sarah, on the other hand, is never called a concubine. This is

---

9. Joseph Blinkinsopp, "The Family in First Temple Israel," in *Families in Ancient Israel*, 58.
10. Jeffrey H. Tigay, *The JPS Torah Commentary: Deuteronomy* (Philadelphia: Jewish Publication Society, 1996), 232n7.
11. Michael Coogan, *God and Sex: What the Bible Really Says* (New York: Twelve, 2010), 84.
12. Stephens, *Polygamy in the Law of Moses*, 109.

obviously because she is Abraham's primary wife. In Jacob's family, Leah (Genesis 32:22), Rachel (Genesis 29:28; Genesis 32:22), Bilhah (Genesis 30:4), and Zilpah (Genesis 30:9) are all called wives, but later Bilhah is also called a concubine (Genesis 35:22). Leah, Rachel, and Zilpah are never called concubines.

Ryan Stephens explains some of the distinctions between a primary wife and a concubine. "Concubines are never recorded as having a formal marriage contract or bringing a dowry into the family. The absence of a formal marriage, which includes payment of a bride price and dowry, means that the primary wife has rights that a concubine does not."[13] If a man divorced his wife, he had to give her a written certificate to that effect, while this was not required in the case of a concubine. The concubine, however, could not be sold as a slave after she was married and had a child, but had to be sent away free. Notwithstanding these ancient distinctions, the union between a husband and a concubine was considered a legal and legitimate marriage with certain rights and protections. Children of a concubine, however, would not inherit unless such a provision was made by the father.[14]

"Raising Up Seed": Patriarchs, Polygamy, and Children

One of the more common reasons for a man to marry an additional wife was the need to produce an heir to whom he could pass on his inheritance and property. The importance that children represented for parents in the ancient world is not fully appreciated today. Leo Perdue writes:

> Barrenness was considered a disgrace and evidence of divine disfavor (Gen. 30:23; 2 Samuel 6:20–23). In addition, the desire to have many children may reflect the extremely high infant mortality in this culture. Divorce and widowhood before any children were born were especially threatening to women, if they did not later remarry. Sons could take care of their mothers, especially in their old age. Pragmatically speaking, the mother produced the children who would provide the labor and the heirs for the household's (and her) survival.[15]

---

13. Stephens, *Polygamy in the Law of Moses*, 109.
14. Stephens, *Polygamy in the Law of Moses*, 109–110.
15. Perdue, "The Israelite and Early Jewish Family," 182.

So, in the world of the biblical patriarchs, "while monogamy was the standard practice, concubinage and polygamy were practiced on occasion to ensure a household's producing of needed progeny."[16] In the surrounding ancient Near Eastern cultures of the day, a wife who was unable to conceive and bear children would sometimes provide a second wife as a surrogate birth mother for her husband so that they could obtain an heir for their family. Ancient Near Eastern texts preserve examples of laws and contracts which explained the rules, rights, and expectations for such arrangements. These laws appear to have varied somewhat in different locales, but in many ways correlate well with what we find in biblical accounts of the patriarchs and their families.

According to Tikva Frymer-Kensky, "the proper intrafamily relationships may have been subject to local customs or individual contract, but it is clear that the concept of a barren wife giving her husband a concubine is well established in the Near East."[17] According to Carol Meyers, "Having an infertile wife was likely grounds for even a peasant man to take a second one [wife]."[18] The prophet Samuel's righteous father Elkanah, a devout Israelite of the tribe of Ephraim, had two wives, Hannah and Peninnah. Vawter states that "Peninnah was probably Elkanah's secondary wife, taken by him in view of Hannah's barrenness; this was the commonest situation leading to bigamy, polygamy, or the recourse to concubines, with or without concurrence of the primary legal wife. As in Mesopotamia, details of this kind were probably spelt out in the marriage contract."[19]

Abraham

Abraham is considered to be the father of the faithful by adherents of three major religious traditions. Latter-day Saints also revere Abraham as an example of strict obedience to God's commandments, and believe that we can be blessed through the blessings of those covenants he made and kept with God. Our understanding of Abraham

---

16. Perdue, "The Israelite and Early Jewish Family," 171.
17. Tikva Frymer-Kensky, "Patriarchal Family Relationships and Near Eastern Law," *Biblical Archaeologist* 44, no. 4 (Autumn 1981): 212.
18. Carol Meyers, *Rediscovering Eve*, 101.
19. Vawter, "The Biblical Theology of Divorce," 226n7.

and polygamy is informed by Latter-day Saint scripture, including Doctrine and Covenants 132 and the Book of Abraham.

The biblical account names three of Abraham's wives: Sarah, Hagar, and Keturah. It also recounts some of the many challenges in Abraham's family, including the rivalries and strife between Sarah, Hagar, and their children. These problems are sometimes viewed by readers as evidence of the evils of polygamy. While there can be no doubt about the challenges that plural marriage arrangements would present, these only show that polygamy was difficult, not that it was sinful. Support for the case that it was not can be seen in how the biblical account unfolds.

Sarah was unable to have children (Genesis 11:30), but the Lord, in spite of this, promised Abraham that he would make of him a great nation and that in him "all the families of the earth would be blessed" (Genesis 12:2–3). When he returned from Egypt, God told him, "And I will make thy seed as the dust of the earth; so that if a man can number the dust of the earth, then shall thy seed be numbered" (Genesis 13:16) and they would also inherit the land (Genesis 13:14–15). He first assumes that his servant Eleazar will be his heir since he had no children of his own (Genesis 15:1–3), but God tells him that his heir would "come forth out of his own bowels" (Genesis 15:4) and that his future seed would be numbered as the stars (Genesis 15:5). "Look now toward heaven, and tell the stars, if thou be able to number them," the Lord says, "so shall thy seed be" (Genesis 15:5). Here we observe that at this point in the text, the Lord has told him nothing about having a child through Sarah, although he is credited for his faith. "And he believed in the Lord; and he counted it to him for righteousness" (Genesis 15:5–6).

Sarah, likely aware of the Lord's promises, asks Abraham to take Hagar as his wife so that she "may obtain children by her" (Genesis 16:2), and after this marriage, Abraham's concubine-wife conceives (Genesis 16:1–4). Given the ordering of the text, Abraham and Sarah appear to act in faith according to their understanding, based upon what God had told them up to this point, in the hope that the Lord will honor his promises to their family through Hagar. Stephens observes, "Abraham apparently has no shame about taking Hagar as a slave wife."[20] While there is friction between the two strong-willed women, there is not a hint of God's disapproval of Abraham's marriage with Hagar.

Then Hagar makes a mistake. "And when she saw that she had conceived, her mistress was despised in her eyes" (Genesis 16:4). Insight into this episode in Abraham's family can be found in other ancient Near Eastern texts in which laws proscribe the status of a concubine. Tikva Frymer-Kensky discusses the laws of Hammurabi, roughly contemporary with the time of Abraham.

> A woman was expected to bear children for her husband. If she could not do so ... he might marry another. Possibly to forestall this, the woman might give her own personal slave to her husband to bear children for her. This hand maiden, although no longer a mere servant, must not become a rival to the original wife nor consider herself her equal.[21]

Under Hammurabi's law, if a concubine tried to do this, the primary wife was permitted to discipline her by again reducing her status to that of a slave, although she could not sell her if she had borne a child.[22] While we cannot say to what extent Abraham was directly aware of or followed this part of Hammurabi's law, this may be the context of the episode when Hagar begins to look down upon Sarah. That would run against the culture of that time, so it is not surprising to read that Sarah "dealt hardly with her" and Hagar ran away (Genesis 16:6). We do not know what Sarah did, but whatever it was, Hagar was very upset and fled.

In spite of this familial conflict, the Lord remains very much involved. There is no condemnation of either Sarah or Abraham in the text, but an angel appears and comforts Hagar, commanding her to go back home and submit to Sarah. The Lord then promises, "I will multiply thy seed exceedingly, that it shall not be numbered for multitude" (Genesis 16:10).

After Ishmael is born, the Lord covenants with Abraham that "I will multiply thee exceedingly" (Genesis 17:2), make him "exceedingly fruitful," a father of many nations and kings (Genesis 17:4, 6), that he

---

20. Stephens, *Polygamy in the Law of Moses*, 92.
21. Frymer-Kensky, "Patriarchal Family Relationships," 211.
22. Frymer-Kensky, "Patriarchal Family Relationships," 211.

would establish his divine covenant with his seed, and that they will inherit the land (Genesis 17:2–8).

It is only then, in the middle of chapter 17, that the Lord tells Abraham that Sarah will be also blessed with a child and that she would become a "mother of nations" (Genesis 17:15–16; Genesis 18:9–15), and that he would establish his covenant with her son Isaac (Genesis 17:19). The Lord also tells Abraham that he has heard his prayer for Ishmael and that the Lord will also make Ishmael "fruitful and will multiply him exceedingly; twelve princes shall he beget, and I will make him a great nation" (Genesis 17:20).

Several years later, when Sarah perceives potential conflict and danger in the family, she asks Abraham to send Hagar and Ishmael away. This troubles Abraham, who does not want to do so. But God tells him to do what Sarah asks of him, repeating his promise that he will make of Ishmael a great nation, because he is of Abraham's seed (Genesis 21:13). In this case, by sending Hagar and Ishmael away, Abraham follows the word of the Lord to hearken to Sarah. There is still not a word of criticism for Abraham or Sarah about polygamy. Stephens observes,

> The text communicates that it was a perceived threat by Sarah due to Ishmael's behavior toward Isaac and the potential for conflict in the distribution of inheritance that prompted the dismissal (21:9–10). There is nothing in the narrative of Abraham that either explicitly or implicitly gives any indication that Abraham's polygamy was displeasing to God.[23]

After they are sent away, the Lord does not forget Hagar. He continues to hear her and Ishmael's prayers, and preserve their lives, repeating the promise to them that Ishmael will be a great nation whose seed will be blessed (Genesis 21:17–21).

The Lord continues to bless Abraham:

> I will multiply thy seed as the stars of the heaven, and as the sand which is upon the sea shore, and thy seed shall possess the gate of his enemies. And in thy seed shall all the nations of the earth be blessed; because thou hast obeyed my voice (Genesis 22:17–18).

The covenant promises that God would multiply and raise up seed unto Abraham were miraculously fulfilled in the children of his wives

---

23. Stephens, *Polygamy in the Law of Moses*, 92.

and concubines. Abraham had six children through his wife Keturah, one through Hagar, and one through Sarah, and the subsequent generations of his seed were multiplied (Genesis 25:1–6, 13–16). The reference to the "sons of the concubines, which Abraham had" (Genesis 25:6) is taken by some scholars to refer to Hagar and Keturah, while others have interpreted this to mean that the concubines mentioned were in addition to those two. Many biblical scholars also believe that the summary genealogy in Genesis 25:1–6 is chronologically out of place and that this marriage and the birth of her children likely occurred while Sarah was still alive.[24] According to Genesis, Sarah lived thirty-seven years after the birth of Isaac (Genesis 17:17; Genesis 23:1–2), so Abraham's marriage to this concubine may have taken place while Sarah was still alive. The genealogy in these verses is thought to be placed at this point in the text as a marker at the end of the Abraham story, just before his death, showing how the Lord's promises about his having children were fulfilled.

As seen in the Lord's later promise to bless Isaac, His judgement of Abraham's worthiness is also significant. "Because that Abraham *obeyed my voice*, and *kept my charge, my commandments, my statutes,* and *my laws*" (Genesis 26:5).[25] To sum up, in the biblical text:

- Abraham throughout his life has at least three wives (Sarah, Hagar, and Keturah).
- Abraham is consistently portrayed as faithful and obedient. He acts in faith, he keeps God's commandments, and the Lord blesses him with prosperity and children.
- Abraham is never reproved, called a sinner, an adulterer, a fornicator, or charged with committing whoredoms or

---

24. Gordon J. Wenham, *Volume 2, Genesis 16–50,* Word Biblical Commentary, ed. David A. Hubbard and Glenn W. Barker, 60–63 vols. (Dallas: Word Books, 1994), 2:160–161; Nahum Sarna, *The JPS Commentary Genesis* (Philadelphia: Jewish Publication Society, 1989), 172; Robert Jamieson, A.R. Fauset, and David Brown, *A Commentary, Critical, Experimental, and Practical on the Old and New Testament*, 3 vols. (Glasgow: William Collins, Queen's Printer, 1863), 1:14-15; E. A. Speiser, *Genesis* (Garden City, NY: Doubleday & Company, 1964), 189.
25. Genesis 18:17–19. He is a prophet with authority to mediate between sinners and God (Genesis 20:7).

- having lustful desires of any kind, in contrast to some of his contemporaries.
- He is repeatedly shown to be one whose relationship with God is such that he can often receive revelation and have confidence conversing with him and having his prayers heard and answered.
- The Lord repeatedly promises Abraham throughout his life that he will raise up seed or children through him and that they will in turn inherit the promises of these covenants.
- The text recounts that the Lord raised up seed to Abraham through each of his wives (Sarah, Hagar, and Keturah). These wives and their children are also blessed in various ways. Notably, his plural wife Hagar is also deemed worthy on several occasions to receive divine manifestations and revelation, with promises specifically for her and her posterity.

Jacob/Israel

As he blessed Abraham, the Lord also blessed Isaac with children (Genesis 26:4–5, 24), although there is no indication in the biblical account that Isaac had more than one wife.[26] In addition, the Lord renewed the promises and blessings given previously to Abraham and Isaac to Jacob. "Thy seed shall be as the dust of the earth ... and in thee

---

26. The passages in Doctrine and Covenants 132:1, 37 could suggest that Joseph Smith had additional revelation about Isaac having plural wives which is not mentioned in the Bible. If so, we do not have an account of this from the Prophet Joseph Smith. Neither the biblical account nor the Joseph Smith translation provides any evidence for Isaac's polygamy. The revelation on marriage may simply be a faithful statement of the Prophet's uncorrected question as first asked of the Lord without necessarily being intended as a matter of historical accuracy. The reference in verse 37, might mean that Isaac, like Abraham and Jacob also received more than one wife at the Lord's direction. Alternatively, in the absence of any additional information in the Bible of modern revelation, could be read as meaning that Isaac too was fully obedient *to all that the Lord commanded him to do,* in spite having only one wife, but that like Abraham and Jacob did none other thing than that which he was commanded and like them has also been exalted. The implication of this would be that a faithful monogamist can be fully obedient to the new and everlasting covenant so long as they do none other thing than that which the Lord commands them in the matter of celestial marriage.

and in thy seed shall all the families of the earth be blessed" (Genesis 28:14).

Jacob married four women while he lived in Haran and labored for his uncle Laban. The seed of these wives would become the children of Israel. He married Leah and Rachel, and then each of his wives provided an additional wife, Bilhah and Zilpah. In spite of many difficulties, the Lord continued to bless and prosper Jacob during these years, and continued to remember him and his covenant concerning his children (Genesis 32:1–2, 24–30; Genesis 35:9–13).

Some readers have suggested that Jacob's plural marriages were not sanctioned by God because Laban tricked him into marrying Leah in order to marry Rachel, but Stephens observes:

> Jacob was tricked into polygamy with Rachel and Leah (29:23–28). Yet Jacob enters into marriage with Bilhah and Zilpah willingly. While the narrative highlights many faults in Jacob's character and behavior, his polygamy is not one of them. Attempts by some scholars to escape the fact that the narrative never condemns Jacob's polygamy are especially strained in the case of Jacob. ...
>
> No case can be made for the assertion that the narrative concerning Jacob or Esau implicitly disapproves of their polygamy. In each case, there are other explicitly stated elements (e.g., foreignness, jealousy, deceit, and favoritism) that account for the negative depiction of Jacob and Esau's conflicts with their wives.[27]

As with Abraham, so can be said of Jacob, that whatever his personal faults or weaknesses, he was also never characterized as an adulterer, a fornicator or charged with committing whoredoms, nor does the Lord ever reprove or condemn any of his plural marriages. In spite of the patriarch's initial preference for Rachel, the divine will is fulfilled by blessing him with many children through all four of his wives who become mothers over the house of Israel. Like Ishmael, Jacob is blessed with twelve sons and at least one daughter. The descendants

---

27. Stephens, *Polygamy in the Law of Moses*, 93, 95. While Esau is portrayed negatively for selling his birthright and his marriages, Isaac and Rebekkah were upset, not about Esau's polygamy, but because they were foreign wives who would not respect the Lord's covenants. When Esau sees that his parents are displeased with his Canaanite wives, he marries another wife who is a daughter of Ishmael (Genesis 28:8–9).

of his children would eventually be led out of Egypt and inherit the land of Canaan.

Latter-day revelation mentions the righteousness and obedience of all three patriarchs (Abraham, Isaac, and Jacob). Each is said to have kept the Lord's law and the everlasting covenant because they "*did none other things than that which they were commanded*" and for this reason, have entered into their exaltation (Doctrine and Covenants 132:37). This may suggest that obedience was the defining issue in the marriage covenant among the patriarchs, rather than the number of wives they had, since Isaac had only one wife according to the biblical account. Eternal blessings were realized as long as they only did that which was specifically commanded or permitted by God and did not usurp privileges that He did not allow.[28]

To summarize, the accounts of the patriarchs Abraham, Isaac, and Jacob show that God sometimes fulfilled his covenants by raising up seed or children to the patriarchs through monogamy and at other times through a plurality of wives.

PART 2: POLYGAMY AND THE LAW OF MOSES

The Law of Moses contained commandments and laws which governed polygamy. While these reflect continuity with ancient Near Eastern culture, they also vary from earlier practices of the patriarchs. Under divine guidance, the prophet Moses, directed adjustments in how marriage practices were to be regulated. In this section, several examples in the Law of Moses which relate to polygamy will be discussed.

The Debt Slave Wife (Exodus 21:7–11)

Exodus 21:7–11 provides legal guidelines regarding the situation where a man purchases a debt slave in order for her to become a wife or concubine.

> If a man sell his daughter to be a maidservant, she shall not go out as the menservants do. If she please not her master, who hath betrothed her to himself, then shall he let her be redeemed: to sell her unto a strange nation he shall have no power, seeing he hath dealt deceitfully with her. And if he have betrothed her unto his son, he shall deal with her after the

---

28. There is also no indication in the Bible that the righteous patriarch Joseph has more than one wife.

manner of daughters. If he take him another wife; her food, her raiment, and her duty of marriage, shall he not diminish. And if he do not these three unto her, then shall she go out free without money (Exodus 21:7–11).

Nahum Sarna explains:

> In the ancient world, a father driven by poverty, might sell his daughter into a well-to-do family in order to ensure her future security. The sale presupposes marriage to the master or his son. Documents recording legal arrangements of this kind have survived from Nuzi. The Torah stipulates that the girl must be treated as a free woman; should the designated husband take an additional wife, he is still obligated to support her. A breach of faith gains her her freedom, and the master receives no compensation for the purchase price.[29]

Sarah Shectman makes the interesting observation that "the woman has been sold into slavery, but the end result seems to be that her interests are protected in much the same way a free primary wife's would be."[30] If the man decided not to consummate the marriage or provide a husband for her as was agreed to, she was to be returned to her family so that they might find an appropriate husband. If he married her to a son, the father is then not allowed to exploit her as a slave laborer, but treat her as a daughter. After the man married her, he is permitted, if he chooses, to take another wife, but if he does so he must continue to fulfill his marriage duties to the first (the wife who was formerly sold because of debt). The law says that "If he take another wife; her food, her raiment, and her conjugal rights he shall not diminish" (Deuteronomy 21:10 JPS).

If the husband failed in these duties, she was permitted to go free. In that case, the man would not be reimbursed what he paid when purchasing her. She could not be sold as a slave, she was to go free.[31] According to Ryan Stephens:

---

29. Nahum Sarna, *The JPS Torah Commentary: Exodus* (Philadelphia: Jewish Publication Society, 1991), 120.
30. Sarah Shectman, "What do we know about marriage in ancient Israel?" in *Reading a Tendentious Bible: Essays in Honor of Robert B. Coote*, ed. M. L. Chaney, et. al. (Sheffield: Phoenix Press, 2014), 171–172.
31. Stephens, *Polygamy in the Law of Moses*, 15, 21–23; Perdue, "The Israelite and Early Jewish Family," 196.

The laws in Exodus provide protection for the slave-wife/concubine, who otherwise could easily be taken advantage of. Embedded in this case law is the obvious assumption that polygamy was a normal and licit practice. Exodus 21:7–11 does not prohibit taking more than one wife. There is no hint in this passage that taking another wife was unlawful or socially unacceptable. What was unlawful and socially unacceptable was to fail to provide for a secondary wife or concubine in favor of another wife.[32]

Polygamy and Sisters (Leviticus 18:18)

The Law of Moses regulated the practice of polygyny in relation to marrying sisters.

> Neither shalt thou take a wife to her sister, to vex her, to uncover her nakedness, beside the other in her lifetime (Leviticus 18:18).

The righteous patriarch Jacob was married to Leah and Rachel who were sisters. The Lord never condemned Jacob or his wives for these marriages, although the situation was understandably a challenging one that fostered rivalries and jealousies within Jacob's family. Perhaps with this history in view, under The law of Moses, a man was forbidden under that law to marry two sisters living at the same time.

"The structure (both formal and literary) of Leviticus 18 indicates that there is no structural break at verse 18 to justify a non-literal reading of 'sister.' Leviticus 18:18 permits a man to marry a woman in addition to his wife so long as the other woman is not a literal sister of his current wife."[33]

Deuteronomy 17:14–20: The Code of the King

Deuteronomy 17:14–20, sometimes referred to as the Code of the King, gives instructions and commandments that Israelite kings were to remember and follow.

> But he shall not multiply horses to himself, nor cause the people to return to Egypt, to the end that he should multiply horses: forasmuch as the Lord hath said unto you, Ye shall henceforth return no more that way. Neither shall he multiply wives to himself, that his heart turn not away: neither shall

---

32. Stephens, *Polygamy in the Law of Moses*, 15.
33. Stephens, *Polygamy in the Law of Moses*, 49–50.

he greatly multiply to himself silver and gold (Deuteronomy 17:16–17).

As the admonition that the king not multiply horses and silver and gold shows, the word translated "multiply" does not forbid plurality (he could have more than one horse) but warns against acquiring these things in excess of what would be proper, so that his heart and that of the people do not turn away from the Lord. This understanding is reflected in many other translations of the passages which read "And he shall not have *many* wives."[34] Richard Nelson states, "He can have military forces, wives, and a treasury, but he is not to 'multiply' them, that is, not acquire too many or too much."[35]

According to David Lamb:

> The limitations placed on royal authority in these verses are restricted to three areas: horses, wives, and wealth in the form of silver and gold. The king is not restricted from having reasonable quantities of these but merely forbidden from acquiring them in excessive amounts. The sense of abundance is communicated by four repetitions of the verb הבר in the hiphil (Deut. 17:15–16) meaning "to multiply."
>
> In terms of wealth, the king is allowed significant amounts, but he is not to multiply wealth for himself "greatly."[36]

Jean-Jaques Bouit states, "The context [of the passage] indicates that it is rather a warning against the abuse of the practice than against polygamy per se."[37] So, how many is "many"? How many is "too many"? This passage doesn't say. It is, according to Jeffrey Tigay, a prohibition

---

34. "And he shall not have **many wives**" (Jewish Publication Society). "And he must not acquire **many wives**" (New Revised Standard Version). "He should not have **many wives**" (New Catholic Bible). "And he shall not acquire **many wives** for himself" (New American Standard Version). "He must not take **many wives**" (NIV). "He shall not acquire **many wives**: (New English Bible). "The king must not take **numerous wives**" (Common English Bible). "The king shall not have **many wives**" (Wycliffe Bible). "He also shall not **have too many wives**" (Coverdale). "Neither shall he take **many wives**" (Geneva Bible).
35. Richard D. Nelson, *Deuteronomy: A Commentary* (Louisville: Westminster John Knox Press, 2004), 222.
36. David T. Lamb, *Righteous Jehu and His Evil Heirs: The Deuteronomist's Negative Perspective on Dynastic Success*ion (New York: Oxford University Press, 2007), 170.
37. Jean-Jaques Bouit, "A Christian Consideration of Polygamy" (DMin Project, Andrews University, 1981), 80.

against having "a large harem," not a prohibition against having more than one wife. Tigay notes that later rabbinic interpretation indicated that a king could have "no more than eighteen wives."[38] No specific number is given in the Law, but the concern was abuse of the practice and that having so many wives would lead the king and Israel astray from God and His commandments.

In practical terms, only a king or a man of significant wealth would have the means to provide for more than one or two wives. Peter Craigie states, "The prohibition probably envisages an increase of foreign wives, which would incur a deviation from true Israelite religion."[39] According to Daniel J. Lewis, the king "must not build a large harem, a usual practice among potentates who wished to establish secure borders by marrying princesses of adjoining countries. Foreign wives, especially, would lead the king away from his pure devotion to Yahweh."[40] Eugene Merrill states that "many wives, with their diverse backgrounds in pagan religions, would induce their husbands to follow after their illicit cults."[41] According to Eugene Carpenter, "the prohibition was political and intended to keep Israel from striking covenants with foreign nations."[42] Jamie Grant states that "the clear implication is that many wives (presumably of foreign origin, cf. Deuteronomy 7:3–6) may lead the king towards the forbidden religious practices of these wives."[43]

Nelson thinks that "it is not actually foreign wives who are forbidden, but too many wives of any sort [Including Israelite wives]. Royal

---

38. Jeffrey Tigay, *The JPS Torah Commentary: Deuteronomy* (Philadelphia: Jewish Publication Society, 2004), 168, emphasis added. This may have been based upon the number of king David's marriages.
39. Peter C. Craigie, *The Book of Deuteronomy* (Grand Rapids: Eerdmans, 1976), 256.
40. Daniel J. Lewis, *The Second Law: The Book of Deuteronomy* (Troy, MI: Diakonos, 2012), 53, emphasis added.
41. Eugene H. Merrill, *The New American Commentary: Deuteronomy* (Nashville: Holman Bible Publishers, 1994), 224, emphasis added.
42. Eugene E. Carpenter, "Deuteronomy," in *Zondervan Illustrated Bible Backgrounds Commentary*, ed. John Walton (Grand Rapids: Zondervan, 2009), 485.
43. Jamie A. Grant, *The King as Exemplar: The Function of Deuteronomy's Kingship Law in the Shaping of the Book of Psalms* (Atlanta: Society of Biblical Literature, 2004), 203n51, emphasis added.

marriages were also important within Israel as a way of consolidating political power. A large number of such marriages would increase the influence of those families so favored at the expense of others."[44] According to Christopher Wright, "The value of a king is assessed solely by the extent to which he will help or hinder that loyalty. A king who will not trust in God but in his own defenses (cf 3:21f.); a king whose heart turns away because of many wives (cf 7:3f.); a king whose great wealth leads to snares of pride (cf 8:13 f.) — such a king will quickly lead the people in the same disastrous directions."[45] Ryan Stephens said that "it seems best to conclude that while foreign wives are largely in view, the direct prohibition is against 'too many' wives of any sort that could compromise the king's loyalty to God, not multiple wives in general."[46]

Law of Inheritance (Deuteronomy 21:15–17)

Deuteronomy 21:15–17 is a commandment relating to inheritance in the case of a man who has children by more than one wife. The purpose of the law was to prevent injustice in the rights of inheritance. It forbids a man with multiple wives from bestowing the birthright inheritance upon the son of a more-favored wife, if the first less-favored wife had provided him a son. He must bestow the birthright upon the son of the first, even if he preferred the second.

> If a man have two wives, one beloved, and another hated, and they have born him children, both the beloved and the hated; and if the firstborn son be hers that was hated: Then it shall be that when he maketh his sons to inherit that which he hath, he may not make the son of the beloved firstborn before the son of the hated, which is indeed the firstborn: But he shall acknowledge the son of the hated for the firstborn, by giving him a double portion of all that he hath: for he is the beginning of his strength ; the right of the firstborn is his (Deuteronomy 21:15–17).

According to Carolyn Pressler, "the law, of course, also assumes the practice of polygamy. It perceives multiple wives as potential threats

---

44. Nelson, *Deuteronomy*, 224, emphasis added.
45. Christopher J. H. Wright, *Deuteronomy* (Peabody, MA: Hendrickson/Paternoster Press, 1996), 209, emphasis added.
46. Stephens, *Polygamy and the Law of Moses*, 59.

to the normal line of succession."[47] Roy Gane observes that "two wives in succession is not the plain sense of the text."[48] Ryan Stephens also concurs that this passage "envisions a polygamous situation."[49]

Rape of an un-betrothed virgin (Deuteronomy 22:28–29)

Under the law of Moses, if a man raped a woman who was betrothed or married, he was put to death. Deuteronomy 22:28–29 sets forth how the rape of an un-betrothed virgin was treated.

> If a man find a damsel that is a virgin, which is not betrothed, and lay hold on her, and lie with her, and they be found. Then the man that lay with her shall give unto the damsel's father fifty shekels of silver, and she shall be his wife; because he hath humbled her, he may not put her away all his days (Deuteronomy 22:28–29).

The law in this case was designed to recompense the father by forcing the perpetrator to pay the bride price, but to also provide future economic security for the woman who had been violated.[50] As Joseph Blenkinsopp observes "the modern reader would tend to think of it as resulting in a thoroughly bad situation for everyone involved except the father, and especially bad for the victim of sexual aggression — one of many examples of the social and psychological gap between the text and reader."[51] This would certainly not have been a happy situation, but it did at least provide a small measure of justice, assuming the victim's family did not first kill the rapist.

> The unavoidable nature of the penalty served as a strong deterrent for such unacceptable behavior. As a result, the implication of Deuteronomy 22:28–29 is that a married man who raped an unmarried woman was forced to marry her and

---

47. Carolyn Pressler, *The View of Women Found in the Deuteronomic Family Laws* (Berlin: De Groyter, 1993), 17.
48. Roy E. Gane, *Old Testament Law for Christians: Original Context and Enduring Application* (Grand Rapids: Baker Academic, 2017), 303.
49. Stephens, *Polygamy in the Law of Moses*, 67.
50. When David's son Amnon raped his half-sister Tamar and cruelly abandoned her, the king failed to enforce the law or punish his son, a matter which would have been abominable to God and lead to murder, rebellion, and misery in David's family.
51. Joseph Blenkinsopp, "The Family in First Temple Israel," in Perdue, Blenkinsopp, Collins, Meyers *Families in Ancient Israel*, 60–61.

provide for her all his days. And he could never divorce her. In such cases, the law would have required polygamy.⁵²

Levirate Marriage (Deuteronomy 25:5–10)

In ancient Israel, a widow could not inherit her dead husband's estate.⁵³ The Law regarding levirate marriage deals with a situation in which a man who was already married could be encouraged to marry his dead brother's wife.⁵⁴ A form of this law existed during the time of the patriarchs. The unrighteous examples of Onan and his father Judah show that failure to keep this law in order to "raise up seed" or children on behalf of the dead brother through his widow at that time was considered unjust and unrighteous behavior (Genesis 38:8–10; 26). Under the Law of Moses, the practice continued and was strongly encouraged.

> If brethren dwell together, and one of them die, and have no child, the wife of the dead shall not marry without unto a stranger: her husband's brother shall go in unto her and take her to him to wife, and perform the duty of an husband's brother unto her.
>
> And if it shall be that the firstborn which she beareth shall succeed in the name of the brother which is dead, that his name be not put out of Israel.
>
> And if the man like not to take a brother's wife, then let his brother's wife go up to the gate unto the elders, and say, My husband's brother refuseth to raise up unto his brother a name in Israel, he will not perform the duty of my husband's brother.
>
> Then the elders of his city shall call him, and speak unto him: and if he stand to it, and say, I like not to take her;
>
> Then shall his brother's wife come unto him in the presence of the elders, and loose his shoe from off his foot,

---

52. Stephens, Polygamy in the Law of Moses, 73.
53. Blenkinsopp, "The Family in First Temple Israel," 72.
54. Perdue, "The Israelite and Early Jewish Family: Summary and Conclusions," 171. While marriage between a man and his sister-in-law is a seeming contraction to the prohibition in Leviticus 18:16 and 20:21, Jeffrey Tigay states that "The Talmudic view is that the prohibition in Leviticus and the present levirate law are, respectively, a generality and an exception. This view is supported by the Hittite Laws, which place the prohibition of relations with one's brother's wife and the levirate law side-by-side, thus making it clear that the latter is an exception to the former." Tigay, *Deuteronomy*, 232.

and spit in his face, and shall answer and say, So shall it be done unto that man that will not build up his brother's house.

And his name shall be called in Israel, The house of him that hath his shoe loosed (Deuteronomy 25:5–10).[55]

Vawter observes that in many cases levirate marriage "would have been impossible without polygamy."[56] Why would the living brother not want to perform the task of the levir? Tigay explains "If already married, he might not want to create a rival for his present wife, or he might calculate that the expense of supporting an extra wife and a child who would not be his own would diminish his estate that he could leave for his own children."[57] Significantly, the law does not exempt a brother who might already be married. While the brother-in-law was not forced to marry his brother's widow, he was *very* strongly encouraged to do so, even to the point of being socially pressured and publicly shamed. The levirate responsibility would be an act against self-interest. Johannes Pedersen states:

> If he is actually the natural heir, it is clear that it is a great sacrifice on his part; for then he might let the deceased be blotted out and take over the inheritance for himself and his progeny. This view, in all probability, underlies the demand of the Deuteronomy to brand with a serious ignominy the man who refuses to fulfil the law. The presupposition is that it is really a great sacrifice he is making.[58]

Apart from providing an heir for his dead brother and his widow, it has also been suggested that another purpose of this law was to provide financial support for the widow by taking her into his family.[59] This again is why the duties of the brother-in-law, as Donald Leggett argues, would have been a sacrifice for him, not to mention other members of his family. Leggett observes:

> Some in Israel were not adequate to the sacrifice of love. Such responsibilities were rejected where love had grown cold. However, because of the close bond of kinship which united

---

55. Perdue, "The Israelite and Early Jewish Family," 188.
56. Vawter, "The Biblical Theology of Divorce," 226n8.
57. Tigay, *Deuteronomy*, 232–233.
58. Johannes Pedersen, *Israel: Its Life and Culture*, 2 vols. (London: Oxford University Press, 1926), 1:91.
59. Raymond Westbrook and Bruce Wells, *Everyday Law in Biblical Israel* (Louisville: Westminster John Knox Press, 2009), 101.

the Israelite clan, the levirate law was one of the concrete ways in which the law of love within the Israelite family often came to expression.⁶⁰

In short, "Deuteronomy 25:5–10 would require polygamy in situations in which a married brother was willing to perform the duties of the levirate marriage."⁶¹

David

Now, the polygamy of Israelite kings in light of Mosaic law will be examined. Since they are mentioned in the prophet Jacob's temple sermon, David and Solomon will be focused on first.

David's first wife was Michal, the daughter of Saul, who was given away after the former had fled for his life (1 Samuel 18:27; 1 Samuel 25:44; 2 Samuel 3:13–14; 2 Samuel 6:20–23). He also had two other wives, Ahinoam and Abigail, before he became king (1 Samuel 25:42–43; 1 Samuel 27:3; 1 Samuel 30:5; 2 Samuel 2:2), and these - not counting Michal - increased to six during the seven years he reigned over Judah at Hebron (2 Samuel 2–5; 1 Chronicles 3:1–4). Stephens provides insight into David's marriage to Abigail in 1 Samuel 25.

> In that account, Abigail was initially the wife of Nabal, a very rich man. After Nabal's death, Abigail becomes one of David's wives. It appears Abigail had no rights to Nabal's wealth after his death. There is no provision in scripture for a wife to inherit her husband's land (Num. 27:8–11). It appears that Abigail had no children and at the death of Nabal, she was left with little means of support. It also seems unlikely that Abigail would leave such wealth to become one of David's wives otherwise. With a dead husband and possibly no children, Abigail would have been left to "join the Levite, the orphan, and the alien as deprived, landless members of society who are entitled to humanitarian aid (Deut. 14:28–29)." David had the means and the willingness to marry Abigail. There is nothing in the narrative to suggest that this was contrary to God's will. Rather, David is able to provide for and protect a woman who was in an otherwise precarious situation.⁶²

---

60. Donald Leggett, *The Levirate and Goel Institutions in the Old Testament with Special Attention to the Book of Ruth* (Cherry Hill, NJ: Mack, 1974), 53–54.
61. Stephens, *Polygamy in the Law of Moses*, 79.
62. Stephens, *Polygamy in the Law of Moses*, 106; Westbrook and Wells, *Everyday Law*, 101.

David married additional wives during the thirty-three years that he dwelt at Jerusalem, although only Bathsheba is specifically named as a wife (2 Samuel 5:13–16; 1 Chronicles 3:5–9; 1 Chronicles 14:3–7). He also had at least ten concubines at the time of Absalom's rebellion (2 Samuel 15:16; 2 Samuel 20:3), and possibly more (2 Samuel 5:13; 2 Samuel 19:5; 1 Chronicles 3:9). Abishag, who is mentioned at the end of David's life, may have also been a concubine (1 Kings 1:3–4; 1 Kings 2:17, 21–22). Andrew Hill argues that some of David's wives and concubines during his reign at Jerusalem may have been political marriages with the Jebusite elite who dwelt at the city in order to strengthen his power there.[63]

Such political marriages - if that is what they were - would be similar to those that his son Solomon would make on a much larger scale, although the text does not indicate from whence these wives and concubines came. It is also not clear *when*, during David's thirty-three years at Jerusalem, these marriages took place. Perhaps they took place over time throughout those years.[64] What is perhaps interesting is that most of these marriages, according to the text, took place at a time when David is portrayed as being highly favored by God (2 Samuel 3:1; 2 Samuel 5:10), praised for his faithfulness and obedience (2 Samuel 8:15), blessed, and received divine promises about his future seed (2 Samuel 7:1–29).

The turning point for David seems to have been the tragedy of Uriah the Hittite and his wife. After committing adultery, David tried to cover it up by having Uriah murdered, a matter that brought sorrow and misery upon both David and his family; he fell under divine condemnation for these crimes. Modern revelation indicates that this was a matter which had eternal consequences. But for which of his crimes did David fall under condemnation?

In his study of Old Testament polygamy, Douglas Welch aptly summarizes, "The charge against David is threefold: adultery, murder,

---

63. Andrew E. Hill, "On David's 'Taking' and 'Leaving' Concubines (2 Samuel 5:13; 15:16)," *Journal of Biblical Literature* 125, No. 1 (Spring 2006): 129–139.
64. The writer of 2 Samuel may have simply mentioned David's Jerusalem marriages and children at this point in the text for convenience before proceeding with the rest of the David story so as not to interfere with the flow of the narrative.

and misuse of power. Polygamy is not implicated at any point."⁶⁵ Stephens notes that,

> Despite David's numerous wives, the text never once mentions David's polygamy in a negative light. This is especially noteworthy when considering that the narrative does not shy away from highlighting David's moral failures.... Most surprising is that the text states that David's many wives are actually blessings from God. When David is confronted about his sin with Bathsheba, the prophet records God's rebuke, "I gave you your master's wives into your bosom and gave you the house of Israel and Judah. And if this were too little, I would add to you much more like these" (2 Sam. 12:8). ... The point of God's rebuke is that there was no reason to steal a man's single wife when God had already given David a number of wives and would have given him more if that was not enough.⁶⁶

The Lord cursed David that "I will raise up evil against thee out of thine own house, and I will take thy wives before thine eyes, and give them to thy neighbor, and he shall lie with thy wives in the sight of this sun. For thou didst do this secretly: but I will do this thing before all Israel, and before this sun" (2 Samuel 12:11–12). Concerning this passage, Thom Stark writes:

> What verse 8 clearly says is that God gave David many wives as a blessing, and what verse 11 clearly says is that God will take away that blessing in order to punish David. ... Yahweh gives and takes away the blessing of many wives. The many wives are assumed here to be a sign of David's greatness. "If

---

65. Douglas E. Welch, "A Biblical Perspective on Polygamy" (ThM Thesis, Fuller Theological Seminary, 1977), 49. See also Stephens, *Polygamy in the Law of Moses*, 98.
66. Stephens, *Polygamy in the Law of Moses*, 97. This is the idea conveyed through most bible translations of 2 Samuel 12:7–8. For example, "I gave you your master's house, and possession of your master's wives ... and if that were not enough, I would give you twice as much more" (Tanakh); "I gave you your master's house, and your master's wives into your bosom ... and if that had been too little, I would have added as much more" (NRSV); "I gave your master's house to you, and your master's wives into your arms. ... And if all this had been too little, I would have given you even more" (NIV); "I gave your master's house to you, and gave his wives into your embrace. ... If that were too little, I would have given even more" (CEB); "I gave thee thy master's house and thy master's wives into thy bosom ... and would if that had been too little: have given thee twice so much more" (Coverdale).

that had been too little," Yahweh says, "I would have added much more!"[67]

David was cursed for his transgressions in the matter of Uriah and his wife, not for the practice of polygamy.

Solomon

In his early reign, Solomon was blessed and able to build the temple in Jerusalem. The biblical account speaks of his later marriages to many wives, under whose influence he tolerated idolatrous practices and turned from righteousness and the Lord's commandments (1 Kings 11:1–11). It also states that he had seven hundred wives and three hundred concubines (1 Kings 11:3)! While these numbers may not be entirely accurate, they no doubt convey the point of the writer, which was that Solomon's excesses were a gross violation of the Code of the King and other laws in Deuteronomy. As Stark notes, in the case of Solomon, "the problems there were outrageous excess, political alliances, and the introduction of foreign cults into Israel."[68]

The portraits of David and Solomon in the Joseph Smith Translation of 1–2 Kings is more negative than that of the biblical account, suggesting that both David and Solomon had times of righteousness and obedience, but also had other periods when they did not fully follow the Lord and keep his commandments. While some of the plural unions of David and Solomon would have been legal and unobjectionable from the perspective of ancient Israel, Solomon's excesses were a clear violation of the Law of Moses.[69] It is difficult to fault David for those marriages that took place when he was in favor before God, but the Joseph Smith Translation may suggest that there is more to David's story than is found in the biblical account. When describing Solomon's marriages to foreign wives, the JST for 1 Kings 11 varies significantly:

> For it came to pass, when Solomon was old his wives turned away his heart after other gods. And his heart was not perfect with the Lord his God, **and it became as the heart of David his father** (JST 1 Kings 11:4).

---

67. Thom Stark, *Is God a Moral Compromiser? A Critical review of Paul Copan's "Is God a Moral Monster?"*, 2nd ed. (n.p., Thom Stark, 2011), 126.
68. Stark, *Is God a Moral Compromiser?*, 120.
69. Stephens, *Polygamy in the Law of Moses*, 98–99.

And Solomon **did evil** in the sight of the Lord, **as David his father**, and went not fully after the Lord (JST 1 Kings 11:6).

The revisions from the Joseph Smith Translation at this place could suggest that Solomon's marriages to foreign women — which led him to tolerate idolatry — were actually repeating the earlier negative example set by his father David (though on a much smaller scale) in marrying foreign wives that led his heart astray in violation of the Law of Moses. Not all of David's wives and concubines are named; is it possible that some of his later marriages were to foreign women, or that some of those marriages were enacted during times when David did not follow the Lord with all his heart or keep His statutes and commandments as he should have?[70]

Positive Aspects of Israelite Polygamy

Some writers grant that polygamy may have been acceptable during Old Testament times, but that the Lord only did so as a concession to a fallen world. This view seems to impose a modern presentist perspective which may not accurately reflect the ancient view. It also ignores more positive aspects of the practice of righteous patriarchs, such as Abraham, and under the commandments of the Law of Moses.

In his recent study, Stephens surveyed passages dealing with polygamy in Exodus, Leviticus, Deuteronomy, the narrative accounts in Genesis, and the books of Samuel and Kings. He also interacts with the work of revisionist biblical scholars, who have recently argued that polygamy was prohibited by the Law of Moses. Although he is an evangelical scholar, who does not believe that polygamy was practiced in the New Testament, his work on Old Testament polygamy resonates in many ways with how members of The Church of Jesus Christ of Latter-day Saints have traditionally interpreted biblical polygamy passages. Interested readers may enjoy comparing his book Polygamy in the Law of Moses (2024) with the arguments of Orson Pratt from the so-called Pratt-Newman debate in 1870.[71]

Stephens highlights some of the positive aspects of the practice in ancient pre-exilic Israel.

---

70. See Appendix 1 at the end of this article.
71. *The Bible and Polygamy: Does the Bible Sanction Polygamy? A Discussion Between Professor Orson Pratt and Rev. Doctor J. P. Newman* (Salt Lake City: Deseret News, 1874).

Women in the ancient world were provided for by their parents, brothers, husbands, or children. As the story of both Ruth and Naomi vividly illustrates, a woman without supporting family had limited options and was an easy target for abuse. It seems that a strong reason for divine permissibility of polygamy could be to provide for such women.

A number of passages examined above had as their focus the protection of vulnerable women. Exodus 21:7–11 describes the situation of a debt-slave being sold for marriage. A woman from a poor and/or indebted family without a dowry to contribute had limited options for marriage. The focus of Exodus 21:7–11 is to provide protection for a woman taken as a secondary wife. The laws concerning the taking of a captive woman as a wife in Deuteronomy 21:10–14 is similar. As men warred, women were often left widowed with little possessions. Deuteronomy 21:10–14 allows for a man to take in a captive woman who otherwise would have had little means for survival. This law elevated such women above the status of a slave and gave the opportunity for a man to care for a woman who was in an extremely vulnerable situation. ...

It seems that the suggestion that polygamy was permitted as a way to *secure offspring and inheritance,* and as a way to *provide for* and *protect vulnerable women* in a fallen world is a sound conclusion that can be reached from the witness of the Hebrew Bible. ...[72]

[S]cripture never speaks of polygamy *per se* negatively. *That polygamy was a regulated practice in the Mosaic Law indicates that God did not "concede" to a fallen society. Instead, polygamy was approved by God and could be used by God as a way to bless (e.g. 2 Sam. 12:8–9), protect, and provide for people (e.g., Exod. 21:7–11; Deut. 22:28–29; 25:5–10). The idea that polygamy was permitted only as a concession to a fallen world should be re-evaluated.* ... The testimony of the Mosaic Law and the narrative accounts consistently show that in the Hebrew Bible polygamy was *permitted and approved of by God under the regulations he provided*... .

It appears that God had a good purpose for allowing it in the Old Testament period. In a fallen world polygamy was necessary as a means to *produce offspring* and *secure inheritance,* and as a means to *provide for and protect vulnerable women.*[73]

---

72. Stephens, *Polygamy in the Law of Moses,* 105–106, emphasis added.
73. Stephens, *Polygamy in the Law of Moses,* 107, emphasis added.

Stephens concludes:

> What remains consistent throughout all the examples of polygamous individuals in the narrative accounts is that there is never any indication that their polygamy was contrary to God's law. ... *Negative assessments of polygamy* in the narrative accounts arrive from *the assumption that polygamy was an illicit practice.* Close examination of these individual cases reveals that trouble and strife often associated with polygamy is in nearly every case explicitly linked to other issues (e.g., jealousy, adultery). The reason there is no negative assessment in the lives of polygamous individuals is because *polygamy was considered a licit practice and regulated as such by the Mosaic Law.* The narrative accounts are consistent with the findings above on the nature of polygamy in the Mosaic Law.[74]

PART 3: JACOB'S CONDEMNATION OF EARLY NEPHITE PRACTICES

With an Ancient Near Eastern cultural context established, we are now in a better position to understand what is going on with early Nephite polygamy. The prophet Jacob introduces his sermon at the temple with a description of the problem:

> And now it came to pass that the people of Nephi, under the reign of the second king, began to grow hard in their hearts, and indulge themselves somewhat in wicked practices, such as like unto David of old desiring many wives and concubines, and also Solomon his son. Yea, and they also began to search much gold and silver, and began to be lifted up somewhat in pride (Jacob 1:15–16).

The Nephites were beginning to be proud, harden their hearts, and become obsessed with riches (gold and silver), and some indulged themselves in taking many wives and concubines. They tried to justify these practices by pointing to the examples of kings David and Solomon, who also had many wives and accomplished notable deeds. Given the history of polygamy in the lives of righteous patriarchs like Abraham and Jacob, and its legal and divine sanction under the law of Moses, what was wrong with Nephite polygamy?

---

74. Stephens, *Polygamy in the Law of Moses*, 99, emphasis added.

Violation of the Law of Lehi

The first problem was that the prophet Lehi received a commandment before his death that his people were to have only one wife unless the Lord should command otherwise (Jacob 2:27–30, 34; Jacob 3:5–6).

> Wherefore, my brethren, hear me, and hearken to the word of the Lord: For there shall not any man *among you* have save it be one wife; and concubines he shall have none. For I the Lord, delight in the chastity of women. And whoredoms are an abomination before me; thus saith the Lord of Hosts. Wherefore, *this people* shall keep my commandments, saith the Lord of Hosts,[75] or cursed be the land for their sakes. For if I will, saith the Lord of Hosts, raise up seed unto me, I will command my people, otherwise they shall hearken unto these things (Jacob 2:30).

I will refer to this commandment as the Law of Lehi, because it was specifically given to Lehi's people in *their* land of promise. Under the Law of Lehi, they were:

- To have only one wife
- To have no concubines[76]
- Not commit whoredoms
- Keep the commandments, including any future commandments of the Lord.

---

75. Perhaps the term "Lord of *Hosts*" (as in Lord of *armies*) is significant. After the division between the Nephites and the Lamanites, there was a constant threat of war. Perhaps the early people of Nephi and their leaders were concerned about the disparity in numbers. Would there be enough Nephites to defend against their enemies? They may have reasoned incorrectly that they would need to increase their numbers over time through plural marriages. If so, the Lord's words indicate that as Lord of armies, God can provide sufficient strength to his people if they are obedient even if such a disparity should exist. A recourse to polygamy was unnecessary; only obedience to what the Lord commands.
76. As noted earlier, in antiquity, concubines were often, though not always, women who had been captives taken in war or those who were slaves. Concubines also appear to have held a secondary class status than a primary wife. Perhaps one reason that the Law of Lehi prohibited concubinage was to establish, at least in ideal, a more egalitarian society. Under later kings such as Mosiah II and during the reign of the Judges slavery was not permitted (Alma 27:9).

As shown, in the days of Abraham and Jacob, having multiple wives, including concubine-wives, was accepted under certain conditions, and later legally sanctioned and regulated under the law revealed to Moses. By contrast, under the commandments of the Law of Lehi, the Nephites were permitted to have one wife, unless the Lord commanded otherwise.

A second problem for the Nephites is the problem of whoredoms. These unholy practices were to be entirely shunned (2 Nephi 9:36; 2 Nephi 26:32; 2 Nephi 28:14). Earlier, under the Law of Moses and the teachings of Israelite prophets, whoredoms could refer to several things, including prostitution. Leviticus warns, "Do not prostitute thy daughter, to cause her to be a whore; lest the land fall to whoredom, and the land become full of wickedness" (Leviticus 19:29). Deuteronomy commands, "there shall be no whore of the daughters of Israel" (Deuteronomy 23:17). Although it was sometimes tolerated among biblical peoples, whoredoms were characterized in entirely negative terms.[77] In addition to prostitution, whoredoms in the Bible could also refer more broadly to *any* unsanctioned sexual activity outside of a legal marriage, such as fornication or adultery. The term could also denote idolatrous worship or apostasy.[78]

A marriage in ancient Israel, whether monogamous or polygamous, would not have been considered adultery (a capital crime), prostitution, or fornication because it was a legally sanctioned sexual relationship with accompanying rights, obligations, and protections. Among Book of Mormon people, from the time of Lehi onward, polygamy — unless specifically commanded by God — would have been contrary to divine commandment and considered an abomination. Possibly, under the Law of Lehi, unsanctioned polygamy was also classified as a whoredom although this is not entirely clear from the

---

77. Elaine Adler Goodfriend, "Prostitution," in *Anchor Bible Dictionary*, 6 vols., ed. David Noel Freedman (New York: Doubleday, 1992), 5:505–510. This is why in biblical accounts prostitutes such as Rahab (Joshua 2:1–22; Hebrew 11:31) and the mother of the baby judged by Solomon (1 Kings 3:16–28) who act in positive ways were considered to be notable since they acted contrary to common expectation. Money or material goods generated from prostitution was not accepted as a temple donation of payment in fulfilment of any vow (Deuteronomy 23:18).

78. Of course, apostasy and sexual transgression do not have to be mutually exclusive.

text. The account of the abominations of King Noah, his priests, and his people may suggest a categorical distinction between whoredoms or harlotry and the abomination of unsanctioned polygamy (Mosiah 11:4, 6, 14; Mosiah 12:29).

Those Nephites who were under divine condemnation in Jacob's sermon sought to justify their "whoredoms" by an appeal to things done by David and Solomon (Jacob 2:23). If we assume that whoredoms, as understood by the Nephites, encompassed unsanctioned plural marriages, that would mean that they were seeking to justify these relationships because David and Solomon were prominent polygamists. Many of Solomon's wives were also of foreign origin, a practice which Nephites may have tried to emulate as they themselves increased in wealth (2 Kings 11:1–8; Jacob 1:15). Possibly through trade with foreign groups, non-Nephite women were brought into Nephite lands as captives, potential laborers, artisans, wives, concubines, or as victims of non-marital sexual exploitation. Under these circumstances, some Nephite men may conceivably have tried to "excuse themselves in committing whoredoms" or prostitution (Jacob 2:23) under the sophistry that these women were not Nephite and therefore not technically violating the law.[79]

Violations of the Law of Moses

In addition to the explicit prohibition under the Law of Lehi, a third problem with Nephite polygamy is that they tried to justify themselves by appealing to the examples of David and Solomon who had "many wives and concubines," a pretext that reflected a poor understanding of the scriptures (Jacob 2:23). Jacob corrects this misunderstanding by citing a part of the Law of Moses which at least one of those kings, Solomon, violated (Deuteronomy 17:14–20). We do not know if the Nephite king was included in this divine reproof, but Jacob expands the application of those passages in the law to his broader Nephite audience.

It was during the reign of the second, unnamed king appointed after the death of Nephi that the Nephites became "lifted up" in pride,

---

79. For additional perspective on the connection between riches and polygamy in light of ancient Mesoamerica, see Brant A. Gardner, *Second Witness: Analytical and Contextual Commentary on the Book of Mormon*, 6 vols. (Salt Lake City: Kofford Books, 2007), 2:488–499, 508.

becoming "hard in their hearts," obsessed with the accumulation of "gold and silver," and desired "many wives and concubines" (Jacob 1:15–16).

Jacob mentions these same points of the Law in his sermon in chapter 2, where he mentions David and Solomon's "many wives and concubines" (Jacob 2:24), the Nephite quest for "gold and for silver" (Jacob 2:12), and reproves them for being "lifted up" in the pride of their "hearts" (Jacob 2:13, 20). Some in Jacob's audience — and this would have been particularly awkward if the king was involved — were doing the very things Israelite kings were warned not to do under the Law of Moses.

Deuteronomy	Jacob
Thou shalt in any wise set him **a king** over thee whom the Lord thy God shall choose, one from among thy brethren shalt thou set **king** over thee (Deuteronomy 17:15).	And now it came to pass that the people of Nephi, under the reign of the second **king** (Jacob 1:15).
And he shall not have **many wives** (Deuteronomy 17:17, JPS).	Like unto David of old desiring **many wives** and concubines, and also Solomon his son (Jacob 1:15). Behold David and Solomon truly had **many wives** and concubines which thing was abominable before me, saith the Lord (Jacob 2:24).
Neither shall he greatly multiply to himself **silver and gold** (Deuteronomy 17:17).	Yea, and they also began to search much **gold and silver** (1:16). You have begun to search for **gold, and for silver** (Jacob 2:12).
That his **heart** turn not away (Deuteronomy 17:17).	[The Nephites] began to grow hard in their **hearts** and indulge themselves somewhat in wicked practices (1:15). Pride of your **hearts** (Jacob 2:13). Ye were proud in your **hearts** (Jacob 2:20).
That his heart be not **lifted up** above his **brethren** (Deuteronomy 17:20).	And began to be **lifted up** somewhat in pride (1:16). Ye are **lifted up** in the pride of your hearts ... and persecute your **brethren** (Jacob 2:13)

Table 1: Comparison of Deuteronomy 17:14–20 and Jacob 1–2

Misreading David and Solomon

Some readers assume that Jacob's condemnation of David and Solomon's abominations is a blanket condemnation of Old Testament polygamy and all those who practiced it. Some even go so far as to throw the prophets Abraham and Jacob "under the bus," but this is unwarranted. Book of Mormon prophets repeatedly reference the covenant promises made to the patriarchs, including Abraham and Jacob, and rehearse the covenants made with God concerning their seed favorably (1 Nephi 15:18; 1 Nephi 22:9; 2 Nephi 27:33–35; 2 Nephi 29:14; 3 Nephi 5:21–26; 3 Nephi 20:25).[80] Only David and Solomon are mentioned by name in these verses, and that is because the Nephites' efforts to justify their actions based upon their scriptural examples are problematic. The Lord states:

> Behold, David and Solomon truly had *many wives* and concubines, which thing was abominable before me, saith the Lord" (Jacob 2:24).

Solomon's marriages were abominable because, under the Law of Moses, kings were forbidden from having "*many wives*" (Deuteronomy 17:17). As noted earlier, the law did not forbid plural marriages but warned that the practice should not be abused, taken to excess, or used unrighteously. Solomon's violation of this commandment is very clear (1 Kings 11:1–11). Solomon's marriages were abominable because they were excessive; they were also abominable because his foreign marriages led him and his people to tolerate idolatry, another violation of the commandments under the Law of Moses (Deuteronomy 7:1–26). They may have been considered sinful in the eyes of God if they were enacted after Solomon's apostasy.

David also had many wives and concubines. The account in 1–2 Samuel indicates that most of these marriages took place at a time in his life when he was highly favored by God and when he was generally obedient and faithful. Latter-day revelation indicates that many of David's wives and concubines were "given" to him as a blessing by God under the hand of righteous prophets who had authority to do so (Doctrine and Covenants 132:38–39). Clearly there is an important distinction between a sacred privilege that is unrighteously usurped on personal and selfish initiative, and a blessing that is divinely bestowed in an authorized and appropriate way. David, however, committed adultery with Uriah's wife and had Uriah murdered to cover it up. These were serious violations of the Law of Moses, and if David had

---

80. Nephi taught, "For the Lord covenanteth with none save it be with them that repent and believe in his Son, who is the Holy One of Israel" (2 Nephi 30:2).

not been king, he could have been put to death. Those crimes, and his poor example before his family and the people, fostered even further abominations and disaster.

It is possible that some of David's marriages to wives and concubines were enacted following his transgressions in the matter of Uriah and were done without prophetic authorization. There is no account of this in the biblical text, but if that were the case, those unauthorized marriages may have also been considered abominable before God.

Latter-day revelation allows us to also deduce that it would *become* abominable before God for a man who has broken the new and everlasting covenant and became a murderer to retain many wives and concubines. The Lord would not accept such unions in eternity. In ancient Israel, David's wives and concubines would have continued to be legally a part of his family and under his protection, but a wife would have no eternal marriage prospects with a murderer, even if he was a king who had once been favored of God. This is why the Lord warns against the transgression of "shedding innocent blood" in a modern revelation (Doctrine and Covenants 132:26), which states that because of the matter with Uriah and his wife, David "hath fallen from his exaltation, and received his portion; and he shall not inherit them out of the world, for I gave them [his wives] unto another, saith the Lord" (Doctrine and Covenants 132:39). Solomon's many wives and concubines were abominable because of his excesses and his toleration of idolatry. David's marriages *became* abominable in the sight of God when he became a murderer to conceal his adultery.[81]

Two Ways of Raising Up Seed unto the Lord

As noted, while most marriages in ancient Israel would have been monogamous, polygamous marriages had legal sanction and were protected under the Law of Moses. The scriptures show examples of righteous children who were raised in polygamous families, as well as

---

81. This only reflects the Lord's view concerning David's status before God as a covenant breaker and murderer and says nothing about the salvation of his wives. We know nothing about the righteousness or unrighteousness of David's wives and concubines, who, of course, would not be held accountable for David's choices in this matter. I assume any of David's wives who were and remained righteous under these terrible circumstances would still be blessed and fully compensated according to their own faithfulness before God, but in terms of eternal marriage, not through David.

monogamous ones. Under the Law of Lehi, however, Book of Mormon peoples were to practice monogamy.

Marriage is pleasing to God and is ordained of Him, but must be governed according to His will, authority, and commandments, in order to endure beyond this life into eternity (Doctrine and Covenants 132:15–21). While polygamous marriages were acceptable and legal under the Law of Moses, the Law of Lehi enjoined monogamy. "Wherefore, thus saith the Lord, I have led this people forth out of the land of Jerusalem, by the power of mine arm, that I might *raise up* unto me a righteous branch from the loins of Joseph" (Jacob 2:25). *They* were to raise up righteous monogamous families in their new land of promise.

Earlier, the Lord had raised up seed or posterity through plural marriages. Old Testament examples show that this could be difficult, but that the Lord would also bless those who remained faithful under these circumstances. Speaking of biblical polygamy, Stephens states:

> Given the importance of preserving family line and property, especially in the context of the Old Covenant, it is likely that one purpose for permitting polygamy was to **secure offspring**. The story of Abraham, Sarah, Hagar, and Jacob discussed above illustrates the importance of securing heirs. As discussed above, the taking of another wife/concubine for the purpose of **securing offspring** was practiced in the Bible and the ANE. **The ability to multiply children** that polygamy affords also had great economic benefits. … From the narrative accounts of Abraham and Jacob, and the Law of the Levirate in Deuteronomy 25:5–10, it seems reasonable that polygamy was permitted to **secure enough heirs** to maintain, protect, and provide for the ancestral name and land."[82]

As family history, this cultural background of polygamy would all have been obvious to Jacob's audience on that day at the temple of Nephi. They would have known that while most of their Israelite ancestors raised up seed through monogamy, others raised up seed through polygamy. They would also be aware that plural marriages had once been a legally sanctioned way to "secure offspring" and even "multiply children."

The issue for the early Nephites was *in what way* they were to "raise up" seed. They were to keep God's commandments (Jacob 2:29).

---

82. Stephens, *Polygamy in the Law of Moses*, 104–105, emphasis added.

Which ones? Jacob's sermon presents these two potential paths of obedience, both of which had precedent in their family history: Raise up seed through polygamy OR Raise up seed through monogamy according to the Law of Lehi.

Jacob 2:30 answers this question. Lehi's people were to obey the Law of Lehi and raise up seed through monogamy (Jacob 2:25–27, 30), but the Lord also taught that there might be rare occasions when it becomes the Lord's will for His people "raise up seed" by having more than one wife, as others of His faithful servants sometimes did in the past.

In those exceptional circumstances, however, He would still provide a commandment to raise up seed in ***that*** way. "For if I will saith the Lord of Hosts, raise up seed unto me [through plural marriages] I will command my people; otherwise, they shall hearken unto these things" meaning the Law of Lehi to have one wife (Jacob 2:30). The Nephites were not to usurp that privilege unto themselves or indulge in such things on their own initiative, as some in Jacob's audience had clearly been doing.

Jacob teaches that both cases, monogamy and polygamy, require strict obedience to God's will, revealed word, and His commandments, mediated through a divinely authorized living prophet, like Moses or Lehi had been. Monogamy was the default rule; polygamy could be the exception, but *only* by specific divine commandment in the Lord's own way.

Revisionist Interpretations of Jacob 2:30

Some have claimed that, contrary to the traditional view of The Church of Jesus Christ of Latter-day Saints, Jacob 2:30 does not really refer to a potential condition under which the Lord might give a commandment for men to have more than one wife. They instead believe it refers to the fate and judgement of those who reject Jacob's warning. One example of this peculiar interpretation was published in 1869 by E. G. Briggs and R. M. Attwood:.

> He commands them that they shall have but one wife, and if they will not keep this commandment, if they will not be subject to this law which he has laid down in order that they may become a righteous people — a seed unto himself — if they will not hearken unto God, then they shall hearken unto these things. What things? Why, the things which were written

concerning David and Solomon his son, by which they seek to excuse themselves in committing whoredoms, and cursed shall be the land for their sakes.[83]

According to this interpretation, those that "hearken" in this passage would be those who are unrighteous. They hearken to and follow the wicked example of David and Solomon's abominations. They will not hearken to God so they will be cursed because they hearken to evil. A similar interpretation is suggested by a recent advocate of polygamy revisionism, based upon an interpretation of the meaning of the word "otherwise."

> [The word otherwise] conveys a condition or choice and the result if that condition is not met. In every usage found in the Book of Mormon, we can observe a consistent pattern where the main statement or action always represents an intended outcome, and the alternative condition or consequence is always an undesirable outcome.[84]

In other words, this writer argues, examples of "otherwise" point to a consequence which is always negative, so the use of "otherwise" in Jacob 2:30 must, contrary to what most Latter-day Saints would maintain, also point to an undesirable outcome, the consequences of hearkening to evil ("otherwise, they shall hearken unto these things"). He then argues, like the first writers cited above, that "Jacob 2:30 implies that if the Lord's words are not heeded, it is inevitable that His people shall instead hearken to the doctrines of men and be swayed by wicked practices and abominations."[85]

This interpretation is too narrow and is problematic. In English, "otherwise" generally means in another way or manner or in different circumstances.[86] The text of Jacob's sermon also shows that the revi-

---

83. E. C. Briggs and R. M. Attwood, *Address to the Saints in Utah and California: Polygamy Proven an Abomination by Holy Writ. Is Brigham Young President of the Church of Jesus Christ or Not?* (Plano: Church of J.C. of L. D. Saints, 1869), 3.
84. Steve Reed, "A Proposed Reinterpretation of Jacob 2:30," *oneClimbs* blog post, January 5, 2017, online at oneclimbs.com.
85. Reed, "A Proposed Reinterpretation."
86. For "otherwise" the *Oxford English Dictionary* has "A. Phrase with *wise*, manner, way, as distinct sb., e.g. *in other wise*.... B. 1. In another way, or in other ways; in a different manner, or by other means; differently. ... 2. In another case; in other circumstances; if the case be not so; if not; else. ... 3. In other respects; with regard to other points. ... 4. On the other hand ... C. Adjectival

sionist reading does not work when applied to the context of Jacob 2:30, because both cases reflect God's will and purposes in raising up seed, although under different circumstances and in different ways. Both ways, however, are governed by divine commandment. "For if I will, saith the Lord of Hosts, raise up seed unto me [through plural marriages] I will command my people; otherwise they shall hearken unto these things." (Jacob 2:30). If it is His will for his people to raise up seed in *that* particular way — and in the context of Jacob's sermon that way would be having more than one wife, as earlier patriarchs like Abraham and Israelite ancestors did under the Law of Moses — then, God will under those particular circumstances command it.

The second possible circumstance to which "otherwise" points is the default condition, namely, that the Lord's people hearken to "these things." What are "these things" to which his people must hearken? Contrary to the revisionist interpretation, they are to hearken to the commandment under the Law of Lehi that they should have one wife and no concubines which Jacob had just cited, and to which he repeatedly points in chapters 2 and 3 ("these commandments", "these things", "the commandment of the Lord", "this commandment") as the following passages show.

> Wherefore, my brethren, **hear me**, and **hearken** to the **word of the Lord**: For there shall not any man among you have save it be one wife; and concubines he shall have none (Jacob 2:27).
>
> Otherwise, ye shall **hearken** unto **these things** (Jacob 2:30)
>
> And now behold, my brethren, ye know that **these commandments** were given unto our father, Lehi; wherefore ye have known them before; and ye have come unto great condemnation; for ye have done **these things** which ye ought not to have done (Jacob 2:34. They have violated the commandments in the Law of Lehi by having multiple wives and concubines).
>
> Behold the Lamanites your brethren ... have not forgotten **the commandment of the Lord**, which was given unto our father that they should have save it were one wife, and concubines they should have none, and there should not be whoredoms committed among them (Jacob 3:5).

---

uses. 1. Predicatively, approaching an adj.; In another state or condition; differently conditioned or existing; not so; different; other. ... 2. As *adj*. That would otherwise be ...; that would otherwise exist.

And now, **this commandment** they observe to keep; wherefore, because of this observance, in keeping **this commandment**, the Lord God will not destroy them, but will be merciful unto them, and one day they shall become a blessed people (Jacob 3:6).

Based upon Jacob's words, the simplest and most straightforward reading of the passage is that *if* the Lord sees fit at a future time, for reasons known only to Him, should want His people to raise up children by having more than one wife, He *will* in those exceptional circumstances command them to do so; otherwise, or unless that be the case, His people are to hearken to the Law of Lehi, the commandment to have save it be one wife.

Conclusion

An understanding of the world of Abraham, Isaac, and Jacob provides perspective that helps us understand the Book of Mormon prophet Jacob's teachings. Abraham and his grandson Jacob were both polygamists and they were righteous. God made covenants with them that He would raise up seed through them and their wives, and He blessed them and their posterity in fulfillment of His word. Their stories show that polygamy was difficult. While their lives were filled with trials and serious challenges, they remained faithful to God and kept His laws and commandments. According to revealed scripture, they have overcome all things and dwell among the redeemed whose garments are "spotless, pure, and white" (Alma 5:24). They "have entered into their exaltation, according to the promises, and sit upon thrones, and are not angels but are gods" (Doctrine and Covenants 132:37).

Polygamy was sanctioned and regulated under the Law of Moses. Through those commandments, the Lord provided ways in which families of that time, under those circumstances, could also be blessed. Jacob and his fellow Nephites would have been familiar with all of this: it was a part of their heritage and informs the setting of his temple sermon.

The Nephites, however, were situated differently than God's people in earlier times, with additional counsel and divine commandments suited to their time and circumstances. *They* were to prioritize the Law of Lehi over earlier practices from their cultural history. "These things" to which Jacob's people were to "hearken" were the commandments to have only one wife (Jacob 2:34; Jacob 3:5–6), unless or until their Lord willed it to be otherwise. And then, only by specific divine commandment in the appropriate and authorized way. They, like us, were not to excuse contemporary disobedience to living prophets by appealing to dead ones.

Appendix A: Different Views of David and Solomon

1 Kings 3	JST 1 Kings 3
And Solomon made affinity with Pharaoh king of Egypt, and took Pharaoh's daughter, and brought her into the city of David until he has made an end of building his own house, and the house of the Lord, and the wall of Jerusalem round about (1 Kings 3:1).	*And the Lord was not pleased with Solomon.* For he made affinity with Pharaoh king of Egypt, and took Pharaoh's daughter, and brought her into the city of David until he had made an end of building his own house and the house of the Lord (JST 1 Kings 3:1).
Only the people sacrificed in high places, because there was not house built unto the name of the Lord, until those days (1 Kings 3:2).	*And the Lord blessed Solomon for the people's sake only.* And the people sacrificed in high places because there was not house built unto the name of the Lord until those days (JST 1 Kings 3:2).
And Solomon loved the Lord, walking in the statues of David his father: only he sacrificed and burnt incense in high places (1 Kings 3:3).	*And because the Lord blessed Solomon as he was* walking in the statues of David his father, *he began* to love the Lord (JST 1 Kings 3:3).
And Solomon said, Thou hast shewed unto thy servant David my father great mercy, according as he walked before thee in truth, and in righteousness, and in uprightness of heart with thee (1 Kings 3:6).	And Solomon said, Thou hast showed unto thy servant David my father great things according to thy mercy **when** he walked before thee in truth and in righteousness and in uprightness of heart with thee (JST 1 Kings 3:6).
And if thou wilt walk in my ways, to keep my statutes and my commandments, as thy father David did walk, then I will lengthen thy days (1 King 3:14).	And if thou walt walk in my ways to keep my statues and my commandments, then I will lengthen thy days. *And thou shalt not walk in unrighteousness as did thy father David* (JST 1 Kings 3:14).

Table 2: Comparison of 1 Kings 3 and the JST of 1 Kings 3

1 Kings 11	JST 1 Kings 11
But Solomon loved many strange women together with the daughter of Pharaoh, women of the Moabites, Ammonites, Edomites, Zidonians, and Hittites. Of the nations concerning which the Lord said unto the children of Israel, ye shall not go in unto them, neither shall they come in unto you: for surely they will turn away your heart after their gods: Solomon clave unto these in love. And he had seven hundred wives, princesses, and three hundred concubines: and his wives turned away his heart (1 King 11:1-3).	
For it came to pass, when Solomon was old, that his wives turned away his heart after other gods: and his heart was not perfect with the Lord his God, as was the heart of David his father (11:4).	For it came to pass, when Solomon was old his wives turned away his heart after other gods. And his hear was not perfect with the Lord his God, *and it became as the heart of David his father* (JST 11:4).
And Solomon did evil in the sight of the Lord, and went not fully after the Lord, as did David his father (1 Kings 11:6).	And Solomon did evil in the sight of the Lord, *as David his father*, and went not fully after the Lord (JST 1 Kings 11:6).
Because that they have forsaken me, and have worshipped Ashtoreth the goddess of the Zidonians, Chemosh the god of the Moabites, and Milcom the god of the children of Ammon, and have not walked in my ways, to do that which is right in mine eyes, and to keep my statutes and my judgments, as did David his father. Howbeit I will not take the whole kingdom out of his hand, but I will make him prince all the days of his life for David my servant's sake, whom I chose, because he kept my commandments and my statutes (1 Kings 11:33-34).	Because that they have forsaken me, and have worshipped Ashtoreth the goddess of the Zidonians, Chemosh the god of the Moabites, and Milcom the god of the children of Ammon, and have not walked in my ways, to do that which is right in mine eyes, and to keep my statutes and my judgments. And his heart is become as David his father, *and he repenteth not as did David his father that I may forgive him.* Howbeit I will not take the whole kingdom out of his hand, but I will make him prince all the days of his life for David my servant's sake whom I chose because he kept my commandment and my statutes *in that day* (JST 1 Kings 11:33-34).
And it shall be if thou wilt hearken unto all that I command thee, and wilt walk in my ways, and do that which is right in my sight, to keep my statutes and my commandments, as David my servant did; that I will be with thee, and build thee a sure house, as I built for David, and will give Israel unto thee (1 Kings 11:38).	And it shall be if thou wilt hearken unto all that I command thee, and wilt walk in my ways, and do that which is right in my sight, to keep my statutes and my commandments, as David my servant did *in the day that I blessed him*, I will be with thee, and build thee a sure house, as I built for David, and will give Israel unto thee. *And for the transgression of David and also for the people, I have rent the kingdom.* (JST 1 Kings 11:38).

Table 3: Comparison of 1 Kings 11 and the JST of 1 Kings 11

1 Kings 14:8	JST 1 Kings 14:8
And rent the kingdom away from the house of David, and gave it thee: and yet thou hast not been as my servant David, who kept my commandments, and who followed me with all his heart, to do that only which was right in mine eyes (1 Kings 14:8).	And rent the kingdom away from the house of David, and gave it thee **because he kept not my commandments**—but thou hast not been as my servant David **when** he followed me with all his heart only to do right in mine eyes (JST 1 Kings 14:8).

Table 4: Comparison of 1 Kings 14:8 and the JST of 1 Kings 14:8

1 Kings 15:5	JST 1 Kings 15:5
Because David did that which was right in the eyes of the Lord, and turned not aside from any thing that he commanded him all the days of his life, save only in the matter of Uriah the Hittite (1 Kings 15:5).	Because David did that which was right in the eyes of the Lord, and turned not aside from any thing that he commanded him to sin against the Lord, **but repented of the evil** all the days of his life, save only in the matter of Uriah the Hittite, **wherein the Lord cursed him** (1 Kings 15:5).

Table 5: Comparison of 1 Kings 15:5 and the JST of 1 Kings 15:5

2 Kings 22:2	JST 2 Kings 22:2
And he did that which was right in the sight of the Lord, and walked in all the way of David his father, and turned not aside to the right hand or to the left (2 Kings 22:2).	And he did that which was right in the sight of the Lord, and walked **not** in all the way of David his father, and turned not aside to the right hand or to the left (JST 2 Kings 22:2).

Table 6: Comparison of 2 Kings 22:2 and the JST of 2 Kings 22:2

8

"EVEN AS MOSES DID"

THE USE OF THE EXODUS NARRATIVE IN MOSIAH 11–18

SARA RILEY

This paper explores the intertextual relationship between the Exodus narrative and Mosiah 11–18. Using Richard Hays's seven criteria for intertextuality, the analysis demonstrates the plausibility of deliberate allusion and examines the theological and literary functions of this intertextual framework. By analyzing structural and thematic parallels, this study argues that the author of Mosiah intentionally employs Exodus motifs to underscore themes of bondage, prophetic authority, deliverance, covenant renewal, and divine deliverance. A close literary and narratological analysis demonstrates how Abinadi and his successor Alma are cast in Mosaic terms to frame their prophetic missions and the deliverance of the Nephites. The analysis highlights how these allusions serve theological and rhetorical purposes, legitimizing Alma's leadership and reinforcing covenant identity among his followers. The intertextual reading also incorporates the role of God as deliverer of his peoples, both with the Israelites and the Nephites.

The account of the Exodus is distributed throughout the biblical books of Exodus, Leviticus, Numbers, Deuteronomy, and portions of Joshua. S. E. Lowenstamm defines the Exodus as "encompassing everything from the bondage in Egypt up to the preparations to cross the Jordan after forty years of wilderness wandering."[1] Similarly, the book of Mosiah narrates analogous themes: the rule of a wicked king, the enslavement and deliverance of a people, covenant-making before the Lord, and eventual arrival in a new land.

---

1. S. E. Lowenstamm, *The Evolution of the Exodus Tradition* (Jerusalem: Magnes Press, 1965), 32n18.

This paper examines how the Exodus narrative operates within Mosiah — both structurally and thematically — and investigates whether these allusions were intentional and, if so, what theological and literary purposes they serve.

Methodological Considerations

While absolute certainty regarding authorial intent is unattainable, it remains plausible that the Exodus parallels in Mosiah were deliberate. Several methodological limitations must, however, be acknowledged.

First, linguistic analysis is constrained by the absence of the Book of Mormon's original language. Since only an English translation is extant, detailed syntactical comparison with the Hebrew Bible is limited. Second, the precise textual sources available to the author(s) of Mosiah remain uncertain, as does the version of the Pentateuch that informed their narrative. Third, both accounts present themselves as historical writings, complicating strict one-to-one correspondence of events. Finally, Mormon's editorial influence as compiler and abridger may have shaped the Exodus motifs that appear in the text.

Despite these limitations, applying Richard B. Hay's criteria for intertextuality can strongly support intentional or allusions and "the more subtle echoes."[2] Hays proposes seven tests for identifying intentional scriptural allusion:

1. Availability: Was the proposed source available to the author and original readers/hearers?
2. Volume: What is the degree of explicit repetition of words or syntactical patterns?
3. Recurrence: Is the same passage or reference used elsewhere?
4. Thematic Coherence: Does the alleged echo fit within the argument of the later text?
5. Historical Plausibility: Is it historically plausible that the author intended this connection?
6. History of Interpretation: Have other readers or interpreters heard a similar echo?
7. Satisfaction: Does the proposed reading make sense?

---

2. Richard B. Hays, *Echoes of Scripture in the Letters of Paul* (New Haven, CT: Yale University Press, 1989), 29–32.

THE AVAILABILITY OF THE EXODUS NARRATIVE

A preliminary question concerns whether the author of the book of Mosiah possessed access to the Exodus text. 1 Nephi 5 records that Lehi's family obtained the brass plates from Jerusalem, which "contained the five books of Moses":

> [My] father, Lehi, took the records which were engraven upon the plates of brass, and he did search them from the beginning. And he beheld that they did contain *the five books of Moses*, which gave an account of the creation of the world, and also of Adam and Eve, who were our first parents (1 Nephi 5:10–11, emphasis added).

The Exodus resonated deeply with Nephi, as he used the example of Moses parting the Red Sea to persuade his brothers that the Lord could help them obtain the brass plates (1 Nephi 4:2–3). Later on, Nephi would admonish his brothers of God's power (1 Nephi 17:23–42).[3] Nephi's younger brother Jacob also references the Exodus as "the provocation in the days of temptation while the children of Israel were in the wilderness." (Jacob 1:7)

Further references in later generations demonstrate continued familiarity with the Exodus narrative. King Limhi brings attention to it when he speaks to his people: "That God who brought the children of Israel out of the land of Egypt, and caused that they should walk through the Red Sea on dry ground, and fed them with manna that they might not perish in the wilderness" (Mosiah 7:19–20).

Lastly, the courts of King Noah had — or at least claimed that they had — an understanding of the Law of Moses as contained in the Exodus narrative, "And they [Noah's priests] said: We teach the law of Moses" (Mosiah 12:28).

Although this brass-plates record may have differed from the present-day Pentateuch, it nonetheless establishes that the Exodus account

---

3. Several scholars have noted the Exodus narrative influence on Nephi's account. See Terrence L. Szink, "Nephi and the Exodus," in *Rediscovering the Book of Mormon*, ed. John L. Sorenson and Melvin J. Thorne (Salt Lake City: Deseret Book and FARMS, 1991), 38–51; S. Kent Brown, "The Exodus Pattern in the Book of Mormon," in *From Jerusalem to Zarahemla: Literary and Historical Studies of the Book of Mormon* (Provo, UT: Religious Studies Center, Brigham Young University, 1998), 75–98; and Noel B. Reynolds, "Lehi as Moses," *Journal of Book of Mormon Studies* 9, no. 2 (2000): 26–35, 81–82.

was known among the Nephites, and the references collectively affirm that the Exodus story was available and significant within the Nephite religious tradition.

STRUCTURAL PARALLELS BETWEEN EXODUS AND MOSIAH

The Exodus narrative opens with an oppressive pharaoh who enslaves Israel; Zeniff's record within the book of Mosiah introduces King Noah, a corrupt monarch who imposes heavy taxation and forced labor. Moses flees Egypt after killing an Egyptian and later returns under divine commission to deliver his people. Abinadi similarly flees and subsequently returns at divine command to prophesy against King Noah's court.

Both Moses and Abinadi confront royal priests, suffer rejection, and precipitate the liberation of their followers. The Israelites' passage through the Red Sea parallels the baptism of Alma's followers at the Waters of Mormon.[4] Both groups then journey through the wilderness, receive divine instruction, and are ultimately delivered to a promised land — Israel to Canaan, and Alma's people to Zarahemla. Lastly, the Israelites begin to establish cities in the land of Canaan, and Alma is authorized to organize churches in the land of the Nephites.

Exodus	*Mosiah*
Oppressive Pharaoh of Egypt	Oppressive and wicked King Noah
Moses kills an Egyptian, and flees to Midian	Abinadi prophesies and flees the people
Moses is commanded to return to deliver Israel	Abinadi is commanded to return and prophesy
Moses and Aaron compete against Pharaoh's court priests	Abinadi withstands King Noah's priests
The firstborns in Egypt die, and Israelites leave Egypt	Abinadi is executed, and Alma escapes with his followers
Israelites pass through the Red Sea	Alma's people are baptized

---

4. George S. Tate also likens the crossing of the Red Sea to the baptisms of Alma's people and adds, "As Christian commentators from the Fathers to the present have consistently pointed out, each individual conversion reenacts the Exodus: under spiritual prompting, the person abandons worldliness (Egypt), experiences a rebirth involving the death of the 'old man' (baptism), and wanders patiently while tried in the wilderness until proven worthy to enter the promised land." See George S. Tate, "The Typology of the Exodus Pattern in the Book of Mormon," in *Literature of Belief: Sacred Scripture and Religious Experience*, ed. Neal E. Lambert (Provo, UT: Religious Studies Center, Brigham Young University, 1981), 245–262.

Exodus	Mosiah
Israelites wander in the wilderness	Alma's people flee into the wilderness
Moses instructs the people and gives laws	Alma organizes and instructs his followers
The Lord chastens the Israelites	The Lord tries the faith of the Nephites
The Lord delivers the Israelites in many instances (hunger, thirst, battles, etc.)	The Lord delivers the people of Alma from the Lamanites
Israelites cross the Jordan river and arrive in the promised land	Alma and his people escape and arrive in the land of Zarahemla
Israelites begin to establish cities	Alma is authorized to organize the church

Table 1: The Books of Exodus and Mosiah

As seen in Table 1, the narrative structure of the book of Mosiah mirrors the Exodus account in several significant ways. These correspondences suggest that the author of Mosiah consciously employed the Exodus pattern as an organizing framework for the narrative of that book. The intertextuality of Exodus is not only supported in the overarching structure, but also sustained in its granularity, of which each chapter will be examined.

Mosiah 11: King Noah and Pharaoh

The book of Mosiah portrays King Noah as the literary counterpart to the oppressive and hard-hearted pharaoh of Egypt (see Table 2). The text begins in verse one by stating that King Noah did not walk in the ways of his father (Mosiah 11:1); likewise "[There] arose up a new king over Egypt, which knew not Joseph" (Exodus 1:8). Both rulers exploit their subjects through forced labor and grand construction projects (Mosiah 11:6–13; Exodus 1:11–14).

Each questions divine authority — Pharaoh asks, "*Who is the Lord*, that I should obey his voice to let Israel go?" (Exodus 5:2), while Noah demands, "Who is Abinadi, that I and my people should be judged of him, or *who is the Lord*, that shall bring upon my people such great affliction?" (Mosiah 11:27). Both harden their hearts despite repeated divine warnings, and both fear rebellion among their subjects (Mosiah 18:33; Exodus 1:10).[5] The cumulative effect of these parallels portrays

---

5. David Rolph Seely also mentions these Moses/Pharaoh comparisons in "Abinadi, Moses, Isaiah, and Christ: 'O How Beautiful Upon the Mountains Are Their Feet,'" in *The Book of Mormon: The Foundation of Faith*, ed. Joseph McConkie, David M. Whitchurch, Fred E. Woods, and Patty A. Smith (Salt Lake City: Deseret Book, 1999), 203.

King Noah as a Pharaoh figure, thereby situating Abinadi in the role of a prophetic deliverer akin to Moses.

Pharaoh in Exodus	King Noah in Mosiah 11
"there arose up a new king over Egypt, which knew not Joseph." (1:8)	King Noah did not walk in the ways of his father (v. 1)
Israelites build "treasure cities," and there lives were "bitter with hard bondage" (1:11–14)	The Nephites labored hard to support King Noah and his building projects (vv. 6–13)
"I the Lord thy God am a jealous God, visiting the iniquity of the fathers upon the children" (20:5)	The Nephites "shall know that I am the Lord their God, and am a jealous God, visiting the iniquities of my people" (v. 22)
"Pharaoh said, Who is the Lord, that I should obey his voice to let Israel go?" (5:2)	King Noah said, "Who is Abinadi, that I and my people should be judge of him, or who is the Lord?" (v. 27)
Pharaoh's heart is hardened (9:12, 34–35)	The Nephites and King Noah harden their hearts (v. 29)
Pharaoh is afraid the Israelites will have an army (1:10)	King Noah is paranoid of Alma creating an uprising (18:33)

Table 2: Pharaoh and King Noah

MOSIAH 12: PROPHETIC PARALLELS AND PLAGUE IMAGERY

Abinadi's prophetic gestures and pronouncements reinforce the Exodus typology. In Mosiah 12:2, the Lord commands Abinadi to "stretch forth thy hand," echoing the repeated command given to Moses to "stretch forth thy hand" over Egypt (Exodus 7:19; Exodus 9:22).[6] Abinadi's prophecies of hail, pestilence, and destruction (Mosiah 12:4–8) parallel the Egyptian plagues (Exodus 7–12), underscoring divine retribution upon a corrupt and unrepentant ruler.

---

6. After originally presenting this paper, Grant Hardy's work "Abinadi as a New Moses," was brought to my attention. All the comparisons between Abinadi and Moses in his work have already been mentioned, but Hardy adds, "It is striking that it is God himself who orchestrates the parallelism through a provocative allusion to Moses in his first command to Abinadi. Readers are to understand here that although Mormon recognizes and highlights this particular reenactment, he seems to be following God's lead rather than imposing a pattern of his own devising." See Grant Hardy, "Providential Recurrence: Parallel Narratives," in *Understanding the Book of Mormon: A Reader's Guide* (New York: Oxford University Press, 2010), 157–158.

Moses	Abinadi
The Lord commands Moses to "stretch forth thy hand" on multiple occasions to afflict Egypt	The Lord commands Abinadi, "Stretch forth thy hand" (Mosiah 12:2)
"And the Egyptians shall know that I am the Lord" (Exodus 7:2)	King Noah "shall know that I am the Lord" (Mosiah 12:3)
Moses sends plagues, including hail, the east wind, locusts, boils, and death of firstborns	Abinadi prophesies hail, the east wind, pestilence, insects to devour grain, sore afflictions, and utter destruction (Mosiah 12:4–8)
Moses and Aaron withstand and confound Pharaoh's court priests (Exodus 7:11–12)	Abinadi withstands and confounds King Noah's priests (Mosiah 12:17–20)

Table 3: Signs of Prophetic Power

Abinadi prophesies that "the life of King Noah shall be valued even as a garment in a hot furnace" (Mosiah 12:3). Beyond serving as a dire warning against the king's impending destruction, this imagery may evoke the theophany at Mount Sinai, where "Mount Sinai was altogether on a smoke, because the Lord descended upon it in fire: and the smoke thereof ascended as the smoke of a *furnace*, and the whole mount quaked greatly" (Exodus 19:18).

Within the Exodus account, the Israelites are instructed to sanctify themselves and wash their garments in preparation to enter the divine presence (Exodus 19:14). By contrast, Abinadi's metaphor suggests that King Noah, being neither sanctified nor righteous, was unworthy to lead his people and incapable of enduring the purifying presence of the Lord. The prophetic declaration thus operates as both a moral indictment and a symbolic warning of divine judgment.[7]

Explicit References to the Exodus

While many allusions to the Exodus are subtle, several explicit references occur in Mosiah 12–13. One of the most explicit comparisons comes in Mosiah 13:5 when Abinadi is testifying to the priests and it is recorded that "[His] face shone with exceeding luster, even as Moses' did while in the mount of Sinai, while speaking with the Lord." This instance recalls the Mosiac theophany in Exodus 34:29, when Moses

---

7. John W. Welch, Gordon C. Thomasson, and Robert F. Smith, "Abinadi and Pentecost," in *Reexploring the Book of Mormon*, ed. John W. Welch (Salt Lake City: Deseret Book and FARMS, 1992), 137. See also Scripture Central, "Did Abinadi Prophesy During Pentecost? (Mosiah 13:5)," *KnoWhy* 90 (October 16, 2019), online at scripturecentral.org.

descends Mount Sinai with the new covenant tables and his face is physically shining from speaking with the Lord.

Additionally, Abinadi specifically references the Exodus several times in his speech, showing that even he had the Exodus in mind while preaching to Noah's court: "I know if ye keep the commandments of God ye shall be saved; yea, if ye keep the commandments which the Lord delivered unto Moses in the mount of Sinai" (Mosiah 12:33).

Abinadi continues and discusses the law's role in preparing the Israelites: "It was expedient that there should be a law given to the children of Israel, yea, even a very strict law; for they were a stiffnecked people, quick to do iniquity, and slow to remember the Lord their God" (Mosiah 13:29), linking his message to the Exodus narrative.

Exodus Motifs in Mosiah 13–16

There are three central Exodus motifs that climax in Mosiah 13–16. These are woven throughout the story of the Exodus: God's divine presence, deliverance from bondage, and the giving of the law — and are equally prominent in the book of Mosiah.

Motif 1: God's Presence with His People

In Exodus, God's continual presence affirms His covenant with Israel. The Lord delivers the Israelites throughout the narrative, even during times of rebellion, and demonstrates His faithfulness to His covenant people. Likewise, Abinadi proclaims that "God himself shall come down among the children of men and shall redeem His people" (Mosiah 15:1), emphasizing divine condescension and covenantal fidelity. As mentioned, Abinadi's face shines as Moses's did, recalling when the prophet descended from Mount Sinai when God's presence was present.

Motif 2: Deliverance from Bondage

The theme of deliverance from slavery in Exodus recounts physical liberation, and even portrays God as the divine warrior. The text mentions that the Israelites were armed for battle, but in Exodus 14, God says, "I the Lord will fight for you." In Exodus 15, the Israelites sing, "The Lord is a warrior, the Lord is his name." Mosiah 14:1 asks "to whom is the arm of the Lord revealed?" David Seely notes that the "arm of the Lord" is a metaphor for the power of God used in delivering the Israelites (see Exodus 15:16).[8]

The book of Mosiah also proclaims deliverance and transforms this theme into spiritual redemption through Christ. Abinadi quotes Isaiah 53 and weaves the Messianic message of Christ overcoming the battle of evil and delivering them from their iniquities. Abinadi further explains the sufferings of Christ, and that God "breaketh the bands of death, having gained the victory over death" (Mosiah 15:8).

Motif 3: The Giving of the Law.

The law is the principal part of the events in Exodus: from the giving of the law, to the reception of the law on Mount Sinai, and special instructions to become a holy nation. Additionally, Abinadi reiterates the Ten Commandments to the king's court, and expounds on the Law of Moses and its purposes as a typological foreshadowing of the Savior's atonement (Mosiah 13:27–31). This motif will continue with Alma the Elder teaching the people in Mosiah 18. George S. Tate notes that the phrase "he commanded them" recurs seven times as Alma is giving the people laws (Mosiah 18:19–24, 27).[9]

John W. Welch, Gordon C. Thomasson, and Robert F. Smith argue that Abinadi's trial likely coincided with the Feast of Weeks (Pentecost), which commemorated the giving of the Law at Sinai (Exodus 19:1). If correct, this temporal setting deepens the theological resonance of Abinadi's discourse on the commandments and his explication of the law's redemptive purpose. The festival's three-day duration (Exodus 19:11) may also correspond to the three days of Abinadi's imprisonment prior to execution (Mosiah 17:6). Another part of the festival was celebrating the conclusion of the grain harvest, which correlates to Abinadi's prophecies of famine (Mosiah 12:6). They also note that the Pentecost celebrated Israel's deliverance from bondage, yet Abinadi prophesied of the Nephites being brought into bondage (Mosiah 11:21, 23; Mosiah 12:2, 5).[10]

---

8. Seely, "Abinadi, Moses, Isaiah, and Christ," 206.
9. Tate, "The Typology of the Exodus Pattern in the Book of Mormon," 245–262, column 6.
10. Welch, Thomasson, and Smith, "Abinadi and the Pentecost," 135–138.

Mosiah 17: Alma as a Joshua Figure

Alma emerges as a prophetic successor figure comparable to Joshua. Described as "a young man" (Mosiah 17:2), Alma mirrors Joshua, the "young man" who served Moses (Exodus 33:11). Both record the teachings of their prophetic predecessors (Mosiah 17:4; Joshua 24:26) and lead their communities into covenantal renewal in a promised land. Through Alma, the Exodus pattern continues within the Nephite narrative. Joshua brings the children of Israel across the Jordan, and the Israelites begin to set up the lands of their inheritance in Israel. Likewise, Alma brings the people safely to the land of Zarahemla and begins to set up churches in the land. S. Kent Brown sees Alma as a Moses figure, noting that:

> Each was a member of a royal court and was forced to flee because of an injustice. Each led his people from the clutches of enslaving overlords. Each led them through the wilderness to the land from which their ancestors had originated. Moreover, each gave the law to his people and placed them under covenant to obey the Lord.[11]

Mosiah 18: Covenant Renewal at the Waters of Mormon

Not long after entering the wilderness, the Israelites made covenants at Sinai. This covenant relationship with God is also reflected in the Mosiah narrative not long after Alma's people fled into the wilderness, beginning in Mosiah 18. The covenant-making at the Waters of Mormon parallels the Israelites' experience at Marah (Exodus 15).[12] Both occur in wilderness settings and involve purification through water and the establishment of divine law. Furthermore, the Israelites passing through the Red Sea has been seen as a baptism-like experience: "All our fathers were under the cloud, and all passed through the sea; And were all baptized unto Moses in the cloud and in the sea" (1 Corinthians 10:1–2).

Not only Paul has seen this parallel, but also others at the beginning of the Christian era in the Jewish community. Besides circumci-

---

11. Brown, "The Exodus Pattern in the Book of Mormon," 114–115.
12. Thanks to Jonathan Riley and Jared Riddick for these connections from consulting over a pre-publication draft of their forthcoming paper, "Marah and Mormon: Covenants at the Waters", where this connection is examined in further detail.

sion, they included a purification rite of initiation, as G. Foote-Moore explains,

> The purpose of this initiation was to cause the proselyte to go through the sacrament received by the people at the time of the crossing of the Red Sea. The baptism of the proselytes was, then, a kind of imitation of the Exodus. This is important in showing us that the link between Baptism and the crossing of the Red Sea existed already in Judaism.[13]

Linguistic Connections

There are some linguistic ties between the Waters of Marah in Exodus 15 and the Waters of Mormon in Mosiah 18 (see Table 4) It begins with Alma gathering his people to a water source in a place called Mormon. The Syriac translation of Exodus 15 shows that Marah was likely pronounced as *Mor-ah*,[14] which is pronounced similarly to the first half of the name Mormon. Furthermore, both groups arrive at a place of water soon after fleeing the wicked rulers.

In the Exodus narrative, the Israelites are traveling in the wilderness of Shur. Shur can mean *to travel* or *to sing* in Hebrew,[15] a connection to when this event immediately precedes the Song of the Sea, or the Song of Miriam (Exodus 15:20–21). This may be an intended pun in Mosiah 18:30: "How blessed are they, for they shall *sing* to his praise forever."

The Waters of Marah is stated as being in the wilderness, and the Waters of Mormon noted in verse 4 as "being in the borders of the land, having been infested by times or at seasons by wild beasts," perhaps indicating a wilderness layout. The Waters of Mormon is described as the fountain of pure water, and the Waters of Marah were purified, or made sweet, when Moses cast a tree into the water. In both accounts, trees play a symbolic role in redemption — Moses purifies bitter waters by casting in a tree (Exodus 15:25), while Alma's people find refuge in a grove of trees.

---

13. G. Foote-Moore, *The Bible and the Liturgy* (Notre Dame, IN: University of Notre Dame Press, 1956), 88–89.
14. William H. C. Propp, *Exodus 1–18: A New Translation with Introduction and Commentary*, Anchor Bible Commentaries, 86 vols. (New York, NY: Doubleday, 1999), 2:576.
15. Ludwig Koehler and Walter Baumgartner, *The Hebrew and Aramaic Lexicon of the Old Testament*, 5 vols. (Leiden: Brill, 2001), 4:1453.

Both episodes culminate in covenantal affirmation and communal rejoicing. In Mosiah 18, Alma invites the people to be "baptized in the name of the Lord, as a witness before him that ye have entered into a covenant with him," to which the people clapped their hands for joy (perhaps in a musical manner similar to the Song of Miriam in Exodus 15). Exodus 15:25 states that at the Waters of Marah, Moses "made for them a law and a judgement, and there he proved them."

There is yet another name pun between the two narratives. In Exodus 15:27, immediately after leaving Marah, the Israelites come to a place called Elim, and the name of the first person Alma baptizes is Helam (Mosiah 18:12). The similarity of these two names becomes even more apparent when one notes that in Mosiah 27:16, the name was originally misspelled as Helim/Helem.[16]

Exodus 15	Mosiah 18
Waters of Marah	Waters of Mormon
Fled from the Pharaoh and his armies	Fled from King Noah and his armies
Shur/Song of the Sea (vv. 1–22)	Sing his praise forever (v. 30)
Trees purify the waters to be drinkable (v. 25)	Grove of trees hides the Nephites
The Israelites covenant with God (v. 25)	The Nephites covenant with God to keep his commandments
Elim (v. 27)	Helam/Helim (v. 12)

Table 4: The Waters of Marah and the Waters of Mormon

ALMA'S PEOPLE AND THE ISRAELITES IN MOSIAH 18 AND 23–24

As the narrative of the book of Mosiah progresses, striking parallels continue to emerge between the experiences of Alma's people and those of the Israelites in Exodus (see Table 5). Alma's organization of his community reflects a distinctly Mosaic model of leadership and governance. For instance, Alma appoints one priest for every fifty members of his people (Mosiah 18:18), echoing Moses's appointment of subordinate leaders to administer judgment and oversee the Israelites (Exodus 18:25).

---

16. Royal Skousen notes that the printer's manuscript reads as *Helem* and was first spelled as *Helim*, but then the *"i"* was overwritten with an *"e."* See Royal Skousen, *Analysis of Textual Variants of the Book of Mormon, Part Three: Mosiah 17 – Alma 20*, 6 vols. (Provo, UT: Foundation for Ancient Research and Mormon Studies, Brigham Young University, 2014), 4:1506.

Similarly, Alma's instruction concerning Sabbath observance, labor, charity toward the poor, and the moral and social order of his community (Mosiah 18:19–29; Mosiah 23:14–18) closely mirrors the legislative and ethical content of the Mosaic law, which governs these same dimensions of Israelite life. In both cases, the establishment of divine law serves as the foundation for covenantal identity and communal stability.

The text further reinforces this typological connection through its portrayal of divine blessing and deliverance. In Mosiah 23:19, Alma's people are described as multiplying and prospering, recalling the Israelites' increase in Egypt (Exodus 1:7), a growth that provoked Pharaoh's anxiety. When confronted by the advancing Lamanite forces, Alma exhorts his people not to fear but to trust in divine deliverance (Mosiah 23:27), a moment that resonates with Moses's assurance to Israel at the Red Sea: "Fear ye not, stand still, and see the salvation of the Lord" (Exodus 14:13).

The motif of divine responsiveness to suffering also unites the two narratives. During the Nephites' bondage under the Lamanites, the Lord is said to hear their cries (Mosiah 24:10–12), just as He hears the Israelites' cries under Egyptian oppression (Exodus 2:23–24). Brown also notes that "the Lord softened the hearts of those who stood in the way of the captives departure and the Lamanite overseers and guards treated their captives more gently and kindly (Mosiah 21:15, 23:29)," similar to when the "Lord gave the people favour in the sight of the Egyptians" (Exodus 11:3; Exodus 12:36).[17] Finally, the account of the Lord's intervention on behalf of Alma's people — "I will stop the Lamanites in this valley" (Mosiah 24:23) — finds a close parallel in the Lord's promise to "trouble the host of the Egyptians" as Israel passes safely through the sea (Exodus 14:24).

Taken together, these narrative correspondences underscore the deliberate evocation of the Exodus pattern, situating Alma's community as a covenantal people whose trials, deliverance, and organization recapitulate Israel's sacred history.

---

17. Brown, "The Exodus Pattern in the Book of Mormon," 114.

The Israelites	Alma's People
Moses appoints men to administer over the people (Exodus 18:25)	Alma organizes one priest to every 50 (Mosiah 18:18)
Moses gives laws concerning the Sabbath, property rights, civil laws, justice, etc.	Alma instructs concerning the Sabbath, labor, charity, social conduct and administration (Mosiah 18:19–29; Mosiah 23:14–18)
Israelites increase and multiply (Exodus 1:7)	The people multiply and prosper (Mosiah 23:19)
Moses tells the people to "Fear ye not, stand still, and see the salvation of the Lord" (Exodus 14:13)	Alma exhorts them not to be frightened, but to remember God's deliverance (Mosiah 23:27)
The Israelites' cries come up to God (Exodus 2:23)	The Lord hears the Nephites' cries (Mosiah 24:12–13)
The Lord "gave the people favour in the sight of the Egyptians" (Exodus 11:3, Exodus 12:36)	The Lord softened the hearts of the Lamanites (Mosiah 21:15, Mosiah 23:29)
The Lord "troubles the host of the Egyptians" (Exodus 14:24)	The Lord promises "I will stop the Lamanites in this valley" (Mosiah 24:23)

Table 5: The Israelites and Alma's People

THE PURPOSE OF EXODUS INTERTEXTUALITY IN THE BOOK OF MOSIAH

If, as the textual parallels suggest, there is intentional allusion and intertextual engagement between the narrative of Mosiah and the Exodus account, the question naturally arises: what purpose does this intertextuality serve? Why does the author(s) of Mosiah invoke the Exodus story?

The Exodus stands at the theological and historical center of Israelite identity, and was used as a reminder of Israel's covenant to God, such as Isaiah (11:16), Micah (7:15), Hosea (2:15; 11:1), Haggai (2:5), and the Psalms (114; 135:8, 9). It represents the formative event in which Israel comes to understand itself as a covenant people in relationship with God. As James Plastaras observes,

> It was the Exodus which shaped all of Israel's understanding of history. It was only in light of the Exodus that Israel was able to look back into the past and piece together her earlier history. It was also the Exodus which provided the prophets with the key to the understanding of Israel's future. In this sense, the Exodus stands at the center of Israel's history.[18]

---

18. James Plastaras, *The God of Exodus: The Theology of the Exodus Narrative* (Milwaukee: Bruce Publishing Company, 1966), 7.

Other scholars have noted that the Exodus was "used as an initial dateline for the Israelites' history" throughout the Hebrew Bible, and was used to compare later events in the narrative, such as 1 Samuel 8:8; 2 Samuel 7:6, and 2 Kings 21:15.[19] The Exodus, therefore, is not merely a narrative of deliverance; it is the interpretive framework through which Israel comprehends divine action in history, both past and future.

Religious and Political Transformation

The Exodus also functions as a paradigm for religious and political transformation within Israel's collective memory. At the dedication of Solomon's Temple, for instance, the construction is explicitly dated to 480 years after the Exodus (1 Kings 6:1).[20] This chronological framing may have served to legitimize the temple as the new center of covenantal worship, positioning it as a divinely sanctioned continuation of the Exodus covenant.

Similarly, the Mosiah narrative records a period of significant religious and political transition. In Mosiah 25:19, "king Mosiah granted unto Alma that he might establish churches throughout all the land of Zarahemla; and gave him power to ordain priests and teachers over every church." The authorization of multiple churches under Alma represents a new religious structure for the Nephite community, just as the institution of judges in place of a monarchy marks a political transformation (Mosiah 29). The deliberate evocation of the Exodus motif in this context may serve to confer legitimacy upon these institutional innovations, situating them within a divinely guided pattern of renewal and deliverance. By invoking the Exodus, the author(s) of Mosiah could be reinforcing the theological authority of these changes — framing them as covenantal developments rather than departures from divine order.

---

19. K. A. Kitchen, "Exodus, the," in *The Anchor Yale Bible Dictionary: D–G*, 6 vols., ed. D. N. Freedman (Doubleday: Yale University Press, 1992), 2:700–708. Kitchen also notes that allusions to "the Exodus-event are relatively numerous across the varied span of Old Testament writings," 2:701.
20. This could possibly be symbolic of "12 × 40." Twelve is often used in God's order, such as the twelve tribes of Israel, and forty typically represents a testing or transformation (forty days of rain during the flood, Israelites wandering forty years).

Moses, Abinadi, and Christ

Ultimately, however, the most profound function of Exodus typology in the book of Mosiah lies in its Christological dimension. The Title Page of the Book of Mormon states that it is written towards "the convincing of Jew and Gentile that Jesus is the Christ, the Eternal God," and within that framework, the Exodus and the figure of Moses operate as types and shadows that prefigure Christ's redemptive work. Abinadi explicitly declares, "all these things were types of things to come" (Mosiah 13:31), while the risen Christ himself tells the Nephites, "Behold, I am he of whom Moses spake, saying: A prophet shall the Lord your God raise up unto you of your brethren, like unto me" (3 Nephi 20:23). As S. Kent Brown insightfully explains,

> All of the words describing Israel's bondage derive from the root *'bd*. It is also a noun from this same root which is translated 'servant' in Isaiah 53, which Abinadi had quoted at length and then immediately linked to Jesus' ministry. What is clear here is that Jesus is the expected servant (*'ebed*) who, by paying the price of redemption, frees all those who will follow him from bondage (*'abōdāh*), the very term used in the Exodus account.[21]

In this light, the Exodus narrative functions not only as a historical or typological precedent but as a theological template for understanding Christ's redemptive act.

Conclusion

The pervasive structural, thematic, and linguistic parallels between the Exodus narrative and the book of Mosiah strongly suggest intentional intertextuality. Collectively applying Hay's seven criteria supports the conclusion that the Exodus motifs in Mosiah were intentionally employed:

1. Availability: The Exodus text was known via the brass plates.
2. Volume: Numerous verbal and thematic parallels exist.
3. Recurrence: Repeated citations and echoes of Exodus appear throughout Mosiah.
4. Thematic Coherence: The Exodus motifs integrate seamlessly with Mosiah's themes of deliverance and covenant-making.

---

21. Brown, "The Exodus Pattern in the Book of Mormon," 75–98.

5. Historical Plausibility: The author could plausibly have intended these allusions.
6. History of Interpretation: Subsequent readers and scholars have recognized similar patterns.[22]
7. Satisfaction: The reading yields coherent theological meaning.

Through its intertextual engagement with the Exodus, the Mosiah narrative reaffirms the enduring covenantal relationship between God and His people, legitimizes moments of institutional and political transformation, and ultimately directs the reader toward Christ as the fulfillment of the Exodus pattern. The result is a deeply layered text that integrates Israelite sacred history into Nephite theology, positioning deliverance, covenant, and divine guidance as the central pillars of its message.

---

22. As previously mentioned, see Hardy, "Providential Recurrence: Parallel Narratives," 157–158; Seely, "Abinadi, Moses, and Christ," 203–206; Tate, "The Typology of the Exodus Pattern in the Book of Mormon," 245–262; Welch, Thomasson, and Smith, "Abinadi and the Pentecost," 135–138; and Brown, "The Exodus Pattern in the Book of Mormon," 75–98.

9

HOLD TO THE ... SERPENT WAND?

JOHN S. THOMPSON

Ancient Egyptian iconography offers a key to understanding scriptural imagery involving serpents and rods in relation to divine words or authority. Archaeological finds, such as serpentine wands and images of serpent-wielding on tomb walls and healing stelae, suggest that holding a serpent in the hand symbolized divine protection and authority, whereas a serpent underfoot represented conquered evil. This cultural backdrop illuminates biblical narratives such as Moses's serpent rod swallowing the serpent rods of the Egyptian priests, the lifted up brazen serpent healing the Israelites from the serpents on the ground, and the dragon of John's Revelation being opposed by the child with a rod in his hand. It also clarifies Book of Mormon imagery wherein an "iron rod" pierces through the "mists of darkness," a traditional symbol of the chaos-serpent. Ultimately, these symbols converge on the Messiah, the divine scepter held in God's hand to vanquish all enemies and heal the faithful.

The ancient Egyptians referred to their own written words as *zš n mdw nṯr*, "the writing of the word of god," and their documents as *mḏꜣwt nt mdw nṯr*, "the scrolls of the word of god."[1] The term *mdw nṯr* "word of god" is attested from the earliest ages of ancient Egypt. For example, a title appearing in some non-royal elite tombs of the Old Kingdom as early as circa 2350 BC includes *ḥr(y)-sštꜣ n mdw-nṯr*, "overseer of the secret of the word of god."[2] The hieroglyphic for *mdw*

---

1. Adolf Erman and Hermann Grapow, eds., *Wörterbuch der ägyptischen Sprache*, 7 vols. (Leipzig, DE: J. C. Hinrichs, 1926–1963), 2:181.
2. Mastaba of Ni-ankh-Re, Fifth Dynasty, in S. Hassan, *Excavations at Gîza, Vol. IV, 1932-1933* (Cairo: Government Press, 1943), 155, fig. 108, pl. XLI.

"word" is written 𓌂 which is a simple rod, walking stick, or staff.³ The equation of "word" with "rod" extends back, well before Nephi, Moses, and even Abraham.

The relationship of God's "word" to a "rod" is probably best understood through the symbolism of divine or royal scepters, maces, swords and similar items. Such handheld objects were often used in texts and imagery to represent the deity's or king's authority, protection, and judgment against enemies.⁴ In fact, scriptures explicitly equate rods with scepters or the act of ruling.⁵

Rods were also used as a standard of measurement or "rule." For example, the apostle John measures the altar, the temple, and "them who worship therein" with a rod, but he leaves unmeasured the temple courtyard as a symbol of protection for those within the measured space and judgment upon that which was not measured (Revelation 11:1–2; compare Jerusalem being measured with respect to divine judgment in 2 Kings 21:13 and Zechariah 2:1–5). The celestial city in Revelation is measured with a rod of gold (Revelation 21:15–17). As items for measuring, rods were natural symbols for the words of a deity or king (the "rule"-ers), because their words were the law, constitution, or standard by which the actions of people or nations were measured.⁶

---

3. Alan H. Gardiner, *Egyptian Grammar: Being an Introduction to the Study of Hieroglyphs*, 3rd edition, revised (Oxford: Griffith Institute, Ashmolean Museum, 1957), 510, sign-list S43.
4. John A. Tvedtnes, "*Rod* and *Sword* as the Word of God," *Journal of Book of Mormon Studies* 5, no. 2 (1996), 148–155.
5. See, for example, Psalm 110:2; Isaiah 14:5; Ezekiel 19:11, 14; Revelation 2:26–27.
6. Measuring rods representing royal or divine authority can be seen in the Mesopotamian "rod and ring (or coil of rope)" motif which were symbols of divine authority gods gave to kings but were also understood to be measuring devices. See Henri Frankfort, *The Art and Architecture of the Ancient Orient* (New Haven: Yale University Press, 1996), 104; E. Douglas Van Buren, "The Rod and Ring," *ArOr* 17, no. 2 (1949): 435; Mary Abram, "A New Look at the Mesopotamian Rod and Ring: Emblems of Time and Eternity," *Studia Antiqua* 10, no. 1 (2011): 15–36. The Egyptian king's role as the divinely appointed measurer is ritually reflected in the "stretching-the-cord" ceremony, attested from the First Dynasty (Palermo Stone). See Corrina Rossi, *Architecture and Mathematics in Ancient Egypt* (Cambridge: Cambridge University Press, 2004), 148–173.

Archaeological examples of physical royal cubit rods from the era of Egypt's New Kingdom have survived. A wooden one, gilded in gold, was given as a gift from king Amenhotep II to a man named Kha, the architect and overseer of works at Deir el-Medina in the eighteenth dynasty. The inscription on it celebrates the king as "the perfect god ... the lord of strength ... strong and heroic ... ruler of Heliopolis ... strong bull in every foreign country ... who plunders in every foreign county."[7] These words connect the king's ability to rule to the object upon which they are written — a measuring rod. Apotropaic inscriptions can also appear on these measuring rods, suggesting the king's ability to combat chaos through measuring: "Cubit as life, strength, health, as a protection that repels the enemy."[8]

The relationship between handheld objects such as rods, scepters, and swords with *words* can be seen in these Old and New Testament passages:

> "And there shall come forth a rod out of the stem of Jesse. ... He shall smite the earth with the rod of his mouth..." (Isaiah 11:1, 4).

> "The Lord's voice crieth unto the city, ... hear ye the rod" (Micah 6:9).

> "And out of his mouth goeth a sharp sword, that with it he should smite the nations: and he shall rule them with a rod of iron" (Revelation 19:15).

Depicting these objects coming out of a mouth or relating to a voice suggests they were understood as symbols for words.

The above review establishes a background for exploring the ancient use of handheld, serpent-related objects, in the ancient world which also appear to symbolize royal or divine words of authority as protection or judgment — not only the words and authority of for-

---

7. Marcella Trapani, "Behind the Mirror: Art and Prestige in Kha's Funerary Equipment," in *Art and Society: Ancient and Modern Contexts of Egyptian Art*, ed. Katalin Anna Kóthay (Budapest: Museum of Fine Arts, 2012), 160–161, 167, Plate 32.1; Barbara Russo, *Kha (TT 8) and his Colleagues: the Gifts in his Funerary Equipment and Related Artefacts from Western Thebes*, GHP Egyptology 18, (London: Golden House Publications, 2012), 10–13, 97.
8. Franck Monnier, Jean-Pierre Petit, and Christophe Tardy, "The use of the 'ceremonial' cubit rod as a measuring tool — An explanation," *Journal of Ancient Egyptian Architecture* 1 (2016): 4-5, fig. 3.

eign divinities or their representatives, but the word and authority of Israel's God and his representatives. This work complements the excellent work undertaken by Andrew Skinner and Neal Rappleye concerning the ancient Near Eastern background of serpent imagery, the symbolic duality of serpents (representing both good and evil), and their "fiery" or "flying" nature as portrayed in Latter-day Saint scripture.[9] In contrast to their work, this study focuses more on the connections between handheld serpent objects such as wands and scepters with divine words in ancient Egypt, providing deeper insight into the serpent imagery found in the Old Testament, New Testament, and Book of Mormon.

Ancient Egyptian Serpents in the Hand

Serpent-shaped implements, varying in style and material, appear in the archaeological record from the Middle Kingdom to the Late Period of ancient Egypt. Some of the objects are likely decorative, but some were likely held in the hand and used as ritual wands.[10]

Robert Ritner noted that, although serpent-wand artifacts are rare, "corresponding depictions of clutched serpents are common and perhaps served as artistic prototype for the actual ritual implement."[11] For example, a scene from the Tomb of Bebi at El Kab, depicts multiple females — one labelled *ḫnmt.t* "nurse-maid" — wielding serpentine wands or staves in one hand and a curved implement in the other, facing a seated couple. Similar curved implements, carved from the tusks of hippopotami, are attested in the archaeological record and labelled by modern scholars as "magical knives," "wands," and "birth tusks" — due to their connection to child-bearing.[12]

---

9. Andrew C. Skinner, "Serpent Symbols and Salvation in the Ancient Near East and the Book of Mormon," *Journal of Book of Mormon Studies* 10, no. 2 (2001): 42–55, 70-71; Neal Rappleye, "Serpents of Fire and Brass: A Contextual Study of the Brazen Serpent Tradition in the Book of Mormon," *Interpreter: A Journal of Latter-day Saint Faith and Scholarship* 50 (2022): 217–297.
10. See Robert Ritner, "The Serpent Wand in Ancient Egypt," in *Through a Glass Darkly: Magic, Dreams and Prophecy in Ancient Egypt* (Swansea, GB: Classical Press of Wales, 2006), 205–226 for a discussion of such artifacts.
11. Ritner, "The Serpent Wand," 212.
12. Georg Steindorff, "The Magical Knives of Ancient Egypt," Journal of the Walters Art Gallery 9 (1946): 41–51, 106–7; Hartwig Altenmüller, *Die Apotropaia und die Götter Mittelägyptens: Eine typologische und religionsgeschichtliche*

Not only are these curved wands grasped in tandem with the serpentine wands in the tomb of Bebi, but the real life examples of the curved wands often have entities grasping-snakes depicted upon them, creating a strong connection between the two objects. Some of the curved wands also have texts written upon them, providing clues to their purposes and, by association, the purposes of the serpent wands or staves used in connection with them. One texts states:

> Recitation by the many protectors: "We have come that we may extend our protection around the healthy child Minhotep, alive, sound, and healthy, born of a noblewoman Sitsobek, alive, sound, and healthy.[13]

These words reveal an apotropaic purpose of providing health and protection for infants and children against inimical forces.[14] The design of at least one curved wand appears to prefigure New Kingdom netherworld scenes relating to the rebirth of the sun-god and protection against his enemies, suggesting these objects are drawing upon the greater cosmic struggles to empower their current specific use with children.[15]

One Middle Kingdom tomb, excavated at the Ramesseum in Thebes, contained a box of papyri that included healing incantations. On the lid of the box is a figure of a jackal reclining on a chest — a

---

Untersuchung der sogenannten „Zaubermesser" des Mittleren Reichs (Munich, 1965); Stephen Quirke, *Birth Tusks: The Armoury of Health in Context – Egypt 1800 BC* (Middle Kingdom Studies 3, Golden House Publications, 2016); Hartwig Altenmüller "Zu den Feindbildern auf den Zauberstäben des Mittleren Reiches und der Zweiten Zwischenzeit," *Études et Travaux* XXX (2017), 73–94.

13. Wand at New York Metropolitan Museum of Art 08.200.19. James P. Allen, *The Art of Medicine in Ancient Egypt* (New York: Metropolitan Museum of Art, 2015), 29.
14. Stephen Quirke, *Birth Tusks: The Armoury of Health in Context – Egypt 1800 BC* (Middle Kingdom Studies 3, Golden House Publications, 2016); Fred Vink, "The Principles of Apotropaic Magic on Middle Kingdom Wands," *Ancient Egypt Magazine* 17, no. 3, iss. 99 (December 2016/January 2017): 12–17.
15. Joshua A. Roberson, "The Early History of 'New Kingdom' Netherworld Iconography: A Late Middle Kingdom Apotropaic Wand Reconsidered," in David P. Silverman, W. K. Simpson, and Josef Wegner (eds.), *Archaism and Innovation: Studies in the Culture of Middle Kingdom Egypt* (New Haven & Philadelphia: Yale University / University of Pennsylvania Museum, 2009), 427–445.

graphic substitution for the title *ḥr(y)-sštȝ*, "overseer of secrets," recalling the previously mentioned title "overseer of secrets of the word of god." Accompanying the box of papyri were: 1) a curved wand depicting the dwarf god Bes and the goddess Beset grasping serpents (the wand and detail of Bes shown on the left below), 2) a bronze statuette of the goddess Beset holding a serpent in each hand (shown center), and 3) a bronze object of a serpent (shown on the right), among other objects.[16] Scholars analyzing this collection have suggested that the papyri and the depictions of the serpent-grasping deities among the artifacts help clarify the use of the serpent-shaped artifact on the right as a wand held in the hand and used for apotropaic purposes, likely while the protective spells on the papyri were spoken.[17]

A point to highlight here is that the context for these wands, whether curved with serpents depicted on them or serpent shaped, suggests they are to be accompanied by words if the healing and protection they provide was to be efficacious.

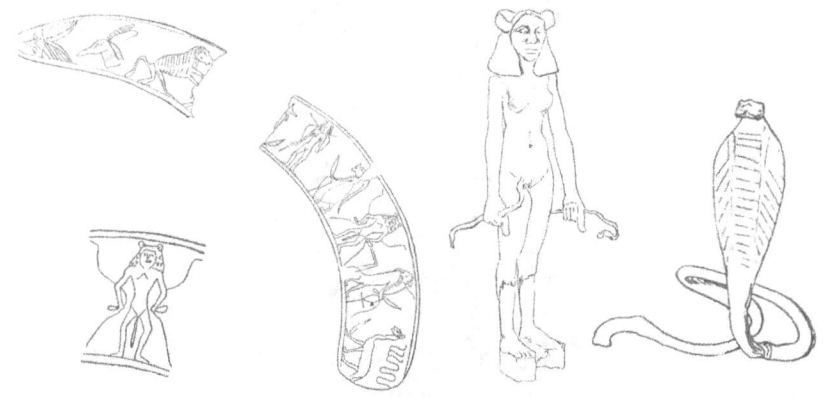

Extracted Line Drawings from Plate III in J. E. Quibell, The Ramesseum

---

16. Tomb 5 in J. E. Quibell, *The Ramesseum*, in *Egyptian Research Account 1896* (London: Bernard Quartich, 1898), 3 and plate III.
17. For discussion of this collection of artifacts see J. Bourriau, *Pharaohs and Mortals: Egyptian Art in the Middle Kingdom* (Cambridge University Press, 1988), 110–111; Robert K. Ritner, *The Mechanics of Ancient Egyptian Magical Practice* (Oriental Institute of the University of Chicago, 1993), 222–232; Ritner, "The Serpent Wand," 206–207; Werner Forman and Stephen Quirke, *Hieroglyphs and the Afterlife in Ancient Egypt* (British Museum Press, 1996), 106–109.

Cippi of "Horus on the crocodiles", from the New Kingdom and later, are comparable artifacts to the aforementioned wands. These depict the god Horus, representative of the king himself, as a child grasping serpents in his hands, along with lions, scorpions, or other dangerous creatures.

Hieroglyphics written on these objects are framed as words or spells spoken by Isis and Thoth to ward off evil from and to heal the child Horus, the divine counterpart of the king himself. The gods' words protecting the child king on a cosmic/mythical level provide impetus for giving a child or others a drink from the waters that are poured over these words, receiving similar protection and healing in their personal lives. This is akin to what was seen earlier in which the spells associated with the curved wands with serpent imagery on them contain the words of deity for protecting a child.

Horus the Child on Crocodiles

A text on one cippus reads: "Words spoken by Isis, the Great, mother of God, mistress of magic. ... She seals the mouth of all reptiles which bite with their mouths and sting with their tails."[18] The words from the goddess's mouth stops the mouths of serpents. The

---

18. László Kákosy and Ahmed M. Moussa, "A Horus Stela with Meret Goddesses" in *Studien zur Altägyptischen Kultur* 25 (1998): 150.

Metternich cippus has Isis describing her efficacy as "powerful speech and chosen words" for countering venom and disease.[19] Again, words of power must be spoken in connection with the serpents and other dangerous creatures grasped in the hand for the healing and protection to be efficacious.

But Horus is not just wielding serpents and other creatures in his hand, he is also standing on top of crocodiles. Depictions of a person standing on dangerous animals like crocodiles provides a Near Eastern cultural context for Old and New Testaments passages from the Psalmist and the Savior, who stated:

> "Thou shalt tread upon the lion and adder: the young lion and the dragon shalt thou trample under feet" (Psalm 91:13).
>
> "Behold, I give unto you power to tread on serpents and scorpions, and over all the power of the enemy: and nothing shall by any means hurt you." (Luke 10:19).

There appears to be an ancient cultural distinction between dangerous animals depicted under the feet versus those that are held higher in the hand. When dangerous animals are depicted beneath the feet, it appears to be a symbolic declaration of divine rule or power over the forces of chaos and danger represented by the creature beneath the feet. When a creature, most often a serpent, is in the hand, they become benevolent tools for combating chaos or evil. Coffin Text 885, states: "the snake is in my hand and cannot bite me," which Ritner interprets as "the deity (or his priestly representative) exerts mastery over the animals and the power they embody, rendering them harmless to the holder but dangerous 'weapons' against inimical forces."[20]

A further connection between the wands and cippi is that the wands preserve images of Bes or Beset holding serpents in their hands, and the cippi often depict Horus grasping serpents in his hand with an image of Bes's face directly overhead. A classic iconographic feature of Bes is his tongue sticking out of his mouth. While such action is usually interpreted by scholars as an apotropaic grimace — driving away evil by distorting the face and sticking out the tongue — no text actually states this is the reason. The ancient Egyptians understood

---

19. Carl Sander-Hansen, *Die Texte der Metternichstele, Analecta Aegyptiaca 7* (Copenhagen: Ejnar Munksgaard, 1956), 56, Spell 6.
20. Ritner, "The Serpent Wand," 213; compare with Ritner, *Mechanics*, 128n583, 224n1041.

the tongue to be the organ of speech,[21] so it is just as valid that Bes's tongue is meant to represent words of power coming out of his mouth in order to repel evil.

In later years, amulets for protection depict the dwarf god Pataikos, standing on crocodiles with serpents in his hands and serpents coming out of his mouth.[22] Serpents — not a tongue — coming out of the mouth heightens the association of serpents with words, akin to rods, or swords, coming out of the mouth mentioned earlier. It is also possible that Pataikos is not hosting benevolent serpents in his mouth, but is instead biting or swallowing malevolent serpents; however, this interpretation would also relate to divine words or authority overcoming forces of chaos.

The relationship between serpents and words of power is further illustrated by iconography of the goddess Weret-hekau, who is depicted as a cobra but whose name means literally "Great of Magic/Spells." Weret-hekau is linked to the serpentine *uraeus* in coronation regalia. The serpentine shaped wands and images likely represent her; in other words, the royal serpent emblem is the symbolic embodiment of spell-power (or words). The personification of Heka — "magic" itself — is a god depicted holding two or four serpents across the chest.

One of the most formal icons representing divine authority in ancient Egypt is the *was*-scepter. Sometimes the *was*-scepter was depicted as serpentine-shaped or enwrapped by a serpent. The fork depicted at the bottom of this scepter had the functional purpose

---

21. The Shabaka Stone inscription includes the line: "As for the tongue, it repeats what the heart has devised.... For every word of god came about through what the heart devised and what the tongue commanded." K. Sethe, *Dramatische Texte zu Altaegyptischen Mysterienspielen*, vol. 1 (Leipzig: Hinrichs, 1928), 4–9; Miriam Lichtheim, *Ancient Egyptian Literature, vol. 1: The Old and Middle Kingdoms* (Berkeley: University of California Press, 1973), 54. See also gold leafed tongue amulet artifacts in Isis Davis-Marks, "Archaeologists in Egypt Discover Mummy with Gold Tongue," *Smithsonian Magazine*, 3 February 2021, online at smithsonianmag.com.
22. Sources listed in Hartwig Altenmüller, "Pataikos" in *Lexikon der Ägyptologie*, vol. 4, edited by Wolfgang Helck and Eberhard Otto (Wiesbaden: Otto Harrassowitz, 1975), see particularly 723 n. 4. See also John A. Wilson, "Pataikos," in *Ancient Egyptian Sculpture and Painting in the Museum of Fine Arts, Boston* (Boston: Museum of Fine Arts, 1975), 77–103; Ephraim Stern, "A Pataikos from Tel Mevorakh," *Israel Exploration Journal* 26 (1976): 183–187.

of pinning a malevolent serpent's head in order to kill it, as noted by Trude Dothan and Robert Ritner.[23] Hence, the serpent wrapped around the scepter itself, held up in the hand, is benevolent, representing the god's word or authority. It, along with the fork, is used to attack a malevolent serpent on the ground "under foot" representing chaos, evil, or death.

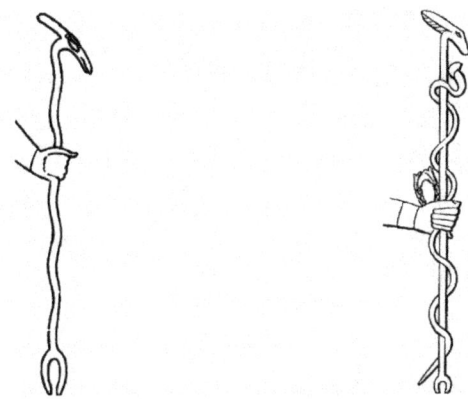

Examples of was-scepters

SCRIPTURAL REFLECTIONS OF SERPENTS AS WORDS OF POWER/ AUTHORITY

Similar to the serpents in the hand accompanied by divine words providing healing and protection against the venom and stings of dangerous animals underfoot in the Egyptian culture, the scriptures are full of God's word/authority being depicted as a benevolent serpent fighting against a false word/authority of a malevolent serpent. The very first sign which the Lord gives Moses of His authority is to cause his handheld rod to turn into a serpent, then back into a rod again, when Moses grasps the serpent's tail (Exodus 4:2–4). This foreshadowed the duel between Moses and the Egyptian priests, each with their rods turning to serpents (Exodus 7:10–13). Moses's serpent, however, would swallow those serpents of the Egyptian priests, and become a rod in the hand again. In the context of ancient cultural understanding outlined above, this story becomes a perfect symbol of God's word and authority bettering the false words and author-

---

23. Trude Dothan, "Forked Bronze Butts from Palestine and Egypt," *Israel Exploration Journal* 26 (1976): 20–34; Ritner, "The Serpent Wand," 218n8.

ity of the apostate priests. Thus, if the images of Pataikos mentioned earlier are biting or swallowing the serpent in his mouth (rather than a serpent emerging from the mouth as a symbol of words), it likely represents the power of the divine mouth or words over the serpent representing chaos or false words, similar to Moses serpent-rod swallowing the Egyptian serpents.

Likewise, the brazen serpent, on a rod or staff held up in the hand, overcomes the venom of those fiery flying serpents. In the Book of Mormon, Nephi understood the cultural context of serpents and declared that the fiery serpents were God's effort to "straiten [the children of Israel] in the wilderness with his rod" (1 Nephi 17:41). This is another example of the benevolent handheld serpent held up high versus the malevolent serpents on the ground. Similar cultural distinction may inform Captain Moroni placing only a "piece" of his coat up on a pole, compared to the remainder of his coat, which was likely cast down and trodden under foot with the coats of his troops (see Alma 46:12, 19, 21-22).

Moses's serpent-wand swallowing the serpent-wands of the Egyptian priests prefigures Revelation 12's depiction of the great serpent seeking to swallow the child who, importantly, is holding a rod in his hand (vv. 4–5). That the being the serpent intended to harm is a child holding a rod echoes the cippi which portray a need to protect the royal child Horus holding serpents from the malevolent forces of chaos.

The serpent in Revelation 12 goes on to persecute the child's mother, the woman with twelve stars on her head, and she flees into the wilderness. The serpent sends a flood of water out of its mouth (suggesting a flood of false words) to prevent the woman from ever coming back, but the Earth opens her mouth and swallows the dragon's flood in order to help the woman return (vv. 15–16). The Book of Mormon fulfills the imagery of this moment perfectly, for it is God's word that literally came from a hole in the ground, the mouth of the earth and voice from the dust, prepared for the purpose of swallowing the false words of the dragon which flooded the Earth as the Church of Christ wandered in the wilderness.

The serpent in the Garden of Eden speaks words that tempt Adam and Eve toward the tree of death. It is in symbolic opposition to the flaming sword–God's word held in the hand–which "keeps the way to the tree of life" (Genesis 3:13, 24). The parallels in Lehi's vision are the mists of darkness or "temptations of the devil" that are in symbolic opposition to the rod of iron, God's word, which may also be flaming (see 1 Nephi 12:17 cf. 1 Nephi 15:30). That Lehi and Nephi speak of a mist of darkness in opposition to the rod of iron when a false rod or serpent would, based on the cultural context above, be expected is interesting because in the ancient world, mists of darkness are often associated with the great cosmic serpent of chaos.

As an example, Apep, the serpent of chaos in Egyptian mythology, each night tries to devour the sun god Ra in the underworld. He is often depicted emerging from darkness or storm clouds, attempting to plunge the cosmos into eternal night. Texts speak of "the storm of Apep"[24] or "the demon of darkness."[25] The Book of Overthrowing Apep mentions

> Apep the foe of Rê is felled in storm by the shining of Rê, Apep is felled in very truth. He is to be burnt in a fire ... and his remains placed in a pot of urine and pounded up into one mass [likely describing some sort of execration ritual on an image of Apep]. Thou shalt do accordingly at the sixth hour of the night and at the eighth hour of the day, placing Apep on the fire and spitting on him very often at the beginning of every hour of the day until the turning of the shadow. After this, at the sixth hour of the day, thou shalt place Apep on the fire, spitting on him and trampling on him with thy left foot.... [note Apep's position underfoot] Thou shalt do accordingly at the eighth hour of the day, driving off Apep that he may not attack the Night-bark. Thou shalt do accordingly when storm brews in the east of the sky and when Rê sets in the west in order to prevent the storm-red from growing in the east of the sky. Thou shalt do accordingly very often in order to prevent bad weather from growing in the sky and to prevent thunderstorms from growing in the sky. Thou shalt do this very often against storm so that the sun may shine and Apep be felled in very truth; it will be well with whoso does it upon earth, and it will be well with him in the realm of the dead, strength shall be given to that man to attain the office of his superior, and it

---

24. Raymond O. Faulkner, *The Ancient Egyptian Book of the Dead* (London: British Museum Press, 1985), 119.
25. Jan Assmann, *The Search for God in Ancient Egypt*, trans. David Lorton (Ithaca, NY: Cornell University Press, 2001), 69?***

will be his salvation from all evil and harmful things in very truth.[26]

In this text, Apep/Apophis appears to be the personification of anything that threatens the sun's light, such as eclipses or clouds. Such ideas caused E. A. Wallis Budge to speak of Apep as "the serpent-devil of mist, darkness, storm, and night. ..."[27]

In light of their cultural context, the serpent in the garden of Eden and the cosmic serpent's mists of darkness in Lehi's/Nephi's visions are symbols of the counterfeit words (false authority or rods like those the magicians wield in the story of Moses), which tempt and blind people, leading them astray (1 Nephi 15:24). They are in opposition to the flaming sword and rod of iron representing the true word and authority of God that guides one to life and salvation at the tree of life.

The serpent in the Garden of Eden is cursed to crawl upon his belly, eat dust, and to eventually have his head crushed (Genesis 3:14–15); though, the tool for crushing the head goes unmentioned. However, "smiting scenes" depicted from the earliest to later periods of Egyptian history, such as on the predynastic palette of Narmer to New Kingdom temple pylons, portray the king using a rod or mace to crush the head of the enemy who is often depicted in a gesture of crawling (one leg extended back, the other forward).

Palette of Narmer

---

26. Book of Overthrowing Apep (Bremner-Rhind Papyrus). Raymond O. Faulkner, "The Bremner-Rhind Papyrus—I." Journal of Egyptian Archaeology 23 (1937): 166–185; "The Bremner-Rhind Papyrus—II." Journal of Egyptian Archaeology 24 (1938): 41–53.
27. E. A. Wallis Budge, *The Gods of the Egyptians: Studies in Egyptian Mythology*, 2 vols. (London: Methuen & Co., 1904), 1:11

The tomb of Menkheperreseneb at Thebes depicts foreign nations appearing before the king. The first nation is depicted crawling on his belly (one leg extends back and the other is tucked up under the body) with his face to the ground, or dust, before the Pharaoh.[28] While it may appear that this nation is merely paying respect to the king, crawling and "licking or eating" dust is linked to curse imagery, as seen in scriptural passages such as Isaiah 49:23, wherein the foreign nations, or kings and queens, lick the dust of Israel's feet. They are to be seen as a cursed people who go upon their bellies and ultimately will be crushed, notwithstanding their furthering the work as "nursing mothers," etc.

This is clarified in the Book of Mormon, wherein Jacob takes the prophecy of Isaiah and interprets it, telling his listeners and latter-day readers that "they [the Gentile nations] that fight against Zion and the covenant people of the Lord shall lick up the dust of their feet ... unto [their] destruction ..." (2 Nephi 6:13–14; compare with Micah 7:16–17, Psalm 72:9). Of course, any Gentile-helpers who repent and make the covenant will be saved, being made into Israel (2 Nephi 6:12). As an aside, snakes literally do lick or eat dust as they crawl as a form of perceiving their environment, so the curse of God as written in the scriptures is poetically framed within the observable behavior of serpents.

The point of these examples is to demonstrate that the king's rod, held in the hand, is in opposition to the serpent-like figures crawling at their feet, and echoes the crawling serpent whose head is to be crushed in the opening chapters of the Bible. God's word and authority prevails over that of Lucifer's false words and authorities in the world.

Conclusion

The use of serpents held in the hand in connection with divine words in the ancient world parallels the long tradition of rods, maces, and swords being utilized as symbols for divine authority and words. Rods and swords in the hand can smite an enemy and protect or guide a friend. Likewise, a venomous serpent in the hand, controlled by

---

28. TT 86, published in Norman de Garis Davies and Alan H. Gardner, eds., *The Tombs of Menkheperrasonb, Amenmose, and Another*, Theban Tombs Series, 5 vols. (London: Egypt Exploration Society, 1933), 5:2–9 and plates 3–7.

divine power, can protect and heal while opposing the forces of chaos often represented by an opposing serpent or dragon.

Consequently, these symbols ultimately become emblematic of the anointed king — or Messiah — in scripture sent to deliver his people. It is His scepter — whether sword, rod, or serpent — that can fully protect, heal, guide, and vanquish every foe. By extension, He is the serpent-scepter held in His Father's hand and lifted up, that He might draw all men unto Him to be healed, and because of His virtue and His charity, His dominion flows unto Him without compulsory means, forever and ever.

10

WHO SHALL ASCEND INTO THE HILL OF THE LORD?

AN OLD TESTAMENT FRAMEWORK FOR UNDERSTANDING THE EXCLUSIVE NATURE OF THE TEMPLE

TYLER GOLIGHTLY

Latter-day Saints occupy a distinctive place in the modern religious landscape. Like other Christians, they hold weekly public worship services open to all, yet their temple worship is reserved for those who meet specific requirements of worthiness. The contrast between the openness of sacrament meetings and the restricted nature of temple ordinances can seem difficult to reconcile in a culture that values transparency and accessibility. In this paper, the concept of sacred space in the Old Testament is examined as a framework for understanding this dynamic. Drawing on passages from Exodus and Leviticus, it explores how ancient Israel viewed holiness, access, and preparation for entering sacred spaces. Through this lens, the Latter-day Saint temple emerges as part of a long-standing divine pattern that defines sacred space as both set apart and deeply meaningful.

The Church of Jesus Christ of Latter-day Saints occupies an awkward space in the religious world. To the casual observer, we appear to be like any other church: there are public worship services in normal-looking chapels, and a liturgy — the Sacrament — which anyone can participate in. This is a practice that we are comfortable talking about because it is something that we do regularly.

In contrast, there are our temples: ornate, beautiful edifices where only those holding a current temple recommend can enter. Here sacred ceremonies are performed which only the initiated can participate in, and whose details are not freely discussed outside the building premises. This part of our worship is something which many Latter-day Saints — myself included — struggle to discuss. We want to communicate the unique nature of the temple, but want to avoid making it sound like we have something to hide. This difficulty is compounded by the temple's seemingly exclusive nature. For some, that nature must mean that there *is* something to hide, such as nefarious, even Satanic, rituals.

On a more personal and serious level, the exclusivity of the temple and its ceremonies can feel isolating to those not of our faith. On the day of a Latter-day Saint sealing, there are often family members and friends of the new couple waiting outside of the temple, because they are either not members of the Church or do not hold a current temple recommend.

Both of these situations lead many to ask the same questions. Why exclusivity? Why not open the temple up to everyone? Why keep people out? The exclusive nature of the temple and the struggle of many Saints to answer questions about it has led some to erroneous (and somewhat hilarious) conclusions:

- The Church is hiding nefarious, Satanic practices where kidnapped people are sacrificed to the devil
- The temple is secret because it's just crazy
- The Church does not want the public to witness their pagan, occultic, and Masonic ceremonies which prove they are not Christian
- The exclusive nature of the temple is fuel for a cultural superiority complex
- The Church intentionally excludes people because they hate sinners, the LGBT community, and/or anyone who isn't a perfect Latter-day Saint

Many members of The Church of Jesus Christ of Latter-day Saints struggle to answer these questions in an informed and sensitive way because we lack the proper framework to consider and talk about the concept of sacred space. After all, in a world where information is readily available and nothing is hidden, religious spaces and closed ceremonies are seen as weird or "cultish." In a society that has no concept of the sacred, how do Latter-day Saints talk about this place that not everyone can enter or participate in?

This is a difficult and unique predicament, but there is an answer, and it can be found in a beloved volume of scripture: the Old Testament. More specifically, in the ritual purity laws of Exodus and Leviticus. The texts of the Old Testament have unconsciously informed the way we view sacred space, which in turn informs the way we restrict access to the temple. The purpose of this paper is to build an initial framework for understanding exclusivity and sacred space based on the writings of the Old Testament.

To begin, we will explore Israelite and Ancient Near Eastern thought on the temple as a dwelling place of a deity. Then the Israelite concept of holiness and how that informed access to sacred space will be examined. Finally, these concepts will be related to the modern temples of The Church of Jesus Christ of Latter-day Saints.

Sacred Space as the Literal Dwelling Place of Deity

Before similarities can be fleshed out between Israelite sacred space theology and Latter-day Saint temple theology, this fundamental question must be answered: how did the ancient Israelites think about sacred space?

The Israelites existed in an Ancient Near Eastern context, and naturally borrowed many ideas from their neighbors. This was especially true for the concept of sacred space. For example, in many societies, a temple was viewed as the dwelling place of whichever deity the temple belonged to. A major portion of the Babylonian creation myth, the *Enuma Elish*, features the gods creating a temple in Babylon as a place where they could dwell and rest:[1]

> Now, lord, seeing you have established our freedom
>
> What favour can we do for you?
>
> Let us make a shrine of great renown:
>
> Your chamber will be our resting place wherein we may repose.
>
> Let us erect a shrine to house a pedestal
>
> Wherein we may repose when we finish (the work).[2]

The Israelites thought of the tabernacle, and later the temple, as literal dwelling places of the Lord.[3] In Exodus 25, Jehovah commands

---

1. Ira Spar, "Mesopotamian Creation Myths," *Timeline of Art History*, Metropolitan Museum of Art, 1 April 2009, online at metmuseum.org.
2. *Enuma Elish*, Tablet VI 49–54, trans. W.G. Lambert, online at etana.org.
3. William J. Hamblin and David Seely, *Solomon's Temple: Myth and History* (London: Thames & Hudson, 2007), 9; see also 2 Samuel 7:5; 2 Chronicles

Moses to "tell the Israelites to take for me an offering; from all whose hearts prompt them to give you shall receive the offering for me. ... And have them make me a sanctuary, that I may dwell among them. In accordance with all that I show you concerning the pattern of the tabernacle and of all its furniture, so you shall make it" (Exodus 25:2, 8–9, NRSV).

In 1 Kings 6, Solomon is in the process of building the temple, and receives a revelation from the Lord. The Lord says to him, "Concerning this house that you are building, if you will walk in my statutes, obey my ordinances, and keep all my commandments by walking in them, then I will establish my promise with you, which I made to your father David. I will dwell among the children of Israel, and will not forsake my people Israel" (1 Kings 6:11–13, NRSV). Later, in his dedicatory prayer for the newly constructed temple in Jerusalem, Solomon said, "I have built you [meaning the Lord] an exalted house, a place for you to dwell in forever" (1 Kings 8:13, NRSV).

The Hebrew for the word "dwell" used in these verses is *šākan*. In this context, it "involves a proper dwelling, a lasting stay, not a passing transition."[4] Thus, when the Lord is said to "dwell" somewhere, it means that He *literally* dwells there. The Israelites considered the tabernacle and the later temple as places where the Lord *literally* dwelt/lived among His people.

Holiness

Because both the tabernacle and the temple were seen as the literal dwelling places of Jehovah, they were considered "holy." In Exodus 29:43–45, it reads:

> I will meet with the Israelites there [meaning the tabernacle], and it shall be sanctified by my glory; I will consecrate the tent of meeting and the altar; Aaron also and his sons I will consecrate to serve me as priests. I will dwell among the Israelites, and I will be their God. (NRSV)

It is the Lord's glory, or more precisely His divine presence (*kabod*), that makes the tabernacle holy, but what is the meaning of

---

 7:11; Isaiah 2:3.
4. Ernst Jenni and Claus Westermann, *Theological Lexicon of the Old Testament*, 3 vols., trans. Mark E. Biddle (Peabody, MA: Hendrickson Publishers, 2023), 3:1328.

the word "holy?" Despite being a near universal idea, it is actually quite a bit difficult to precisely define.⁵ The Hebrew root for holy, *qodeš*, denotes something as being set apart from the world.⁶ Kurt Goldammer describes the holy as "the entirely different," writing that "[the holy] is not just different from all things human, it is also different from the normal world and the temporal [or profane]."⁷ If something is holy, it is (sometimes literally) set apart entirely from the rest of the world, and it must be kept that way. According to the *Theological Dictionary of the Old Testament*, "What is holy and what is profane are to be strictly distinguished, with the latter not allowed to come into contact with the former."⁸

This concept of holiness was central to how the Israelites thought about and dealt with sacred space. It is also the most important concept for Latter-day Saints to understand as we interact with the relevant Old Testament texts dealing with sacred space.

In the minds of the Israelites and other Ancient Near Eastern peoples, the primary way that the outside/profane world interacted, or came into contact, with the holy was through impurity. Jacob Milgrom writes, "Impurity is the implacable foe of holiness wherever it exists; it assaults the sacred realm even from afar."⁹ If the profane were to come into contact with the holy, whether directly or indirectly, the consequences would be catastrophic for the offender and the community. What exactly were those consequences? Three episodes in the Old Testament shed light on the subject.

---

5. Mircea Eliade, *Patterns in Comparative Religion*, trans. Rosemary Sheed (Lincoln, NE: University of Nebraska Press, 1996; orig. New York: Sheed & Ward, Inc., 1958), 1.
6. G. Johannes Botterweck, Helmer Ringgren, and Heinz-Josef Fabry, eds., *Theological Dictionary of the Old Testament*, 17 vols., trans. Douglas W. Scott (Grand Rapids: Wm. B. Eerdmans, 2003), 7:523; Jenni and Westermann, *Theological Lexicon*, 3:1104.
7. Kurt Goldammer, *Die Formenwelt des Religiösen* (Stuttgart, DE: A. Kröner, 1960), 53.
8. Botterweck, Ringgren, and Fabry, *Theological Dictionary*, 7:534; Othmar Keel, *The Symbolism of the Biblical World: Ancient Near Eastern Iconography and the Book of Psalms*, trans. Timothy J. Hallett (Winona Lake, IN: Eisenbrauns, 1997), 123.
9. Jacob Milgrom, *Leviticus: A Book of Ritual and Ethics*, Continental Commentaries (Minneapolis: Fortress Press, 2004), 256–257.

CONSEQUENCES OF PROFANING SACRED SPACE
Exodus 19

In Exodus 19, the Israelites are far beyond the Red Sea, and have reached Sinai. The Lord reveals to Moses that He wants to make Israel a "kingdom of priests, and an holy nation" by covenanting with them and giving them a law (Exodus 19:6, KJV).

Not only would He give Israel a law, but the Lord would also "come down upon Mount Sinai in the sight of all people" (Exodus 19:11, KJV). This was a momentous occasion, which is why the children of Israel had to prepare for it by washing their clothes and abstaining from sexual contact for three days (Exodus 19:10–11, 15). There was another very important commandment which they had to keep while at the mountain: "Be careful not to go up the mountain or to touch the edge of it. Any who touch the mountain *shall be put to death*. No hand shall touch them, but they shall be stoned or shot with arrows, whether animal or human being, they shall not live" (Exodus 19:12–13).

Eventually, the Lord would invite the Israelites to join Moses on the mountain, but any uninvited crossing of the threshold between sacred and profane warranted immediate execution at the hands of the people (Exodus 19:13). For God to come down to Sinai and converse with Moses, no one could contaminate the mountain, and the people were to enforce this prohibition.

Leviticus 10

At the time recorded in Leviticus 10, the tabernacle had just been dedicated and, as signified by the appearance of the glory (*kabod*) of the Lord in the sight of all Israel, was now considered holy (Leviticus 9:23). For the Israelites, this theophany surely was a wonderful and awesome (in the literal sense) experience, one which no one would forget.

Except two rather important individuals seem to have forgotten: Nadab and Abihu, sons of Aaron and members of the priestly caste. In their enthusiasm to officiate in their priestly office, they seemingly forgot the now holy nature of the sanctuary and the need to exclude the profane. They "took [their censers] ... and ... offered *unholy* fire before the Lord, such as he had not commanded them" (Leviticus 10:1, NRSV, emphasis added). Nadab and Abihu brought coals from an outside or "profane" source *into* the tent itself, thereby contaminating it.[10]

The universal order had just been violated. What was the consequence for such a crime?

"And there went out fire from the Lord, and devoured them, and they died before the Lord" (Leviticus 10:2, NRSV). For the individual offender (or offenders, in this case), the consequence of profaning the holy sanctuary could be immediate death by the hand of God.

However, the Israelites did not believe that the impure had to physically violate the bounds of the sacred in order for contamination to occur. The sins of the people could also indirectly contaminate the sanctuary, and thus the sanctuary itself would have to be purified.[11] This belief was the motivation behind the various purification or "sin" offerings prescribed by the Torah.[12]

Why did the sanctuary itself have to be purified? Jacob Milgrom writes: "God will not abide in a polluted sanctuary. To be sure, the Merciful One would tolerate a modicum of pollution. *But there is a point of no return.* If the pollution levels continue to rise, the end is inexorable. God abandons the sanctuary and leaves the people to their doom."[13]

It should be noted that, in the view of the Israelites, Jehovah was not a strict god who arbitrarily smote the people for the smallest of inadvertent ethical or ritual wrongs. The contamination brought upon the sanctuary by such wrongs was cleansed through the regular "sin" offerings described in Leviticus 4.[14] If the sanctuary was not purified quickly or was profaned repeatedly, the wellbeing and prosperity of the entire community and civilization was at risk.[15] Continual profanation through intentional wrongdoing would bring the judgment of God upon the people.

---

10. Milgrom, *Leviticus*, 93–94.
11. Milgrom, *Leviticus*, 42–43.
12. Jacob Milgrom, *Leviticus 1–16*, Anchor Yale Bible Commentary, 3 vols. (New Haven: Yale University Press, 2008), 1:254–261; see also Leviticus 4 and Leviticus 16.
13. Milgrom, *Leviticus*, 32; Milgrom, *Leviticus 1–16*, 1:258–261.
14. Milgrom, *Leviticus*, 147.
15. Milgrom, *Leviticus*, 262.

Ezekiel

In Ezekiel, the prophet is shown in vision the idolatrous practices and worship of foreign deities ("abominations," as the prophet refers to them) taking place within the temple complex at Jerusalem. The children of Israel had violated the sanctity of the temple by building and worshipping idols, as well as worshipping deities/objects that were certainly not related to Jehovah (Ezekiel 8:3, 7–16).

The Lord says to Ezekiel, "Mortal, do you see what they are doing, the great abominations that the house of Israel are committing here, to drive me far from my sanctuary?" (Ezekiel 8:6, NRSV). Ultimately, God's presence departs from the temple, and the people are delivered to destruction as a result of their continual sin.[16] The people had polluted the sanctuary with their ethical and — more importantly — their ritual sins to the point that it was impossible for the presence of the Lord to remain.

Hopefully, it is obvious that, in the Israelite worldview, holiness could be a life or death matter for the people. Contact between the holy and the impure or profane meant, at best, almost certain death to the offending party, and at worst, the contact between the two would lead to the divine presence of Jehovah being driven from sacred space. Such an action would bring cataclysmic levels of death and destruction to the community.

ACCESS TO SACRED SPACE

Improper interaction with the holy brought death, either by the hand of God or man, and thus access to the holy was strictly controlled and limited.[17] In some Ancient Near Eastern cultures, one would have to pass by a set of guardian statues in order to enter the temple complex. These guardians were thought to ward off demons and protect the sanctuary from being defiled.[18]

The tabernacle, and later the temple at Jerusalem, did not have such measures, but there were other means of protecting the sanc-

---

16. Ezekiel 10; Ezekiel 8:18; Ezekiel 22:31.
17. Philip Peter Jenson, *Graded Holiness: A Key to the Priestly Conception of the World*, Journal for the Study of the Old Testament Supplement Series 106, ed. David J. A. Clines and Philip R. Davies (Sheffield, GB: Sheffield Academic Press, 1992), 55.
18. Keel, *Symbolism of the Biblical World*, 123.

tuary. To illustrate this, we turn to the Psalms. Psalms 15 and 24 are thought to be part of a gate liturgy; where a festival procession would make its way to the gates of the temple complex and a priest would ask the leader of the procession if the members of that company met the ritual *and* ethical requirements to enter the temple complex. The leader of the procession would then affirm that they did indeed meet the requirements.[19] This liturgy served as a way to both admit the prepared to receive their blessings and prevent those who were impure from being cursed at the hand of God.[20]

Psalm 24 reads:

> Who shall ascend into the hill of the Lord? or who shall stand in his holy place? He that hath clean hands, and a pure heart; who hath not lifted up his soul unto vanity [or "what is false"], nor sworn deceitfully. He shall receive the blessing from the Lord, and righteousness from the God of his salvation. This is the generation of them that seek him, that seek thy face, O Jacob" (Psalm 24:3–6, KJV).[21]

And in a similar vein, Psalm 15 reads:

> O Lord, who may abide in thy tabernacle? who shall dwell in thy holy hill? He that walketh uprightly, and worketh righteousness, and speaketh the truth in his heart. He that backbiteth not with his tongue, nor doeth evil to his neighbor, nor taketh up a reproach against his neighbor (Psalm 15:1–3, KJV).

As stated, only those who met certain conditions (moral and ritual purity) could pass through the gates and be admitted into the sacred space. As illustrated by these Psalms, these conditions involved not just ritual purity, but also the correct treatment of others. As Othmar Keel put it, "the chief wall which separates God and man is (ethical) misconduct toward one's coreligionists."[22]

However, being able to enter the complex did not guarantee access to the sanctuary or its rituals. Only the priests could perform sacrifices on the altar in the courtyard or access the sanctuary itself, a regulation

---

19. Sigmund Mowinckel, *The Psalms in Israel's Worship*, Biblical Resource Series, 14 vols., trans. D. R. Ap-Thomas, ed. Astrid B. Beck and David Noel Freedman (Grand Rapids: William B. Eerdmans Publishing Company, 2004), 3:177–179.
20. Keel, *Symbolism of the Biblical World*, 183.
21. In the NRSV, it is rendered "that seek the face of the God of Jacob."
22. Keel, *Symbolism of the Biblical World*, 126.

that was enforced under penalty of death.[23] Although the common layperson had access to the courtyard, there were still restrictions on where they could go and what they could do in that space. Even if an Israelite was a male descendant of Aaron, there were further rituals to be performed and requirements that needed to be met in order to officiate. Potential officiants needed to be washed, anointed, and clothed in priestly garments before they could begin to offer sacrifices or enter the sanctuary.[24] In addition, per Leviticus 21, they had to live by additional requirements not imposed upon the laypeople.

Even being a priest did not grant one automatic access to all areas of the temple. The Holy of Holies was limited to the high priest alone, and accessed only once a year. If the high priest were to either enter more often, access the space improperly clothed, or without incense, he would die, since that was where the Lord's presence resided (Leviticus 16:2–4, 12–13). The high priest was also required to wear additional clothing and follow stricter purity laws than those of the normal priestly class.[25] All of this was to avoid the high priest defiling both himself and the sanctuary.

Ritual and ethical preparation was necessary to approach or encounter sacred space; encountering the holy was serious business to ancient Israel. Even within the sanctuary complex itself, there were grades of holiness with additional requirements and preparation necessary.[26] Only if one was prepared to enter sacred space and met the necessary requirements, would they participate in what Keel calls the "wholly other energy active within the temple."[27]

What Does this Mean for Latter-day Saints?

Latter-day Saints will find that they have a great deal in common with ancient Israelites when it comes to the ways in which they view sacred space. As signified by the engraving found on nearly every temple of The Church of Jesus Christ of Latter-day Saints, temples are viewed as the literal dwelling places of God, where one can go

---

23. Numbers 1:50–54; see also Jacob Milgrom, *Numbers,* The JPS Torah Commentary, 5 vols. (Philadelphia: Jewish Publication Society, 2003), 4:342.
24. Exodus 40:12–15; see also Exodus 28:42–43; Exodus 30:17–21, 30.
25. See Exodus 28; also Leviticus 21:10–15.
26. Jenson, *Graded Holiness,* 63.
27. Keel, *Symbolism of the Biblical World,* 123.

to encounter Him. The Lord says as much in modern revelation. In Doctrine and Covenants 97, He states:

> And inasmuch as my people build a house unto me in the name of the Lord, and do not suffer any unclean thing to come into it, that it be not defiled, my glory shall rest upon it; yea, and my presence shall be there, for I will come into it, and all the pure in heart that shall come into it shall see God. But if it be defiled I will not come into it, and my glory shall not be there; for I will not come into unholy temples (Doctrine and Covenants 97:15–17).[28]

Elder James E. Talmage writes:

> A Temple is more than chapel or church, more than synagogue or cathedral; it is a structure erected as the House of the Lord, sacred to the closest communion between the Lord Himself and the Holy Priesthood, and devoted to the highest and most sacred ordinances characteristic of the age or dispensation to which the particular Temple belongs.[29]

The Lord wants His covenant people to think about the temple in the same way the Old Testament Israelites did. Access to a place imbued with holiness must be limited to those who have prepared themselves for such an occasion, for a lack of preparation (or, more precisely, worthiness) on the part of an individual brings spiritual danger.

It is interesting to note that, similar to the Israelite tabernacle and temple, access to holier areas of a Latter-day Saint temple requires that one be initiated into a priestly class of sorts by being washed, anointed, and clothed in priestly garments. However, in contrast with the Old Testament priestly caste, the initiatory rite in Latter-day Saint temples today is not limited to those of a specific lineage. Rather, all members of the Church who have the requisite capacity and worthiness are able to be initiated into and participate in rituals in the holier spaces of the temple.[30] While initiation into a "priestly class" is still required to

---

28. This idea is also extended in Doctrine and Covenants 94:8–9 to the office of the First Presidency that was to be built next to the Kirtland Temple.
29. James E. Talmage, *The House of the Lord: A Study of Holy Sanctuaries, Ancient and Modern* (Salt Lake City: The Church of Jesus Christ of Latter-day Saints, 1912), 14.
30. Compare with Robert S. Boylan, *After the Order of the Son of God: The Biblical and Historical Evidence for Latter-day Theology of the Priesthood*, ed. Ranyane Melo (self-published; printed by CreateSpace Independent Publishing

"ascend" to the temple, this initiatory ordinance is available to every member of God's covenant people that are willing to live the additional requirements that come with it.

Latter-day Saints do not have a concept of ritual purity in the same way as the ancient Israelites did. This is a very important distinction to keep in mind when drawing parallels between modern revealed beliefs and practices and those of the Old Testament. Latter-day Saints do not need to cleanse themselves after bodily emissions, avoid pork and shellfish, or avoid those with skin diseases in order to be able to enter the house of the Lord.

Instead, access to the temple is determined by a willingness to demonstrate "worthiness," a comparatively abstract concept signified by worthily holding a current temple recommend. This worthiness entails not just moral righteousness and obedience to revealed laws, but also a belief in the foundational claims of The Church of Jesus Christ of Latter-day Saints.[31]

In his book *The Holy Temple*, the late President Boyd K. Packer writes:

> After a temple is dedicated we do not feel we own it. It is the Lord's house. He directs the conditions under which it may be used. He has revealed the ordinances that should be performed therein and has established the standards and conditions under which we may participate in them. ... It should not be surprising that there should be limitations as to those who may receive [these ordinances] and those who may witness them. It should not, therefore, seem strange that the temples are held sacred, for all who will prepare themselves by repentance, by baptism, by preparation in worthiness to meet the qualifications, may enter therein to participate in the ordinances offered in the house of the Lord.[32]

Every person willing to join the Lord's covenant people and live by the requisite worthiness standards is able to enter and participate in the ordinances of the temple. The Lord will deny entry to no one

---

Platform, 2018), 31–32.

31. *General Handbook: Serving in The Church of Jesus Christ of Latter-day Saints* (Salt Lake City: The Church of Jesus Christ of Latter-day Saints), 26.3.3.1, online at churchofjesuschrist.org.
32. Boyd K. Packer, *The Holy Temple* (Salt Lake City: Deseret Book, 1980), 35.

that comes to His house with a broken heart and a contrite spirit (2 Nephi 26:25–28, 33).

Conclusion

"Holiness to the Lord. The House of the Lord."

These two pronouncements are engraved on nearly every temple of The Church of Jesus Christ, and we take them literally. The Lord has told His Saints that – like the tabernacle and temple of the Old Testament – the latter-day temple is His dwelling place that contains his actual divine presence, or his "glory" (Doctrine and Covenants 88:119). This is what makes these edifices holy. That holiness requires us to maintain a distinction and separation between the holy and unholy, just as in times of old. As Latter-day Saints, we do not need to struggle to explain the limited access to our temples. Our beliefs about sacred space have been shaped and informed by the Old Testament, and we can and should turn there to explain the holy nature of our temples. Holiness is not about keeping people out, it is about ensuring that they are prepared to encounter God in His house. The Lord wants all of His children to choose holiness.

The General Handbook of The Church of Jesus Christ of Latter-day Saints states: "The temple is the house of the Lord. Entering the temple and participating in ordinances there is a sacred privilege. This privilege is reserved for those who are spiritually prepared and striving to live the Lord's standards, as determined by authorized priesthood leaders."[33] Let us all strive to have "clean hands and a pure heart", and invite others to do the same, that we may all be made holy by encountering the Lord in His house (Psalms 24:4).

---

33. *General Handbook*, 26.3.3, online at churchofjesuschrist.org.

11

IN THE BEGINNING

GROUNDING JOSEPH SMITH'S COSMOLOGY IN GENESIS 1

STEPHEN O. SMOOT

This paper explores how Genesis 1 can be read as a theological foundation for key elements of Latter-day Saint cosmology. Challenging the traditional Christian doctrine of creatio ex nihilo, Genesis 1 is shown to support a creation from pre-existing matter, consistent with early Israelite cosmologies and affirmed in Latter-day Saint teachings. The imago Dei *concept of Genesis 1:26 is interpreted to include not only moral or spiritual likeness but also a physical or anthropomorphic dimension, aligning with Latter-day Saint understandings of embodied divinity. Finally, the plural language of Genesis 1:26 is examined in light of ancient parallels and modern revelation, offering a basis for a divine plurality rather than strict ontological monotheism. Together, these readings situate Genesis 1 as a scriptural and theological anchor for distinctively Latter-day Saint views on creation, divine embodiment, and the nature of God.*

INTRODUCTION: JOSEPH SMITH AND GENESIS 1

Few scriptural texts occupied Joseph Smith's attention as consistently as the opening chapters of the book of Genesis. From the earliest stages of his prophetic ministry, Joseph repeatedly returned to Genesis 1, not merely to comment on its content, but to reframe, expand, and retranslate its meaning within a broader theological vision. This sustained engagement reveals how central the themes of creation, divine order, and human purpose were to Joseph's revelatory project. Through translation efforts, prophetic teaching, and liturgical innovation, the opening verses of Genesis became for the Prophet a springboard for profound doctrinal developments.[1]

Joseph's first major engagement with Genesis 1 came through his inspired revision of the Bible, known today as the Joseph Smith Translation (JST).[2] In 1830, immediately after the publication of the Book of Mormon, Joseph began reworking the Genesis creation narrative, introducing expanded cosmological insights and theological emphases. This effort was later formalized in the canon of The Church of Jesus Christ of Latter-day Saints as the Book of Moses in the Pearl of Great Price — a product of this Bible revision or translation in which Joseph reframed the creation story in explicitly revelatory terms, depicting God's voice speaking directly to Moses about the spiritual as well as physical dimensions of creation. This version additionally highlights the pre-mortal council, divine planning, and the agency of humanity, laying a foundation for the Prophet's later revelations.[3]

Joseph's revelatory engagement with Genesis 1 also took new shape in the Book of Abraham, a scriptural text he produced after acquiring a collection of Egyptian papyri.[4] Abraham chapters 4 and 5 parallel the Genesis creation narrative but introduce significant innovations. In this account, for instance, *the Gods* rather than a singular

---

1. See generally Kent P. Jackson, *The Restored Gospel and the Book of Genesis* (Salt Lake City: Deseret Book, 2001); Jeffrey M. Bradshaw, *In God's Image and Likeness: Creation, Fall, and the Story of Adam and Eve* (Salt Lake City: Eborn Books, 2014). See additionally Kent P. Jackson, comp., *Joseph Smith's Commentary on the Bible* (Salt Lake City: Deseret Book, 1994), 1–26; Andrew F. Ehat and Lyndon W. Cook, comps., *The Words of Joseph Smith: The Contemporary Accounts of the Nauvoo Discourses of the Prophet Joseph* (Provo, UT: Religious Studies Center, Brigham Young University, 1980), 421.
2. Robert J. Matthews, *"A Plainer Translation": Joseph Smith's Translation of the Bible — a History and Commentary* (Provo, UT: Brigham Young University Press, 1975); Kent P. Jackson, *Understanding Joseph Smith's Translation of the Bible* (Provo, UT: Religious Studies Center, Brigham Young University; Salt Lake City: Deseret Book, 2022).
3. Aaron P. Schade and Matthew L. Bowen, *The Book of Moses: From the Ancient of Days to the Latter Days* (Provo, UT: Religious Studies Center, Brigham Young University; Salt Lake City: Deseret Book, 2021).
4. See generally John Gee, *An Introduction to the Book of Abraham* (Provo, UT: Religious Studies Center, Brigham Young University; Salt Lake City: Deseret Book, 2017); Stephen O. Smoot, John Gee, Kerry Muhlestein, and John S. Thompson, *A Guide to the Book of Abraham*, in *BYU Studies Quarterly* 61, no. 4 (2022).

deity undertake the work of creation, emphasizing a plurality of divine beings acting in council. By revisioning Genesis through Abraham's prophetic lens, Joseph presented the creation not merely as a past event but as an eternal pattern tied to divine authority and human potential.

Joseph's focus on Genesis 1 reemerged again in the temple endowment he introduced in Nauvoo in May 1842.[5] The endowment ritual begins with a dramatized retelling of the creation of the world, following the narrative arc of Genesis 1 but expanding it in scope and purpose. Here, the creation account serves not only as a cosmogonic myth but as a sacred liturgy through which participants ritually reenact the journey of the soul — from pre-mortal beginnings to mortal probation and, ultimately, exaltation. For Joseph, Genesis 1 was not a static text but a living revelation, continually opened anew by prophetic insight and adaptable to different settings and contexts.

The Prophet's return to the themes of Genesis 1 culminated in his final general conference sermon, the King Follett Discourse, delivered in April 1844.[6] In this bold and sweeping address, Joseph directly engaged the Genesis phrase "in the beginning," arguing that it had been mistranslated and misunderstood. Rather than referring to the absolute beginning, Joseph taught that the opening phrase *berēšît bara' 'elōhîm* in Genesis 1:1 should be rendered "the head one of the Gods brought forth the Gods" in a divine council,[7] thus framing the creation as a deliberative act of divine organization among exalted beings. He also taught that the verb *bara'* did not mean to create from nothing, but to fashion preexisting materials into something new. This reinterpretation also advanced his doctrine that God was once a mortal man who progressed to godhood, and that humanity is of the

---

5. Joseph Smith, "Journal, May 4, 1842," p. 94, and Joseph Smith, "History, 1838–1856, Volume C-1, May 4, 1842," *Joseph Smith Papers*, online at josephsmithpapers.org; Matthew McBride, *A House for the Most High: The Story of the Original Nauvoo Temple* (Salt Lake City: Greg Kofford Books, 2007), 100–103.
6. The discourse was delivered on April 7, 1844, and was recorded by four secretaries. See "Accounts of the 'King Follett Sermon'," *Joseph Smith Papers*, online at josephsmithpapers.org. The first published account of the King Follett Discourse appeared after Joseph's death on August 15, 1844 ("Conference Minutes," *Times and Seasons* 5, no. 15 [August 15, 1844]: 612–617).
7. Joseph Smith, "Discourse, 7 April 1844, as Reported by Willard Richards," p. 68, *Joseph Smith Papers*, online at josephsmithpapers.org, spelling standardized.

same divine species with the potential to follow that path. The King Follett Discourse thus tied Joseph's expansive cosmology and theology of divine plurality directly back to Genesis 1, underscoring how central the creation narrative was to his final and most theologically audacious teachings.

Strictly speaking, Joseph Smith's grammatical claims in the King Follett Discourse concerning the opening verse of the Bible do not align with standard Hebrew syntax. As a result, scholars have generally understood the Prophet's remarks as a form of prophetic expansion or commentary rather than a precise linguistic analysis. Writing in the 1960s, Jewish scholar Louis Zucker observed how "the syntax [Joseph] imposes on [Genesis 1:1] is impossible," yet he also acknowledged that this "free-handling of Hebrew grammar and the language of the Hebrew Bible" was not evidence of ineptitude or deception. Rather, Zucker argued, it showed that Joseph "did not [care] to appear before the world as a meticulous Hebraist. He used the Hebrew as he chose, as an artist, inside his frame of reference, in accordance with his taste, according to the effect he wanted to produce, as a foundation for theological innovations."[8] Recent analysis by Latter-day Saint scholar Matthew Grey reaffirms this view, emphasizing that Joseph's engagement with Hebrew reflects a creative and theological but not strictly technical use of the language.[9]

Nevertheless, Joseph's broader theological insights in the King Follett Discourse resonate in striking ways with what modern biblical scholarship has uncovered about the deep past of ancient Israel. Hebrew scholars since the Middle Ages, for instance, have avowed that *berēʾšît* functions as a temporal clause. Modern studies in bib-

---

8. Louis C. Zucker, "Joseph Smith as a Student of Hebrew," *Dialogue: A Journal of Mormon Thought* 3, no. 2 (1968): 52–53.
9. Matthew J. Grey, "'The Word of the Lord in the Original': Joseph Smith's Study of Hebrew in Kirtland," in *Approaching Antiquity: Joseph Smith and the Ancient World*, edited by Lincoln H. Blumell, Matthew J. Grey, and Andrew H. Hedges (Provo, UT: Religious Studies Center, Brigham Young University; Salt Lake City: Deseret Book, 2015), 249–302; Matthew J. Grey, "Approaching Egyptian Papyri through Biblical Language: Joseph Smith's Use of Hebrew in His Translation of the Book of Abraham," in *Producing Ancient Scripture: Joseph Smith's Translation Projects in the Development of Mormon Christianity*, ed. Michael Hubbard MacKay, Mark Ashurst-McGee, and Brian M. Hauglid (Salt Lake City: University of Utah Press, 2020), 390–451.

lical cosmology further reveal that the earliest strata of the Hebrew Bible often depict God operating within a divine council — a heavenly assembly of divine beings or lesser gods. Several texts in the Hebrew Bible portray divine deliberation and plurality in the heavenly realm, suggesting that Israelite monotheism developed over time from an earlier, more pluralistic theological framework. In addition, the structure and themes of Genesis 1 reflect key elements found in Mesopotamian, Egyptian, and Canaanite material, where the cosmos is organized from a preexisting chaotic substance (typically water) rather than summoned from nothing. Joseph's insistence that matter is eternal and that God "organized" the world rather than created it *ex nihilo* mirrors these ancient conceptions.

Furthermore, Joseph Smith's reading of Genesis 1:26, where God declares "let us make man in our image, after our likeness," illustrates his alignment with ancient conceptions of divinity and humanity. Whereas traditional Christian theology often interprets the *imago Dei* in spiritual or moral terms, Joseph emphasized a literal, embodied likeness between God and humankind, teaching that God possesses a tangible, glorified body (compare to Doctrine and Covenants 130:22–23). This view of divine embodiment was central to Joseph's theology and stood in contrast to the abstract, incorporeal deity of post-Nicene Christianity. His interpretation resonates strongly with certain ancient Near Eastern and early Israelite notions of the image of God, in which kings or humans function as divine representatives and bear a functional or even physical resemblance to deity. Modern biblical scholarship increasingly recognizes *imago Dei* as denoting not only spiritual or moral attributes but also humanity's royal vocation and embodied role within the created order — insights that echo Joseph's expansive vision of divine corporeality and human exaltation.

Though the Prophet's linguistic justifications for his Hebrew interpretations are difficult to sustain under technical scrutiny, his theological instincts and revelatory insights nevertheless anticipated a return to pre-creedal patterns of creation in striking and profound ways — something even non-Latter-day Saint writers have noticed and appreciated. Harold Bloom famously praised Joseph for his "imaginative recapture of crucial elements in the archaic Jewish religion, elements evaded by normative Judaism and by the Church after it." Bloom went on to write how the Prophet's "religious genius always manifested itself through what might be termed his charismatic accuracy," and, further, of "his uncanny recovery of elements in ancient Jewish theurgy that had ceased to be available either to normative Judaism or Christianity."[10] In short, Joseph's teachings align with what many scholars now identify as authentic remnants of ancient concepts embedded within biblical cosmology. His revelatory expansions, though certainly unorthodox by the standards of modern creedal Christianity, situate his teachings in closer continuity with ancient cosmological thought than many of his contemporaries, or even later critics, may have recognized.

Building on Kevin L. Barney's foundational work,[11] this study revisits Joseph Smith's interpretations of Genesis 1 in light of what current scholarship reveals about ancient Near Eastern and biblical cosmology. It examines how the Prophet's teachings align with modern biblical scholarship on three key fronts: the structural ordering of the cosmos in Genesis 1, the *imago Dei* concept with particular emphasis on divine embodiment, and the presence of divine plurality within early Israelite religion. By situating Joseph's insights within these larger scholarly frameworks, this study seeks to show how his theological innovations reflect a meaningful recovery of ancient conceptual patterns, thereby deepening our understanding of his contributions to Latter-day Saint thought.

How Does Genesis 1 Envision Creation?

Genesis 1 presents an intensely structured and theologically rich account of creation. Rather than offering a mythological drama of divine conflict or a modern scientific description of material origins, the narrative unfolds as a deliberate imposition of order, function, and purpose upon a chaotic and formless cosmos. Through patterned language, repeated refrains, and the sequential use of divine speech, the narrative presents creation not merely as a physical act, but as a liturgical and cosmic ordering, culminating in rest and sanctification.

---

10. Harold Bloom, *The American Religion: The Emergence of the Post-Christian Nation* (New York: Touchstone, 1992), 99, 101.
11. Kevin L. Barney, "Examining Six Key Concepts in Joseph Smith's Understanding of Genesis 1:1," *BYU Studies* 39, no. 3 (2000): 107–124; cf. Kevin L. Barney, "Joseph Smith's Emendation of Hebrew Genesis 1:1," *Dialogue: A Journal of Mormon Thought* 30, no. 4 (1997): 102–135.

The creation account begins not with absolute nothingness but with a scene of pre-existent chaos. As will be explored more below, a close reading of the Hebrew syntax in Genesis 1:1–2 supports the translation of verse 1 as a dependent temporal clause: "When God began to create the heavens and the earth...." This reading implies that verse 2 sets the scene of primordial disorder before divine ordering begins in verse 3. Here, in verse 2, the earth was "without form and void" (*tōhû wa bōhū*), darkness (*ḥōšek*) covered the primeval ocean (*těhôm*), and a wind or spirit of God (*rûaḥ 'elōhîm*) hovered over the waters. These terms unmistakably evoke a formless, uninhabitable state, a motif common in ancient Near Eastern cosmogonies.[12] But unlike Babylonian or Canaanite myths, which depict creation as the outcome of divine combat (*Chaoskampf*),[13] Genesis 1 offers a radically different model. God does not struggle with cosmic monsters; he speaks, and creation responds. Divine fiat, not divine warfare, is the instrument of order.

The first act of creation in this framing introduces light and time (Genesis 1:3–5). God declares "let there be light," and it appears. Notably, light is not tied to a physical source — the sun and moon are created only on day four. This prioritization of light underscores its foundational role in this cosmology: it initiates time itself, dividing day from night and setting the rhythm upon which all subsequent

---

12. Menahem Kister, "*Tohu wa-Bohu*, Primordial Elements and *Creatio ex Nihilo*," *Jewish Study Quarterly* 14 (2007): 229–256.
13. See Hermann Gunkel, *Schöpfung und Chaos in Urzeit und Endzeit: Eine religionsgeschichtliche Untersuchung über Gen 1 und Ap Joh 12* (Göttingen: Vandenhoeck and Ruprecht, 1895); David Toshio Tsumura, *Creation and Destruction: A Reappraisal of the Chaoskampf Theory in the Old Testament* (Winona Lake, IN: Eisenbrauns, 2005); Joann Scurlock and Richard H. Beal, eds., *Creation and Chaos: A Reconsideration of Hermann Gunkel's Chaoskampf Hypothesis* (Winona Lake, IN: Eisenbrauns, 2013). Jeffrey M. Bradshaw and Ronan James Head, in their article "The Investiture Panel at Mari and Rituals of Divine Kingship in the Ancient Near East" (from *Studies in the Bible and Antiquity* 4 [2012]: 1–42), argue that Babylonian and Canaanite creation accounts are centrally concerned with the establishment of temples or sacred space. These texts often feature the *Chaoskampf* motif, which bears a general resemblance to the Latter-day Saint concept of a premortal war in heaven (cf. Moses 4:1–4; Abraham 3:27–28; Revelation 12:7–12). While the characters and narrative details differ, the overarching themes align in ways that resonate with Latter-day Saint teachings.

acts of creation depend.[14] By naming "day" and "night," God establishes dominion through language, a theme that recurs throughout the narrative.

On the second day, God creates the *raqiaʿ*, typically translated "firmament" or "expanse" (Genesis 1:6–8). This structure divides the chaotic waters, creating the waters above and waters below the firmament. In the ancient Israelite conception, influenced by broader Near Eastern cosmology, this *raqiaʿ* was envisioned as a solid dome holding back celestial waters.[15] While some modern interpreters have tried to reinterpret the *raqiaʿ* as atmospheric sky, the cultural-linguistic evidence supports understanding it as a firm vault.[16] The division of the waters introduces the vertical ordering of the cosmos, establishing layered space within which life can be sustained.

The third day brings a pivotal transformation: the gathering of the lower waters into seas and the appearance of dry land (Genesis 1:9–13). For the first time, the earth becomes a stable, inhabitable realm. Vegetation emerges, not through planting or cultivation, but by divine command. Importantly, the earth is now portrayed as fertile and self-generating, capable of sustaining life "according to its kind."[17] The theme of fruitfulness is introduced, prefiguring human-

---

14. See the discussion in Cory Crawford, "Light and Space in Genesis 1," *Vetus Testamentum* 68 (2018): 556–580. Since antiquity, interpreters of the Bible have noticed this issue, and one of the more common solutions has been to see the light of Genesis 1:3 as a manifestation of God's glory. See the sources and discussion in James Kugel, *Traditions on the Bible: A Guide to the Bible as It Was at the Start of the Common Era* (Cambridge: Harvard University Press, 1998) 47–48; Elaine H. Pagels, "Exegesis of Genesis 1 in the Gospels of Thomas and John," *Journal of Biblical Literature* 118, no. 3 (1999): 484–486.
15. Paul H. Seely, "The Firmament and the Water Above, Part I: The Meaning of *raqiaʿ* in Gen. 1:6–8," *The Westminster Theological Journal* 53 (1991): 227–240; "The Firmament and the Waters Above, Part II: The Meaning of 'The Water Above the Firmament' in Gen 1:6–8," *The Westminster Theological Journal* 54 (1992): 31–46.
16. Samuel L. Boyd, "A Double-Plated Cosmos? Gen. 1's Cosmology, the Baal Stele, and the Logic of a Firmament of the Earth," *Journal of Ancient Near Eastern Religions* 20, no. 2 (2020), 87–112.
17. The term translated as "kind" (*mîn*) in Hebrew does not have an exact English equivalent (E. König, "Die Bedeutung des hebräischen מִין," *Zeitschrift für die alttestamentliche Wissenschaft* 31 [1911]: 133–46; A. Rahel Davidson Schafer, "The 'Kinds' of Genesis 1: What is the Meaning of *Mîn*?" *Journal of*

ity's own commission. This day also introduces the first signs of ecological function, not just form: the land and plant life are designed to perpetuate themselves.

On the fourth day, God populates the *raqiaʻ* with celestial luminaries — the sun, moon, and stars — designated to govern time (Genesis 1:14–19). These are "for signs, and for seasons, and for days, and years." The Hebrew word *môʻădîm*, translated "seasons," often refers to liturgical festivals, hinting at a theological calendar.[18] The decision to avoid naming these luminaries (for example, using "greater light" and "lesser light") may subtly demythologize ancient astral deities.[19] Here, celestial bodies are not divine but subordinate instruments in God's ordering of sacred time.

With space now structured, life begins to fill it. On the fifth day (Genesis 1:20–23), God creates creatures of the sea and sky. The narrative notes the creation of "great sea creatures" (*tannînîm*; KJV "great whales"), a term often associated with mythological sea monsters in ancient Near Eastern literature.[20] Yet here, these beings are not cha-

---

the *Adventist Theological Society* 14, no. 1 [Spring 2003]: 86–100). Probably the closest modern approximation would be something like "species" in the sense of broad taxonomic likeness, but modern readers would do well to avoid anachronistically imposing modern scientific categories onto pre-scientific cultures such as ancient Israel. See the discussion in Paul H. Seely, "The Meaning of *Mîn*, 'Kind'," *Science and Christian Belief* 9, no. 1 (1997): 47–56; C. John Collins, *Reading Genesis Well: Navigating History, Poetry, Science, and Truth in Genesis 1–11* (Grand Rapids, MI: Zondervan, 2018), 155–156.

18. Bill T. Arnold, "Genesis 1 as Holiness Preamble," in *Let us Go up to Zion: Essays in Honour of H. G. M. Williamson on the Occasion of his Sixty-Fifth Birthday*, ed. Iain Provan and Mark J. Boda, Vetus Testamentum Supplements, 153 (Leiden: Brill, 2012), 339–340.
19. Ronald Hendel, *Genesis 1–11: A New Translation with Introduction and Commentary*, Anchor Yale Bible Commentaries, Genesis Series, 2 vols. (New Haven: Yale University Press, 2024), 1:124.
20. John Day, *God's Conflict with the Dragon and the Sea: Echoes of a Canaanite Myth in the Old Testament* (Cambridge: Cambridge University Press, 1985). At Ugarit, *tnn* (*tu-un-na-nu*) are a class of sea drakes (Gregorio del Olmo Lete and Joaquín Sanmartín, ed. *A Dictionary of the Ugaritic Language in the Alphabetic Tradition*, trans. Wilfred G. E. Watson [Leiden: Brill, 2015], 860; Mark S. Smith and Wayne T. Pitard, *The Ugaritic Baal Cycle: Introduction with Text, Translation and Commentary of KTU/CAT 1.3–1.4*, Supplements to Vetus Testamentum 114 [Leiden: Brill, 2009], 2:248–249, 253–255; J. A. Emerton, "Leviathan and LTN: The Vocalization of the Ugaritic Word for the Dragon,"

otic threats but part of God's harmonious order. All creatures are commanded to be fruitful and multiply, echoing the command soon given to humans. This marks the first explicit blessing in the narrative, emphasizing God's desire for the perpetuation of life.

Day six represents the climax of creation (Genesis 1:24-31). Land animals are created in broad categories such as livestock, creeping things, and," wild beasts, all fitting into the increasingly structured taxonomy of creation. But the true apex is humanity. Unlike other creatures, humanity is not made "according to its kind," but in the *image* (*ṣelem*) and *likeness* (*dĕmût*) of God. This sets humankind apart both ontologically and functionally (more on this below). Humans are tasked with "subduing" the earth and "having dominion" over all living creatures, roles reminiscent of royal ideology in the ancient Near East where kings were described as the image of the gods. The *imago Dei* thus conveys both form and function: humans resemble God in form and they represent him in authority.[21] Unlike other creatures, humans are addressed directly by God, blessed, and given stewardship over creation. The command to "be fruitful and multiply" extends the theme of sacred generativity. Humanity becomes the divinely appointed steward of an ordered cosmos.

The creation narrative concludes not with another act of forming or filling, but with divine rest (Genesis 2:1-4a). God "rests" (*šāvat*) on the seventh day, blesses it, and sanctifies it. The focus changes from space to time. The seventh day is set apart as holy, signaling that the culmination of creation is not merely function but communion. In this theology, creation becomes a cosmic temple — a sacred space-time matrix into which God invites humanity, the Sabbath marking fulfillment and consecration.[22]

Vetus Testamentum 32 [July 1982]: 327-331).

21. David Noel Freedman, "The Status of Humanity in the Cosmos According to the Hebrew Bible," in *On Human Nature: The Jerusalem Center Symposium*, ed. Truman G. Madsen, David Noel Freedman, and Pam Fox Kuhlken (Ann Arbor, MI: Pryor Pettengill Publishers, 2004), 9-25.

22. Modern scholarship widely recognizes Genesis 1:1-2:4a as essentially a narrative about God inaugurating his cosmic temple through creation. Moshe Weinfeld popularized this interpretation in "Sabbath, Temple and the Enthronement of the Lord — The Problem of the Sitz im Leben of Genesis 1:1-2:3," in *Mélanges Bibliques et Orientaux en L'Honeur de M. Henri Cazelles*, ed. Mathias Delcor and André Caquot (Neukirchen-Vluyn: Neukirchner

Genesis 1 thus presents a thoroughly ordered, hierarchical cosmos in which God systematically differentiates, assigns roles, and brings structure to a chaotic beginning. Each creative act unfolds in sequence, marked by divine speech and concluded with judgment ("it was good") and closure. The emphasis throughout is on the transformation of disorder into a meaningful, life-sustaining world where each element has a place and purpose. What's more, "the results of each day of Creation are symbolically reflected in temple furnishings," so that "what came of it was an earthly temple that was laid out and furnished in symbolic likeness of the heavenly temple."[23] The narrative is thus not primarily concerned with how the material universe came into being, but rather with how it came to function as an ordered, sacred space.[24] Humanity stands at the center of this hierocentric vision, not as an afterthought, but as God's image-bearers, stewards, and covenant partners. And at the summit of the structure is the Sabbath, a sign that creation is not

---

Verlag, 1981), 501–512. See additionally Jon D. Levenson, "The Temple and the World," *Journal of Religion* 64, no. 3 (1984): 275–298; Howard N. Wallace, "Genesis 2:1–3 — Creation and Sabbath," *Pacifica: Australasian Theological Studies* 1 (1988): 235–250; Jon D. Levenson, *Creation and the Persistence of Evil: The Jewish Drama of Divine Omnipotence* (Princeton, NJ: Princeton University Press, 1988), 78–99; Walton, *Genesis 1 as Ancient Cosmology*, 100–119, 178–192; William P. Brown, *The Seven Pillars of Creation: The Bible, Science, and the Ecology of Wonder* (New York: Oxford University Press, 2010), 33–79; L. Michael Morales, *The Tabernacle Pre-Figured: Cosmic Mountain Ideology in Genesis and Exodus*, Biblical Tools and Studies 15 (Leuven: Peeters, 2012), 76–85; Kivatsi Jonathan Kavusa, "Creation as a Cosmic Temple: Reading Genesis 1:1–2:4a in Light of Willie van Heerden's Ecological Insights," *Journal for Semitics* 30, no. 1 (2021): 1–23; Matthijs de Jong, "The Seventh Day in Genesis 2:2–3 and the Change from Kingship to Sabbath," in *Congress Volume Aberdeen 2019*, ed. Grant Macaskill, Christl M. Maier, and Joachim Schaper, Supplements to Vetus Testamentum 192 (Leiden: Brill, 2022), 17–49; Christopher D. Kou, "God's Statue in the Cosmic Temple: צֶלֶם and דְמוּת in Genesis and the Plural Cohortative in Genesis 1:26 in Light of the Sanctuary Setting and Christological Telos," *Journal of the Evangelical Theological Society* 66, no. 1 (2023): 11–31.

23. Jeffrey M. Bradshaw, *The First Days and the Last Days: A Verse-by-Verse Commentary on the Book of Moses and JS-Matthew in Light of the Temple* (Orem, UT: The Interpreter Foundation, 2021), 30.
24. See especially John H. Walton, *Genesis 1 as Ancient Cosmology* (Winona Lake, IN: Eisenbrauns, 2011).

just functional but also holy. The cosmos is a temple; time is sacred; and creation is the stage upon which God and humanity meet.

CREATION FROM NOTHING

Latter-day Saints are familiar with this creation narrative through both the Bible and its dramatized retelling in the temple. The narrative, however, is far more theologically rich and structurally intricate than a surface reading in translation might suggest. This is evident even from the very first verse: "In the beginning God created the heaven and the earth" (KJV). The underlying Hebrew of the opening phrase — *berēšît bārā' 'elōhîm* — is notoriously ambiguous. While traditional readings render this as an absolute beginning followed by a complete action, many scholars since at least the Middle Ages have argued that *berēšît* is perhaps best understood as a construct form, meaning "in the beginning of ..." rather than "in the beginning."[25] This would make the phrase an adverbial temporal clause, rendering the passage something like "when God began to create the heavens and the earth ..." or "at the beginning of God creating the heavens and the earth" rather than asserting a definitive beginning point.[26] The next verse then introduces the primordial state of the cosmos at the time of God's inauguration of the creation. This reading emphasizes that Genesis opens not with absolute nothingness, but with an existing chaotic state awaiting divine organization, a feature that parallels ancient Near Eastern cosmogonies like the Babylonian Enuma Elish, where creation begins with the taming and structuring of primordial waters.[27]

The verb *bārā'*, traditionally translated "to create," has likewise received renewed scrutiny.[28] It occurs exclusively with God as its sub-

---

25. As early as the twelfth century, Ibn Ezra interpreted *bārā'* as being in construct with *berēšît*. H. Norman Strickman and Arthur M. Silver, trans., *Ibn Ezra's Commentary on the Pentateuch: Genesis (Bereshit)* (New York, NY: Menorah Publishing, 1988), 21–22.
26. Mark S. Smith, *The Priestly Vision of Genesis 1* (Minneapolis: Fortress Press, 2010), 43–45; Hendel, *Genesis 1–11*, 107–109.
27. Nahum Sarna, *Genesis*, JPS Torah Commentary, 5 vols. (Philadelphia: The Jewish Publication Society, 1989), 1:5.
28. Ellen Van Wolde, "Why the Verb ברא Does Not Mean 'to Create' in Genesis 1.1–24a," Journal for the Study of the Old Testament 34, no. 1 (2009): 4–23; "Separation and Creation in Genesis 1 and Psalm 104: A Continuation of the

ject in the Hebrew Bible, but its semantic range does not necessarily denote creation from nothing (*ex nihilo*). Instead, modern scholars argue that *bārā'* often refers to acts of differentiation and separation, or otherwise creative activity.[29] Genesis 1 repeatedly describes God separating elements — light from darkness, waters above from waters below, sea from dry land — suggesting that *bārā'* emphasizes God's role in assigning boundaries, roles, and purposes rather than bringing material entities into being from nonexistence. This is reinforced by the fact that many of the entities named in Genesis 1 (for example, "the deep," "waters," "earth") appear already present in verse 2. Thus, creation in Genesis 1 is depicted less as a moment of ontological origin and more as a divine ordering of space, time, and life into a harmonious and functioning cosmos. This view of creation as ordering and assigning function also explains the literary structure of Genesis 1. The narrative follows a precise pattern, as we have seen: over six days, God establishes distinct realms (light/darkness, sky/sea/land) and then populates them (celestial bodies, birds and fish, land animals and humans). The pairing of realms and their inhabitants over two triads of days (Days 1–3 forming the environments, Days 4–6 filling them) reflects a sophisticated literary and theological organization. Each day's activity is introduced by divine speech, followed by a command, its execution, a declaration that it was good, and the naming of the day. The result is a liturgically stylized and theologically loaded vision of the cosmos — not a scientific blueprint, but a theological proclamation of divine sovereignty, cosmic order, and the goodness of creation.

This reading of Genesis 1, which enjoys broad acceptance among modern biblical scholars across denominational lines, naturally calls into question the notion that Genesis 1 teaches *creatio ex nihilo* — one of the most enduring theological assumptions about the text. This view, dominant in much of Jewish and Christian tradition, hinges largely on the traditional reading of Genesis 1:1 as a standalone, absolute statement. However, the grammatical shift discussed above significantly alters the theological implications of the passage, aligning it

---

Discussion of the Verb ברא," *Vetus Testamentum* 67, no. 4 (2017): 611–647; Ellen van Wolde and Robert Rezetko, "Semantica and the Semantics of ברא: A Rejoinder to the Arguments of Advanced by B. Becking and M. Korpel," *Journal of Hebrew Scriptures* 11 (2011): 2–39.

29. Walton, *Genesis 1 as Ancient Cosmology*, 127–133.

more closely with ancient Near Eastern creation accounts where gods shape a preexisting, chaotic cosmos into order, rather than bringing matter into existence from nothing.[30] This is reinforced by the second verse of Genesis. The elements in this verse appear to exist prior to God's first creative act of calling forth light. The text, in other words, presumes the presence of chaotic, unstructured matter before divine ordering begins. "Primeval stuff already exists in verses 1–2," notes Marc Zvi Brettler, "and the text shows no concern for how it originated."[31] Instead, the focus is on what God does with it: separating, assigning roles, and bringing it into a structured, purposeful existence. This literary and theological architecture suggests that Genesis 1 is primarily concerned with the establishment of cosmic order, not the metaphysical origins of matter.

While later Jewish and Christian theology did develop the concept of creation *ex nihilo*, this occurred well after the composition of Genesis.[32] Articulation of the doctrine appears no earlier than in Second Temple literature, such as apparently 2 Maccabees 7:28,[33] and was further developed by early Christian thinkers like Theophilus of Antioch in the second century CE.[34] These later theological developments were often formulated in dialogue with Greek philosophical metaphysics and in opposition to competing cosmologies, such as Gnosticism, that

---

30. It should be further noted that some who accept the traditional reading of Genesis 1:1 nevertheless question whether such mandates a view of creation *ex nihilo* (for example, John Day, *From Creation to Babel: Studies in Genesis 1–11* [London: Bloomsbury, 2013], 8.)
31. Marc Zvi Brettler, *How to Read the Bible* (Philadelphia: The Jewish Publication Society, 2005), 41.
32. Gerhard May, *Schöpfung aus dem Nichts: Die Entstehung der Lehre von der Creatio ex Nihilo*, Arbeiten zur Kirchengeschichte 48 (Berlin: De Gruyter, 1978); Gary A. Anderson and Markus Bockmuehl, eds., *Creation ex Nihilo: Origins, Development, Contemporary Challenges* (Notre Dame, IN: University of Notre Dame Press, 2018); Nathan J. Chambers, *Reconsidering Creation ex Nihilo in Genesis 1*, Journal of Theological Interpretation Supplements 19 (University Park, PA: Eisenbrauns, 2020).
33. Note Robert Doran, *2 Maccabees: A Critical Commentary*, Hermeneia (Minneapolis: Fortress Press, 2012), 161, who questions whether this passage actually teaches creation *ex nihilo*.
34. James Noel Hubler, "Creatio ex Nihilo: Matter, Creation, and the Body in Classical and Christian Philosophy Through Aquinas," (PhD diss., University of Pennsylvania, 1995).

proposed eternal matter independent of God.³⁵ The creation narrative in Genesis 1 thus does not teach creation from nothing. Rather, it presents a theological vision in which God brings order, structure, and purpose to a preexistent, chaotic world. The emphasis is on functional ontology — how things work and what roles they play — rather than on the material origins of the cosmos as such. This reading is not only consistent with the text itself but also with broader ancient Near Eastern cosmological frameworks. Genesis 1, then, should be read as a hymn of divine sovereignty and order, not a metaphysical treatise on the origin of matter.

Imago Dei — Humans in the Likeness of God

Genesis 1:26–27 presents one of the most profound theological declarations in all of scripture: "Let us make man in our image, after our likeness. ... So God created man in his own image, in the image of God created he him; male and female created he them." Few verses in the Bible have provoked as much sustained theological and scholarly reflection as this passage.³⁶ Across Jewish and Christian history, schol-

---

35. May, *Schöpfung aus dem Nichts*, 40–63, 151–182; Keith Norman, "Ex Nihilo: The Development of the Doctrines of God and Creation in Early Christianity," *BYU Studies* 17, no. 3 (1977): 301–303; Frances Young, "'Creatio Ex Nihilo': A Context for the Emergence of the Christian Doctrine of Creation," *Scottish Journal of Theology* 44, no. 1 (1991): 139–151; Blake T. Ostler, "Out of Nothing: A History of Creation *ex Nihilo* in Early Christian Thought," *FARMS Review* 17, no. 2 (2005): 253–320; J. C. O'Neill, "How Early is the Doctrine of 'Creatio Ex Nihilo'?" *Journal of Theological Studies* 53, no. 2 (2002): 449–465.
36. See J. Richard Middleton, *The Liberating Image: The Imago Dei in Genesis 1* (Grand Rapids, MI: Brazos Press, 2005); Andreas Schüle, "Made in the ›Image of God‹: The Concepts of Divine Images in Gen 1–3," *Zeitschrift für die alttestamentliche Wissenschaft* 117 (2005): 1–20; Brent A. Strawn, "Comparative Approaches: History, Theory, and the Image of God," in *Methods Matter: Essays on the Interpretation of the Hebrew Bible in Honor of David L. Petersen*, ed. Joel M. LeMon and Kent Harold Richards, SBL Resources for Biblical Study 56 (Atlanta, GA: SBL Press, 2009), 117–142; C. L. Crouch, "Genesis 1:26–7 as a Statement of Humanity's Divine Parentage," *Journal of Theological Studies* 61 (2010): 1–15; Catherine L. McDowell, *The Image of God in the Garden of Eden: The Creation of Humankind in Genesis 2:5–3:24 in Light of the mīs pî pīt pî and wpt-r Rituals of Mesopotamia and Ancient Egypt* (Winona Lake, IN: Eisenbrauns, 2015); Tyson L. Putthoff, *Gods and Humans in the Ancient Near East* (Cambridge: Cambridge University Press, 2020); David M. Carr, "Competing Construals of Human Relations with 'Animal' Others in the

ars and theologians have pondered the meaning of the *imago Dei* and what it implies about the nature of humanity, the nature of God, and the purpose of creation itself.[37]

The word translated as "image" (*ṣelem*) in Genesis 1:26–27 commonly refers in other biblical and ancient Near Eastern contexts to statues, figures, and effigies meant to visibly represent a deity or king. Similarly, the word for "likeness" (*dĕmût*) reinforces a sense of resemblance or similitude, whether in form or function. The term *ṣelem* appears seventeen times in the Hebrew Bible, often referring to carved or cast images such as statues or effigies (as in Numbers 33:52; 1 Samuel 6:5; 2 Kings 11:18; Ezekiel 7:20; Ezekiel 16:17). Its counterpart *dĕmût*, used twenty-five times, similarly denotes form, shape, or likeness, and is used to describe modeled patterns or visual resemblances (as in 2 Kings 16:10; Ezekiel 1:5, 10, 20, 22, 28). Thus the most immediately apparent reading of the Hebrew of Genesis 1:26–27 points to something visual and even perhaps tangible.[38] As Richard J. Clifford explains, "the most natural explanation" of this language "is that humans resemble God because they resemble heavenly beings who resemble God."[39] Benjamin Sommer concurs, emphasizing that these terms "pertain specifically to the physical contours of God," especially when viewed through the lens of their broader Semitic usage.[40] So too does David Noel Freedman, who comments, "Certainly the intention [of Genesis 1:26] is to say that God and man share a common physical

---

Primeval History (Genesis 1–11)," *Journal of Biblical Literature* 140, no. 2 (2021): 251–269.

37. D. J. A. Clines, "The Image of God in Man," *Tyndale Bulletin* 19, no. 1 (1968): 53–103; Daniel Simango, "The Imago Dei (Gen 1:26–27): A History of Interpretation from Philo to the Present," *Studia Historiae Ecclesiasticae* 42, no. 1 (2016): 172–190; Yair Lorberbaum, *In God's Image: Myth, Theology, and Law in Classical Judaism* (Cambridge: Cambridge University Press, 2015).
38. Phillis A. Bird, "'Male and Female He Created Them': Gen 1:27b in the Context of the Priestly Account of Creation," *Harvard Theological Review* 74, no. 2 (1981): 139–144; Henri Cazelles, "Selem et demût en Gn 1,26–28," in *La vie de la Parole: De l'Ancien au Nouveau Testament* (Paris: Desclée, 1987), 103–106.
39. Richard J. Clifford, "The Divine Assembly in Genesis 1–11," in *Sibyls, Scriptures, and Scrolls: John Collins at Seventy*, ed. Joel Baden, Hindy Najman, and Eibert Tigchelaar, Supplements to the Journal for the Study of Judaism (Leiden: Brill, 2017), 278–279.
40. Benjamin D. Sommer, *The Bodies of God and the World of Ancient Israel* (Cambridge: Cambridge University Press, 2009), 69.

appearance."[41] W. Randall Garr goes so far as to say the language in these verses suggests how "angelic gods ... look like God, and they look like men; the gods' shape is intermediate between the two worlds they connect."[42] The two terms are thus essentially synonymous and "indicate that human beings resemble God," even if they do not on their own define the precise nature of that resemblance.[43]

That nature is clarified somewhat by Genesis 5:3, which provides a compelling analogy. There, Seth is said to have been begotten "in [Adam's] own likeness, after his image," using the same Hebrew terms *děmût* and *ṣelem*. Just as Seth physically and spiritually resembles his father Adam, so too do human beings resemble their divine Parent. The logic is generational: divine similitude is passed down as a parent's image is passed to a child. This suggests not only a relational bond between God and humanity, but a real continuity of nature and form.[44] As sons and daughters inherit the form and features of their earthly parents, so too do they bear the imprint of divine parentage. God's image is thus transmitted not metaphorically, but through the very structure of humanity's spiritual and physical being.[45]

The declaration in Genesis that humanity was created "in his image" and "according to his likeness" most likely draws upon a conception in which God is understood to possess a discernible, even visible form that humans were made to resemble. The use of the first-person plural in this verse (more on this below) additionally implies that God, divine beings, and humans all share this common morphology.[46] In this light, the text suggests more than metaphor or

---

41. Freedman, "The Status and Role of Humanity," 16.
42. W. Randall Garr, *In His Own Image and Likeness: Humanity, Divinity, and Monotheism*, Culture and History of the Ancient Near East 15 (Leiden: Brill, 2003), 88.
43. Paul Sands, "The Imago Dei as Vocation," *Evangelical Quarterly* 82, no. 1 (2010): 29.
44. Catherine McDowell, "Human Identity and Purpose Redefined: Gen 1:26-28 and 2:5-25 in Context," *Advances in Ancient, Biblical, and Near Eastern Research* 1, no. 3 (Autumn 2021): 29-44.
45. Crouch, "Genesis 1:26-7 as a Statement of Humanity's Divine Parentage," 1-15.
46. Sommer, *The Bodies of God and the World of Ancient Israel*, 69. Garr, *In His Own Image and Likeness*, 88, states how Genesis 1:26-27 "recalls a morphological characteristic of gods," suggesting "the concrete, corporeal reality of human beings in a concrete, physical world suggests that the representation implied

abstraction; it strongly points toward divine embodiment or corporeality. J. Maxwell Miller acknowledges how it is "difficult to avoid" the anthropomorphic implications of these verses, while Yair Lorberbaum puts an even finer point on it by writing how "the passage in Genesis [1:26] confronts the deniers of anthropomorphism with an almost insurmountable barrier."[47] Indeed, throughout the Hebrew Bible, God is regularly described in explicitly anthropomorphic terms: he has a face (Exodus 33:11), hands (Isaiah 65:2), and feet (Exodus 24:10). These are not isolated poetic devices but part of a foundational biblical conception in which God appears so overtly human in form that he is at times even mistaken for a human being (for example, in Genesis 18:1–2; Genesis 32:24–30; Judges 13:6, 20).[48]

One particularly vivid example of this is found in Ezekiel 1:26–28, where the prophet describes a vision of God enthroned above the firmament. The figure Ezekiel sees is said to have "the likeness [děmût] of the appearance of a human being." As scholar Patrick D. Miller observes, this passage "very effectively" demonstrates that děmût can convey anthropomorphic shape and visible form.[49] While later Jewish and Christian theology increasingly moved toward abstract, incorporeal conceptions of God, the cosmology in Genesis maintains a view that allows for a God with a form, and a humanity that reflects that form. This further reinforces the view that the *imago Dei* includes literal morphological dimensions. Human beings are not only spiritually akin to God but are patterned after his physical appearance, both body and countenance.

The second key element of the *imago Dei* in Genesis 1:26 pertains to status and function. That humanity is made in God's image distinguishes human beings from all other creatures and signals their elevated role in creation. In ancient Mesopotamian and Egyptian con-

---

in v. 26 include a physical one."
47. J. Maxwell Miller, "In the 'Image' and 'Likeness' of God," *Journal of Biblical Literature* 91, no. 3 (1972): 291; Lorberbaum, *In God's Image*, 48.
48. See further Sommer, *The Bodies of God and the World of Ancient Israel*; Putthoff, *Gods and Humans in the Ancient Near East*; Charles Halton, *A Human-Shaped God: Theology of an Embodied God* (Louisville, KY: Westminster John Knox Press, 2021); Francesca Stavrakopoulou, *God: An Anatomy* (New York: Knopf, 2022).
49. Miller, "In the 'Image' and 'Likeness' of God," 291–292.

texts, kings were frequently described as bearing the image or likeness of the gods as a justification for their rule.[50] Genesis extends this royal imagery beyond monarchs to encompass all of humanity, so that every man and woman is made in the image of God and therefore shares in a divine commission to govern the world. "According to the meaning of the Hebrew word ṣelem," note Karl Löning and Erich Zenger, "human beings are to be in the world as a kind of living image or statue of God," and are thereby the agents of his power in a kingly role on the earth. They explain:

> A look into Egyptian and Mesopotamian culture, where the duties of the royal office were often represented by the concept of the king as the image of the creator God, opens up another nuance involved in calling the human being an image of God. Understood in this way, the primary responsibility of the royal office is to defend the order of society against external and internal enemies as well as to help the weak, above all, to attain their rights. While in the Egyptian tradition the *king* is the "image of God" on the basis of his royal office, in the biblical story of creation this dignity and responsibility belong to *all* human beings without distinction. The concept is here practically "democratized": not because of *extraordinary* achievement or responsibilities, but as *human beings* all are royal images of God.[51]

This idea is made explicit in the dominion mandate of Genesis 1:28, where humanity is commanded to "subdue" (*kābaš*) the earth and "have dominion" (*rādâ*) over all living things. Humanity's role is not merely passive; it is an active participation in divine rule that includes a call to stewardship over the earth.[52] "Being the image of God

---

50. Middleton, *The Liberating Image*, 93–145.
51. Karl Löning and Erich Zenger, *To Begin With, God Created...: Biblical Theologies of Creation*, trans. Omar Kaste (Collegeville, MN: The Liturgical Press, 2000), 108.
52. Freedman, "The Status and Role of Humanity," 17, offers an important reflection on the language of this passage: "Humanity has achieved dominance and control [of the earth], and the time has now come to exercise responsibility and care for the creation over which we have been placed as agents of the Most High. Surely with authority goes an equal measure of answerability, and the time has come with urgency for showing guardianship and nurture for creation and creatures, for renewal and restoration that formerly was used in destruction and devastation, in conquest and abandonment."

determines Adam's role and place within the cosmos," notes Andreas Schüle, and this image is integrally connected to humanity's divinely ordained rulership over the earth.[53] Similarly, Crouch argues that the concept of *imago Dei* is rooted in the ideology of kingship and that being made in God's image authorizes humans to uphold cosmic and moral order as God's stewards on earth.[54] Thus, taken together, these two dimensions of the *imago Dei* — corporeality and status — present a holistic view of humanity in Genesis 1. Human beings are depicted as both physically resembling God and functionally representing him. While later interpreters have tended to emphasize one aspect over the other, the cosmology of Genesis 1 appears to hold both in balance. The account affirms that humans are at once embodied reflections of the divine and vicegerents over the created order.

Divine Plurality in Israelite Cosmology

The opening clause of Genesis 1:26 has attracted theological and linguistic scrutiny due to its plural construction.[55] The English "let us make" of verse 26 is a single Hebrew verb — *naʿăśeh*. It is a cohortative in the first-person plural, clearly indicating that God is addressing more than one party. (This is further confirmed by the plural possessive pronoun "our" also used in the verse.) Yet the identity of this audience is not specified within the text, inviting a range of interpretive possibilities. One traditional explanation that goes back to at least the Middle Ages posits that God is using the *pluralis majestatis* or "royal we," a rhetorical device in which monarchs or sovereigns speak in the plural to reflect majesty, dignity, or authority.[56] However, this explanation is problematic from a philological standpoint. There is scant evidence that such a linguistic convention existed in ancient

---

53. Schüle, "Made in the ›Image of God‹," 5.
54. C. L. Crouch, "Made in the Image of God: The Creation of אדם, the Commission of the King and the *Chaoskampf* of YHWH," *Journal of Ancient Near Eastern Religions* 16 (2016): 9.
55. Jürg Hutzli, *The Origins of P: Literary Profiles and Strata of the Priestly Texts in Genesis 1–Exodus 40*, Forschungen zum Alten Testament 164 (Tübingen: Mohr Siebeck, 2023), 51–52.
56. Matthew Oseka, "History of Jewish Interpretation of Genesis 1:26, 3:5, 3:22 in the Middle Ages," *Scriptura* 117, no. 1 (2018): 15; Jarl Fossum, "Gen 1,26 and 2,7 in Judaism, Samaritanism, and Gnosticism," *Journal for the Study of Judaism* 16, no. 2 (1985): 202–239.

Hebrew.[57] Paul Joüon and Takamitsu Muraoka declare bluntly that "the *we* of majesty does not exist in Hebrew" verbs, although they do point out that Hebrew recognizes a plural of majesty in nouns.[58] The only plausible example of a *pluralis majestatis* in the entire biblical corpus appears in Aramaic, not Hebrew, in a letter from the Persian king (Ezra 4:18). Nowhere in the Hebrew Bible does God consistently or demonstrably speak in this manner, and thus the *pluralis majestatis* fails to provide a satisfactory account for the grammar of Genesis 1:26.

Gerhard F. Hasel rejects this common explanation and proposes the concept of a "plural of fullness," meaning the phrase reflects an inner complexity within the divine being.[59] According to Hasel, this plural form "supposes that there is within the divine Being the distinction of personalities, a plurality within the deity" and thus anticipates, in embryonic form, the Christian doctrine of the Trinity.[60] For Hasel and others working within a Trinitarian framework, this interpretation offers theological continuity with later Christian orthodoxy by retrojecting divine plurality into the inner life of a singular deity. However, this reading is problematic from a historical-critical perspective. As John Day points out, this proposal involves "reading back into the text a Christian theological idea which evolved only much later."[61] The doctrine of the Trinity was a product of centuries of post-biblical theological reflection and ecumenical controversy. To assert that the author of Genesis embedded this idea within Genesis 1:26 is to anachronistically impose a fully developed Christian dogma onto an Israelite text that predates these theological developments by several centuries.

A more plausible and widely accepted view among modern biblical scholars is that the plural speech of Genesis 1:26 reflects a consultation with the divine council, a well-established concept across

---

57. Patrick D. Miller, *Genesis 1-11: Studies in Structure and Theme*, Journal for the Study of the Old Testament Supplement 8 (Sheffield: Department of Biblical Studies, University of Sheffield, 1978), 10–11.
58. Paul Joüon and Takamitsu Muraoka, *A Grammar of Biblical Hebrew*, 2nd rev. ed. (Rome: Gregorian and Biblical Press, 2011), 347, 469.
59. Gerhard F. Hasel, "The Meaning of 'Let Us' in Gn 1:26," *Andrews University Seminary Studies* 13, no. 1 (1975): 58–66.
60. Hasel, "The Meaning of 'Let Us' in Gn 1:26," 65.
61. John Day, *From Creation to Babel: Studies in Genesis 1–11* (London: Bloomsbury, 2013), 11.

numerous passages in the Hebrew Bible.[62] The divine council refers to the assembly of heavenly beings, subordinate to the high God, who serve as messengers, advisors, and participants in the administration of the cosmos. This celestial bureaucracy is not unique to Israelite religion; it reflects a broader ancient Near Eastern cosmological pattern where chief deities preside over divine assemblies.[63] In the Israelite context, the divine council appears in vivid and unmistakable terms. 1 Kings 22:19–22 presents perhaps the clearest depiction: the prophet Micaiah recounts a vision in which he "saw the Lord sitting on his throne, and all the host of heaven standing by him." In this scene, God consults his court on how to entice King Ahab, and a spirit who "stood before the Lord" volunteers a plan. This narrative demonstrates divine deliberation and agency among the heavenly host, even as God retains ultimate sovereignty. Similarly, Job 1:6 and 2:1 portray "the sons of God" (*bene 'elōhîm*) assembling before the Lord, with Satan or "the adversary" (*ha śāṭān*) among them. These scenes underscore the hierarchical and judicial nature of the council, where decisions about earthly affairs are weighed and administered.

Psalm 82 adds a further layer of complexity to this notion of the divine council. It opens with the striking statement: "God [*'elōhîm*] has taken his place in the divine council; in the midst of the gods [*'elōhîm*] he holds judgment" (verse 1, NRSV). Here, *'elōhîm* appears to

---

62. Gerald Cooke, "The Sons of (the) God(s)," *Zeitschrift für die alttestamentliche Wissenschaft* 35, no. 1 (1964): 22–23; Miller, *Genesis 1–11*, 9–27; David M. Carr, *The Formation of Genesis 1–11: Biblical and Other Precursors* (New York: Oxford University Press, 2020), 21–22, 25; Hendel, *Genesis 1–11*, 128–129; Day, *From Creation to Babel*, 12–13; Ellen van Wolde, *Reframing Biblical Studies: When Language and Text Meet Culture, Cognition, and Context* (Winona Lake, IN: Eisenbrauns, 2009), 192–196; Mark S. Smith, *The Early History of God: Yahweh and the Other Deities in Ancient Israel*, 2nd ed. (Grand Rapids, MI: Eerdmans, 2002), 143–144; Garr, *In His Own Image and Likeness*, 88. See also Stephen O. Smoot, "The Divine Council in the Hebrew Bible and the Book of Mormon," *Interpreter: A Journal of Latter-day Saint Faith and Scholarship* 27 (2017): 155–180.

63. E. Theodore Mullen, Jr., *The Divine Council in Canaanite and Early Hebrew Literature*, Harvard Semitic Monographs 24 (Chico, CA: Scholars Press, 1980); Lowell K. Handy, *Among the Host of Heaven: The Syro-Palestinian Pantheon as Bureaucracy* (Winona Lake, IN: Eisenbrauns, 1994); John Day, *Yahweh and the Gods and Goddesses of Canaan*, Journal for the Study of the Old Testament Supplement Series 265 (Sheffield, GB: Sheffield Academic Press, 2000).

refer both to the God of Israel and to other divine beings who are held accountable by him. The psalm portrays God as presiding over a council of lesser divinities, criticizing their injustice, and declaring their mortality as an assertion of divine supremacy within a structured heavenly order. Isaiah 6:1–8 likewise reflects divine council imagery. The prophet sees the Lord enthroned in the temple, surrounded by seraphim who proclaim his holiness. The Lord's question in verse 8, "Whom shall I send, and who will go for us?" echoes the plural language of Genesis 1:26 and evokes the deliberative dynamic of the divine council. The structure of the scene follows the pattern of a divine sovereign addressing his court before commissioning a task.

Seen in this light, the plural speech of Genesis 1:26 and elsewhere in Genesis, such as in the Babel account (Genesis 10:32–11:9), can be understood as a moment of divine deliberation within the heavenly court. Richard J. Clifford has commented on "the persistent presence of heavenly beings in the creation of 'heaven and earth'" in the book of Genesis. He identifies no fewer than seven instances in Genesis 1–11 that suggest the involvement of a divine "entourage," as he calls it.[64] These references, while sometimes subtle, point to a recurring motif in the early chapters of Genesis: God's creative and administrative actions unfold in dialogue with a populated celestial realm, reinforcing the notion that divine plurality was integral to the religious imagination of ancient Israel.

This does not necessarily imply that the members of the council in Genesis share in the actual act of creation, since verse 27 shifts decisively to singular verbs and pronouns: "So God created man in his own image." The creation itself is God's alone, but the consultation acknowledges the reality of a populated heavenly realm in which God acts in relationship to other divine beings.[65] This literary structure —

---

64. Clifford, "The Divine Assembly in Genesis 1–11," 276, identifying the following passages: Genesis 1:26; Genesis 3:5, 22–24; Genesis 6:2, 4; Genesis 11:7; and "arguably" Genesis 5:22–24.

65. Michaela Bauks, "Gottesbild und Menschenbild: Zum Spannungsverhältnis von priesterschriftlichem Monotheismus und mythischen Versatzstücken in Gen 1," in *Gott und Mensch im Alten Testament: Zum Verhältnis von Gottes- und Menschenbild*, ed. Jürgen van Oorschot and Andreas Wagner, Veröffentlichungen der Wissenschaftlichen Gesellschaft für Theologie 52 (Leipzig: Evangelische Verlagsanstalt, 2018), 105–122, argues that the plural language in verse 26 reflects residual elements of divine council imagery

plural deliberation followed by singular execution — reinforces the concept of a sovereign God presiding over a populated divine court.

Grounding Joseph Smith's Cosmology in Genesis 1

We can now turn to examining Joseph Smith's cosmology in light of this review of the biblical record. This reevaluation has significant implications not only for understanding the biblical worldview but also for situating the revelations of Joseph Smith within the world of the Bible. As we have seen, key themes in Genesis 1 — such as divine council imagery, creation as ordering rather than origination from nothing, and the *imago Dei* as a functional and relational status — closely align with the theological framework Joseph Smith articulated. Rather than being outliers, his teachings often resonate with and even anticipate modern scholarly insights into ancient Israelite cosmology. Exploring these points of convergence allows us to appreciate the Restoration's doctrinal depth while also placing it in meaningful conversation with contemporary biblical studies.

One of the clearest points of agreement is the rejection of *creatio ex nihilo*. Although Christian orthodoxy insists on this dogma to preserve divine transcendence, the text of Genesis 1 simply does not explicitly teach such. The Hebrew syntax of Genesis 1:1–2 strongly suggests that the earth already existed in an unordered state at the moment God called forth light in verse 3. Thus, God's creative work consists in organizing and assigning roles to various elements of the cosmos, as we have seen. The emphasis throughout is not on material origination but on function, order, and purpose — a view of creation that scholars like John Walton have described as "functional ontology."[66] In this framework, to "create" means to give structure to a previously unordered world, not necessarily to summon it into existence from non-being. This model of creation aligns closely with Joseph Smith's teachings. In the King Follett Discourse, the Prophet explicitly rejected *creatio ex nihilo*, affirming instead that "God had materials to organize the world."[67] Furthermore, according to Joseph "the mind of man," meaning "the intelligence part" of the human creature, is

---

adapted into a monotheistic framework.
66. Walton, *Genesis 1 as Ancient Cosmology*, 162, 165, 169, 183, 190, 193.
67. Smith, "Discourse, 7 April 1844, as Reported by Willard Richards," p. 68, spelling standardized.

"coequal with God himself," effectively eliminating the notion of the generation of souls *ex nihilo* with the other elements.[68] Indeed, Joseph was emphatic that "God never had power to create the spirit of man" out of absolute nothing as his Christian contemporaries insisted, and thus the "human soul, man, existed in spirit and mind coequal with God himself."[69] In this doctrinal framework, matter is eternal, and God's creative work is understood as organizing eternal elements according to divine law.

This understanding is consistent with the growing scholarly consensus that Genesis 1 reflects a worldview of divine order rather than spontaneous creation. The implications of this alignment are profound. Genesis 1 offers a vision of the cosmos as a divinely structured reality, governed by speech and law, with each component serving a defined role. Joseph Smith's revelations, along with his sermons and temple teachings, recover this ancient perspective by emphasizing eternal matter, divine intelligences, and a cosmos ordered according to divine purpose (see Abraham 3:22–28). For Latter-day Saints, the Genesis creation account is not merely the beginning of the world; it is the beginning of a divine project aimed at exalting God's children by revealing their eternal identity, role, and destiny within the cosmos.

This theological harmony continues in the Latter-day Saint reading of humanity's creation in the image of God. In the Latter-day Saint tradition, where divine embodiment and eternal purpose are central doctrines, the vision in Genesis 1:26–27 of the human person as both image-bearer and ruler aligns well with Restoration theology and opens up expansive possibilities for understanding our identity, purpose, and divine potential.[70] For centuries, traditional Christian

---

68. Joseph Smith, "Discourse, 7 April 1844, as Reported by William Clayton," p. 16, *Joseph Smith Papers,* online at josephsmithpapers.org.
69. Joseph Smith, "Discourse, 7 April 1844, as Reported by Wilford Woodruff," p. 137, *Joseph Smith Papers,* online at josephsmithpapers.org, spelling standardized.
70. Stephen Webb, in *Mormon Christianity: What Other Christians Can Learn from the Latter-day Saints* (New York: Oxford University Press, 2013), offers a compelling example of how Latter-day Saint metaphysics can contribute serious and substantive insight to the broader Christian theological conversation. As a Catholic philosopher deeply engaged with classical theism, Webb recognized in the teachings of Joseph Smith a bold, cohesive, and philosophically rich vision of God, creation, and human potential — one that challenges traditional

interpretations have spiritualized the *imago Dei*, defining it in terms of rationality or morality. Far from such dogmatically motivated abstractions, the belief that human beings are literally created in the image of God stands as a cornerstone of Latter-day Saint anthropology. Joseph Smith taught that God the Father is an exalted, glorified being with a tangible, perfected body of flesh and bone. As he told his listeners during the King Follett Sermon, God "is a man like one of yourselves," possessing "the person, image, and very form of man" (compare to Doctrine and Covenants 130:22).[71] He additionally taught that human beings are God's begotten offspring (see Doctrine and Covenants 76:18–24).[72] This celestial parentage provides the theological foundation for the Latter-day Saint doctrine that men and women are of the same species as God, differing only in degree and glory, not in kind. As Parley P. Pratt memorably captured in his 1855 classic *Key to the Science of Theology*, "Gods, angels, and men, are all of one species, one race, one great family widely diffused among the planetary systems."[73] As such, to be made in God's image is not merely to function as his representative on earth but to participate in his very nature, with the potential to become like him in every meaningful sense.[74]

---

assumptions without abandoning core Christian commitments. Webb argues that Latter-day Saint teachings on divine embodiment, eternal matter, and human deification provide a coherent alternative metaphysical framework.

71. Smith, "Discourse, 7 April 1844, as Reported by William Clayton," p. 17, spelling and punctuation standardized.
72. Brian C. Hales, "'A Continuation of the Seeds': Joseph Smith and Spirit Birth," *Journal of Mormon History* 38, no. 4 (Fall 2012): 105–130.
73. Parley P. Pratt, *Key to the Science of Theology* (Liverpool: F. D. Richards; London: Latter Day Saints' Book Depot, 1855), 33.
74. The doctrine of theosis or deification is a foundational aspect of Restoration theology. While Joseph Smith expressed this doctrine most explicitly and forcefully during the final years of his life, it would be a mistake to assume that the idea emerged only in that late period. In reality, the theological foundations for deification are already present in some of the Prophet's earliest revelations. From the beginning, Joseph taught a vision of human potential that pointed toward divine likeness and exaltation, a trajectory that would reach full expression in Nauvoo but that was rooted in his earliest theological intuitions. See Jordon T. Watkins and Christopher James Blythe, "Christology and Theosis in the Revelations and Teaching of Joseph Smith," in *How and What You Worship: Christology and Praxis in the Revelations of Joseph Smith*, ed. Rachel Cope, Carter Charles, and Jordan T. Watkins (Provo, UT: Religious

The Latter-day Saint emphasis on divine embodiment also contributes a unique dimension to this theology. Because God is embodied, our own physical bodies are not obstacles to spirituality but essential instruments in the process of divine progression. As taught in modern revelation, "the spirit and the body are the soul of man" (Doctrine and Covenants 88:15), and "man is spirit" (Doctrine and Covenants 93:33). Thus, the body is not a temporary shell to be discarded in the future eschaton but a vital component of eternal identity. This high view of the body that resoundingly rejects the ancient but flawed notion of *soma sema* finds its roots in Genesis 1's depiction of a God who creates embodied beings in his own likeness. Moreover, the divine image is manifest not only individually but relationally. Genesis 1:27 states that God created humanity "male and female," suggesting that gendered, embodied partnership is itself part of what it means to be in the image of God. This idea dovetails with the Latter-day Saint doctrine that exaltation requires eternal marriage and the union of male and female as the model for divine parenthood and creative power (Doctrine and Covenants 131:1–4; Doctrine and Covenants 132:15–20).

Ultimately, the Restoration's reading of the *imago Dei* transforms a foundational biblical idea into a comprehensive theology of eternal identity. To be created in God's image is to possess divine origin, divine form, divine destiny, and divine stewardship. It is to recognize that mortality is not a detour from the divine path but the very arena in which divine nature is nurtured and fulfilled. In this light, Genesis 1 does more than introduce the human story — it sets forth the pattern of God's own work: to create beings in his image and guide them back into his presence, not as mere subjects, but as exalted sons and daughters of God (Moses 1:39; Abraham 3:25–26).

This vision also helps clarify the plural language of Genesis 1:26 and elsewhere. While later readers sought to resolve this plurality through a variety of (often strained) interpretive strategies, modern scholarship recognizes this as a reference to the divine council. As

---

Studies Center, Brigham Young University; Salt Lake City: Deseret Book, 2020), 123-156; Mark A. Mathews, "'Then Shall They Be Gods': The Restoration of the Doctrine of Exaltation," in *Doctrine and Covenants Insights: Capstone of Doctrinal Understanding*, ed. Kenneth L. Alford, Mary Jane Woodger, Mark A. Mathews (Provo, UT: Religious Studies Center, Brigham Young University; Salt Lake City: Deseret Book, 2025), 241-252.

mentioned, the Hebrew Bible unmistakably depicts a heavenly assembly surrounding God. These divine beings are not competitors but participants in the divine governance of the cosmos. Joseph Smith's revelations likewise affirm a populated heaven — not only with angels, but with exalted beings, Gods, and intelligences. As Joseph taught in the King Follett Sermon, "The head one called the Gods together in grand council. ... In the beginning, the head of the Gods called a council of the Gods and concocted a scheme to create this world."[75] Restoration scripture such as Abraham 4–5 also recounts creation in the plural voice, speaking of *the Gods* organizing and forming the heavens and the earth. This reflects the same divine plurality that Genesis 1 preserves.[76] God does not act in isolation but within a divine society, counseling and directing creation through unity and order. This perspective restores a more ancient Israelite cosmology, one that resonates with both the biblical text and the teachings of the Prophet Joseph. When God says "let us make man in our image," he is therefore not speaking metaphorically, nor is he speaking in the manner of a haughty Persian potentate. He is addressing his divine council, a society of exalted beings, of which he is chief. The image of God into which humanity is created thus reflects not only the nature of God the Father but the likeness of this glorified society (compare to Doctrine and Covenants 130:1–2). This expands the theological horizon of the *imago Dei* and invites every human being into a divine narrative of belonging, potential, and exaltation.

In sum, Genesis 1 offers a remarkably rich theological vision — a structured, purposeful cosmos created by a God who speaks order into being and who creates humanity in his image to share in his work. Joseph Smith's revelatory cosmology does not stand apart from or in contrast to this vision but magnifies it. Through Restoration scripture

---

75. Smith, "Discourse, 7 April 1844, as Reported by Willard Richards," p. 68, spelling and punctuation standardized.
76. Stephen O. Smoot, "Council, Chaos, and Creation in the Book of Abraham," *Journal of the Book of Mormon and Other Restoration Scripture* 22, no. 2 (2013): 28–39; Smoot, "The Divine Council in the Hebrew Bible and the Book of Mormon," 155–180; Smoot, "'I am a Son of God': Moses' Prophetic Call and Ascent into the Divine Council," in *Tracing Ancient Threads in the Book of Moses: Inspired Origins, Temple Contexts, and Literary Qualities*, 2 vols., ed. Jeffrey M. Bradshaw, David Rolph Seely, John W. Welch, and Scott A. Gordon. (Orem, UT: Interpreter Foundation, 2021), 2:923–942.

and prophetic teaching, Latter-day Saints are invited to see Genesis 1 not as an ancient curiosity or a scientific puzzle, but as a divine blueprint for understanding God, creation, and ourselves.

Conclusion

The opening chapter of Genesis offers a remarkably rich and multilayered vision of creation — one that speaks less to the material origins of the universe and more to the ordering of the cosmos according to divine will and purpose. Far from describing creation *ex nihilo*, the text assumes the presence of chaotic elements — formless earth, dark waters, and deep abyss — and portrays God as the grand architect of the universe who fashions structure, function, and meaning into existence. Through successive acts of separation, naming, and blessing, God transforms an unordered world into a habitable cosmos, culminating in the creation of humanity. At the center of this vision stands the doctrine of the *imago Dei* — the declaration that humankind is made in the image and likeness of God. While this has historically been interpreted in metaphysical terms, modern biblical scholarship increasingly recognizes it as a declaration of humanity's shared ontology with the divine and its divine vocation and appointment: to rule, steward, and reflect God's character within the created order. This vocational reading reframes human identity as inherently relational, purposeful, and representative of divine sovereignty on earth.[77]

Notably, many of the insights emerging from contemporary scholarship harmonize in striking ways with the theological framework restored by Joseph Smith in the nineteenth century. Joseph's rejection of *creatio ex nihilo*, once viewed as radical, now finds growing support among critical scholars who read Genesis 1 as describing the organization of preexistent chaos, not the spontaneous generation of matter. Joseph's understanding of the *imago Dei* also aligns with these scholarly developments. Rather than viewing the image of God as an abstract spiritual quality, Joseph's insights restore a concrete, embodied interpretation to Genesis 1:26–27, consistent with how the biblical terminology (*ṣelem* and *děmût*) was understood in ancient Semitic contexts. His teachings reinforce the idea that to be created in God's

---

77. McDowell, "Human Identity and Purpose Redefined," 29–44.

image is not only to bear his form but to participate in his divine work of stewardship, governance, and ultimately, exaltation.

Joseph Smith's teachings on the divine council likewise resonate with what modern biblical scholars increasingly recognize as a core feature of ancient Israelite religion. Far from being a theological novelty, the Prophet's articulation of a populated heaven composed of exalted beings, angels, and divine intelligences mirrors the divine assemblies depicted in texts like Psalm 82 and Job 1–2. Joseph's revelations affirm the existence of such a council and expand on its composition and function, describing it as a society of divine beings working in unity with God. This aligns well with critical scholarship that views Genesis 1:26 as a remnant of this divine council worldview — an understanding that Joseph restored and developed into a robust cosmology consistent with the biblical text.

It should be clarified that this analysis is not merely "arguing from consensus," as if the majority view alone establishes truth. Appeals to scholarly consensus, when used fallaciously, can obscure the need for careful evaluation of evidence and interpretation. However, recognizing where Joseph Smith's teachings intersect with well-supported scholarly findings invites a more nuanced and constructive conversation. Rather than relying on consensus as "proof," the goal here is to highlight meaningful areas of convergence between the Prophet's revelatory insights and contemporary biblical scholarship. In doing so, Joseph's contributions can be properly recognized not as mere curiosities or theological oddities, but as substantive perspectives in the broader theological discourse surrounding Genesis 1. His expansive cosmology, rejection of *creatio ex nihilo*, understanding of the divine council, and view of humanity's divine potential all deserve serious consideration in light of evolving scholarly paradigms.[78]

Genesis 1 does more than recount the beginning of the world — it unveils a divine design grounded in purpose, order, and eternal identity. For Latter-day Saints, this text resonates with prophetic power. It reveals a God who organizes the cosmos not from nothing, but from eternal elements, who speaks light and life into being, and who creates his children in his own image with divine potential. When

---

78. See Terryl L. Givens, *Wrestling the Angel: The Foundations of Mormon Thought: Cosmos, God, Humanity* (New York: Oxford University Press, 2015) for a full treatment of this topic.

read through the lens of ancient Near Eastern cosmology, modern biblical scholarship, and the revelations of the Restoration, especially the teachings of the Prophet Joseph Smith, Genesis 1 becomes more than a fusty creation myth from antiquity unfit for the sensibilities of the modern scientific world — it becomes a testament to God's eternal work "to bring to pass the immortality and eternal life of man" (Moses 1:39).

12

OUT OF THE DUST RE-EXAMINED

THE LITERARY FUNCTION OF NECROMANTIC IMAGERY IN THE BOOK OF MORMON

AMANDA COLLEEN BROWN-MATHER

Isaiah 29:4 describes a voice whispering "out of the dust" like a "familiar spirit," imagery traditionally interpreted by Latter-day Saints as a prophecy of the Book of Mormon's translation. However, historically, this language draws directly from ancient Near Eastern necromancy, the prohibited practice of summoning the dead for esoteric knowledge. While the Hebrew Bible originally employed these terms to condemn unauthorized divination and depict spiritual silence, the Book of Mormon radically reinterprets the metaphor. Prophets Lehi, Nephi, and Moroni transform the imagery this unlawful practice into a symbol of God's redemption. In their hands, the "voice from the dust" is no longer a familiar spirit summoned by an outlawed medium, but a sanctioned record of a fallen people speaking to the living through a divinely empowered translator. This literary reclamation underscores a profound theological claim: God's power allows for the prophetic word to transcend the grave.

> And thou shalt be brought down, and shalt speak out of the ground, and thy speech shall be low out of the dust, and thy voice shall be, as of one that hath a familiar spirit, out of the ground, and thy speech shall whisper out of the dust.[1]
> Isaiah 29:4

Interpreted by Latter-day Saints as a prophecy of the early Restoration, Isaiah 29:4 acts as a cornerstone of Book of Mormon self-proph-

---

1. To best match Book of Mormon verses, all Hebrew Bible verses in this paper are taken from the King James Version.

ecy.² The image of a voice whispering from the dust like a familiar spirit evokes the moment the Gold Plates were unearthed and the translation process from mute artifact into sacred text began. It asks the reader to connect with a record emerging from its grave to speak again, thus framing the Book of Mormon as a liminal, yet prophetic, text between the living and the dead.³

Yet Isaiah's imagery and the Book of Mormon's expansion of it also carry an original meaning and context. When read in its wider ancient Near Eastern and biblical *sitz im leben*, the verse's language draws upon concepts associated with necromancy, the practice of communing with the dead to receive esoteric knowledge from beyond the grave.

Reading this verse through the lens of the original historical context allows modern readers to fully appreciate how multiple Book of Mormon authors reinterpreted Isaiah's original metaphor at various points in the record. What begins with Isaiah's oracle of siege on Jeru-

---

2. Book of Mormon commentaries show a general preference for an eisegetical reading of Isaiah 29:4. In 1987, Joseph F. McConkie and Robert L. Millet argued that Nephi applied Isaiah 29:4 to his people, who would "cry from the dust" as a voice of warning. Joseph F. McConkie and Robert L. Millet, *Doctrinal Commentary on the Book of Mormon*, 4 vols. (Salt Lake City: Bookcraft, 1987), 2:306. That same year, D. Michael Quinn examined the meaning of "familiar spirit" before 1830, but did not link it directly to Book of Mormon exegesis. D. Michael Quinn, *Mormonism and the Magic World View* (Salt Lake City: Signature Books, 1987), 152–153. Brant A. Gardner's six-volume *Second Witness: Analytical and Contextual Commentary on the Book of Mormon* further explored possible associations between necromancy and specific passages. Brant A. Gardner, *Second Witness: Analytical and Contextual Commentary on the Book of Mormon*, 6 vols. (Salt Lake City: Greg Kofford Books, 2007), 2:55–61, 2:352–375, 2:456–461, 6:109–126, 6:410–425. In 2008, Paul Y. Hoskisson compared 2 Nephi 26:16 and Isaiah 29:4 as a case study for distinguishing exegetical from eisegetical readings of scripture. Paul Y. Hoskisson, "The 'Familiar Spirit' in 2 Nephi 26:16," *Insights* 28, no. 6 (2008): 7. Hoskisson also considered the interpretive ramifications of reading necromancy into a Book of Mormon text. Hoskisson, "The Familiar Spirit," 7. More recently, Tad R. Callister read these in Nephi's use of Isaiah 29:4 in Tad R. Callister, *A Case for the Book of Mormon* (Salt Lake City: Deseret Book, 2019), 189.
3. Thank you to Dr. Val Sederholm, Dr. Jonathon Riley, and Ryan Schnell for their consultation on different aspects of this paper. Our conversations have been invaluable.

salem becomes a prophecy of a fallen people speaking to future generations "out of the dust."

Reexamining the development of this metaphor, beginning with the Hebrew Bible and continuing within the Book of Mormon, highlights a deeper theological claim: God's power and prophecy transcend death. In both textual traditions, the voice from the dust is not one of forbidden foreign divination but of the prophesied survival of the word of God though His prophets.

Necromancy in the Ancient Near East

A general survey of necromancy, as it appears in both the Hebrew Bible and the broader ancient Near East, lays a cultural and historical foundation to base a discussion on the theme's development in the Book of Mormon. Necromancy is "the practice of consulting the dead, usually with the help of a medium,"[4] and was used "to obtain information from [the dead], generally regarding the revelation of unknown causes or the future course of events."[5] Ancient necromancy sought to enlist or manipulate the spirits of deceased ancestors[6] to reveal knowledge of the future — knowledge believed to be uniquely accessible to them because they had transcended one world into another.[7]

The following excerpts from Egypt, Mesopotamia, Hattusha, and Ugarit are by no means exhaustive, but they do provide additional context to the cultural world of the Hebrew Bible in which this metaphor developed.

Egyptian

Although the ancient Egyptians did not have a distinct term for

---

4. Philip J. King and Lawrence E. Stager, *Life in Biblical Israel* (Louisville, KY: Westminster John Knox Press, 2001), 380.
5. Brian B. Schmidt, *Israel's Beneficent Dead: Ancestor Cult and Necromancy in Ancient Israelite Religion and Tradition* (Winona Lake, IN: Eisenbrauns, 1996), 11; Fred Miller, "Prophecy in Judaism and Islam," *Islamic Studies* 17 (1978): 28; Edmund B. Keller, "Hebrew Thoughts on Immortality and Resurrection," *International Journal for Philosophy of Religion* 5 (1974): 20–21; Harry A. Hoffner Jr., "Second Millennium Antecedents to the Hebrew 'Ôḇ," *Journal of Biblical Literature* 86, no. 4 (1967): 395–396.
6. For further discussion of the relationship between ancestor cults and necromancy, see Schmidt, *Israel's Beneficent Dead*.
7. Theodore J. Lewis, *Cults of the Dead in Ancient Israel and Ugarit* (Atlanta: Scholars Press, 1989), 2.

"necromancy," the practice of communicating with the dead was deeply embedded in their understanding of the worlds of the living and the dead. Robert K. Ritner observes that "permeating funerary cult, literature, judicial practice and theology, 'necromancy' in ancient Egypt is perhaps far too pervasive a phenomenon to deserve marginalization by a term still tinged with ill repute."[8]

In this worldview, the dead could act as intercessors and sources of hidden knowledge, accessible through incantations as well as dreams, ritual letters, or temple oracles. These communications extended to sacred animals, whose mummified bodies were believed to possess divine agency. While the term "necromancy" is anachronistic in an Egyptian context, the consultation of the dead fits seamlessly within Egypt's cosmic hierarchy.

Mesopotamian

Mesopotamian necromancy centered on the consultation of the *eṭemmu* (the ghost or shade) through rituals to bring the deceased into a state of communication with the living. Although necromancy was not as popular a revelatory method as dreams or extispicy in Mesopotamia, it consistently appears across periods and regions, and its rites were closely tied to the ancestor cult. Some Mesopotamian rituals explicitly labeled "incantation ... to see a ghost in order to make a decision," direct the practitioner to use topical applications or incantations to compel communication from underworld spirits. In other cases, ritual pits (*išibzu*) served as vertical conduits through which underworld deities or ghosts were summoned upward by filling pits with offerings and smearing them with blood to attract semi-divine beings. While these rites differ from Israelite descriptions of necromancy in form, the conceptual model where the dead are contacted using a mediated ritual space is familiar.[9]

---

8. Robert K. Ritner, "Necromancy in Ancient Egypt," in *Magic and Ritual in the Ancient World*, ed. Paul Mirecki and Marvin Meyer (Leiden, NL: Brill, 2002), 95.
9. Gregorio del Olmo Lete, "The Marzeaḥ and the Ugaritic Magic Ritual System: A Close Reading of KTU 1.114," *Aula Orientalis* 33, no. 2 (2015): 221–222, JoAnn Scurlock, *Magico-Medical Means of Treating Ghost-Induced Illnesses in Ancient Mesopotamia* (Leiden, NL: Brill, 2006), 156–157. Billie Jean Collins, "Necromancy, Fertility and the Underworld in Hittite Thought," in *Magic and Ritual in the Ancient World*, ed. Paul Mirecki and Marvin Meyer (Leiden, NL:

Hittite

Parallel to the more ancestral spirit-focused examples, Hittites used ritual pits as portals connecting the living world to the underworld, to invoke deities. These pits served in a variety of rituals, but were also access points for summoning underworld gods and chthonic forces such as the Sun Goddess of the Earth and the Primordial Deities.

Offerings, including libations of wine and oil and the sacrifice of pigs or lambs, were deposited into these openings to nourish the beings whom a worshipper wished to contact. These rites reflect a Hittite worldview in which the earth was animate, and these pits acted as liminal zones where communication with the dead or divine could occur through ritual sacrificial offerings.[10]

Ugaritic

Gregorio del Olmo Lete's reading of the *marzeaḥ* banquet situates necromancy within the broader Ugaritic ritual system. He argues that the *marzeaḥ* banquet was "devoted to the magic, namely necromantic praxis for contacting the Underworld through the altered state of consciousness reached by drunkenness."[2] Here, food, wine, and incantations were used to contact the dead through pits or ritual containers.[3] In Israel, we see a linguistic and material parallel between the pit, or ritual container, and necromancy, denoting a cultural memory potentially linking these texts to other necromantic texts with the ancient Near East.[11]

WORDS DENOTING NECROMANCY

Three Hebrew nouns are associated with necromantic practice: אוֹב (*'ōb*), עָפָר (*'āphār*), and יִדְּעֹנִי (*yidde'ōnî*). The *hapax legomenon* אִטִּים

Brill, 2002), 231–233. Francesca Stavrakopoulou, "Pit, Spirit, Necromancer or Instrument Used in Necromancy? A Diachronic Study of 'ōb and Related Terms," *Hebrew Bible and Ancient Israel* 2 (2013): 11–17; Tzvi Abusch and Daniel Schwemer, *Mesopotamian Magic: Textual, Historical, and Interpretive Perspectives* (Groningen, NL: Styx, 1999), 82–84.

10. Billie Jean Collins, "Necromancy, Fertility, and the Dark Earth: The Use of Ritual Pits in Hittite Cult," in *Magic and Ritual in the Ancient World*, ed. Paul Mirecki and Marvin Meyer (Leiden, NL: Brill, 2002), 224–243.
11. Gregorio del Olmo Lete, "The Marzeaḥ and the Ugaritic Magic Ritual System: A Close Reading of KTU 1.114," *Aula Orientalis* 33, no. 2 (2015): 221–241.

(*'iṭṭîm*) is also referenced in Isaiah 19:3. All of these words together link the underworld, the dead, and their speech.

אוֹב (*'ōb*)

ōb appears in the Hebrew Bible sixteen times and is usually, though not exclusively, paired with *yidde'ōnî*. *'ōb* is translated "familiar spirit" or "ghost", and may refer to an ancestral spirit, given the root's close proximity to *av*, translated as "father." Sometimes it refers to the spirit itself, but it can also reference the medium.

Some scholars have suggested that the word's etymology is derived from a Semitic root meaning "hollow space" or "skin bottle," signifying an empty bottle that makes a noise when air passes through it, mimicking the muttering or whispering sounds of the dead through a medium. The Septuagint renders *'ōb* as ἐγγαστρίμυθος, "ventriloquist", preserving and association between necromantic speech and the resonance of a hollow body or vessel as well as the role a medium played in helping the dead speak.[12]

יִדְּעֹנִי (*yidde'ōnî*)

While *'ōb* references the vessel or voice, *yidde'ōnî* concerns itself with the practitioner. Derived from the root *yd'*, "to know", the word translates to "knower." Morphologically, it is a noun of agency formed with the *ōnî* ending, parallel to designations for skilled professionals.[13] Additionally, the word may have mimicked the chirping sound that proceeded forth out of the practitioners as they communed with the dead.[14]

עָפָר (*'āphār*)

The noun *'āphār*, can be translated as "dust" or "loose earth."[15] From Genesis 2:7 ("dust of the ground") to Job 10:9 ("unto dust shalt

---

12. Philip S. Johnston, *Shades of Sheol: Death and Afterlife in the Old Testament* (Downers Grove, IL: IVP Academic, 2002), 161.
13. For an in-depth analysis of the word's etymology, see Hoffner, "Second Millennium Antecedents," and Irving L. Finkel, "Necromancy in Ancient Mesopotamia," *Archiv für Orientforschung* 29–30 (1983): 14.
14. Hugo Enrique Mendez, "Condemnation of Necromancy in the Hebrew: An Investigation of the Rational" (unpublished master's thesis, University of Georgia, 2009), 5; Keller, "Hebrew Thoughts," 16.
15. G. Johannes Botterweck, Helmer Ringgren, Heinz-Josef Fabry, eds., *Theological Dictionary of the Old Testament*, 17 vols., (Grand Rapids, MI:

thou return"), *'āphār* transcends the commonplace and holds creation and death. When paired with *'ōb or yiddeʿōnî,* the dust evokes the state of those being summoned for information. It is the substance that separates the living from the dead. For the ancient Mesopotamians, the dead were imagined as dwelling in the dust, inhabitants of a dim underworld, a characterization readily reflected in these texts.

אטים *('iṭṭîm)*

This word — only found once in the Hebrew Bible in Isaiah 19:3 — is likely a cognate with Akkadian eṭemmu, and is "spirit of the dead." Alinda Damsma expands eṭemmu's meaning to not only include "ghost" but also "medium" in a necromantic context. This parallels the Hebrew ambiguity of *'ōbôt* and *yiddeʿōnîm* and highlights a possible philosophical collapse of boundaries between the dead and the one who speaks for them.[16]

NECROMANCY IN THE HEBREW BIBLE

The Hebrew Bible references to necromancy indicate that it was present, or at least known, in ancient Israel; however, determining the extent of the practice's influence within mainstream Israelite society is difficult given the limited evidence available.[17] Texts provide little indication that ritual implements beyond the enigmatic *'ōb* were required for necromantic practice in Israel. The absence of clear material evidence dating to Iron Age II (1,000-586 BCE) further complicates an assessment on how widespread necromancy was in ancient Israel or what instruments may have been used. As a result, the biblical texts themselves remain the primary witnesses through which necromantic practice can be understood.

Additionally, the texts of the Hebrew Bible do not denounce necromancy as frequently as they do the cults surrounding Baal or Asherah, likely because necromancy was less widely practiced within popular Israelite religion.[18] Nevertheless, by the time of their redaction, the

---

Eerdmans, 2001), 11:259–260.

16 Alinda Damsma, "'Spirits of the Dead' or 'Necromancers'? The *eṭemmū* in an Old Assyrian Letter Reinterpreted in Light of Hebrew *'ōbôt, yiddeʿōnîm,* and *'iṭṭîm,*" *Religions* 16, no. 5 (2025): 614.

17 Douglas W. Mackenzie, "Faith and Superstition," *Bibliotheca Sacra and Theological Review* 27, no. 6 (1906): 412.

18 Johnston, *Shades of Sheol,* 153.

texts that address it clearly position necromancy outside the bounds of sanctioned Israelite worship.[19]

Law Texts

The Holiness Code, of which Leviticus 19:31 is a part, condemns seeking after those who "have familiar spirits" or "are wizards," (ōbôt and yiddeʿōnîm) rather than explicitly describing the practice itself.[20] Leviticus 20: 6, 27 strengthen the Code's prohibition by declaring that those who engage in necromancy are to be put to death by stoning. This is an indication that the state cult regarded such activity as blasphemous against YHWH.

Deuteronomy 18:10–12 reiterates this condemnation, listing necromancers and diviners among those whom YHWH will drive out from the land.[21] These laws effectively set Yahwistic prophecy in direct opposition to necromancy. This tension reflects the authors' and redactors' intent to elevate YHWH's sanctioned channels of revelation above all competing sources of divine knowledge.[22]

Additionally, Deuteronomy 26:14 should not be overlooked in this study. When paying the produce portion every third year to support the Levites and the poor, a dweller within the gates had to explicitly state that none of the food was offered to the dead.[23] This speaks more largely to a house or ancestor cult, but can also refer to necromancy as an aspect of said worship.

These prohibitions also suggest that necromancy (and related forms of divination) retained some popular appeal within the context of Israelite religion. The persistence of such practices, despite prohibitions, underscores the human impulse to seek knowledge of the future, particularly in moments of crisis.

---

19. Lewis, *Cults of the Dead*, 104; Johnston, *Shades of Sheol*, 153.
20. Mendez, "Condemnation of Necromancy," 4.
21. King and Stager, *Life in Biblical Israel*, 196–198.
22. Jonathan Stökl, "How Unique Was Israelite Prophecy?," in *The Wiley-Blackwell History of Jews and Judaism*, ed. Alan T. Levenson (Malden, MA: John Wiley & Sons, 2012), 54.
23. Johannes Unsok Ro and Diana Edelman, eds., *Collective Memory and Collective Identity: Deuteronomy and the Deuteronomistic History in Their Context* (Berlin, DE: De Gruyter, 2021), 53.

Saul and the Woman Medium (ba'alat-'ôb) of Endor

Necromancy's tension with covenantal fealty is best highlighted in Saul's encounter with the Medium of Endor in 1 Samuel 28. On the eve of his final battle against the Philistines and David's ascension to the Israelite throne, the once-divinely-chosen King Saul finds himself isolated from every legitimate channel of prophecy provided by the Israelite cult.[24] The text emphasizes the completeness of Saul's spiritual desolation: YHWH no longer answers him "by dreams, nor by Urim, nor by prophets" (v. 6).

This divine silence is the culmination of a long trajectory of disobedience, Saul's unsanctioned sacrifice at Gilgal (1 Samuel 13), his failure to destroy Amalek (1 Samuel 15), and his increasingly erratic jealousy toward David. By the time Saul turns to a necromancer, his estrangement from YHWH is complete.[25] The act of seeking a battle oracle from the dead thus emerges not as an isolated lapse in divine fealty but as the culmination of the king's total spiritual collapse and subsequent inability to rule.

Disguised and under cover of night, Saul visits the Medium at Endor, a woman who, like her practice, operates at the margins of Israelite society. Having previously expelled these practitioners from the land, Saul now seeks the very power he outlawed and condemned to death. His request: "Bring me up Samuel." The woman, terrified when she realizes the identity of her visitor, protests, refusing to perform the requested ritual before extracting an oath that she will not be killed for doing so. She successfully "brings up" Samuel, whose appearance is described in language evocative of necromantic scenes: he is an old man rising, wrapped in a robe, emerging from the earth.

The narrative intentionally blurs the line between forbidden ritual and prophetic encounter, forcing the reader to wrestle with what exactly this woman has conjured for Saul and whether this is indeed

---

24. Hoffner, "Second Millennium Antecedents," 396.
25. The Chronicler attributes Saul's downfall to his act of necromancy: "So Saul died for his transgression ... for asking counsel of one that had a familiar spirit, to enquire of it" (1 Chronicles 10:13–14). For a literary analysis of Saul's portrayal as the prototype of failed kingship, see Matthew Michael, "The Prophet, the Witch and the Ghost: Understanding the Parody of Saul as a 'Prophet' and the Purpose of Endor in the Deuteronomistic History," *Journal for the Study of the Old Testament* 38, no. 3 (2014): 316–346.

an encounter with one of YHWH's prophets from beyond the grave. Is it the real Samuel, or a divine apparition permitted by YHWH to pronounce judgment one final time?[26]

Samuel's rebuke cuts to the heart of the story: "Why hast thou disquieted me, to bring me up?" (v. 15). His tone underscores that Saul's desperate act violates both divine order and prophetic hierarchy. Saul's reply exposes his inner crisis: "I am sore distressed; for the Philistines make war against me, and God is departed from me ... therefore I have called thee, that thou mayest make known unto me what I shall do." The king's words reveal not only fear but the theological confusion Saul's reign instigated for the Israelites. He still seeks YHWH's will, but through a medium explicitly forbidden by YHWH's law. Samuel's response seals Saul's fate: his kingdom has been given to David, and the next day he and his sons will die in battle. The narrative's conclusion is grimly symmetrical; having crossed the boundary between life and death in search of guidance, Saul will enter the realm of the dead before nightfall.

This account functions as both historical tragedy and theological allegory. Saul's death is not merely a military defeat but a spiritual consequence of a king's misplaced dependence on unsanctioned revelation. Necromancy, in this story, is the physical manifestation of his severed relationship with YHWH, the final act of a king who can no longer discern divine will. Saul's end thus becomes a cautionary mirror for Israel as a nation, illustrating how reliance on alternative sources of revelation, no matter how desperate the circumstance, leads only to divine withdrawal and death for not only the king, but a covenant people.

Isaiah

Another instance of necromancy's metaphorical use appears in Isaiah 8:19–20, where YHWH's response to Judah's political and

---

26. This question finds a parallel in a Roman-period Demotic cycle of wisdom tales, "The Tales of Petese," where a widow consults a medium at her husband's tomb. The god Re animates her husband's corpse and speaks through it in a form of divine ventriloquism, transforming the mouth of the dead into a divine oracle, thus affirming Re's control of even the spirits of the underworld. For more on this, see K. S. B. Ryholt, *The Story of Petese, Son of Petetum, and Seventy Other Good and Bad Stories (P. Petese)* (Copenhagen, DK: Carsten Niebuhr Institute of Near East Studies, University of Copenhagen, 1999).

spiritual crisis transforms necromantic language into a critique of misplaced trust. The context for this oracle arises during the Syro-Ephraimite War (circa 734 BCE), when King Ahaz of Judah faced pressure to join a coalition against Tiglath-Pileser III's Assyrian empire. Rather than trusting in YHWH's prophetic assurances through his prophet, Isaiah, Ahaz turned toward political alliances with Syria and Israel and foreign counsel. In this moment of national anxiety, the prophet's warning addresses not only Ahaz's diplomacy but the people's temptation to turn toward other sources of revelation when divine communication appears withdrawn.[27]

The text reads:

> And when they shall say unto you, Seek unto them that have familiar spirits, and unto wizards that peep and that mutter: should not a people seek unto their God? for the living to the dead? To the law and to the testimony: if they speak not according to this word, it is because there is no light in them (Isaiah 8:19–20).

As so often is the case, Isaiah's rhetoric fuses political and religious critique. The language of "peeping and muttering" evokes the strange, hollow sounds associated with necromantic rituals, emphasizing the contrast between the incoherent whispers of the dead and the reliability of Yahwistic prophecy, spoken through Isaiah. The Hebrew *'ōbôt* and *yiddeʿōnîm* (translated "familiar spirits" and "wizards") describe practices that rely on the voices of the dead or their intermediaries, but Isaiah recasts them as symbols of spiritual blindness. His question, "for the living to the dead?" asks: why should those who serve the living God seek counsel from the dead in the underworld?

Isaiah's words condemn both literal necromancy and figurative dependence on illegitimate prophecy. His warning extends beyond ritual practice to encompass all misplaced trust, whether in political alliances, false prophets, or foreign cult systems. The command to return "to the law and to the testimony" (v. 20) redirects the people's attention to YHWH's revealed word as the only valid source of foreknowledge within Israel.[28] By invoking necromancy, Isaiah exposes how Judah's pursuit of alternative oracular manifestations mirrors

---

27. Mendez, "Condemnation of Necromancy," 36, 42–43; Lewis, *Cults of the Dead*, 130.
28. Mendez, "Condemnation of Necromancy," 20.

the necromancer's attempt to access hidden knowledge. The passage also implies historical continued efforts by the Jerusalem priests to suppress popular divinatory practices that competed with the temple's prophetic authority.

Isaiah's use of necromancy as a political and theological metaphor continues in Isaiah 19:3, where the prophet expands his critique to Egypt, portraying necromancy as emblematic of a foreign nation's inferiority before YHWH:

> And the spirit of Egypt shall fail in the midst thereof; and I will destroy the counsel thereof: and they shall seek to the idols, and to the charmers, and to them that have familiar spirits, and to the wizards.

This oracle forms part of a larger prophetic collection that envisions the downfall of Egypt under Assyrian invasion. For Isaiah, Egypt's turning to necromancers and idols underscores the same pattern as seen in Judah: a search for divine foreknowledge that YHWH has cut off. The futility of such efforts reinforces the theological conviction that only YHWH can provide prophecy, even to other nations.[29]

Whereas Egyptian religion viewed communication with the dead as an integral part of maintaining cosmic order and divine favor, Isaiah depicts it as a sign of decay, an attempt to recover wisdom from sources already silenced. The prophet's contrast between Egypt's failed diviners and the divine word of YHWH recasts necromancy as a literary shorthand for the supremacy of Judah's deity.

The theme reaches its most striking and paradoxical expression in Isaiah 29:4, where the necromantic image is inverted and applied to Jerusalem herself:

> And thou shalt be brought down, and shalt speak out of the ground, and thy speech shall be low out of the dust, and thy voice shall be, as of one that hath a familiar spirit, out of the ground, and thy speech shall whisper out of the dust.

This oracle, addressed to *Ariel* (a poetic name for Jerusalem meaning "Lion of God") belongs to a section reflecting the Assyrian siege of 701 BCE under Assyria's King Sennacherib.[30] To describe YHWH's

---

29. Christopher B. Hays, "The Covenant with Mut: A New Interpretation of Isaiah 28:1–22," *Vetus Testamentum* 60, no. 2 (2010): 234; Mendez, "Condemnation of Necromancy," 45–46.
30. For a discussion on the evidence of Sennacherib's influence in Isaiah, see Robin

holy city as one "that hath a familiar spirit" appears jarring and counterintuitive. The comparison between Zion and the voice of a dead spirit reinvents necromancy, not as ritual, but as metaphor: Jerusalem has become like the dead, its voice reduced to a whisper from the grave.[31] The city that once proclaimed YHWH's word is now silenced, its prophets asleep, its revelation buried under layers of the people's wickedness and disbelief. Scholars have observed that the passage "portrays the cessation of Yahwistic prophecy as coincident with the adoption of necromancy,"[32] suggesting that Isaiah's imagery reflects divine judgment over the corruption of prophecy obtained through unauthorized channels.

When read through a literary lens, this verse renders Jerusalem itself as a kind of necromantic figure. It transforms into a city so devastated through siege, famine, and war that it speaks only from the dust. Taken together with verse 10 ("For the LORD hath poured out upon you the spirit of deep sleep, and hath closed your eyes: the prophets and your rulers, the seers hath he covered"), the imagery tells us who is responsible for this transformation. YHWH has silenced his city, withholding prophecy from those who refused to hear it at its utterance. The people's "deep sleep" parallels the grave; yet their city whispers "out of the dust" in anticipation of the moment when YHWH will reanimate the city through the remembrance of His covenant.

Throughout Isaiah, necromantic imagery functions not to describe the ritual but to reveal the consequences of divine absence and reliance on other forms of revelation outside of those prescribed by the Israelite cult. Each passage transforms the language of necromancy into a literary and theological device.[33] Whether applied to Judah, to foreign

---

Routledge, "The Siege and Deliverance of the City of David in Isaiah 29:1–8," *Tyndale Bulletin* 43 (1992): 181–190.

31. One possible interpretation suggests a demolition of the city so complete that its inhabitants' only recourse is to communicate with future generations through a practice such as necromancy. Johnston, *Shades of Sheol*, 111.
32. Schmidt, *Israel's Beneficent Dead*, 164.
33. Stökl offers an interpretive nuance on Isaiah's use of necromantic idiom: "It is easier to assume that idioms from the polytheistic past are still being used in a monotheistic environment." Jonathan Stökl, "Divination as Warfare: The Use of Divination Across Borders," in *Divination, Politics, and Ancient Near Eastern Empires*, ed. Jonathan Stökl and Amar Annus, Ancient Near Eastern Monographs 7 (Atlanta: Society of Biblical Literature, 2013), 61.

nations, or even to Zion itself, necromancy becomes a metaphor for the consequences of non-Yahwhistic prophecy. In this inversion lies the Hebrew Bible's enduring message: sanctioned prophecy cannot be coerced from the dead.

Necromancy in the Book of Mormon

The Book of Mormon interprets Isaiah 29:4 as a prophecy of the coming forth of the Book of Mormon. The verse's description of a voice "whispering out of the dust" finds a natural parallel in the image of a buried record brought forth from the ground to speak as the voices of the dead calling to future generations. The Book of Mormon thus transforms Isaiah's warning to a silenced Jerusalem into a promise of restoration.

Lehi's Commentary

The first development of this motif appears in 2 Nephi 3:19–20, where Lehi, in his final blessing to his son Joseph, introduces the idea that the "fruit of [his] loins" will one day "cry from the dust." He prophesies:

> And it shall be as if the fruit of thy loins had cried unto them from the dust; for I know their faith. And they shall cry from the dust; yea, even repentance unto their brethren, even after many generations have gone by them. And it shall come to pass that their cry shall go, even according to the simpleness of their words.

Lehi's dying words merge a patriarch's final blessing with prophecy. His language situates the coming forth of the Book of Mormon between revelation and death, speech and silence. In this way, Lehi becomes the first Book of Mormon prophet to cast the future book as a medium through which the dead will yet communicate. His image of descendants "crying from the dust" transforms the traditional boundary between life and death into a prophetic act. Writing itself becomes sacred mediation, an assurance that even if the prophets' voices are silenced through death, their words will speak to future generations.

Nephi's Commentary

Nephi later builds upon his father's language in 2 Nephi 26:15–16, where he directly interacts with Isaiah's prophecy and applies it to his own unique circumstances, creating a sort of proto-*pesher*.³⁴ The passage reads:

> After my seed and the seed of my brethren shall have dwindled in unbelief, and shall have been smitten by the Gentiles; yea, after the Lord God shall have camped against them round about, and shall have laid siege against them with a mount, and raised forts against them; and after they shall have been brought down low in the dust, even that they are not, yet the words of the righteous shall be written, and the prayers of the faithful shall be heard, and all those who have dwindled in unbelief shall not be forgotten.
>
> For those who shall be destroyed shall speak unto them out of the ground, and their speech shall be low out of the dust, and their voice shall be as one that hath a familiar spirit; for the Lord God will give unto him power, that he may whisper concerning them, even as it were out of the ground; and their speech shall whisper out of the dust.

Here, Nephi's reinterpretation of Isaiah 29:4 serves multiple purposes. On one level, Nephi claims Isaiah's metaphor, aligning it with a branch of Israel's diverging story. The Nephites, whose destruction he foresees, will become the "familiar spirit" that speaks from the dust. Adding to the metaphor, Nephi introduces a divinely empowered "him" who will "whisper concerning them." Though unnamed, this individual functions as a medium between the dead authors and the living audience. In the Latter-day Saint interpretive tradition, this figure has been understood as a redactor or translator, who serves as the medium through whom the voices of the dead are made intelligible.³⁵

By integrating Isaiah's imagery into his own prophecy, Nephi constructs a layered typology: the Nephite destruction mirrors Jerusalem's fall, while the record that survives them parallels the resurrected city's future restoration. The people who once refused prophetic revelation become, in death, the source of it, echoing Isaiah's paradox of revelation emerging from the dust.

---

34. It is worth noting that Nephi's interpretive technique parallels the pesher style later found at Qumran, where scriptural prophecy is applied to contemporary or eschatological contexts. 4Q161–4Q164 contains interpretive fragments of the same Isaianic passage, though the section corresponding to Isaiah 29:4 is lost. Despite the missing context from the Dead Sea Scrolls pesher, its existence demonstrates a shared interpretive impulse regarding this passage.
35. Quinn, *Mormonism and the Magic World View*, 152–153.

Nephi concludes his development of this metaphor in 2 Nephi 33:13, where he personalizes the imagery and places himself within the context of the prophecy:

> And now, my beloved brethren, all those who are of the house of Israel, and all ye ends of the earth, I speak unto you as the voice of one crying from the dust: Farewell until that great day shall come.

This passage functions as Nephi's farewell address. Having witnessed the destruction of his descendents in vision, Nephi writes with the awareness that his words will outlive not only him, but an entire people. His "cry from the dust" is a final testimony that binds the living reader to the dead prophet through his words' translator/medium. Through this reimagined metaphor of a prohibited ritual invocation, there is one glaring difference from the Hebrew Bible passages' approach: this time, the dead prophets are sanctioned by God and His appointed prophet to speak out of the dust.

Moroni's Commentary

After narrative silence from the Large Plates, the "voice from the dust" theme reemerges in the writings of Moroni, who serves as the final redactor of the Nephite record. In Mormon 8:23, Moroni invokes both Isaiah's and the Nephite interpretation:[36]

> Search the prophecies of Isaiah. Behold, I cannot write them. Yea, behold I say unto you, that those saints who have gone before me, who have possessed this land, shall cry, yea, even from the dust will they cry unto the Lord; and as the Lord liveth he will remember the covenant which he hath made with them.

With the perspective of a suvivor of genocide, Moroni evolves the image from a dualistic prophecy of destruction and translation, to a plea for covenantal remembrance. The dead saints now "cry unto the Lord," transforming the necromantic metaphor into a scene of divine restoration.

Salvation is made possible for the dead who remember their God as they cry from the dust. God hears the voices of the departed and acts

---

36. Moroni is most likely quoting Nephi's version of Isaiah and its surrounding context, rather than the original text of Isaiah 29:4. See Gardner, *Second Witness*, 6:109–126.

upon their behalf, ensuring that the promises made to ancient Israel will yet be fulfilled. Moroni's use of Isaiah's language thus places God at the center of the metaphor, recasting what was once condemned in the Hebrew Bible as an image of sacred reconciliation.

Moroni employs necromantic imagery a final time in the last chapter of the Book of Mormon. Moroni 10:27 reads:

> And I exhort you to remember these things; for the time speedily cometh that ye shall know that I lie not, for ye shall see me at the bar of God; and the Lord God will say unto you: Did I not declare my words unto you, which were written by this man, like as one crying from the dead, yea, even as one speaking out of the dust?

Here, Moroni collapses the temporal and spiritual distance between author and reader originally preserved in Nephi's interpretation of the verse. The "voice from the dust" becomes both literal and eschatological: not only will the prophets speak from the dust, but Moroni anticipates a future meeting between himself and his readers before the judgment bar of God. In this final act, the metaphor comes full circle. The once-forbidden act of communing with the dead is reimagined as a divine reunion where all are joined through their interaction with prophecy.

The Book of Mormon's engagement with the necromancy metaphor thus mirrors the Hebrew Bible's theological development from prohibition to literary redefinition. What the Biblical authors rejected as a threat to prophetic authority is, in the hands of Isaiah, Lehi, Nephi, and Moroni, transfigured into a literary expression of revelation and redemption.[37] Furthermore, these Book of Mormon prophets build upon Isaiah's redevelopment to illustrate that God alone governs the boundaries between the living and the dead, and that through his appointed medium, even the dust may speak.

Conclusion

The Hebrew Bible and other ancient Near Eastern texts reference the ancient practice of divination through communion with the dead, a motif that the Book of Mormon later expands upon. Although the Hebrew Bible repeatedly prohibits necromancy, it also develops its imagery and terminology into powerful literary devices. The bibli-

---

37. Gardner, *Second Witness*, 6:410–425.

cal authors used these references not to endorse the practice, but to underscore YHWH's supremacy over all revelatory systems, providing prophecy through His appointed prophets.

Similarly, Book of Mormon prophets adapt this imagery to frame the book's discovery, translation, and affect upon its readers within the same theological construct. While the focus shifts from prohibition to divine fulfillment, both traditions affirm YHWH as the omniscient source of revelation concerning the future. The metaphor of necromancy, grounded in real ancient practice and reimagined through literary transformation, thus serves to contrast YHWH's sanctioned revelation with unauthorized or popular modes of divination, reaffirming His exclusive authority in both the Hebrew Bible and the Book of Mormon.

13

MASTER MAHAN

LEGEND(S) OF CAIN IN THE LATTER DAY SAINT TRADITION

CHRISTOPHER JAMES BLYTHE

Genesis depicts Cain as a simple exile, but Latter-day Saint tradition has cultivated a complex mythology around the first murderer. Joseph Smith's revelations reimagined him as "Master Mahan," the architect of a secret pact with Satan, sparking a trajectory of folklore regarding his cosmic status. Some traditions even asserted that Cain's physical body allowed him to outrank the devil in the hierarchy of evil. These legends intensified within schismatic fundamentalist movements, which popularized theories about Cain's monstrous parentage — identifying him as the literal offspring of the Serpent — and his prophesied return as an apocalyptic antiChrist. Ultimately, this evolving lore illustrates the dynamic nature of scriptural reception, where canonical gaps are continually filled with imaginative theological narratives.

In Genesis, Cain is the first murderer. He was cursed, exiled, and marked as a warning to others who might harm him. This was the end of his story in the Bible but, over the centuries, many additional readings of Cain, his crime, and his punishment developed.[1] Cain became the father of monsters. In the words of the medieval Jewish text, the Zohar, "from [Cain] originate all the evil habitations and demons and goblins and evil spirits in the world."[2] The Old English poem *Beowulf*

---

1. See the first three chapters in Robert C. Gregg, *Shared Stories, Rival Tellings: Early Encounters of Jews, Christians, and Muslims* (New York: Oxford University Press, 2015), 7–40, 41–74, 75–113.
2. Quoted in Stephen T. Asma, *On Monsters: An Unnatural History of Our Fears* (New York: Oxford University Press, 2009), 89.

identifies Cain as the progenitor of the monstrous Grendel.[3] The same era produced a tradition that Cain himself was not a son of Adam at all, but the child of Eve and the serpent. He was not fully human, but monstrous in his nature.

Retellings of Genesis are not uncommon in the ancient or modern world. In the Latter Day Saint[4] Book of Moses, Joseph Smith's expansion of the early chapters of Genesis, Cain murders his brother not out of jealousy alone, but at the behest of Satan. In turn, Satan grants him the title of "Master Mahan," placing him at the head of his mortal followers. While Moses was the last of Joseph Smith's scriptural productions to discuss Cain in any depth, Latter-day Saints quickly began exploring the significance of the first murderer by developing legends recounting his experience post-exile. Cain became a wandering immortal, the progenitor of a cursed race, and part of a Satanic hierarchy in which he outranked Satan himself.[5]

The early Latter Day Saint tradition was marked by this kind of scriptural innovation, both in the production of new texts (such as the Book of Mormon) and in oral speculation. As literary critic Harold Bloom has stated, Joseph Smith's "religious genius" was in his ability to be "a great reader, or creative misreader, of the Bible."[6] The creative impulse (as it comes to traditional narratives) has become rare among theologians and leaders in the Church of Jesus Christ of Latter-day Saints since the close of the nineteenth century. This is partly what Bloom meant when he insisted, "Mormonism no longer *is* Joseph

---

3. R. D. Fulk, Robert E. Bjork, and John D. Niles, eds., *Klaeber's Beowulf*, 4th ed. (Toronto: University of Toronto Press, 2008), 7, lines 106–107.
4. Members of the Church of Jesus Christ of Latter-day Saints are sometimes referred to as "Mormons," although they have recently discouraged this moniker. In this article, I use "Latter Day Saint," instead of "Latter-day Saint," to describe believers in the Latter Day Saint tradition, which encompasses several churches and groups, as well as independent believers. I use the term "Latter-day Saint" only when speaking directly of those who belong to The Church of Jesus Christ of Latter-day Saints.
5. Elder Bruce R. McConkie of the Quorum of the Twelve Apostles taught that Cain "will rule over Satan himself when the devil and his angels are cast out everlastingly." See Bruce R. McConkie, *A New Witness for the Articles of Faith* (Salt Lake City: Deseret Book, 1985), 658.
6. Harold Bloom, *The American Religion: The Emergence of the Post-Christian Nation* (New York: Simon & Schuster, 1992), 84.

Smith, but it was from 1830 to 1890, the sixty years of its spiritual greatness."[7] As the new faith became institutionalized, its creative and free-ranging interpretation of scripture likewise stabilized.

Those stories preserved in canonized scripture remain, but the faithful have come to view expansive scriptural interpretations skeptically. This is not true of those saints belonging to heterodox or schismatic movements, particularly among those Latter Day Saints typically referred to as Mormon Fundamentalists. This article documents the reception and expansion of Cain's biblical narrative in early Latter-day Saint thought, and the later reception of Cain to the present. Those of you familiar with my work will not be surprised to see that I include schismatic Latter Day Saint communities and their interpretive tradition in my analysis.

Latter-day Saint additions to Cain's narrative fall into two broad categories. First, are stories that describe encounters with an immortal, beastlike wanderer. This trope has its origins in a legend that early apostle David W. Patten met the first murderer in 1835 while travelling in Tennessee. Historian Matt Bowman has done an excellent job analyzing this legend cycle in an essay entitled, "A Mormon Bigfoot: David Patten's Cain and the Conception of Evil in Latter-day Saint Folklore." Bowman considers how Cain became associated with the most famous of American cryptids while also arguing that these stories had shifting racial implications.[8] Here, I am focused on the second category of Cain lore, which had its origins with Joseph Smith himself: folk theology concerning Cain's place in a Satanic hierarchy.

NINETEENTH CENTURY LEGENDS OF CAIN

The story of Cain is one of many singular expansions that held significance to early Latter-day Saints. Cain first appeared in Latter-day Saint texts in the Book of Mormon, a scriptural work translated by Joseph Smith and published in 1830. There, a shadowy conspiracy known as the Gadianton Robbers initiated others into "oaths" and ceremonies "which had been handed down even from Cain" (Ether 8:15).

---

7. Bloom, *American Religion*, 82.
8. Matthew Bowman, "A Mormon Bigfoot: David Patten's Cain and the Conception of Evil in LDS Folklore," in W. Paul Reeve and Michael Scott Van Wagenen, *Between Pulpit and Pew: The Supernatural World in Mormon History and Folklore* (Logan, UT: Utah State University Press, 2011), 17–39.

While in the book of Genesis, there is no discussion of the devil's involvement in Abel's murder, the Book of Mormon states that the devil "did plot with Cain, that if he would murder his brother Abel it should not be known unto the world. And he did plot with Cain and his followers from that time forth" (Helaman 6:27). Both of these threads — Cain as the founder of an ancient occult conspiracy and Cain's plot with the devil — would become prominent themes in Joseph's second scriptural project, the "new translation" of the Bible.[9]

In 1830, Joseph Smith revised and expanded major portions of the book of Genesis with a penchant toward clarifying difficult passages. For instance, he doubled down on the perennial question of Mosaic authorship by inserting a preface to Genesis that presents the creation account as a vision seen and experienced by Moses. The Book of Moses settled questions stemming from the two conflicting creation accounts of Genesis 1 and 2 by explaining that the book described a spiritual creation, followed by a physical creation. The Book of Moses also placed seemingly anachronistic ideas about Jesus and the devil within the Garden narrative.

While the book of Genesis provides no hint that the serpent was a devil or fallen angel, Latter Day Saints inherited a Christianized reading of the text. Through their reading of the King James Version of the Bible, they interpreted the book of Revelation's identification of Satan as "the old serpent" as an allusion to his role there (Revelation 12:9). The Book of Mormon echoed the same language: "And because he [an angel of God] had fallen from heaven, and had become miserable forever, he sought also the misery of all mankind. Wherefore, he said unto Eve, yea, even that *old serpent*, who is the devil, who is the father of all lies, wherefore he said: Partake of the forbidden fruit, and ye shall not die, but ye shall be as God, knowing good and evil" (2 Nephi 2:17–18). When Joseph Smith recorded his expanded version of Genesis, later referred to as the Book of Moses, he made the devil's presence in the garden explicit, much as other rewritings of Genesis

---

9. "Smith called his work 'translation,' but the term is a misnomer here, since he did not use original manuscripts in his work of revision, expansion, and correction and went well beyond rendering ancient words and concepts into English equivalents." See Terryl L. Givens, with Brian M. Hauglid, *The Pearl of Greatest Price: Mormonism's Most Controversial Scripture* (New York: Oxford University Press, 2019), 32.

had done — the first of which seems to have been the *Life of Adam and Eve*, a text dating to sometime between the second and fifth centuries.[10] Unlike the Book of Mormon, Moses distinguishes the serpent from Satan: "Satan put it into the heart of the serpent, (for he had drawn away many after him,) ... And he said unto the woman: Yea, hath God said — Ye shall not eat of every tree of the garden? (And he spake by the mouth of the serpent)" (Moses 5:6–7).

In the Book of Moses, Satan's involvement with humanity continued after the fall. While Adam and Eve sought to teach their descendants that which they had received from God, "Satan came among them, saying: I am also a son of God; and he commanded them, saying: Believe it not; and they believed it not, and they loved Satan more than God" (Moses 5:13). Cain particularly "loved Satan more than God," and it is at Satan's command that Cain brings his agricultural offering to sacrifice at an altar. In both the original text and Joseph Smith's expansion, deity accepts the animal sacrifice offered by Cain's brother, Abel, but rejects Cain's offering. The Book of Moses provides a new passage, with an angel clarifying the importance of animal sacrifice to Adam, thus explaining the "mysterious reason one sacrifice is deemed unacceptable while the other is well-received."[11] In the words of Terryl Givens, "Cain's offering is presented as a deliberate sacrilege rather than innocent misstep."[12]

Joseph Smith's retelling of the Genesis account expands on Deity's short response following His rejection of Cain's offering. In the King James Version, the relevant text reads simply, "If thou does well, shalt thou not be accepted? And if thou doest not well, sin lieth at the door. And unto thee shall be his desire, and thou shalt rule over him" (Genesis 4:7). Keeping in mind that Jewish commentators and scholars do not believe this passage alludes to a demonic figure, the Book of Moses pulls this initial text apart and stitches it back together with additional language, clarifying that God had referenced just such a being:

> If thou doest well, thou shalt be accepted. And if thou doest not well, sin lieth at the door, and Satan desireth to have thee;

---

10. See, "Life of Adam and Eve," in *The Old Testament Pseudepigrapha*, 2 vols., ed. James H. Charlesworth (New York: Doubleday, 1985), 2:249–295.
11. Regina M. Schwartz, *The Curse of Cain: The Violent Legacy of Monotheism* (Chicago: University of Chicago Press, 1997), 2.
12. Givens and Hauglid, *The Pearl of Greatest Price,* 70.

and except thou shalt hearken unto my commandments, I will deliver thee up, and it shall be unto thee according to his desire. And thou shalt rule over him.

Moses's expansion literalizes the passage:

For from this time forth thou shalt be the father of his lies; thou shalt be called Perdition; for thou wast also before the world. And it shall be said in time to come — That these abominations were had from Cain; for he rejected the greater counsel which was had from God; and this is a cursing which I will put upon thee, except thou repent (Moses 5:23–25).

At this point, the Genesis account immediately moves from Deity's censure of Cain to the murder of his brother. In the Book of Moses, Cain next encounters Satan, to whom he swears an oath of fidelity and secrecy, with the fallen angel promising he would "deliver thy brother Abel into thine hands." The passage continues, "And Satan sware unto Cain that he would do according to his commands." Between this covenant and the murder of Abel, Cain declares his new position: "Truly I am Mahan, the master of this great secret, that I may murder and get gain. Wherefore Cain was called Master Mahan, and he gloried in his wickedness" (Moses 5:30–31).

After killing Abel, God curses Cain with much the same wording as appears in the book of Genesis, along with a fascinating interpolation: Cain declares that "Satan tempted me because of my brother's flocks. And I was wroth also; for his offering thou didst accept and not mine" (Moses 5:38). His words seem to echo Adam and Eve's defense after eating the forbidden fruit, with Adam pointing to Eve's temptation and Eve pointing to the serpent's beguilement (Genesis 3:12–13).

Latter-day Saints have offered two interpretations of what came from the contract between Cain and Lucifer. The first interpretation, championed by the theologian Hugh Nibley, held that Cain entered into a typical devil's pact. Like Christopher Marlowe's Dr. Faustus, Cain would "rule over" the devil as his servant throughout his life in exchange for his immortal soul.[13] This would be a temporary relationship in which Cain gets what he desires in mortality but not in eternity when he is subject to Satan. Satan's promise to "do according

---

13. Hugh W. Nibley, "Lecture 19," in *Teachings of the Pearl of Great Price* (Provo, UT: Foundation for Ancient Research and Mormon Studies, Brigham Young University, 2002), 243–244.

to [Cain's] commands" and God's warning that Satan "desires to have you" suggests this as a plausible reading. In fact, I should confess this is my preferred reading.

A second, and vastly more influential interpretation, is that Cain permanently came to outrank Lucifer in an infernal hierarchy by virtue of his having a body. Lucifer had apparently — for reasons undisclosed to the reader — selected a mortal to become his superior. In the words of Latter-day Saint apostle Joseph Fielding Smith,

> As far as Cain is concerned, the information given is definite that he became Perdition, and that Lucifer who is Satan, became subject to him. It appears that the reason Satan desired to have him was due to the fact that Cain had obtained a body of flesh and bones and therefore had superior power, and Satan was willing to accept and be obedient to him because of that condition. The natural conclusion is, therefore, that a devil with a body of flesh and bones has some power greater than one who was denied the physical body.[14]

This second interpretation ties into the elaborate Latter Day Saint mythology involving a time before the creation of the earth. Based on the teachings of Joseph Smith, Latter-day Saints believe that humans, angels, and gods are all one species in different states of development.[15] Before mortal birth, humankind existed as a vast family of spirits headed by a benevolent "Heavenly Father" and "Heavenly Mother." These divine parents had already lived as mortals on a world sometime in the distant past. They had died, been resurrected, and after being deified, now prepared their spirit children to become like them. As Joseph Smith had declared only months before his death, "God himself, who sits enthroned in yonder heavens, is a man like unto one of yourselves, that is the great secret. ... You have got to learn how to be Gods yourselves ... the same as all Gods have done."[16]

During this pre-mortal era, God announced that one of his children would serve as a savior to redeem the others. In Moses 4, in a

---

14. Joseph Fielding Smith, *Answers to Gospel Questions*, 5 vols. (Salt Lake City: Deseret Book Company, 1958), 2:170–172. Scripture citations within the quotation silently removed.
15. Parley P. Pratt, *Key to the Science of Theology* (Liverpool: F. D. Richards, 1855), 33.
16. Joseph Smith, "Discourse, 7 April 1844, as Published in Times and Seasons," pp. 613–614, *Joseph Smith Papers,* online at josephsmithpapers.org.

passage leading up to the garden narrative, and without a parallel in Genesis, this scene is described:

> [Satan] came before me, saying — Behold, here am I, send me, I will be thy son, and I will redeem all mankind, that one soul shall not be lost, and surely I will do it; wherefore give me thine honor. But, behold, my Beloved Son, which was my Beloved and Chosen from the beginning, said unto me — Father, thy will be done, and the glory be thine forever. Wherefore, because that Satan rebelled against me, and sought to destroy the agency of man,[17] which I, the Lord God, had given him, and also, that I should give unto him mine own power; by the power of mine Only Begotten, I caused that he should be cast down (Moses 4:1–3).

The most fundamental purpose of mortality was for spirits to obtain bodies. Lucifer and those who sided with him instead of the pre-mortal Jesus would forever be deprived of a body. On 5 January 1841, Joseph Smith stated, "We came to this earth that we might have a body and present it pure before God in the Celestial Kingdom. The great principle of happiness consists in having a body. The Devil has no body, and herein is his punishment. He is pleased when he can obtain the tabernacle of man and when cast out by the Savior he asked to go into the herd of swine showing that he would prefer a swines body to having none. All beings who have bodies have power over those who have not."[18] In the Latter-day Saint cosmos, the vast majority of sons of perdition are unembodied coming from the premortal realm, but there is a presumably small minority who have been born, become sons of perdition in mortality, and died. By virtue of their births, they will be resurrected and, thus, possess bodies in the afterlife.

Brigham Young built on this idea in a way that would leave most current Latter-day Saints puzzled. He taught that a devil needed to have lived a mortal life. For instance, Young approved of those "not worthy" to receive the sacred temple rituals of the faith, known as the

---

17. See Philip L. Barlow, "Shards of Combat: How Did Satan Seek to Destroy the Agency of Man?" *BYU Studies Quarterly* 60, no. 3 (2021): 113–125.
18. Joseph Smith, "Discourse, 5 January 1841, as Reported by William Clayton," in *Documents, Volume 7: September 1839–January 1841*, ed. Matthew C. Godfrey, Spencer W. McBride, Alex D. Smith, and Christopher James Blythe, Vol. 7 of the Documents series of *The Joseph Smith Papers* (Salt Lake City: The Church Historian's Press, 2018), 495.

endowment, so that they would become devils. "A person, to become an angel of the Devil, has first to be a good Saint, and then deny the Lord who bought him. Do you query why we give endowments to A., B., and C.? It is to make devils of those who will deny the faith, for that is also necessary, as a host of devils will be needed."[19] On another occasion he stated that "we have to get our devils from this earth, for the worlds that are to be created."[20] This teaching likely paved the way for later speculation about the position of devils in eternity. However, the only mortal devil ever identified by a prophet appears to be Cain. Commentators have wrestled whether such a position (a "son of perdition") extends also to Judas Iscariot.[21]

NEUTRAL SPIRITS AND THE OFFSPRING OF CAIN

Traditionally to identify mortals as the descendants of Cain is to allege that they share in his nature and in his curse. While the Book of Moses did characterize the descendants of Cain as black (Moses 7:22), there were likely no institutional restrictions on black members during the lifetime of Joseph Smith. This changed in 1852, when Brigham Young first taught that the descendants of Cain would be deprived of the priesthood until all of Abel's descendants had the opportunity to receive it. This was the beginning of a policy of The Church of Jesus Christ of Latter-day Saints denying individuals of black African descent lack priesthood ordination and access to the temple rites crucial to individual and familial practice within the tradition. This policy was officially ended in 1978, and The Church of Jesus Christ of Latter-day Saints has come to disavow the theology on race that existed in this early period.[22]

---

19. Brigham Young, "Discourse, Salt Lake City, 9 September 1860," in *The Complete Discourses of Brigham Young*, 5 vols., ed. Richard S. Van Wagoner (Salt Lake City: Smith-Pettit Foundation, 2009), 3:1649.
20. Brigham Young, "Historian's Office Journal, Salt Lake City, 27 August 1859," in *The Complete Discourses of Brigham Young*, 3:1494.
21. See Ogden Kraut, *Judas Iscariot* (Dugway, UT: Pioneer Press, 1980).
22. "Today, the Church disavows the theories advanced in the past that black skin is a sign of divine disfavor or curse, or that it reflects unrighteous actions in a premortal life; that mixed-race marriages are a sin; or that blacks or people of any other race or ethnicity are inferior in any way to anyone else. Church leaders today unequivocally condemn all racism, past and present, in any form." The Church of Jesus Christ of Latter-day Saints, "Race and the

One of the narratives used to justify limits on black participation within the faith was a myth that they had sinned while still spirits in the premortal world. This story seems to have originated with the Latter-day Saint apostle Orson Hyde in the year following Joseph Smith's death. He presented two versions of the story that year. In a published version of a sermon delivered on 27 April 1845, he wrote:

> At the time the devil was cast out of heaven, there were some spirits that did not know who had the authority, whether God or the devil. They consequently did not take a very active part on either side, but rather thought the devil had been abused, and considered he had rather the best claim to the government. These spirits were not considered bad enough to be cast down in hell, and never have bodies; neither were they considered worthy of an honorable body on this earth. ... [Hyde then explained the idea of the curse of Canaan's lineage based on the events of Genesis 9.] Now, it would seem cruel to force pure celestial spirits into the world through the lineage of Canaan that had been cursed. This would be ill appropriate, putting the precious and the vile together. But those spirits in heaven that rather lent an influence to the devil, thinking he had a little the best right to govern, but did not take a very active part any way, were required to come into the world and take bodies in the accursed lineage of Canaan; and hence the negro or African race.[23]

Hyde argued that God's justice would prevent Him from placing the spirits of the righteous in the inferior bodies of Canaan's descendants. Thus, it could be presumed that those of African descent were less righteous. In a second telling of this narrative, Hyde abandoned the idea that black people had been neutral, with slight leanings towards Satan, in this primordial war, and instead posited that they had sided with Lucifer but were not leaders in his cause. In this account, they were not simply given black physical bodies, according to this second statement, but were black spirits.

> [I]n the council in heaven when Satan rebelled there were some who took an active part in the rebellion but yet were too

---

Priesthood," *Gospel Topics Essays*, online at churchofjesuschrist.org.
23. Orson Hyde, *Speech of Elder Orson Hyde Delivered Before the High Priests Quorum in Nauvoo, April 27th, 1845, Upon the Course and Conduct of Mr. Sidney Rigdon, and Upon the Merits of His Claim to the Presidency of the Church of Jesus Christ of Latter-day Saints* (Nauvoo, IL: John Taylor, 1845), 30.

cowardly to be leaders in the rebellion with Lucifer and others. The leaders in the rebellion were hurled from heaven to hell and were doomed to remain without bodies, but the others whose crimes were not so great were cursed with blackness and became black spirits. When Cain murdered his brother Able on the earth the Almighty cursed him and put a mark on him, or rather turned him black to give the black spirits a chance to come and take bodies like themselves, and the black spirits taking the black bodies made the negroes.[24]

Both accounts make the same basic claim: spirits with sympathy or even allegiance to Satan would be born in black bodies. In the second account, Hyde interestingly shifted his genealogical starting point from Canaan to Cain.

While this narrative was crucial for future stories of Cain, there was pushback among Church leaders and others. For instance, Brigham Young openly rejected these ideas, insisting that it was not pre-mortal behavior that deprived mortals of the privilege but simply their descent from the first murderer. At a meeting of the Salt Lake School of the Prophets, on Christmas Day 1869, in response to a question as to if blacks were neutral in the war in heaven, President Young said:

> No, they were not, there were no neutral spirits in Heaven at the time of the rebellion, all took sides. If any one says they heard the Prophet Joseph say that the spirit of the blacks were neutral in Heaven, he would not believe them, for he heard Joseph say to the contrary. All spirits are pure that came from the presence of God. The posterity of Cain are black because he committed murder. He killed Abel and God set a mark upon his posterity. But the spirits are pure that enter their tabernacles and there will be a chance for the redemption of all the children of Adam, except the sons of perdition.[25]

The recent scholarship of Paul Reeve, Christopher Rich, and LaJean Caruth, demonstrates how even Young's position on African descent from Cain was not a consensus opinion. They cite Orson Pratt's speech, declaring "we have no proof that the Africans are the

---

24. Orson Hyde, "Minutes, 22 March 1845," in *Council of Fifty, Minutes, March 1844–January 1846, The Joseph Smith Papers*, edited by Matthew J. Grow, Ronald K. Esplin, Mark Ashurst-McGee, Gerrit J. Dirkmaat, Jeffrey D. Mahas (Salt Lake City: Church Historian's Press, 2016), 360.
25. See *Salt Lake School of the Prophets, 1867–1883*, edited by Devery S. Anderson (Salt Lake City: Signature Books, 2018), 44.

descendants of old Cain who was cursed, and even if we had that evidence we have not been ordered to inflict that [curse] upon that race."[26] Historicizing the priesthood ban and its justifying theology is significant, but our purpose is to understand what the material tells us about Cain himself. In short, this set of stories builds on the claim that Cain is the head of Satan's followers by moving from his leadership over an ancient secret society to become the progenitor of Satan's followers (or at least the neutral spirits) in this life.

Importantly, descent from Cain has not always been a racial question — or at the very least, someone seemingly of Caucasian descent could also be accused of being descended from Cain. For instance, years before Brigham Young asserted that black people would be deprived the priesthood because of their lineage, he became the target of a similar claim by William Smith, a prophetic rival. In Smith's newspaper, *The Melchizedek and Aaronic Herald*, he reported that Young had once received a blessing from Joseph Smith which identified his lineage: "Joseph the Prophet placed his hands upon Brig Ham Young's head and pronounced these words, "you are of the lineage of Cain through the loins of Ham."[27]

MORMON FUNDAMENTALISM AND CAIN'S BIRTH

Mormon Fundamentalism built on the myths of Cain's monstrous origins. Fundamentalism was a revitalization movement that coalesced in the early twentieth century among those continuing to advocate for plural marriage. The Church of Jesus Christ of Latter-day Saints had publicly disavowed the practice in 1890. In the twenty-first century, most of the tens of thousands of contemporary adherents trace their beliefs to the ministry of Lorin C. Woolley who, in 1929, organized a council to perpetuate plural marriages outside of the mainstream Restored Church. The movement had already come to revere Woolley as a revealer of secrets and a teacher of mysteries. Early Fundamentalists considered one of Woolley's stories so crucial that

---

26. Orson Pratt, March 22, 1856, quoted in W. Paul Reeve, Christopher B. Rich Jr., and LaJean Purcell Carruth, *This Abominable Slavery: Race, Religion, and the Battle over Human Bondage in Antebellum Utah* (New York: Oxford University Press, 2024), 202.
27. William Smith, "B. Young's Lineage," *The Melchizedek and Aaronic Herald* 1, no. 8, February 1850.

they referred to it simply as the "Lorin Woolley story." Woolley, as a young man, had served as a bodyguard for President John Taylor, who was then in hiding from federal marshals eager to prosecute him for polygamy. He claimed to have been present in 1886 when a resurrected Joseph Smith, along with Jesus Christ, supposedly appeared to John Taylor and others to commission them to make sure that new children were born every year to plural families.[28]

This was just one of the mysteries that Woolley shared with his followers. He frequently spoke as if he had knowledge of the personal lives of Latter-day Saint leaders and the proceedings of the hierarchy's confidential meetings. Woolley also shared singular interpretations of scripture. For instance, he told early Fundamentalists that Adam had three wives and Jesus had eight; Seth started constructing the Great Pyramid of Giza, which Shem completed; and Abraham was required to sacrifice Isaac for his mistreatment of Hagar.[29]

Woolley also taught an idea that is typically referred to as the "serpent seed" doctrine, which has come to be most associated with the white-supremacist Christian Identity movement, but has a much older origin. The idea usually suggests that Eve's two sons, Cain and Abel, had two different fathers. Whereas Adam had fathered Abel, the Serpent had fathered Cain. Often it was suggested they were born as a most unusual set of half-twins. The earliest allusion to this teaching among fundamentalists seems to be found in a special notebook belonging to Joseph Musser, titled Book of Remembrance, in which he kept notes of Lorin Woolley's teachings. In an entry for 23–25 January, 1933, he wrote simply: "Nature of forbidden fruit: Sexual."[30] The note does not explain what it means for a serpent to give something sexual to a woman. The next reference is from 17 February, 1938, and appears in the journal of Joseph Lyman Jessop. On that day, Jessop spent time with his "Uncle Rone" (Moroni Jessop) and others "discuss[ing] points

---

28. See Brian C. Hales, "John Taylor's 1886 Revelation," in *The Persistence of Polygamy: Fundamentalist Mormon Polygamy from 1890 to the Present*, ed. Newell G. Bringhurst and Craig L. Foster (Independence, MO: John Whitmer Books, 2015), 58–111.
29. *Reminiscences of John W. Woolley and Lorin C. Woolley*, 3rd ed. (Payson, UT: Latter Day Publications, 2007), 229, 233, 286.
30. Joseph W. Musser, *Book of Remembrance*, January 23–25, 1933. Copy in author's possession.

of remembrance of the sayings and instructions of John W. and Lorin C. Woolley." By this time, Lorin had been dead for close to four years, and his father had been deceased for a decade. Individuals like Moroni Jessop, who had known them both, were often asked to recall their teachings. According to the journal entry, "Uncle Rone retold us of Grandpa (John W.) Woolley telling that Cain was a catch colt [illegitimate child]. Our thots are that Adam is not the father of Cain, nor does Abel and Cain have the same mother."[31]

In 1942, Arnold Boss recorded an interview he conducted with Jessop. When he asked Jessop what the Woolleys had taught him about "Father Adam," Jessop recalled that they both taught "Father Adam was the God of this earth." This was the so-called Adam-God doctrine. But, he recalled, "On several occasions grandpa told me, 'Oh my boy, Oh my boy, I would like to tell you certain things, but I can't, I can't. I expect that I will have to go over to the otherside with my lips sealed.' ... I was told 'When you once get the facts about the Garden of Eden, it will be all clear as mud, Did you ever heard about a catch colt?' I said, 'yes'. 'Well', he said, 'that is the kind of man Cain is. He was a catch colt. Father Adam was not the father of Caine, the Devil was.'"[32]

A few years later, Arnold Boss, then incarcerated with other polygamists, spent an evening discussing Cain with Joseph Musser, then the leading fundamentalist theologian.

> In place of going outside after supper to walk around, I spent most of the time in Joseph's cell. I asked him what the forbidden fruit was that Eve had partaken of? I said, some in early days claim it was the sex life, others say it is not so? Joseph answered me saying, "It is the first; and that Cain was not the son of Seth's mother. He was another woman's son. The father being the negative power. As Adam and Eve came here resurrected beings and begat flesh and bones for their children, so the negative power (Devil — not Lucifer who fell) an immortal being came and multiplied. Cain was a catch colt. There are two powers; there are two eternal powers, both over there and here. And so they exist upon all worlds. Two powers exert themselves to exalt and try man.[33]

---

31. *Diary of Joseph Lyman Jessop*, 3 vols., (privately published, 2000), 2:147.
32. *Testimony of Moroni Jessop*, p. 34, unpublished. Copy in author's possession.
33. *Prison Diary of Arnold Boss*, privately published, June 21, 1945, p. 12.

This seems to be the earliest reference to a physical evil being that Musser separates from the fallen Lucifer. He calls this being simply "the devil." These entries provide us with little detail about what early Fundamentalists believed to have happened in the Garden. In this regard, they are much like kernel narratives, which assume that the reader will be able to complete the story without it being clearly articulated. This usually hints that the author believes the reader will be familiar with a more substantial narrative. What we do get from these entries — beyond interpretations of the serpent fathering Cain — is first, the suggestion of multiple evil beings and, second, that the mother of Cain is not the mother of Abel (according to Moroni Jessop) and not the mother of Seth (according to Musser). That Adam had multiple wives further complicates the story.

While these ideas circulated informally among Fundamentalists, they rarely appeared in print. The first time this legend formed the basis of a theological tract was in 1955, with Francis M. Darter's *The Origin of the Temple Veil*. This would not have been without controversy. Darter had long alienated himself from other Fundamentalists, in part due to his speculative publications. He began his "extremely rare lecture" with the promise that he would "identify the Mystery Father and Mother of Cain."[34] Darter believed that until then, "God evidently saw fit to keep this story out of print."[35] He pointed readers to the legend of neutral spirits who "truly loved Lucifer and his gospel plan of force as much as they loved their own Father Michael, if not more."[36]

After what Darter suggested was "tens of thousands of years (according to Joseph Smith) supporting and preparing them for their mortality... these neutrals to turn their faces toward Lucifer and their backs upon Him, withdrawing their love and support from their God Father, when he needed them most, and they Him, was truly enough to cause Him to lose all interest or desire to Fatherhood or to Sire, them into mortality."[37] Adam was the mortal incarnation of deity, who

---

34. Francis Michael Darter, *The Origin of the Temple Veil* (Salt Lake City: Self-published, 1955), 3.
35. Darter, *Origin of the Temple Veil*, 3.
36. Darter, *Origin of the Temple Veil*, 4.
37. Darter, *Origin of the Temple Veil*, 4.

became mortal to provide bodies for his posterity. As a result, God devised a plan to avoid having a genetic relationship with them.

> So our Father conceived a way, thru His beloved Eve, and her sister wives, Sarah and Lilith, who, i.e. Lilith, according to records, was the world's most beautiful mortal woman. ... Now it was through Lilith, that these neutral spirits were divinely planned to be born into mortality. In plain words: God gave them Satan and their co-father Lucifer the so-called Serpent, for their basic mortal Father: the one they most honored. But Lucifer the Devil was greatly handicapped in his becoming their mortal Father; for he too, was only a spirit man, in his first Estate' unable to have children, having no tangible body. ... [However,] Lucifer can enter the body of a mortal or animal and can control their actions. ... Therefore: spirit Lucifer and mortal Satan knowing Father Michael Adam's desire not to be the mortal Father of these unworthy neutral spirits, who later became the black race of our earth, sought a way, say holy records, thru a very subtle, intelligent creature, also called the Serpent. One who walked on legs, and had hands, and could speak the Adamic language. A creature that he, Lucifer, found favor with, and greatly desired himself becoming the Co-father with this creature, of their proposed son Cain, and his lineage.
>
> This creature was no other than Satan, the Father mortal Devil of the Eloheim Kingdom; who still lived in mortality and was forced to roam about. His position was the same as the Father devil of our earth — Cain — the Satan of our world who still lives. Hence: this mortal Satan of the Eloheim Kingdom, (where Michael, the Arch-angel, Father God of our earth, came from), is the actual Father in person of Cain and Lucifer the Co-father. (We have Co-pilots.) ... Now Devils are not resurrected. When God makes full use of them — they eventually face death and dissolution. Hence, it took this mortal Satan of the Eloheim Kingdom to be the actual Father of the devil of our world, known as Cain. And Cain will be forced to live until he becomes the Father of Devils of other worlds of Michael's Kingdom.[38]

According to Darter's narrative, while Adam approved of the relationship between the serpent and Lilith in that it allowed him not to father "neutral spirits,"[39] he was angered by the serpent's subsequent

---

38. Darter, *Origin of the Temple Veil*, 4–5.
39. Darter, *Origin of the Temple Veil*, 5.

attempt to beguile Eve.[40] This was the impetus of the serpent's curse in which he "turned this mortal Satan's spirit into the body of a crawling Serpent, forcing death in due time, upon Satan's mortal body."[41]

Darter had more to say about the "Goddess Lilith." He argued that Genesis's depiction of Adam and Eve as monogamists was intended to hide the practice of plural marriage from an unworthy world.[42] Darter identified Adam's three wives as Eve, Sarah, and Lilith, replacing Lorin Woolley's Phoebe with Lilith, Adam's wife in Hebrew folklore.[43] Lilith did not knowingly have an affair, but "her divine mind was closed leaving only mortality, hence she could not see as clear, in that certain mortal act."[44] Curiously, Darter also claims that "Cain was evidently the spirit child of Lilith."[45] She was redeemed of her sin by raising up these spirits. It is probable that Darter is implying what another Mormon Fundamentalist, Fred Collier, stated directly: that Lilith had once been the bride of Satan (or perhaps Lucifer in Darter's cosmology). Collier explained, "Of course, now for those of us in Mormon theology, we can believe that Satan lost his wife, Adam was God so, you know, Satan lost his wife to Adam and through that preserved this race on the earth for a purpose."[46]

This idea of premortal coupling drew from the text of a vision reported by Mosiah Hancock that had circulated among Latter-day Saints in the late nineteenth century.[47] This vision held that all beings were first created with soul mates. When a third of the male spirits fell, the remaining women selected husbands from the remaining male spirits. Thus, in this reading, Satan came to the garden as the serpent, in part, to reclaim his wife. This detail does not appear in any other accounts I have located.

Darter may have been the first to write on Cain's strange parentage but he was not the last. Alexander Joseph, a prominent fundamentalist

---

40. Darter, *Origin of the Temple Veil*, 5–6
41. Darter, *Origin of the Temple Veil*, 5.
42. Darter, *Origin of the Temple Veil*, 16.
43. Darter, *Origin of the Temple Veil*, 6.
44. Darter, *Origin of the Temple Veil*, 18.
45. Darter, *Origin of the Temple Veil*, 7
46. Fred C. Collier, "Gospel Doctrine Class-Cain," February 5, 1993, in Fred C. Collier Speeches (Unpublished), 584-585. Copy in author's possession.
47. Mosiah Lyman Hancock, "Mosiah L. Hancock autobiography," undated, 54–56, *Church History Library*, online at catalog.churchofjesuschrist.org.

of the 1970s, used the language of "arc-angel" for Michael "because he arced from another place to this earth." He similarly called the serpent an "arch-devil," who "followed [Michael] to this earth." Joseph names the serpent Cain, acknowledging his identity on this earlier world. The serpent Cain (who Darter had called Satan and Musser called simply the devil) "seduced Lilith who was an 'Eve' and generated a child after his kind. ... Cain's offspring received his father's name (i.e. Cain)." By including two Cains in this version, Joseph was able to make sense of an accounting of Cain's death in the Book of Jasher 2:26–28, in which "he was mistaken for a wild animal and killed." As in Darter's telling, the serpent was able to die because he had been cursed in connection with tempting Eve. However, Alexander Joseph explained that the biblical Cain "is still alive. He mostly goes about at night and keeps his eye on the moon."[48] While I am uncertain why Joseph comments on Cain's attention to the moon, his nocturnal lifestyle points to his monstrous nature.

Joseph's understanding of the story followed Darter's narrative closely with only small variations. Adam had three wives, although all held the title of Eve. He wrote specifically of Sarah and Lilith, as Darter had, and he presumably held Woolley's doctrine that Adam's third wife was Phoebe. Rather than emphasize the neutral spirits, Joseph wrote of Cain's offspring as "the kind that kills God's offspring and seduces women and lies about it."[49] Remembering that Joseph believed God's offspring were Anglo-Saxons, Joseph seemed to be claiming that black people were defined by an alleged bloodlust for white people. His writings also suggest that he brought the serpent seed idea in an anti-semitic direction (as was characteristic of the non-Latter-day Saint Christian Identity movement.)

Fundamentalists have not always been comfortable with the idea that Cain was the offspring of a devil. Nathan Taylor, who spent over a decade associated with the Apostolic United Brethren, recalled that while "there was a clique in the AUB who believed the idea that there was a separate line descended from Lucifer (with maybe Lilith as his wife) — but these weren't ideas the majority of those I associated with accepted — someone told me they thought Satan was a fallen

---

48. Alexander Joseph, *Joseph Talks to Himself*, 50–51. Undated, unpublished. Copy in the author's possession.
49. Joseph, *Joseph Talks to Himself*, 55.

god — these concepts seemed to be on the fringe of Fundamentalism though."[50] Rulon Allred, the head of the AUB from 1954 to 1977, had reportedly declared it a false doctrine. His successor, Owen Allred, likewise considered it an offense to Eve, who was a divine being.

This perspective was repeated by Marianne Watson — a historian affiliated with the Apostolic United Brethren, one of the most well-established Fundamentalist communities — who answered my query on whether the devil fathered Cain simply with: "We in the AUB group certainly do NOT believe it. For me, it is a subject hardly worth my attention--doctrinally or historically."[51] Interestingly, Fundamentalists often accept the idea that the devil has a body, even when he is not considered the father of Cain. It has more to do with incorporating Brigham Young's statements on an embodied devil than it does explaining anything about Cain.

The idea that Satan came from an earlier creation on another world is widely accepted in Mormon Fundamentalism. Marianne Watson explained, "As far as Lucifer (as the devil) having a body, we believe that he was of the same generation as Adam--both having had immortal bodies before Adam came to this earth."[52] However, another Mormon Fundamentalist, Drew Briney, suggested that "it is not a common doctrine at all — mostly, it is held in disrepute by fundamentalists."[53]

Members of the True and Living Church of Jesus Christ of Saints of the Last Days believe Lucifer's embodiment is obvious, considering "Joseph Smith clearly defined an 'angel' as a resurrected being, having a body. He was most clear on this point. So, Lucifer, when he rebelled, was actually 'a [resurrected being] who was in authority in the presence of God.' To be a 'resurrected being in authority in the presence of God' would have made Lucifer a God himself at that time."[54] Drew

---

50. Nathan Taylor, personal communication to author, November 4, 2022, copy in author's possession.
51. Marianne Watson, email message to author, November 9, 2022, copy in author's possession.
52. Marianne Watson, email message to author, November 9, 2022.
53. Drew Briney, personal communication to author, November 6, 2022, copy in author's possession.
54. John Pratt, "Treatise on Perdition," in possession of the author.

Briney pointed to a poetic interpretation of Joseph Smith's vision of the heavens, which states:

> 21. And I saw and bear record of warfare in heav'n;
> For an angel of light, in authority great,
> Rebell'd against Jesus, and sought for his pow'r,
> But was thrust down to woe from his Godified state.[55]

Continuing he explained that Joseph Smith's belief that "Lucifer was a spirit is not considered conflicting, because Lucifer is in a state of dissolution and so that merely suggests that his body had been dislodged by the time Joseph said that." He also explained that it was only because Lucifer's body was regressing to "native intelligence" that Cain "after the millennium will be superior over him because Cain will have a resurrected body."

THE MAN OF SIN

Some Fundamentalists were not only concerned with Cain's origin story. They also believed scripture hinted that he would again emerge in the last days as an anti-Christ figure. The passage is 2 Thessalonians 2:3–4:

> Let no man deceive you by any means: for that day shall not come, except there come a falling away first, and that man of sin be revealed, the son of perdition; Who opposeth and exalteth himself above all that is called God, or that is worshipped; so that he as God sitteth in the temple of God, shewing himself that he is God.

Fundamentalists frequently read this passage to mean that the devil (or another head villain) would claim to be God from within a Latter-day Saint temple. This point was explained by Rulon Allred. "Our head temple will have the devil there … we will have a complete fulfillment of it when Cain himself sits as God in one of those temples and says, 'I am he.'"[56] Fred Collier likewise wrote of Cain as an apocalyptic dictator in his scriptural work, *Book of Revelations*. "The Anti-Christ is and shall be Satan, the son of Satan, even as he is and shall be the Devil, and the son of the Devil. … And if you will receive

---

55. Drew Briney, November 6, 2022, copy in author's possession. See also Joseph Smith, "The Answer," *Times and Seasons* 4, no. 6 (February 1, 1843): 83.
56. Rulon C. Allred, *Treasures of Knowledge: Selected Discourses and Excerpts from Talks* (Hamilton, MT: Bitterroot Publishing Co., 1982), 2: 294.

it, this is the Anti-Christ that seeketh the Throne of My Beloved Son."[57] Curiously, the figure of the anti-Christ has rarely made a significant impact in Latter-day Saint discourse, but it seems an obvious extension of the idea of "Master Mahan," Satan's man on earth.

Conclusion

The importance of the legend of Cain's parentage was an example of the oral gnosis that set apart early Fundamentalist leaders and, in turn, the movement as a whole. It was a subject to be discussed privately with leaders and recorded cryptically in diary entries. When Darter wrote of it publicly, he did so professing to be the first to reveal the secret publicly. Later, it would become a topic in fundamentalist revelatory works such as Fred Collier's Book of Revelations and Robert Crossfield's Second Book of Commandments.

This article only scratches the surface of Cain lore, particularly among schismatic movements. For instance, Julie Rowe, excommunicated visionary and energy healer, speaks of being harassed by Cain at an airport.[58] On her podcasts, she has called him a "shapeshifter." The nineteenth-century schismatic prophet Charles B. Thompson claimed that Cain was literally the incarnation of Lucifer.[59] Later, the Morrisites would profess that Cain was reincarnated as Judas Iscariot and, finally, George A. Smith, a contemporary Latter-day Saint general authority.[60]

There is a great deal we can learn about Latter Day Saint biblical expansion and speculative theology through Cain lore. In reality, while Cain is an idiosyncratic example, he is illustrative of a common phenomenon in our biblical reception. While we rarely tell Cain lore in formal settings, we regularly speak of our unique understanding of figures like Adam, Abraham, Moses, or Elijah. These figures demonstrate how our understanding of such figures typically begins with an

---

57. Fred C. Collier, *The Book of Revelations* (Hanna, UT: Colliers Publishing, 2006), 34.
58. "A Plague Spreading Through Many Families," *Truth Matters* blogpost, May 31, 2019, online at ldstruthmatters.blogspot.com.
59. Charles B. Thompson, ed., *Zion's Harbinger and Baneemy's Organ* 2, no. 10 (October 1852): 77.
60. Joseph Morris, "The 'Spirit Prevails'" (San Francisco: J.A. Dove & Co., 1886), 12.

original expansion by Joseph Smith that is subsequently developed in future speculation by Latter Day Saint leaders and laity.

14

"THEY DID CONTAIN THE FIVE BOOKS OF MOSES"

SOURCE CRITICISM AND THE CONTENTS OF THE PLATES OF BRASS

NEAL RAPPLEYE

The Book of Mormon's claim of a 600 BC record containing the "five books of Moses" creates a direct conflict with prevailing biblical scholarship. Many scholars argue the Pentateuch was not compiled until centuries later, making the "plates of brass" a historical impossibility. However, substantial evidence from archaeology, linguistics, and epigraphy challenges this late-dating trend. This alternate view places the primary composition of the Hebrew Bible, including the core of the Pentateuch, firmly in the pre-exilic period (especially the eighth to seventh centuries BC). Linguistic analysis shows the texts use Standard Biblical Hebrew, not the later language from after the exile. Furthermore, archaeological finds and internal textual clues—such as later books referencing earlier ones—suggest that these narratives and legal codes were already being compiled into an authoritative corpus before 600 BC. This framework makes the existence of a proto-Old Testament, as described in the Book of Mormon, historically plausible.

Few subjects are as hotly contested in biblical studies today than questions regarding when and how the texts in the Hebrew Bible (or Old Testament) were written and compiled. Traditional ascriptions of authorship and dating are widely questioned in favor of complicated theories proposing multiple layers of composition and editing spanning centuries. Increasingly, many biblical scholars are pushing the dates of final composition to progressively later periods, with some favoring dates as late as the fourth to second centuries BC — only shortly before the earliest copies of biblical texts are attested among the Dead Sea Scrolls.[1] Latter-day Saint theology rejects scriptural inerrancy, so is not *inherently* threatened by historical-critical theories about the composition of biblical texts.[2] However, an important wrinkle is Nephi's summary of the contents of the plates of brass, a record compiled sometime before 600 BC.

According to Nephi, when his father examined the records engraved upon the brass plates, he found that "they did contain the five books of Moses, which gave an account of the creation of the world, and also of Adam and Eve, who were our first parents" (1 Nephi 5:11). In other words, they contained a version of the first five books of the Old Testament — Genesis, Exodus, Leviticus, Numbers, and Deuteronomy — commonly called by the Hebrew name *Torah* (meaning law or teaching) or the Greek name *Pentateuch* (meaning five books). Nephi also said they contained "a record of the Jews from the beginning, even down to the commencement of the reign of Zedekiah, king of Judah" (1 Nephi 5:12). A version of this same history appears in Judges through 2 Kings 24, and presumably this constituted an early form of that same history, or one based on similar sources. It also had "the prophecies of the holy prophets, from the beginning, even down to the commencement of the reign of Zedekiah" (1 Nephi 5:13). In terms of biblical prophets, this includes at least Jeremiah — mentioned specifically by Nephi here in 1 Nephi 5:13 — and Isaiah, quoted extensively in the Book of Mormon (see 1 Nephi 20–21; 2 Nephi 12–24; Mosiah 14). Others, such as Amos, Hosea, Micah, Zephaniah, and Nahum, hypothetically could have been on the plates as well. This substantial overlap between the likely contents of the plates of brass and what we have today as the Old Testament presents a potential problem

---

1. Niels Peter Lemche, "The Old Testament — A Hellenistic Book?," in *Did Moses Speak Attic? Jewish Historiography and Scripture in the Hellenistic Period*, ed. Lester L. Grabbe (Sheffield, GB: Sheffield Academic Press, 2001), 287–318; Niels Peter Lemche, "Is the Old Testament Still a Hellenistic Book?," in *Biblical Interpretation Beyond Historicity*, ed. Ingrid Hjelm and Thomas L. Thompson (New York: Routledge, 2016), 61–75.
2. See David Rolph Seely, "'We Believe the Bible to Be the Word of God, as Far as It Is Translated Correctly': Latter-day Saints and Historical Biblical Criticism," *Studies in the Bible and Antiquity* 8 (2016): 64–88; Philip Barlow, *Mormons and the Bible: The Place of the Latter-day Saints in American Religion* (New York: Oxford University Press, 1991), 103–147.

for the Book of Mormon, in light of modern theories favoring exilic or post-exilic composition for much of the Hebrew Bible.

Some critics view this problem as insurmountable. According to Alex Douglas, "Scholars do not know everything about the world of the Old Testament, but everything they do know indicates that the brass plates could not have existed as Nephi describes them."[3] He further explains, "The Book of Mormon supposes that a kind of proto-Old Testament — a compilation of everything dealing with life before the exile — existed in 600 BCE, but over and over again modern scholarship shows this supposition to be highly unlikely, if not impossible."[4] He singles out the Torah, specifically, as a problem. "The 'five books of Moses' clearly refer to the Pentateuch, but the Pentateuch was not compiled — nor indeed was the Priestly source even written — until well after Lehi would have left Jerusalem. There could not, therefore, have been 'five books.' Furthermore, the earliest indication that these books were ascribed to Moses does not surface until after the exile."[5]

Contrary to these strong statements, however, all is not lost for the Book of Mormon. In contrast to literary and textually-based biblical scholars, many archaeologists, epigraphers, and historical linguists — whose opinions tend to be more firmly grounded in dateable comparative data from archaeology and inscriptions — are inclined to see the Iron II period (circa 1000–586 BC), and especially the Iron IIC (circa 720–586 BC), as the primary setting for the composition and initial compilation of many biblical texts. This paper will briefly review archaeological, epigraphic, and linguistic evidence that suggests much of the Hebrew Bible was written in the pre-exilic period and brought together and edited in the eighth to seventh century BC. It will then focus a more detailed — though far from complete or comprehensive — discussion specifically on the dating of Pentateuchal texts, making the case that much of the Torah was written and compiled before 600 BC.

It is important to note that this paper will not deal with questions regarding the *historicity* of the biblical texts under discussion. The only consideration for this study is whether or not some form of the

---

3. Alex Douglas, *The Old Testament for Latter-day Saints* (Salt Lake City: Signature Books, 2023), 176.
4. Douglas, *Old Testament for Latter-day Saints*, 175.
5. Douglas, *Old Testament for Latter-day Saints*, 174.

texts were written sometime prior to 600 BC and could thus be plausibly available to be copied onto the plates of brass.

A Reference Guide to Chronological Periods Mentioned in This Paper

Levantine Archaeological Periodization

Middle Bronze Age	2000–1550 BC
Late Bronze Age	1550–1200 BC
Iron Age I	1200–1000 BC
Iron Age IIA	1000–925 BC
Iron Age IIB	925–720 BC
Iron Age IIC	720–586 BC

Ancient Near Eastern Imperial Ages

Neo-Assyrian Period	911–612 BC
Neo-Babylonian Period	626–539 BC
Persian Period	539–332 BC
Hellenistic Period	332–63 BC
Maccabean Period	167–37 BC

Israelite History Periodization

Pre-Exilic	1200–586 BC
Pre-Monarchic	1200–1000 BC
Monarchic/First Temple	1000–586 BC
Exilic	586–539 BC
Post-Exilic	539–400 BC
Second Temple	516 BC–70 AD

All dates should be considered approximations and may differ somewhat from those found in other sources

THE COMPOSITION AND COMPILATION OF THE HEBREW BIBLE

Evidence from inscriptions and other archaeological finds indicates that Hebrew writing and literature grew out of the wider Northwest Semitic literary tradition, which already exhibited considerable complexity and sophistication by the Late Bronze Age (circa 1550–1200 BC).[6] A handful of biblical texts possess archaic features and

---

6. Richard S. Hess, "Literacy in Iron Age Israel," in *Windows into Old Testament History: Evidence, Argument, and the Crisis of "Biblical Israel"*, ed. V. Philips Long, David W. Baker, and Gordon J. Wenham (Grand Rapids: Eerdmans, 2002), 83–85; William M. Schniedewind, *How the Bible Became a Book: The Textualization of Ancient Israel* (Cambridge: Cambridge University Press,

literary motifs attested in Canaanite inscriptions from the mid to late second millennium BC.[7] This suggests that they were composed (at least orally) sometime between Late Bronze II and early Iron I (circa 1300–1100 BC). By the Iron IIA period (circa 1000–925 BC), Hebrew inscriptions are directly attested in the archaeological record, and the corpus of Hebrew inscriptions grows considerably in the Iron IIB (circa 925–720 BC) and especially the Iron IIC (circa 720–586 BC) periods, when many scholars believe literacy had become widespread.[8] Epigrapher Matthieu Richelle notes that some inscriptions from the Iron IIA period attest to a "semi-cursive" script that was created "due to the practice of scribes writing fast, because they were writing long texts."[9] Seal impressions from a late ninth-century-BC context, but dated by iconography to as early as the mid-eleventh century BC, bear evidence of the papyrus documents they were once attached to, demonstrating the use of papyrus scrolls for writing long documents during this period.[10] Richelle thus concluded that "the conditions for the production of literature were already present in the 10th and 9th

---

2004), 56–57; Christopher A. Rollston, "Epigraphic Evidence from Jerusalem and its Environs at the Dawn of Biblical History: Methodologies and a Long Durée Perspective," *New Studies in the Archaeology of Jerusalem and its Region* 11 (2017): *10–*12.

7. Hess, "Literacy in Iron Age Israel," 84–85; Schniedewind, *How the Bible Became a Book*, 52–56; Ronald Hendel and Jan Joosten, *How Old is the Bible? A Linguistic, Textual, and Historical Study* (New Haven: Yale University Press, 2018), 45.

8. Hess, "Literacy in Iron Age Israel," 86–94; Christopher A. Rollston, *Writing and Literacy in the World of Ancient Israel: Epigraphic Evidence from the Iron Age* (Atlanta, GA: Society of Biblical Literature, 2010); William M. Schniedewind, *A Social History of Hebrew: Its Origins Through the Rabbinic Period* (New Haven: Yale University Press, 2013), 99–122; Shira Faigenbaum-Golovin, Arie Shaus, Barak Sober, et al., "Algorithmic Handwriting Analysis of Judah's Military Correspondence Sheds Light on Composition of Biblical Texts," *PNAS* 113, no. 17 (2016): 4667.

9. Matthieu Richelle, "Elusive Scrolls: Could Any Hebrew Literature Have Been Written Prior to the Eighth Century BCE?," *Vetus Testamentum* 66 (2016): 590.

10. Matthieu Richelle, "Literacy in the Kingdom of Judah: A Typology of Approaches and a Criticism of Quantitative Perspectives," *Jerusalem Journal of Archaeology* 7 (2024): 116; William G. Dever, *Beyond the Texts: An Archaeological Portrait of Ancient Israel and Judah* (Atlanta: SBL Press, 2017), 406.

centuries [BC]."[11] Christopher A. Rollston emphatically states, "There was writing and reading in Jerusalem and its environs in Iron IIA," which was not "something *de novo*," but rather was "part of a long and deep tradition."[12] He thus concluded that "the intellectual infrastructure was certainly present in the southern Levant during the ninth century BCE for writing texts of substance and sophistication, and this is as true of scribes in Israel and Judah as it was for scribes in Moab, Ammon, and Damascus."[13] Thus, books were likely being written in Israel during the early monarchy, perhaps including some of the biblical books or at least sources that were later incorporated into biblical writings.[14]

Like any language, Hebrew underwent various stages of development, which makes it possible to approximate a general date for a biblical text based on the historical stage of Hebrew the text reflects. The bulk of the Hebrew Bible is written in what scholars call "Standard Biblical Hebrew" (SBH) or "Classic Biblical Hebrew" (CBH). Linguists Ron Hendel and Jan Joosten have noted the close similarity to the stage of Hebrew reflected in Iron II inscriptions and Classic Biblical Hebrew: "The language of Judean inscriptions from the eighth to sixth centuries BCE stands close to CBH." Thus, "in regard to the essential linguistic system ... epigraphic Hebrew and CBH are essentially identical."[15] Various inscriptions from the eighth to seventh centuries BC, including those from Khirbet el-Qom, Kuntillet Ajrud, Beit Lei, Arad, and Ḥorvat ʿUza display literary features reminiscent of biblical literature.[16] Three biblical-like psalms, including a version of Psalm 20, were part of a literary corpus belonging to the Israelite/Judean community found in Elephantine in Egypt.[17] Although found in Egypt

---

11. Richelle, "Elusive Scrolls," 592.
12. Rollston, "Epigraphic Evidence from Jerusalem," *16.
13. Christopher A. Rollston, "Inscriptional Evidence for the Writing of the Earliest Texts of the Bible: Intellectual Infrastructure in Tenth- and Ninth-Century Israel, Judah, and the Southern Levant," in *The Formation of the Pentateuch*, ed. Jan C. Gertz, Bernard M. Levinson, Dalit Rom-Shiloni, and Konrad Schmid (Tübingen, DE: Mohr Siebeck, 2016), 19.
14. Alan Millard, "The Knowledge of Writing in Iron Age Palestine," *Tyndale Bulletin* 46, no. 2 (1995): 207–217.
15. Hendel and Joosten, *How Old is the Bible*, 71.
16. Dever, *Beyond the Texts*, 495–496, 588; Millard, "Knowledge of Writing," 216.
17. Karel van der Toorn, "Egyptian Papyrus Sheds New Light on Jewish History,"

and transcribed in Aramaic using a Demotic Egyptian script, the texts were originally composed in Hebrew language somewhere in ancient Israel by or before the eighth century BC.[18] Silver scrolls from the late seventh century BC found in Jerusalem contain variations of Deuteronomy 7:9–10 and Numbers 6:24–26, leading William G. Dever to state that they "belong clearly to a literary tradition that is close to, almost identical with, the biblical tradition."[19] William M. Schniedewind combines this evidence with the increased evidence for literacy and greater social complexity in the Iron IIC period to suggest that "social conditions favored the flourishing of Hebrew literature in the eighth through seventh centuries BCE."[20]

In contrast, according to Israel Finkelstein "there is almost no evidence for Hebrew writing in Yehud [Judah] in *c.* 586–350 BCE, and very little evidence until *c.* 200 BCE. This should serve as a warning signal to those who tend to place much biblical material in Persian period Yehud."[21] The destruction and devastation by the Babylonians left Judah as a depopulated and culturally impoverished region ill-suited to the large-scale production of literary works.[22] Furthermore, Hebrew writing that appears in inscriptions *after* this period represents a distinctly different stage of the Hebrew language. Even attempts to imitate Classical Biblical Hebrew in writings found among the Dead Sea Scrolls bear the tell-tale signs of their later composition.[23] Moreover, the Classical Biblical Hebrew writings generally reflect an Iron Age setting and show little to no Persian or Greek cultural influence.[24]

Biblical Archaeology Review 44, no. 4 (2018): 32–39, 66, 68.

18. Karel van der Toorn, *Becoming Diaspora Jews: Behind the Story of Elephantine* (New Haven: Yale University Press, 2019), 83–86.
19. Dever, *Beyond the Texts*, 588.
20. Schniedewind, *How the Bible Became a Book*, 67.
21. Israel Finkelstein, "Jerusalem and Judah 600–200 BCE: Implications for Understanding Pentateuchal Texts," in *The Fall of Jerusalem and the Rise of the Torah*, ed. Peter Dubovský, Dominik Markl, Jean-Pierre Sonnet (Tübingen, DE: Mohr Siebeck, 2016), 14.
22. Schniedewind, *How the Bible Became a Book*, 139–147, 165–171; Dever, *Beyond the Texts*, 603–608.
23. Hendel and Joosten, *How Old is the Bible*, 85–97; Schniedewind, *How the Bible Became a Book*, 171–182.
24. William G. Dever, "Can Archaeology Serve as a Tool in Textual Criticism of the Hebrew Bible?," in *Sacred History, Sacred Literature: Essays on Ancient Israel,*

Collectively, all of this evidence points to the Iron II period, and especially the late eighth to seventh centuries BC, as the time period in which the majority of the Hebrew Bible was written, edited, and brought together into an authoritative collection of writings.[25] Schniedewind explains, "The Bible as we know it began to take shape in Jerusalem in the late eighth century BCE.... Powerful social and political forces converged at that time resulting in the collection of earlier, mostly oral, traditions and the writing of new texts." Events such as "the exile of the northern kingdom and the urbanization of the rural south — particularly Jerusalem — set into motion the collection and editing that resulted in the writing of extended portions of the Hebrew Bible. This began in the court of King Hezekiah in the late eighth century BCE ... but it would spread and reach its apex in the latter days of the Judean monarchy."[26] Israel Finkelstein and Neil Asher Silberman similarly argue that "archaeology has provided enough evidence ... that the historical core of the Pentateuch and the Deuteronomistic History [i.e., Genesis–2 Kings] was substantially shaped in the seventh century BCE."[27]

Amassing impressive libraries of culturally and religiously important texts, along with legal and administrative documents, was also part of the zeitgeist of the era. "The number of archives and libraries in the Near East rose sharply beginning in the eighth century [BC] and reached its apex in the seventh century [BC]."[28] Neo-Assyrian kings like Sennacherib (circa 705–681 BC) and Ashurbanipal (circa 668–627 BC) boasted of their impressive libraries. "A similar phenomenon seems to have occurred in Egypt" under Pharaoh Shabaqa (circa 716–702 BC).[29] Egyptologist James K. Hoffmeier explains, "[The] Saite period (the late seventh and sixth century [BC]) has been called the 'Saite Renaissance,' in which ancient texts were copied and utilized."[30]

---

the Bible, and Religion in Honor of R. E. Friedman on his Sixtieth Birthday, ed. Shawna Dolansky (University Park, PA: Eisenbrauns, 2008), 225–237.
25. Dever, "Can Archaeology Serve as a Tool," 235–237.
26. Schniedewind, How the Bible Became a Book, 64, 89–90.
27. Israel Finkelstein and Neil Asher Silberman, The Bible Unearthed: Archaeology's New Vision of Israel and the Origin of Its Sacred Text (New York: Touchstone, 2001), 14.
28. Schniedewind, How the Bible Became a Book, 74.
29. Schniedewind, How the Bible Became a Book, 75.
30. James K. Hoffmeier, "The Discovery of the Book of the Law in 2 Kings 22:8–10

Thus, the collection of older texts and traditions, along with writing of new literature, under the reign of Hezekiah and his successors, "fits in with the general desire of kings to build a library as an accoutrement of royalty."[31] As Hoffmeier notes, "Concerning the late eighth century BC in Judah ... king Hezekiah was caught up in the spirit of the times and actively preserved earlier Hebrew literature."[32]

In Assyria, libraries were not limited to the king, but other royal and religious officials and even merchants maintained libraries within their own homes.[33] The writings kept within these private libraries were not limited to a given individual's professional background, "but could include hundreds of works outside their field of specialization" suggesting "the broad education and, in some cases, deep learning of the individuals in question."[34]

The evidence for libraries and archives in Judah is limited to a few collections of seals and ostraca, but the evidence does suggest that document collections were being kept in both royal administrative contexts and private domestic settings.[35] Copies of more substantive works

---

in the Light of the Literary Renaissance of the Eighth to Seventh Centuries in the Ancient Near East," in *Write That They May Read: Studies in Literacy and Textualization in the Ancient Near East and in the Hebrew Scriptures, Essays in Honour of Professor Alan R. Millard*, ed. Daniel I. Block, David C. Deuel, C. John Collins, Paul J. N. Lawrence (Eugene, OR: Pickwick Publications, 2020), 291.

31. Schniedewind, *How the Bible Became a Book*, 84.
32. Hoffmeier, "Discovery of the Book of the Law," 293.
33. Nadav Na'aman, "Sources and Composition in the History of David," in *Ancient Israel's History and Historiography: The First Temple Period* (University Park, PA: Eisenbrauns, 2006), 32–33; Millard, "Knowledge of Writing," 213–214.
34. Simo Parpola, "Assyrian Library Records," *Journal of Near Eastern Studies* 42, no. 1 (1983): 10.
35. Yigal Shiloh and David Tarler, "Bullae from the City of David: A Hoard of Seal Impressions from the Israelite Period," *Biblical Archaeologist* 49, no. 4 (1986): 196–209; Anson F. Rainey, "The Saga of Eliashib: Office Files Found of Commander of Fort at Arad," *Biblical Archaeology Review* 13, no. 2 (1987): 36–39; André Lemaire, "Writing and Writing Materials," in *The Anchor Bible Dictionary*, 6 vols., ed. David Noel Freedman (New York: Doubleday, 1992), 6:1004; Margreet Steiner, "Jerusalem in the Tenth and Seventh Centuries BCE: From Administrative Town to Commercial City," in *Studies in the Archaeology of the Iron Age in Israel and Jordan*, ed. Amihai Mazar (Sheffield, GB: Sheffield Academic Press, 2001), 284; Dana M. Pike, "Israelite Inscriptions from the Time of Jeremiah and Lehi," in *Glimpses of Lehi's Jerusalem*, ed. John W. Welch,

were typically written on perishable materials that simply have not survived well in the regions of Israel and Judah.[36] In southern Egypt, however, where the drier conditions have resulted in better preservation of papyri documents, a corpus of 35 literary texts — including historical narratives, ritual songs, and laments — was found among the mixed community of diaspora Jews/Israelites, Syrians, and Babylonians living in Elephantine and Syrene. This collection of writings as a whole pre-dates this community's arrival in Egypt, likely coming from the eighth to seventh centuries BC. They are not exclusively Israelite, but rather reflect the diverse background of this eclectic group. Nevertheless, these writings stand as direct evidence that Judeans and Israelites far outside the royal administration were participating in the literary culture and aggregation of written material common to the Neo-Assyrian period (circa 911–612 BC).[37]

The full size and scope of the impressive Assyrian libraries was certainly more expansive than anything in Judah at the time. In terms of what eventually made it into the biblical canon, however, Schniedewind argues the collection of material was already fairly comprehensive in Hezekiah's day. It would have included the eighth century BC prophetic works (such as Amos, Hosea, Micah, and parts of Isaiah), some of the wisdom writings attributed to David and Solomon in Psalms and Proverbs, an early version of the history recorded in Joshua–2 Kings culminating in the fall and exile of the northern kingdom of Israel, and some of the priestly codes and other traditions found in Genesis, Exodus, and Leviticus.[38] This foundational collection would have continued to be edited and expanded by Hezekiah's successors in the seventh century BC, and copies certainly would have circulated among the scribes and possibly other royal and priestly officials and other elites.

This broadly overlaps with the reported contents of the plates of brass (1 Nephi 5:11-13), and suggests that, at least in general terms, it is plausible that an official such as Laban could have possessed a copy of this early proto-Bible. Much of the Pentateuch — or at least the

---

David Rolph Seely, and Jo Ann H. Seely (Provo, UT: Foundation for Ancient Research and Mormon Studies, Brigham Young University, 2004), 203–210.
36. Richelle, "Elusive Scrolls," 556–594.
37. Van der Toorn, *Becoming Diaspora Jews*, 61–88, 149–187.
38. Schniedewind, *How the Bible Became a Book*, 89–90.

traditions and writings that would later be included in the Pentateuch — is included amongst the materials Schniedewind argues were being compiled and edited in the eighth century BC. Nonetheless, since the dating and composition of the Torah is a highly contested topic within biblical studies, a closer look at the evidence for its pre-exilic composition is necessary.

THE COMPOSITION OF THE PENTATEUCH

Understanding exactly *how* and *when* the Torah was written has long been one of the most complicated and controversial questions in modern biblical studies. In Judeo-Christian tradition, it is conventionally believed that Moses wrote the Torah. In contrast, biblical scholars generally posit a long and complicated process of composition for the Pentateuch that post-dates the time of Moses by centuries. For roughly a hundred years, the prevailing academic paradigm for understanding the origins of the Torah was the "documentary hypothesis" — the idea that, in its present form, the Torah was composed from various source "documents" which had been spliced together to form one grand narrative.[39] Using apparent narrative seams, unnecessary repetitions, and contradictory details in the present text, advocates for this theory slice the accounts from Genesis through Numbers up into various hypothetical source documents.[40]

In the classical formulation of the documentary hypothesis, there are four main sources: (1) the J-source, so-called because of its preference for the divine name *Jehovah*; (2) the E-source, named for its preference for the divine title *Elohim*; (3) the P-source, a label applied to the body of laws, customs, rituals, and narratives focused on priestly matters; and (4) the D-source, which is essentially the book of Deuteronomy. Many scholars would also recognize Leviticus 17–26 as a fifth

---

39. Joseph Blenkinsopp, *The Pentateuch: An Introduction to the First Five Books of the Bible* (New York: Doubleday, 1992), 1–28; Thomas B. Dozeman, *The Pentateuch: Introducing the Torah* (Minneapolis: Fortress Press, 2016), 33–199; Joel S. Baden, *Source Criticism* (Eugene, OR: Cascade Books, 2024).
40. Richard Elliott Friedman, *Who Wrote the Bible?*, 2nd ed. (New York: HarperCollins, 1997); David Bokovoy, *Authoring the Old Testament: Genesis–Deuteronomy* (Salt Lake City: Greg Kofford Books, 2014), 1–122; Baruch J. Schwartz, "The Documentary Hypothesis," in *The Oxford Handbook of the Pentateuch*, ed. Joel S. Baden and Jeffrey Stackert (New York: Oxford University Press, 2021), 165–187.

source embedded within P, called the "Holiness Code," or simply H for short.[41] Over time, various scholars have modified and adapted this basic model, adding layers, redactions, and sources in rather complex and unwieldy ways.[42] As Shawna Dolansky observed, "The lack of a clear and consistent source-critical method applied universally has led ... to a proliferation of unwieldy and ultimately untenable arguments for overly complicating and fragmenting the Documentary Hypothesis."[43] Others have challenged the veracity of this model altogether.[44] By the end of the twentieth century, critiques had become so prevalent that Joseph Blenkinsopp declared: "There is no longer a consensus on the existence of identifiable, continuous narrative sources covering the entire range of the Pentateuch."[45] To be sure, many scholars still adhere to and defend some form of the documentary hypothesis.[46] Yet a variety of alternatives have also been proposed, and no theory presently holds widespread acceptance in the field.[47]

---

41. Antony F. Campbell and Mark A. O'Brien, *Sources of the Pentateuch: Texts, Introductions, Annotations* (Minneapolis: Fortress Press, 1993); Richard Elliot Friedman, *The Bible with Sources Revealed: A New View into the Five Books of Moses* (New York: HarperOne, 2003).
42. Baden, *Source Criticism*, 78–97.
43. Shawna Dolansky, "Deuteronomy 34: The Death of Moses, Not of Source Criticism," *Journal of Biblical Literature* 133, no. 3 (2014): 676.
44. R. N. Whybray, *The Making of the Pentateuch: A Methodological Study* (Sheffield, GB: Sheffield Academic Press, 1994); John S. Bergsma and Jeffrey L. Morrow, *Murmuring Against Moses: The Contentious History and Contested Future of Pentateuchal Studies* (Steubenville, OH: Emmaus Academic, 2023), 3–78, 173–253; Dozeman, *Pentateuch*, 136–179; Blenkinsopp, *Pentateuch*, 19–25; Baden, *Source Criticism*, 98–120.
45. Blenkinsopp, *Pentateuch*, 25.
46. Baruch J. Schwartz, "Does Recent Scholarship's Critique of the Documentary Hypothesis Constitute Grounds for its Rejection?," in *The Pentateuch: International Perspectives on Current Research*, ed. Thomas B. Dozeman, Konrad Schmid, and Baruch J. Schwartz (Tübingen, DE: Mohr Siebeck, 2011), 3–17; Joel S. Baden, *The Composition of the Pentateuch: Renewing the Documentary Hypothesis* (New Haven: Yale University Press, 2011); Friedman, *Who Wrote the Bible*; Bokovoy, *Authoring the Old Testament*.
47. Rolf Rendtorff, *The Problem of the Process of Transmission in the Pentateuch*, trans. John J. Scullion (Sheffield, GB: Sheffield Academic Press, 1990); David M. Carr, *Reading the Fractures of Genesis: Historical and Literary Approaches* (Louisville, KY: Westminster John Knox, 1996); Anthony F. Campbell and Mark A. O'Brien, *Rethinking the Pentateuch: Prolegomena to the Theology of*

The interest of this paper, however, is more with *when* the Torah was written rather than *how*. Even more specifically, the question is (at least in broad outlines) how much of the Pentateuch was part of the literature that was being either written, edited, or compiled from earlier sources during the eighth and seventh centuries BC? In the classical formulation of the documentary hypothesis, J is thought to be the earliest source, generally dating to the United Monarchy (circa tenth–ninth centuries BC); E is thought to come from northern Israel and date to early in the divided monarchy (circa ninth–eighth centuries BC); D is linked to Josiah's reforms (see 2 Kings 22–23) and thus dated to the seventh century BC; and then P (including H) is dated to the Babylonian exile or even later (circa sixth–fifth centuries BC). The sources were then integrated together into the Pentateuch, as we know it today, sometime after P was written.[48]

Like the documentary hypothesis itself, these traditional dates have been challenged, especially as regards the late dating of P/H.[49] One of the major critiques has been that the classical documentary hypothesis and the dates of the sources were initially formulated in a literary vacuum, when very little ancient Near Eastern literature (outside the Bible itself) had been discovered and studied.[50] Theories about the development and dating of the sources were thus based on

---

Ancient Israel (Louisville, KY: Westminster John Knox, 2005); Konrad Schmid, *Genesis and the Moses Story: Israel's Dual Origins in the Hebrew Bible*, trans. James D. Nogalski (University Park, PA: Eisenbrauns, 2010).

48. Norman K. Gottwald, *The Hebrew Bible: A Brief Socio-Literary Introduction* (Minneapolis: Fortress Press, 2009), 82–84, 184–188, 200–201, 221–223, 273–279; David Noel Freedman, "The Pentateuch," in *Eerdmans Commentary on the Bible*, ed. David Noel Freedman (Grand Rapids: Eerdmans, 2003), 25–31.

49. Benjamin Kilchör, "Wellhausen's Five Pillars for the Priority of D over P/H: Can They Still Be Maintained?," in *Paradigm Change in Pentateuchal Research*, ed. Matthias Armgardt, Benjamin Kilchör and Markus Zehnder (Wiesbaden, DE: Harrassowitz, 2019), 101–113; Moshe Weinfeld, *The Place of the Law in the Religion of Ancient Israel* (Leiden, NL: Brill, 2004), 16–33; Ziony Zevit, "Converging Lines of Evidence Bearing on the Date of P," *Zeitschrift für die alttestamentliche Wissenschaft* 94, no. 4 (1982): 481–511.

50. K. A. Kitchen, *On the Reliability of the Old Testament* (Grand Rapids: Eerdmans, 2003), 484–497; David M. Carr, *The Formation of the Hebrew Bible: A New Reconstruction* (New York: Oxford University Press, 2011); Joshua A. Berman, *Inconsistency in the Torah: Ancient Literary Convention and the Limits of Source Criticism* (New York: Oxford University Press, 2017).

modern, anachronistic literary expectations. In recent years, many scholars have advocated for greater use of ancient Near Eastern literature, inscriptions, and archaeology in models for understanding the composition and development of the Torah.[51] Using this rationale, several lines of evidence indicate that, on the whole, the Pentateuch was primarily written, compiled, and edited during the time before the Babylonian exile of 586 BC.

First, historical linguistics indicates that essentially all of the Torah is written in Standard Biblical Hebrew, not Late Biblical Hebrew as would be expected if it were written, or even heavily edited, in the fifth century BC or even later. As Gary A. Rendsburg summarized, "the main body of the Torah is written in Standard Biblical Hebrew, which represents the language of Judah during the monarchy (both early and late) … [and] there are no indications of Late Biblical Hebrew."[52] This is true of *all* the putative sources or literary layers within the Torah, including the material attributed to P.[53] Jan Joosten explains, "The Pentateuch is, from a linguistic point of view, remarkably unified. It is hard to detect developments from book to book or from one stratum to another. The Priestly code stands out for its religious cast and its literary presentation, but it reflects roughly the same type of Hebrew as the non-P sections."[54] Recall that Standard (or Classical) Biblical Hebrew

---

51. Jeffrey H. Tigay, ed., *Empirical Models for Biblical Criticism*, 2nd ed. (Eugene, OR: Wipf and Stock, 2005); Raymond F. Person Jr. and Robert Rezetko, ed., *Empirical Models Challenging Biblical Criticism* (Atlanta: SBL Press, 2016); Joshua A. Berman, "A Critical Intellectual History of the Historical-Critical Paradigm in Biblical Studies," in *Exploring the Composition of the Pentateuch*, ed. L. S. Baker Jr., Kenneth Bergland, Felipe A. Masotti, and A. Rahel Wells (University Park, PA: Eisenbrauns, 2020), 7–25.
52. Gary A. Rendsburg, "Pentateuch, Linguistic Layers in the," in *Encyclopedia of Hebrew Language and Linguistics*, 4 vols., ed. Geoffrey Khan (Leiden, NL: Brill, 2013), 3:62–63.
53. Avi Hurvitz, "The Evidence of Language in Dating the Priestly Code: A Linguistic Study in Technical Idioms and Terminology," *Revue Biblique* 81, no. 1 (1974): 24–56; Gary Rendsburg, "Late Biblical Hebrew and the Date of 'P'," *Journal of Ancient Near Eastern Society* 12, no. 1 (1980): 65–80; Linda Petersson, "The Linguistic Profile of the Priestly Narrative of the Pentateuch," in *Paradigm Change in Pentateuchal Research*, 243–264. See Hendel and Joosten, *How Old is the Bible*, 129 for additional studies on the early linguistic dating of P.
54. Jan Joosten, "Diachronic Linguistics and the Date of the Pentateuch," in

is closely related to the Hebrew language found in inscriptions from the early first millennium BC, as Frank Polak observed: "In general, the language of the Pentateuch largely fits the profile of the texts from Kuntillet 'Ajrud and Judahite administrative texts."[55]

Furthermore, the meanings of rare and difficult to interpret words that occur in the Torah (and other SBH texts) are best determined by finding related words (known as *cognates*) in Akkadian and Ugaritic inscriptions, languages that were unknown by the post-exilic period.[56] As William M. Schniedewind explains, "Akkadian was essentially unknown outside of scholastic circles by the fifth century BCE, and Ugaritic disappeared as a language around 1200 BCE." He further observes that "the languages prevalent in the Near East during the Persian and Hellenistic periods — namely, Aramaic, Persian, and Greek — play little role in the philological problems related to the difficult [to interpret words]."[57] These rare words likely became difficult to interpret because they represent an earlier stage of Hebrew, and fell out of use "when the scribal tradition of Hebrew suffered a disjunction by the end of the sixth century BCE."[58] This dovetails with the evidence of early Hebrew inscriptions to date the language of the Pentateuch and other biblical texts to the time before the exile.

In fact, some evidence indicates that Hebrew of the Pentateuch is even earlier than the rest of the SBH corpus.[59] Yoel Elitzur has analyzed when dozens of specific words and expressions appear and disappear in SBH writings, and how their usage changes across these same books; taking external archaeological and historical data into

---

Formation of the Pentateuch, 336, 338.
55. Frank Polak, "The Identification of Preexilic Material in the Pentateuch," in *Oxford Handbook of The Pentateuch*, 319.
56. William M. Schniedewind, "Linguistic Dating, Writing Systems, and the Pentateuchal Sources," in *Formation of the Pentateuch*, 352–354.
57. Schniedewind, "Linguistic Dating," 353.
58. Schniedewind, "Linguistic Dating," 353–354.
59. Yoel Elitzur, "Diachrony in Standard Biblical Hebrew: The Pentateuch via-à-vis the Prophets/Writings," *Journal of Northwest Semitic Languages* 44, no. 2 (2018): 81–101; Aaron D. Hornkohl, *Diachronic Diversity in Classical Biblical Hebrew* (Cambridge: Faculty of Asian and Middle Eastern Studies, University of Cambridge; Cambridge: Open Book Publishers, 2024).

consideration, Elitzur found that the Hebrew of the Torah consistently fit better with the earlier external data.[60]

Of course, there still could have been multiple stages of development, expansion, and editing over a long period of time — but the writing and compilation process likely culminated sometime before the mid-sixth century BC, since "all the strata were composed during the period when [Classical Biblical Hebrew] was in use."[61] This view is further strengthened by the fact, noted by Schniedewind, that "there are striking similarities between Pentateuchal literary genres (especially treaties and legal texts) and ancient Near Eastern literature of the preexilic period" and yet "no convincing or extended comparisons in the Pentateuch with Persian or Hellenistic literary genres."[62] Indeed, many parallels come from Egyptian, Canaanite, and Mesopotamian literature dating from the Iron IIC all the way back into the Middle and Late Bronze Ages.[63] The social contexts of the Torah also largely reflects the archaeology of the Bronze and Iron Ages, rather than the later (and more cosmopolitan) Hellenistic era.[64]

In broad strokes, then, the linguistic, epigraphic, and archaeological evidence points to the pre-exilic period for the origins, development, and compilation of the Pentateuch. This can be illustrated with greater detail by considering the evidence related to the individual books or sections of the Torah. As previously noted, the emphasis here is on how this kind of evidence helps determine *dating* of the texts, not necessarily the *historicity* of the events and people described in the texts.

Deuteronomy

Within the canonical order, Deuteronomy is the final of the five books of the Torah. Yet it is widely regarded as the "linchpin" for dating the entirety of the Pentateuch, and thus it makes for the most reason-

---

60. Yoel Elitzur, "The Interface between Language and Realia in the Preexilic Books of the Bible," *Hebrew Studies* 59 (2018): 129–147; Yoel Elitzur, "Emergence and Disappearance of Words and Expressions in Pre-Exilic Biblical Hebrew," *Revue Biblique* 129, no. 4 (2022): 481–504.
61. Joosten, "Diachronic Linguistics," 342.
62. Schniedewind, "Linguistic Dating," 352.
63. David P. Wright, "Ancient Near Eastern Literature and the Pentateuch," in *Oxford Handbook of the Pentateuch*, 379–398.
64. Dever, "Can Archaeology Serve as a Tool," 236–237.

able starting point for our discussion of specific sections.⁶⁵ Scholarship has traditionally linked Deuteronomy (or at least a version of it) to the "book of the law" mentioned in 2 Kings 22:8.⁶⁶ This not only dates some form of the book to the seventh century BC, but also assumes it was an especially influential text at this time. William M. Schniedewind called it "the Magna Carta of Josiah's political and religious reforms."⁶⁷ This hypothesis has been supported by several lines of archaeological and inscriptional evidence in recent years.

Perhaps the most widely accepted evidence connecting the composition of at least parts of Deuteronomy to the seventh century BC are the parallels between Deuteronomy 13 and 28 and the obligations and curses found in Esarhaddon's Succession Treaty (EST), dated to about 672 BC.⁶⁸ As Polak notes, "the Deuteronomic use of such Neo-Assyrian phraseology would lack sociopolitical context" if it were written and adapted long after the destruction of Ninevah in 612 BC.⁶⁹ In fact, Jeffrey Stackert has shown that Assyrian succession treaties had a short shelf life, as they were typically replaced by an accession treaty of the new king shortly after he arose to power — as happened with Ashurbanipal in 669 BC.⁷⁰ Stackert thus reasons that "the literary, epigraphic, archaeological, and other historical evidence combine" to point to a date close to 670 BC for the integration of the EST into Deuteronomy.⁷¹ Jeffrey Tigay also observes that several details in the book reflect the imperial age of the eighth–seventh centuries BC.⁷²

---

65. Jeffrey Stackert, *Deuteronomy and the Pentateuch* (New Haven: Yale University Press, 2022), 1–2; Gordon Wenham, "The Date of Deuteronomy: Linch-Pin of Old Testament Criticism," parts 1 and 2, *Themelios* 10, no. 3 (1985): 15–20 and 11, no. 1 (1985): 15–18.
66. Jack R. Lundbom, *Deuteronomy: Law and Covenant* (Eugene, OR: Cascade Books, 2017), 2–5; Dozeman, *Pentateuch*, 507–508.
67. Schniedewind, *How the Bible Became a Book*, 112.
68. Stackert, *Deuteronomy and the Pentateuch*, 94–108; Wright, "Ancient Near Eastern Literature," 389–392.
69. Polak, "Identification of Preexilic Material," 330; Udo Rütersworden, "The Place of Deuteronomy in the Formation of the Pentateuch," in *Oxford Handbook of the Pentateuch*, 288.
70. Stackert, *Deuteronomy and the Pentateuch*, 145–158.
71. Stackert, *Deuteronomy and the Pentateuch*, 158.
72. Jeffrey H. Tigay, *Deuteronomy*, The JPS Torah Commentary (Philadelphia: Jewish Publication Society, 1996), xxi.

Schniedewind cites the centrality of writing in Deuteronomy as further evidence linking it to the seventh century BC:

> Writing is central to the revelation in Deuteronomy. ... In contrast to Exodus, Deuteronomy makes a repeated point of the fact that the revelation on Sinai was written down (4:13; 5:19; 9:10; 10:4; 27:3, 8; 31:24). Not only was the Torah written, but Moses' teachings needed to be written again "when you have crossed over to enter the land, *you shall write down all the words of this teaching/Torah*" (27:3). Even the king needs to make a copy himself so that he may read it and consult it (17:18). Moreover, bits and pieces of the *Torah* should appear in every house. Deuteronomy repeatedly enjoins the people to "inscribe them on the doorposts of your house" (6:9; 11:20). In this way, every Judahite would be reminded of the written injunctions of the teaching, or *Torah*. It was written on the doorposts of the house.[73]

This emphasis on writing, according to Schniedewind, best reflects the social situation of the seventh century BC, when archaeology indicates the spread of writing through Judahite society. That these injunctions about writing the law were being taken seriously in the late seventh century BC is indicated by the attestation of language similar to Deuteronomy 7:9–10 on a small silver scroll dated to this period.[74]

This, of course, does not mean that there were no earlier versions of Deuteronomy that pre-date this time. The passages based on EST "appear to be somewhat secondary" to the larger Deuteronomic legal corpus,[75] suggesting that they represent late scribal revision of an earlier existing text.[76] Some scholars believe that an earlier version of Deuteronomy was preserved in the northern kingdom of Israel, and that this was one of the texts brought to Judah by northern refugees.[77]

---

73. Schniedewind, *How the Bible Became a Book*, 109.
74. Schniedewind, *How the Bible Became a Book*, 105–106; Hendel and Joosten, *How Old is the Bible*, 123.
75. Wright, "Ancient Near Eastern Literature," 391.
76. Bill T. Arnold and Brian T. Shockey, "Deuteronomy 13 and the Succession Treaty of Esarhaddon," in *"Now These Records are Ancient": Studies in Ancient Near Eastern and Biblical History, Language and Culture in Honor of K. Lawson Younger, Jr.*, ed. James K. Hoffmeier, Richard E. Averbeck, J. Caleb Howard, and Wolfgang Zwickel (Münster, DE: Zaphon, 2022), 1–14.
77. Lundbom, *Deuteronomy*, 5–6; Schniedewind, *How the Bible Became a Book*, 83.

This is consistent with the apparent influence of early Deuteronomic traditions in the writings of Hosea, a prophet in northern Israel in the eighth century BC.[78] It would also make sense of why the text was apparently lost or unknown in Judah until it was rediscovered during the reign of Josiah.

Sandra L. Richter found that the so-called "name theology" of the Deuteronomic core (chapters 5–27) borrowed the idiom "to place his name" from Akkadian sources attested as early as the third millennium BC, and first appearing in Northwest Semitic in the ninth century BC. This idiom was "consistently associated with the royal act of making inscriptions, the installation of inscribed monuments, and, in non-monumental contexts, the fame resulting from such monuments."[79] The children of Israel are instructed to establish monuments with the words of the law written upon them at Mt. Ebal, in the northern kingdom near Shechem (Deuteronomy 27:1–8). According to Richter, this points to Mt. Ebal — not Jerusalem — as the centralized "place which the Lord your God shall choose ... to put his name" (Deuteronomy 12:5).[80] Excavations at Mt. Ebal have determined that it was an active worship site for only a very brief period of time in the early Iron Age, circa 1250–1100 BC.[81] Thus, one of the central motifs of the early core of Deuteronomy stems from a *very* early tradition. Richter suggests "some form of Deuteronomy encompassing chapters v–xxvii [5–27] is premonarchic and pro-Ebal."[82] Richter strengthened this conclusion through economic analysis of Deuteronomy 5–27.[83] Comparing economic realities reflected in Deuteronomy's

---

78. Cartsen Vang, "When a Prophet Quotes Moses: On the Relationship of the Book of Hosea and Deuteronomy," in *Sepher Torath Mosheh: Studies in the Composition and Interpretation of Deuteronomy*, ed. Daniel I. Block and Richard Schultz (Peabody, MA: Hendrickson, 2017), 277–303.
79. Sandra L. Richter, "The Place of the Name in Deuteronomy," *Vetus Testamentum* 57, no. 3 (2007): 344.
80. Richter, "Place of the Name," 342–366.
81. Sandra L. Richter, "The Archaeology of Mount Ebal and Mount Gerizim and Why It Matters," in *Sepher Torath Mosheh*, 311–315; Richter, "Place of the Name," 361–364.
82. Richter, "Place of the Name," 366.
83. Sandra Lynn Richter, "The Question of Provenance and the Economics of Deuteronomy," *Journal for the Study of the Old Testament* 41, no. 1 (2017): 23–50; Sandra L. Richter, "The Question of Provenance and the Economics

legal corpus to the archaeologically recoverable economies in Israel and Judah throughout the Iron Age and into the post-exilic period, Richter found that "the evidence points us to a period astride the Iron I/IIA transition in the Central Hill Country."[84] This early dating for the Deuteronomic core is also reflected in the confession recorded in Deuteronomy 26:5: "A wandering Aramean was my ancestor" (NRSV). According to Yoel Elitzur, historical and archaeological evidence pertaining to the social development of the Arameans indicates that they were known for a nomadic ("wandering") and pastoral way of life in the second millennium BC, but no longer after the eleventh century BC. As such, "the plain meaning of the phrase convincingly links it to the pre-eleventh century BCE."[85]

Even the one part of the core Deuteronomic law which mentions the king — the so-called "law of the king" in Deuteronomy 17:14–20 — "appears to stem from a period where Israel has not yet [had] any direct experience with monarchy as [a] governmental system."[86] Historian and archaeologist Baruch Halpern argues that the "law of the king," along with the rest of the legislation of Deuteronomy 17:8–18:22 "erecting a central judiciary, a priestly order, and a prophetic office as positions independent of the monarchy," effectively served as the Israelite constitution adopted at the beginning of the monarchy — thereby requiring its origins to be in the pre-monarchic period.[87]

Deuteronomy 32–33 reflects an archaic stage of biblical Hebrew which also dates to this very early period (late second millennium BC), though they may not have been attached to the book of Deuteronomy until a later date.[88] Other parts of the book, such as Deuteronomy 1–4,

---

of Deuteronomy: The Neo-Babylonian and Persian Periods," *Catholic Biblical Quarterly* 82, no. 4 (2020): 547–566; Sandra Lynn Richter, "Economics and *Urdeuteronomium*: A Response to Kare Berge, Diana Edelman, Philippe Guillaume, and Benedetta Rossi," *Journal for the Study of the Old Testament* 48, no. 1 (2023): 84–104.

84. Richter, "Question of Provenance" (2017), 48. See also Tigay, *Deuteronomy*, xxi–xxii.
85. Elitzur, "Interface between Language and Realia," 131–133 (quote on p. 133).
86. Carsten Vang, "The Non-Prophetic Background for the King Law in Deuteronomy 17:14–20," in *Paradigm Change in Pentateuchal Research*, 208.
87. Baruch Halpern, *The Constitution of the Monarchy in Israel* (Chico, CA: Scholars Press, 1981), 225–235, quote on p. 234.
88. Hendel and Joosten, *How Old is the Bible*, 127–128; Tigay, *Deuteronomy*, xxiv.

29–31, and 34, are typically thought to be later expansions, but they nonetheless appear to be largely pre-exilic.[89] Some scholars argue that the overall structure of the whole book reflects the structure of Hittite treaties and law codes dated to the late second millennium BC.[90] Such conclusions are based on comprehensive analysis of approximately 100 attested ancient Near Eastern law codes and treaty documents dated from the late third millennium up through the first millennium BC.[91] As K. Lawson Younger and Neal A. Huddleston concluded, "When one compares the overall structure of Deuteronomy with all the ancient Near Eastern treaty materials, it is evident that Deuteronomy bears a closer resemblance to the late second-millennium [BC] Hittite treaty form than any other treaty tradition."[92]

Beyond the overall structural analysis, scholars have noted similarities in the conceptual worldview, modes of discourse, and the rhetorical uses of retold (and revised) history in both Deuteronomy and Hittite treaties and legal texts.[93] According to Ada Taggar-Cohen, "there are too many similarities to dismiss the possibility of an inherited knowledge of the [Hittite] political-treaty tradition."[94]

---

89. Tigay, *Deuteronomy*, xxv–xxvi.
90. Kitchen, *Reliability of the Old Testament*, 283–307; Paul Lawrence, *The Books of Moses Revisited* (Eugene, OR: Wipf and Stock, 2011), 47–94; George E. Mendenhall and Gary A. Herion, "Covenant," in *Anchor Bible Dictionary*, 1:1180–1188.
91. Kenneth A. Kitchen and Paul J. N. Lawrence, *Treaty, Law and Covenant in the Ancient Near East*, 3 vols. (Wiesbaden, DE: Harrassowitz Verlag, 2012); Neal A. Huddleston, "Ancient Near Eastern Treaty Traditions and Their Implications for Interpreting Deuteronomy," in *Sepher Torath Mosheh*, 30–77. See also Noel Weeks, *Admonition and Curse: The Ancient Near Eastern Treaty/Covenant Form as a Problem in Inter-Cultural Relationships* (London: T & T Clark International, 2004).
92. K. Lawson Younger Jr. and Neal A. Huddleston, "Challenges to the Use of Ancient Near Eastern Treaty Forms for Dating and Interpreting Deuteronomy," in *Sepher Torath Mosheh*, 104.
93. Berman, *Inconsistencies in the Torah*, 63–103; Neal A. Huddleston, "Deposit and Read! A Discursive Explanation of Peripheral Akkadian Treaty Traditions and their Implications for Deuteronomy," in *"Now These Records are Ancient"*, 243–265; Billie Jean Collins, *The Hittites and Their World* (Atlanta: Society of Biblical Literature, 2007), 109–111.
94. Ada Taggar-Cohen, "Biblical *Covenant* and Hittite *Išḫiul* Reexamined," *Vetus Testamentum* 61, no. 3 (2011): 462.

Joshua Berman likewise concluded, "Taken as a whole, the similarities between the Sinai covenant [as represented in Deuteronomy] and the Hittite treaties are too striking to be dismissed as coincidence."[95] Such compelling parallels with comparative material from the late second millennium BC imply that although it likely underwent revision and expansion in later centuries, the broad outlines of the book took shape very early on.

In sum, much of Deuteronomy appears to be based on fairly early source material, and indeed a substantially complete version of the book may very well have existed by the early Iron Age. It was evidently lost or neglected in Judah until northern refugees brought a version to Jerusalem in the late eighth century BC. It then underwent editing and expansion resulting in an essentially final form of the book that reflects an Iron IIC setting as it became part of the larger efforts to compile and aggregate the historical traditions of Israel and Judah underway at this time.

Outside of Deuteronomy, three other legal collections were incorporated into the Pentateuch: (1) The Ten Commandments (or "Decalogue") and so-called "Covenant Code" (or "book of the Covenant") and narrative context around them, essentially comprising of Exodus 19–24, a literary unit source critics have often had difficulty trying to parse.[96] (2) The Priestly Code, making up the bulk of the P source, including parts of Exodus, essentially all of Leviticus, and parts of Numbers. (3) The Holiness Code, embedded within P as Leviticus 17–26.

The Decalogue and Covenant Code

Both the Decalogue and the Covenant Code were used as source material for Deuteronomy, so much of Exodus 19–24 necessarily predates the final editing and compiling of Deuteronomy in the early to

---

95. Joshua A. Berman, "God's Alliance with Man," *Azure* 25 (2006): 95.
96. T. D. Alexander, "The Composition of the Sinai Narrative in Exodus XIX 1–XXIV 11," *Vetus Testamentum* 49, no. 1 (1999): 2–20; James K. Hoffmeier, *Ancient Israel in Sinai: The Evidence for the Authenticity of the Wilderness Tradition* (New York: Oxford University Press, 2005), 181–183; Richard E. Averbeck, "Pentateuchal Criticism and the Priestly Torah," in *Do Historical Matters Matter to Faith? A Critical Appraisal of Modern and Postmodern Approaches to Scripture*, ed. James K. Hoffmeier and Dennis R. Magary (Wheaton, IL: Crossway, 2012), 159–177.

mid-seventh century BC.[97] Schniedewind has also pointed out that the revelation on Sinai is primarily portrayed as an oral revelation; writing does not play a major role there like it later does in Deuteronomy. It thus originates from before the Iron IIC, early in the history of Israel when they were still a primarily oral culture.[98]

According to William S. Morrow, the Lord's self-declaration in the opening formula of the Decalogue (Exodus 20:2) reflects the opening formula used in northwest Semitic royal inscriptions that primarily date to the ninth to eighth centuries BC. These inscriptions present various monarchs as the ideal king who executes justice. Thus, in its present form, the Decalogue in Exodus 20 is framed to represent the Lord as the ideal divine king within an Iron IIB setting.[99] Yet the commandments themselves were not limited to the Iron Age.

The first and second commandments of the Decalogue (Exodus 20:3–6), requiring Israel to maintain an exclusive relationship with the Lord and only worship him and no other gods, are similar to the loyalty rhetoric of ancient Near Eastern treaties from both the Neo-Assyrian and Late Bronze Age Hittite traditions.[100] The nearest antecedent, in terms of an exclusive relationship to a *deity* (rather than a king or overlord), is the short-lived religious reforms of Pharaoh Akhenaten in the fourteenth century BC.[101] As Nahum M. Sarna explained, "The exclusive worship of Aten became the official state religion, and the worship of other gods seems to have been outlawed. Extraordinarily, the god Aten was not allowed to be represented in either human or animal form."[102] Although not *depicted* in human form, Aten was imagined "and described with a face, heart, mouth, and limbs ... [and] referred to as father and Akhenaten is his son."[103] Egyptian Atenism was probably not true monotheism, but neither was the earliest form of Israelite region, nor does the first commandment of the Decalogue

---

97. Dozeman, *Pentateuch*, 511–515.
98. Schniedewind, *How the Bible Became a Book*, 12, 121–128.
99. William S. Morrow, *An Introduction to Biblical Law* (Grand Rapids: Eerdmans, 2017), 51–54.
100. Morrow, *Introduction to Biblical Law*, 60–62.
101. Richard S. Hess, *Israelite Religion: An Archaeological and Biblical Survey* (Grand Rapids: Baker Academic, 2007), 162–164.
102. Nahum M. Sarna, *Exploring Exodus: The Origins of Biblical Israel* (New York: Schocken Books, 1996), 151.
103. Hess, *Israelite Religion*, 164.

require it.[104] Richard S. Hess thus reasons that this "Egyptian model provides a Late Bronze Age antecedent" to Israel's exclusive relationship with the Lord, "especially in light of the close connection between Egypt and earliest Israel in biblical tradition [i.e., the Exodus]."[105]

The Sabbath law (Exodus 20:8–11) is unique in that no other ancient Near Eastern text mandates the ritual observance of a seven-day "week," but there are seven-day ritual cycles attested throughout the ancient Near East going back to the third millennium BC.[106] Closely approximating a seven-day week is the concept known from mid-second millennium BC Assyrian sources, where every seventh day of the lunar month was considered unlucky and therefore "marked by special fasts and prayers."[107] This same calendrical practice was attested in Assurbanipal's library from the seventh century BC.[108]

The moral injunctions of the Decalogue (Exodus 20:12–17) are common across various societies, including some noteworthy parallels in Babylonian and Egyptian texts from the second millennium BC.[109] Each of the Ten Commandments thus has ties back to early material, and could very well represent some of earliest stipulations in Israel's legal and religious traditions. In the view of Moshe Weinfeld, the earliest version of the Decalogue went back to "the dawn of Israelite history … as the foundation document of the Israelite community."[110]

Many of the laws in the Covenant Code (Exodus 21–23) have parallels to various ancient Near Eastern legal collections, all of which date to the second millennium BC.[111] Frank Polak explains, "The Covenant Code (Exodus 21–22) shares features with the Old Babylonian

---

104. Hess, *Israelite Religion*, 163–164.
105. Hess, *Israelite Religion*, 165.
106. Sarna, *Exploring Exodus*, 147–148.
107. S. H. Hooke, *Babylonian and Assyrian Religion* (London: Hutchinson's University Library, 1953), 61. The "middle of the second millennium BC" is described as "the period under consideration" in Hooke's book on p. xi.
108. Robert B. Coote and David Robert Ord, *In the Beginning: Creation and the Priestly History* (Minneapolis: Fortress Press, 1991), 80.
109. Sarna, *Exploring Exodus*, 139.
110. Moshe Weinfeld, "The Decalogue: Its Significance, Uniqueness, and Place in Israel's Tradition," in *Religion and Law: Biblical-Judaic and Islamic Perspectives*, ed. Edwin B. Firmage, Bernard G. Weiss, and John W. Welch (University Park, PA: Eisenbrauns, 1990), 32.
111. Sarna, *Exploring Exodus*, 162–168.

Eshnunna Code (§53//Exodus 21:35); with Codex Hammurabi (§117//Exodus 21:2–4); with the Hittite Laws (§105–6/107//Exodus 22:4–5), and with legal deeds from Late Bronze Emar."[112] There is an especially strong relationship to the Laws of Hammurabi, which were experiencing a resurgence in Neo-Assyrian scribal circles around the same time Hebrew literature was being gathered and edited under Hezekiah's direction.[113] On the whole, however, the laws reflect a second millennium BC milieu.

Jay W. Marshall analyzed the Covenant Code in light of an anthropological model of law, and concluded "this is a pre-monarchial society rather than a well-organized central government." Compared with the level of society reflected in the archaeology of Israel, Marshall suggested the "Book of the Covenant regulates Israel in the early to middle Iron I period" (circa twelfth century BC).[114] Shalom M. Paul similarly concluded that the biblical laws in Exodus 21–23 generally reflect a pre-monarchic social setting after studying the relationship between the Covenant Code and Late Bronze Age cuneiform legal collections.[115] The Covenant Code, Paul concluded, was "the distinctive Israelite contribution to jurisprudence ... of second millennium [BC] legal collections."[116]

The overall literary unit of Exodus 19–24 possesses additional ties to the second millennium BC. For instance, toward the beginning Israel is identified as the Lord's "peculiar treasure" (Exodus 19:5), an

---

112. Polak, "Identification of Preexilic Material," 330. Compare the examples given in Lawrence, *Books of Moses Revisited*, 102–106.
113. Bernard M. Levinson, "Is the Covenant Code an Exilic Composition? A Response to John Van Seters," in *In Search of Pre-Exilic Israel*, ed. John Day (London: T&T Clark, 2004), 288–297; David. P. Wright, *Inventing God's Law: How the Covenant Code of the Bible Used and Revised the Laws of Hammurabi* (New York: Oxford University Press, 2009); Wright, "Ancient Near Eastern Literature," 385–389.
114. Jay W. Marshall, *Israel and the Book of the Covenant: An Anthropological Approach to Biblical Law* (Chico, CA: Scholars Press, 1993), 178–179; note that I have silently replaced Marshall's abbreviation BC with the full title "Book of the Covenant."
115. Shalom M. Paul, *Studies in the Book of the Covenant in the Light of Cuneiform and Biblical Law* (Leiden, NL: Brill, 1970), 44–45, 102; Sarna, *Exploring Exodus*, 161–162.
116. Paul, *Studies in the Book of the Covenant*, 105.

expression paralleled in mid-second millennium BC political and diplomatic texts.[117] When taken as a whole, the presentation of the Sinai covenant in Exodus 19–24 reflects Levantine treaty making procedures documented in inscriptions from Mari, dated to the early second millennium BC.[118] This squares well with the analysis of T. Desmond Alexander, who detected hints that this literary unit (or at least its earliest core) dates back to "as early as the pre-monarchic period."[119]

To put it briefly, the Decalogue and Covenant Code were based on early material, and some form of Exodus 19–24 may have already existed in the early Iron Age. This corpus then underwent some editing and revision in the Iron IIB-C period, prior to the final editing of Deuteronomy, and may have even been used as a source for Hezekiah's reform measures.[120] This places it firmly within the body of material being compiled and edited in the eighth–seventh centuries BC.

The Priestly and Holiness Codes

Some scholars have argued that Exodus 20 through the end of Leviticus should be taken holistically as a single unit representing a covenant making event at Sinai patterned after the Hittite treaties of the late second millennium BC, similar to Deuteronomy.[121] Most scholars, however, believe that Exodus 19–24 is from a separate source, as discussed above. The legal texts, ritual prescriptions, and the detailed descriptions of the tabernacle that make up most of Exodus 25–40 belong to the Priestly Code, as does the legal and ritual material of Leviticus and Numbers 1–9, along with a handful of other passages in parts of Exodus and Numbers.

---

117. Sarna, *Exploring Exodus*, 130–131.
118. Frank H. Polak, "The Covenant at Mount Sinai in the Light of Texts of Mari," in *Sefer Moshe: Studies in the Bible and the Ancient Near East, Qumran, and Post-Biblical Judaism*, The Moshe Weinfeld Jubilee Volume, ed. Chaim Cohen, Avi Hurvitz, and Shalom M. Paul (University Park, PA: Eisenbrauns, 2004), 119–134.
119. Alexander, "Composition of the Sinai Narrative," 20.
120. Rainer Albertz, *A History of Israelite Religion in the Old Testament Period*, 2 vols., trans. John Bowden (Louisville, KY: Westminster John Knox, 1994), 1:180–186.
121. Kitchen, *Reliability of the Old Testament*, 283–307; Hoffmeier, *Ancient Israel in Sinai*, 183–192; Lawrence, *Books of Moses Revisited*, 47–94.

Embedded within this block of text is the Holiness Code, mainly consisting of Leviticus 17–26, which is typically understood as either a subset of P or a supplement to it. The dating of the laws and ritual instructions of P and H is highly contested. They are traditionally viewed as the latest material within the Pentateuch and dated to the exilic or post-exilic periods.[122] A sizable (and growing) contingent of scholars, however, have contended that P/H belongs to the pre-exilic period.[123] As already mentioned, the language of most texts attributed to the P source is consistent with Classical Biblical Hebrew.[124] Other lines of evidence are also indicative of an earlier date.

The most direct evidence that at least part of the P source is pre-exilic is the attestation of the so-called "priestly blessing" of Numbers 6:24–26 on two silver scrolls dated to the late seventh or early sixth century BC.[125] This does not prove that all of P had been written and compiled before the exile, but it does establish what scholars call a *terminus ante quem* (the *latest possible date*) for at least part of the P source as being the late seventh century BC. All the key expressions used in the blessing are also attested as early as the second millennium BC in Ugaritic and Mesopotamian texts, so the blessing could originate within a much earlier context.[126] Gabriel Barkay, the archaeologist who discovered the inscriptions, has noted, "Our two texts seem

---

122. Gottwald, *Hebrew Bible*, 273–279.
123. Dozeman, *Pentateuch*, 179–185.
124. Avi Hurvitz, "Once Again: The Linguistic Profile of the Priestly Material in the Pentateuch and its Historical Age," *Zeitschrift für die alttestamentliche Wissenschaft* 112, no. 2 (2000): 180–191; Frank H. Polak, "Syntactic-Stylistic Aspects of the So-Called 'Priestly' Work in the *Torah*," in *Le-ma'an Ziony: Essays in Honor of Ziony Zevit*, ed. Frederick E. Greenspahn and Gary A. Rendsburg (Eugene, OR: Cascade Books, 2017), 345–382.
125. Jeremy D. Smoak, *The Priestly Blessing in Inscription and Scripture: The Early History of Numbers 6:24–26* (New York: Oxford University Press, 2016), 13–16; Gabriel Barkay, Marilyn J. Lundberg, Andrew G. Vaughn, and Bruce Zuckerman, "The Amulets from Ketef Hinnom: A New Edition and Evaluation," *Bulletin of the American Schools of Oriental Research* 334 (2004): 41–71.
126. Ada Yardeni, "Remarks on the Priestly Blessing on Two Ancient Amulets from Jerusalem," *Vetus Testamentum* 41, no. 2 (1991): 176–185; Gabriel Barkay, "The Priestly Benediction on Silver Plaques from Ketef Hinnom in Jerusalem," *Tel Aviv: Journal of the Institute of Archaeology of Tel Aviv University* 19, no. 2 (1992): 176–181.

to support those who contend that the Priestly Code was already in existence, at least in rudimentary form, in the First Temple period."[127]

Passages in Deuteronomy also adopt and adapt material from the Holiness Code.[128] Other parts of P, coming from nearly all of Leviticus 1–15 and parts of Exodus and Numbers, are presupposed by the Deuteronomic laws.[129] For instance, when struck with a skin disease, Deuteronomy 24:8 instructs the children of Israel to "do according to all that the priests the Levites shall teach you: as I commanded them, so ye shall observe to do." This clearly alludes to the priestly instructions concerning skin diseases found in Leviticus 13–14.[130] According to Benjamin Kilchör, the Levirate marriage laws of Deuteronomy 25:5–10 presupposes the prohibition in Leviticus 20:21 (from H) and "picks up on the topic of daughters' right to an inheritance (Num 27:1–11) and the related problem that when a daughter marries, the inheritance of her father might transfer to another family (Num 36:6–12)," both usually attributed to P.[131] Thus, some form of P/H must pre-date the final composition of Deuteronomy in the early to mid-seventh century BC.

Furthermore, William M. Schniedewind has noted that — in contrast to Deuteronomy — writing is not an important component in P, nor is P self-conscious of its status as a written text. This indicates that it was primarily written and compiled *before* the emergence of the "orthodoxy" of the written word in the seventh century BC.[132] Frank Polak slightly modifies that conclusion, as he does see evidence for "the authority of the written text" in parts of P, indicating a seventh century BC editorial layer. On the whole, however, Polak detects oral

---

127. Gabriel Barkay, "The Riches of Ketef Hinnom," *Biblical Archaeology Review* 35, no. 4 (2009): 34–35, 122–126.
128. Jacob Milgrom, "The Antiquity of the Priestly Source: A Reply to Joseph Blenkinsopp," *Zeitschrift für die alttestamentliche Wissenschaft* 111, no. 1 (1999): 14–19; Kilchör, "Wellhausen's Five Pillars," 101–113.
129. Benjamin Kilchör, "The Reception of Priestly Laws in Deuteronomy and Deuteronomy's Target Audience," in *Exploring the Composition of the Pentateuch*, 213–225.
130. Zevit, "Converging Lines," 502; Kilchör, "Reception of Priestly Laws," 214–215.
131. Benjamin Kilchör, "Levirate Marriage in Deuteronomy 25:5–10 and Its Precursors in Leviticus and Numbers: A Test Case for the Relationship between P/H and D," *Catholic Biblical Quarterly* 77, no. 3 (2015): 429–440.
132. Schniedewind, *How the Bible Became a Book*, 115, 120.

roots that point to the ninth–eighth centuries BC for its earliest written form.[133] Ziony Zevit similarly believes P's legal material dated to this time period. "Historical, geographical, social, and political considerations suggest a ninth century BCE setting for the law [in P]."[134] Jan Joosten's analysis of the historical and social setting of H led to a similar conclusion: "the historical conditions addressed by H are those of the pre-exilic period ... this almost certainly implies an origin in Judah in the monarchic period."[135]

This dovetails well with the analysis of the material culture reflected in P/H passages by archaeologist Avraham Faust.[136] Faust found that various passages in P/H reflect an Iron Age material culture, with some passages of H best fitting within an Iron IIC setting. He thus concluded, "It is the Iron Age world, as expressed in the archaeological record, which is also reflected in the Priestly writings." H, Faust suggested, might date more specifically "to the very late 8th–early 6th centuries BCE," but "P covers a longer period of time, beginning before H, and continuing alongside it, toward the end of the Iron Age."[137] When the description of altars found in Leviticus's purification rituals are compared to archaeological findings in Israel, according to Zevit, they are describing Iron Age altars from as early as the end of the tenth century BC.[138] Another study, by David S. Vanderhooft, analyzed the kinship terminology used throughout P and found that it conformed to Iron Age realities (and not those of the Babylonian

---

133. Polak, "Syntactic-Stylistic Aspects," 373, 376–377.
134. Zevit, "Converging Lines," 509.
135. Jan Joosten, *People and Land in the Holiness Code: An Exegetical Study of the Ideational Framework of the Law in Leviticus 17–26* (Leiden, NL: Brill, 1996), 90, 91.
136. Avraham Faust, "The World of P: The Material Realm of Priestly Writings," *Vetus Testamentum* 69, no. 2 (2019): 173–218. See also Avraham Faust, "Cities, Villages, and Farmsteads: The Landscape of Leviticus 25:29–31," in *Exploring the Longue Durée: Essays in Honor of Lawrence E. Stager*, ed. J. David Schloen (University Park, PA: Eisenbrauns, 2009), 103–112.
137. Faust, "World of P," 204–205.
138. Ziony Zevit, "Philology, Archaeology, and a Terminus a Quo for P's ḥaṭṭāʾt Legislation," in *Pomegranates and Golden Bells: Studies in Biblical, Jewish, and Near Eastern Ritual, Law, and Literature in Honor of Jacob Milgrom*, ed. David P. Wright, David Noel Freedman, and Avi Hurvitz (University Park, PA: Eisenbrauns, 1995), 29–38.

and Persian period), as attested in archaeology, inscriptions, and other Iron Age biblical texts.[139] Thus, as written in their current form, significant portions of P and H reflect an Iron II setting, generally pre-dating the final form of Deuteronomy.

Additional evidence indicates that, even if their current form reflects the Iron II period, the laws and rituals of P/H have their roots in even earlier laws and customs going back to the late second millennium BC. As Bernhard W. Anderson concluded, "A good deal of the old tradition, which developed out of the cultic practice of the time of Moses and the Tribal Confederacy, has been preserved in the Priestly Work by the Jerusalem priesthood."[140] The absence of pig bones, for example, is a common identity marker of Israelite archaeological sites going back to the early Iron I period (circa 1200 BC), indicating that the taboo on pork (see Leviticus 11:7) is among the earliest customs of ancient Israel.[141] Essentially all of the legal material in this large literary unit is predominantly paralleled by second millennium BC law collections.[142] As Richard S. Hess explains, "Whatever traditions lay behind Levitical laws as now preserved, in various cases the existing evidence witnesses to a great antiquity to these laws within the context of ancient Near Eastern jurisprudence."[143] The detailed tabernacle description, priesthood order, sacrifices and offerings, and ritual calendar with its festival regulations — all typically considered part of the Priestly work — each fit comfortably within the broader milieu of the Late Bronze Age.[144] Jacob Milgrom, one of the foremost

---

139. David S. Vanderhooft, "The Israelite *Mišpaḥâ*, the Priestly Writings, and Changing Valences in Israel's Kingship Terminology," in *Exploring the Longue Durée*, 485–496. Compare Faust, "World of P," 195–202.
140. Bernhard W. Anderson, *Understanding the Old Testament*, 4th ed. (Hoboken, NJ: Prentice-Hall, 1986), 452.
141. Avraham Faust, *Israel's Ethnogenesis: Settlement, Interaction, Expansion and Resistance* (New York: Routledge, 2006), 35–40.
142. Kitchen and Lawrence, *Treaty, Law and Covenant*, 3:139–142.
143. Richard S. Hess, *The Old Testament—A Historical, Theological, and Critical Introduction* (Grand Rapids: Baker Academic, 2016), 86.
144. On the tabernacle, see Michael M. Homan, *To Your Tents, O Israel! The Terminology, Function, Form, and Symbolism of Tents in the Hebrew Bible and the Ancient Near East* (Leiden, NL: Brill, 2002), 89–128; Kenneth A. Kitchen, "The Tabernacle—A Bronze Age Artefact," *Eretz-Israel: Archaeological, Historical and Geographical Studies* 23 (1993): 119*–129*; Richard Elliott

authorities on the Priestly source, dated the editing and compilation of P/H to circa 750 BC, but argued that the original setting of the rituals and customs was at pre-monarchic Shiloh. There, archaeological digs uncovered a sanctuary that served as an interregional and multi-tribal religious center in the early to mid-eleventh century BC. According to Milgrom, "The basic presuppositions of P fit the archaeological data of Shiloh to perfection."[145]

The Narratives of Genesis, Exodus, and Numbers

Having reviewed evidence relating to the composition of each of the legal codes, it remains to survey the data relevant to the narrative portions of the Torah. This essentially comprises all of Genesis, roughly the first half of Exodus, and parts of Numbers 10–36. This material tells a sweeping narrative, beginning with the creation of the world, the flood, the lives of Israel's patriarchs and matriarchs, and culminating with the story of Moses, the exodus and the traditions about the wilderness wandering. In the traditional model of the Documentary Hypothesis, three sources (J, E, and P) telling roughly the same story have been interwoven into one overarching narrative.[146] As previously discussed, the J/E material was typically thought to be fairly

---

Friedman, *The Exodus: How It Happened and Why It Matters* (San Francisco: HarperOne, 2017), 53–54. On priesthood order, see Daniel Fleming, "The Biblical Tradition of Anointing Priests," *Journal of Biblical Literature* 117, no. 3 (1998): 401–414; Hess, *Israelite Religion*, 53–54, 113–114; Jacob Milgrom, "The Shared Custody of the Tabernacle and a Hittite Analogy," *Journal of the American Oriental Society* 90, no. 2 (1970): 204–209. On sacrifices and rituals, see Moshe Weinfeld, "Traces of Hittite Cult in Shiloh, Bethel and in Jerusalem," in *Religionsgeschichtliche Beziehungen Zwischen Kleinasien, Nordsyrien und dem Alten Testament*, ed. Bernd Janowski, Klaus Koch, and Gernot Wilhelm (Göttingen, DE: Vandenhoeck and Ruprecht, 1993), 455–472; Hess, *Israelite Religion*, 104–108. On the calendars and festivals, see David T. Stewart, "A Brief Comparison of the Israelite and Hittite Festival Calendars," in Jacob Milgrom, *Leviticus 23–27: A New Translation and Commentary*, The Anchor Bible, vol. 3B (New York: Doubleday, 2001), 2076–2080; Bryan C. Babcock, *Sacred Ritual: A Study of the West Semitic Ritual Calendars in Leviticus 23 and the Akkadian Text Emar 446* (University Park, PA: Eisenbrauns, 2014).

145. Jacob Milgrom, "Priestly ('P') Source," in *Anchor Bible Dictionary*, 5:459–460, quote on p. 460.

146. See either Friedman, *Bible with Sources Revealed* or Campbell and O'Brien, *Sources of the Pentateuch* for examples of this.

early, from the tenth to eighth centuries BC, while the P narrative was a later recapitulation of the story written during or after the exile.

This general model still has its advocates, but many of the details, including the dating of the different narrative strands, have been disputed, as mentioned earlier. Most scholars, however, still support the division of these materials into at least two strands: P and non-P (sometimes called JE).[147] Since the late 20th century, some scholars have pushed for exilic or post-exilic composition for most of this material, including the non-P/JE portions, though they acknowledge that traditions and sources from the First Temple period were used.[148] Considerable evidence, however, indicates that not only the so-called JE material, but also the portions attributed to P should be dated to the monarchic period.

First, as previously noted, the language of the Torah is by and large Classical Biblical Hebrew (CBH) and consistent with the version of Hebrew attested in inscriptions from the time of the Israelite and Judahite kingdoms. In a recent study, Cambridge linguist Aaron D. Hornkohl found several linguistic features that actually distinguish the Pentateuch slightly from the rest of the CBH corpus. Based on comparisons with Hebrew and other Northwest Semitic inscriptions, Hornkohl argued that the CBH of the Torah should be dated earlier than other CBH texts, proposing a tentative date range of 1000–800 BC.[149] Naturally, this remains the case when individual strands of material are examined on their own. For instance, Richard M. Wright systematically studied the passages in Genesis, Exodus, and Numbers typically attributed to the so-called J-source. He concluded, "The 'J' source reflects substantially a pre-exilic linguistic background. *We may therefore conclude that 'J' is (most likely) a product of the pre-exilic period.*" In fact, Wright found a "total absence of late features in 'J'," which can show up in texts from the end of the pre-exilic period (Iron

---

147. See Dozeman, *Pentateuch*, 218–229, 243–251, 260–267, 270–277, 294–298, 303–313, 319–326, 331–333, 349–357, 448–455, 464–470.
148. See David M. Carr, *An Introduction to the Old Testament: Sacred Texts and Imperial Contexts of the Hebrew Bible* (Hoboken, NJ: Wiley-Blackwell, 2010), 187–206; John Van Seters, *The Yahwist: A Historian of Israelite Origins* (University Park, PA: Eisenbrauns, 2013); Schmid, *Genesis and the Moses Story*.
149. Hornkohl, *Diachronic Diversity*.

IIC). Thus, he reasoned, "one should look to a period antedating the late pre-exilic period" for the origins of the J material.[150]

Richard Elliott Friedman came to similar conclusions based on his own linguistic analysis. "From this evidence, J [and] E ... come from the earliest stage of Biblical Hebrew (BH). ... *It is linguistically impossible for J to be exilic or post-exilic.*" In response to scholars who argue for a later date, Friedman states, "The texts that they call late are written in the earliest, 'classical,' stage of biblical Hebrew: J and E come before the Deuteronomist. J, E, D, and P *all* come before Ezekiel."[151] Frank Polak detected linguistic features in "the main strands of the patriarchal narrative; the Joseph narrative and the exodus-Sinai-desert cycle; as well as some sections of the Primeval History" which point primarily to an Iron IIB setting (circa nineth–eighth century BC).[152] Polak's analysis does reveal editorial expansions in a more intricate writing style, but these are still generally dated to the late Judean monarchy (approximately seventh century BC), not the Exile or Persian period.[153] J. A. Emerton essentially corroborates these linguistic dates using inscriptional evidence. According to Emerton, J is consistent with "the literary tradition seen in North-West Semitic inscriptions of the ninth–seventh centuries [BC]."[154]

---

150. Richard M. Wright, *Linguistic Evidence for the Pre-exilic Date of Yahwistic Source* (London: T&T Clark, 2005), 161–162, 164.
151. Richard Elliott Friedman, *The Hidden Book in the Bible: The Discovery of the First Prose Masterpiece* (New York: HarperSanFrancisco, 1998), 359, 362. Emphasis in the original.
152. Polak, "Identification of Preexilic Material," 333.
153. For his full analysis, see Frank H. Polak, "Oral Substratum, Language Usage, and Thematic Flow in the Abraham-Jacob Narrative," in *Contextualizing Israel's Sacred Writings: Ancient Literacy, Orality, and Literary Production*, ed. Brain B. Schmidt (Atlanta: SBL Press, 2015), 217–238; Frank H. Polak, "Oral Platform and Language Usage in the Abraham Narrative," in *Formation of the Pentateuch*, 405–441; Frank H. Polak, "Storytelling and Redaction: Varieties of Language Usage in the Exodus Narrative," in *Formation of the Pentateuch*, 443–475.
154. J. A. Emerton, "The Date of the Yahwist," in *In Search of Pre-Exilic Israel*, 128. See John A. Emerton, "The Kingdoms of Judah and Israel and Ancient Hebrew Writing," in *Biblical Hebrew in Its Northwest Semitic Setting: Typological and Historical Perspectives*, ed. Steven E. Fassberg and Avi Hurvitz (Jerusalem: Hebrew University Magnes Press; University Park, PA: Eisenbrauns, 2006), 44–49 for discussion of the inscriptional evidence Emerton has in mind.

This is consistent with William M. Schniedewind's observation that, in contrast to Deuteronomy, "Writing and written texts do not play a significant role in Genesis, Exodus, Leviticus, or Numbers. ... This observation has significant implications. It suggests that the first four books of the Pentateuch were written when writing was not self-consciously important." According to Schniedewind, this fits the early First Temple period, prior to the seventh century BC when writing became commonplace.[155] Furthermore, Deuteronomy itself alludes to several of the narrative episodes recorded in other parts of the Torah, attesting to their earlier date of composition. As Joshua Berman succinctly summarizes: "Deuteronomy adapts and freely rewrites several major accounts from the books of Exodus and Numbers: the appointment of officials (Exod 18:13–27+Num 11:10–25\\Deut 1:9–18); the sin of the spies (Num 13–14\\Deut 1:19–46); the conquest of the Transjordan (Num 20:14–21:35\\Deut 2:2–3:11); the revelation of Sinai (Exod 19:1–20:23\\Deut 5:2–30); and the sin of the gold calf (Exod 32:1–34:35\\Deut 9:8–21)."[156]

For the most part, these stories are typically attributed to J or E.[157] Friedman explains, "The opening chapters of Deuteronomy are filled with allusions to the JE stories. Deuteronomy is Moses' farewell address, and he refers to many of the events of his forty years with the people. His reminiscences — all but one — are to events from JE stories, not to P stories."[158] The one exception, according to Friedman, is the story of the spies found in Numbers 13–14 and 32:8–13. In its retelling, Ziony Zevit demonstrates that Deuteronomy draws on both P and non-P material from Numbers 13–14 and 32:8–13.[159] The clear implication is that the narratives of Exodus and Numbers — especially those typically attributed to JE — were written before Deuteronomy took on its final form in the early to mid-seventh century BC.

It is not just the so-called JE material that appears to be early, however. There are at least a few brief allusions to the narratives attributed to P in Deuteronomy, in addition to the story of the spies from Numbers 13–14 already mentioned. Berman notes that Deuter-

---

155. Schniedewind, *How the Bible Became a Book*, 81–82.
156. Berman, *Inconsistencies in the Torah*, 81–82.
157. Tigay, *Deuteronomy*, xxiv.
158. Friedman, *Who Wrote the Bible*, 207.
159. Zevit, "Converging Lines," 503–509.

onomy makes passing allusion to "the idolatry of Baal Peor (Deut 4:3 [cf. Num 25:1–19]); rebellions at Taberah, Massah, and Kibroth-Hattaavah (9:22 [cf. Num 11:1–3, 31–34; Exod 17:1–7]); the death of Aaron (10:6; 32:50 [cf. Num 20:22–29]); the rebellion of Dathan (11:6 [cf. Num 16]); Balaam (23:4–5 [cf. Num 22–24]); Miriam's leprosy (24:8–9 [cf. Num 12:1–15]); and the rebellion at Meribah (32:51 [cf. Num 20:1–13])."[160] Several of these stories — such as the rebellion at Meribah, death of Aaron, and the idolatry at Baal Peor — are stories typically attributed to P in whole or in part.[161] Deuteronomy 10:6–7, according Bernard M. Levinson, "seem[s] to quote a wilderness itinerary from the Priestly literature (cf. Num 33:30–38)."[162] Zevit also noticed that Deuteronomy 29:12 references the promise to the Patriarchs (Genesis 17:7–8; Genesis 22:16–18; Genesis 26:24) and the children of Israel (Exodus 6:7; Leviticus 26:12) in a way that combines strands from JE and P/H.[163] The present version of Deuteronomy, then, draws on accounts in Genesis, Exodus, and Numbers from across each of the hypothetical sources. As Berman concludes, "Deuteronomy seems to rely on the reader's familiarity with the accounts as they appear in the Tetrateuch [i.e., Genesis–Numbers]; indeed, at no point does Deuteronomy reference an event not found in Tetrateuch."[164]

Much has already been said about the evidence for a pre-exilic date of the so-called P-source when discussing the legal and ritual material. When Hornkohl subjected his recent linguistic studies of the Pentateuch to source critical analysis, he found that P largely shares the same early (circa 1000–800 BC) CBH profile generally found in the non-P material.[165] According to Hornkohl, many scholars find that "P's pre-exilic linguistic profile stands as insurmountable evidence of its early date."[166] Some evidence even indicates that the P narrative *preceded* the non-P narrative material, providing the foundational

---

160. Berman, *Inconsistencies in the Torah*, 82, brackets added.
161. See Friedman, *Who Wrote the Bible*, 253–254.
162. Bernard M. Levinson, "Deuteronomy," in *The New Oxford Annotated Bible: An Ecumenical Study Bible*, 5th ed., ed. Michael D. Coogan (New York: Oxford University Press, 2018), 267, note on 10.6–9.
163. Zevit, "Converging Lines," 502.
164. Berman, *Inconsistencies in the Torah*, 82, brackets added.
165. Hornkohl, *Diachronic Diversity*, 21, 206.
166. Hornkohl, *Diachronic Diversity*, 13.

backbone of the Pentateuch. Gordon J. Wenham scrutinized all the passages typically attributed to P in Genesis and found "that the P-material throughout Genesis is not a late insertion into an essentially J-composition, rather that it is one of the sources used by J to form our book of Genesis."[167] If the P-source's narrative predates that of JE, then it follows that like JE it dates to sometime before the seventh century BC.

Another indication of the early origins of the narratives in Genesis, Exodus, and Numbers is the inclusion and prominence of the northern Israelite tribes throughout the accounts.[168] "Examples of the prominence of the northern tribes abound in the Pentateuch," according to Schniedewind. It is not telling the origin story of *Judah* alone, but of all Israel. "The stories of Genesis, for example, are the stories of the twelve tribes of Israel. Although Genesis privileges the tribe of Judah as the tribe from which the kings of Israel should emerge, the book is a story about all of the twelve brothers. ... the Book of Exodus also tells a story of all the tribes of Israel that will become the people of Israel. ... The Book of Numbers begins with a census of *all Israel*, and so on."[169] Deuteronomy also heavily reflects northern traditions, leading some scholars to conclude that the pre-seventh century BC edition of the book was primarily preserved in the northern kingdom.[170] "The stories in the Pentateuch tell the origins of the people of Israel — both north and south."[171]

This inclusion and emphasis on the tribes of the northern kingdom make very little sense if it was written in post-exilic Judah. As Schniedewind explains, "These twelve tribes are essentially a pre-exilic concept. The concept does not appear, for example, in the Persian books of Ezra and Nehemiah. Those were books written in the fifth or fourth century B.C.E. when the northern tribes were not only lost — as a result of the Assyrian exile — but also irrelevant."[172] It was not

---

167. Gordon J. Wenham, "The Priority of P," *Vetus Testamentum* 49, no. 2 (1999): 258. Note that Wenham uses J to refer to the combined JE or non-P writings.
168. Bergsma and Morrow, *Murmuring Against Moses*, 125–143.
169. Schniedewind, *How the Bible Became a Book*, 82–83.
170. Schniedewind, *How the Bible Became a Book*, 83; Lundbom, *Deuteronomy*, 5–6.
171. Schniedewind, *How the Bible Became a Book*, 83–84.
172. Schniedewind, *How the Bible Became a Book*, 83.

very long after the demise of the northern kingdom that its relevance would have begun to fade. "The northern kingdom had disappeared in the eighth century B.C.E. and by the end of the seventh century B.C.E. was the pariah of the religious and political orthodoxy. ... But in the days of Hezekiah, the northern tribes were still on the minds of the people in Judah. Indeed, many of them were refugees living in Jerusalem. Hezekiah dreamed of reincorporating their territory."[173] Thus, the reign of Hezekiah — when Judah was striving to integrate many people from the northern kingdom — is the logical timing for the compilation and integration of these northern-oriented Torah narratives into the Judahite corpus of literature.

The *origins* of these accounts, however, necessarily pre-date the demise of the northern kingdom. Much of what was integrated into the Pentateuch with a northern perspective likely stems from traditions and writings brought to Judah by the northern Israelite refugees.[174] Some scholars, such as Friedman, argue that the northern traditions can predominately be attributed to the E source, which they surmise was written in northern Israel prior to its demise in the late eighth century BC.[175] Others argue these northern-inclusive stories go back to before the division of Israel into two kingdoms.[176] Furthermore, it is likely that some additional northern writings were brought to Jerusalem which were ultimately excluded from the biblical corpus: "It is only natural to assume that there were northern prophets ... who were closer to the royal institutions in Samaria. This kind of material could not possibly have entered the Bible as we know it today."[177]

Just as is the case with other parts of the Torah, a substantial body of evidence from archaeology and comparative ancient Near Eastern data indicates that these accounts — though compiled, edited, and committed to written form in the Iron II period — have deep roots

---

173. Schniedewind, *How the Bible Became a Book*, 82–83.
174. Israel Finkelstein, *The Forgotten Kingdom: The Archaeology and History of Northern Israel* (Atlanta: Society of Biblical Literature, 2013), 3, 65, 140–151. Compare David M. Carr, *Writing on the Tablet of the Heart: Origins of Scripture and Literature* (New York: Oxford University Press, 2005), 76–77.
175. Friedman, *Who Wrote the Bible*, 62–69, 86–88; Friedman, *Hidden Book*, 358–359.
176. Bergsma and Morrow, *Murmuring Against Moses*, 125–143.
177. Finkelstein and Silberman, *Bible Unearthed*, 223.

going back to the second millennium BC. In many cases, the primeval history (Genesis 1–11), the ancestral narratives (Genesis 12–50), the exodus (Exodus 1–15), and the wilderness wandering (Exodus 16–18, Exodus 31–34; Numbers 10–36) preserve accurate information about the Middle and Late Bronze Ages or reflect ideas attested in these early eras.[178] For our present purposes, however, it is enough to have demonstrated that the Pentateuchal narratives likely pre-date the seventh century BC.

"Five Books of Moses"

To be clear, the claim is not that the entirety of the Pentateuch existed exactly as it does today by 600 BC. Indeed, evidence from the Book of Mormon suggests that there were some differences in what the Nephites had on the plates of brass, most notably the inclusion of additional material that aligns with the later revealed book of Moses and other JST materials.[179] There likely continued to be edits and revisions to this material into the exilic and post-exilic period. But, in the words of respected biblical scholar and source critic Menaham Haran, a substantial body of evidence suggests that "all the sources of the Pentateuch — the most sacred part of the Old Testament canon — did in fact attain literary crystallization during the First Temple period."[180] A remaining question is what *form* this material existed

---

178. See Kitchen, *Reliability of the Old Testament*, 241–312, 421–447; James K. Hoffmeier, *Israel in Egypt: The Evidence for the Authenticity of the Exodus Tradition* (New York: Oxford University Press, 1997); Hoffmeier, *Ancient Israel in Sinai*.
179. Noel B. Reynolds, "The Brass Plates Version of Genesis," in *By Study and also By Faith: Essays in Honor of Hugh W. Nibley*, 2 vols., ed. John M. Lundquist and Stephen D. Ricks (Salt Lake City: Deseret Book; Provo, UT: Foundation for Ancient Research and Mormon Studies, 1990), 2:136–173; Jeff Lindsay and Noel B. Reynolds, "'Strong Like Unto Moses': The Case for Ancient Roots in the Book of Moses Based on Book of Mormon Usage of Related Content Apparently from the Brass Plates," in *Tracing Ancient Threads in the Book of Moses: Inspired Origins, Temple Contexts, and Literary Qualities*, 2 vols., ed. Jeffrey M. Bradshaw, David Rolph Seely, John W. Welch, and Scott A. Gordon (Orem, UT: Interpreter Foundation; Salt Lake City: Eborn Books, 2021), 1:315–420.
180. Menaham Haran, *Temples and Temple-Service in Ancient Israel: An Inquiry into Biblical Cult Phenomena and the Historical Setting of the Priestly School* (University Park, PA: Eisenbrauns, 1985), 6.

in. Had it been compiled into something resembling the Pentateuch as we have it today — the "five books" of Genesis, Exodus, Leviticus, Numbers, and Deuteronomy? Had it achieved its authoritative status at this point, and even been attributed to Moses already?

Nephi's statement, that the plates of brass contained "the five books of Moses" would seem to imply that the answer to these questions is *yes* (1 Nephi 5:11). This is not *necessarily* so, however. A quarter century ago, Kevin Barney suggested that this expression could be a translator's gloss for another expression Nephi might have used for this material as it existed and was known in his day.[181] Furthermore, if the basics of the classic Documentary Hypothesis are accepted, the source material could have existed in the form of "five books" — J, E, D, P, and H — before the final compilation into the Torah as it is known today. This could be reduced to only four sources if either JE or P/H are taken to be a single source by 600 BC. But since the Book of Mormon indicates the existence of additional material not attested in the current Pentateuch with a seemingly northern kingdom bias (such as 2 Nephi 3), one could still hypothesize a fifth source (call it *N* for "northern source") on the plates of brass.

That said, there is some evidence to suggest that the source material had been compiled into something closely resembling the Torah, as it stands today, by the seventh century BC. First, as already noted, Deuteronomy, more or less as presently constituted, essentially dates to the early to mid-seventh century BC, with much of the core, and even the overall structure, going back even earlier; and Deuteronomy shows awareness of both the narrative and legal material from Genesis to Numbers. To quote, again, from Berman, "Deuteronomy seems to rely on the reader's familiarity with the accounts as they appear in the Tetrateuch [i.e., Genesis–Numbers]."[182] Benjamin Kilchör concluded from a detailed study of the legal material in the Pentateuch, that "Deuteronomic law pre-supposes Exodus, Leviticus, and Numbers more or less in their present shape and in quasicanonical prestige."[183]

---

181. Kevin L. Barney, "Reflections on the Documentary Hypothesis," *Dialogue: A Journal of Mormon Thought* 33, no. 1 (2000): 74.
182. Berman, *Inconsistencies in the Torah*, 82, brackets added.
183. Kilchör, "Reception of Priestly Laws," 213, summarizing the findings of his book *Mosetora und Jahwetora: Das Verhältnis von Deuteronomium 12–26 zu Exodus, Levitikus und Numeri* (Wiesbaden, DE: Harrassowitz, 2015).

Deuteronomy, then, the "linchpin" of Pentateuchal dating, attests to the existence of the rest of the Torah, essentially in its current form, no later than the mid-seventh century BC.

In addition to Deuteronomy, the prophetic works of Jeremiah and Ezekiel, written in the late seventh and early sixth centuries BC, demonstrate familiarity with material traditionally attributed to both P and D.[184] The ways these prophetic works interact with (and sometimes blend) the laws of P and D can only be explained if *both* the P and D sources pre-dated the composition of Jeramiah.[185] It further suggests that both legal codes were part of an established, authoritative corpus together. Georg Fischer goes even further, arguing that the book of Jeremiah betrays familiarity with the Pentateuch *as a whole*, in essentially the same form as it exists today. "Overall, the links between the books of the Torah and Jeremiah are too many and too strong to be accidental. They span the whole range, from the first chapter of Genesis to the final frame of Deuteronomy.... No book of the Torah is missing. ... The author of Jeremiah was obviously very closely acquainted with the whole Torah."[186] Passages of Ezekiel, too,

---

184. Menahem Haran, "The Law-Code of Ezekiel XL–XLVIII and its Relation to the Priestly School," *Hebrew Union College Annual* 50 (1979): 45–71; Rise Levitt Kohn, "A Prophet Like Moses? Rethinking Ezekiel's Relationship to the Torah," *Zeitschrift für die alttestamentliche Wissenschaft* 114, no. 2 (2002): 236–257; Kenneth Bergland, "Jeremiah 34 Originally Composed as a Legal Blend of Leviticus 25 and Deuteronomy 15," in *Paradigm Change in Pentateuchal Research*, 189–205.

185. Bergsma and Morrow, *Murmuring Against Moses*, 81–124; Dalit Rom-Shiloni, "The Forest and the Trees: The Place of Pentateuchal Materials in Prophecy of the Late Seventh/Early Sixth Centuries BCE," in *Congress Volume Stellenbosch 2016*, ed. Louis C. Jonker, Gideon R. Kotzé, and Christl M. Maier (Leiden, NL: Brill, 2017), 56–92.

186. George Fischer, "ותפשי התורה לא ידעוני: The Relationship of the Book of Jeremiah to the Torah," in *Formation of the Pentateuch*, 903–904. Note that Fischer dates both the Torah and the composition of Jeremiah to late dates, in the Persian period, but one need not accept his assumptions about dating to find his arguments for literary connection persuasive. The realia of Jeremiah accords with the archaeology of the seventh century BC, suggesting it is in fact contemporary with the prophet himself. See Philip J. King, *Jeremiah: An Archaeological Companion* (Louisville, KY: Westminster John Knox, 1993); Dever, *Beyond the Texts*, 615. Linguistically, Jeremiah belongs to the late seventh to the sixth century BC. See Aaron D. Hornkohl, *Ancient Hebrew Periodization*

indicate knowledge of all parts (JE, P/H, and D) of the Torah, sometimes in their combined form.[187]

Some have even argued that the earlier prophet Hosea reflects knowledge of the whole Pentateuch.[188] After a careful study of several passages, Umberto Cassuto concluded, "There is nothing in the entire Book of Hosea to compel us to suppose that the Pentateuchal material existed in his day in a form different from that before us today. On the contrary the Book of Hosea contains passages that cause us to believe that much of what read in the Torah today already existed in its present form in Hosea's time and was known to broad circles of the people."[189] The writings of Hosea and other early eighth century BC prophets, according to Schniedewind, show evidence of editing and redacting from the reign of Hezekiah.[190] Thus, the presence of all parts of the Torah in Hosea points to the compilation and editorial activity of Hezekiah's reign as the latest possible period for the formation of an initial version of the Pentateuch, based on earlier sources combined with some new editorial expansions from the late eighth century BC.

None of this means there was *no* revision, editing, and even expansion of the Pentateuch after the eighth–seventh century BC. The texts no doubt continued to be modified during the exilic and post-exilic

---

and the Language of the Book of Jeremiah (Leiden, NL: Brill, 2014).

187. Millar Burrows, *The Literary Relations of Ezekiel* (Philadelphia: Jewish Publication Society, 1925), 3–15, 19–25, 28–36, 47–68; Ben Zion Katz, "The Pentateuch Quoted Intact: Evidence from Ezekiel and Psalms," *Jewish Bible Quarterly* 44, no. 1 (2016). Note that Burrows dates Ezekiel to the very late Maccabean period, but as with Fischer, this late dating needn't be accepted to find the intertextual arguments hold merit. Linguistically, Ezekiel is securely dated to the sixth century BC. See Mark F. Rooker, *Biblical Hebrew in Transition: The Language of the Book of Ezekiel* (Sheffield, GB: JSOT Press, 1990).

188. Umberto Cassuto, "The Prophet Hosea and the Books of the Pentateuch," in *Biblical and Oriental Studies*, trans. Israel Abrahams (Jerusalem: Magnes Press, Hebrew University, 1973), 79–100; Mark F. Rooker, "The Use of the Old Testament in the Book of Hosea," *Criswell Theological Review* 7, no. 1 (1993): 51–66. As with Jeremiah and Ezekiel, some scholars will date Hosea to a later period, but the realia of Hosea and other eighth century prophets reflects the Iron II period. See Philip J. King, *Amos, Hosea, Micah: An Archaeological Commentary* (Louisville, KY: Westminster Press, 1988).

189. Cassuto, "The Prophet Hosea and the Books of the Pentateuch," 100.

190. Schniedewind, *How the Bible Became a Book*, 76, 84–85.

periods. But an extensive body of evidence — only cursorily reviewed here — suggests that a fairly complete proto-Torah existed no later than the late eighth century BC. The writing, editing, and compiling of this material was an ongoing process that likely began early in the Iron Age, and culminated during the major period of literary activity in the Iron IIC. Some may note that this precludes Moses as the *direct* author of this material, but it should not be overlooked that even in its final form, almost every portion of the Torah contains hints of material traceable to the pre-monarchic period of the late second millennium BC. This places much of the foundational traditions in or close to the so-called "Mosaic Age" (circa thirteenth century BC). It cannot be proven that Moses was the originator of this material, but given that Moses looms larger than any other figure within the corpus, it is not hard to imagine how his name would have been linked to it as the founder of, and source of authority for, these traditions, even in their rewritten and adapted form.[191]

Conclusion

This paper has tried to lay out a preliminary case for dating the primary period of composition for a large portion of the Hebrew Bible, and especially the Pentateuch, to the Iron II period, particularly the eighth–seventh centuries BC. Much of what was being composed and compiled during this period corresponds in general terms with the contents described as being on the plates of brass (see 1 Nephi 5:11–16), and it is proposed that the existence of this collection of texts in the possession of Laban generally fits with the picture of this period as a time of literary flourishing as reconstructed by William Schniedewind and other scholars.

Of necessity, only a fraction of the relevant evidence and scholarship could be highlighted here. No pretense is made of having settled all questions relative to the presence of "the five books of Moses" in a collection of texts engraved on metal plates in early sixth century BC Jerusalem. Biblical scholars will probably never come to a consensus on the dating and composition of the Pentateuch, and so questions

---

191. See Bill T. Arnold, *Encountering the Book of Genesis* (Grand Rapids: Baker Books, 2003), 167–179; John H. Walton and D. Brent Sandy, *The Lost World of Scripture* (Downers Grove, IL: IVP Academic, 2013), 17–74.

will always persist as to how much and which specific passages could have been accessible by 600 BC.

Even as questions remain, however, Latter-day Saints need not consider this an insurmountable problem for the historicity of the Book of Mormon. Several lines of evidence — from linguistics, epigraphy, archaeology, history, and intertextual relationships — have led many scholars to believe that the Torah was written, in large measure, before Lehi departed from Jerusalem. It therefore remains plausible for Lehi to have found that the plates of brass obtained from Laban "did contain the five books of Moses" (1 Nephi 5:11).

15

DOES ISAIAH'S DESCRIPTION OF THE RIGHTEOUS SERVANT REFER TO JESUS CHRIST?

JEFFREY M. BRADSHAW

The description of the Righteous Servant in Isaiah 53 is by far the most important and widely cited chapter in the New Testament and in modern scripture testifying of the life and atonement of Jesus Christ. That said, it may be surprising to many Bible readers to know that the New Testament attests a climate of uncertainty and speculation at the time of Jesus regarding several prophetic figures whose comings were anticipated by His people. The cumulative effect of such well-known biblical uncertainties — combined with a modern tendency to doubt the possibility of prophetic foresight in general — threatens to erode confidence that Isaiah — or any other Old Testament prophet — could have known so much about Jesus Christ long before His birth. The hope is that this essay will help Latter-day Saints — and others who are willing to accept Isaiah's word as divine prophecy — to understand why their belief in Isaiah's poignant prophecy as an authentic witness of Jesus Christ is well-founded in light of both ancient Jewish and Christian traditions of biblical interpretation and the best of modern scholarship.

Since I was a young boy, I have loved Isaiah 53. There are three reasons that I like to call it the "crown jewel" of the Old Testament:

1. Its literary beauty — both in the original, sometimes obscure, Hebrew text and in its magnificent King James Bible translation — best experienced musically in listening to Handel's *Messiah*;
2. Its key role within the writings of Isaiah — the most important and widely cited prophet in the New Testament and in modern scripture — as the last of his four "Servant Songs"; and
3. Its unparalleled clarity and poignancy as an ancient witness of

Jesus Christ long before His birth, a truth frequently affirmed in modern Latter-day Saint scripture and teachings.

So much has been written and so much can be said about Isaiah 53 that I will need to be selective. So, in this essay, I will focus on just three questions:

1. Why, in contrast to many who study this chapter, can Latter-day Saints and other believers in Old Testament prophecy be confident that Isaiah's description of the Righteous Servant refers to Jesus Christ?
2. What is the big picture being painted by Isaiah 53 (and its preface at the end of Isaiah 52)?
3. How might we understand some of the difficult-to-comprehend details in these verses?

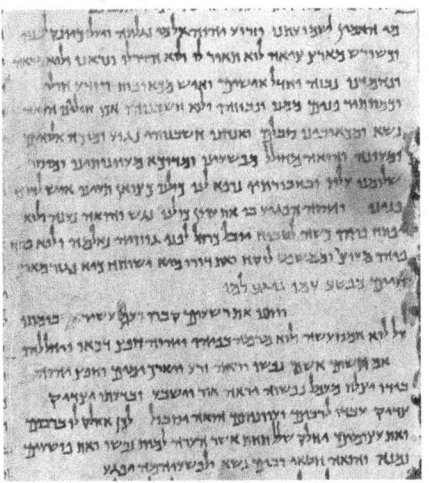

Isaiah 53 in the Great Isaiah Scroll (1QIsaª), found among the Dead Sea Scrolls, circa first century BCE.

1. Who is the Righteous Servant in Isaiah 53?

Why is it so hard to pinpoint the identity of the Servant?

John W. Welch has mentioned some of the reasons that readers differ on the identity of the "righteous servant" in Isaiah 53.[1] His

---

1. John W. Welch, "Isaiah 53, Mosiah 14, and the Book of Mormon," in *Isaiah in the Book of Mormon*, ed. Donald W. Parry and John W. Welch (Provo, UT: Foundation for Ancient Research and Mormon Studies, 1998), 309–310.

thoughts on these difficulties can be summarized in the following three points:

1. *The servant is never specifically identified.* The pronoun "he," as well as the "we," "our," and "thou" have all been variously interpreted. Fortunately, the Book of Mormon makes it clear that the "he" refers to Christ. Abinadi says plainly: "I would that ye should understand that God himself shall come down among the children of men and shall redeem his people" (Mosiah 15:1).
2. *The time-frame — past, present, or future — is unclear.* Again, the Book of Mormon helps us out, making it clear that the passage is written in the "prophetic past tense." In other words, it is speaking "of things to come *as though they have already come*" (Mosiah 16:6, emphasis added).
3. *The nature of the suffering of the servant is difficult to understand.* At first the people despise him, but later they conclude that He has borne their griefs. Again, Abinadi's plain prose removes the mystery from the meaning of these verses when he says that the servant "shall be led, crucified, and slain.... Thus God breaketh the bands of death, ... giving the Son power to make intercession for the children of men" (Mosiah 15:7–8).

In addition to the witness of the Book of Mormon, "modern apostles of the restored Church of Jesus Christ, such as James E. Talmage, Joseph Fielding Smith, and Bruce R. McConkie, have also stated that Jesus is the subject of Isaiah 53."[2] And, more recently, President Russell M. Nelson has taught the same truth.[3]

It may be surprising to some to learn that the New Testament attests a climate of uncertainty and speculation at the time of Jesus regarding *several* prophetic figures whose comings were anticipated by His people. For example, the gospel of John reported that "priests and

---

2. Victor L. Ludlow, *Isaiah: Prophet, Seer, and Poet* (Salt Lake City: Deseret Book, 1982), 448. See, for example, Joseph Fielding Smith, *Doctrines of Salvation*, 3 vols., comp. Bruce R. McConkie (Salt Lake City: Bookcraft, Inc., 1954–1956), 1:23–24; James E. Talmage, *Jesus the Christ* (Salt Lake City: Deseret News, 1915), 47; Bruce R. McConkie, *The Promised Messiah: The First Coming of Christ*, The Messiah, 6 vols. (Salt Lake City: Deseret Book, 1978), 1:234–235.
3. Russell M. Nelson, *Teachings of Russell M. Nelson* (Salt Lake City: Deseret Book, 2018), 20.

Levites from Jerusalem" were sent to ask John the Baptist which one of three such figures he was:[4] the Messiah,[5] Elijah,[6] or "that prophet" — the latter usually either associated with the "Prophet ... like unto [Moses]" mentioned in Deuteronomy 18:15[7] or else with Moses himself.

As another example of the uncertainty surrounding this figure, note that after Herod beheaded John the Baptist, he feared that Jesus might be John "risen from the dead" (Mark 6:14–16). Then, as now, mapping biblical prophecy to precise timeframes, circumstances, and individuals is a notoriously risky business. As a Danish parliamentarian once obtusely opined: "It is difficult to make predictions, especially about the future."[8]

With specific respect to Isaiah 53, the lack of a settled interpretation at the time of Jesus for the identity of the righteous servant is witnessed in the question the Ethiopian eunuch asked Philip: "I pray thee, of whom speaketh the prophet this? of himself, or of some other man?" (Acts 8:34). Even Jesus's disciples, to whom He had explained that He must needs "suffer many things, and be killed, and be raised again the third day," failed to recognize these events as Messianic necessities (Matthew 16:21). When a horrified Peter rebuked Jesus, saying: "Be it far from thee, Lord: this shall not be unto thee," the Lord was obliged to forcefully disavow His chief apostle's error with these words: "Get thee behind me, Satan: thou art an offence unto me" (Matthew 16:22–23; Mark 9:31–32; Mark 16:10–11; John 20:9).

---

4. See John 1:19–23. Also see Gerland L. Borchert, *The New American Commentary: John 1–11: An Exegetical and Theological Exposition of Holy Scripture* (Nashville: B&H Publishing Group, 1996), 127–128.
5. See Borchert, *John 1–11*, 127.
6. Malachi 3:1; Malachi 4:5–6. Compare with Sirach 48:10–11.
7. Quoted by Peter in Acts 3:22. Compare with 1 Maccabees 4:46 and Testament of Benjamin 9:2. Robert J. Utley, *The Beloved Disciple's Memoirs and Letters: I John, the Gospel of John, II John, and III John* (Marshall, TX: Kindred Publications, 1999), 24, wrote: "There are two distinct ways this term was used in the NT: (1) as an eschatological figure distinct from the Messiah (cf. 7:40–41) or (2) as a figure identified with the Messiah (cf. Acts 3:22)."
8. The original Danish read, *"Det er vanskeligt at spaa, især naar det gælder Fremtiden."* Karl Kristian Steincke, *Farvel Og Tak: Og saa en Tilvaerelse IV (1935–1939)* (Eau Claire, WI: Fremad Publishing, 1948), 227. A Danish politician, Steincke presented the saying as one of "a couple of parliamentary howlers" that was made during the parliamentary year 1937–1938.

What were the different guesses about the identity of the Servant of Isaiah 53 in Jesus's day and afterward? Below we summarize some of the common identifications in three, roughly chronological, phases.

Common Identifications for the Servant in History

The Servant as the Messiah in Second Temple and Early Rabbinic Judaism. Many Jewish interpreters in Second Temple and early rabbinic Judaism understood Isaiah's servant in Isaiah 53 as the Messiah. Elsewhere, Kent Brown and I have written at length about the earliest known Second Temple sources.[9] However, there are several impressive examples of the servant of Isaiah 53 being understood in Jewish tradition messianically that come from early rabbinic sources, including the *Targum*, the *Talmud*, and the later rabbinic literature.[10] Some examples include:

---

9. S. Kent Brown and I have written at length on this subject (S. Kent Brown and Jeffrey M. Bradshaw, "Man and Son of Man: Probing Theology and Christology in the Book of Moses and in Jewish and Christian Tradition," in *Tracing Ancient Threads in the Book of Moses: Inspired Origins, Temple Contexts, and Literary Qualities*, 2 vols., ed. Jeffrey M. Bradshaw, David R. Seely, John W. Welch, and Scott Gordon (Orem, UT: Interpreter Foundation; Springville, UT: Book of Mormon Central; Redding, CA: Foundation for Apologetic Information and Research; Tooele, UT: Eborn Books, 2021), 2:1257–1332). In addition, Hengel and Bailey have made a careful survey of pre-Christian sources relating to Isaiah 53. See Martin Hengel and Daniel P. Bailey, "The Effective History of Isaiah 53 in the Pre-Christian Era," in *The Suffering Servant: Isaiah 53 in Jewish and Christian Sources*, ed. Bernd Janowski and Peter Stuhlmacher (Grand Rapids: William B. Eerdmans Publishing Company, 2004), 146. In the English translation of Florentino García Martínez, Qumran Dead Sea Scroll 4Q541, fragment 9, column 1 reads: "They will utter many words against him, and an abundance of lies; they will fabricate fables against him. His generation will change the evil, and [] established in deceit and violence." Florentino Garcia Martinez, "Messianic Hopes in the Qumran Writings," in *LDS Perspectives on the Dead Sea Scrolls*, ed. Donald W. Parry and Dana M. Pike (Provo, UT: Foundation for Ancient Research and Mormon Studies, Brigham Young University, 1997), 136–137, as cited in Welch, "Isaiah 53," 308. The translator "sees in this text an important confirmation that the messianic interpretation of Isaiah 53 'not an innovation of purely Christian origin,' but rather was already 'the result of previous developments.'" See Welch, "Isaiah 53," 308; Martinez, "Messianic Hopes," 137.
10. See Michael L. Brown, "Jewish Interpretations of Isaiah 53," in *The Gospel According to Isaiah 53: Encountering the Suffering Servant in Jewish and Christian Theology*, ed. Darrell L. Bock and Mitch Glaser (Grand Rapids:

- The *Targum of Jonathan ben Uzziel*[11] (composed between 70 and 135 AD) for Isaiah 52:13 reads: "Behold my servant Messiah shall prosper; he shall be high, and increase and be exceedingly strong";
- The *Babylonian Talmud*[12] (codified in the sixth century AD) asks: "The Messiah — what is his name? The Rabbis say, 'the leprous one': Those of the house of Rabbi say, 'the sick one,' as it is said, 'surely he hath borne our sickness'" (Isaiah 53:4);
- *Midrash Rabbah*,[13] speaking with reference to Ruth 2:14, explains the verse in terms of "the Messiah," explaining it as follows: "'Come hither': approach to a royal state. 'And eat of the bread' refers to the bread of royalty; 'And dip thy morsel in the vinegar' refers to his sufferings, as it is said, 'But he was wounded because of our transgressions'" (Isaiah 53:5);
- *Midrash Tanhuma*[14] applies Isaiah 52:13 and 53:3 to the Messiah;
- In the *Yalkut Shimoni*, a thirteenth-century compilation of earlier commentary, it reads:

Kregel, 2012), 62–64, 79–83; Victor Buksbazen, "Of Whom Does the Prophet Speak? (Isaiah 53)," *Israel My Glory* blog, March/April 2017, online at israelmyglory.org.

11. Michael Maher, ed., *Targum Pseudo-Jonathan, Genesis*, Aramaic Bible, 22 vols. (Collegeville, MN: Liturgical Press, 1992), 1.B:52:13. One of the most interesting features of the *Targum* is how it bifurcates the figure of the Servant — ascribing the descriptions of the Servant's exaltation in the passage to the Messiah while applying the descriptions of the Servant's suffering and death to the wicked, "with some application of the text to the nation of Israel as a whole." Brown, "Jewish Interpretations," 62. See Jostein Adna, "The Servant of Isaiah 53 as Triumphant and Interceding Messiah: The Reception of Isaiah 52:13–53:12 in the Targum of Isaiah with Special Attention to the Concept of the Messiah," in *The Suffering Servant: Isaiah 53 in Jewish and Christian Sources,* ed. Bernd Janowski and Peter Stuhlmacher (Grand Rapids: William B. Eerdmans, 2014), 189, 224.
12. *Babylonian Talmud*, Sanhedrin 98b.
13. *Ruth Rabbah* 5:6, as cited in *Midrash Rabbah*, 3rd ed., 10 vols., ed. H. Freedman and Maurice Simon (London: Soncino Press, 1983), 8:64.
14. John T. Townsend, ed., "Parasha Toldot 14," in *Midrash Tanhuma*, 3 vols. (Jersey City: Ktav Publishing, 1989–2003), 1:166.

"Who art thou, O great mountain?"[15] This refers to the King Messiah. And why does he call him "the great mountain?" Because He is greater than the patriarchs. As it is said, "My servant shall be high and lifted up and lofty exceedingly." He will be higher than Abraham, who says, "I raise high my hand unto the Lord."[16] Lifted up above Moses, to whom it is said, "Lift it up into thy bosom."[17] Loftier than the ministering angels, of whom it is written, "Their wheels were lofty and terrible."[18]

Such rabbinic teachings clearly identify the servant described in Isaiah 52–53 as the Messiah, the anointed one. However, what was not settled among all Jewish believers anciently — and is still not settled today — is the nature and role of this prophesied messiah.

The Servant as Jesus Christ in the New Testament and Later Christianity. Though, as mentioned previously, mapping scriptural prophecies to specific events typically carries risks, both ancient and modern Christians affirm with confidence that Jesus Christ is the Servant of Isaiah 53.[19] When the Ethiopian eunuch asked Philip, "Of whom speaketh the prophet?," the reply was unequivocal: "Philip began at the same scripture, and preached unto him *Jesus*" (Acts 8:35, emphasis added).[20]

Moreover, as Mikeal Parsons insightfully argues, Luke's account of Philip's reply to the eunuch in Acts 8, "is given content by the precursor text in Luke 24."[21] When the resurrected Jesus spoke to the

---

15. Zechariah 4:7.
16. Genesis 14:22.
17. Numbers 11:12.
18. Ezekiel 1:18.
19. Buksbazen: "Some of the medieval scholars who interpreted this passage in an individual sense applied it either to Jeremiah or to Isaiah, others to Hezekiah, and some to any righteous person who suffers innocently." Buksbazen, "Of Whom."
20. For more on how Isaiah 53 is used in Acts 8, see Darrell L. Bock, "Isaiah 53 in Acts 8," in *The Gospel According to Isaiah 53: Encountering the Suffering Servant in Jewish and Christian Theology*, ed. Darrell L. Bock and Mitch Glaser (Grand Rapids: Kregel, 2012), 133–144.
21. Mikeal C. Parsons, "Isaiah 53 in Acts 8: A Reply to Professor Morna Hooker," in *Jesus and the Suffering Servant: Isaiah 53 and Christian Origins*, ed. William H. Bellinger and William R. Farmer (Eugene: Wipf and Stock, 2009), 117.

disciples on the road to Emmaus, He was doubtless alluding in part to Isaiah 53 when He said: "O fools, and slow of heart to believe all that *the prophets have spoken*: Ought not Christ *to have suffered these things*, and *to enter into his glory*?" (Luke 24:25–26, emphasis added). Likewise, when the Lord spoke to the apostles, He said: "All things must be fulfilled, which were written in the law of Moses, and *in the prophets*, and in the psalms, concerning me. And said unto them, Thus it is written, and thus it behoved Christ *to suffer*, and *to rise from the dead* the third day: And that *repentance and remission of sins* should be preached in his name" (Luke 24:44, 46–47, emphasis added).

The included tables show how Matthew, John, Peter, and Paul each apply various verses of Isaiah 53 to Christ.[22]

---

22. Matthew 8:17; John 1:29, John 12:38; Acts 3:13, Acts 4:27, 30, Acts 10:36, 43; 1 Peter 1:11; 1 Peter 2:21–25; Romans 4:25, Romans 5:29, Romans 10:15–16, Romans 15:21; 1 Corinthians 2:9, 1 Corinthians 5:7, 1 Corinthians 15:3; 2 Corinthians 5:20; Hebrews 9:28; 1 John 3:5. For more on Isaiah 53 as it appears or influences these and other related passages, see Michael J. Wilkins, "Isaiah 53 and the Message of Salvation in the Gospels," in *The Gospel According to Isaiah 53: Encountering the Suffering Servant in Jewish and Christian Theology*, ed. Darrell L. Bock and Mitch Glaser (Grand Rapids: Kregel, 2012), 133–144; Craig A. Evans, "Isaiah 53 in the Letters of Peter, Paul, Hebrews, and John," in *The Gospel According to Isaiah 53*, 145–170. Specifically, the table is recreated from Evans, "Isaiah 53," 144.

Quotations and Echoes of Isaiah 52:13–53:12 in Peter	
Isaiah	1 Peter and Peter in Acts
52:13	Acts 3:13 (Peter), 4:27, 30 (Peter)
53	1 Peter 1:11
53:4	1 Peter 2:24
53:5	1 Peter 2:24
53:1, 5–6 (+ 52:7)	Acts 10:43 (Peter) (+ Acts 10:36)
53:6	1 Peter 2:25
53:7	1 Peter 2:23
53:9	1 Peter 2:21–22, 4:1
53:12	1 Peter 2:24

Quotations and Echoes of Isaiah 52:13–53:12 in Paul	
Isaiah	Paul
52:15	Rom. 15:21; 1 Cor. 2:9
53:1 (+ 52:7)	Rom. 10:16 (+ Rom. 10:15; 2 Cor. 5:20)
53:4–5	Rom. 4:25
53:7	1 Cor. 5:7
53:8–9	1 Cor. 15:3
53:11	Rom. 5:19

Quotations and Echoes of Isaiah 52:13–53:12 in Hebrews and John	
Isaiah	Hebrews and Johannine Writings
53:1	John 12:38
53:6–7	John 1:29
53:10	1 John 3:5
53:12	Heb. 9:28

One significant note about the above included table: though Isaiah 52:13–15 is rightfully seen as a single piece with chapter 53, there is also a good reason to consider the two passages separately: Unlike Isaiah 53, Isaiah 52:13–15 has a wider application beyond Jesus Christ alone. For more details, see the discussion about the end of Isaiah 52 below.

The Servant as Jesus Christ and the People of Israel in the Book of Mormon. As mentioned at the beginning of this essay, Abinadi's exposition and commentary on Isaiah 53 in Mosiah 14–15 is one of the clearest witnesses that this prophecy refers to the life and atoning mission of Jesus Christ. However, as Matthew L. Bowen argues:[23]

> The Jews as the Messiah's own people — described to Nephi as "mine ancient covenant people" as covenant Israel — also fit the typology of Isaiah's suffering servant. A common modern Jewish reading of the servant song of Isaiah 53 is that the servant is the Jewish people.[24] Latter-day Saints should neither be adverse to, nor dismissive of this reading. In fact, Nephi himself records an oracle from the Lord using language that draws on the servant songs of Isaiah, including Isaiah 53, to condemn Gentile antisemitism and ingratitude for the Jewish production, transmission, and preservation of the biblical writings:
>
>> But thus saith the Lord God: O fools, they shall have a Bible; and it shall proceed forth from the Jews, mine ancient covenant people. And **what thank they the Jews for the Bible which they receive from them?** Yea, what do the Gentiles mean? Do they remember <u>the travails, and the labors, and the pains of the Jews, and their diligence unto me, in bringing forth salvation unto the Gentiles</u>? O ye Gentiles, have ye remembered the Jews, mine ancient covenant people? Nay; **but ye have cursed them, and have hated them, and have not sought to recover them.** But behold, I will return all these things upon your own heads; for **I the Lord have not forgotten my people.** Thou fool, that shall say: A Bible, we have got a Bible, and we need no more Bible. **Have ye obtained a Bible save it were by the Jews?** (2 Nephi 29:4–6)
>
> When Nephi records the Lord's scathing question, "what thank they [the Gentiles] the Jews for the bible which they receive from them?" the use of the verb "thank" — Hebrew *ydy* or *ydh* — cleverly plays on the names Judah (*yĕhûdâ*, "praise, thanks") and its tribal derivative, "Jews"[25] (*yĕhûdîm*,

---

23. Matthew L. Bowen, *'The Travail of His Soul': The Narratological Use of Isaiah's Suffering Servant Typology in Mosiah 14–24* (n.p., 2025): 16–18. Manuscript in the possession of the author. This paper will be published in early 2026, and page numbers will differ from the published manuscript.
24. David Noel Freedman, Allen C. Myers, and Astrid B. Beck, eds., entry for "Servant of the Lord," in *Eerdmans Dictionary of the Bible* (Grand Rapids: William B. Eerdmans, 2000), 1189–1190.
25. Matthew L. Bowen, "'What Thank They the Jews?'" in *Name as Key-Word:*

those who are to be "thanked" or "praised out of a feeling of gratitude"),[26] similar to the etiological wordplay on Judah in the birth report in Genesis 29:35 ("And she [Leah] conceived again, and bare a son: and she said, Now will I praise the Lord [ôdeh 'et-yhwh]: therefore she called his name Judah") and Jacob's blessing on Judah in Genesis 49:8: "Judah [yĕhûdâ], thou art he whom thy brethren **shall praise** [yôdûkā, literally, thy brethren **shall thank thee**]; thy hand shall be in the neck of thine enemies; thy father's children shall bow down before thee."

When the Lord asks another pointed question, "Do they [the Gentiles] **remember the travails, and the labors, and the pains of the Jews**, and their diligence unto me, in **bringing forth salvation unto the Gentiles?**" he has reference to several of the servant songs of Isaiah.

Firstly, "travails" in the triad "the travails, and the labors, and pains of the Jews" recalls the "travail" (ʿămal) of the servant's "soul" in Isaiah 53:11; "labors" recalls, the servant's exclamation in Isaiah 49:4: "I have laboured [yāgaʿtî] in vain, I have spent my strength for nought, and in vain: yet surely my judgment is with the Lord, and my work [ûpĕʿullātî] with my God"; and "pains" recalls the "man of pains" and "the pains" borne in Isaiah 53:3–4.

Secondly, the phrase "diligence in bringing salvation unto the Gentiles" clearly and deliberately alludes to Isaiah 49:3, 6. In Isaiah 49:3 expressly designated the people of Israel as his servant, "Thou art my servant, O Israel, in whom I will be glorified" (Isaiah 49:3) and further foretold, "I will also give thee for a light to the Gentiles, that thou mayest be my salvation [yĕšûʿatî] unto the end of the earth" (Isaiah 49:6). Thus, in 2 Nephi 29:4, the Lord duly notes the "diligence" of the Jews, implicitly as "my servant, O Israel," in "bringing salvation unto the Gentiles."

Going further, Bowen notes that "Alma and his people's fulfillment of the messianic suffering servant typology of Isaiah 53/Mosiah 14, which gave them experiential knowledge to 'stand as witnesses' (com-

---

Collected Essays on Onomastic Wordplay and the Temple in Mormon Scripture, ed. Matthew L. Bowen (Orem, UT: Interpreter Foundation; Salt Lake City: Eborn Books, 2018), 69–81.

26. Moshe Garsiel, *Biblical Names: A Literary Study of Midrashic Derivations and Puns*, trans. Phyllis Hackett (Ramat Gan, IL: Bar-Ilan University Press, 1991), 171.

pare Mosiah 24:14 with Mosiah 18:29), helps us better appreciate how covenant Israel at other times fulfills this typology."[27]

Representation of a massacre of the Jews in 1349. Antiquitates Flandriae (Royal Library of Belgium manuscript, circa 1376–1377).

The Servant as the People of Israel in Rabbinic Judaism. Although the identification of the Servant as the people of Israel is attested in one account from the early third century,[28] there is currently no evidence that this identification took hold firmly (and, eventually, decisively)

---

27. Bowen, *'The Travail of His Soul'*: 1.
28. See Christoph Markschies, "Jesus Christ as a Man Before God: Two Interpretive Models for Isaiah 53 in the Patristic Literature and Their Development," in *The Suffering Servant: Isaiah 53 in Jewish and Christian Sources,* ed. Bernd Janowski and Peter Stuhlmacher (Grand Rapids: William B. Eerdmans, 2004), 284–292, for a full account of Origen's dialogue. Here is a key paragraph from Celsus's "arguments against Christianity in the figure of an imaginary Jew" (Markschies, "Jesus Christ as a Man Before God," 285, citing *Contra Celsum* 1:55, trans. Henry Chadwick): "At this the Jew said that these prophecies referred to the whole people as though of a single individual, since they were scattered in the dispersion and smitten, that as a result of the scattering of the Jews among the other nations many might become proselytes. In this way he explained the text: 'Thy form shall be inglorious among men' (Isaiah 52:14); and 'those to whom he was not proclaimed shall see him' (Isaiah 52:15); and 'Being a man in calamity' (Isaiah 53:3)." Walther Zimmerli and Joachim Jeremias, *The Servant of God: Studies in Biblical Studies, First Series, No. 20* (London: SCM Press, 1965), 53–55, attribute the rise of the identification of the Servant as a collective people rather than as an individual to grammatical deviations (plural vs. singular) in the Greek Septuagint translation of the Hebrew Bible. Consequently, they "assume that the informants of Origin were Hellenistic Jews."

among authoritative commentators until much later. Indeed, Walther Zimmerli and Joachim Jeremias go so far as to say that "there is not to be found a definitely non-messianic exegesis of Isaiah 53 in the rabbinic literature of the first millennium."[29] Victor Buksbazen explains the historical context for the change from an individual (typically messianic) identity to a corporate identity of the Servant in Isaiah 53 as follows:[30]

> Behind this change lies the tragic Jewish experience during the Crusades. During the First Crusade in AD 1096, when the Crusaders, in their misguided zeal, attempted to wrest the Holy Sepulchre from the Muslims, they became aware that the infidels were not only "the pagan Muslims" in faraway Palestine, but also "the Christ-killing Jews" who were living in their very midst, in so-called Christian Europe. Encouraged by their fanatical leader and frequently incited by high-ranking clerics, the Crusaders committed massacres of the Jews, especially of those who lived in France, Italy, and Germany. Thousands were butchered, their synagogues burned, and their possessions pillaged.
>
> This horrible experience, which lasted for almost two centuries, left a traumatic impact on the Jews comparable only to their later experience under Hitler. From that time on, their revulsion against everything that the Christians believed or represented became more violent and hostile than ever before.
>
> Since that time, the question of Isaiah 53 took on a heated polemical and emotional character. And since the Christians in their frequent disputes with the Jews used Isaiah 53 as one of their main arguments for the Messiahship of Jesus, the Jews felt impelled to reinterpret this prophecy in such a way as to blunt the Christian argument. Since that time, the question of Isaiah 53 took on a heated polemical and emotional character.
>
> ...[For example, during] that period the outstanding Jewish scholar Joseph Ben Kaspi (1280–1340) warned the rabbis that "those who expounded this section of the Messiah give occasion to the heretics [Christians] to interpret it of Jesus." About this statement Rabbi Saadia ibn Danan observed, "May God forgive him for not having spoken the truth."[31]

---

29. Zimmerli and Jeremias, *Servant of God*, 76.
30. Buksbazen, "Of Whom."
31. As cited in Samuel R. Driver and Adolf Neubauer, *The 'Suffering Servant' of Isaiah, According to Jewish Interpreters* (New York: Herman Press, 1969), 203.

In any case, since AD 1096, Jewish interpreters began to teach that Isaiah's suffering servant was not the Messiah but persecuted and suffering Israel, "who was led to the slaughter like a sheep and opened not his mouth" (Isaiah 53:7).

In the light of the Crusaders' atrocities, this interpretation took on a semblance of [truth] and found much favor among the majority of Jews, but not among all of them. Still the original Messianic interpretation of Isaiah 53 persisted and survived even to the present day. It is preserved in Jewish liturgy for the Day of Atonement in a prayer attributed to Eliezer Ha-Kallir (eighth century AD):[32]

> We are shrunk up in our misery even until now! Our rock hath not come to us; Messiah, our righteousness, hath turned from us; we are in terror, and there is none to justify us! Our iniquities and the yoke of our transgressions he will bear, for he was wounded for our transgressions: he will carry our sins upon his shoulder that we may find forgiveness for our iniquities, and by his stripes we are healed. O eternal One, the time is come to make a new creation, from the vault of heaven bring him up, out of Seir draw him forth that he may make his voice heard to us in Lebanon, a second time by the hand of Yinnon.

From the prayer it is obvious that the Jews of that era believed that the Messiah had already come and were praying that He may come "a second time." Some of the medieval scholars who interpreted this passage in an individual sense applied it either to Jeremiah or to Isaiah, others to Hezekiah, and some to any righteous person who suffers innocently.

Many of the ancient rabbis were aware of the seemingly divergent elements in the Messianic prophecies. One stream of thought spoke of the suffering Messiah.[33] The other described a triumphant Messiah who will subdue the rebellious nations and establish His kingdom.[34] To resolve this problem the rabbis have resorted to the theory of the two Messiahs, the suffering one, called Messiah ben Joseph, who died in battle against Edom (Rome). He is followed by the triumphant Messiah, Messiah ben David, who establishes His kingdom of righteousness after defeating the Gentile nations.[35]

---

32. As cited in Driver and Neubauer, *Suffering Servant*, 445.
33. Isaiah 50:5–7; Isaiah 53.
34. Psalms 2; Psalms 110.
35. Isadore Epstein, ed., *The Soncino Hebrew-English Talmud (Babylonian)*, 30

Another attempt to resolve the seeming contradiction of a suffering and triumphant Messiah is mentioned in *Pesikta Rabbati*.[36] According to this, the Messiah ben David suffers in every generation for the sins of each generation. Other rabbinical authorities sought to find a solution to this puzzle in various ingenious ways, which did not commend themselves to most Jewish people.

Some rabbinical authorities have postponed the solution of this and all other perplexing questions to the coming of the prophet Elijah, the forerunner of the Messiah, who will make all things clear.[37]

Not surprisingly, acrimonious debates with Christians seems to have been an important factor in leading an increasing number of Jewish scholars (starting as early as the third century) to disavow previous traditions that had supported the idea that selected mortals, notably including Jacob, Moses, Elijah, and Enoch,[38] had ascended to

---

vols. (London: Soncino Press, 1948), Sukkah 16:246; Joseph Klausner, *The Messianic Idea in Israel: From Its Beginning to the Completion of the Mishnah*, trans. W. F. Stinespring, 3rd Hebrew ed. (New York: Macmillan Publishing Company, 1955), 483–501.

36. *Pesikta Rabbati* 35–36.
37. *Baba Metzia* 6.
38. See Abraham Joshua Heschel, *Heavenly Torah as Refracted Through the Generations*, trans. Gordon Tucker (New York: Continuum International, 2007) at the following pages: Jacob, 343; Moses, 342–343; Elijah, 354; and Enoch, 349. Regarding **Jacob**, Heschel notes: "The patriarch Jacob sees in his dream 'a ladder set on the ground...' but only 'the angels of God were going up and down on it' (Genesis 28:12)." For Latter-day Saint perspectives on this event and the ladder of heavenly ascent, see Jeffrey M. Bradshaw, "Faith, Hope, and Charity: The 'Three Principal Rounds' of the Ladder of Heavenly Ascent," in *"To Seek the Law of the Lord": Essays in Honor of John W. Welch*, ed. Paul Y. Hoskisson and Daniel C. Peterson (Orem, UT: Interpreter Foundation, 2017), 59–112, esp. 62–77; Jeffrey M. Bradshaw, "Now That We Have the Words of Joseph Smith, How Shall We Begin to Understand Them? Illustrations of Selected Challenges Within the 21 May 1843 Discourse on 2 Peter 1," *Interpreter: A Journal of Mormon Scripture* 20 (2016): 47–150, esp. 61–70; Jeffrey M. Bradshaw, *Creation, Fall, and the Story of Adam and Eve*, In God's Image and Likeness, 3 vols. (Salt Lake City: Eborn Books, 2009; rep. 2014), 1:34, caption to Figures 1–2 and 1–3; 1:39, caption to Figure 1–8; 1:43–44, commentary 1:1c; 1:351, caption to Figure 5–13; 1:479, commentary 6:5a; Excursus 11, 1:548; Excursus 50, 1:654; and Jeffrey M. Bradshaw and David J. Larsen, *Enoch, Noah, and the Tower of Babel*, In God's Image and

heaven. Gordon Tucker and Leonard Levin explain that the intensified rabbinical opposition was:[39]

> with good reason, for a safe ascent to heaven, it would seem, could be successfully accomplished by someone who is, at least in part, of heaven. Thus it is that the idea of the ascent of a human to heaven brings close on its heels the idea of a descent to earth of a heavenly being. The latter, of course, is *the* central tenet of Christianity. This is not the first time we have seen parallels between Akivan ideas in the second century and roughly contemporaneous ideas characteristic of early Christians (and especially Jewish Christians). Nor is this the first (or the last) time we see controversy over Akivan views being raised and energized by that very parallelism.

Importance of appreciating the ongoing diversity of viewpoints in Jewish scholarship. Of course, the brief overview of identifications for the Servant of Isaiah 53 given above, with its overly sharp demarcations of Jewish historical interpretive trends, does not do justice to the spirit of the Jewish exegetical tradition. Unlike traditional ways of Western thinking with which most members of The Church of Jesus Christ of Latter-day Saints are most familiar and comfortable

---

Likeness, 3 vols. (Orem, UT: Interpreter Foundation; Salt Lake City: Eborn Books, 2014), 2:382–388; 2:395, caption to Figure G11–12. Regarding **Moses**, see Jeffrey M. Bradshaw, David J. Larsen, and Stephen T. Whitlock, "Moses 1 and the Apocalypse of Abraham: Twin Sons of Different Mothers?" in *Tracing Ancient Threads in the Book of Moses: Inspired Origins, Temple Contexts, and Literary Qualities*, 2 vols., ed. J. M. Bradshaw et al. (Orem, UT: Interpreter Foundation; Springville, UT: Book of Mormon Central; Redding, CA: FAIR; Tooele, UT: Eborn Books, 2021), 2:789–921; and Jeffrey M. Bradshaw, *Temple Themes in the Book of Moses* (Salt Lake City: Eborn Books, 2014), 23–50. Regarding **Elijah**, Doctrine and Covenants 110:13 speaks of "Elijah the prophet, who was taken to heaven without tasting death." Regarding **Enoch**, see Jeffrey M. Bradshaw, David J. Larsen, and Stephen T. Whitlock, "Moses 1 and the Apocalypse of Abraham: Twin Sons of Different Mothers?" *Interpreter: A Journal of Latter-day Saint Faith and Scholarship* 38 (2020): 179–290; Jeffrey M. Bradshaw, "Moses 6–7 and the Book of Giants: Remarkable Witnesses of Enoch's Ministry," in *Tracing Ancient Threads* (2021), 2:1041–1256; and Jeffrey M. Bradshaw, *Enoch and the Gathering of Zion: The Witness of Ancient Texts for Modern Scripture* (Orem, UT: Interpreter Foundation; Springville, UT: Book of Mormon Central; Salt Lake City: Eborn Books, 2021)..

39. See the translator's introduction to chapter 18 in Heschel, *Heavenly Torah*, 341–342.

— ways that usually hunger to find single, correct, unambiguous, and authoritative answers for complex doctrinal questions — generations of Jewish scholars are usually not "troubled by a multiplicity of rabbinic views on central theological questions; on the contrary, [they are] pleased to find differing viewpoints."[40] It would mischaracterize the rabbinic tradition to say merely that such differences, including details of debates on questions such as the interpretation of Isaiah, are carefully documented, when the more complete truth is that they are, in addition, lovingly cherished and preserved so that future generations can appreciate the wrestle as much as the results. Speaking of the ability of the great twentieth-century Jewish scholar and teacher Abraham Joshua Heschel to appreciate the richness made available through diverse rabbinic views, his daughter Susannah Heschel, herself a professor of Jewish Studies at Dartmouth College, wrote:[41]

> For him, the school of Akiva was mystical, apocalyptic, radical, uncompromising, enthusiastic, strong, militant, deep, paradoxical, and sweeping, whereas the school of Ishmael was critical, rationalistic, self-limited, clear, dry, measured, balanced, careful, and patient.
>
> A [Latter-day Saint] philosopher I came to know twenty years ago was very taken with Heschel's work. In a letter he sent me after he began integrating some of Heschel's theology into his teaching at Brigham Young University, he noted that "Heschel sings rather than argues" — intending that assessment not pejoratively but descriptively.

The confluences and divergences of Jewish and Christian beliefs about the Messiah have sometimes led to contentious misunderstandings. In this regard, Shirley Lucass provides a helpful perspective on why the ideas discussed in this paper may offer a path to continued, respectful dialogue:[42]

> If Jesus' first coming is accepted as the inauguration of the messianic era (based on the acceptance that his messiahship was authentically Jewish), and if at his Second Coming all of the expected conditions of the Age to Come were to prevail,

---

40. Heschel, *Heavenly Torah*, xix.
41. Heschel, *Heavenly Torah*, xix, xxv.
42. Shirley Lucass, *The Concept of the Messiah in the Scriptures of Judaism and Christianity*, Library of Second Temple Studies 78, ed. Lester L. Grabbe (London: T&T Clark, 2011; rep. London: Bloomsbury, 2013), 209.

then there is nothing in this proposition that would jeopardize the integrity of Judaism as it now stands. Effectively, therefore, this invalidates the statement of [Jacob Neusner: "Is Jesus the Christ? If so, then Judaism falls. If not, then Christianity fails."[43] We hope that our broader conception of the issue will allow] a move away from the assertion and denial that has plagued dialogue from the "parting of the ways" (ca. 70 CE), opening up fresh possibilities and a new foundation on which dialogue can be built.

Admittedly, however plausible this may be, it cannot wipe out 2,000 years of persecution, mistrust, and hatred. Even so, if [this] premise …. is accepted — namely, that the messiahship of Jesus as portrayed in the New Testament can be rooted in antecedent Jewish tradition — then I believe that this will provide a bridge to dialogue that has hitherto not existed.

2. What Is the Big Picture Being Painted in Isaiah 53?

Rhetorical structure. Zooming out to understand the context of chapter 53, we should understand that it is only one part of the four passages in Isaiah that are classed by scholars as "servant songs."[44] S. Kurt Neumiller has described the larger rhetorical structure that both surrounds and is found within Isaiah 53:[45]

> Using the theme from the preceding 49–52 block, which [in turn is] built upon the theme from chapters 40–48, Isaiah now summarizes and terminates the line of thought and symbolism of the intercessory servant with a block of four chapters which forcefully present the Lord as the epitome of Israel's savior and [describe] what He will do to redeem Israel. The four-chapter block is presented in an alternating A–B–C fashion based upon general subject:
>
> A — The condescending intercessory servant (Grace, Mercy) (53:1–12)
> B — Redeemed Israel, bride of the Lord (Natural Israel) (54:1–13)
> C — Fight against Zion and [failure] (Enemies outside) (54:14–17)

---

43. Jacob Neusner, *Jews and Christians: The Myth of a Common Tradition* (Binghampton, NY: Global Publications at SUNY Binghampton, 2001), 49.
44. See others in Isaiah 42:1–9; Isaiah 49:1–7; and Isaiah 50:4–9.
45. S. Kurt Neumiller, "Comments on Isaiah 53," *Latter-day Saint Seminar*, online at ldsgospeldoctrine.net.

A — The exalted saving Lord (Justice) (55:1–13)
    B — All righteous brought to His House (All nations) (56:1–8)
        C — Wicked among Israel consumed (Enemies within) (56:9–12)

The parallelism informs us of the unity of the Lord's experience and mission [as well as the planning that took place long before]. He is both the lowly suffering servant and the exalted powerful Lord. He saves both Israel and the Gentiles who worship Him, and he destroys His enemies both inside and outside of Zion.

The textual structure of this chapter can be structured as a chiasm starting with the last three verses from the preceding chapter. The structure is robust enough to be spotted and commented on by the author of the Westminster Bible commentary, which normally does not give much regard to rhetorical structures.

  A — (v. 52:13–15) Lord speaks of exalting His servant because of his actions
   B — (v. 1) Who can believe the arm of the Lord is revealed?
    C — (v. 2–3) Servant was not appealing to man and is rejected
     D — (v. 4–5) We thought he was cursed, he took upon himself our sins
      E — (v. 6a–b) We have gone astray like sheep do
       F — (v. 6c) And the Lord visited upon him,
       F — (v. 6d) the iniquity of us all
      E — (v. 7) Servant is meek and submissive as sheep are
     D — (v. 8) Servant is judged and killed, by the sins of His people
    C — (v. 9) Servant is counted among wicked though he was not wicked
   B — (v. 10–11b) Lord chose him that His purposes are achieved
  A — (v. 11c–12) Lord speaks of exalting His servant because of his actions

Parallels with Isaiah 14. Avraham Gileadi found specific parallels and contrasts between Isaiah's descriptions of the righteous servant in chapter 53 and the wicked servant in chapter 14, the former tracing a path from humiliation to exaltation and the latter following precisely the opposite course:[46]

Isaiah 14	Isaiah 53
13. The Tyrant ascends ('lh) the heavens.	1–2. The Servant grows up ('lh) out of the earth
14. The Tyrant aspires to be like the Most High.	3. The Servant submits to being the lowliest of men.
15. The Tyrant's ignominy is irrevocable.	4–5b. The Servant's ignominy is redemptive.
16–17b. The Tyrant causes havoc and destruction.	5cd. The Servant causes peace and healing.
17c. The Tyrant keeps men in bondage.	6. The Servant atones [frees men from the bondage of sin].
18. The kings of the nations are honorable in death.	7. The Servant goes like a lamb to the slaughter.
19. The Tyrant is slain for his own crimes.	8. The Servant is slain for the crimes of his people.
20ab. The Tyrant is unburied because he did violence.	9. The Servant buried because he did no violence.
20c–21. The Tyrant's offspring are wiped out.	10. The Servant's offspring continue.
22. All in Babylon are condemned.	11. The Servant vindicates many.
23. Babylon is an inheritance for noxious birds.	12. The Lord's great ones inherit with the Servant.

Overview of the four-part structure of Isaiah 52:13–53:12. Readers should keep the three structural aspects of the chapter presented previously in mind for further study. However, for the purposes of examining the meaning of the verses in more detail, the four-part breakdown of Kurt Neumiller will be useful background. As mentioned previously, Isaiah 52:13-15, which contains God's proclamation of the Servant's exaltation, is of a piece with the chapter that follows. Here are the four parts of Neumiller's description of the big picture:[47]

---

46. Avraham Gileadi, ed., *The Literary Message of Isaiah* (New York: Hebraeus Press, 1994), 164–170. For a scholarly assessment of Gileadi's extensive writings on Isaiah, see David R. Seely, "Avraham Gileadi, *The Literary Message of Isaiah*," FARMS Review of Books 8, no. 1 (1996): 69–79. Though Seely notes that Gileadi's discussions of a latter-day David have been controversial (see pp. 75–76), he has also found "much of value" in Gileadi's in-depth studies (p. 79)..
47. The four-part structure and the general description of each part has been

1. *The Servant's success and eventual exaltation, a summarizing preface to chapter 53 (52:13–15).* These verses assure the reader up front that God's intent "from the beginning"[48] is to end the suffering of the Servant with a glorious finish. From the Book of Mormon[49] we learn that these verses apply not only to Jesus Christ, but also to "the Lord's prophetic servants (i.e., types of Christ)," with "their vindication being concurrent with the Second Advent."[50] Specifically, Moses is both a type of the Messiah and also of Joseph Smith.[51] Some argued that the Book of Mormon is also personified as the Servant described in these verses by Jesus Christ in 3 Nephi 21.[52]
2. *The people's confessional, describing the events of Christ's mortal life and atonement (53:1–6).* "Here [Israel] is speaking in something of a confessional. They admit they [wrongfully judged] the Servant and [rebelled] against [God's] will."[53] Now sorrowful for having despised and rejected the Servant, they openly declare that His sufferings included not only their derision but also, more poignantly, His atoning sacrifice on their behalf.
3. *The Servant's suffering, describing Christ's trial and crucifixion (53:7–9).* The suffering that leads to the Servant's death is described in a poignant series of images: He was "oppressed" and "afflicted" and at last "brought as a lamb to the slaughter" and "cut off from the land of the living," in company with "the wicked." Notwithstanding all this, and in pointed contrast to the evil tyrant,[54] God assures the righteous Servant a burial

---

adapted from Neumiller, "Isaiah 53."
48. Isaiah 40:21; Isaiah 41:4, 26; Isaiah 46:10; Isaiah 48:3, 5, 7, 16.
49. 3 Nephi 20:43–45; 3 Nephi 21:10–11.
50. Neumiller, "Isaiah 53."
51. David Rolph Seely, "'A Prophet Like Moses': Deuteronomy 18:15–18 in the Book of Mormon, the Bible, and the Dead Sea Scrolls," in *"To Seek the Law of the Lord": Essays in Honor of John W. Welch*, ed. Paul Y. Hoskissen and Daniel C. Peterson (Orem, UT: Interpreter Foundation, 2017), 359–374.
52. Gaye Strathearn and Jacob Moody, "Christ's Interpretation of Isaiah 52's 'My Servant' in 3 Nephi," *Journal of the Book of Mormon and Other Restoration Scripture* 18, no. 1 (2009): 4–15.
53. Neumiller, "Isaiah 53."
54. Isaiah 14:18–22.

(v. 9) and the ultimate preservation of His spiritual offspring (v. 10).

4. *The Servant's reward, describing Christ's post-mortal glory (53:10–12).* Verses 10–12 present an answer to the question of why God would allow "an innocent Servant [to be] mercilessly and unjustly killed at the hands of oppressors. [We learn] that the Lord chose to [bruise] the Servant [as an offering for sin to] redeem His offspring, grant life, and ultimately prosper [the Servant, thus revealing] the arm of the Lord in the act of salvation."[55]

3. How Might We Understand Some of the Difficult-to Comprehend Verses?

Though the King James English used in our Bible translation is beautiful, it is sometimes unclear — both because of its archaic vocabulary and, at times, its shaky sense of obscure Hebrew terms. Below, I will draw on the work of various Isaiah scholars to get at the plain sense of some of these difficult words and phrases.

The Servant Shall Be Exalted (Isaiah 52:13–15)

13 ¶ Behold, my servant shall deal prudently,
he shall be *exalted* and *extolled*,
and *be very high*.

my servant shall deal prudently. Or, better, "my servant shall become wise."[56] Thus, "the Servant's wisdom is an aspect of his exaltation."[57]

he shall be exalted. In this verse, Isaiah describes both the suffering and the exaltation of Jesus Christ. In addition, however, in the Book of Mormon the resurrected Jesus Christ Himself applies Isaiah's description of a "suffering servant" to the Prophet Joseph Smith, and the Book of Moses applies similar language to Enoch.[58] Moreover,

---

55. Neumiller, "Isaiah 53."
56. Margaret Barker, entry for 52:13, "Isaiah," in *Eerdmans Commentary on the Bible*, ed. James D. G. Dunn and John W. Rogerson (Grand Rapids: William B. Eerdmans, 2003), 534.
57. Barker, "Isaiah," 534.
58. Regarding the application of this prophecy to Joseph Smith, see 3 Nephi 20:43; and Doctrine and Covenants 10:43. Compare 3 Nephi 21:10. Gaye Strathearn

Moses is both a type of the Messiah and also of Joseph Smith.[59] These

---

and Jacob Moody observe that 3 Nephi 21:10, using the language of Isaiah 52:13–15, appears to reference not only the prophet Joseph Smith but also the Book of Mormon; see Strathearn and Moody, "Christ's Interpretation," 7–8. Like Joseph of Egypt, who was unknown to his brethren until he revealed himself as their temporal savior (Genesis 45:5), Alma was the sole priest of Noah "to whom" (*'al-mî*) the Lord "revealed" his arm as Abinadi's prophetic successor (Mosiah 17:2; 14:1, quoting Isaiah 53:1). See Matthew L. Bowen, "Alma—Young Man, Hidden Prophet," *Interpreter: A Journal of Mormon Scripture* 19 (2016): 343–53; Matthew L. Bowen, "Young Man, Hidden Prophet: Alma," in *Name as Key-Word: Collected Essays on Onomastic Wordplay and the Temple in Mormon Scripture*, ed. Matthew L. Bowen (Orem, UT: Interpreter Foundation; Salt Lake City: Eborn Books, 2018), 91–100; and Aaron P. Schade and Matthew L. Bowen, "'To Whom is the Arm of the Lord Revealed?'," *Religious Educator* 16, no. 2 (2015): 91–111. There is a textual affinity between Isaiah's prophecy and Enoch traditions. Enoch's "faith" and "righteousness" (Moses 7:13, 19) resulted in him being "high and lifted up" (Moses 7:24), paralleling the Son of Man being "lifted up on the cross" (Moses 7:55; cf. Isaiah 52:13; John 3:14; 8:28). This "lifting up" may imply initiation into heavenly mysteries (Moses 7:59). In 1 Enoch 71:3, Michael initiates Enoch into "all the secrets of mercy," and later (71:14) Enoch is proclaimed "Son of Man." See George W. E. Nickelsburg and James VanderKam, *1 Enoch 2: A Commentary on the Book of 1 Enoch, Chapters 37–82*, Hermeneia: A Critical and Historical Commentary on the Bible (Minneapolis: Fortress Press, 2012), 320–321. While the "Son of Man" title may startle some, it fits Latter-day Saint theology regarding the ordinance of becoming a "son of God" administered by God's own voice (see JST Genesis 14:29). See also the overview for Moses 7 in Jeffrey M. Bradshaw and David J. Larsen, God's Image 2, 117; and Jeffrey M. Bradshaw, *Temple Themes in the Oath and Covenant of the Priesthood* (Salt Lake City: Eborn Books, 2014), 59–65.

59. Seely, "Prophet Like Moses," 359–374. Of course, though Moses's career as a prophet can be mapped to Isaiah 52–53 and undisputedly paralleled that of the Savior in many respects, even to the point of "atoning for the sins of his people (verbal stem *kpr*) and even offering his life to God (Exodus 32:30–34), [Moses] does not die, not at that point at any rate, and we are not told that his sufferings had a salvific effect on others." Joseph Blenkinsopp, *Isaiah 40–55: A New Translation with Introduction and Commentary*, Anchor Yale Bible Commentaries, 89–92 vols., ed. William Foxwell Albright and David Noel Freedman (New Haven: Yale University Press, 2002), 19A:119. It seems therefore that if Moses was a model for the servant of Isaiah 52–53, he served as a type rather than as the ultimate fulfillment of Isaiah's prophecy. Jesus was a prophet "like" Moses (Deuteronomy 18:15). See also John W. Welch, *The Sermon on the Mount in the Light of the Temple* (Farnham, GB: Ashgate, 2009),

examples make it evident that others in addition to Jesus Christ also can be "lifted up" — becoming *sons* of Man[60] and receiving "everlasting life" (John 3:16) — through unwavering faithfulness in "the trial of [their] faith" (Ether 12:6).[61]

14 As many were astonied [astonished[62]] at thee;
his visage [appearance[63]] was so marred <u>more than any man</u>,
and *his form* <u>more than the sons of men</u>:

many were astonished at thee. The people would gape in astonishment and disdain at the Servant,[64] just as the crowd had been filled "with wonder and amazement" — "and with anger" at Abinadi (Alma 13:8).

his visage was so marred. The King James Version, translated from the Hebrew Masoretic text, agrees with the wording of the Book of Mormon.[65] That said, agreement with the Book of Mormon should not be regarded as definitive evidence of correctness for Latter-day Saints, since Joseph Smith later revised the wording Old Testament passages from the Book of Mormon in later translations and sermons — including, for example, his later substitution of "gathering" for "sprinkling in JST Isaiah 52:15 (see discussion below).[66]

Intriguingly, the Dead Sea Great Isaiah Scroll has a variant reading of "I have anointed him."[67] Though there seems to be no disagree-

---

22; Sharon Haddock, "Sistine Chapel art illustrates parallels between Moses and Christ," *Deseret News* (September 3, 2011), online at deseret.com.
60. See the extensive discussion of the plurality of "sons of man" in the mystical sense of the term in *Gospel of Thomas,* Logion 106, in Samuel Zinner, *The Gospel of Thomas: Exploring the Semitic Alternatives, A Textual-Philological Commentary with an Emended and Reconstructed Version of the Thomas Gospel* (London: Matheson Trust, 2011), 305.
61. Compare with 1 Peter 1:7. Here, Moroni is speaking specifically of the sure witness that came when Christ personally "showed himself unto our fathers" (Ether 12:7).
62. Isaiah 52:14a in *The Holy Bible* (Salt Lake City: The Church of Jesus Christ of Latter-day Saints, 1979/2003), consistent with 3 Nephi 20:44.
63. Isaiah 52:14b in the Latter-day Saint edition of the Bible (1979/2003).
64. Compare Isaiah 53:3.
65. 3 Nephi 20:44; 3 Nephi 21:10.
66. For more on this topic, see Jeffrey M. Bradshaw, "Foreword," in Bowen, *Name as Key-Word,* xxii–xxiv; Bradshaw, *Now That We Have the Words,* 14–15.
67. Entry for 52:14 in Barker, "Isaiah," 534; Margaret Barker, *Temple Mysticism: An Introduction* (London: Society for Promoting Christian Knowledge, 2011),

ment that the transcription of this phrase in the scroll is correct,[68] most scholars reject this variant and instead translate it as if it were identical to the Masoretic text.[69] However, if the literal translation were to be accepted as a possibility, it would be consistent with the *Targum Jonathan's Isaiah*'s reference in 52:13 to "my servant, the Messiah"[70] (that is, the "anointed one") and to the description of his "brightness" as a "holy brightness" (that is, a brightness due to his divine anointing) in 53:3.[71] "The verse then [would describe] not a human being unrecognizable because he has been disfigured, but *one whose appearance has*

155–157. Barker's reading follows the Great Isaiah Scroll (1QIsaa), which reads *mishty* (משחתי = "I anointed," from the root מ-ש-ח or *m-sh-ch*) instead of *mishat* (משחת = "marred," "ruined," or "disfigured," from the root ש-ח-ת or *sh-ch-t*) in the Masoretic text. Compare with the description of David's anointing in Psalm 89:19–20. More pointedly, see the description of Enoch's anointing and clothing in the Book of Moses, *2 Enoch*, and *3 Enoch* (Bradshaw and Larsen, *God's Image 2*, 103–105).

68. See Moshe Henry Goshen-Gottstein, ed., *The Book of Isaiah*, The Hebrew University Bible 10, 3 vols. (Jerusalem: Magnes Press, 1995), 3:241n3, for a comparison of an authoritative transcription from the Aleppo Codex (a Masoretic text) and the Great Isaiah Scroll.

69. See, for example, Isaiah 52:14 in "English Translations of the Book of Isaiah (The Great Isaiah Scroll, trans. Peter W. Flint and Eugene Ulrich vs. the Masoretic version, New JPS Electronic Edition)," *The Digital Dead Sea Scrolls*, Israel Museum, online at dss.collections.imj.org.il; Isaiah 52:14 in Donald W. Parry, *The Book of Isaiah: A New Translation (Preliminary Edition)* (Springville, UT: Book of Mormon Central, 2022), 128n197. Martin Abegg Jr., et al., admit the possible reading of "my marring" in 1QIsaa in their notes but reject the variant in their English translation, instead favoring the Masoretic "marring." See Martin Abegg Jr., Peter Flint, and Eugene Ulrich, eds., *The Dead Sea Scrolls Bible: The Oldest Known Bible Translated for the First Time into English* (New York: HarperCollins Publishers, 1999), 359n1152. For a detailed rationale for a "marred" Messiah, see Loren Blake Spendlove, "There Is No Beauty That We Should Desire Him," *Interpreter: A Journal of Latter-day Saint Faith and Scholarship* 53 (2022): 1–30.

70. See the entry for Isaiah 52:13 in Bruce D. Chilton, trans., *The Isaiah Targum: Introduction, Translation, Apparatus and Notes*, The Aramaic Bible: The Targums, 19 vols., ed. Kevin Cathart, Michael Maher, and Martin McNamara (Wilmington, DE: Michael Glazier, Inc., 1987), 11:103; "Isaiah 52:13," *Targum Jonathan on Isaiah*, online at sefaria.org; Isaiah 52:14 in Barker, "Isaiah," 534; Barker, *Temple Mysticism*, 156.

71. "Isaiah 53:3," *Targum Jonathan on Isaiah*, online at sefaria.org; Chilton, *Isaiah Targum*, 103, Isaiah 53:3: "his brilliance will be a holy brilliance."

changed because he has been exalted and made wise, and the Lord has anointed him.[72] This fits the context of the previous verses, where the theme is exaltation, not ruination. Demonstrating that this interpretation is neither outlandish nor novel, Peter J. Gentry not only cogently argues for it on the basis of several considerations,[73] but also cites the work of Dominique Barthélemy. Barthélemy "discusses five Jewish interpreters from the 12th to 19th centuries who adopted 'anointing' as the best interpretation, and two Christian interpreters from the 16th to 17th centuries who held such a view."[74]

Going further in this line of thinking from a theological perspective, Pseudo-Clement's *Recognitions* 1:45:2 defines the Greek title "Christ" with reference to an anointing of oil administered by God Himself: "Although indeed He was the Son of God, and the beginning of all things, He became man; Him first God anointed with oil which was taken from the wood of the Tree of Life: from that anointing therefore He is called Christ."[75]

C. S. Lewis succinctly expressed the principle behind the practice of anointing all Christians: "Every Christian is to become a little 'christ.' The whole purpose of becoming a Christian is simply nothing else."[76]

15 So shall he sprinkle[77] [or "gather"[78]] many nations;

---

72. Isaiah 52:14 in Barker, "Isaiah," 534; Psalm 89:19–20.
73. Peter J. Gentry, "Part 1: The Servant Sprinkles Many as Anointed Priest," *Text & Canon Institute*, 30 March 2022, online at textandcanon.org.
74. Dominique Barthélemy, *Critique Textuelle de L'Ancien Testament: 2. Isaïe, Jérémie, Lamentations* (Fribourg, CH: Éditions Universitaires; Göttingen, DE: Vandenhoeck & Ruprecht, 1986), 387–395.
75. Pseudo-Clement, "Recognitions of Clement," in *The Ante-Nicene Fathers (The Writings of the Fathers Down to AD 325)*, 10 vols., ed. Alexander Roberts and James Donaldson (Buffalo: Christian Literature Company, 1886; rep. Peabody, MA: Hendrickson Publishers, 2004), 8:89. Compare with F. Stanley Jones, *An Ancient Jewish Christian Source on the History of Christianity: Pseudo-Clementive Recognitions 1.27–71*, Society of Biblical Literature Text and Translations 37/Christian Apocrypha Series 2, ed. Jean-Daniel Dubois and Dennis R. MacDonald (Atlanta: Scholars Press, 1995), 76–77.
76. C. S. Lewis, *Mere Christianity* (New York: Touchstone, 1996), 154.
77. Ezekiel 36:25; 1 Peter 1:2, as referenced in Isaiah 52:15a in the Latter-day Saint edition of the Bible (1979/2003).
78. Isaiah 52:15a in the Latter-day Saint edition of the Bible (1979/2003), citing JST Isaiah 52:15. See Scott H. Faulring, Kent P. Jackson, and Robert J. Matthews,

So shall he sprinkle many nations. Margaret Barker observes that many versions of the Bible have substituted another word for "sprinkle," because they did not understand the context of the passage, and so they have obscured the meaning from all their readers.[79] So what is the correct context for the puzzling phrase "sprinkle many nations"? Remember that "the atonement blood that was *sprinkled*[80] was the blood sprinkled, *nāzâ*, on the Day of Atonement to cleanse and consecrate,[81] and also the blood sprinkled by the Servant on many nations, so that they would be able to see and understand."[82] Gentry also concludes that the "priestly function" of the term is plausible in context and convincingly addresses grammatical objections to the use of "sprinkle" and argues against alternative reading of "startle," "astonish," or "astound."[83]

So shall he gather many nations. As an alternative to "sprinkle," the Joseph Smith translation of this verse changes the word to "gather."[84] The Prophet's translation is fitting in light of both *Targum Jonathan Isaiah* 52:12, "the God of Israel is about to gather your exiles,"[85] and John 12:32. "And I, if I be lifted up from the earth, will draw all men unto me." Bruce D. Chilton understands the *Targum* to mean that "the gathering of exiles (v. 12) is associated with a victorious 'Messiah' (vv. 13–15)."[86]

While there is no obvious etymological connection between "sprinkle" and "gather" that would suggest that a scribal error could

---

eds., *Joseph Smith's New Translation of the Bible: Original Manuscripts* (Provo, UT: Religious Studies Center, Brigham Young University, 2004), 827, as found in "Old Testament Manuscript 2," 110.
79. Margaret Barker, *King of the Jews: Temple Theology in John's Gospel* (London: Society for Promoting Christian Knowledge, 2014), 560n118.
80. Hebrews 10:22; Hebrews 12:24.
81. Leviticus 16:19.
82. Barker, *King of the Jews*, 560.
83. Gentry, "Part 1," online at textandcanon.org. See also Barthélemy, *Critique Textuelle*, 386–387.
84. Isaiah 52:15a in the Latter-day Saint edition of the Bible (1979/2003), citing JST Isaiah 52:15; Faulring, Jackson, and Matthews, *Original Manuscripts*, 827, as found in "OT 2," 110. See also Isaiah 52:15 in Parry, *Book of Isaiah*, 128.
85. Chilton, *Isaiah Targum*, 103, Isaiah 52:12. Compare with *Targum Jonathan on Isaiah*, Isaiah 52:12: "He that shall gather your captivity is the God of Israel."
86. Chilton, *Isaiah Targum*, 103n52:1–52:15.

have confused these terms, perhaps there is another kind of connection between them. Since the Messiah's victory is spiritual as much as temporal, the "gathering" to the kingdom of God accomplished by the "sprinkling" of atoning blood is as real and essential as the "literal gathering of Israel"[87] — suggesting that these two unrelated terms may in fact be "telling you different dimensions of one unified idea."[88]

> the kings shall shut their mouths at him:
> for *that which had not been told them* shall they see;
> and *that which they had not heard* shall they consider.

kings shall shut their mouth at him. Both appalled by the Servant's debasement, and astonished at His eventual vindication and exaltation, "kings shall purse their mouths closed,"[89] left speechless in wonderment.

that which had not been told them they shall see. The end of this verse introduces the theme of the unexpected humiliation of the Servant described in 53:1–3. With closed mouths and open eyes, the earthly elite will see a truth they had never learned. How could they have imagined that the "greatest" of all would come as a "servant" (Matthew 23:11); that he who would "ascend up on high" must needs first descend "below all things" (Doctrine and Covenants 88:6)?

The People's Confessional (Isaiah 53:1–6)[90]

> 1 *Who* hath <u>believed</u> our report?
> And *to whom* is the arm of the Lord <u>revealed</u>?

Who hath believed our report? The JPS Version gives an alternate reading: "Who can believe what we have heard?"[91] Like the kings and

---

87. Articles of Faith 1:10.
88. Rabbi Daniel Lapin and Susan Lapin, *Buried Treasure: Secrets for Living from the Lord's Language* (Mercer Island, WA: Lifecodex, 2012), 16.
89. Robert Alter, *The Hebrew Bible: A Translation with Commentary*, 3 vols. (New York: W. W. Norton, 2019), 2:801n. *kings shall seal their lips.*
90. For the commentary on Isaiah 53, I will rely heavily on the insightful work of S. Kurt Neumiller, in Neumiller, "Isaiah 53." I have taken the liberty to insert my own edits to his commentary in brackets and to add scripture references in endnotes. I also draw liberally on quotations from Donald W. Parry, Jay A. Parry, and Tina M. Peterson, eds., *Understanding Isaiah* (Salt Lake City: Deseret Book, 1998), among others.
91. Jewish Publication Society, *Tanakh: The Holy Scriptures* (Philadelphia: Jewish

nations referred to in 52:15, the surprising form in which the Lord's arm is revealed through Christ's ministry results in general astonishment and unbelief. "Behold, here is the agency of man, and here is the condemnation of man; because that which was from the beginning is plainly manifest unto them, and they receive not the light" (Doctrine and Covenants 93:31). "And the light shineth in darkness; and the darkness comprehended it not" (John 1:5).

the arm of the Lord. The faithful and observant among God's people will recognize the "arm of the Lord" revealed in the report of His servants. The "arm of the Lord" is "previously mentioned in 51:9 and 52:10 as the agent of salvation. See also John 12:37–38 [as a reference to this prophecy's fulfillment in] Jesus's mortal ministry, and 1 Nephi 22:10–11 and Doctrine and Covenants 45:47 [regarding its ultimate fulfillment in the Second Coming]."[92]

Margaret Barker notes that "'arm' and 'seed/son' are similar in Hebrew, therefore the phrase is better read as "to whom has the seed/son of the Lord been revealed" (cf. *Septuagint* Isaiah 48:14). This makes better sense of [Isaiah] 53:2, literally 'sucking child' (cf. *Septuagint*, 'little child'), not 'young plant.'"[93]

2 For he shall grow up before him as a *tender plant,*
and as a *root out of dry ground:*
he hath *no form nor comeliness;* and when we shall see him
there is *no beauty* that we should desire him.

he shall grow up before him. Throughout the chapter, we understand Isaiah "to be speaking of two divine beings: '*He* [the Son] shall grow up before *him* [the Father]' (verse 2); '*the Lord* [God the Father] laid on *him* [the Son] the iniquities of us all' (verse 6); 'it pleased *the Lord* to bruise *him*' (verse 10); '*he* hath put *him* to grief' (verse 10); '*he* shall see the travail of *his* soul, and shall be satisfied' (verse 11); '*I* will divide *him* a portion' (verse 12)."[94] Such an interpretation requires us to take the Hebrew term 'Jehovah' (usually translated as 'Lord' in the King James version) as referring to the Father. Though this is at odds with

---

Publican Society, 1985), 732.
92. Neumiller, "Isaiah 53."
93. Barker, "Isaiah," 534; Barker, *Temple Mysticism,* 157.
94. Welch, "Isaiah 53," 302–303.

the more standard use of 'Jehovah' to refer to the Son in Latter-day Saint sources, it is not without precedent:

> "Divine names and titles, especially in the Bible, are occasionally ambiguous. The distinction between the Father and the Son is sometimes unclear. For example, the Hebrew term *Elohim* — a title usually applied to the Father by Latter-day Saints — often refers to Jehovah in the Bible.[95] Furthermore, people prayed to Jehovah as if he were the Father. In some cases, ambiguity may be due to the transmission of the text; in others it may be explained by divine investiture wherein Christ is given the authority of the Father."[96]

as a root out of dry ground. "The image [is that] of a dry plant growing in a desert. Desert plants are [typically] scrubby [and] scraggly. [Figuratively speaking,] the servant grows up in a spiritual desert as he is among those who [generally] reject Him and His message.[97] Note that the plant grows despite the ground being dry, indicating a 'water' source other than the parched earth. The [plant] grows by the Lord's favor [rather than by earthly sustenance]." Luke writes, "The child grew, and waxed strong in spirit, filled with wisdom: and the grace of God was upon him."[98] [The references to the tender plant also make clear that], unlike any other intercessory servant described in scripture, the servant's mission spans "his entire lifetime from start to finish," from his initial growth as a seedling to his being prematurely 'cut off' (v. 8).[99] The deletion following the word 'root' is based on the text in Mosiah 14:2.

no beauty that we should desire him. "That the servant has no outward form or beauty ['that we should desire him' seems a contrastive allusion to] Absalom son of David who was popular among Israel because of his considerable physical beauty and charisma."[100] Joseph Fielding Smith writes that: "it is expressed here by the prophet that he had no form or

---

95. For example, Isaiah 12:2.
96. David R. Seely, "Jehovah, Jesus Christ," in *Encyclopedia of Mormonism*, 4 vols., ed. Daniel H. Ludlow (New York: Macmillan Publishing Company, 1992), 2:720–721. See also James R. Clark, ed., *Messages of the First Presidency*, 6 vols. (Salt Lake City: Bookcraft, 1965–1975), 5:32.
97. Compare with Amos 8:11–13.
98. Luke 2:40.
99. Neumiller, "Isaiah 53."
100. Neumiller, "Isaiah 53"; 2 Samuel 14:24–25; 2 Samuel 15:1–6.

comeliness, that is, he was not so distinctive, so different from others that people would recognize him as the son of God. He appeared as a mortal man."[101]

> 3 He is *despised*
> and *rejected* of men;
> a *man of sorrows,*
> and *acquainted with grief*:
> and *we hid as it were our faces* from <u>him;</u>
> <u>he</u> was *despised,* and *we esteemed him not.*

He is despised and rejected of men. Compare John 1:11: "He came unto his own, and his own received him not." See also Isaiah 49:7.

we hid as it were our faces from him. The concept is "the Semitic custom of not showing your face to (that is, turning away from) those whom you despise or reject."[102] "Not only did people refuse to follow him but they shunned him. The Servant will be viewed with the same disdain as the Jews viewed a leper."[103]

> 4 Surely he hath *borne* <u>our griefs,</u>
> and *carried* <u>our sorrows:</u>
> yet we did esteem him *stricken,*
> *smitten* of God,
> and *afflicted.*

Surely he has borne our griefs and carried our sorrows. Matthew 8:16–17 applies this reference to Jesus's healing of the sick; 1 Peter 2:24 applies it to His bearing of our sins.

yet we did esteem him stricken. "This statement [recalls] the story of Job where the innocent man is afflicted, and his friends consider him cursed by God. In that case, [as] in this one, the [people judge him unrighteously]. Peter describes the situation in its true light: 'For Christ also hath once suffered for sins, the *just* for the *unjust,* that he might bring us to God.'"[104]

> 5 But he was *wounded* <u>for our transgressions,</u>

---

101. Smith, *Doctrines of Salvation,* 1:23; Doctrine and Covenants 93:11–17.
102. Neumiller, "Isaiah 53."
103. Parry, Parry, and Peterson, *Understanding Isaiah,* 474.
104. Neumiller, "Isaiah 53"; 1 Peter 3:18.

He was *bruised* <u>for our iniquities:</u>
The <u>chastisement</u> of *our peace* was <u>upon him;</u>
And with <u>his stripes</u> *we are healed.*

he was wounded for our transgressions.

> "Verses 5–6 [are a clear] reference to the intercessory act of vicarious atonement. Here we have a righteous one, who delivers salvation to those who cannot save themselves — a type of all God's servants whose mission it is to carry His message and His love to all nations.[105] In the Old Testament, we see prophets such as] Moses who pled on Israel's behalf many times, [and Abraham who appealed for mercy on behalf of] the possible righteous in Sodom and Gomorrah. [At the same time, though they were afflicted by the wicked and suffered as a result of them], none of these preceding intercessors actually participated in a vicarious expiation of sins. [In this respect Christ's atonement was unique]."[106]

This verse is paraphrased in Romans 4:25 and 1 Peter 2:24.

with his stripes we are healed. "When Jesus was scourged by Pilate's men, the whip left stripes on his back."[107] Paradoxically, we are healed by wounds and our garments made white by red blood: "Blood ordinarily produces stains, even indelible stains. But acceptance of the blood of Christ symbolically and actually does just the opposite. Our garments may be made white in the blood of the Lamb. 'By the blood [of Christ] ye are sanctified.'"[108]

6 All *we* like sheep have <u>gone astray;</u>
we have <u>turned every one to his own way;</u>
and the Lord hath laid on him the iniquity of us all.

All we like sheep have gone astray.

> The image of scattering sheep, each going in his own way, shows how foolish the people were in rejecting the servant. [This depiction of the straying sheep is also meant to recall] the [wandering] that preceded the entrance [of the children of Israel]

---

105. Isaiah 43:22–28; Isaiah 46:3–4.
106. Neumiller, "Isaiah 53."
107. Parry, Parry, and Peterson, *Understanding Isaiah*, 475; Matthew 27:24–26.
108. Truman G. Madsen, "The Suffering Servant," in *The Redeemer: Reflections on the Life and Teachings of Jesus the Christ* (Salt Lake City: Deseret Book, 2000), p. 232. Compare with Moses 6:60; 1 Nephi 12:10; Alma 5:21; Ether 13:10.

into the promised land. This wandering about and failing to heed the [law of the] Lord was specifically [warned of] by Moses.[109] As Jesus was the incarnation of the Law,[110] the rejection of Jesus would be the ultimate rejection of the Law.[111]

the Lord hath laid upon him the iniquities of us all. "This passage harks back to the meaning of the ritual of the Day of Atonement (Leviticus 16), when the high priest laid his hand on the head of the victim and, in essence, transferred to him the sins of the people."[112] "[This phrase is the emotional center of the chapter] and leaves no doubt that the subject here is the vicarious expiation of sins. Especially note the singular 'him' and the very inclusive 'guilt of all of us.' Attempting to [arrive at an interpretation that takes 'him'] as referring to anyone besides Jesus Christ is most difficult [since] no other single intercessor has suffered for 'all of us.'" Compare this with Isaiah 43:24–25, where "it is stated that the Lord is forced into the position of servant because of Israel's sins and He must expiate them Himself in order to vindicate His name."[113]

Josefa de Ayala (circa 1630–1684): The Sacrificial Lamb, circa 1670–1684..

---

109. Deuteronomy 12:8; Ezekiel 34:6; Zecharaiah 13:7. New Testament parables also speak of sheep who have gone astray (for example, Matthew 10:6; Matthew 18:12). See also Doctrine and Covenants 1:16: "They seek not the Lord to establish his righteousness, but every man walketh in his own way, and after the image of his own god, whose image is in the likeness of the world, and whose substance is that of an idol, which waxeth old and shall perish in Babylon, even Babylon the great, which shall fall."
110. John 1:1–3; 3 Nephi 15:9.
111. Neumiller, "Isaiah 53."
112. Parry, Parry, and Peterson, *Understanding Isaiah*, 475.
113. Neumiller, "Isaiah 53."

> 7 He was <u>oppressed</u>,
> and *he was* <u>afflicted</u>,
> yet *he openeth not his mouth:* he is brought as a <u>lamb to the slaughter</u>,
> and as a <u>sheep before her shearers</u> is dumb, so *he [opened] not his mouth.*

He was oppressed and he was afflicted. "Jesus was oppressed and afflicted throughout his ministry [b]ut this passage seems to refer particularly to the legal trials he suffered immediately before his crucifixion."[114] "[T]he Hebrew *nagas* employed here implies the use of physical violence."[115]

yet he opened not his mouth. "[M]ore than [just a prophecy of the Lord's refusal to speak to Herod,[116] the phrase] indicate[s] the meek and submissive nature of the servant [to] the task [he is to perform]. The servant [does not return] railing for railing [to] his oppressors, nor does he [submit to the temptation to 'curse God and die']."[117]

he is brought as a lamb to the slaughter, and as a sheep before her shearers. "The sheep [theme] is altered [from verse 6]. Rather than a group of shepherdless wandering sheep, we have here a single docile sheep that submits [silently to its shearing and slaughter as a literal 'offering for sin.'"[118]

> 8 He was taken from prison and from judgment: and who shall declare his generation?
> for *he* was <u>cut off out of the land of the living</u>:
> for the transgression of my people was *he* <u>stricken</u>.

He was taken from prison and from judgment. A plainer translation would be "[h]e was taken by force (Hebrew *'utser*) and without justice (Hebrew *mish'pat*)."[119]

---

114. Parry, Parry, and Peterson, *Understanding Isaiah*, 475; Matthew 26:67–68; Matthew 27:29–30.
115. Neumiller, "Isaiah 53"; Isaiah 58:3; Exodus 3:7.
116. Luke 23:9.
117. Neumiller, "Isaiah 53"; Job 2:9.
118. Neumiller, "Isaiah 53," commentary on v. 10; compare with Jeremiah 11:19; Psalms 38:14.
119. Parry, Parry, and Peterson, *Understanding Isaiah*, 476.

who shall declare his generation? "The New International Version renders this phrase as 'who can speak of his descendants?' implying that because he was 'cut off from the land of the living' he had none. But Jesus did indeed have descendants, those who become his children through righteousness."[120]

he was cut off from the land of the living. Compare Lamentations 3:54.

for the transgressions of my people he was stricken. A version of Isaiah found in the Dead Sea Scrolls (1QIsa) renders the term "my people" as "his people." Such a rendering would favor "the servant as being the condescending Lord as it would say the servant was [stricken] for his own people. Note the irony [in the fact that the] servant was killed as a result of the people's sinning, and he was [also] killed for the people's sins."[121] The idea that the Servant was not merely "stricken," but rather "stricken *to death*," is evident not only from the parallel to the slaughtered lamb in verse 7, but also is attested in the *Septuagint* — arguably the best extant textual witness for the meaning of this verse, according to John D. Meade.[122]

> 9 And he made his *grave* with the wicked,
> and with the rich in his *death;*
> because *he had* done no violence [evil],
> neither was any deceit *in his mouth.*

And he made his grave with the wicked, and with the rich in his death. In 1 Corinthians 15:3–4, Paul avers that Jesus Christ died and was buried "according to the scriptures." No doubt Isaiah 53:9 was one of the scriptures he had in mind. However, the KJV wording of the verse is the reverse of what is expected: "his grave with the wicked, and with the rich in his death." According to the New Testament, he was crucified ("in his death") between two thieves ("the wicked") and buried ("his grave") in Joseph of Arimathea's tomb ("with the rich") — not vice versa.

---

120. Parry, Parry, and Peterson, *Understanding Isaiah*, 476; Mosiah 15:10–13; and v. 10 of the present commentary.
121. Neumiller, "Isaiah 53."
122. John D. Meade, "Part 2: Does Isaiah's Servant Really Die for the People?," *Text & Canon Institute*, 5 April 2022, online at textandcanon.org.

Highlighting the antithetical relationship between the passages describing the wicked tyrant and those describing the righteous servant,[123] Avraham Gileadi writes:

> Isaiah 14:20 represents the Tyrant as unburied because of his wickedness — a covenant curse. Isaiah 53:9, however, represents the Servant as buried, implying his innocence of wickedness; the statement, "he had done no violence," confirms this. Further, 53:9, as it stands, contains an anomaly: biblical tradition generally associates violence (*hamas*) with wickedness[124] and deceit (*mirma*) with wealth,[125] not vice versa. Isaiah 53:9 should thus read, "He was appointed among the wicked in death; among the rich was his burial"[126]

Another solution to this problem is suggested by conjectural emendation of the Hebrew *'ose ra'* (meaning 'rich') to *'asir'* (meaning 'evildoers'), which would heighten the parallelism in the two pairs of terms (grave-wicked, evildoers-death).[127] Finally, Gentry argues for similar phrasing consistent with scripture, based on arguments for the priority of 1QIsa[a]: "And they assigned his burial with wicked men and with a rich man *his tomb*" (ויתנו את רשעים קברו ועם עשירים בומתו).[128]

Some translations also render the Hebrew term *'bamah'* as 'high place' rather than 'grave,' which gives the image of Christ being 'lifted up among the wicked' (that is, crucified between thieves). This would be an explanation for where Abinadi got the term 'crucified' in what appears to be an interpretation of Isaiah in Mosiah 15:7.[129]

because he had done no evil. Mosiah 14:9 changes the term "violence" to "evil," consistent in general meaning with the Jewish Publication Society (JPS) translation that renders this term as "injustice."

10 Yet it pleased *the Lord* to <u>bruise him;</u>
he hath <u>put him to grief:</u>

---

123. Isaiah 14:20–21. See also Barker, *Temple Mysticism,* 157 regarding the cherub in Ezekiel 28.
124. Genesis 6:11–13.
125. Psalms 52:2–7.
126. Gileadi, *Literary Message,* 167.
127. Neumiller, "Isaiah 53."
128. Peter J. Gentry, "Part 3: The Servant's Burial according to the Scriptures," *Text & Canon Institute,* 6 April 2022, online at textandcanon.org.
129. Neumiller, "Isaiah 53."

when thou shalt make his soul an offering for sin, *he* shall <u>see his seed,</u>
he shall <u>prolong his days,</u>
and the pleasure of the Lord shall <u>prosper</u> in *his hand.*

Yet it pleased the Lord to bruise him. The term 'pleased' can be interpreted simply to signify that the servant's suffering was consistent with the Lord's will. The JPS translation is: 'But the Lord chose to crush him' and the AB reads: 'Yahweh decided to crush him.' "Certainly the Father took no pleasure in the suffering of his Son. But the Father was pleased that his Son would obediently offer such a sacrifice, meaning the sacrifice was according to the Father's wishes and his will. The Father was pleased further because of the love manifest by his Son and also because of the blessings that would come to the rest of his children."[130]

he hath put him to grief. 1Qisa offers the reading 'he pierced [him].'[131]

when thou shalt make his soul an offering for sin. "The AB states: 'The guilt offering (see Leviticus 4) is a type of sacrifice intended to atone for involuntary ritual offenses. The use of the term here has no particular reference to the rite of the guilt offering; the servant is compared to the victim of an atonement sacrifice.'"[132]

he shall see his seed. Rather than being bereft of descendants (verse 8) the servant will enjoy a spiritual posterity without number.

> Abinadi interpreted this expression in Mosiah 15:10–13, saying that the seed of Christ are the righteous who have heard the good word of salvation and believed and obeyed: 'These are his seed, or they are the heirs of the kingdom of God. For these are they whose sins he has borne; these are they for whom he has died, to redeem them from their transgressions.' Elsewhere we learn that the seed of Christ are those who are 'spiritually begotten' as his sons and daughters (Mosiah 5:7), born of water and the Spirit (Moses 6:64–68). Beginning with this expression, we move from Isaiah's prophecy of the Lord's suffering to his prophecy of the Lord's triumph.[133]

---

130. Parry, Parry, and Peterson, *Understanding Isaiah*, 476.
131. Neumiller, "Isaiah 53"; Psalm 22:16.
132. Neumiller, "Isaiah 53."
133. Parry, Parry, and Peterson, *Understanding Isaiah*, 477.

he shall prolong his days. In a second unexpected reversal of fortune, the servant who was prematurely 'cut off out of the land of the living' will actually have His life lengthened as He exercises His power to break the bands of death. The blessings of immortality through the resurrection and "eternal lives" through sealings to posterity which are here promised to the righteous servant are also extended to all the faithful who follow Him (Doctrine and Covenants 132:24).

11 *He* shall see of the travail of his soul, and shall be <u>satisfied:</u> by his knowledge shall *my righteous servant* <u>justify many;</u> for he shall bear their iniquities.

He shall see the travail of his soul and shall be satisfied. The Prophet Joseph Smith promised, "All your losses will be made up to you in the resurrection provided you continue faithful [to Christ]. By the vision of the Almighty I have seen it."[134] For the servant, as well as for all the righteous, the day will come when the sufferings of life and the pain of death "shall be sweet unto them," whereas for the unrepentant not only death but also the memory of life's pleasures will be tainted with deep sorrow and bitterness (Doctrine and Covenants 42:46–47; Luke 16:25). Wrote C. S. Lewis:

> [Both] good and evil, when they are full grown, become retrospective. Not only this [Heavenly] valley but all this earthly past will have been Heaven to those who are saved. Not only the twilight in that [spirit prison], but all their life on earth too, will then be seen by the damned to have been Hell. That is what mortals misunderstand. They say of some temporal suffering, "No future bliss can make up for it," not knowing that Heaven, once attained, will work backwards and turn even that agony into a glory. And of some sinful pleasure they say "Let me but have *this* and I'll take the consequences": little dreaming how damnation will spread back and back into their past and contaminate the pleasure of the sin. Both processes begin even before death. The good man's past begins to change so that his forgiven sins and remembered sorrows take on the quality of Heaven: the bad man's past already conforms to his badness and is filled only with dreariness. And that is why, at the end of all things, when the sun rises here [in the place of God's glory] and the twilight turns to blackness

---

134. Joseph Smith Jr., *Scriptural Teachings of the Prophet Joseph Smith*, comp. Joseph Fielding Smith (Salt Lake City: Deseret Book, 1969), 296.

down there [where Satan reigns], the Blessed will say, "We have never lived anywhere except in Heaven," and the Lost, "We were always in Hell." And both will speak truly.[135]

He shall see the travail of his soul. According to Anthony Ferguson, the best textual witnesses to this phrase add the term "light" to the phrase — for example, "From the anguish of his soul, *he shall see light* and he shall be satisfied."[136] In light of the Servant's death, this small addition is significant. This is because the Hebrew phrase "see light" (יראה אור) "is an idiom for describing life [or the revival of life] while the phrase "not seeing light" is an idiom of death."[137]

by his knowledge shall my righteous servant justify many. The literal rendering of the Hebrew term 'knowledge' is problematic; some emend it to read 'suffering,' 'experience,' 'humiliation,' or 'affliction.'[138] This alteration, combined with a more literal translation of the rest of the phrase would suggest the reading: 'by his suffering my righteous servant makes the many righteous.'

for he shall bear their iniquities. See Isaiah 43:22–25.

> 12 Therefore will I *divide* him a <u>portion with the great,</u>
> and he shall *divide* the <u>spoil with the strong;</u>
> because he hath poured out his soul unto death:
> and he was *numbered* with <u>the transgressors;</u>
> and he *bare* the <u>sin of many,</u>
> and *made intercession* for <u>the transgressors.</u>

bare the sin of many. John Meade argues for the priority of the plural "sins" in 1QIsa^a, 1QIsa^b, 4QIsa^d, LXX, Symmachus, Peshitta, and the Targum over the singular "sin" in the Masoretic text and Vulgate — a difference of a single *yod*.[139]

---

135. C. S. Lewis, *The Great Divorce* (New York: Macmillan Publishing Company, 1946), 68.
136. Anthony Ferguson, "Part 5: The Servant Who Sees Light after Anguish," *Text & Canon Institute,* 16 April 2022, online at textandcanon.org.
137. Ferguson, "Part 5," online at textandcanon.org. See, for example, Job 33:28, 30; Psalm 36:9 vs. Proverbs 13:14, Proverbs 14:27; Job 3:16; Psalm 49:19.
138. Parry, Parry, and Peterson, *Understanding Isaiah,* 477.
139. John D. Meade, "Part 4: Who Does the Servant Intercede For?," *Text & Canon Institute,* 13 April 2022, online at textandcanon.org.

and made intercession for the transgressors. Meade also argues for the strength of the Dead Sea Scrolls witnesses for transgressions/rebellions over transgressors/rebels.[140] Since the phrase "made intercession" can have a negative sense (for example, torture, attack),[141] the Scrolls' witness that the Savior is standing against sin rather than standing against sinners is important.

> [In this context the Hebrew verb denoting the process of intercession] means "to intervene," as in Isaiah 59:16. [Thus this phrase] does not mean, as some editors imagine, that he made prayers of intercession for [the transgressors], but that with his life, his suffering, and his death, he took their place and underwent their punishment in their stead.[142]

Conclusion

This concludes our brief discussion of this incomparable chapter. For Latter-day Saints, reflecting on the redeeming sacrifice of Jesus Christ brings life changing renewal each week when we take the sacrament. Including Isaiah 53 as part of that reflection can enrich our understanding of His love and example. Indeed, my wife Kathleen silently repeats portions of Isaiah 53 in her mind each Sunday (along with other verses and portions of the ordinances) as part of her sacrament devotional.

George Herbert (3 April 1593–1 March 1633),[143] a Welsh poet, orator and priest, has beautifully captured the unstinting invitation of the Lord that repeatedly calls us back to the sacrament table to feel his forgiveness and taste his goodness. The central character in the verse below is "Love," a personified virtue who, of course, represents the Savior. It has been set to moving music by Ralph Vaughan Williams. Christopher Palmer comments on the song as follows:[144]

---

140. Meade, "Part 4," online at textandcanon.org.
141. Meade, "Part 4," online at textandcanon.org.
142. Neumiller, "Isaiah 53."
143. Many of Herbert's poems were included in a posthumously published volume, George Herbert, *The Temple: Sacred Poems and Private Ejaculations*, 2nd ed. (London: Pickering, 1838).
144. Christopher Palmer, *Vaughan Williams: Serenade to Music, Flos Campi, Five Mystical Songs, Fantasia on Christmas Carols*, CD liner, CDA86420, Hyperion, 1990.

Both what Herbert said and the way he said it appealed to the Christian agnostic (or "disappointed theist") in Vaughan Williams, "Love bade me welcome" looks both more inward and far further forward than the other songs. The rapt stillness at its center — the Act, at which point, in the traditionally Edenic key of E, wordless voices intone the *O sacrum convivium* [— used within a liturgy on the Sacrament of the Lord's Supper[145] —] is one of the great moments in Vaughan Williams.

Here is the poem, which invites us to think about the invitation to accept the Atonement of Jesus Christ generally, and specifically when we are given the privilege of taking the sacrament:[146]

> Love bade me welcome: yet my soul drew back,
>   Guilty of dust and sin.
> But quick-eyed Love, observing me grow slack
>   From my first entrance in,
> Drew nearer to me, sweetly questioning,
>   If I lack'd anything.
>
> A guest, I answer'd, worthy to be here:
>   Love said, you shall be he.
> I the unkind, ungrateful? Ah my dear,
>   I cannot look on thee.
> Love took my hand, and smilingly did reply,
>   Who made the eyes but I?
>
> Truth Lord, but I have marr'd them: let my shame
>   Go where it doth deserve.
> And know you not, says Love, who bore the blame?
>   My dear, then I will serve.
> You must sit down, says Love, and taste my meat:
>   So I did sit and eat.

---

145. *O sacrum convivium* is a liturgical reflection on the Sacrament of the Lord's Supper: "O sacred banquet! / in which Christ is received, / the memory of his Passion is renewed, / the mind is filled with grace, / and a pledge of future glory to us is given. / Alleluia." As the words make it clear, however, the sacrament is only a foretaste of the celestial feast. Thus, in the musical setting for Herbert's dialogue with Deity, one might further imagine the culminating encounter of Divine acceptance, the wordless refrain in the crucial instant at once expressing both the ineffable joy of the penitent soul and the magnitude of the love freely offered through the sufferings of our Lord.

146. Herbert, "162. Love," in *The Temple*, 200.

A version of this paper with expanded footnotes and a full bibliography, removed here for length, is available at https://tinyurl. com/Bradshaw-isaiah-53. This essay has been adapted from a blog post by Jeffrey M. Bradshaw, "Why Is Isaiah 53 the Crown Jewel of the Old Testament? (Two-Part Reflection on the Come, Follow Me Study Selection for Isaiah 50–57," Interpreter Foundation blog, 26 and 29 September 2022, online at interpreterfoundation.org, with some material drawn from S. Kent Brown and Jeffrey M. Bradshaw, "Man and Son of Man: Probing Theology and Christology in the Book of Moses and in Jewish and Christian Tradition," in Tracing Ancient Threads in the Book of Moses: Inspired Origins, Temple Contexts, and Literary Qualities, *2 vols., ed. Jeffrey M. Bradshaw, David R. Seely, John W. Welch, and Scott Gordon (Orem, UT: Interpreter Foundation; Springville, UT: Book of Mormon Central; Redding, CA: Foundation for Apologetic Information and Research; Tooele, UT: Eborn Books, 2021), 2:1257–1332.*

16

THE HISTORICAL JONAH

JOHN GEE

Most modern scholarship dismisses the book of Jonah as a late-date fable, but a strong case exists for its historicity. The book's core claim — the mass repentance of Nineveh — offers a unique explanation for a documented, yet unexplained, "imperial hiatus" in eighth-century BC Assyria. Precisely during Jonah's lifetime, the notoriously cruel Assyrian empire entered a sudden decline, halting expansion and reversing its aggressive policies. This historical anomaly aligns directly with the book's narrative. Furthermore, common arguments for a late date, such as supposed linguistic errors or the naming of Nineveh as capital, are unconvincing. Linguistic evidence suggests the text's unique words are archaic or markers of Jonah's northern Hebrew dialect, not a later era. Archaeological evidence also confirms Nineveh was indeed the Assyrian capital at that exact time, making the book surprisingly consistent with the historical record.

The main point of the book of Jonah is that Jonah preached to Nineveh and "they turned from their evil way" (Jonah 3:10). Under these circumstances, Jonah has to be viewed as one of the most — if not the most — spectacular success stories of the Old Testament. If this is not the principal way that most people view Jonah, it might be because of how Jesus cited him:

> For as Jonas was three days and three nights in the whale's belly; so shall the Son of man be three days and three nights in the heart of the earth. The men of Nineveh shall rise in judgment with this generation, and shall condemn it: because they repented at the preaching of Jonas; and, behold, a greater than Jonas is here (Matthew 12:40–41; compare with Luke 11:30–32).

In modern times, the focus has generally been on the fish (*dāg*, Jonah 2:1) or whale (*kētous*, Matthew 12:40) swallowing Jonah. Both ancient Judah and ancient Israel were land-locked countries, and it is not clear that they would have made a distinction between a fish and a whale.

Jonah was a northern Israelite prophet who lived in the time of Jeroboam II (circa 791–750 BC).[1] If he was a real historical person, then "Jonah was the earliest, in point of time, of all the prophets whose labours and predictions have been recorded in separate books."[2] "Since the first appearance of the story of Jonah, its truth has been called into question."[3] The book of Jonah has "been called a fable, legend, and fictional tale."[4] Others think of him as a parable against the United States of America,[5] or "the modern church" which "is in retreat."[6] For most authors, the default assumption is that Jonah is ancient fiction. They often place the book of Jonah within the Hellenistic period. The situation, however, is more complicated than that. We will argue here that a solid case can be made for Jonah being historical and that the major event narrated in the book of Jonah actually took place.

The Historical Situation

The book of 2 Kings assigns Jonah to the reign of Jeroboam II (circa 791–750 BC):[7]

> Jeroboam, son of Joash, reigned in Samaria forty-one years and he did evil in the eyes of Jehovah. He did not turn away from the sins of Jeroboam, son of Nebat, which he sinned with Israel. He restored the borders of Israel from the entrance to Hamath to the sea of the plain according to the word of the

---

1. Kenneth A. Kitchen, *On the Reliability of the Old Testament* (Grand Rapids, MI: William B. Eerdmans, 2003), 31.
2. Patrick Fairbairn, *Jonah: His Life, Character, and Mission* (Grand Rapids, MI: Baker Book House, 1980), 3.
3. Edgar James Banks, *Jonah in Fact and Fancy* (Reading, PA: Frank J. Boyer, 1899), 37.
4. Vanessa Lovelace, "Jonah," in *The Oxford Handbook of the Minor Prophets*, ed. Julia M. O'Brien (Oxford: Oxford University Press, 2021), 457.
5. Miguel A. de la Torre, *Liberating Jonah* (Maryknoll, NY: Orbis Books, 2007), 25–58.
6. R. T. Kendall, *Jonah: An Exposition* (Grand Rapids, MI: Zondervan, 1978), 11.
7. Kenneth A. Kitchen, *On the Reliability of the Old Testament* (Grand Rapids, Michigan: William B. Eerdmans, 2003), 31.

Lord God of Israel which he spoke by the hand of Jonah, son of Amittai, the prophet from Gath-Hepher (2 Kings 14:23–25).

Four Assyrian kings' reigns overlap with the reign of Jeroboam II:

- Adad-nirari III (810–783 BC)
- Shalmaneser IV (782–773 BC)
- Assur-dan III (772–755 BC)
- Assur-narari V (754–745 BC)

Originally, Assyria was a city state with only a couple of tributaries to the north. It lies under the 300 millimeters isohyet (that is, it receives, on average, less than 300 millimeters of rain a year)[8] and so, like Israel and Judah, the rainfall is not sufficient for consistent crops. Its tributary cities, however, were in the zone where there was enough rain, so they could load their crops on barges and send them down the Tigris, and then drag the unloaded barges back up the river. Assyria first rose to prominence in the early second millennium through trade. Textiles and metals were sent between depots of Assyria and Kanesh and then to associated settlements. Assyria annexed various territories to increase the amount of food available. Later, they attempted to control the trade routes by seizing various points along the routes and levying tolls.[9]

On the surface, it appears as though Adad-nirari III continued the expansion of the Assyrian empire by planting boundary stones on the Orontes river near Antakya at the border of the ancient kingdom of Hamath,[10] and between the borders of Kummuh and Gurgum.[11] He even put Jeroboam's predecessor, Joash II (806–791 BC), under trib-

---

8. Bleda S. Düring, *The Imperialisation of Assyria* (Cambridge: Cambridge University Press, 2020), 27–29.
9. Susan Frankenstein, "The Phoenicians in the Far West: A Function of Neo-Assyrian Imperialism," in *Power and Propaganda*, ed. Mogens Trolle Larsen (Copenhagen: Akademisk Forlag, 1979), 269–273.
10. Adad-narari III A.0.104.2, in A. Kirk Grayson, *Assyrian Rulers of the Early First Millennium BC II*, The Royal Inscriptions of Mesopotamia: Assyrian Periods, 3 vols., ed. A. Kirk Grayson, Ronald F. G. Sweet, and Dietz O. Edzard (Toronto: University of Toronto Press, 1996), 3:203–204.
11. Adad-narari III A.0.104.3, in Grayson, *Assyrian Rulers of the Early First Millennium BC II*, 3:205.

ute,[12] and Shalmaneser IV went as far as Damascus to extract tribute.[13] When we look more closely, however, we see some nuance is required.

Adad-nirari III said that his grandfather was "the king of the four quarters, who slew all his enemies, and flattened them like a flood."[14] In doing so, the Assyrians gained a justifiable reputation for cruelty that surely lies behind Jonah's initial reluctance to go there (Jonah 1:3). Ashurnasirpal II (883–859 BC) brags about burning the prisoners of war of his battles.[15] These sorts of exploits, however, are not ones that Adad-nirari III claims for himself. Thus, "in his titles and epithets we find recognition of a gap between the royal duty to expand the empire and Adad-nīrārī's achievements as a military leader."[16]

Adad-nirari's reign can be divided into three periods. The first period "focused on re-establishing Assyrian control of the west." It lasted from 810 to 803 BC. "A total of four out of the first seven years were spent campaigning in the west ... to crush a rebellion that arose during his father's reign."[17] The second period lasted from about 804 to 796 BC. At that time Adad-nirari installed governors in regions liable to revolt.[18] The third period talks about the submission of foreign states without military action.[19]

Adad-nirari says, in his Tell al-Rimah stele:

> I levied chariots, troops, and soldiers and commanded that they go to the land of Hatti. In one year I placed the whole land of Amurru and Hatti in my hands. I placed tax and tribute upon them until the last day. ... He received the tribute

---

12. Adad-narari III A.0.104.7 7–8, in Grayson, *Assyrian Rulers of the Early First Millennium BC II*, 3:211; Adad-narari III A.0.104.8 12, in Grayson, *Assyrian Rulers of the Early First Millennium BC II*, 3:213.
13. Shalmanesar IV A.0.105.1, in Grayson, *Assyrian Rulers of the Early First Millennium BC II*, 3:240.
14. Adad-narari III 1, in Grayson, *Assyrian Rulers of the Early First Millennium BC II*, 3:202.
15. Ashurnasirpal II 1, A. Kirk Grayson, *Assyrian Rulers of the Early First Millennium BC I (1114–859 BC)*, The Royal Inscriptions of Mesopotamia: Assyrian Periods, 3 vols., ed. A. Kirk Grayson, Ronald F. G. Sweet, and Dietz O. Edzard (Toronto: University of Toronto Press, 1991), 2:201.
16. Luis Robert Siddall, *The Reign of Adad-nirari III* (Leiden, NL: E. J. Brill, 2013), 177.
17. Siddall, *The Reign of Adad-nirari III*, 57.
18. Siddall, *The Reign of Adad-nirari III*, 58.
19. Siddall, *The Reign of Adad-nirari III*, 58–59.

of Joash of the Samaritan land and of the land of Tyre and the land of Sidon.[20]

At the end of the campaign, he says that there were "In total 331 small cities which Nergal-eriš started to rebuild at the command of his lord."[21] It has been suggested that captives that Adad-nirari deported from his campaigns were responsible for the rebuilding,[22] but this is an inference that is not present in the text. It has also been suggested that Adad-nerari settled captives in the capital as well,[23] but on closer inspection, evidence for this is missing. Granted, "most of the instances of mass deportation are from the reign of Tiglathpileser III up to that of Ashurbanipal."[24] The Tell Rimah stele dates to the second period of Adad-nerari's reign.[25] This action dates before the reign of Jeroboam II (circa 791–750 BC),[26] and thus before the time of Jonah. The eponym chronicle indicates that there were no more campaigns principally against the west after 796 BC.[27]

On the other hand, we do have a series of decrees from Adad-nirari III granting land, people, and tax-exempt status to a group of individuals and institutions.[28] Only three of these decrees have their dates preserved: 792 BC, 788 BC, and 786 BC.[29] All of these date to the third

---

20. Adad-narari III 7 4–8, in Grayson, *Assyrian Rulers of the Early First Millennium BC II*, 3:211.
21. Adad-narari III 7 20, in Grayson, *Assyrian Rulers of the Early First Millennium BC II*, 3:211; Bustenay Oded, *Mass Deportations and Deportees in the Neo-Assyrian Empire* (Wiesbaden, DE: Ludwig Reichert, 1979), 4: "In an inscription of Adad-nerari III found at Tell al-Rimah, reference is made to 331 settlements which were rebuilt in the region under the control of the Assyrian governor Nergal-eresh."
22. Oded, *Mass Deportations and Deportees in the Neo-Assyrian Empire*, 20.
23. Oded, *Mass Deportations and Deportees in the Neo-Assyrian Empire*, 55.
24. Oded, *Mass Deportations and Deportees in the Neo-Assyrian Empire*, 19.
25. Siddall, *The Reign of Adad-nirari III*, 58.
26. Kitchen, *On the Reliability of the Old Testament*, 31.
27. Eponym chronicle 809–782, in Alan Millard, *The Eponyms of the Assyrian Empire 910–612 BC* (Helsinki: The Neo-Assyrian Text Corpus Project, 1994), 35–38.
28. SAA 12 1–12, in L. Kataja and R. Whiting, *Grants, Decrees and Gifts of the Neo-Assyrian Period* (Helsinki: Helsinki University Press, 1995), 4–15.
29. SAA 12 10, in Kataja and Whiting, *Grants, Decrees and Gifts of the Neo-Assyrian Period*, 13–14; SAA 12 1, in Kataja and Whiting, *Grants, Decrees and Gifts of the Neo-Assyrian Period*, 4–7; SAA 12 11, in Kataja and Whiting, *Grants,*

period of Adad-nerari's reign. We also have a boundary stele that he erected near Antakya establishing peace between Zakur of Hamath and Ataršumki, son of Adramu, and establishing the Orontes River as the boundary between the two countries from this time as well.[30]

In the last part of his reign,[31] Adad-nerari claimed to have "established in my hands from the bank of the Euphrates, the land of Hatti, the entire land of Amurru, the land of Tyre, the land of Sidon, the land of Omri, the land of Edom, and the land of Palastine, to the great sea of the west. I imposed tax and tribute upon them."[32] He may have imposed tribute, but that is different than conquering them.

By the end of his reign, Adad-nerari III had "made the captive peoples return to their home and granted them permanent inheritances and food."[33] This is an abrupt about-face on a fundamental aspect of the Assyrian Empire. Because of this, "in the first half of the 8th century the two Israelite states experienced a period of calm."[34] Thus, "a central problem is how to understand the imperial hiatus and its effect on the overall perception of Assyrian imperialism."[35] The book of Jonah explains this.

The book of Jonah says that the Assyrians repented (Jonah 3:5–9) and from the surviving record it appears that they did. Ashur-dan III (772–755 BC) is known only for building activities.[36] Ashur-nirari V (754–45 BC) stopped collecting taxes from foreign tributaries.[37] Instead of war, we have "the Assyrian king arbitrating between

---

Decrees and Gifts of the Neo-Assyrian Period, 14.
30. Adad-narari III 2, in Grayson, *Assyrian Rulers of the Early First Millennium BC II*, 3:203–204.
31. Siddall, *The Reign of Adad-nirari III*, 58.
32. Adad-narari III 8 11–14, in Grayson, *Assyrian Rulers of the Early First Millennium BC II*, 213.
33. Synchronistic Chronicle iv.15–20, in A. Kirk Grayson, *Assyrian and Babylonian Chronicles* (Locust Valley, NY: J. J. Augustin, 1975), 169; Jean-Jacques Glassner, *Mesopotamian Chronicles* (Atlanta: Society of Biblical Literature, 2004), 182.
34. Benedikt Otzen, "Israel under the Assyrians," in *Power and Propaganda*, 251.
35. Siddall, *The Reign of Adad-nirari III*, 7.
36. Aššur-dan III A.0.106, in Grayson, *Assyrian Rulers of the Early First Millennium BC II*, 3:245.
37. Aššur-narari V A.0.107, in Grayson, *Assyrian Rulers of the Early First Millennium BC II*, 3:247.

local dynasts — with no visible inclination to annex their territory."[38] For two generations, Israel had peace from the Assyrians. By the end of this period, "Urartu had complete control of all of the territory [north] of the Assyrian heartland stretching from the Iranian plateau to the [east] to [north] Syria and the Mediterranean in the [west]. Assyria was on the verge of extinction when Tiglath-pileser III came to the throne"[39] with a policy that could be styled as to make Assyria great again.

DATING THE BOOK OF JONAH

The book of Jonah is told in the third person and does not necessarily need to be a contemporary account. In other words, the date of Jonah and the date of the book of Jonah's composition do not need to be the same. This, of course, raises the issue of when precisely the book of Jonah was written.

Scholars are divided on the date of Jonah. Some say that "determining the date for the composition of Jonah is such an elusive and probably impossible task."[40] Others state that "all competent critics agree that it is post-exilic."[41] "Dating the book is problematic," says another, "because there is virtually no direct information and everything has to be derived by internal evidence of varying degrees of trustworthiness."[42]

The twelve prophets, which includes Jonah, are mentioned in Sirach (49:10) and therefore the text existed in the second century BC.[43] Jonah is also attested in the Dead Sea Scrolls (4QXII).[44] The second century BC forms the *terminus ante quem* and the eighth cen-

---

38. J. N. Postgate, "The Land of Assur and the Yoke of Assur," *World Archaeology* 23 (1992): 251.
39. A. Kirk Grayson, "Mesopotamia, History of (Assyria)," in *Anchor Bible Dictionary*, 6 vols., ed. David Noel Freedman (New York: Doubleday, 1992), 4:743–744.
40. James Limburg, *Jonah: A Commentary* (Louisville, KY: Westminster/John Knox Press, 1993), 31.
41. Edgar James Banks, *Jonah in Fact and Fancy* (Reading Pennsylvania: Frank J. Boyer, 1899), 160.
42. Jonathan Magonet, "Jonah, Book of," in *Anchor Bible Dictionary*, 3:940.
43. Limburg, *Jonah: A Commentary*, 28.
44. Eugene Ulrich, *The Biblical Qumran Scrolls* (Leiden, NL: Brill, 2013), 2:610–614.

tury BC forms the *terminus post quem*, providing a six to seven century span in which Jonah might have been written.

Anachronisms

In the book of Jonah, the capital of Assyria is Nineveh. This is seen as an anachronism:

> The book's references to Nineveh are anachronistic, and geographically implausible, suggesting the use of a symbolic 'evil place' such as is found in other late prophets, and also interestingly in the Hellenistic world after 600 BCE.[45]

Other scholars observe, "The statement in 3:3 that Nineveh 'was' a great city, suggests that it was no longer in existence at the time of composition, i.e., after 612 B.C."[46] In the nineteenth century, a compelling argument for the date of Jonah was that "some wandering exiled Jew may have seen the impressive ruins of Nineveh, and was inspired to teach his fellow countrymen a lesson in Yahveh's ever-present power."[47] Many readers of the Bible may be unaware that the capital of Assyria changed throughout history. If one consults Wikipedia, one might have the impression that from the time of Ashurnasirpal II until Sargon II founded Dur-Sharrukin, that Nimrud was the capital. The book of Jonah would thus have had an anachronistic capital for the Assyrian empire. This view is complicated when we look at the locations in which texts were found.

The capital of Tiglath-pileser III was at Nimrud. If we look at where the royal inscriptions of Tiglath-pileser III were found (as shown in the table),[48] the greatest number come from the capital, Nimrud (Kalhu).

Location	Number of Inscriptions
Nimrud (Kalhu)	109
Ashur	20

---

45. Alastair G. Hunter, *The Judgement of Jonah: Yahweh, Jerusalem and Nineveh* (London: T&T Clark, 2022), 3.
46. Magonet, "Jonah, Book of," 3:940.
47. Banks, *Jonah in Fact and Fancy*, 155.
48. Hayim Tadmor and Shiego Yamada, *The Royal Inscriptions of Tiglath-pileser III (744–727 BC) and Shalmaneser V (726–722 BC), Kings of Assyria* (Winona Lake, IN: Eisenbrauns, 2011).

Location	Number of Inscriptions
Arslan Tash	1
Mila Mergi	1
Western Iran	1
Unknown	1

Royal Inscriptions of Tiglath-pileser III

Of the royal inscriptions of Shalmaneser V, all nine come from Nimrud (Kalhu), the capital.

Sargon II moved the capital to Dur-Sharrukin (Khorsabad). Of his royal inscriptions (as shown in the table), the vast majority come from Dur-Sharrukin.[49]

Location	Number of Inscriptions
Dur-Sharrukin	284
Ashur	113
Nineveh	60
Uruk	26
Babylon	18
Nimrud	14
Carchemish	13
Tell Tayinat	5
Persepolis	5
Arslantepe	4
Kish	3
Tag	2
Djigan	2
Karamles	2
Ashdod	2
Nahrawan	1
Tepe Gawra	1
Tell Baradan	1
Acharneh	1

---

49. Grant Frame, *The Royal Inscriptions of Sargon II, King of Assyria (721–705 BC)* (University Park, PA: Eisenbrauns, 2021).

Location	Number of Inscriptions
Tell Ahmar	1
Tell Hadad	1
Qal'eh-i Imam	1
Tang-i Var	1
Najafabad	1
Tell Amarna (Syria)	1
Kition (Cyprus)	1
Unknown origin	34

Royal Inscriptions of Sargon II

We therefore expect that most of the royal inscriptions will come from the capital. Let us then consider the Assyrian rulers of the time of Jonah and the aftermath, starting with Adad-nirari III.[50]

Location	Number of Inscriptions
Nineveh	29
Ashur	23
Nimrud (Kalhu)	19
Antakya	1
Dur-Katlimmu (Tell Sheik Hammad)	1
Kızkapanlı	1
Saba'a	1
Tell al-Rimah	1
Unknown provenance	1

Royal inscriptions of Adad-nirari III

If the greatest number of the royal inscriptions come from the capital, then Adad-narari's capital was in Nineveh. Nineveh was also known for its hanging gardens.[51]

Of the royal inscriptions of Shalmaneser IV (782–773 BC), one was found at Kızkapanlı, one was found at Tell Abta, and one is purportedly from Nineveh but has been argued to be from Ashur.[52] The only royal

---

50. Grayson, *Assyrian Rulers of the Early First Millennium BC II*, 3:200–224.
51. Mario Liverani, *Assyria: The Imperial Mission* (Winona Lake, IN: Eisenbrauns, 2017), 69–70.
52. Grayson, *Assyrian Rulers of the Early First Millennium BC II*, 3:239–244.

inscription of Ashur-dan III (772–755 BC) is from Ashur.[53] The only inscription from Ashur-narari V (754–45) is of unknown provenance.[54]

What looks to be a strike against Jonah, the capital being at Nineveh, turns out to be an argument in its favor.

Language

All the book of Jonah leaves us with to date it is the language used in the text. There are two problems with that procedure: one chronological and the other geographical. The chronological problem is in some ways the most straightforward. The Hebrew language changed over time and linguistic features are generally divided between those that are early or late. The problem generally is that the dates of the biblical books are almost all disputed. One text may be designated as early by one scholar, but late by another. This complicates determining which features of the language themselves are early or late. Some books, however, claim to be late and no one argues that they were written earlier than they claim to be. These provide examples of indisputably late features of the language. Earlier forms appear by contrast with known late features.

The geographic problem stems from where Jonah came from. Jonah is a prophet from the northern kingdom of Israel. The Hebrew Bible is a record of those from the southern kingdom of Judah. Only in exceptional cases were northern prophets mentioned in the southern record: Elijah, Elisha, Amos, and Jonah. These northern stories were brought south after the ten tribes were scattered, and the refugees fled south and settled in the land of Jerusalem. The Hebrew Bible is mostly written in the Judean dialect of Hebrew, and we know relatively little about the Hebrew dialect or dialects from Israel.

Like the accounts of Elijah and Elisha, Jonah is a third-person narrative. One is left with three general possible scenarios for a northern account being included in the Hebrew Bible. The first possibility is that Jonah was written in the north, in the northern dialect and then brought with the northern refugees into the south. The second is that the story was brought by the northern refugees and written by someone in the southern dialect. The third is that the story was invented

---

53. Grayson, *Assyrian Rulers of the Early First Millennium BC II*, 3:245.
54. Grayson, *Assyrian Rulers of the Early First Millennium BC II*, 3:246–247.

and has no basis in reality but was written by someone in the southern dialect at a later time.

One critic helpfully gives a list of supposedly late vocabulary in Jonah.[55] Granted, this was from the nineteenth century before many epigraphic sources were known, but modern critics do not feel the need to bother about citing much evidence. Some more recent arguments for post-exilic language usage are less than convincing.[56] Each of these vocabulary elements can be examined in turn:

The term for sailors used is *hammallāḥîm* (Jonah 1:5). This term is only used in the Hebrew Bible in Ezekiel 27:9, 27, 29, which happens to be the only other time when sailors are mentioned in the Hebrew Bible. It is also the Phoenician term for sailor[57] with the Targum using a different term (*sapnayā'*) for the sailors.[58]

The term for ship used is *hassəpînāh* (Jonah 1:5). This is a *hapax legomenon* in the Hebrew Bible, which alone does not tell us whether it is early or late, because it is otherwise unattested in the Bible. It is, however, attested outside the Bible in other pre-exilic inscriptions.[59] It is difficult, if not disingenuous, to argue that a term is an indication of a post-exilic date when it appears in preexilic texts. The Targums use a different term (*'îlpā'*) for boat, which indicates that the earlier term was no longer in common usage and a more up-to-date term needed to be used.

The term for the captain of the ship is *rab haḥḥobēl*, "chief of the sailors" (Jonah 1:6), and both of the terms in the phrase are supposedly late. The construction with *rb* followed by a title is abundantly attested in Ugarit (which was destroyed around the time of Moses),[60] and other preexilic Northwest Semitic languages.[61] The term *ḥbl* is a

---

55. Banks, *Jonah in Fact and Fancy*, 158.
56. Limburg, *Jonah*, 29.
57. J. Hoftijzer and K. Jongeling, *Dictionary of the North-West Semitic Inscriptions* (Leiden, NL: E. J. Brill, 1995), 632.
58. Targum Jonathan Jonah 1:5, in Alexander Sperber, *The Bible in Aramaic*, 5 vols. (Leiden, NL: E. J. Brill, 2004), 1:437.
59. Hoftijzer and Jongeling, *Dictionary of the North-West Semitic Inscriptions*, 797.
60. Georgio del Olmo Lete and Joaquín Sanmartín, *A Dictionary of the Ugaritic Language in the Alphabetic Tradition*, 2 vols. (Leiden, NL: Brill, 2015), 2:747–748.
61. Hoftijzer and Jongeling, *Dictionary of the North-West Semitic Inscriptions*, 1049–1050.

Punic term for sailor.⁶² Although Punic — the form of Phoenician used in the Phoenician colony at Carthage — is attested later, it still derives from Phoenician, and just because it is not attested in the smaller Phoenician corpus does not mean that it was not Phoenician. The term *ḥbl* derives from a term that means "mooring rope" that is attested at least as early as Ugaritic.⁶³ Given the rather scanty coverage of nautical terminology in most preexilic Semitic languages, we can only say that this is not attested early but that it cannot be ruled out. The Targum uses a different term (*rab səpanyā'*) for captain.

The term used for the sea being calm is *yištoq* (Jonah 1:11–12). This is attested in Old Aramaic.⁶⁴ As has been noted, "some of the words relating to the sea voyage may be technical maritime terms, possibly Phoenician in origin, which could have been available at any period."⁶⁵ The Targum uses a different verb (*ynûaḥ*) for the sea being calm.

The verb for consider or regard is *yitʿaššēt* (Jonah 1:6). This particular form is also a *hapax legomenon* in the Hebrew Bible, although the root appears in Jeremiah (5:28). It is attested in Old Aramaic.⁶⁶ Since the term only appears once, and is attested in preexilic times, there is no particular reason to consider it late. The Targum uses a different term here (*yitraḥêm*), meaning that it was not in common usage later.

The book of Jonah has fourteen relative pronouns. Twelve are *'ašer*,⁶⁷ and three are *še*.⁶⁸ Normally, the use of *še* is a sign of a post-exilic book⁶⁹ as the pronoun *še* was borrowed from Akkadian *ša* during the exile.⁷⁰ Three terms show the use of the relative *še*. These are *bašellamî* (Jonah 1:7), *bašellî* (Jonah 1:12), and *šebin-laylāh* (Jonah 4:10). It is difficult to imagine that any of these were the result of linguistic updating. On the other hand, Rendsburg claims that they are a normal form of the relative pronoun in the Hebrew grammar of the northern kingdom,

---

62. Hoftijzer and Jongeling, *Dictionary of the North-West Semitic Inscriptions*, 345.
63. del Olmo Lete and Sanmartín, *Dictionary of the Ugaritic Language*, 1:347.
64. Hoftijzer and Jongeling, *Dictionary of the North-West Semitic Inscriptions*, 1200.
65. Magonet, "Jonah, Book of," 3:940.
66. Hoftijzer and Jongeling, *Dictionary of the North-West Semitic Inscriptions*, 895.
67. Jonah 1:5, 8, 9, 14; Jonah 2:10; Jonah 3:2, 8, 10; Jonah 4:5, 10, 11 (2x).
68. Jonah 1:7; Jonah 4:10.
69. Limburg, *Jonah*, 29.
70. Ronald Hendel and Jan Joosten, *How Old Is the Hebrew Bible?* (New Haven: Yale University Press, 2018), 29–30, 43.

and thus preexilic.[71] The Targum uses different expressions here: *bədîl māh*, *bədîlî*, and *bəlêlyā'*, respectively. If constructions with *še* were the use of late vernacular, we would not expect them to be replaced.

The term used for appointing or preparing the fish, the gourd, and the worm is *yəman* (Jonah 1:17; Jonah 4:6, 7, 8). This is attested in Old Aramaic[72] and Ugaritic.[73] The Targum uses a different verb (*zamîn*) here.

The term used for the king of Nineveh laying aside his garments is *ya'abēr* (Jonah 3:6). The term is so common that it is hard to credit this argument. The Targum uses a different verb here (*'a'dî*).

The term for the royal decree is *ṭa'am* (Jonah 3:7). This, of course, is cognate with the Akkadian term for decree, and is common in the Persian period.[74] It genuinely looks like a late usages. The Targum, however, uses a different word (*migzêrat*) for decree.

The term in Jonah for labor is *'āmaltā* (Jonah 4:10). This term also appears in Old Aramaic.[75] This is the only word on the list for which the Targum uses the same word.

The term for ten thousand in Jonah is *ribû* (Jonah 4:11). This appears in Official Aramaic and thus appears late.[76] The Targum uses a related term, *ribwān*.

None of the vocabulary items appears in the Late Biblical Hebrew lexicon,[77] and only one of them appears in the Targum of Jonah. This indicates that the supposed Aramaisms in Jonah were considered archaic by Aramaic speakers, and therefore not used. This also makes a Hellenistic date for the book of Jonah unlikely.

Other proposals are less than convincing. For instance, "The expression, God of heaven," we are told, "is very late."[78] This is, of course, an assertion that does not particularly hold up well since the

---

71. Gary A. Rendsburg, "A Comprehensive Guide to Israelian Hebrew: Grammar and Lexicon," *Orient* 38 (2003): 12–13.
72. Hoftijzer and Jongeling, *Dictionary of the North-West Semitic Inscriptions*, 660.
73. del Olmo Lete and Sanmartín, *Dictionary of the Ugaritic Language*, 2:554.
74. Hoftijzer and Jongeling, *Dictionary of the North-West Semitic Inscriptions*, 427.
75. Hoftijzer and Jongeling, *Dictionary of the North-West Semitic Inscriptions*, 870–871.
76. Hoftijzer and Jongeling, *Dictionary of the North-West Semitic Inscriptions*, 1052.
77. Avi Hurvitz, *A Concise Lexicon of Late Biblical Hebrew* (Leiden, NL: E. J. Brill, 2014).
78. Banks, *Jonah in Fact and Fancy*, 158.

expression appears in Genesis (24:3, 7). It was more popular in later times, but its use earlier cannot be ruled out. We are also told that "the compound Yahveh-Elohim, iv. 6, is a certain sign of the post-exilic origin of the book"[79] except that it also shows up on the preexilic Lachish ostraca.[80]

The arguments for dating based on language are less than conclusive.

Conclusion

Direct evidence for the existence and effectiveness of all the Old Testament prophets outside the Old Testament is wanting. We currently lack direct evidence for the existence of almost all individuals who lived in ancient Israel or Judah. Absence of evidence, however, is not evidence of absence.

What Jonah, like the other northern prophets Elijah and Elisha, has is indirect evidence of effectiveness. In the ninth century, Elijah and Elisha preached against the worship of Baal. By the eighth century the vast majority of theophoric names from the northern kingdom of Israel found archaeologically used Jehovah rather than Baal as an element in the names. Sixty-seven percent of the theophoric names use some form of Jehovah, as opposed to seventeen percent using Baal, and fifteen percent using El. This is an indication of the effectiveness of the ministries of Elijah and Elisha.

According to the Old Testament, Jonah went to the Assyrian capital, Nineveh, and preached repentance, and for the next couple of generations there is genuine evidence that the Assyrians changed their ways. We can date Jonah's ministry sometime between about 796 and 783 BC, probably in the earlier part of those years because Assyrian policy changed so dramatically at that time. Some explanation for the change in Assyrian policy during Jonah's lifetime is in order and no explanation is forthcoming from the Assyrian records. The book of Jonah provides both an explanation and an ancient one.

The date of the book of Jonah cannot be determined at our present state of knowledge. Most of the vocabulary items that have been

---

79. Banks, *Jonah in Fact and Fancy*, 158.
80. Lachish 6 12–13, in F. W. Dobbs-Allsopp, J. J. M. Roberts, C. L. Seow, and R. E. Whitaker, *Hebrew Inscriptions* (New Haven: Yale University Press, 2005), 322–323.

argued to be late cannot be excluded from being preexilic. The book is not autobiographical, and may not have been written in his lifetime. One can suppose that there would be no reason to include it among the records of the southern kingdom unless it were brought from the north and already had some sort of status when it entered the southern kingdom. This gives a date for the book of Jonah sometime in the eighth century.

All of these arguments hardly qualify as absolute proof. As a counter-argument against a logical fallacy, however, they may be worth paying attention to.

17

"TO SEAL THE CHILDREN TO THE FATHERS"

ANCIENT AND MODERN TRADITIONS OF ELIJAH'S RETURN

SPENCER KRAUS

In Malachi 4, a prophecy is given that before the great and dreadful day of the Lord, Elijah would return to turn the hearts of children and parents toward one another. This prophecy was also elaborated upon by both Moroni and Joseph Smith in the latter-day dispensation, often in light of the sealing power restored on 3 April 1836 in the Kirtland Temple. This paper will do two things. First, I will discuss how Moroni's and Joseph's repetition of this prophecy is best understood as a prophetic commentary, and not necessarily the restoration of a lost or corrupted text. Second, I will discuss various Jewish and Christian traditions surrounding Elijah's return that can shed light on Moroni's commentary and the fulfilment of this prophecy in the Kirtland Temple in 1836. Both Moroni's and Joseph Smith's prophetic expansions, then, could be understood better in this ancient context, including how these ancient expectations were dramatically and completely fulfilled as Elijah came to the Kirtland Temple.

The book of Malachi ends with a prophecy well known to Latter-day Saints: "Behold, I will send you Elijah the prophet before the coming of the great and dreadful day of the Lord: and he shall turn the heart of the fathers to the children, and the heart of the children to their fathers, lest I come and smite the earth with a curse" (Malachi 4:5–6, KJV).

Malachi's prophecy is found throughout the canon of the Church of Jesus Christ of Latter-day Saints; in fact, it is included in every single volume of scripture. Beyond the Old Testament, it is cited in the New Testament repeatedly. This was a prophecy often connected with John the Baptist from the outset of his life. At the annunciation of John, the angel Gabriel recited this prophecy, with some key differences not attested in either the Hebrew or Greek versions, to highlight John's own future ministry: "With the spirit and power of Elijah he will go before him, to turn the hearts of parents to their children *and the disobedient to the wisdom of the righteous, to make ready a people prepared for the Lord*" (Luke 1:17).[1] During John's life, people asked him if he was Elijah, which he denied (John 1:21). However, John lived his life in a way that evoked the image of that prophet, even down to the type of garment he wore (Matthew 3:4; 2 Kings 1:8). Furthermore, when Jesus spoke about John, he did so by referring to him as Elijah — John had, after all, come in the spirit and power of Elijah as Gabriel had promised — while still promising the disciples that Elijah had not yet come, but would one day do so (Matthew 11:14; 17:12–13; Mark 9:13). Others believed Jesus was Elijah (Matthew 16:14).[2]

It is also important to recognize that the Savior's promise that Elijah would one day come followed His experience on the Mount of Transfiguration, in which Elijah (or another prophetic figure coming in his spirit and power) and Moses visited Jesus, Peter, James, and John. This shows that, in Jesus's mind, Elijah's coming had not been completely fulfilled through either the ministry of John or the divine visitation that He and His apostles had just received (Mark 9:2–13).[3]

---

1. Unless otherwise noted, all biblical citations will come from the New Revised Standard Version updated edition (NRSVue).
2. Like Elijah, Jesus performed miracles and invited followers to leave everything to follow him. Some scholars have also observed that many of the miracles Jesus performed recalled the miracles of Elijah and Elisha, such as reviving a widow's son, feeding the multitude with a few loaves, curing lepers, and miraculously ascending into heaven (in this case, after his resurrection). See Daniel C. Matt, *Becoming Elijah: Prophet of Transformation* (New Haven: Yale University Press, 2022), 117. For Jesus and Elijah calling others to forsake everything to follow them, see 1 Kings 19:19–21; Matthew 4:18–22; Luke 9:57, 61–62. Expectations of Elijah's return (as prophesied by Malachi) would continue to be seen throughout Jesus's life. Even when Jesus was crucified, many mistakenly believed his call for *Eli*, "my God," was directed to *Eliyahu*, Elijah (Matthew 27:46).
3. Regarding the identification of the "Elias" (as rendered in the King James Version) that appeared on the Mount of Transfiguration and the Joseph Smith Translation, which appears to identify him as John the Baptist, see Richard Neitzel Holzapfel, Eric D. Huntsman, and Thomas A. Wayment, *Jesus Christ*

Thus, Malachi's prophecy was significant for Jews and Christians in the first century AD and it shaped many of their beliefs surrounding the Savior's ministry and second coming.

This was also a prophecy that the resurrected Jesus believed the Nephites (who had separated from the main body of Israelites at least two centuries before Malachi was born) needed to have. The Savior cited the ending of the Book of Malachi in full, found as two separate chapters in the King James Version, but still listed together as a single chapter in the Hebrew Bible.[4] With only a few minor exceptions, the version of Malachi cited in 3 Nephi 24–25 matches almost identically with the King James Version.

It is also found in both the Doctrine and Covenants and the Pearl of Great Price. On three occasions, this prophecy is cited almost verbatim as it is found in the King James Version (see Doctrine and Covenants 27:9; Doctrine and Covenants 110:14–15; Doctrine and Covenants 128:17), and on two occasions the prophecy is cited as it was quoted by the angel Moroni to Joseph Smith, which varied greatly from the received text (see Doctrine and Covenants 2; Joseph Smith—History 1:38–39).[5] Furthermore, no changes to Malachi 4 were made in the Joseph Smith Translation of the Bible.

---

and the World of the New Testament: An Illustrated Reference for Latter-day Saints (Salt Lake City: Deseret Book, 2006), 73–74 for the argument that John appeared alongside Elijah and Moses. For the converse, the JST appears to state John was the Elias and may therefore shed light on the Elias of Doctrine and Covenants 110, see Kevin L. Barney, "Who was the Elias of D&C 110?" *By Common Consent*, online at bycommonconsent.com.

4. The division of Malachi 3 into two smaller chapters dates to the thirteenth century and was more thematic than literary on the part of Christian editors. Thus, Malachi 4:5–6 would be found as Malachi 3:23–24 in Hebrew editions of the Bible and some translations today. For the ease of Latter-day Saints, who would most likely be familiar with the four-chapter division of Malachi, I will cite Malachi as such. Suffice it to note that the inclusion of both Malachi 3 and 4 in the Book of Mormon is best understood as Jesus sharing all of a single chapter or oracle from Malachi, with its own versification inserted at a later point to match the King James Version.
5. It is worth noting that the instance in Doctrine and Covenants 128:17 is followed by the next verse with the statement, "I might have rendered a plainer translation to this, but it is sufficiently plain to suit my purpose as it stands." This will be discussed in more detail further below.

Given the prominence of this prophecy in scripture, it is no surprise that Latter-day Saints have repeatedly focused on it. This is also shaped by how this prophecy was introduced at the outset of the Restoration, which has provided Latter-day Saints with more interpretive light to understand its meaning and fulfillment in this dispensation.

Elijah's Return According to Moroni and Joseph Smith

I would like to focus our attention on Moroni's recitation of this passage. When the angel appeared to Joseph Smith in 1823, the Prophet recalled that he cited this passage with significant variation to the text:

> Behold, I will *reveal unto you the Priesthood, by the hand of* Elijah the prophet, before the coming of the great and dreadful day of the Lord.
>
> And he shall *plant in the hearts of the children the promises made to the fathers*, and the hearts of the children shall turn to their fathers. *If it were not so, the whole earth would be utterly wasted at his coming.*

As it was cited by Moroni, no known text supports this reading of Malachi. Rather, the extant manuscript evidence supports the received text. The Book of Mormon itself cites Malachi 4 with little to no variation from the received Hebrew text, perhaps because the underlying Nephite text was functionally equivalent to the Hebrew text as it has been received.[6] Moroni's version of Malachi appears to be something other than a lost urtext. It is perhaps best explained as a prophetic midrash, or commentary, on the scriptures to help explain how this prophecy was about to be fulfilled.[7] This is not a new idea, as other

---

6. While the translation of the Book of Mormon is not fully understood, and while the Lord spoke to Joseph Smith according to his own understanding, keep in mind that Joseph's own understanding would, by this point, include Moroni's altered text.
7. This is not unlike Nephi's own prophetic midrash on Isaiah, connecting passages of Isaiah to the coming forth of the Book of Mormon as Nephi universalized a prophecy from its original, limited context in 2 Nephi 29. It is also possible that Moroni's midrash may have been known to the Nephites generally, as after Jesus had read Malachi, "he expounded them unto the multitude; and he did expound all things unto them, both great and small" (3 Nephi 26:1). Because Mormon did not include what Jesus said when he did so, however, we are left only to speculate.

Latter-day Saint scholars have variously referred to Doctrine and Covenants Section 2 as Moroni's commentary or paraphrase.[8]

Understanding Moroni's words as a prophetic commentary also makes sense in the light of Gabriel's annunciation of John. It will be recalled that rather than citing the Septuagint, which generally aligns with the Masoretic text in this case, Gabriel's reference to Malachi also differed greatly from his recorded prophecy.[9] No early Christian argued that Gabriel had restored a proper reading of Malachi, but rather they read the two passages side by side for greater insight and clarity into Elijah's future ministry and John the Baptist's role as Christ's forerunner during his ministry.[10] Moroni would simply be engaging in the same practice here — introducing this passage in a way that highlights how Joseph Smith and the Latter-day Saints should expect to see this prophecy fulfilled in their current dispensation.

---

8. See, for example, Casey Paul Griffiths, *The Scripture Central Commentary on the Doctrine and Covenants*, 4 vols. (Springville, UT: Cedar Fort, 2024), 1:39; Richard O. Cowan, "Instructions on Baptism for the Dead (D&C 127 and 128)," in *The Doctrine and Covenants*, Studies in Scripture, 8 vols., ed. Robert L. Millet and Kent P. Jackson (Salt Lake City: Deseret Book, 1984), 1:494. Stephen E. Robinson and H. Dean Garrett, *A Commentary on the Doctrine and Covenants*, 4 vols. (Salt Lake City: Deseret Book, 2000), 1:30–31 also notes that because the KJV rendering is utilized in 3 Nephi and other passages of the Doctrine and Covenants it would be wrong to view the received text as incorrect. However, while they simply argue that Moroni's recitation involved "different shades or levels of meaning" to Malachi's prophecy, I argue it is best understood as Moroni's own prophetic commentary, as others have in less detail.
9. For reference, the Septuagint reads, "And behold I am sending to you Elias the Thesbite before the great and notable day of the Lord comes, who will restore the heart of the father to the son and the heart of a person to his neighbor so that I will not come and utterly strike the land." Translation taken from Albert Pietersma and Benjamin G. Wright, eds., *A New English Translation of the Septuagint* (New York: Oxford University Press, 2007), 822. Thus, while one clause is different, the overall meaning of the Greek and Hebrew texts is the same.
10. In making this claim, I have consulted every passage where Malachi 4:5–6 is cited in the *Biblia Patristica*, a helpful index of each biblical passage cited by the Church Fathers. None of them claimed that Gabriel offered a better rendition of Malachi's prophecy that had somehow been corrupted since Malachi's ministry. Many of these passages will also be cited below regarding patristic interpretations of Malachi's return.

In Moroni's midrash, two phrases appear to be unique, specifically, that the Priesthood would be revealed by the hand of Elijah, and the children would have the promises made to the fathers — or, in other words, the covenants — planted in their hearts. The final clause, that the whole earth would be utterly wasted at the Lord's coming, actually better reflects the underlying Hebrew of Malachi 4.[11] Malachi ends his prophecy by stating that Elijah would come to prevent the earth being struck as *ḥerem*, or something ritually proscribed to be utterly destroyed.[12] Even then, Moroni adapts the language to refer to the Lord in the third person — something more befitting a midrashic explanation than the first-person oracle delivered by Malachi.

The other two aspects of Moroni's commentary appear to have been especially significant to Joseph Smith throughout his life. In fact, Joseph appears to have made similar prophetic commentaries on Malachi 4 that were informed by Moroni's own midrash. When he cited Malachi 4:5–6 in his letter regarding baptisms for the dead, Joseph introduced the citation as "a quotation from one of the prophets, who had his eye fixed on the *restoration of the priesthood*" and the restoration of proxy ordinances — something best understood through Moroni's midrash of Elijah revealing the Priesthood (Doctrine and Covenants 128:17).

After citing Malachi 4:5–6 as it is found in the King James Version of the Bible, Joseph also wrote, "I might have rendered a plainer translation to this, but it is sufficiently plain to suit my purpose as it stands. It is sufficient to know, in this case, that the earth will be smitten with a curse *unless there is a welding link of some kind or other between the fathers and the children*" (Doctrine and Covenants 128:18). Thus, while acknowledging that Joseph could have rendered a plainer translation (either through his own study of Hebrew or through his

---

11. This is also evident in modern translations of the Bible. For instance, the English Standard Version (ESV) renders the conclusion to this verse as "strike the land with a decree of utter destruction." Even though the NRSVue maintains in its translation proper wording close to the King James Version, the translators do include a footnote that shows the verse could end as "strike the land with a ban of utter destruction."
12. Ludwig Koehler and Walter Baumgartner, *The Hebrew and Aramaic Lexicon of the Old Testament*, trans. M. E. J. Richardson, 2 vols. (Leiden, NL: Brill, 2001), s.v. חרם. Hereafter cited as *HALOT*.

own prophetic midrash), the biblical text itself could suffice. But Joseph offered another piece of prophetic commentary to help Latter-day Saints understand Malachi: the covenants made to the fathers that Moroni spoke of would offer a welding link between generations through the ordinances of the temple.

In a later sermon delivered on 13 August 1843, Joseph Smith taught that this passage in Malachi "should read and he shall turn the hearts of the children to the <u>covenant</u> made with their fathers."[13] Joseph again connected these covenants to temple ordinances when he taught, on multiple occasions, that this passage dealt with the sealing power. Wilford Woodruff, for instance, recorded on 10 March 1844 that Joseph cited the biblical text of Malachi 4:5–6 before offering his own interpretation: "He should send Elijah to *seal* the children to the fathers & fathers to the children." Furthermore, "We want the power of Elijah to seal those who dwell on earth to those which dwell in heaven."[14]

Woodruff also noted, in a sermon delivered on 21 January 1844, that Joseph stated the word translated as "turn" should be rendered "bind or seal."[15] In this case, the verb Malachi uses is the hiphil construction of *šûv*, which could mean to bring back, turn around, or restore.[16] In context of this verse, scholars have also noted it has covenantal connotations that involve "bonding the current generation ... to the Mosaic covenant of their ancestors. ... The call for reconciliation between the ancestors (lit. 'fathers,' *ʾābôt*) and the 'descendants' (lit. 'sons,' *bānîm*) is really a call for covenantal renewal with Yahweh."[17] Thus, Joseph's translation of bind or seal also appears to be a prophetic interpretation to clarify the covenantal aspect of Malachi's prophecy:

---

13. "Discourse, 13 August 1843–A, as Reported by William Clayton," p. 87, *Joseph Smith Papers*, online at josephsmithpapers.org. Underlining in original.
14. "Discourse, 10 March 1844, as Reported by Wilford Woodruff," p. 208, *Joseph Smith Papers*, online at josephsmithpapers.org; see also "Discourse, 10 March 1844, as Reported by Thomas Bullock," p. 3, online at josephsmithpapers.org. In context, the "power" of Elijah is best understood as the Priesthood keys restored by Elijah in the Kirtland Temple, which again hearkens back to Moroni's midrash.
15. "Journal (January 1, 1843 – December 31, 1844)," January 21, 1844, *Wilford Woodruff Papers*, online at wilfordwoodruffpapers.org.
16. *HALOT*, s.v. שׁוב.
17. Andrew E. Hill, *Malachi*, in *The Anchor Bible*, vol. 25D (New York: Doubleday, 1998), 387–388.

as the hearts of the children are brought back or restored to the covenants made to their fathers, they will be bound or sealed in that same covenant in "a whole and complete and perfect union, and welding together of dispensations" all the way back to our father Adam (Doctrine and Covenants 128:18).

Each of these sermons would have also been referring to the fulfillment of Elijah's return that Joseph Smith witnessed in the Kirtland Temple. After the Savior appeared and accepted the temple on 3 April 1836, Moses, a prophet bearing the name-title of Elias, and Elijah each appeared in subsequent visions to Joseph Smith and Oliver Cowdery, and delivered sacred priesthood keys and powers.[18] Moses "committed

---

18. Regarding the identity of Elias, Joseph appears to have used this name as a title for various prophets who acted as a forerunner to Christ's first or second coming, and so it is hard to ascertain his identity with any precision. See Griffiths, *Doctrine and Covenants*, 4:34; Robinson and Garrett, *Doctrine and Covenants*, 4:65; "Journal, 1835–1836," p. 193, *Joseph Smith Papers*, note 416, online at josephsmithpapers.org. Elsewhere, Joseph noted that "Elias is a forerunner to prepare the way" and "the Spirit of Elias is a forerunner same as John the Baptist," separating this from "the Spirit of Elijah is the sealing power—to seal the hearts of the Fathers to the children—and the children to the Parents." See "Discourse, 10 March 1844, as Reported by Wilford Woodruff," p. 211, *Joseph Smith Papers*, online at josephsmithpapers.org; "Discourse, 10 March 1844, as Reported by Thomas Bullock," p. 3, *Joseph Smith Papers*, online at josephsmithpapers.org. An Elias is mentioned in Doctrine and Covenants 27:6 who holds "the keys of bringing to pass the restoration of all things spoken by the mouth of all the holy prophets since the world began, concerning the last days." The following verse also indicates this Elias visited Zacharias and "and gave promise that he should have a son, and his name should be John, and he should be filled with the spirit of Elias," linking him with the angel Gabriel (Doctrine and Covenants 27:7). This has led to some speculation that Noah is the Elias mentioned in Doctrine and Covenants 110, as Joseph had elsewhere identified Gabriel as the prophet Noah. See "Discourse, between circa 26 June and circa 4 August 1839–A," as published in Clayton, Revelations, p. 3, *Joseph Smith Papers*, online at josephsmithpapers.org. For the argument that the Elias who visited the Kirtland Temple was Noah, see Joseph Fielding Smith, *Answers to Gospel Questions*, 5 vols., comp. Joseph Fielding Smith Jr. (Salt Lake City: Deseret Book, 1960), 3:138–141. While the two Elias figures of Doctrine and Covenants 27 and 110 are both described in similar terms, it is worth noting that the priesthood keys in each section are described using different language and may or may not refer to the same keys. Thus, the Elias that is mentioned in Section 27 may be a completely separate individual from the one mentioned in Section 110. An Elias is also mentioned in Section 77:9, 14

unto us the keys of the gathering of Israel from the four parts of the earth, and the leading of the ten tribes from the land of the north," Elias "committed the dispensation of the gospel of Abraham," and Elijah declared that "the time has fully come, which was spoken of by the mouth of Malachi," before he, too, delivered the sealing keys (Doctrine and Covenants 110:11–16).

Seen in this light, the covenants that would be planted in the hearts of the children may refer not only to temple covenants, but also to the covenants that were actually made to former prophets. These would include the Abrahamic covenant, which is itself fully realized only in the temple, and the covenant God has made to remember Israel and gather them in the last days. The keys delivered by Moses and Elias would therefore work in tandem with those restored by Elijah to the fulfilment of the Lord's covenants. Furthermore, with the Lord's return near at hand, the imperative to utilize these keys and restore temple ordinances weighed heavily on Joseph's mind during the last few years of his life, which may have led to his more frequent references to Malachi 4 and the keys of Elijah.

Viewing Joseph's and Moroni's comments regarding Elijah's return as prophetic commentaries on Malachi can also be supported by President Joseph F. Smith's vision of the redemption of the dead, now canonized as Doctrine and Covenants 138. According to Joseph F. Smith,

> The Prophet Elijah was to plant in the hearts of the children the promises made to their fathers, foreshadowing the great work to be done in the temples of the Lord in the dispensation of the fulness of times, for the redemption of the dead, and the sealing of the children to their parents, lest the whole earth be smitten with a curse and utterly wasted at his coming (Doctrine and Covenants 138:47–48).

Here, the versions of Malachi's prophecy as recorded in the King James Version, Moroni's words to Joseph in 1823, and Joseph Smith's own teachings on this subject are all synthesized together (see the

---

in reference to John the Revelator, highlighting how Joseph applied this name to various individuals, even within the Doctrine and Covenants. Given these references, it seems likely that Joseph similarly applied this title to a prophet and Elias should be best understood as a title in the Doctrine and Covenants rather than a given name.

included table). This suggests that each text sheds light on the other, and that one is not more or less correct than another.

Rather, Moroni's teachings that the promises made to the fathers would be planted in the children's hearts, Joseph's teachings about the temple and the sealing keys, and Malachi's warning about the curse or utter destruction that awaited the world if Elijah had not come all come together as three prophetic witnesses.[19]

Doctrine and Covenants 138:47–48	Source Material	Prophet
The Prophet Elijah was to **plant in the hearts of the children the promises made to their fathers,**	And he shall **plant in the hearts of the children the promises made to the fathers,** and the hearts of the children shall turn to their fathers. (Doctrine and Covenants 2:2)	Moroni
foreshadowing **the great work to be done in the temples of the Lord** in the dispensation of the fulness of times, **for the redemption of the dead,**	"I will give you a quotation from one of the prophets, who had his eye fixed on the restoration of the priesthood, the glories to be revealed in the last days, and in an especial manner this most glorious of all subjects belonging to the everlasting gospel, **namely, the baptism for the dead**" (Doctrine and Covenants 128:17)	Joseph Smith
and **the sealing of the children to their parents,**	"He should send Elijah to **seal the children to the fathers & fathers to the children.** ... We want the power of Elijah to seal those who dwell on earth to those which dwell in heaven."[20]	Joseph Smith
lest the **whole earth** be **smitten with a curse**	"And he shall turn the heart of the fathers to the children, and the heart of the children to their fathers, lest I come and **smite the earth with a curse.**" (Malachi 4:6; cf. Doctrine and Covenants 128:18)	Malachi (and subsequently paraphrased by Joseph Smith)
and **utterly wasted at his coming.**	"If it were not so, the **whole earth** would be **utterly wasted at his coming.**" (Doctrine and Covenants 2:3)	Moroni

---

19. While Doctrine and Covenants 138:48 utilizes language from both Malachi 4 and Doctrine and Covenants 2, as noted earlier, each would be referring to the same Hebrew phrase. The fact that both are used by Joseph F. Smith, however, only further underscores my point.

20. "Discourse, 10 March 1844, as Reported by Wilford Woodruff," p. 208, *Joseph Smith Papers*, online at josephsmithpapers.org; see also "Discourse, 10 March 1844, as Reported by Thomas Bullock," p. 3, *Joseph Smith Papers*, online at josephsmithpapers.org; see also Doctrine and Covenants 128:17–18.

Thus, two important details regarding the coming of Elijah are gained from Moroni and Joseph Smith:

1. Elijah's return is closely connected with Priesthood keys critical to performing ordinances in the temple, especially the sealing ordinance to bind children to ancestors and vice versa.
2. The turning of the hearts of the children would be focused on the covenants God has made with their ancestors. These would include not only covenants made by individuals as they go through the temple for themselves or for the dead, but the covenants made anciently to Abraham, Moses, and other prophets regarding the gathering of Israel and the reception of the eternal blessings promised to God's covenant people.

Both of these points can be better understood when viewed with the added context of Jewish and early Christian interpretations regarding the return of Elijah.

Jewish Beliefs Regarding Elijah's Return

Outside of Malachi's prophecy, one of the first mentions of Elijah's return is found in the book of Ben Sirach, generally dated to the early second century BC and named for its author, Joshua son of Eleazar son of Sirach.[21] After recounting a series of great deeds and miracles which Elijah performed throughout his life, Ben Sirach then referred back to Malachi's prophecy, stating Elijah was "prepared at the appointed time to calm wrath before it breaks out in fury, to turn the hearts of parents to their children and to restore the tribes of Jacob" (Sirach 48:10).

From this passage, Elijah is said to do three things when he returns: 1) to calm wrath, 2) to turn the hearts of parents to their children, and 3) to restore the tribes of Jacob. While the first and second duties come directly from Malachi, the third responsibility comes entirely from Ben Sirach. In making this declaration, Ben Sirach inseparably connected Malachi's prophecy with the ultimate restoration of the tribes of Israel, and set the stage for how future interpreters would understand Elijah's future ministry.

---

21. In Greek, the name Joshua is rendered *Jesus*, and as the book has largely survived through its Greek translation performed by Joshua's grandson, the book is commonly referred to by the Greek name *Jesus ben Sirach*. It is also referred to as *Ecclesiasticus* based on Latin Vulgate manuscripts.

In following centuries, various traditions regarding Elijah would arise which focused on his future role as a restorer of the tribes of Israel. Various rabbis also reported having been visited by Elijah, who would travel between heaven and earth to help the righteous in times of need and even help lead people to repent and turn to the Lord until the Messiah came.[22] Whatever important work Elijah would do prior to the Messianic age, however, he would ultimately be the Messiah's herald and assist in His work of redeeming Israel.

According to the apocalypse known as *Sefer Zerubbabel*, for instance, Elijah is twice associated with the Messiah, and is even stated to assist Him in resurrecting the dead prior to the descent of the celestial temple for the Israelites to resume temple worship.[23] This

---

22. Latter-day Saints may compare this idea, and the reported visitations of Elijah, to the Three Nephites or John the Beloved, who were translated so they could continue to minister to the people until the Messiah returned. See 3 Nephi 28:4–24; John 21:21–23; Doctrine and Covenants 7. Folklore surrounding purported appearances of the Three Nephites to faithful Latter-day Saints also abounds in much the same way as tales of Elijah visiting with rabbinic sages abound. For a discussion on the folklore surrounding these appearances of the Three Nephites in particular, see Julie Swallow, Christopher James Blythe, Eric A. Eliason, and Jill Terry Rudy, *The Three Nephites: Saints, Service, and Supernatural Legend* (Urbana, IL: University of Illinois Press, 2025). For a discussion on the rabbinic accounts of visits with Elijah, see generally Matt, *Becoming Elijah*, 50–71. One visit, reported on pp. 59–60 of Matt's treatment, would also be of interest to Latter-day Saints. After infringing a moral law of heaven, Elijah stopped visiting with Rabbi Yehoshu'a for thirty days, and he only resumed his visits after Yehoshu'a had repented and fasted for that time. Similarly, the Three Nephites were reported in the Book of Mormon to visit frequently with the righteous, but these visits stopped as soon as the Nephite nation became morally corrupt and had apostatized from the truth, as reported in Mormon 1:13.
23. This text, lacking traditional versification, can be found in John C. Reeves, *Trajectories in Near Eastern Apocalyptic: A Postrabbinic Jewish Apocalypse Reader* (Leiden, NL: Brill, 2006), 61, 63; John C. Reeves, "Sefer Zerubbabel: The Prophetic Vision of Zerubbabel ben Sheatiel," in *Old Testament Pseudepigrapha: More Noncanonical Scriptures*, 2 vols., ed. Richard Bauckham, James R. Davila, and Alexander Panayotov (Eerdmans, 2013), 1:462, 464. This latter volume will hereafter be cited as *More Noncanonical Scriptures* to avoid confusion with Charlesworth's collection *Old Testament Pseudepigrapha* (itself cited below). This is also repeated in a later medieval apocalypse known as *Sefer Elijah*, as found in Reeves, *Trajectories in Near Eastern Apocalyptic*,

apocalypse explicitly connects this great work of resurrection to the gathering of Israel, inscribing "the genealogical lists [of the Israelites] according to their families."²⁴ The work of the Messiah ultimately focused on the salvation and gathering of Israel on both sides of the veil, and Elijah would closely assist the Messiah in these efforts.

Because of his close association with the Messiah, Elijah also became associated with the Passover, the Israelite festival celebrating Israel's redemption from Egypt. In Jewish seders today, a place is still set for Elijah, who is expected to arrive for the Passover to herald in the redemption the Messiah will bring.²⁵ Other Jewish traditions also state that when Elijah returns, he may be accompanied by Moses, who had saved Israel from Egyptian bondage and gathered them into a nation during his own mortal ministry. According to *Deuteronomy Rabbah*, a midrash compiled sometime during the fifth through eighth centuries AD, "The Holy One blessed be He said to him: 'Moses, as you live, just as you devoted your life to them in this world, so, in the future, when I bring Elijah the prophet, both of you will come as one.'"²⁶

A key part of Israel's redemption also involved the reconstitution of proper temple worship, and various traditions closely associate

---

31–39. My thanks to Allen Hansen for pointing out these sources. It should be noted that in antiquity and in Joseph Smith's teachings, the temple was closely associated with the resurrection of the dead. I have previously written on many of these correspondences and would refer the reader to my previous work as well as the sources I cited. See Spencer Kraus, "'God Hath Shown unto Me a Vision': The Sacred Handclasp and the Resurrection of the Dead," in *The Temple: Seership, Craftsmanship, and Fellowship*, The Temple on Mount Zion, 8 vols., ed. Jeffrey M. Bradshaw and Stephen D. Ricks (Orem, UT: Interpreter Foundation; Salt Lake City: Eborn Books, 2025), 8:369–393, pagination based on a pre-print edition.

24. Reeves, *Trajectories in Near Eastern Apocalyptic*, 57–58; Reeves, "Sefer Zerubbabel," 460.
25. For a discussion regarding these traditions, which date back centuries, see Matt, *Becoming Elijah*, 78–79, 128–146.
26. *Devarim Rabbah* 3:17; translation taken from sefaria.org. One reason Moses and Elijah may have been linked together may not only be because Elijah's ministry echoed Moses's in certain aspects, as discussed in Matt, *Becoming Elijah*, 80–82, but also because Malachi urged the people to "remember the teaching of my servant Moses, the statutes and ordinances that I commanded him at Horeb for all Israel" immediately before he stated that Elijah would return (Malachi 4:4).

Elijah with this task. These traditions date exceptionally early, at least to the early centuries AD and perhaps even earlier. In the Tractate Eduyot of the Mishnah, for instance, Rabbi Joshua related that "Elijah will come … to keep distant those that were forcibly brought near, and to bring near those that were forcibly kept distant."[27] Earlier, this tractate includes debates among the rabbis regarding those who are fit "for marriage into the priesthood," or in other words, who is "fit to declare impure or pure, to keep at a distance or to bring near."[28] Over the years, as some genealogies became unclear, Elijah would correct these genealogies so that those who were proper heirs of the Levitical priesthood could be identified. Those who wrongly claimed Levitical descent, or those who "were forcibly brought near," would ultimately be kept from serving in the temple, while those who were rightful heirs of this priesthood but kept from their station by others would be restored to their position in the temple.

This idea was repeated throughout the years, well into the Medieval era. The eighth-century text *Tanna debe Eliyyahu*, for instance, expands upon this tradition as two rabbis debated over the qualifications for temple service in the age to come. Rabbi Akiva ultimately noted that, "Because the Ten Tribes had been absorbed by the heathen Cutheans, proselytes will not be accepted from the Cutheans until Elijah and the Messiah come and clear up their ancestry."[29] That is, in order for the Cuthean proselytes to participate in any capacity in the covenantal family of Israel, there would need to be some divine guide to ascertain who was qualified to act in a Levitical or priestly capacity among them before they could do so.

Other early traditions preserved in the Babylonian Talmud also state that Elijah may "establish prophetically that [certain offerings in the temple are] not ritually impure, and render it ritually pure."[30]

---

27. *Mishanh Eduyot* 8:7. Translation taken from Shaye J. D. Cohen, "Tractate Eduyot," in *The Oxford Annotated Mishnah: A New Translation of the Mishnah with Introduction and Notes*, 3 vols., ed. Shaye J. D. Cohen, Robert Goldenberg, and Hayim Lapin (New York: Oxford University Press, 2022), 2:677. See also *Tosefta Eduyyot* 3:4; Babylonian Talmud, Kiddushin 71a, 72b.
28. *Mishnah Eduyot* 8:3. Translation taken from Cohen, "Tractate Eduyot," 675.
29. William G. Braude and Israel J. Kapstein, *Tanna debe Eliyyahu: The Lore of the School of Elijah* (Philadelphia: Jewish Publication Society, 1981), 363.
30. Babylonian Talmud, Pesachim 13a. Translation taken from Sefaria, online at sefaria.org. See also Babylonian Talmud, Pesachim 34a.

In either case, where doubt has entered the collective thought regarding the worthiness of some families or even ritual offerings from the temple, Elijah will come to make things right. In short, he will authorize individuals to exercise the Priesthood and play a role in the offerings or ordinances of the temple.

ELIJAH'S RETURN IN PATRISTIC THOUGHT

The belief that Elijah would return before the Second Coming can also be traced through Christian literature from the early centuries AD.[31] While many modern commentators of Malachi 4 will often view its fulfilment solely through the life and ministry of John the Baptist, such was not the case among the Church Fathers and earliest Christian commentators of the scriptures.[32] Rather than seeing John the Baptist as the ultimate fulfilment of this passage, they saw in John the same thing Jesus saw: a forerunner of His mortal ministry who came with the same power, authority, and spirit of Elijah. Cyprian, for instance, speaks of John as being "sustained with the spirit and power of Elijah," but he was not Elijah redivivus.[33] Origen similarly

---

31. Much of the literature cited below will be found in Alexander Roberts and James Donaldson, eds., *The Ante-Nicene Fathers: Translations of the Writings of the Fathers Down to A.D. 325*, 10 vols. (Buffalo, NY: Christian Literature Publishing Co., 1885–1887), hereafter cited as *ANF*.
32. This interpretation is especially common among Protestant commentators, as seen in Elizabeth Achtemeier, *Nahum–Malachi*, in *Interpretation: A Bible Commentary for Teaching and Preaching* (Atlanta: John Knox Press, 1986), 197–198; Douglas J. Stewart, "Malachi," in *Zephaniah, Haggai, Zechariah, and Malachi*, The Minor Prophets: An Exegetical and Expository Commentary, 3 vols., ed. Thomas Edward McComisky (Grand Rapids: Baker Book House, 1998), 3:1394–1395. Ralph L. Smith, *Micah–Malachi*, Word Biblical Commentary, 62 vols. (Grand Rapids: Zondervan, 1984), 32:342 also simply identifies John the Baptist as Elijah in the New Testament without any note regarding expectations of Elijah's actual return. David W. Baker, *Joel, Obadiah, Malachi*, in The NIV Application Commentary, 44 vols. (Grand Rapids: Zondervan, 2006), 36:304–305 primarily identifies this fulfillment through John the Baptist, but does also note Elijah's appearance on the Mount of Transfiguration. However, Baker fails to identify Jesus's statement that John would yet come in the future after that event. A better treatment that does note Christian interpretations while acknowledging this statement is found in Hill, *Malachi*, 383–384.
33. The Epistles of Cyprian, 72:25, in *ANF* 5:385.

maintained that John came only in the spirit and power of Elijah, similar to Elisha's ministry in the Old Testament.[34] Thus, John could be seen as *a* fulfilment, but he was ultimately only a type and shadow of things to come — a viewpoint consistent with the New Testament's references to Elijah.[35]

Though some variance is found among the early Church Fathers, each typically believed that Elijah's coming would occur at an integral point of time before the Savior's Second Coming. Because the earth is threatened with being struck as *ḥerem*, Elijah would come to help correct this course in a dark and dangerous world, as the devil's power would be great.[36]

---

34. See Origen, *Commentary on John*, 6.62–69, 112, 125; Origen, *Commentary on Matthew*, 13.1–2.

35. Perhaps in a similar vein, Hippolytus of Rome also commented on this passage in light of multiple angelic forerunners to the second coming: "It is a matter of course that His forerunners must appear first, as He says by Malachi and the angel [Gabriel]. ... These, then, shall come and proclaim the manifestation of Christ that is to be from heaven; and they shall also perform signs and wonders, in order that men may be put to shame and turned to repentance for their surpassing wickedness and impiety." Hippolytus of Rome, *Treatise on Christ and Antichrist*, 46; in *ANF* 5:213. In the ellipses is a quotation of Luke 1:17, which was itself a proof text of Malachi 4:5–6 by the angel Gabriel.

36. In the Sibylline Oracles, for instance, one early Christian wrote "The Tishbite, speeding the heavenly chariot and descending to earth, shall show three signs to all the world, signs of a life that is perishing." Translation taken from *Sibylline Oracles* book 2, line 187–89; translation taken from Ursula Treu, "Christian Sibyllines," in *Writings Related to the Apostles; Apocalypses and Related Subjects*, New Testament Apocrypha, 2 vols., rev. ed., trans. William Schneemelcher and R. McL. Wilson (Louisville: John Knox Press, 1992), 2:659. A related belief that manifests in some of the writings of the Church fathers was that the two prophets spoken of in Revelation 11:3–12 were Enoch and Elijah, as both were prophets who had not tasted death during their ministries in the Bible. See, for instance, *Apocalypse of Elijah* 4:7–19, 5:32, in O. S. Wintermute, "Apocalypse of Elijah," in *Apocalyptic Literature and Testaments*, The Old Testament Pseudepigrapha, 2 vols., ed. James H. Charlesworth (Doubleday, 1983), 1:747–748, 752; *The Tiburtine Sibyl* 214–219, in Rieuwerd Buitenwerf, "The Tiburtine Sibyl (Greek)," in *More Noncanonical Scriptures*, 187; Hippolytus of Rome, *Fragment on Daniel* 2.22, in *ANF* 5:182; Hippolytus of Rome, *Treatise on Christ and Antichrist*, 43, in *ANF* 5:213. A text attributed to Hippolytus that also contains this idea is also found in the "Appendix to the Works of Hippolytus," 21, 29, in *ANF* 5:249.

Tertullian saw the promised coming of Elijah as a future event, when in a list of events that would need to happen before the Eschaton, he stated, "No one has yet fallen in with [Elijah]."[37] Elsewhere, in his treatise *Against Marcion*, Tertullian commented on the appearance of Moses and Elijah on the Mount of Transfiguration, stating that while Moses was "the initiator of the Old Testament," Elijah was "the consummator of the New." In other words, Elijah would have a future role in fulfilling Christ's New Covenant that had not been fulfilled by the third century AD.[38] Justin Martyr also referred to the expectation among both Jews and Christians that Elijah would need to return before the Messiah's advent.[39]

---

37. Tertullian, *On the Resurrection of the Flesh*, 22; translation taken from *ANF* 3:561. See also Tertullian, *Against Marcion*, Book 4, Chapter 39, which lists this event as a sign preceding the eschaton. Elias is the Greek form of the name Elijah, and as such is the name utilized by the early Church Fathers, as the two names referred to the same person in the Septuagint and many New Testament passages. However, Latter-day Saints also believe Elias to be a title held by multiple prophets, one of whom also appeared alongside Moses and Elijah in the Kirtland Temple. Distinguishing between the spirit of Elijah (or Elias) as a forerunner and the prophet Elijah himself is also critical to understanding Latter-day Saint doctrine and interpretation of the appearances of Elias in both the New Testament and restoration scripture. For convenience to Latter-day Saints and to avoid confusion, I have elected to adapt the translation from each Church Father (where applicable) to utilize the name Elijah.
38. Tertullian, *Against Marcion*, Book 4, Chapter 22; translation taken from *ANF* 3:383.
39. Justin Martyr also wrote in his *Dialogue with Trypho* under the assumption that Malachi's promise had not yet been fulfilled, and this is an assumption that the Jew Trypho maintains as well. According to Trypho, Jesus could not be the Messiah because Elijah had not returned as Malachi promised. For Justin, and for Christians as a whole, the solution is simple: Malachi was clearly speaking about the eschaton, so Elijah's return would be an event preceding Jesus's second advent and his return to the earth in glory. However, to show Jesus was the Messiah, John the Baptist was sent with the prophetic spirit of Elijah to serve as a forerunner for Christ. Justin Martyr, *Dialogue with Trypho*, 8, 49; for a translation of this text, see Thomas B. Falls, trans., *The Writings of Saint Justin Martyr* (Washington, D.C.: Catholic University of America Press, 1948), 161, 221–223. Tertullian, *Against Marcion*, Book 3, Chapter 16 also notes that Jews of the early centuries AD believed that Elijah would come before the Messiah.

Commenting on the angel declaring the fulness of the Gospel in Revelation 7:2, Victorinus believed this angel to be "[Elijah] the prophet, who is the precursor of the times of Antichrist, for the restoration and establishment of the churches from the great and intolerable persecution."[40] Thus, even though there would be great and intolerable persecution before Jesus returned, Elijah would ultimately help the Saints recover from this persecution and be restored together.

Victorinus also provided an interpretive proof text of Malachi 4, perhaps not unlike what Moroni would later offer, to highlight his interpretation of Elijah as the angel with the fulness of the Gospel: "Lo, I will send to you [Elijah] the Tishbite, to turn the hearts of the fathers to the children, *according to the time of calling, to recall the Jews to the faith of the people that succeed them.*"[41] This proof text also matches the angel Gabriel's interpretation, viewing this prophecy in terms of evangelization to the Christian message.

Thus, for early Christians, the return of Elijah was viewed similarly to Jewish interpretations. Just as Ben Sirach claimed that Elijah would calm wrath and help restore the tribes of Jacob, Elijah was understood to gather God's covenant people into His church. Elijah is the messenger of God's covenant in both traditions, restoring the means whereby true worship of God can commence in a covenant community.

Conclusion

When the Jewish and Christian interpretations are considered alongside Moroni's and Joseph Smith's own prophetic commentaries, it is possible to see how this commentary reflects a deeper, more ancient tradition.

Beginning with the account found in Ben Sirach, all three of Elijah's goals fit in neatly with Moroni's interpretation. According to Ben Sirach, Elijah would calm wrath, turn the hearts of parents to their children, and restore the tribes of Jacob. The angel Moroni taught that when Elijah came to reveal the Priesthood, it would be used to turn the hearts of children to their parents so the earth would not be declared *ḥerem* — thereby calming the Lord's wrath. This Priesthood would

---

40. Victorinus of Pettau, *Commentary on the Apocalypse of the Blessed John*, 7:2, in *ANF* 7:351.
41. Victorinus, *Commentary on the Apocalypse*, 7:2, in *ANF* 7:352; emphasis added.

ultimately be critical in the Lord's work of restoring the tribes of Jacob to the Lord, allowing God's children to return to His presence.

This is especially clear when the events of 3 April 1836 are considered. When Malachi's prophecy was fulfilled in the Kirtland Temple, Joseph Smith and Oliver Cowdery received the sealing keys from Elijah. These keys would not only allow living individuals to be sealed together and therefore become heirs of exaltation, but they would allow the Latter-day Saints to perform proxy ordinances for their ancestors, restoring the dead to the covenant family of God.

Alongside the sealing keys, it is noteworthy that Moses appeared alongside Elijah to deliver the keys of the gathering of Israel. Though not delivered by Elijah himself, the close association of the sealing keys with the gathering of Israel is apparent in both the ancient traditions observed previously and prophetic fulfillment. It is also worth remembering some Jewish traditions that stated Moses would appear alongside Elijah before the Messianic age was brought in. The timing of Elijah (and Moses) appearing in the House of the Lord is also significant, as it occurred during the Passover season in 1836 — a time when Elijah is expected to come to Jewish families.[42]

Traditions of Elijah as a "divine genealogist" are also inseparably connected to temple work — only when the tribes of Israel are organized according to their family lines can the priests and Levites be identified, which will in turn allow temple work to commence.[43] Furthermore, just as Elijah would ultimately authorize certain individuals and families to utilize the Priesthood in these traditions, Elijah revealed the Priesthood to Joseph Smith and Oliver Cowdery, just as Moroni promised. In doing so he authorized them to utilize Priesthood keys critical to performing temple ordinances in this dispensation.

Elijah was said to have a role in revealing which offerings of the temple could be pure or impure. While Latter-day Saint temples do not operate under the Levitical priesthood and do not engage in burnt offerings as did the ancient Israelites, the ordinances performed in our

---

42. See Stephen D. Ricks, "The Appearance of Elijah and Moses in the Kirtland Temple and the Jewish Passover," *BYU Studies Quarterly* 23, no. 4 (1983): 483–486.
43. It is also noteworthy that Latter-day Saint leaders have connected family history and genealogy to the spirit of Elijah as well. See, for example, Russell M. Nelson, "The Spirit of Elijah," *Ensign* 24, no. 11 (November 1994): 84–86.

temples are only made possible through Elijah's sealing keys. Without Elijah's visit to the Kirtland temple in 1836 and the priesthood Moroni promised he would reveal, we could not perform these ordinances today.

The association between the gathering of Israel and the resurrection in some Jewish apocalypses is likewise heavily temple-centric, associated with worship in the celestial temple.[44] Joseph Smith taught, "In the resurrection some are raised to be angels, others are raised to become Gods. These things are revealed in the most holy place in a temple prepared for that purpose."[45] The ordinances of the temple were also associated with the resurrection in antiquity; the temple was, as Jon D. Levenson explained, "the antipode of Sheol, as life is the opposite of death, and praise is the opposite of oblivion."[46] Through the temple and its ordinances, Israel can be gathered for time and for eternity, allowing all of God's children to regain His divine presence.

Later Christian interpretations in the centuries following the Apostles did not tend to focus on the temple itself, but they still focused on covenants and gathering Israel. Maintaining the belief that Elijah would come before the Second Coming to herald the Messiah's return, the Church Fathers taught that Elijah would return at a time of great contention to restore and protect the Saints. They also taught that Elijah would help convert the Jews in the last days into the covenantal body of Christ, necessitating they receive ordinances such as baptism. While they emphasized evangelization of the living, which could be understood in light of the keys restored by Moses in the Kirtland

---

44. In addition to the sources cited above such as *Sefer Zerubbabel*, Kraus, "'God Hath Shown unto Me a Vision,'" 382–385 notes how throughout the ancient Near East and Mediterranean, depictions of individuals clasping the dead by the hand were made in light of the temple rituals of the ancient world that could represent being reunited with the dead in the resurrection or a continual link between the dead and the living. Given Joseph Smith's teachings and the sealing ordinances performed through Elijah's keys today in temples prepared for that purpose, these depictions will be of especial interest to Latter-day Saints.
45. "History, 1838–1856, volume D-1 [1 August 1842–1 July 1843]," p. 1575, *Joseph Smith Papers*, online at josephsmithpapers.org.
46. Jon D. Levenson, *Resurrection and the Restoration of Israel: The Ultimate Victory of the God of Life* (New Haven: Yale University Press, 2006), 95.

temple, the keys of Elijah are deeply connected to the evangelization of the dead.

In order for proxy ordinances to be performed for our ancestors, they must first be taught the gospel. The evangelization of the dead is therefore a significant aspect to proxy ordinances — and was understood as such anciently as well. In the *Shepherd of Hermas*, an early second century Chirstian text included in some early compilations of the New Testament, the angel instructs Hermas that "apostles and teachers who preached the name of the Son of God" preached the Gospel not only while they were living, but after they had died as well, preaching to those who had "fallen asleep" before them. Other apostles and teachers then "went down with [the dead] into the water and came up again. But these went down alive and came up again alive; whereas those who had previously fallen asleep went down dead and came up alive."[47]

This passage provides a clear conceptual link between the evangelization of the dead, showing it was more significant than a one-time event following Christ's crucifixion, and proxy ordinances even if it did not mention the role of Elijah as does latter-day revelation.[48] This

---

47. *Shepherd of Hermas, Parables*, 9.16.5–7 (93:5–7); translation taken from Michael W. Holmes, *The Apostolic Fathers: Greek Texts and English Translations*, 3rd ed. (Grand Rapids, MI: Baker Academic, 2007), 653. Regarding this passage's reference to both baptisms for the dead and the evangelization of the dead, Carolyn Osiek notes, "These verses, without saying so, present a good argument in favor of baptism in the name of the dead, apparently already an act of piety in first-century Corinth. ... Here with the pre-Christian dead, the problem is ... they practiced virtue in their lives, but had not received baptism. Through the apostles and teachers, this problem is solved." Carolyn Osiek, *Shepherd of Hermas: A Commentary*, Hermeneia: A Critical and Historical Commentary on the Bible, 50–55 vols. (Minneapolis, MN: Fortress, 1999), 29:238. Archbishop Hilarion Alfeyev of the Eastern Orthodox faith has likewise noted that this verse is often understood in the context of proxy baptisms and preaching the gospel to the dead in Metropolitan Hilarion Alfeyev, *Christ the Conqueror of Hell: The Descent into Hades from an Orthodox Perspective* (Crestwood, NY: St. Vladimir's Seminary Press, 2009), 25n33. See also Hugh Nibley, "Two Ways to Remember the Dead," in *The World and the Prophets* (Provo, UT: Foundation for Ancient Research and Mormon Studies; Salt Lake City, UT: Deseret Book, 1987), 169–171.
48. Archbishop Hilarion Alfeyev has argued that Christ's ministry to those who had died between His death and resurrection is significant "not only to past

is likewise found in modern revelation, with Joseph F. Smith being shown how a key teaching in the spirit world is the ability of spirits to receive proxy ordinances (Doctrine and Covenants 138:33–34).

In the Church of Jesus Christ of Latter-day Saints, the restoration of the tribes of Jacob has been a key focus from the beginning. And, for the living and the dead, the Priesthood revealed by Elijah makes that possible. As we take the Gospel to the world, we invite others to prepare to enter the temple and make sacred covenants with God, effected through ordinances performed under those Priesthood keys. In life, we can bind or seal the hearts of children to parents and parents to children. Likewise, as our faithful ancestors take the Gospel to those in the spirit world, they prepare others to accept those temple ordinances that are needed to seal us all together into a covenantal family and prevent the earth from being utterly wasted. It is no surprise that President Russell M. Nelson declared, "*Anytime* you do *anything* that helps *anyone*—on either side of the veil—take a step toward making covenants with God and receiving their essential baptismal and temple ordinances, you are helping to gather Israel. It is as simple as that."[49]

In short, Moroni and Joseph Smith each provided prophetic commentary regarding Elijah that conceptually aligned with how ancient Jewish and Christian authors viewed Elijah's return. True to prophetic word, Elijah returned to the earth prior to the Messiah's glorious advent, restoring the Priesthood keys necessary to tie all of God's children together through the covenants made to the fathers.

---

generations but also to all those who followed. ... The teaching that Christ granted to *all* the possibility of salvation and opened for *all* the doors to paradise should also be considered general church doctrine." Alfeyev, *Christ the Conqueror of Hell*, 205, 208; italics in original. Latter-day Saints agree with this observation, with the clearest revelation on the matter being recorded in Doctrine and Covenants 138.

49. Russell M. Nelson, "Hope of Israel," worldwide devotional for youth, June 3, 2018. Emphasis in original.

About the Contributors

Kerry Muhlestein is a professor of Ancient Scripture at BYU, where he teaches several classes on the Old Testament, Isaiah, the Pearl of Great Price, the Ancient Near East, and other scripture courses. He has a PhD from UCLA in Egyptology and Hebrew Language and Literature, and has been teaching Old Testament at the university level for over thirty years. He is also the author of several books, including many about the Old Testament. His newest book is called Inspirations and Insights from the Old Testament. He is also the host and creator of the podcast *The Scriptures Are Real*. Both the book and the podcast are designed to help you get more out of your "Come, Follow Me" studies.

T. Benjamin Spackman is a historian working at the intersection of science, religion, and scriptural interpretation in the ancient and modern worlds. He holds a PhD in American Religious History, as well as a MA (and completed PhD coursework) in Near Eastern Languages and Civilizations, and a BA in Near Eastern Studies from BYU. His dissertation investigated the historical and intellectual roots of Latter-day Saint creationism/evolution conflict in the twentieth century, and he served as co-editor (and contributor) to the recent BYU volume, *The Restored Gospel of Jesus Christ and Evolution*. He writes at BenSpackman.com.

Daniel Ellsworth is a Latter-day Saint writer and researcher. He is a contributor to Public Square Magazine, Interpreter, and the YouTube channel Latter-day Presentations. He writes on subjects with a focus on modern faith and epistemology, and Latter-day Saint paradigms of scripture and prophetic authority.

Allen Hansen is an independent researcher. He was born and raised in northern Israel. He served a mission in Russia, and married Kateryna from Ukraine. They are parents to a daughter. His research interests include the Bible, ancient, medieval and early modern Jewish literature,

Book of Mormon translation, and the meeting points between the church, Judaism, and the history of Israel.

Jennifer Roach Lees holds a Master in Divinity as well as a Masters in Counseling Psychology. She is best known for her research into how the Church of Jesus Christ of Latter-day Saints handles cases of sexual abuse. She has spoken at the annual FAIR conference on this topic, as well as on the dynamics involved in Bishops interviewing teenagers alone. Jennifer is a licensed mental health therapist and lives in Utah.

Paul Bryner is a second-year law student at the University of Utah's S.J. Quinney College of Law with a bachelor's degree in Ancient Near Eastern Studies and Minor in Philosophy from Brigham Young University, where he studied Hebrew, Aramaic, Greek, and Egyptian. Paul is a former research assistant at Scripture Central, where he took the lead on writing 20 articles. Paul is particularly interested in researching the problem of evil and gave a presentation on it at Berkeley's Graduate Theological Union last year. In his spare time Paul enjoys spending time with his wife, playing the piano, and translating the Bible.

Matthew Roper (MA, Brigham Young University) is currently a researcher and writer at Scripture Central and has been a research scholar at the Neal A. Maxwell Institute for Religious Scholarship. He has published in *Literary and Linguistic Computing, BYU Studies Quarterly, Mormon Studies Review, Interpreter: A Journal of Latter-day Saint Faith and Scholarship* and the *Journal of Book of Mormon Studies*.

Sara Riley has a B.A. in Ancient Near Eastern Studies from Brigham Young University, and a Masters in Library and Information Science from the University of Maryland. Since then she has worked at the Utah State Archives, the Smithsonian, and the National Archives. She is currently the Digital Imaging Lab Manager at the Brigham Young University Library. Her journey of loving the Book of Mormon began at a young age bedridden from illness and turning to the scriptures. When Sara is not spending time with her husband and two children, she can be found reading, hiking, and playing the piano. She is passionate about using technology to stimulate and deepen gospel learning.

John S. Thompson obtained his BA and MA in Ancient Near Eastern Studies (Hebrew Bible) from BYU and UC Berkeley respectively and completed a PhD in Egyptology at the University of Pennsylvania, with a dissertation emphasis on ancient priesthood. He was an employee of the Seminaries & Institutes of Religion for 28 years, most recently as a Coordinator and the Institute Director in the Cambridge, Massachusetts, area. John is now very happy to research and write full time for Scripture Central, a nonprofit organization that focuses on ancient and modern historical-cultural contexts of the Bible, Book of Mormon, and other Latter-day Saint scripture. He is married to Stacey Keller from Orem, Utah, and they have nine children and six grandchildren.

Tyler Golightly hails from American Fork, UT. He served his mission in Austin, Texas; and is currently studying Mechanical Engineering with an Aerospace Emphasis at Brigham Young University. He and his wife Elizabeth live in Provo, UT, and have been married for two years. He loves reading, studying Latter-day Saint history and theology, and airplanes.

Stephen O. Smoot is a doctoral candidate in Semitic and Egyptian Languages and Literature at the Catholic University of America. He previously earned a master's degree from the University of Toronto in Near and Middle Eastern Civilizations, with a concentration in Egyptology, and bachelor's degrees from Brigham Young University in Ancient Near Eastern Studies, with a concentration in Hebrew Bible, and German Studies.

Amanda Colleen Brown-Mather holds a MA in Bible and the Ancient Near East from The Hebrew University at Jerusalem and a BA in Ancient Near Eastern Studies from Brigham Young University. She currently spends her time leading a large-scale event production team, writing for the @comefollowme_women Instagram account, and competing in Scottish Highland dance competitions.

Christopher James Blythe is an assistant professor of Folklore at Brigham Young University. He holds a PhD in American Religious History from Florida State University. Blythe is the author of *Terrible Revolution: Latter-day Saints and the American Apocalypse* which was awarded the Best First Book Award from the Mormon History Association. With his wife, Christine, he co-hosts *Angels and Seerstones: A Latter-day Saint Folklore Podcast.* They live with their three boys in Salem, Utah.

Neal Rappleye is currently working as a researcher for the Ancient America Foundation. His primary research interests include ancient Jerusalem, ancient Arabia, the ancient Near East, pre-Columbian Mesoamerica, the 19th century witnesses to the discovery and translation of the Book of Mormon. His work has been published by The Interpreter Foundation, BYU Studies, Religious Educator, Book of Mormon Central, Greg Kofford Books, and Covenant Communications, and he has presented at several conferences. He was previously at Scripture Central (2015–2025) where he wrote over 200 KnoWhy and Evidence articles, and oversaw and contributed to a number of other research projects as the director of research.

Jeffrey M. Bradshaw holds a PhD in Cognitive Science from the University of Washington, is a Senior Research Scientist at the Florida Institute for Human and Machine Cognition (IHMC), where his work spans a wide range of topics in human and machine intelligence, garnering several awards and patents, and leading to advisory roles in science, defense, and academia worldwide. Complementing his technical career, Jeff has authored detailed commentaries on the Book of Moses, Genesis, and temple themes in scripture, and he currently serves as a Church service missionary writing histories of temples in the Democratic Republic of Congo and the Republic of the Congo, having previously served full-time missions with his wife, Kathleen, in France/Belgium and the DR Congo Kinshasa Mission and Temple.

John Gee is the William (Bill) Gay Research Professor at Brigham Young University, where he integrates history, archaeology, and ancient languages into his teaching and research on scripture. His work emphasizes connecting the gospel of Jesus Christ and the scriptures with students' existing knowledge and experiences. As holder of the William (Bill) Gay Research Chair, Dr. Gee advances scholarship in fields directly related to ancient scripture, including Egyptology and other ancient languages, with the goal of deepening understanding and appreciation of the scriptural heritage of The Church of Jesus Christ of Latter-day Saints. His research bridges the study of the ancient world with the study of scripture, bringing together disciplinary insights to illuminate the sacred texts of the Restoration.

Spencer Kraus graduated from Brigham Young University with a Bachelor's degree in Computer Science, Modern Hebrew, and Ancient

Near Eastern Studies. He is a researcher for the Ancient America Foundation and works with Lincoln Blumell on topics relating to early Christianity and the Greek New Testament.

Image Credits

Main Cover: "Open Thou Mine Eyes: Psalm 119:18" by Amberlea Erekson Smoot, used by permission.

Background on Front and Back Cover: page 529 of the Aleppo Codex, via Wikimedia Commons. Images in the public domain.

Page 5: Front cover of *Inspirations and Insights from the Old Testament* by Kerry Muhlestein. Used by permission.

Page 251: Extracted line drawings from Plate III in J. E. Quibell, *The Ramesseum* (London: Bernard Quartich, 1898). Images in the public domain.

Page 252: *Horus the Child on Crocodiles* via Wikimedia Commons.

Page 255: *Was*-scepters via Wikimedia Commons.

Page 258: *Palette of Narmer* via Wikimedia Commons

Page 389: Great Isaiah Scroll (1QIsaa), circa first century BCE, Israel Museum, Jerusalem via Wikipedia Commons.

Page 399: *Antiquitates Flandriae*, attributed to Gilles Li Muisis, Royal Library of Belgium, circa 1376–1377 via Wikimedia Commons.

Page 420: Josefa de Ayala (circa 1630–1684): *The Sacrificial Lamb*, circa 1670–1684. The Walters Art Museum, Baltimore, Maryland. Available in the public domain via a Creative Commons 1.0 license.

Subject Index

A

Aaron (brother of Moses)
    and Miriam challenge Moses, 20
    death of, 379
    priestly consecration of, 264
Abel
    murder of, 323, 327–328, 331, 333, 336
    offering accepted, 327
Abinadi
    as Moses figure, 234–235, 238
    death of, 233, 240
    on Isaiah 53, 390, 394, 397–399, 422–424
    prophecies against King Noah, 233–235, 238
    typology of Christ, 244
Abraham
    covenant of, 22, 136–138, 191–196, 454
    faithfulness of, 191–195, 224
    plural marriage of, 191–196
    sacrifice of Isaac, 180–181, 335
Accommodation, divine
    concept defined, 43–44, 164–165
    in conquest of Canaan, 164–168, 182
    in Law of Moses, 165
    and scripture, 42–45
Adam
    and Eve, 133, 275, 289–290, 323, 326–327
    and Lilith (fundamentalist theory), 338–340
    creation of, 289–293
    in Mormon Fundamentalist thought, 335–340
    pre-mortal role (Michael), 337–340
Adultery
    ancient definition of, 188n8, 215
    David's sin of, 208–209, 219
Ahab, King, 295
Akhenaten
    and monotheism, 92, 367
Alma (the Elder)
    as Moses/Joshua figure, 238
    covenant at Waters of Mormon, 238–240
    organization of church by, 240–241
    people of, delivered, 240–242
Amalekites
    destruction of, 150
Anointing
    of Jesus as Christ, 411–413
    priestly, 270–271

Anthropomorphism
    in Genesis 1, 290–291
    in Hebrew Bible, 291
    Joseph Smith's teachings on, 277, 298–300
Apocalyptic literature
    Jewish, 457–458, 465
    and necromancy, 342
Apostasy
    and covenant corruption, 26
    in ancient Israel, 4, 15, 29
    in Book of Mormon (King Noah), 216
    and temple pollution, 267–268
Ark of the Covenant
    in Josiah's time, 127
Asherah
    in Josiah's reforms, 98–99, 102
    symbolism of, 98n73
Assyria
    decline of, 89–90, 435–436
    influence on Israel/Judah, 3, 85–88, 96
    imperial policy of, 86–87, 432–434
    and Jonah, 432–436
    libraries of, 352–353
    and necromancy metaphors, 316–317
Atenism, 367–368
Atonement, Day of
    and Isaiah 53, 420
    in Leviticus, 266n12, 272
    omission in Deuteronomy, 112
    priestly ritual of, 272

B

Baal
    worship of, 98, 444
    confrontation with Elijah, 444
Babylon
    conquest of Judah, 90–91, 117
    creation myths (Enuma Elish), 263, 280
Baptism
    link to Red Sea crossing, 134–135, 238–239, 246
    for the dead, 162–163, 451–452, 466–467
    of proselytes, 239
Baruch, Second Book of, 121–122
Ben Sira (Sirach)
    on Elijah, 456
    on Josiah, 119–120
Bethel
    altar destroyed by Josiah, 100

Bible. See also Old Testament; New Testament; specific books
  infallibility of, questioned, 47–48, 159–162
  Joseph Smith Translation of, 8, 9, 11, 40–41, 126–127, 210–211, 275
  proto-Old Testament on Brass Plates, 346–349, 353–354
Book of Mormon
  brass plates, contents of, 346, 353–354, 381–383
  Exodus pattern in, 232–42
  Isaiah 53 in, 397–399
  necromantic imagery in, 318–321
  polygamy condemned in, 213–224
  view of American colonization, 168–170
Brass Plates
  contents of, 346–347, 354, 381–383
  dating of, 345–387
  source for Exodus narrative, 231

C

Cain
  curse of, 323, 331–333
  descendants of, 331–333, 338–340
  in Book of Moses, 326–329
  in folklore and legend, 323–325
  Master Mahan title, 328, 343
  in Mormon Fundamentalism, 334–341
  parentage theories (Serpent seed), 335–341
  sacrifice rejected, 327
Canaanites
  identity of, 172–173
  wickedness of, 147, 171–175
Chaoskampf (divine conflict), 13, 280
Chariots
  Assyrian religious use, 87–88
  sun worship, 87–88, 99
Christ. See Jesus Christ
Chronicles, Books of
  account of Josiah, 95–96
  on death of Josiah, 117
  Deuteronomist history, 113–114
Cippi (Horus on crocodiles), 252–253, 256
Colonization, American
  compared to Canaanite conquest, 168–170
Commandments, Ten. See Decalogue
Concubines
  definition and status in antiquity, 189–190, 214n76
  legal protections for, 198–200
Conquest of Canaan
  archaeological evidence for, 154–156
  divine command for, 143–184
  gradual vs. rapid conquest, 153–158
  theodicies regarding, 148–179
Covenants
  Abrahamic, 136–138, 191–196, 454, 458
  corruption cycle, 26
  Davidic, 134, 196
  definition and nature of, 22–27
  hesed (mercy/loyalty) in, 24–25
  Mosaic, 138–141, 165
  Noahic, 134–135
  renewal of (Josiah), 104–105
  restoration of, 132, 135–136
  and temple sealing, 452–453
Creation
  ex nihilo (rejection of), 279, 285–288, 297–298
  functional ontology of, 284, 287
  in Genesis 1, 279–285, 290–293
  Joseph Smith's teachings on, 276–277, 297–298
  structure of days, 281–283

D

David, King
  and Bathsheba/Uriah, 208–209, 218–219
  covenant with, 134
  marriages/polygamy of, 207–210
  condemnation of, 208–209, 218–219
Dead Sea Scrolls
  Isaiah scroll (1QIsaa), 389, 411–412, 423, 426
  Pentateuch manuscripts, 346
Death
  as spiritual transition, 15
  of Josiah, 117–119, 121–124
Decalogue (Ten Commandments)
  dating of, 366–368
  in Exodus 20, 139
  and Hittite treaties, 367
Deification (Theosis)
  and imago Dei, 299–300
  Joseph Smith's teachings on, 276–277, 299
Deuteronomist
  as historian/redactor, 114
  view of kingship, 94–95
Deuteronomy, Book of
  composition and dating, 113, 360–366
  connection to Josiah, 103–104, 108–110
  discovery of the law, 103–104
  law of the king, 200–203

Subject Index

structure of, 365
Divine Council
    in Genesis 1, 293–297
    in Hebrew Bible, 111, 295–296
    Joseph Smith on, 276, 301
Documentary Hypothesis. See Source criticism

E

Egypt
    Atenism, 367–368
    influence on Judah, 90–91
    necromancy in, 307–308, 316
    symbolism of rod/serpent in, 246–255
Elephantine Papyri, 350, 354
Elijah
    appearance in Kirtland Temple, 453–454, 464–465
    expectation of return, 446, 456–460
    and John the Baptist, 447, 460–461
    keys of sealing, 452–453, 464–465
    role in restoring tribes, 456–457, 464
Enoch
    lifted up, 410n58
    in Mormon Fundamentalist thought, 335
Evil, problem of (Theodicy), 144–146
Exodus (event)
    as literary motif in Mosiah, 230–242
    intertextuality of, 230
    typology of, 244

F

Fallibility of scripture, 47–49, 159–162
Family history
    Old Testament as, 6
    work for the dead, 162–163, 466–467
Flood, The (Noah)
    as baptism of earth, 134–135
    in Book of Mormon, 49
    covenant following, 134
    Joseph Smith's translation (Book of Moses), 9–10, 160–161
Fundamentalism, Mormon
    and Cain mythology, 334–341
    Lorin Woolley, 334–335

G

Gathering of Israel
    Elijah's role in, 457–458, 464–465
    and Gentile nations, 398
    Old Testament lens of, 29–30
    restoration of keys for, 454

Genesis, Book of
    Creation narrative, 279–285
    dating of narratives, 375–378
    Joseph Smith's engagement with, 274–277
Gentiles
    and the Book of Mormon, 397–398
    colonization of Americas, 168–170
God
    anger and mercy of, 9–11, 146
    embodiment of, 290–291, 298–300
    nature of, 9–12
    plurality of (Divine Council), 293–297

H

Hammurabi, Code of, 193, 203, 368–369
Herem (utter destruction)
    archaeological evidence, 154–155
    definition and usage, 149–151, 451
    ethical challenges of, 143–144, 166
    as hyperbole, 153, 157
    as ritual devotion, 149
Hezekiah
    literary activity under, 353, 381
Holiness
    concept of (qodeš), 265
    Code (H source), 371–374
    and sacred space, 264–268
Holy Ghost
    as guide in reading scripture, 163
Horus
    on the crocodiles (cippi), 252–253

I

Idolatry
    in Canaan, 172–173
    Josiah's removal of, 97–100
Image of God (Imago Dei)
    embodiment, 288–291, 298–300
    functional/royal status, 291–293
    Joseph Smith's interpretation, 298–300
Inerrancy, biblical
    Latter-day Saint rejection of, 47, 61, 346
Inheritance, laws of, 203–204
Intertextuality
    criteria for, 230
    Exodus in Mosiah, 230–242
Isaiah
    authorship questions, 72
    necromantic imagery in, 314–318
    Servant Songs, 388, 405
    chapter 53 (Suffering Servant), 388–427
Israel

gathering of, 29–30, 457–458
northern kingdom traditions, 380–382

J

Jacob (Patriarch)
    covenant renewal, 196–197
    polygamy of, 196–198
Jacob (Book of Mormon prophet)
    condemnation of polygamy, 213–224
    sermon at temple, 186, 213
Jeremiah
    and Deuteronomy, 384
    and Josiah, 115–116, 124
Jerusalem
    as "Ariel", 316
    siege of (701 BC), 316
Jesus Christ
    as fulfillment of Exodus typology, 244
    as Suffering Servant, 394–396, 409
    typology in Mosiah, 244
    visit to Spirit World, 14–15, 162
John the Baptist
    as Elias/Elijah figure, 447, 460–461
Jonah, Book of
    anachronisms in, 437–439
    dating of, 436–437
    historicity, 430–445
    language of, 440–444
    repentance of Nineveh, 430, 436
Joseph Smith
    cosmology of, 274–304
    King Follett Discourse, 276–277, 301
    teachings on Elijah, 451–454
    translation of the Bible (JST), 8, 40–41, 126–127, 210–211, 275
Josiah, King
    apocryphal traditions of, 119–126
    death of, 117–119, 124
    finding of the Law, 103–105
    reforms of, 79–80, 97–102
    viewed by Latter-day Saints, 126–129

K

Kingship
    divine/sacral nature of, 91–95, 292
    law of the king (Deuteronomy), 200–203, 364

L

Laban (biblical figure), 196
Law of Moses
    composition of, 355–375
    in Book of Mosiah, 237
    polygamy regulations in, 198–206
Levirate marriage, 205–207, 372
Leviticus
    Holiness Code, 371
    purity laws, 265–67, 373–374
Lilith
    in fundamentalist folklore, 338–340
Literacy
    in ancient Israel, 349–350, 362

M

Malachi
    prophecy of Elijah, 446–455
Marriage
    levirate, 205–207
    polygamous. See Polygamy
Master Mahan
    origin of title, 328, 343
Messiah. See also Jesus Christ
    Jewish expectations of, 401–402
    Suffering Servant as, 392–394
    two Messiahs theory, 401
Miracles
    historicity of, 67–68
Mormon Fundamentalism
    Cain mythology, 334–341
Moroni (Angel)
    midrash on Malachi, 449–451
    on "voice from the dust", 320–321
Moses
    authorship of Pentateuch, 386
    Book of (JST), 275, 326–328
    comparison to Abinadi, 234–235
    comparison to Alma, 238
    appearance in Kirtland Temple, 453–454
Mosiah, Book of
    Exodus typology in, 230–242

N

Necromancy
    in ancient Near East, 307–309
    biblical condemnation of, 311–313
    terminology (ob, yidde'oni), 309–311
    transformed in Book of Mormon, 318–321
Nephi
    on brass plates, 346
    on colonization of Americas, 168–170
    on "voice from the dust", 318–320
    view of Canaanite destruction, 174
Nineveh

repentance of, 430–431, 436
  as capital of Assyria, 437–439
Noah (Patriarch)
  covenant of, 134–135
  flood of, 160–161
Noah, King (Book of Mormon)
  as Pharaoh figure, 233–234

P

Pentateuch
  composition and dating, 355–382
  Documentary Hypothesis, 355–356
  linguistic evidence for dating, 358–360
  Mosaic authorship, 386
Peter (Apostle)
  use of Isaiah 53, 396
Polygamy
  biblical practice of, 187–213
  Jacob's condemnation of, 213–224
  Law of Lehi regarding, 214–216
  in Mormon Fundamentalism, 334
  social function in antiquity, 190–191, 211–213
Priesthood
  Levitical, 459
  restoration by Elijah, 450, 453
  lineage restrictions (historical), 331–334
Prophecy
  fulfillment of, 391
  nature of, 69

Q

Qumran. See Dead Sea Scrolls

R

Race
  and priesthood restriction, 331–334
  folklore regarding Cain, 331–334
Repentance
  of Nineveh, 430, 436
Restoration
  of covenants, 132, 135–136
  of priesthood keys, 453–454
Resurrection
  connection to temple, 465
Ritual
  purity, 265–267
  in Leviticus, 373
Rod
  symbolism of, 246–248
  and serpent imagery, 255–256

S

Sabbath
  in creation narrative, 283–284
  in Decalogue, 368
Sacred space
  access to, 268–270
  concept of, 263–264
  consequences of profaning, 266–268
  Latter-day Saint temples as, 270–273
Sacrifice
  child sacrifice (Molech), 99, 173
  Cain and Abel, 327–328
Satan
  as father of Cain (folklore), 335–341
  in Garden of Eden, 326–327
  pact with Cain, 328–329
  premortal rebellion, 330
Saul, King
  and Medium of Endor, 313–314
Sealing power
  Elijah's return, 452–453
  Joseph Smith's teachings on, 452
Serpent
  brazen, 256
  in Garden of Eden, 256–257, 326
  symbolism in Egypt, 249–255
  symbolism in scripture, 255–258
Servant, Suffering (Isaiah 53)
  identity of, 389–405
  Jewish interpretations, 392–394, 399–402
  Christian interpretations, 394–396
Shema (Deuteronomy 6)
  and Josiah's death, 117–118
Solomon, King
  polygamy of, 210–211, 218–219
  temple dedication, 264
Source criticism
  Documentary Hypothesis, 355–356
  dating of Pentateuch sources, 357–379
Spirit world
  evangelization of dead, 162–163, 466
Symbolism
  in Old Testament, 18–21
  Egyptian (rod/serpent), 246–255

T

Tabernacle
  as dwelling place of God, 263–264
  pollution of, 267
Temple
  exclusivity of, 261–273
  Kirtland Temple, 453–454, 464–465

as sacred space, 263–270
in Ezekiel, 268
Theodicy
for conquest of Canaan, 144–146
skeptical theism, 178–179
Torah. See Pentateuch

V

Violence
divine command for, 143–184
in Josiah's reforms, 105–106

Voice from the dust
metaphor in Isaiah and Book of Mormon, 305–322

W

War in Heaven
neutral spirits theory, 332–333
Women
concubines, 189–190
protection of in biblical law, 212
Woolley, Lorin C., 334–335

Z

Zion
and Jerusalem, 317